The
Symbols
of Art

Quarto

First published in 2026 by Frances Lincoln,
an imprint of The Quarto Group.
One Triptych Place, London, SE1 9SH,
United Kingdom
T (0)20 7700 9000
www.Quarto.com

EEA Representation, WTS Tax d.o.o., Žanova ulica 3, 4000 Kranj, Slovenia
www.wts-tax.si

A catalogue record for this book is available from the British Library.

ISBN 978-1-80570-035-7
Ebook ISBN 978-1-80570-036-4

10 9 8 7 6 5 4 3 2 1

Design by Leonardo Collina

Publisher: Philip Cooper
Editor: Isabella Toner
Managing Editor: Laura Bulbeck
Senior Designer: Isabel Eeles
Senior Production Controller: Rohana Yusof

Printed in Guangdong, China TT012026

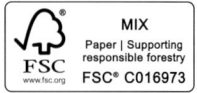

Susie Hodge

The Symbols of Art

Decoding the Hidden Meanings of Art

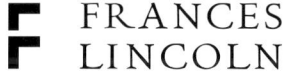

FRANCES LINCOLN

Contents

Introduction

Have you ever noticed an object in a work of art and wondered why it was there? An object that seems to have been put there for a reason beyond its appearance. It might be an oversized shell, a woman holding a flower, a halo or a cross. Even a wild sea, a dark cloud or a book. You can generally guess that these items have been incorporated to represent something else, and you can often work out what that symbolism is. But what about a window, a light bulb, a banana or a colour? An umbrella, a daisy or a butterfly? Do you always know what the artwork is really saying? Are you aware of the signs that an artist has hidden a deeper message, and do you know that the messages can change depending on the time, place and reasons the artwork was created?

When objects or other elements in a work of art do not particularly stand out - or even if they do - you may be missing some extra information that the artist was or is trying to impart. This book aims to help with that.

With meanings that extend beyond straightforward appearances, symbols in art have served as vehicles for emotion, belief, culture and philosophy throughout the history of art. From the earliest cave paintings to the most avant-garde installations, artists have frequently imbued their work with symbols that often shift in relation to geography, time and personal context. These symbols can be either unique to the artist or more universal.

It may seem contradictory, but long ago, when most populations were generally illiterate, symbols in art, including objects, motifs or inanimate objects, were easily 'read' by most viewers. Over time, as we have become better educated, interpreting and decoding symbols in art has become more complex and less widely understood. Once, artists across cultures shared a symbolic vocabulary that was understood by their contemporaries. Now, however, the meanings and metaphors are multiplying and can vary widely. Artists incorporate them to convey spiritual, cultural and social messages, ideas and emotions, and yet, often, we are unable to interpret them. Yet being able to comprehend what an artist meant can hugely enhance our appreciation and understanding of the artwork.

Throughout history, symbolism has been one of the most powerful tools in an artist's visual language. By using elements of their art metaphorically, artists can give us so much more than meets the eye. They can evoke emotions, express ideas and communicate values or beliefs. While the forms and meanings of symbols vary widely across periods and places, their presence has been constant. Even so, traditional or original meanings have sometimes mutated, been recontextualized, or completely renewed.

Multiple functions

Historically, symbolism has served multiple functions. In religious and spiritual art, symbols offered access to divine or moral truths. They enabled artists to convey philosophies and other concepts to a large number of viewers. In political or social contexts, symbolism serves as a method of expressing disagreement, dissension or hope. In the Western world, during the Renaissance (c. 1400-1600), the revival of classical learning profoundly influenced theological studies, which nurtured a rich symbolic vocabulary. Objects, animals, plants and colours became loaded with meaning. For instance, a lily came to represent purity, a dog fidelity, a halo sanctity, a fig tree knowledge or rebirth and a bee industriousness or chastity. Skulls, withered flowers and hourglasses soon began to populate still-life paintings, deliberately reminding the viewer of the transience of earthly life. After movable-type printing was developed in Europe during the fifteenth century, literacy expanded, and artists began incorporating more secular and even satirical symbolism. Symbols such as balloons, umbrellas, the colour orange, or a pair of shoes, for example, could be incorporated into a work of art to convey something more personal to the artist and to reveal more about the image to the viewer.

Symbolism was present in all artistic movements, including the Baroque, Rococo, Romanticism and Impressionism, but it also had its own distinct movement. The late nineteenth century witnessed the rise of Symbolism as an explicit movement, with artists such as Gustave Moreau (1826-98) and Odilon Redon (1840-1916) rejecting realism in favour of dreamlike, poetic imagery, using myth, metaphor, and mood to express philosophical ideas.

Much earlier, in ancient Egypt, symbols such as the Eye of Horus and the scarab beetle represented fundamental concepts, including life, protection and rebirth. These symbols featured in Egyptian art, providing visual cues into the society's religious beliefs and values. Similarly, in ancient Greece, artists used symbols to explore human nature, morality and the relationship between gods and mortals.

In many other cultures, symbols have often carried communal, spiritual or ancestral meanings, transmitted across generations through both oral and visual traditions and practices. Islamic art incorporated geometric and floral motifs, as well as calligraphy, symbolizing divine perfection and the infinite nature of God. African art, such as that found in the Akan, Yoruba or Dogon traditions, utilized masks, textiles and figurative sculpture as symbolic tools in rituals. In Chinese painting, the natural world, including specific trees, the sun, cranes, pine and plum blossoms, carried a range of established meanings, such as longevity or resilience. Japanese ukiyo-e paintings and prints often incorporated symbolic elements within scenes of daily life. For instance, a wave, a colour, a shape, a parasol, rain or a flower could convey layered poetic or philosophical meanings.

Handy guide

Neither fixed nor universal, symbolism depends on context, interpretation and intent. What may be a sacred emblem in one culture could be a decorative motif in another, or a tool for insurrection in a third. Symbolism in art has always reflected our enduring need and desire to create meaning, to share secrets, to connect images with ideas and to express complex concepts in simple ways. By using familiar forms and elements in unconventional ways, artists have long encouraged viewers to question their assumptions and discover new ideas. Ultimately, artists use symbolism to convey meaning without words. Symbolism bridges the gap between the visible and the invisible.

Considering a vast range of artworks, this book serves as your comprehensive guide to the symbolism of the past and present. It is divided thematically into sections, such as the Natural World, the Manmade World, Colours and Shapes, and subsections, including Plants, the Home, Food, Clothing and Colours. It gives an introduction into how certain symbols have been interpreted by different artists over time, unpicking and exploring individual meanings and the reasons artists have included them, with specific examples. It aims to give you the confidence to explore a wide range of art, spanning time and cultural boundaries, and to interpret the symbolism embedded within it.

The Natural World

From cave paintings to contemporary installations, the natural world has been represented artistically across the globe. Comprising flora, fauna, landscapes, water, weather and the universe, the natural world has been used as a visual metaphor across the globe.

Nature is both universal and intimate. A river may mean life in one culture and death in another. A cherry blossom may evoke joy and beauty in one century, and transience and loss in the next. Artists across the millennia have drawn inspiration from these natural forms to express a range of emotions and secondary meanings, from spiritual transcendence to political power, or from eroticism to mourning.

The natural world, represented as symbolism, can be traced back to Palaeolithic cave paintings, where animals and natural cycles were depicted for their material importance and metaphysical associations. Aurochs, bulls, horses and stags painted on the walls of Lascaux or Chauvet caves in France are invocations, mythic presences and sometimes, perhaps, even early prayers. These animals inhabited both the physical landscape and the symbolic consciousness of early humans, a dual presence that has persisted throughout art history.

In many early civilizations, the natural world itself was symbolic and divine. Rivers were deities, the Sun a god, the harvest a cycle of birth and death, and animals could be deities, companions or sources of nourishment. In ancient Egyptian art, the Nile was not only a geographic feature, but also represented life, fertility and the regenerative power of the gods. Similarly, mountains in many Asian and ancient Greek traditions were regarded as homes of the gods.

Plants and flowers have frequently carried layered meanings, often developing symbolic languages within specific cultures or religions. For example, in Christian art, the lily became synonymous with the Virgin Mary's purity, and the rose with divine love or martyrdom. In Islamic and Persian miniature painting, garden imagery represented paradise. In East Asia, flowers like the plum blossom, peony and lotus carried their own cultural meanings, such as perseverance, wealth and spiritual purity.

Artists did not simply record the beauty of a flower; they invoked its underlying significance, creating works that conveyed emotional, spiritual or political meaning.

Food, too, has often held more than aesthetic interest in visual art. Fruit and vegetables appear in still lifes to display technical virtuosity, and also to signal moral, sensual or allegorical themes. The strawberry, for example, might represent purity and humility in medieval devotional art, yet signify sensual pleasure or the transience of beauty in a Rococo still life. Cherries, pomegranates, apples and grapes appear frequently across various cultures and throughout the centuries.

The elements of sky, sea, clouds and storms have long been metaphors for the emotions and the unknown. In the Romantic period (c. 1780–1830), for instance, turbulent seas and brooding skies express inner anxiety or awe. In Japanese ukiyo-e prints, the delicate depiction of rain and shifting clouds evokes a sense of seasonal change, tying human emotion to the rhythms of nature.

Meanwhile, celestial imagery, such as stars, the Sun and the Moon, has consistently bridged the physical and the mystical. In medieval Christian manuscripts, stars guided saints or illuminated God's will. In Aboriginal Australian painting, constellations map ancestral stories. For many cultures, the sky has been a canvas of fate, prophecy and sacred geometry.

The forest may represent danger, mystery or inner confrontation, as seen in European folklore or Renaissance or Romantic allegory. A mountain may symbolize spiritual ascent or earthly challenge. The river may be life-giving or boundary-forming.

Ultimately, the symbolic use of nature in art reveals not only how we see the world, but how we understand ourselves within it. As ecological consciousness grows in contemporary art, the natural world is being reimagined in different ways, often as an active participant in human fate.

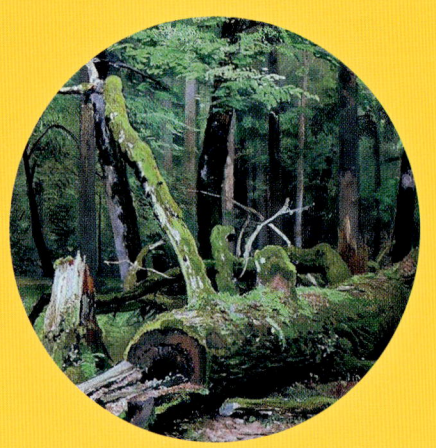

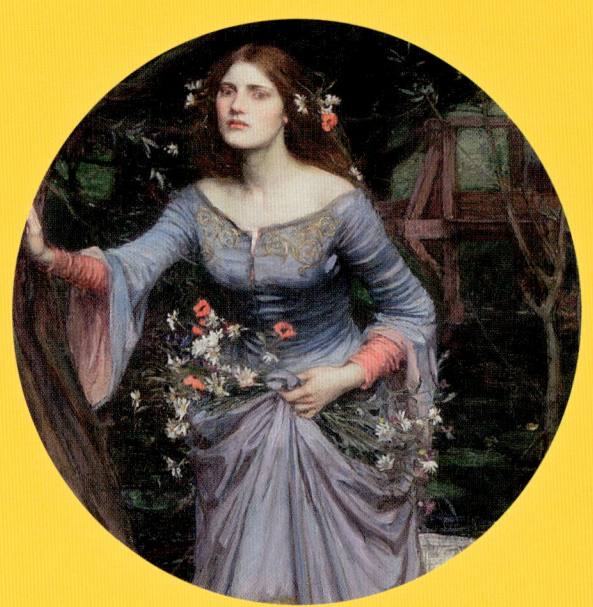

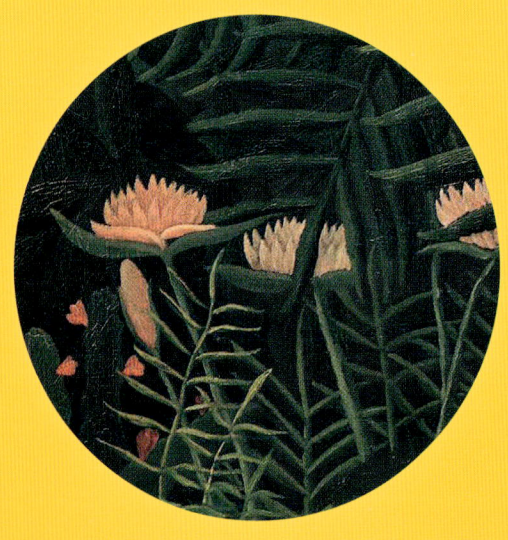

Plants

Sunflower

Throughout history, the bright, sun-facing nature of sunflowers has made them enduring symbols of hope, vitality, devotion and resilience. The flower was only introduced to Europe from the Americas in the sixteenth century, but from then on, in Christian iconography, it has often represented unwavering faith, mirroring the believer's constant turning towards divine light. In his self-portrait of 1632-33, Anthony van Dyck (1599-1641) is almost engulfed by a massive yellow-gold sunflower, representing both Charles I and van Dyck's fidelity to his king. Perhaps the most famous artistic treatment of sunflowers is *Sunflowers*, a series of paintings by Vincent van Gogh (1853-90), in which he captured their vibrancy and expressive potential, symbolizing hope, creativity and his own emotional turmoil. In Chinese and Japanese art, sunflowers are associated with longevity and good fortune, appearing in decorative motifs and traditional paintings. The sunflower continues to be depicted in a wide range of art as a powerful representation of joy, perseverance and the fleeting nature of existence.

1

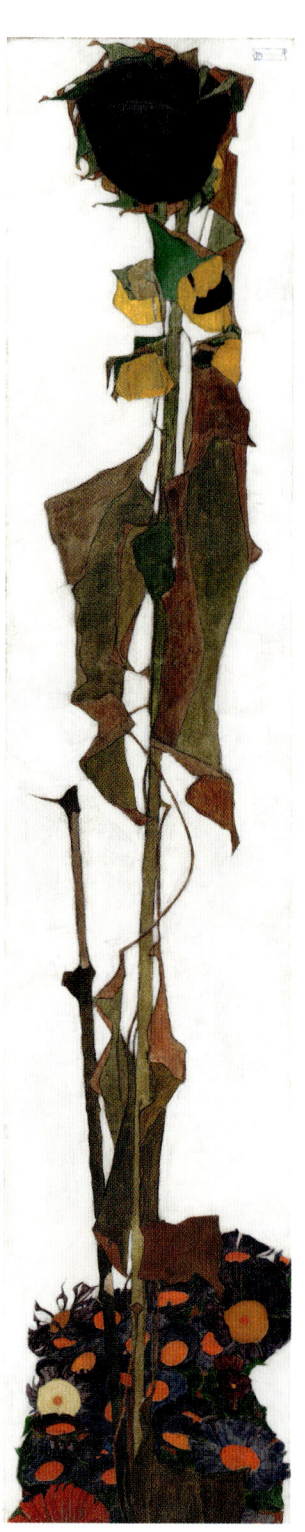

2

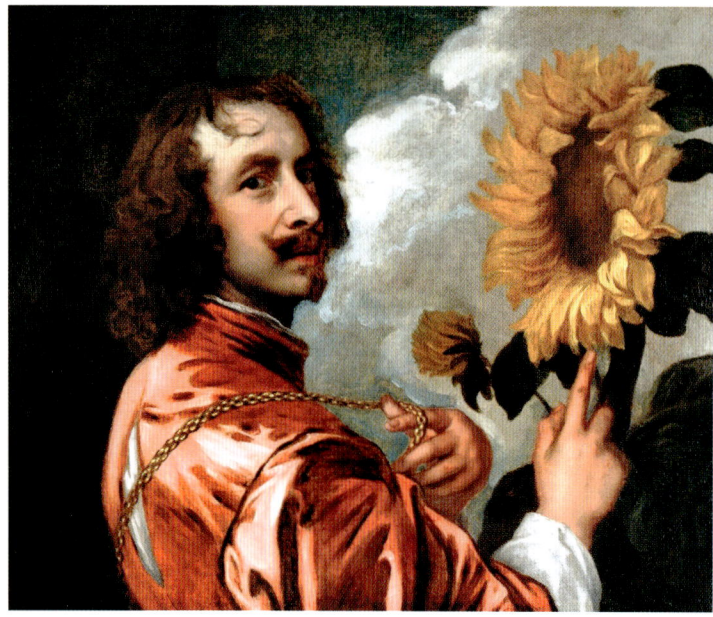

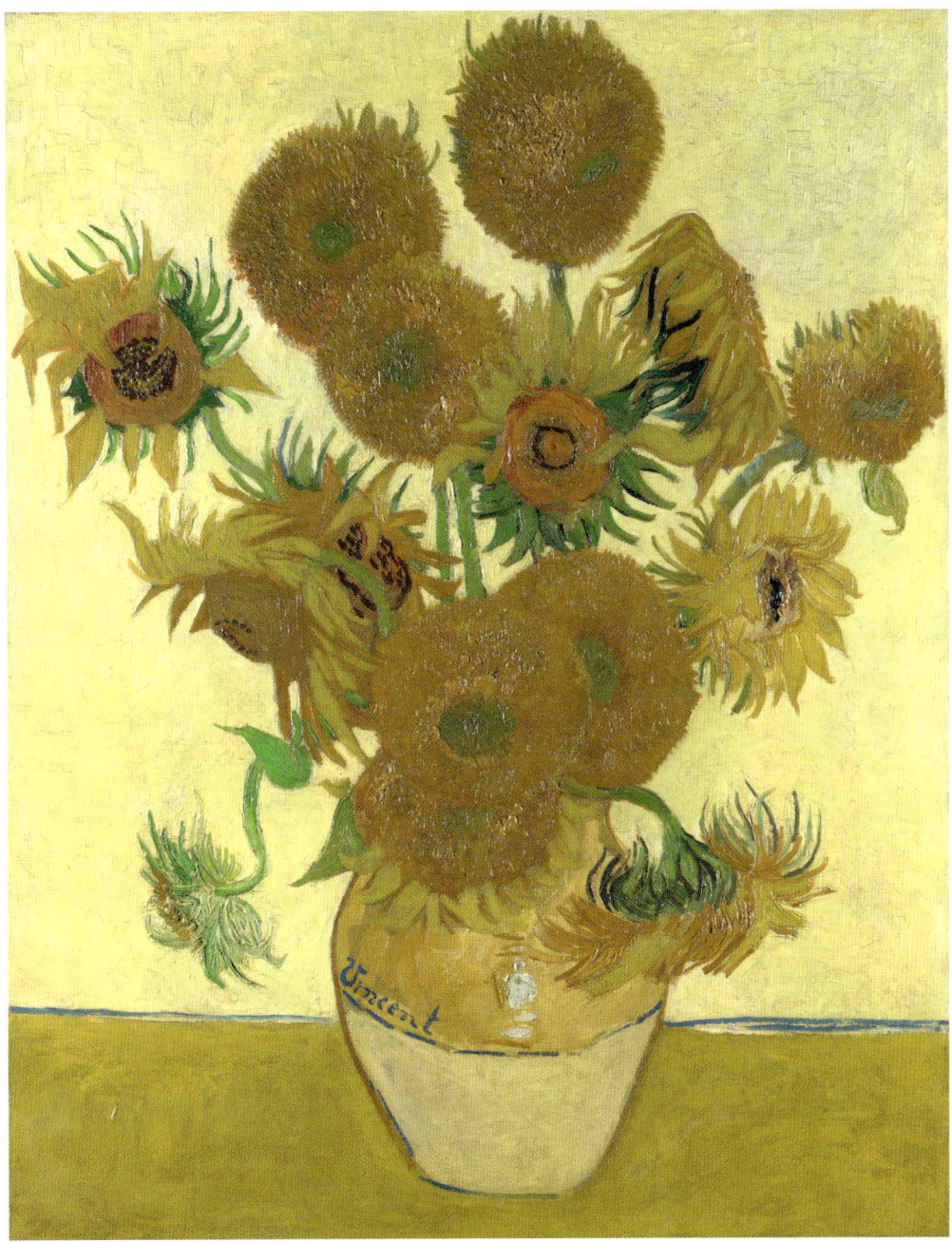

3

1. *Sunflower II,* Egon Schiele, 1910
2. *Self-Portrait with Sunflower,* Sir Anthony van Dyck, 1632-33
3. *Sunflowers,* Vincent van Gogh, 1888

Jasmine

In Indian art, jasmine garlands embellish both gods and lovers, symbolizing divine beauty and romantic devotion. Mughal and Rajput miniature paintings often feature jasmine in scenes of courtship, with its blossoms evoking themes of longing and sensuality. In Chinese brush paintings, jasmine is usually depicted to suggest feminine elegance, purity, virtue and refinement. Jasmine motifs are woven into geometric and floral patterns in Islamic art, representing beliefs about paradise and divine order. Meanwhile, in European art, particularly during the Renaissance, jasmine was linked to the Virgin Mary, symbolizing chastity and spiritual innocence. Artists such as Albert Moore (c. 1841–1893), Leonardo da Vinci (1452–1519), Raphael (1483–1520) and Fra Filippo Lippi (c. 1406–69) used jasmine to highlight themes of grace and divine love. Modern and contemporary artists often portray the jasmine, connecting it to themes of memory and identity.

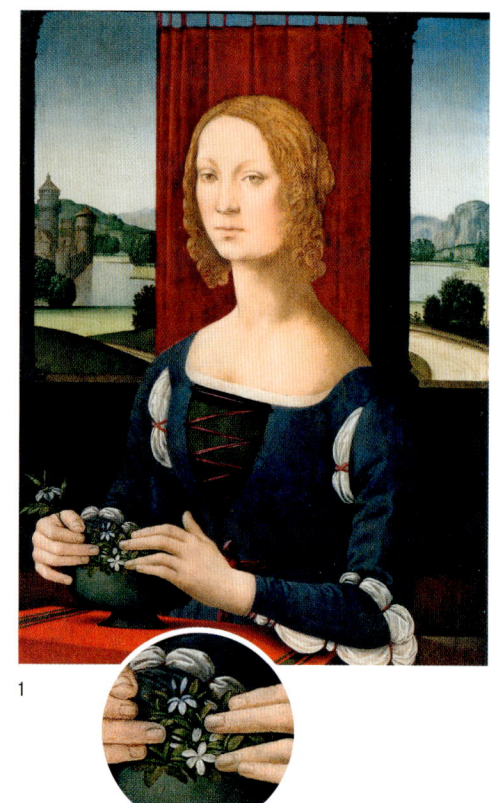

1

2

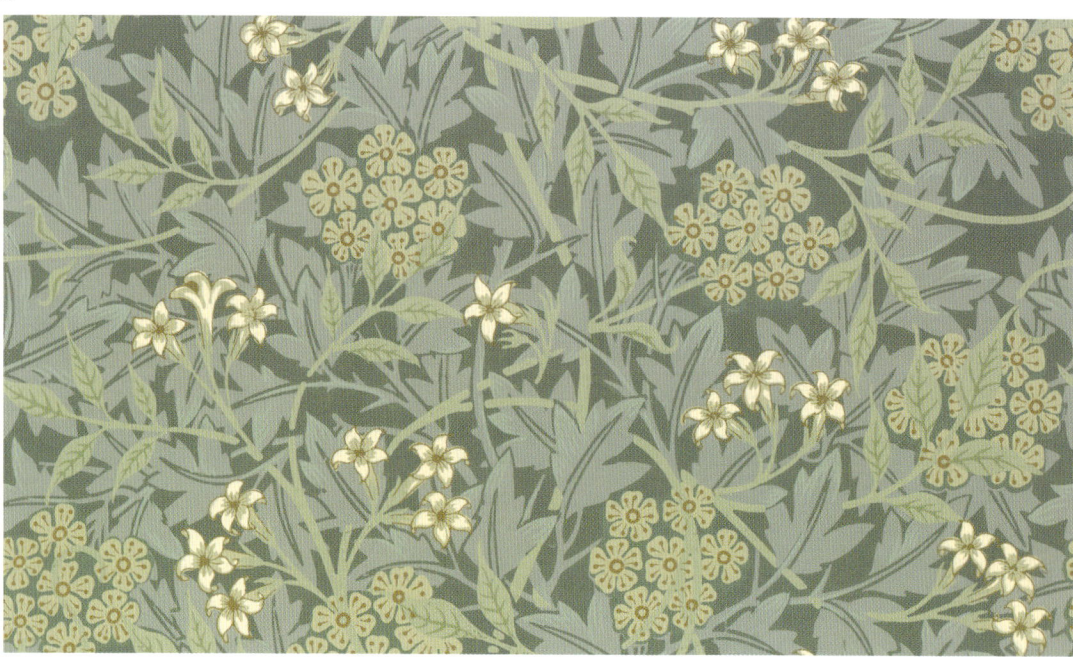

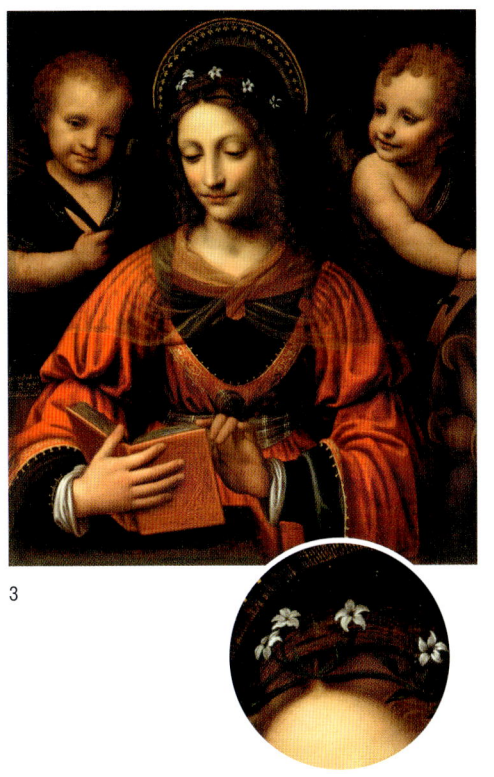

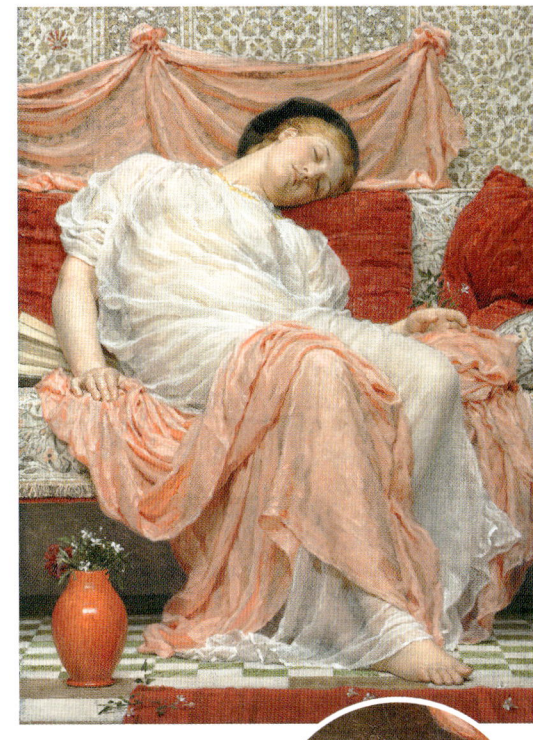

3

4

5

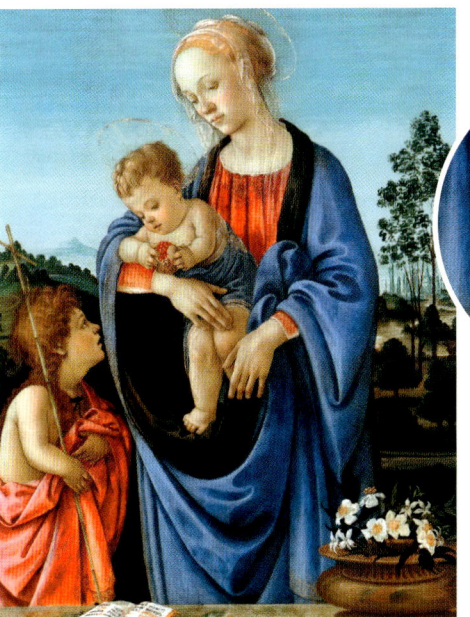

1. *Portrait of a Girl (The Lady of the Jasmine Flowers)*, Lorenzo di Credi, 1485–90
2. *Jasmine*, William Morris, 1872
3. *St Catherine*, Bernardino Luini, 1527–31
4. *Jasmine*, Albert Moore, 1893
5. *Madonna and Child with Young St John the Baptist*, Filippino Lippi, c. 1480

Poppy

The depiction of poppies in art dates back centuries, but some of the most well-documented examples come from the nineteenth century. Due to their sedative properties, they were often associated with sleep, death and remembrance, and were linked to Morpheus, the god of dreams, and Hypnos, the god of sleep in ancient Greek and Roman art. During the nineteenth century, artists such as John Singer Sargent (1856–1925) and the Pre-Raphaelites depicted poppies to suggest ideas about beauty intertwined with mortality. After the First World War, the red poppy became an especially poignant symbol, inspired by the poem *In Flanders Fields* by the Canadian John McCrae (1872–1918), which describes them as representing the blood of fallen soldiers. This led to its prominent use in memorial artworks and war commemorations. In modern and contemporary art, poppies have continued to evoke reflection on conflict, loss and the passage of time.

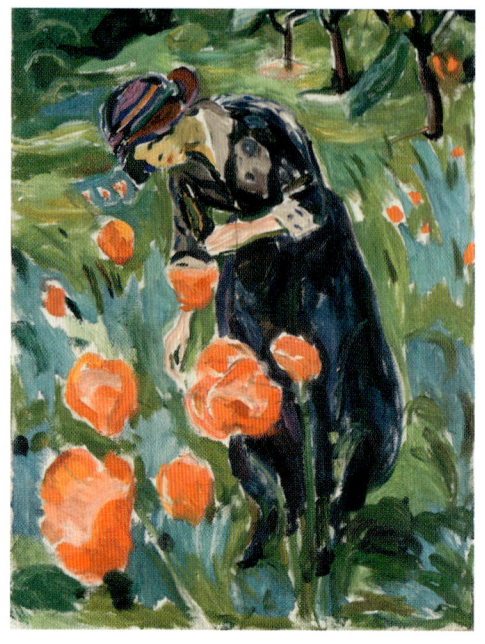

1

2

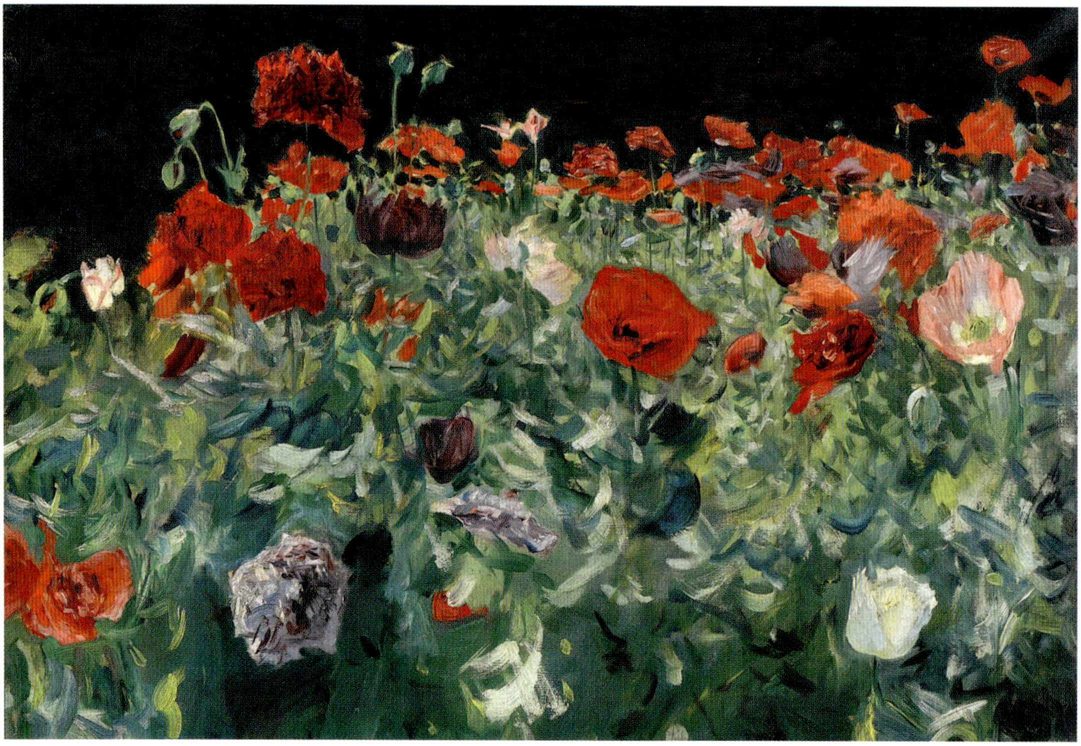

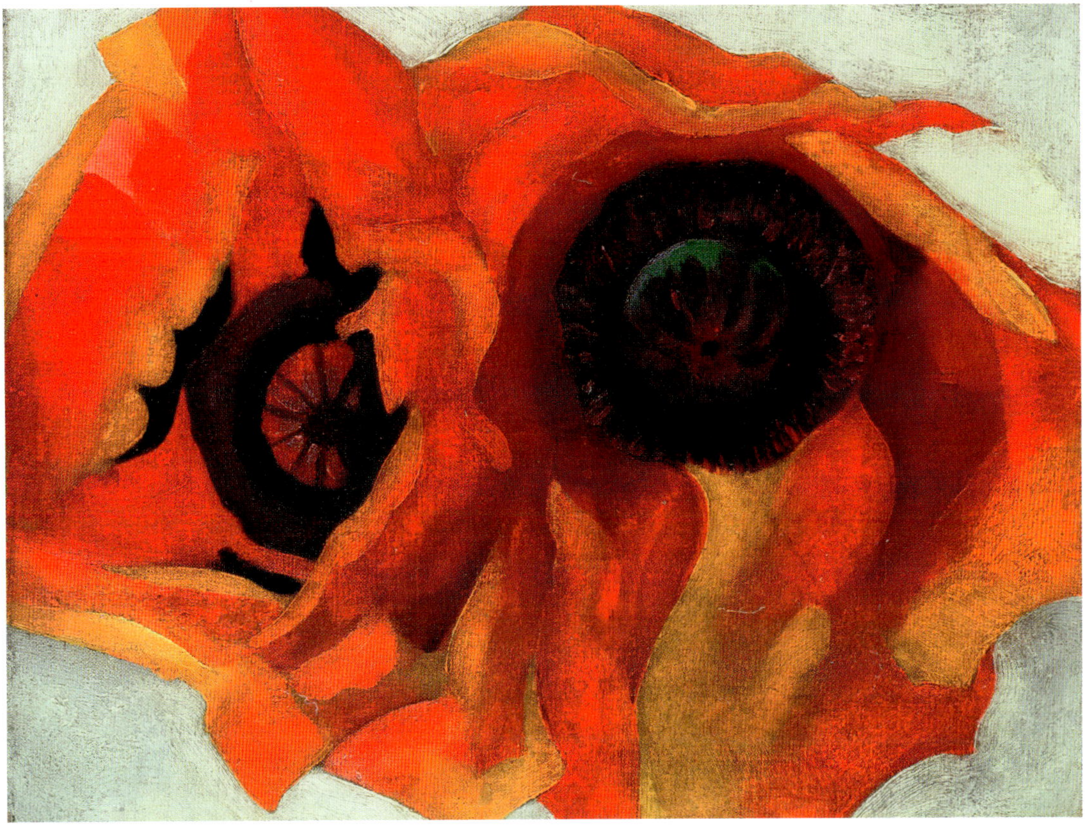

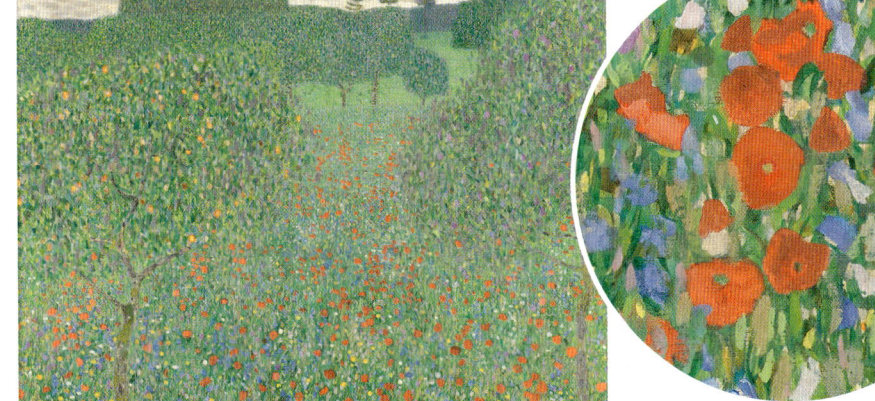

3

4

1. *Woman with Poppies,* Edvard Munch, 1919
2. *Poppies,* John Singer Sargent, 1886
3. *Poppies,* Georgia O'Keeffe, 1926
4. *Flowering Poppies,* Gustav Klimt, 1907

Forget-me-not

With a name that reveals its symbolism, the small blue forget-me-not has long been an enduring emblem of remembrance, love and connection in art. In medieval and Renaissance art, it often appeared in illuminated manuscripts and portraits to signify fidelity and eternal love. In the nineteenth century, particularly in the Victorian era, it was commonly included in mourning art, symbolizing true love and remembrance beyond death. For example, in *Ophelia* (1851–52) by John Everett Millais (1829–96), forget-me-nots are on the riverbank. During the Romantic era, artists frequently incorporated the forget-me-not into portraits and still lifes, emphasizing themes of nostalgia and devotion. Delicate blue flowers resembling

forget-me-nots have appeared in Japanese art, symbolizing transience and beauty, and in Chinese art, representing loyalty and memory. Intricate floral patterns in Persian miniature paintings sometimes include blue flowers, which can symbolize spiritual devotion and the passage of time. Similarly, in Indian Mughal art, floral decorations often carry meanings of impermanence, divine beauty, remembrance and devotion.

1. *Insects with Common Hawthorn and Forget-Me-Not,* Jan van Kessel the Elder, 1654

2. *Forget-Me-Not,* John Everett Millais, 1883

3. *Irises, roses, fritillaries and forget-me-nots in a Wanli vase with two shells and a beetle on a ledge, Balthasar van der Ast, 1622*

4. *Ophelia,* John Everett Millais, 1851–52

1

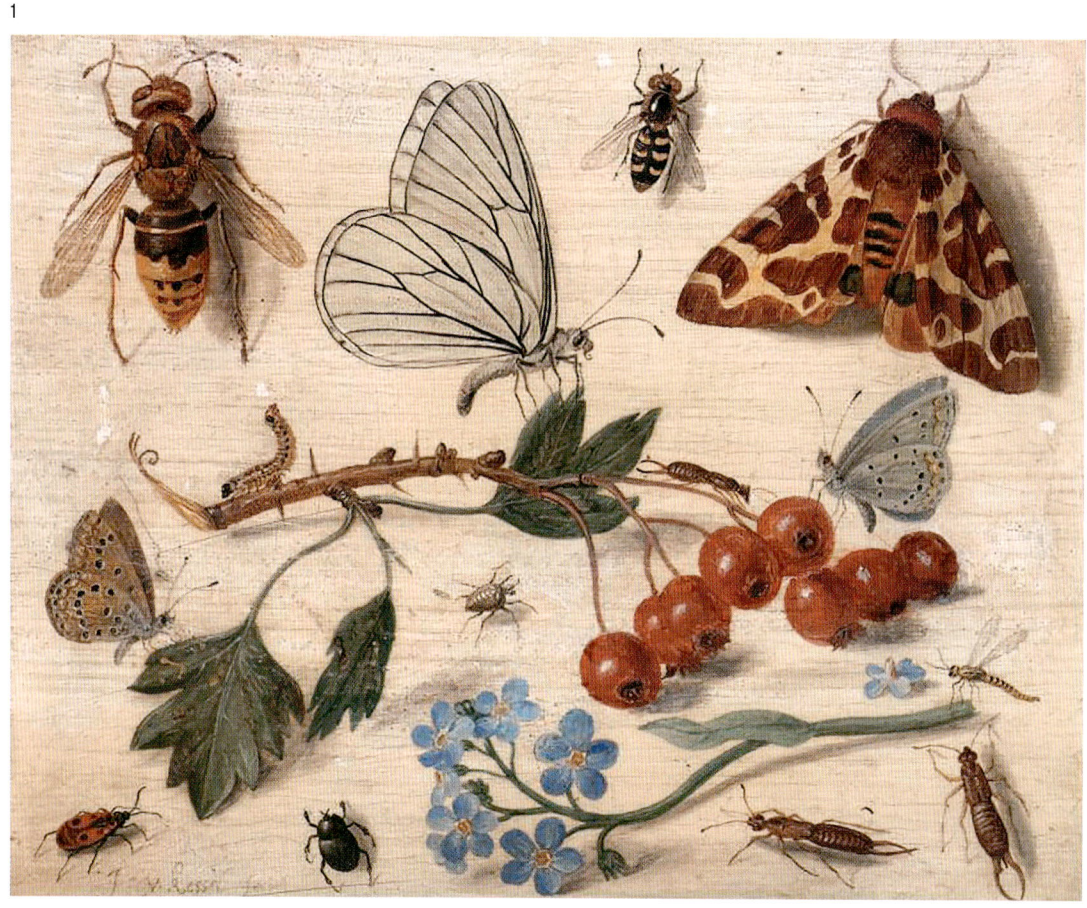

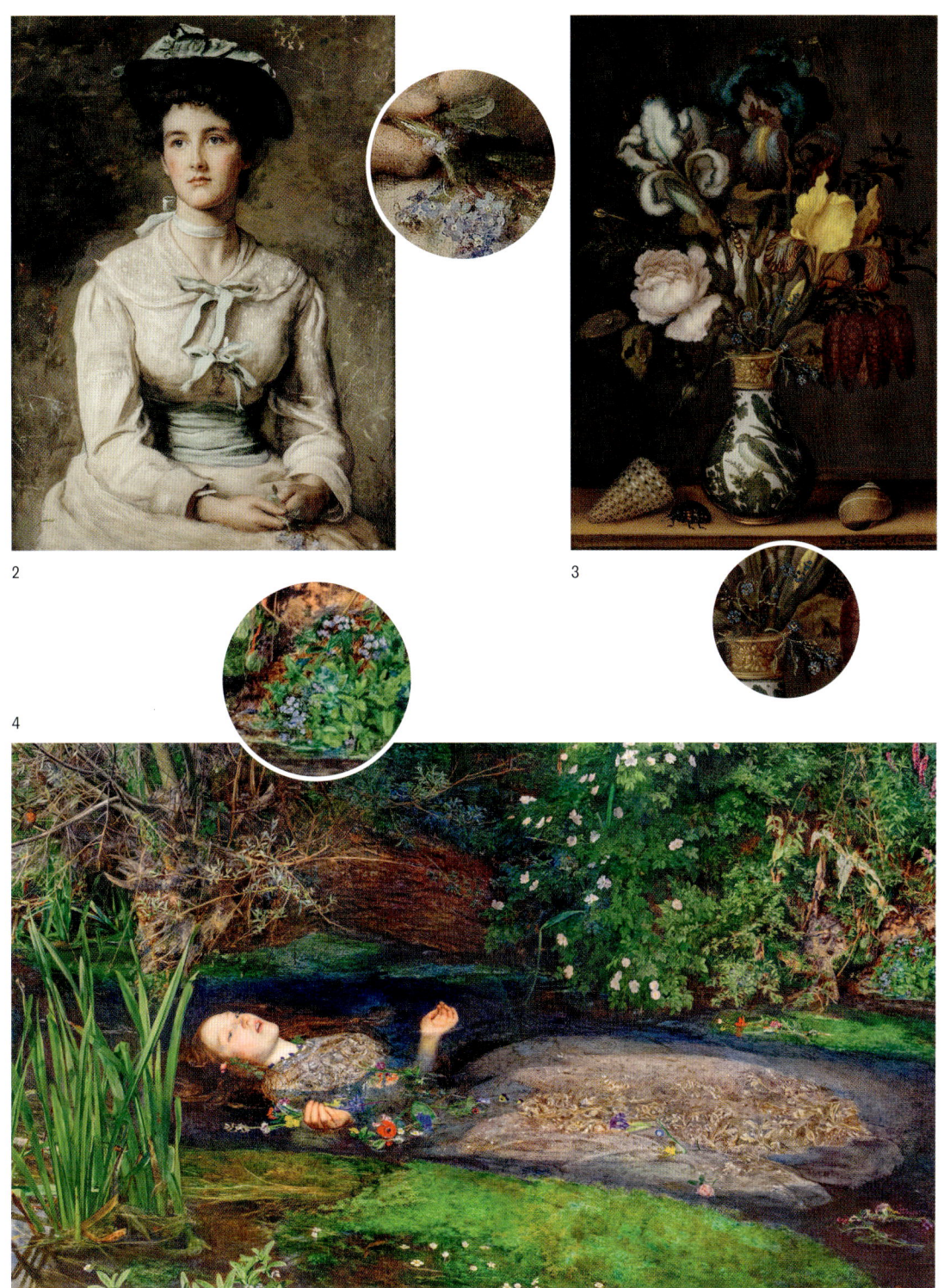

2

3

4

Daisy

Whether woven into crowns in Pre-Raphaelite paintings or scattered across Impressionist landscapes, daisies remain an enduring emblem of purity, renewal and nature's quiet elegance. Frequently associated with innocence, purity and simplicity, daisies have been featured by artists to symbolize childhood, innocence and freshness. In early Christian paintings, daisies were often depicted in scenes featuring the Virgin Mary to highlight her chastity and grace. The daisy has also frequently been included in portraits of younger sitters to convey youthfulness, a lack of artifice and innocence. From the eighteenth century, artists sometimes featured the daisy to symbolize love and nostalgia. In Victorian floral symbolism, daisies represented loyalty and new beginnings, making them popular subjects in decorative arts and still-life compositions. John William Waterhouse (1849–1917) painted *Ophelia* in 1910, incorporating the daisies mentioned in Shakespeare's text to symbolize innocence, purity, remembrance and unrequited love. More modern artists have used the daisy's bright, unassuming form to evoke themes of optimism and resilience.

1

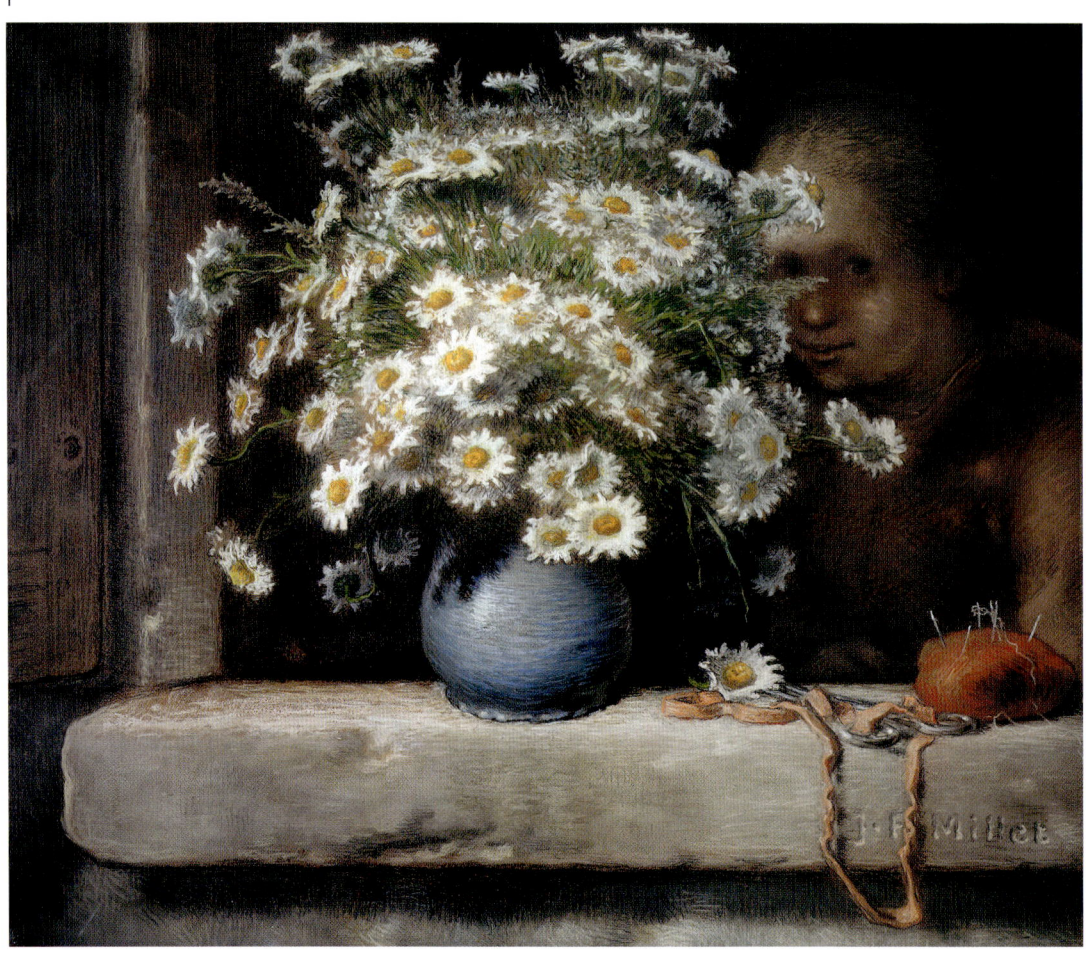

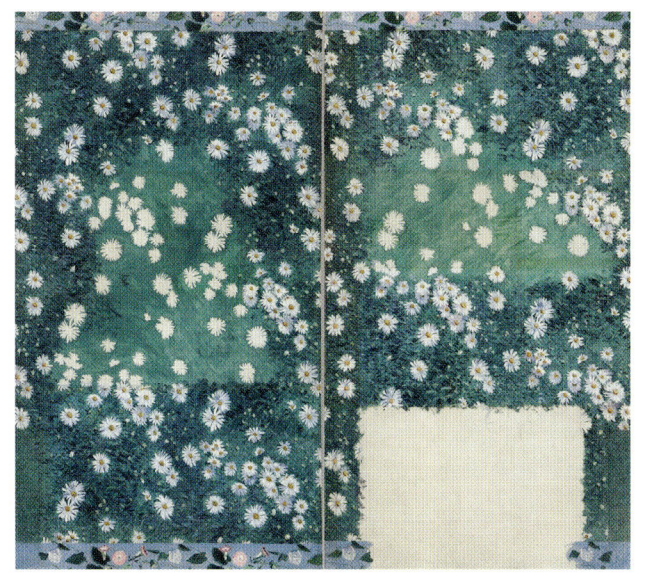

2

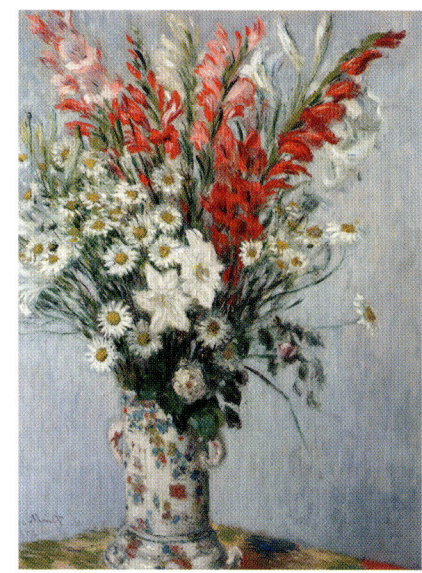

3

4

5

1. *Bouquet of Daisies,* Jean-François Millet, 1866
2. *Bed of Daisies,* Gustave Caillebotte, 1893
3. *Bouquet of Gladiolas, Lilies and Daisies*, Claude Monet, 1878
4. *Ophelia,* John William Waterhouse, 1910
5. *A Young Girl with Daisies,* Pierre Auguste Renoir, 1889

Iris

Across time and cultures, irises have served as compelling visual metaphors for optimism, resilience, insight, transformation and the connection between earthly and spiritual realms. In ancient Greece, the iris was associated with the goddess Iris and, thanks to its pointed petals, often featured in memorial art to guide souls to the afterlife. In Christian iconography, the sword-like leaves came to be associated with the Virgin Mary's sorrows and suffering. The flower also represented purity or the Holy Trinity because of its three-petaled form. In Japan, the iris has long symbolized protection and renewal, appearing in woodblock prints by artists including Katsushika Hokusai (c. 1760-1849). In the nineteenth century, Van Gogh painted irises, conveying his beliefs, hope and resilience. The iris also inspired Alphonse Mucha (1860-1939), who painted it to express natural beauty, elegance and the harmony between humans and nature, which were core ideals of the Art Nouveau movement. In his 1898 panel *Iris*, the flower serves as an allegorical extension of the female figure, embodying grace and organic fluidity.

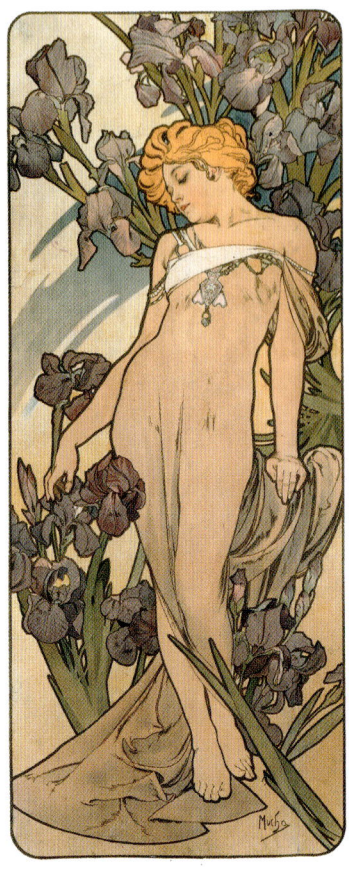

1

2

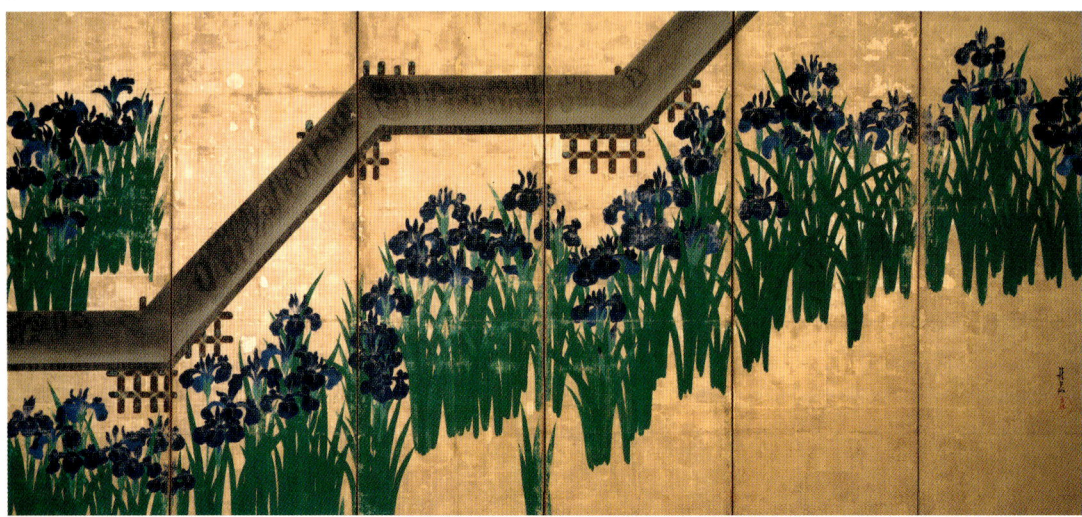

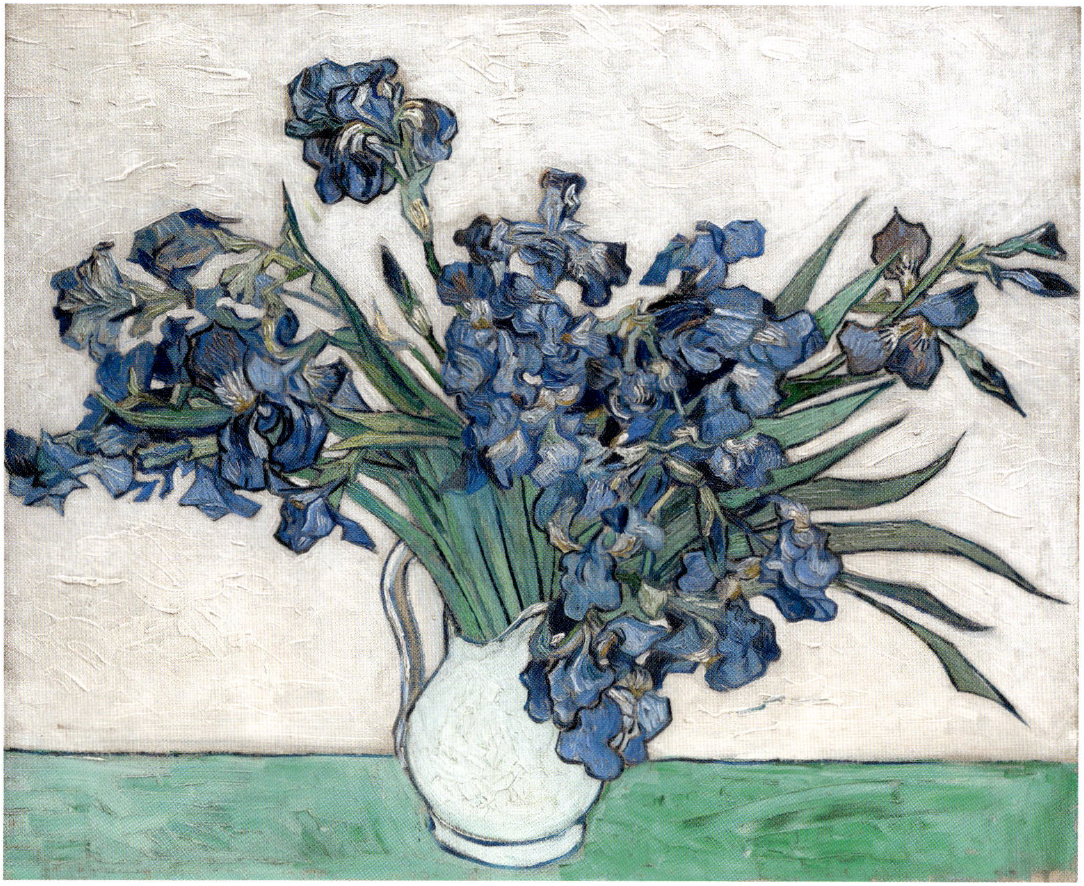

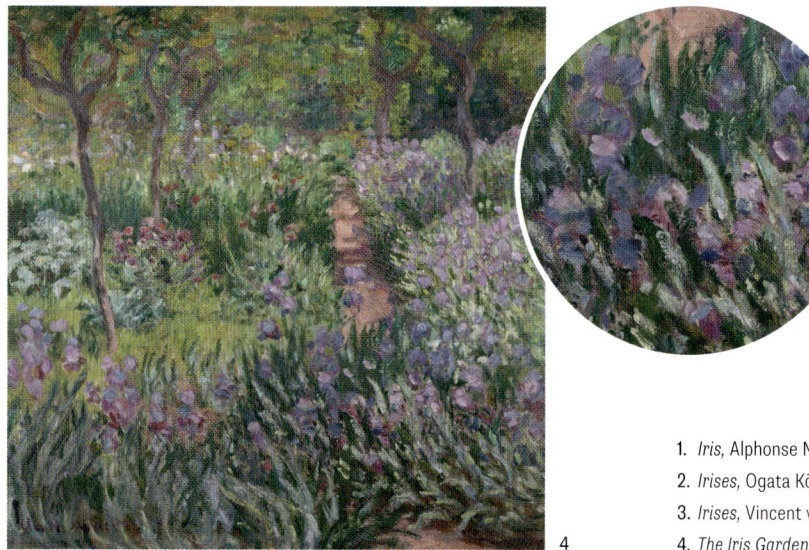

3

4

1. *Iris,* Alphonse Mucha, 1898
2. *Irises,* Ogata Kōrin, early eighteenth century
3. *Irises,* Vincent van Gogh, 1889
4. *The Iris Garden at Giverny,* Claude Monet, 1899-90

Rose

One of the most enduring symbols in art, the rose has also long been associated with love, beauty, passion and secrecy. Ancient Greek and Roman artists connected it with Aphrodite/Venus to symbolize love and devotion. Within Christian iconography, the rose has long signified divine grace, with red roses often associated with Christ's sacrifice and white roses symbolizing purity. Reinforcing themes of transience and mortality, they have frequently appeared in still-life paintings. During the nineteenth century, several artists featured roses to convey meanings based on their colours: red for deep love; pink for admiration; and yellow for friendship. Many artists have embraced the rose as an ethereal symbol, weaving it into portraits and allegorical compositions, such as *The Roses of Heliogabalus* (1888) by Lawrence Alma-Tadema (1836-1912), *The Soul of the Rose* (1908) by John William Waterhouse (1849-1917) and *Roses in a Blue-Green Vase* (1942) by Helene Schjerfbeck (1862-1946).

1. *Roses in a Blue-Green Vase,* Helene Schjerfbeck, 1942
2. *The Soul of the Rose,* John William Waterhouse, 1908
3. *Roses, Convolvulus, Poppies, and Other Flowers in an Urn on a Stone Ledge,* Rachel Ruysch, c. 1680
4. *The Roses of Heliogabalus,* Lawrence Alma-Tadema, 1888

1

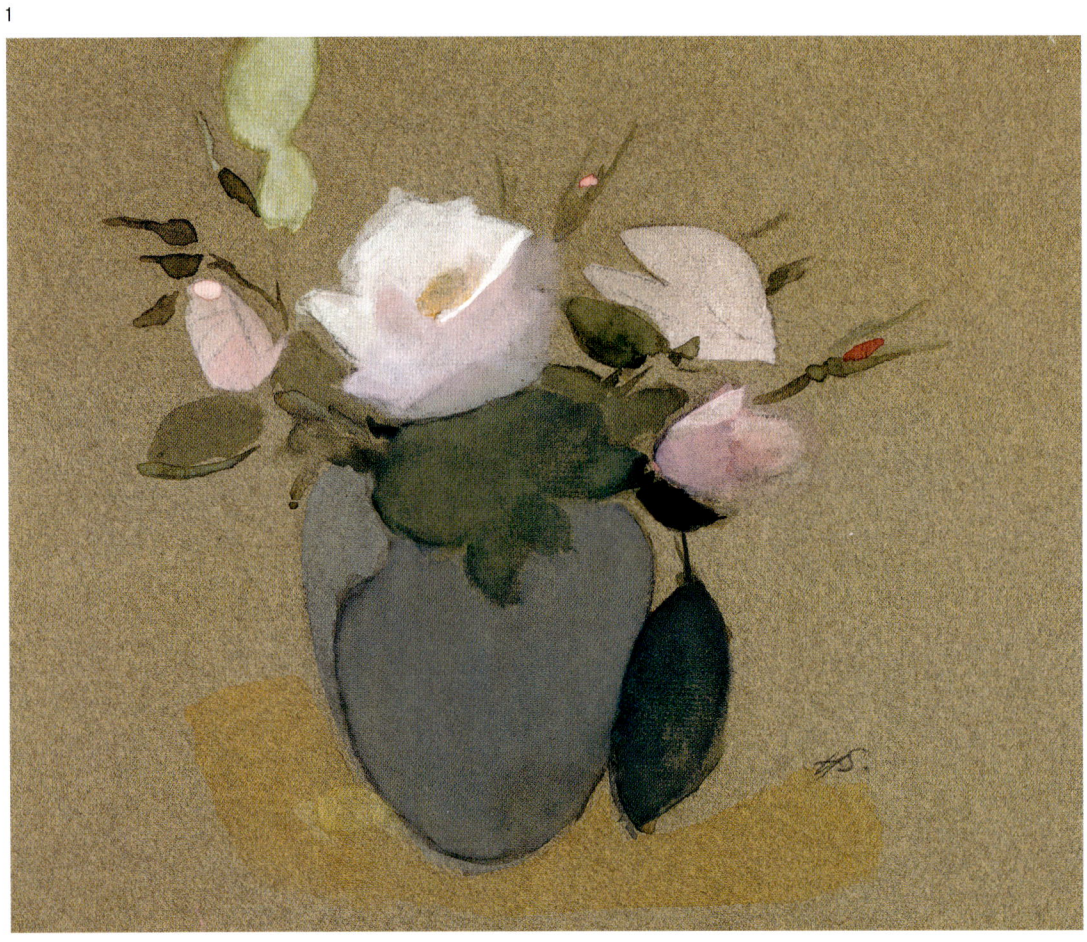

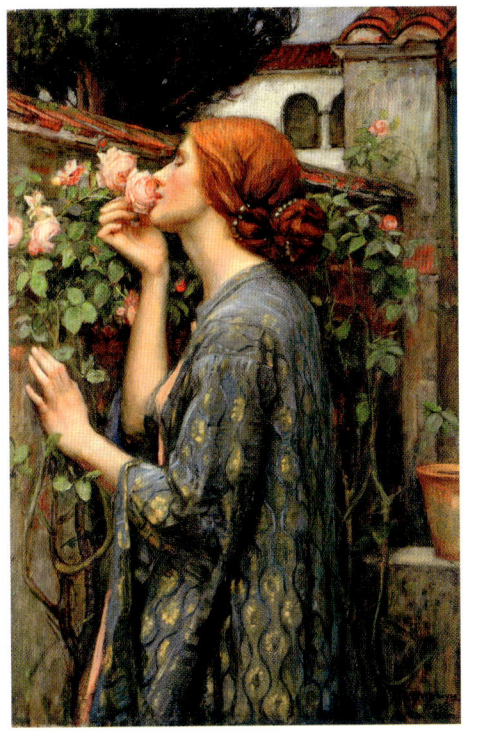

2

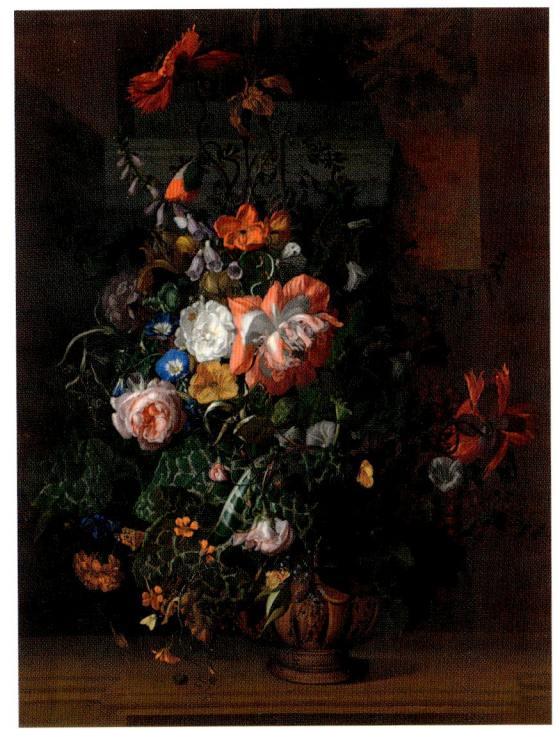

3

4

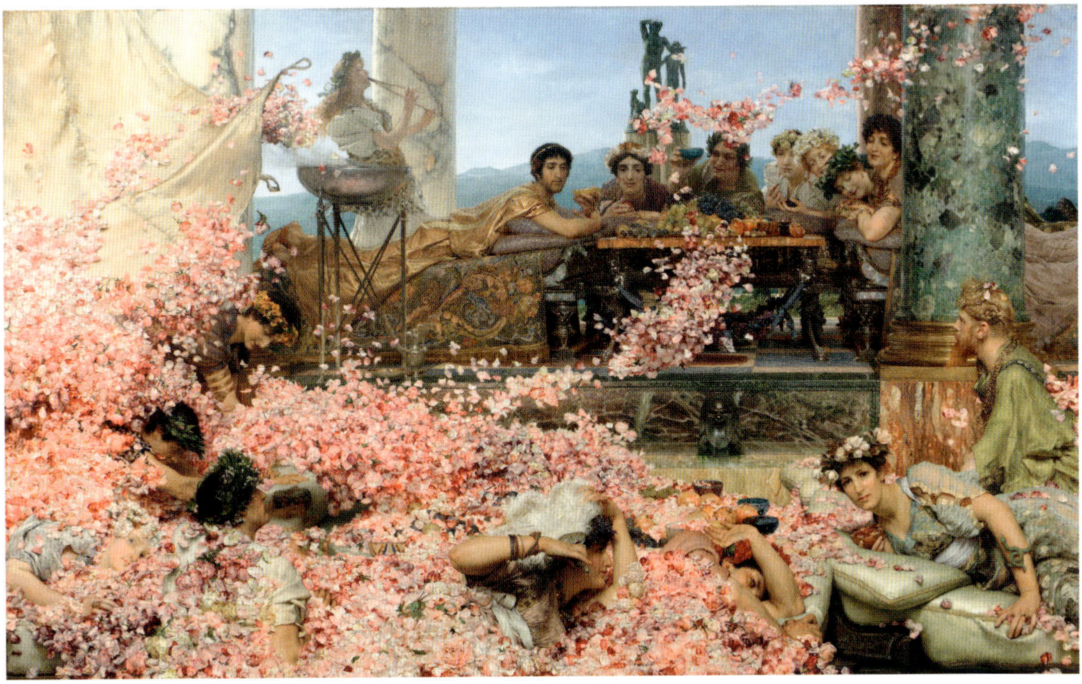

Lotus

The lotus is often depicted as embodying purity, enlightenment, personal transformation and spiritual awakening. In ancient Egyptian art, the lotus symbolized creation and rebirth, frequently appearing in depictions of the afterlife. Chinese and Japanese paintings have used lotus flowers to convey harmony, inner peace and resilience. In Hindu and Buddhist traditions, the lotus represents divine beauty and spiritual growth, and has often been depicted beneath the Buddha and deities such as Vishnu and Lakshmi. It is frequently intricately carved into temple walls, pillars and ceilings, and embedded into paintings and pottery, also symbolizing cosmic harmony. The flower's ability to surface from murky waters intact and beautiful has made it a symbol for the ability to rise above adversity. In Western art, the lotus has occasionally been linked to themes of renewal and femininity, particularly in Art Nouveau designs. Its elegant form and deep symbolic resonance make it a common feature in religious iconography, decorative arts, and contemporary interpretations.

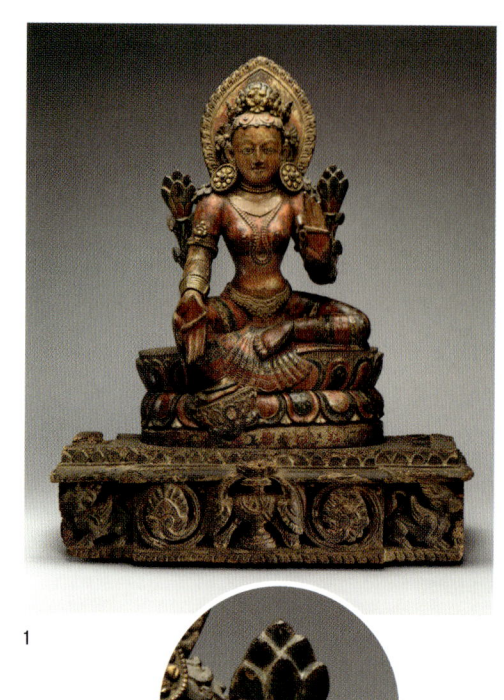

1

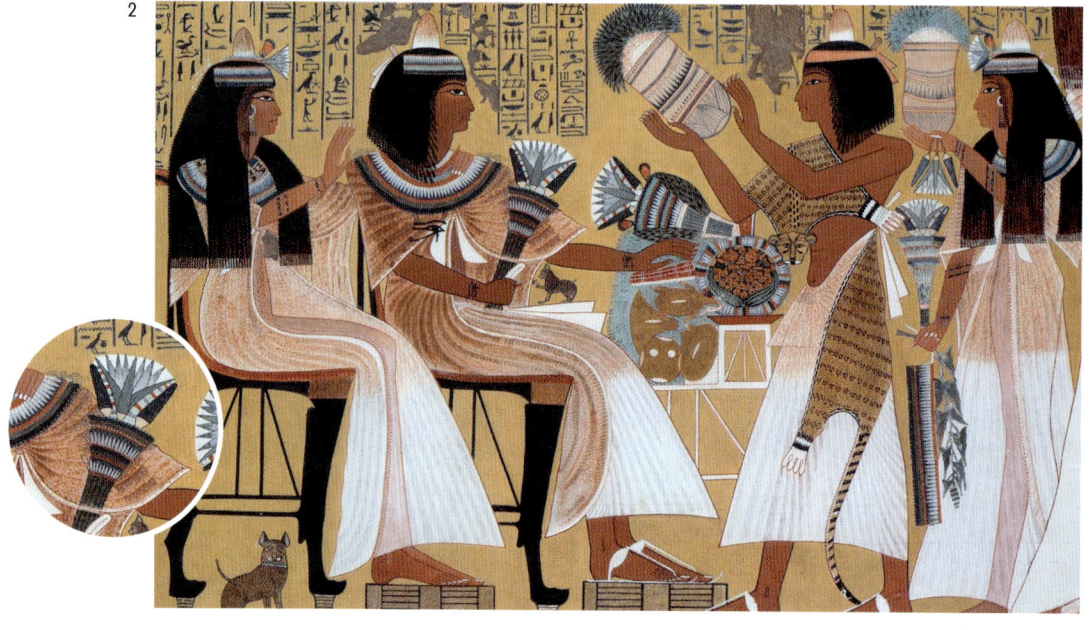

2

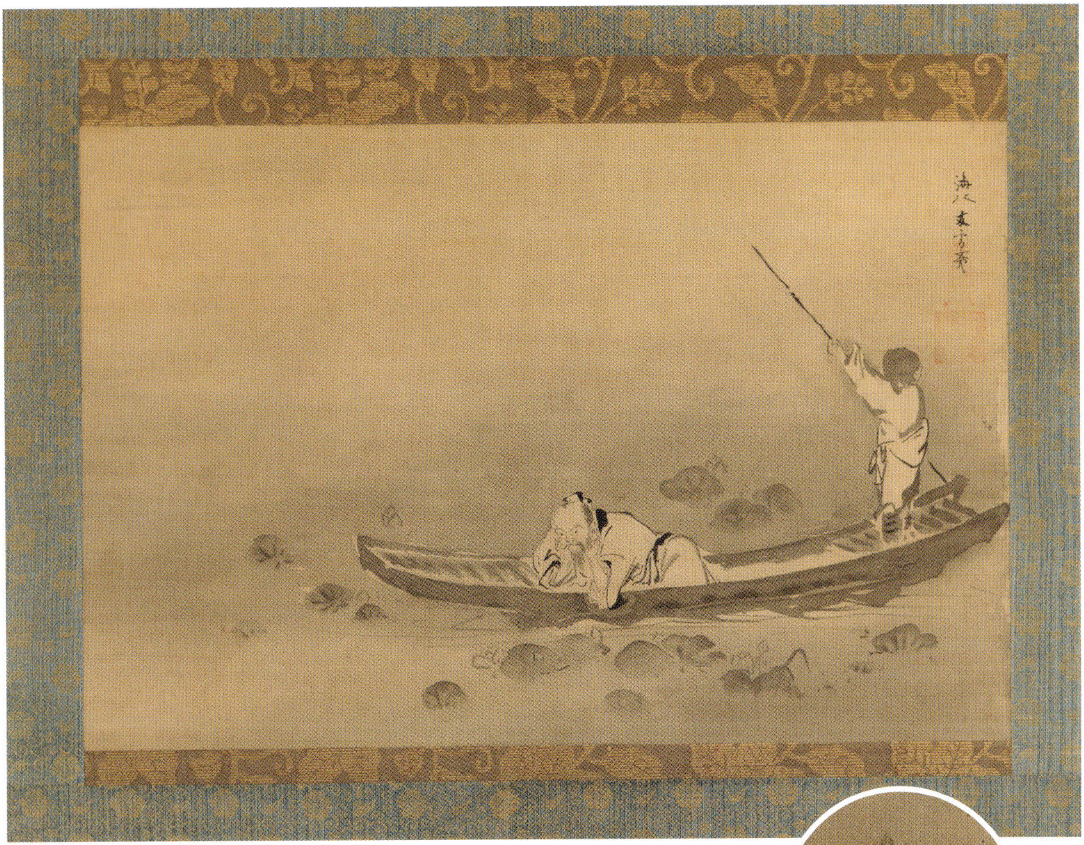

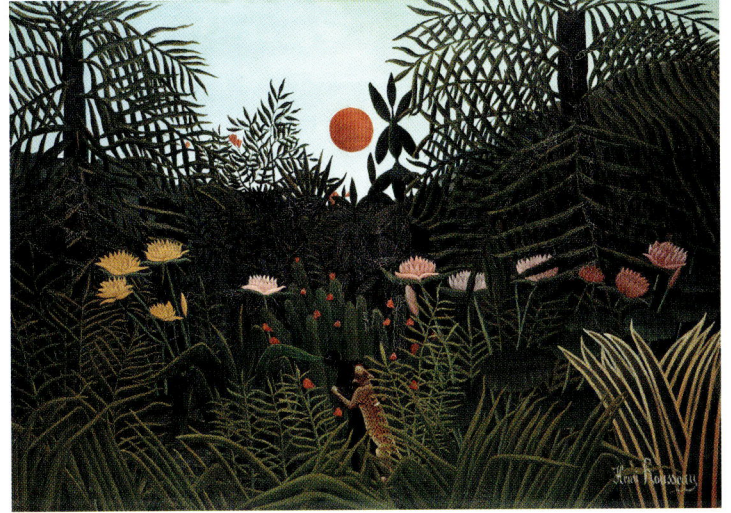

3

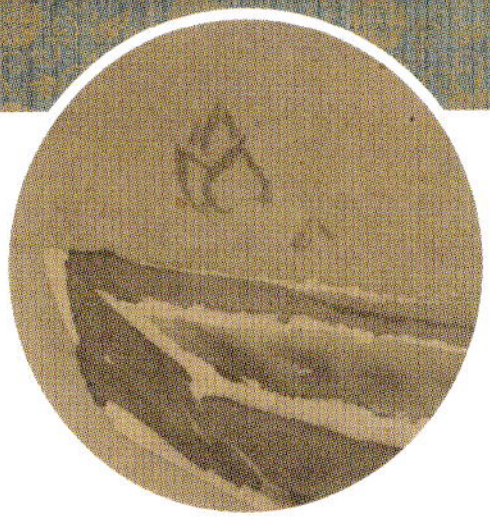

4

1. *Lotus Goddess, Lakshmi,* Nepal,
   seventeenth century
2. *Ipuy and Wife Receive Offerings from
   Their Children,* Egypt, c. 1279–1213 BCE
3. *Zhou Maoshu Admiring Lotuses,* Kaihō
   Yūsetsu, mid-seventeenth century
4. *Man Attacked by a Jaguar,*
   Henri Rousseau, 1910

Lily

Across time and cultures, the lily has represented purity, beauty and spirituality in a vast range of art. In ancient Egypt, lilies were associated with fertility and rebirth, often appearing in stylized form in tomb paintings. Greek and Roman art depicted lilies in connection with the goddess Hera/Juno, who was seen as the 'ideal woman', the goddess of marriage and the family and protector of women in childbirth. In Christian art, the white lily symbolizes the Virgin Mary's purity. The flowers emphasize divine grace, so they were often included in paintings of the Annunciation, such as that by Domenico Veneziano (c. 1410-61) in c. 1442-48. This tradition continued even into the early twentieth century. Although not depicted as a specific emblem, Claude Monet painted water lilies for most of his later life, including in his vast and ambitious series, *Nymphéas*. To him, they represented tranquillity, calm, light and artistic experimentation.

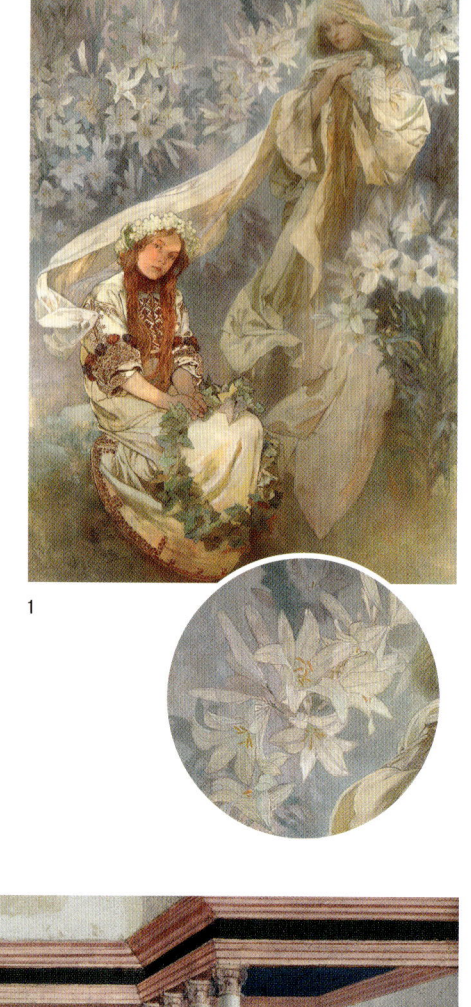

1

2

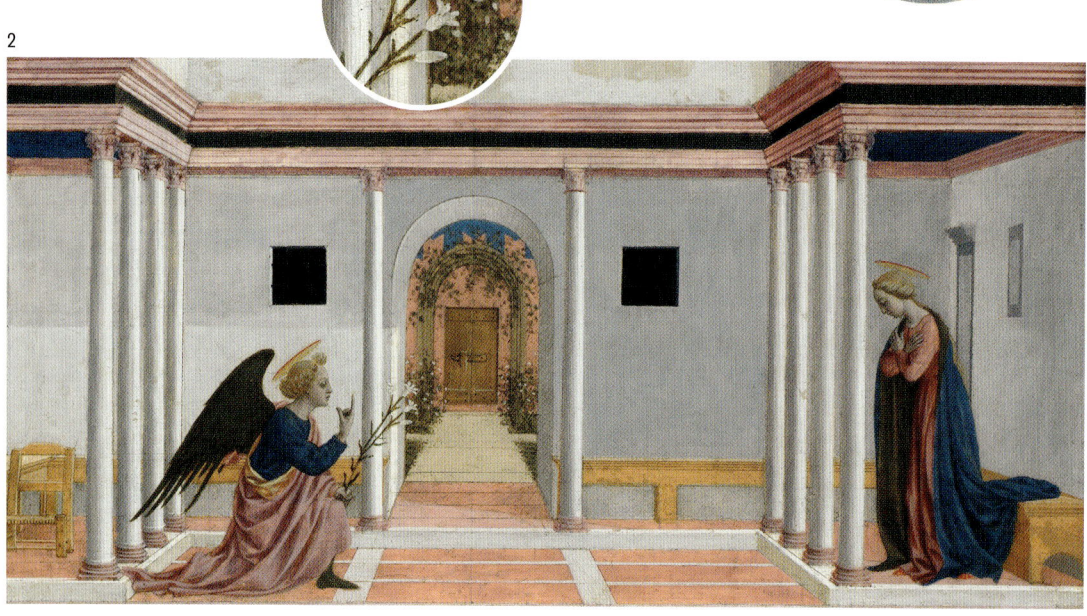

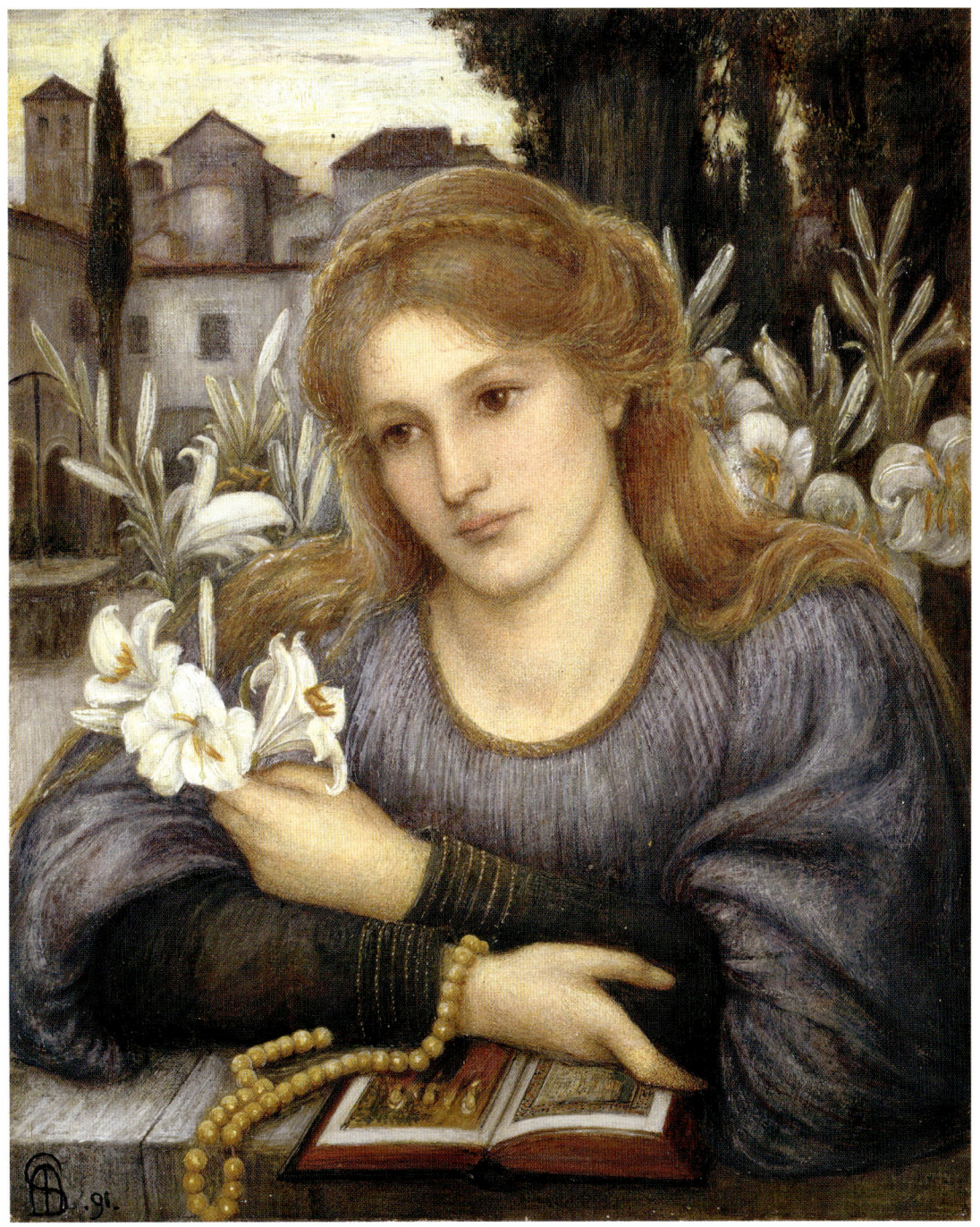

3

Carnation

First mentioned by the Greek botanist Theophrastus in the fourth century BCE as Dianthus or 'God's flower' the carnation was probably imported to the Western world at the end of the thirteenth century. According to a medieval legend, when the Virgin Mary saw her son crucified, her tears fell to the ground and grew into carnations. In some paintings, the Virgin Mary or Jesus is portrayed holding a carnation. In the *Madonna of the Pinks* (1507) by Raphael and *Madonna of the Carnation* (1478-80) by Leonardo da Vinci, the carnation symbolizes divine and maternal love, as well as future suffering, foreshadowing the Crucifixion. In Northern European traditions, the carnation is a symbol of marriage. In portraiture, especially during the sixteenth and seventeenth centuries, carnations could be symbols of engagement or the promise of love. In Dutch still-life painting, the carnation sometimes appeared as a vanitas symbol, suggesting the fleeting nature of beauty and life. In *Portrait of Georg Gisze* (1532) by Hans Holbein the Younger (c. 1497-1543), the carnation may be symbolic of love, beauty or the fragility of life.

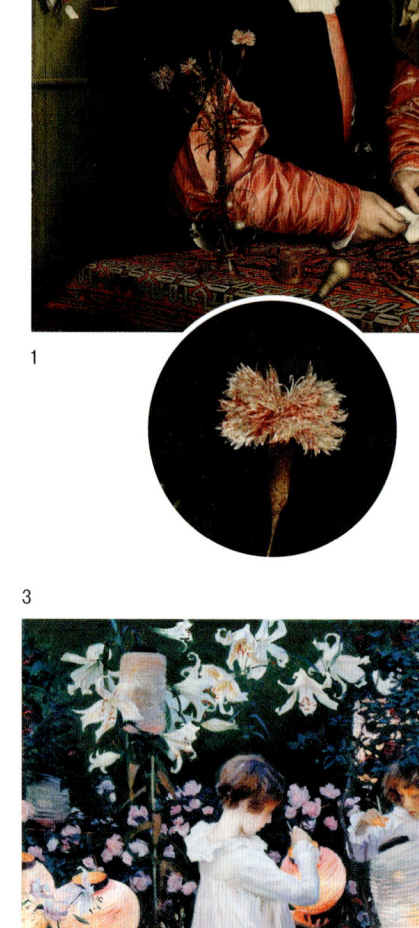

1

2

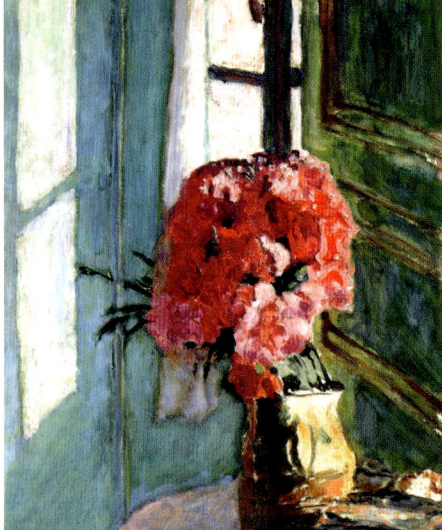

3

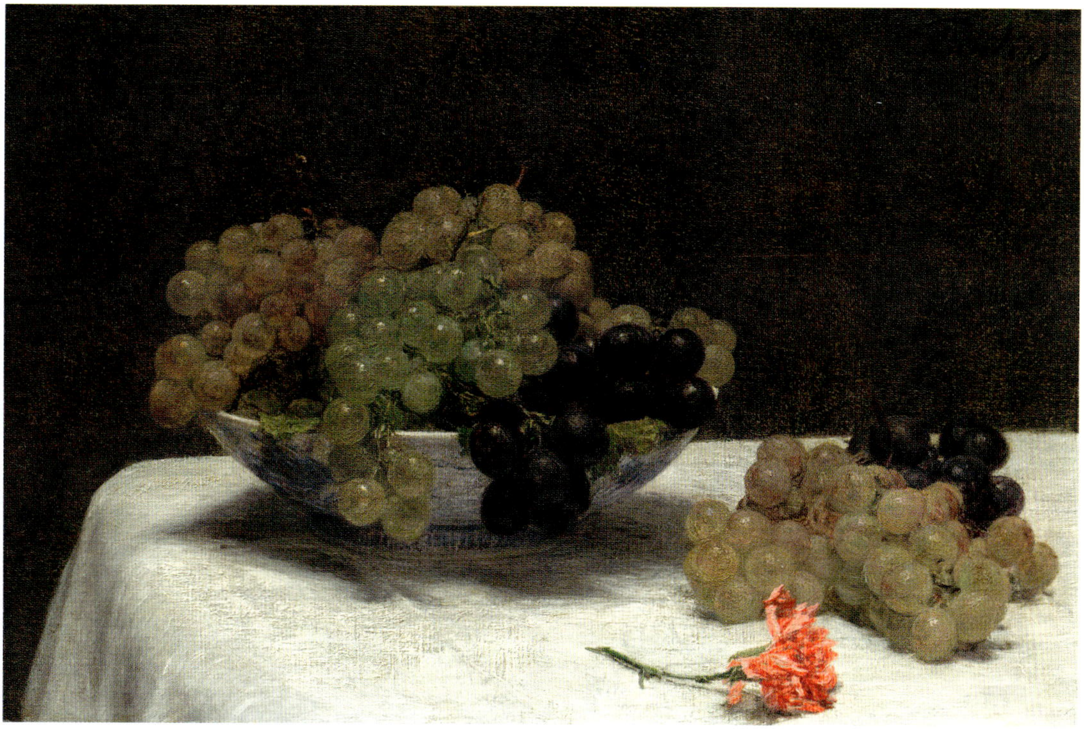

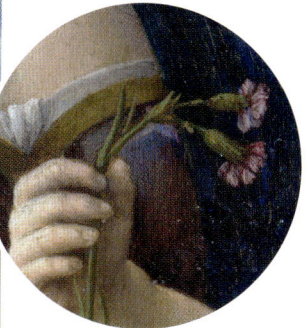

4

5

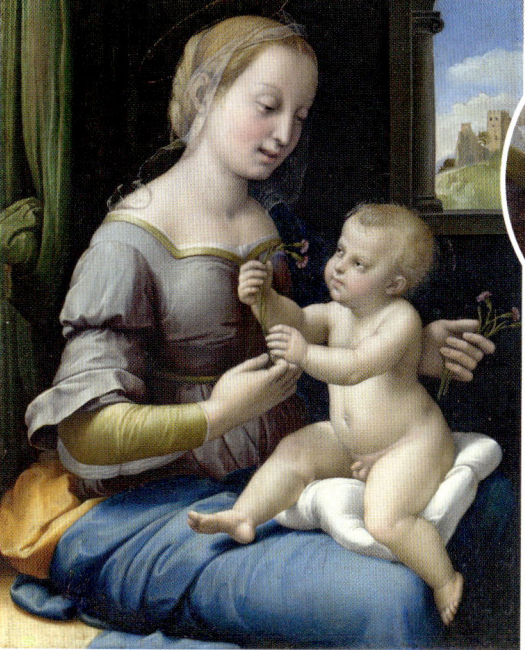

1. *Portrait of Georg Gisze*, Hans Holbein the Younger, 1532
2. *Carnations*, Pierre Bonnard, c. 1921
3. *Carnation, Lily, Lily, Rose*, John Singer Sargent, 1885-86
4. *Still Life with Grapes and a Carnation*, Henri Fantin-Latour, c. 1880
5. *Madonna of the Pinks*, Raphael, 1507

Cypress

Originating in ancient Greece and Rome, the cypress became associated with cemeteries and mourning, due to its evergreen nature and its height, which appears to point towards the heavens. This tradition continued in Christian art, where the cypress was often featured to represent the soul's perpetuity and the promise of eternal life. It frequently appeared in the backgrounds of Crucifixion scenes or religious landscapes to evoke solemnity and spiritual hope. In Renaissance and Baroque paintings, the cypress added emotional gravity to religious and mythological scenes, serving as a visual indication of loss or the passage into the hereafter. In nineteenth-century art, particularly among artists like Vincent van Gogh, cypress trees assumed a more expressive and emotional role, often featured to convey his inner turmoil or loneliness. In the *Isle of the Dead* series by Arnold Böcklin (1827-1901), cypress trees symbolize death, mourning and the transition to the afterlife.

1

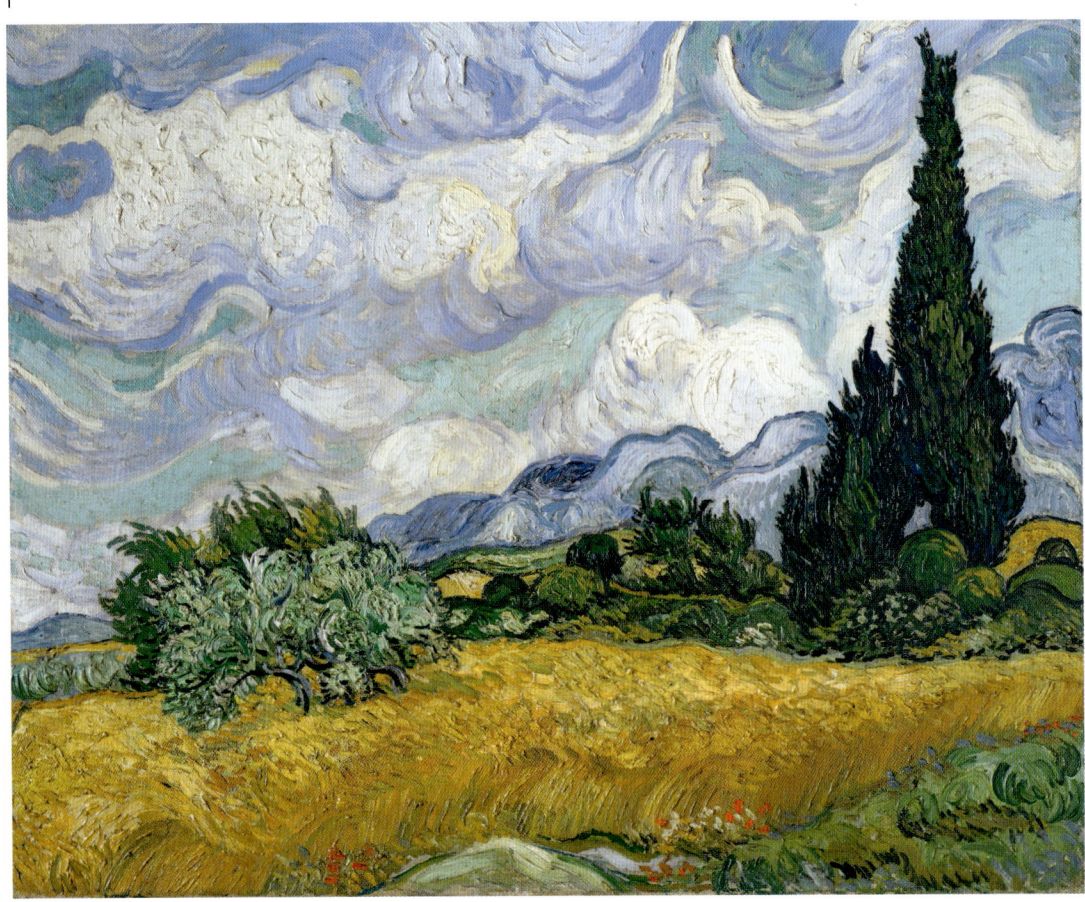

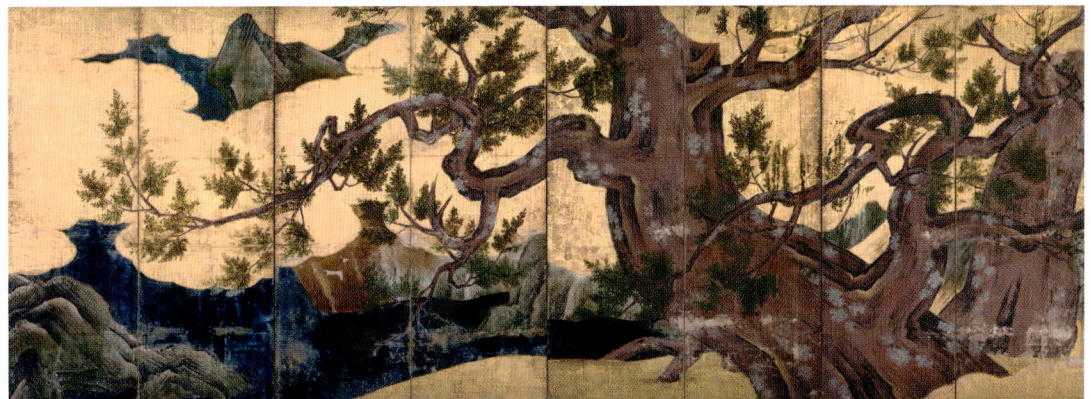

2

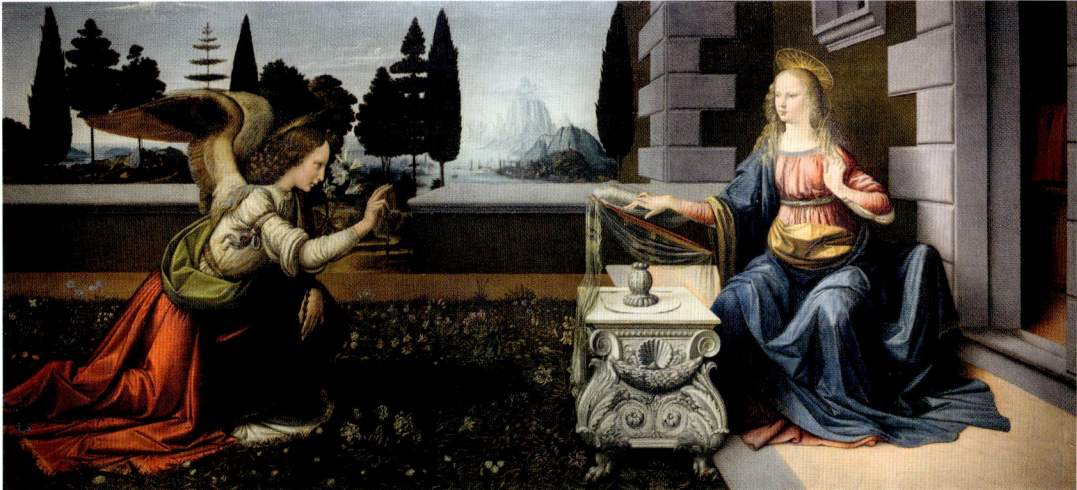

3

4

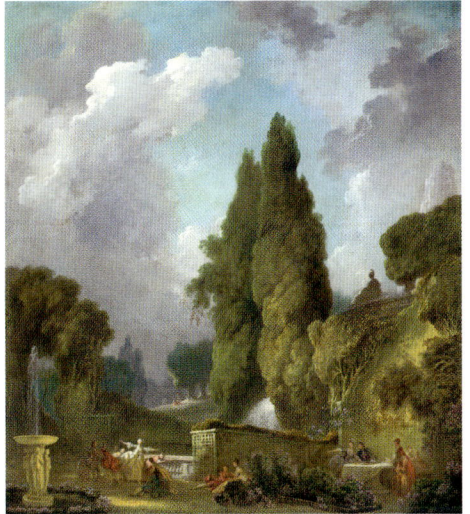

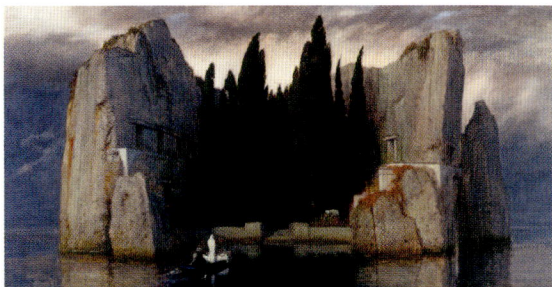

5

1. *A Wheatfield with Cypresses,* Vincent van Gogh, 1889
2. *Cypress Trees screen,* Kanō Eitoku, sixteenth–seventeenth century
3. *Annunciation,* Leonardo da Vinci, c. 1472–76
4. *Blindman's Buff,* Jean-Honoré Fragonard, c. 1775–80
5. *Isle of the Dead,* Arnold Böcklin, 1883

Laurel

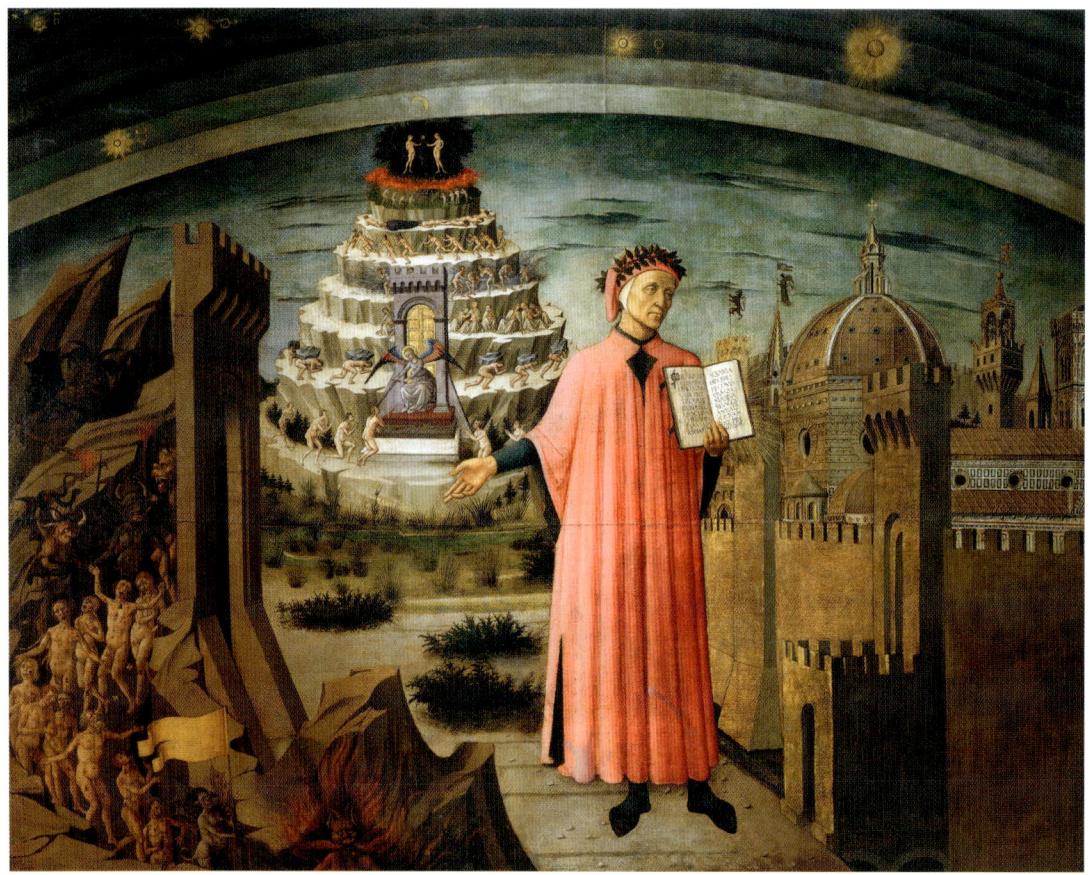

1

Since antiquity, the laurel has been a potent symbol of victory, achievement, divine power and poetic excellence, particularly when its leaves are fashioned into wreaths. In Greco-Roman art, laurel crowns were awarded to victorious athletes, generals and poets, embodying honour and glory. Statues abounded of gods or heroes carrying laurel wreaths on their heads. The god Apollo, often depicted wearing a laurel wreath, further cemented the plant's association with divine inspiration and artistic triumph. During the Renaissance, artists revived classical motifs, and laurel wreaths began to appear in the portraits of scholars, humanists and poets, signifying their intellectual stature and moral virtue. In *Napoleon I on his Imperial Throne* (1806), by Jean-Auguste-Dominique Ingres (1780–1867), the emperor wears a golden laurel crown. Beyond crowns, the laurel's presence in allegorical scenes and emblems reinforced messages of excellence, enduring fame and the rewards of virtuous striving, making it a recurrent motif in both secular and religious art.

1. *Dante Alighieri with Florence and the Realms of the Divine Comedy,* Domenico di Michelino, 1465
2. *Pandora,* Alexandre Cabanel, 1873
3. *Napoleon I on his Imperial Throne,* Jean-Auguste-Dominique Ingres, 1806
4. *The Apotheosis of the Slavs,* from the 'Slav Epic', Alphonse Mucha, 1926

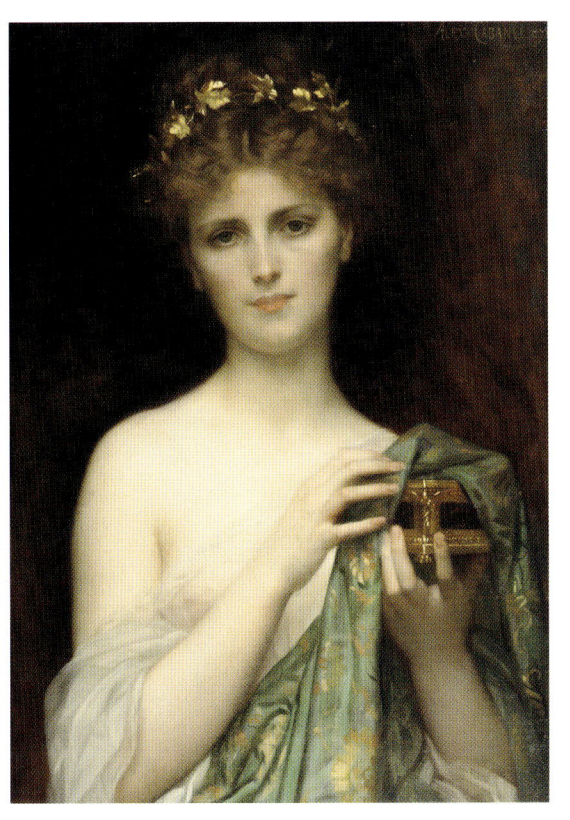

2

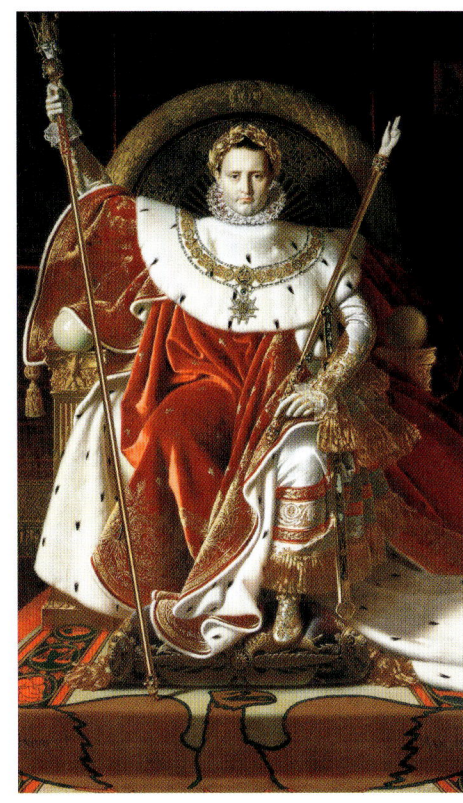

3

4

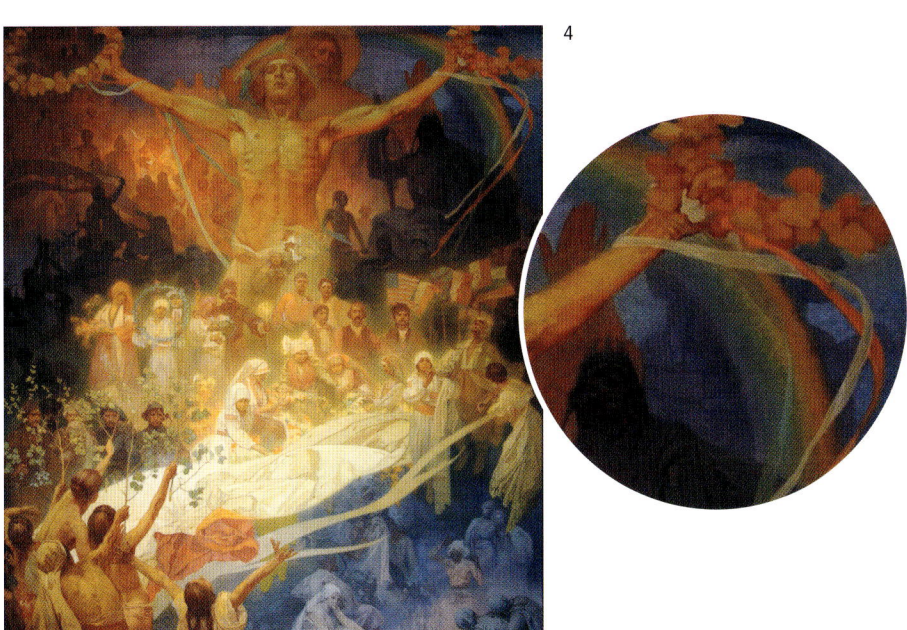

Palm

Often associated with victory, peace and eternal life, or triumph, faith and hope, the depiction of the palm varies depending on the religious, historical and mythological contexts. Often associated with the Tree of Life, the palm has both spiritual and artistic significance in Jewish, Islamic and Christian traditions, symbolizing grace, elegance, victory, wealth and productivity. It is frequently associated with paradise in medieval and Renaissance art. In Christian iconography, palm leaves are commonly seen in scenes of Christ's entry into Jerusalem, commemorating triumph and foreshadowing sacrifice. Christian martyrs are often depicted holding palms to signify their spiritual victory over death. Ancient Roman emperors and victorious gladiators were often depicted with palm branches, reinforcing their association with conquest and honour. Palm trees also appear in landscapes showing paradise, representing divine refuge and immortality. In Renaissance and Baroque paintings, some artists infused palm symbolism into allegorical compositions, reinforcing themes of resurrection and transcendence.

1. *Palm Trees at Bordighera*, Claude Monet, 1884
2. *Entry of Christ into Jerusalem,* Sir Anthony van Dyck, 1617.
3. *The Palm Leaf,* William-Adolphe Bouguereau, 1894
4. *The Girlhood of Mary Virgin,* Dante Gabriel Rossetti, 1848-49

1

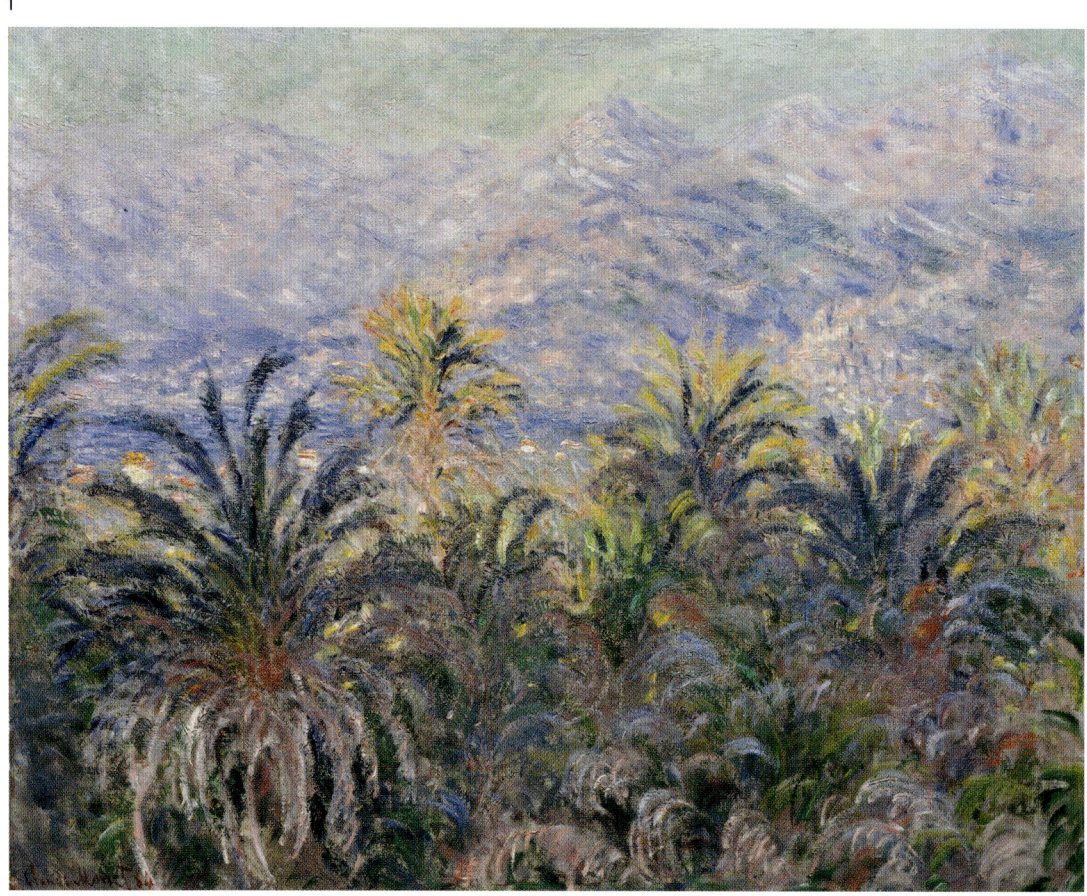

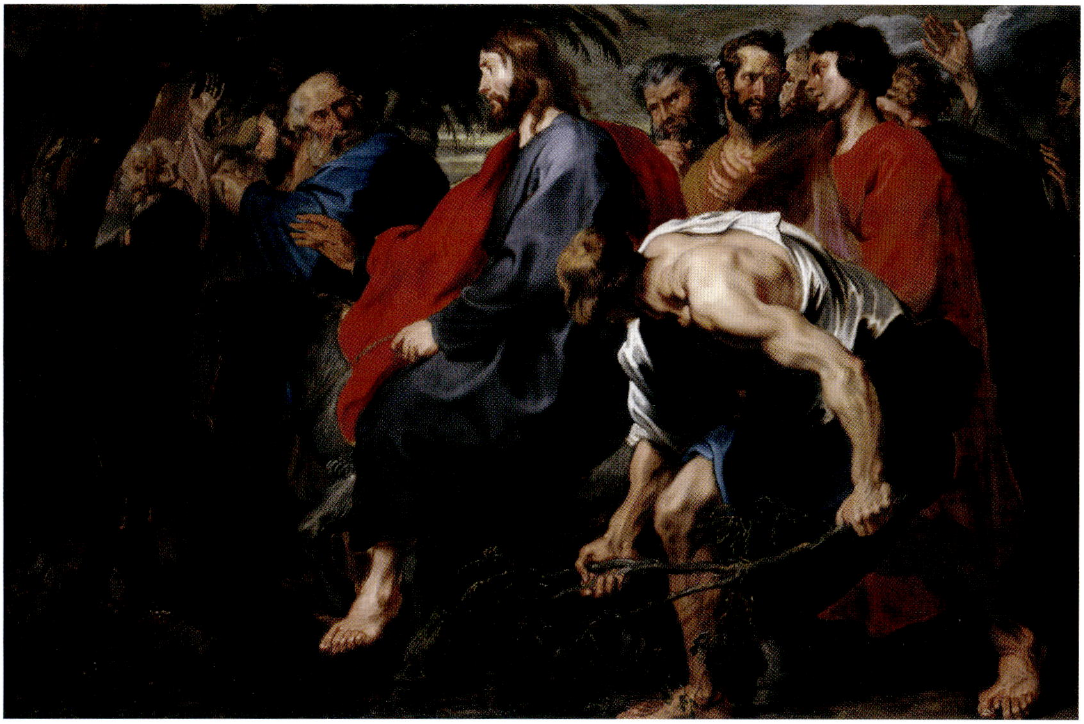

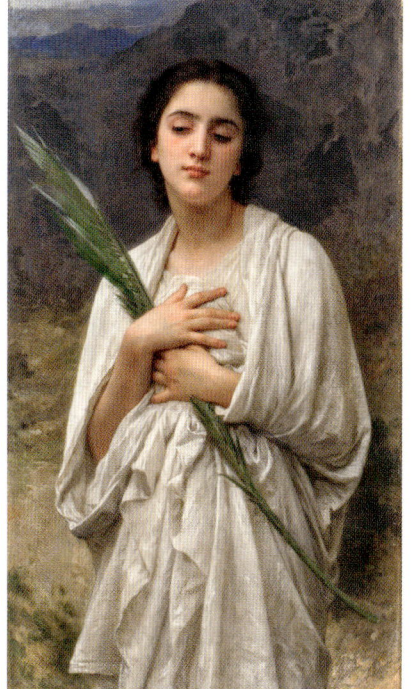

2

3

4

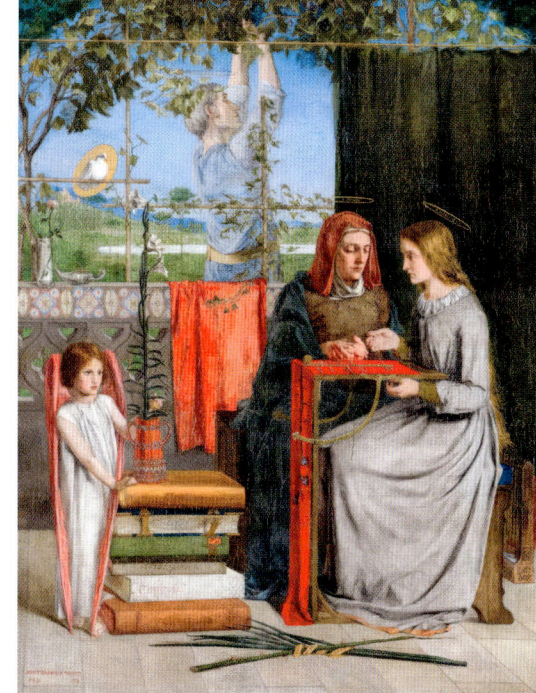

Oak

The towering presence and longevity of the oak tree have made it a powerful artistic symbol of strength, endurance, wisdom and connection to the divine and natural world. In the Celtic world, the oak was sacred to the Druids. The tree appears in Celtic knotwork and illuminated manuscripts, symbolizing wisdom, protection and the axis between earth and sky. In Greek and Roman art, the oak was sacred to Zeus/Jupiter. In *The Holy Family under an Oak Tree* (c. 1518), designed by Raphael and completed by Giulio Romano (c. 1499–1546), the oak tree represents strength, endurance and divine protection. Romantic painters, such as Caspar David Friedrich (1774–1840), used gnarled oaks in their landscapes to evoke the power of nature. In Indigenous American traditions, the oak represents resilience and ancestral wisdom, often depicted in carvings and ceremonial art. Modern artists frequently use the oak to symbolize ecology, endurance and a reminder of our place in the natural order.

1. *The Great Oak*, Jacob van Ruisdael, c. 1648
2. *The Oak Tree in the Snow,* Caspar David Friedrich, c. 1829
3. *The Holy Family under an Oak Tree,* Raphael & Giulio Romano, c. 1518
4. *Cut Down Oak in the Białowieża Forest,* Ivan Shishkin, 1892

1

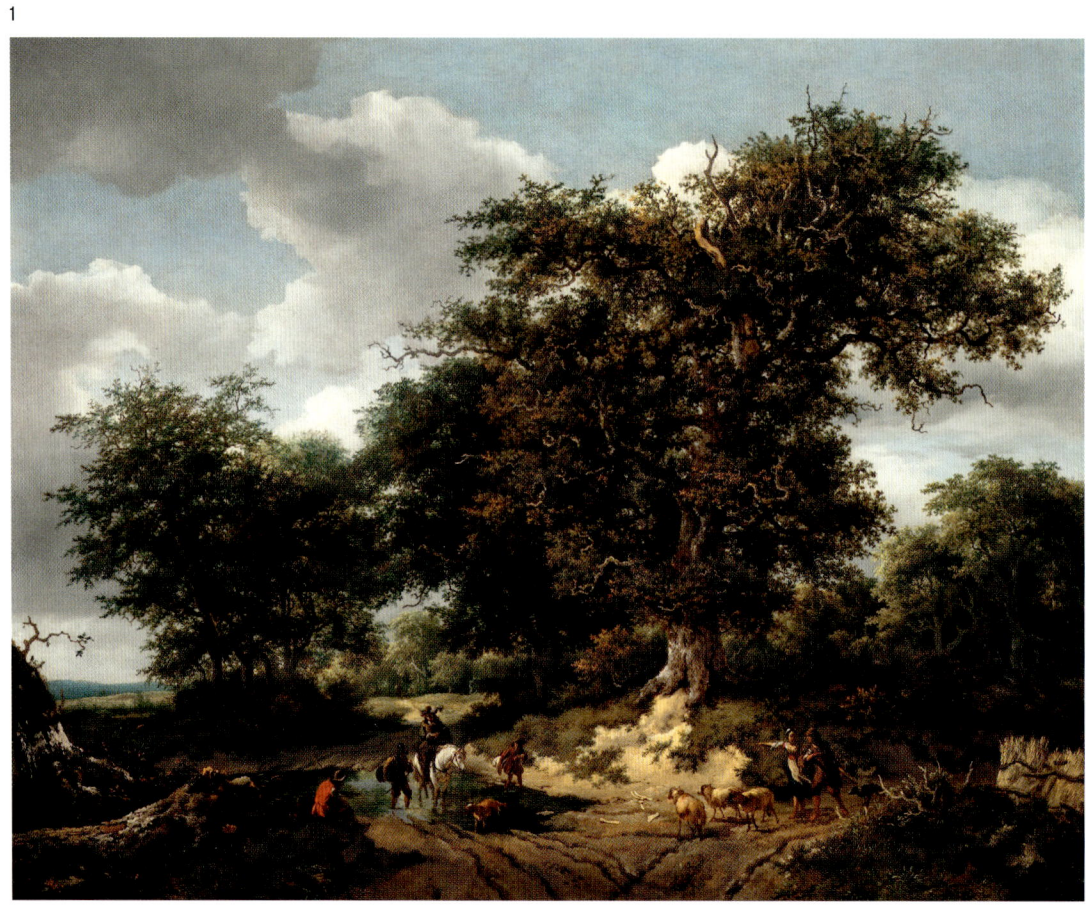

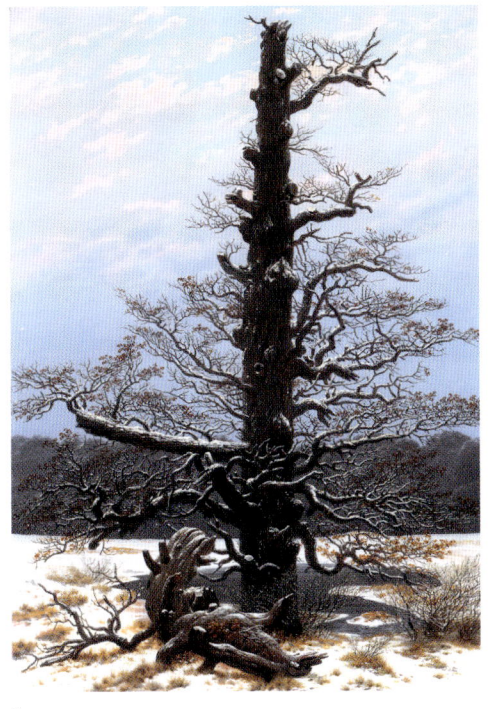

2

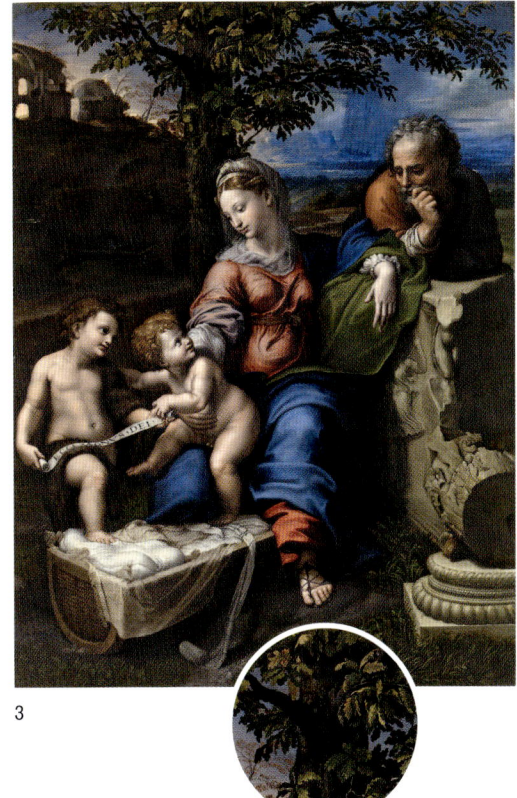

3

4

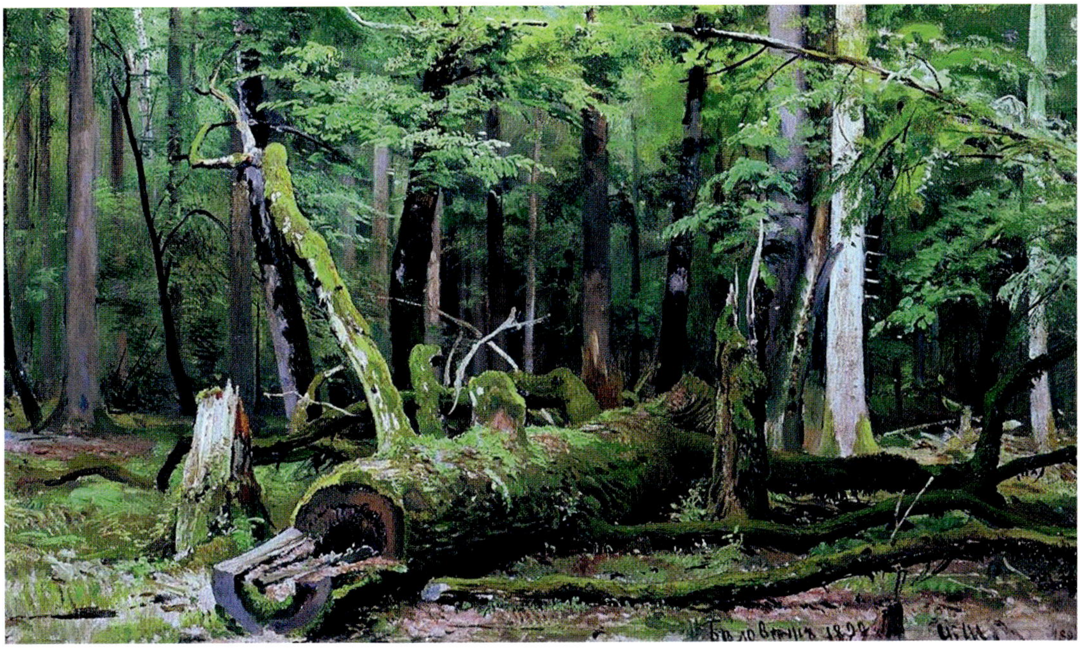

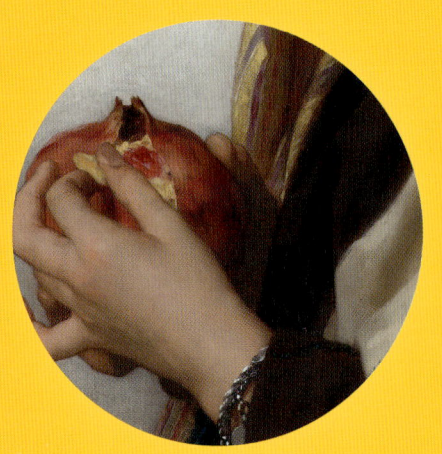

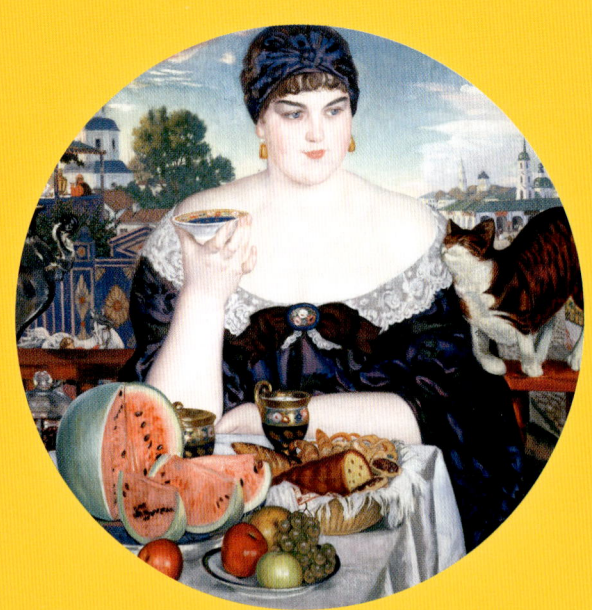

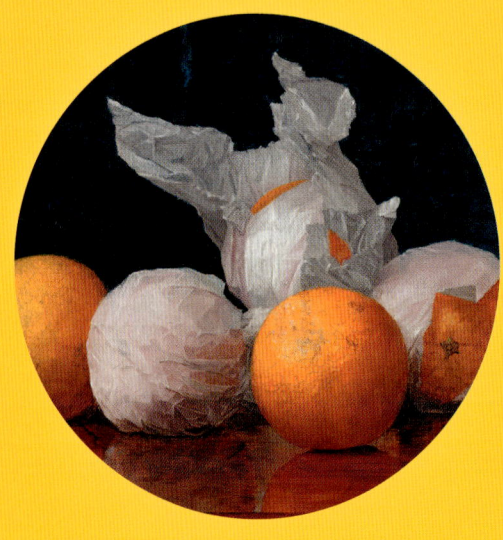

Fruit

Apple

The apple has long been used to embody themes of temptation, knowledge, sin, mortality and love in art. In Christian iconography, it often represents the fruit of the Tree of Knowledge in the Garden of Eden, signifying humanity's fall from grace, original sin and human frailty, as seen in *Adam and Eve* (1504) by Albrecht Dürer (1471–1528). In classical mythology, the golden apple played a crucial role, sparking the events that led to the Trojan War. This has been depicted in numerous works of art, such as *The Judgement of Paris* (1632–35) by Peter Paul Rubens (1577–1640). In Dutch still-life paintings, apples often symbolized transience and the fleeting nature of life, sometimes appearing partially decayed to emphasize mortality. The Surrealist René Magritte (1898–1967) painted apples in several works, such as *The Son of Man* (1964), where a large apple obscures a man's face, to question identity and perception. Apples also symbolize scientific discovery, famously linked to Newton's theory of gravity.

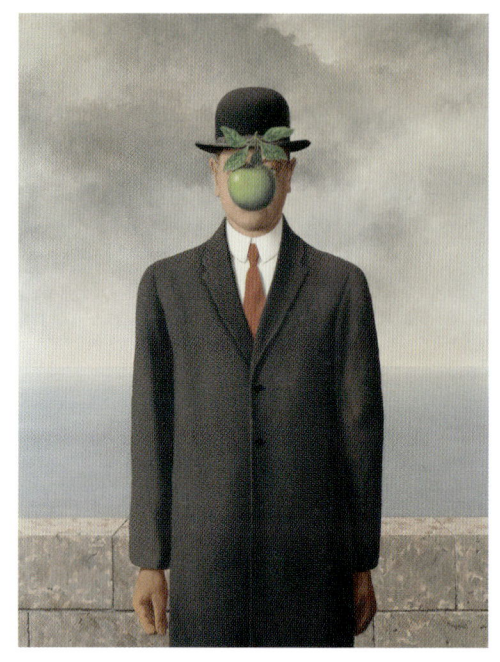

1

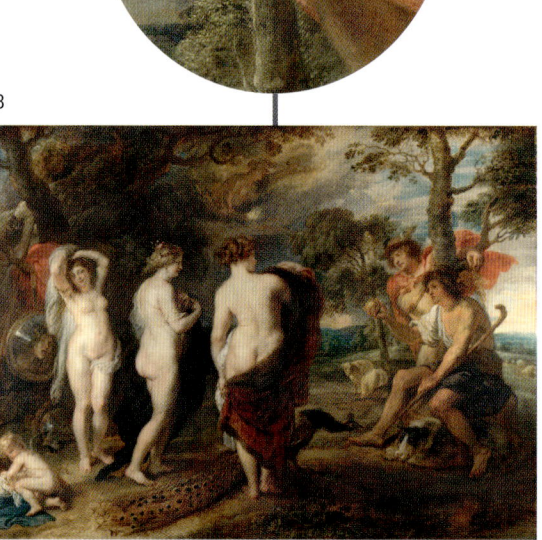

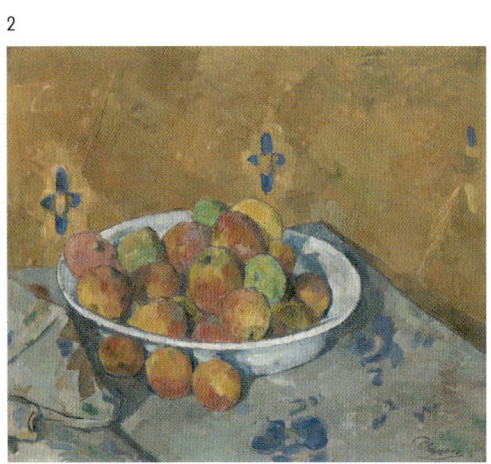

2

3

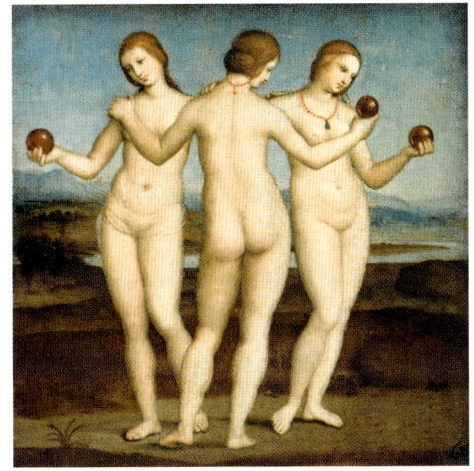

4

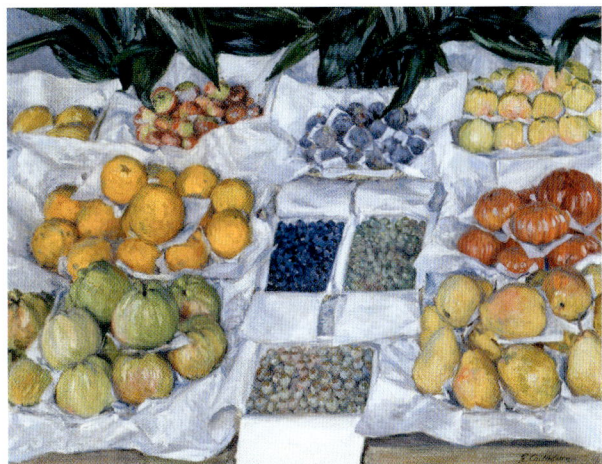

5

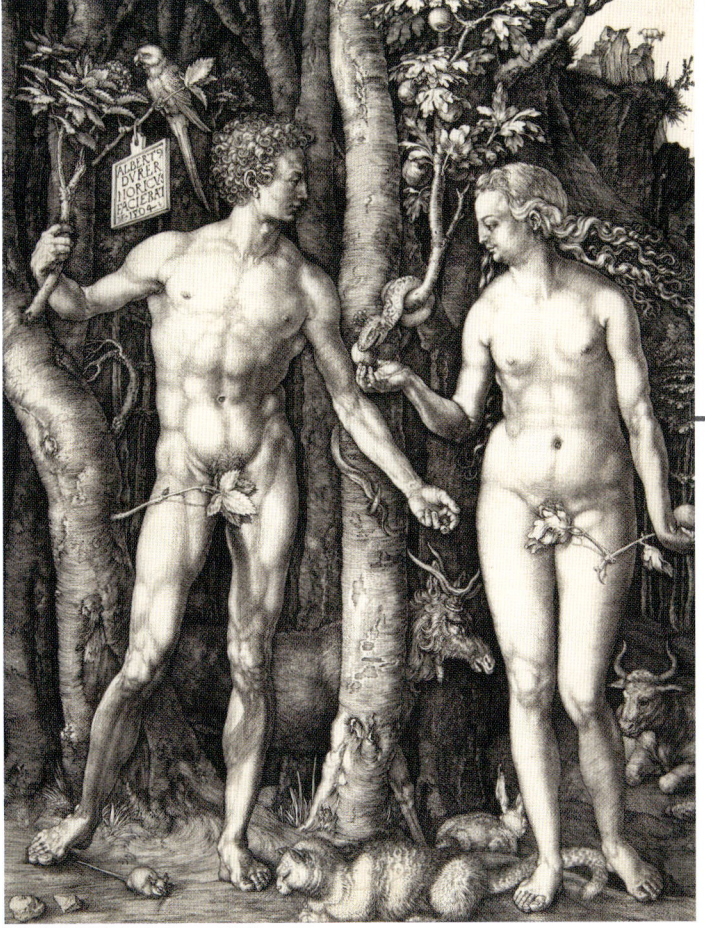

6

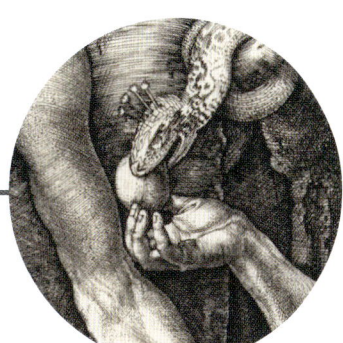

1. *The Son of Man,* René Magritte, 1964
2. *The Plate of Apples,* Paul Cézanne, c. 1877
3. *The Judgement of Paris,* Peter Paul Rubens, 1632-35
4. *The Three Graces,* Raphael, 1500-05
5. *Fruit Displayed on a Stand,* Gustave Caillebotte, c. 1881-82
6. *Adam and Eve,* Albrecht Dürer, 1504

Vine and Grapes

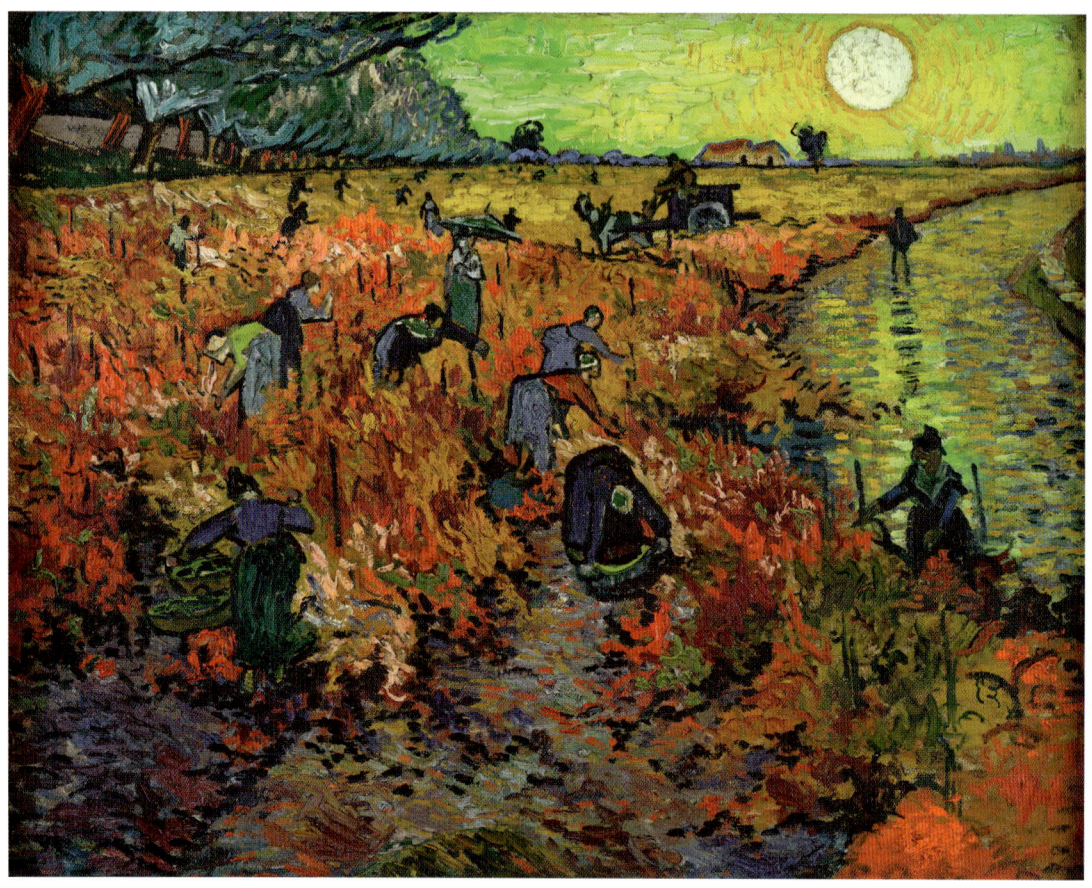

1

Greco-Roman imagery associated grapes and vines with Bacchus/Dionysus, the god of wine, revelry and transformation, representing abundance, pleasure and celebration. Artists such as Caravaggio (1571–1610) and Titian (c. 1488/90–1576) incorporated grapes into still life or mythological scenes to evoke sensuality or divine intoxication. In Christian iconography, grapes represent the blood of Christ and are closely tied to themes of sacrifice, salvation and communion. Vines, often intertwined, seen in medieval manuscripts, stained glass and altarpieces, signify the Church and the unity of believers, after Christ's declaration, 'I am the vine, you are the branches' (John 15:5). Some medieval and Renaissance paintings included grapevines to emphasize themes of spiritual nourishment and divine grace. In contrast, some Dutch still-life compositions feature grapes to represent wealth, indulgence and life's transience. Beyond Western traditions, vines have appeared in Persian miniatures, and Indian and Chinese paintings, symbolizing prosperity and cyclical renewal. Grapevines' twisting forms have also been widely used in decorative arts, such as in Baroque and Art Nouveau designs.

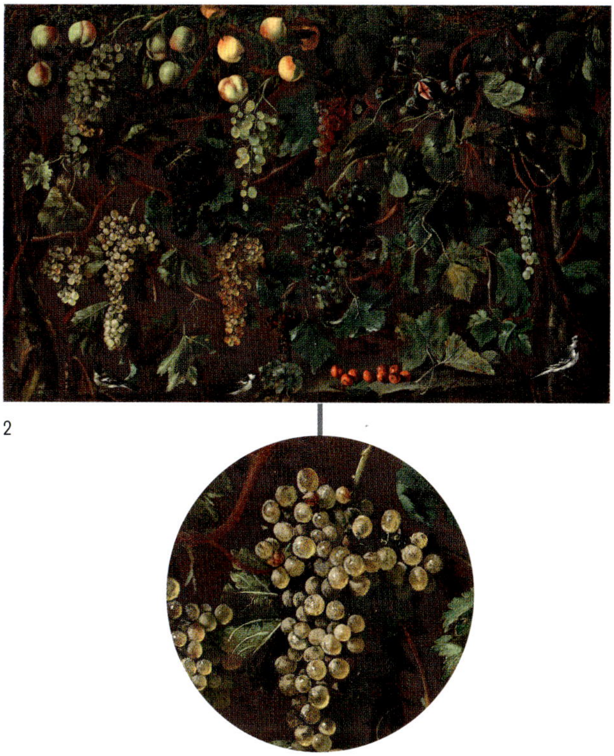

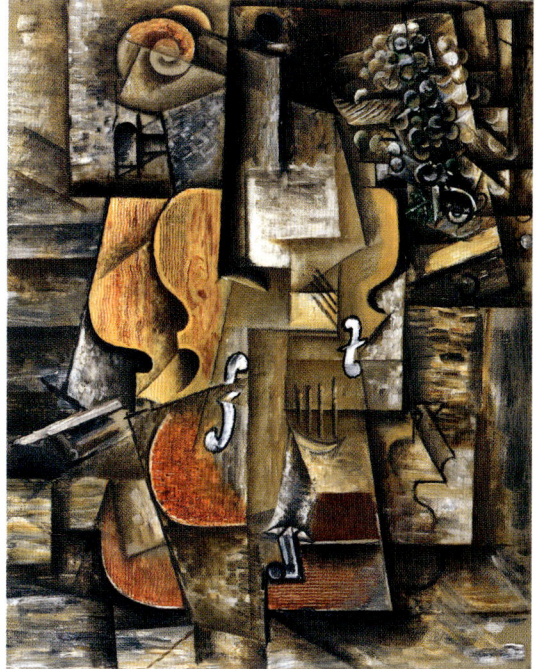

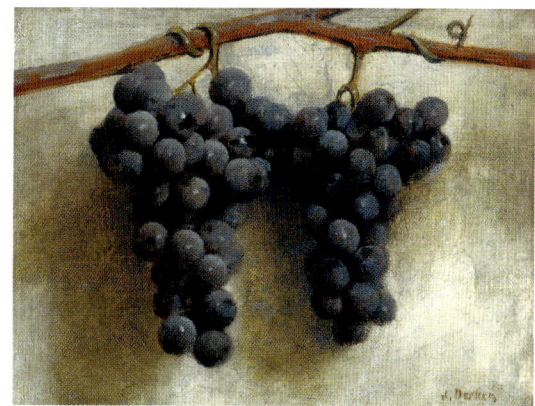

2

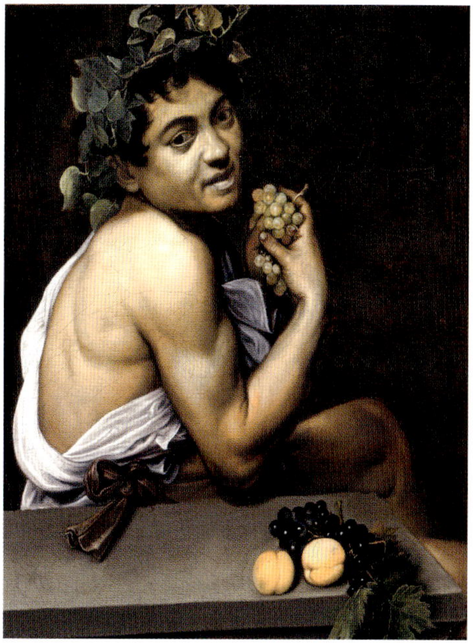

3

4

5

1. *The Red Vineyard,* Vincent van Gogh, 1888
2. *Grape Vines and Fruit, with Three Wagtails,*
   Bartolomeo Cavarozzi, c. 1615–18
3. *Young Sick Bacchus,* Caravaggio, c. 1593
4. *Violin and Grapes,* Pablo Picasso, 1912
5. *Grapes,* Joseph Decker, c. 1890/95

Olive and Olive Tree

Among other things, olives and olive trees in art symbolize peace, wisdom, endurance and prosperity. In ancient Greek and Roman art, the olive tree, sacred to the goddess Athena/Minerva, represented victory and peace. Renaissance paintings often featured olive branches as a symbol of peace, renewal and divine promise, inspired by the biblical story of Noah's Ark. The Sistine Chapel ceiling (1508-12) by Michelangelo (1475-1564) includes a depiction of a dove taking an olive branch to Noah. Also in the Bible, the Sermon in the Garden and Christ's ascension to heaven both take place on the Mount of Olives.

Vincent van Gogh produced at least 15 olive tree paintings, conveying the resilience, mysticism and spirituality of nature, which reflected his emotional struggles. During his stay in northern Italy in early 1884, Claude Monet painted five scenes featuring olive trees. Throughout his career, Pablo Picasso (1881-1973) depicted doves, often carrying an olive branch as a symbol of peace.

1. *Olive Trees in the Moreno Garden,* Claude Monet, 1884
2. *Old Olive Tree,* Ernst Schiess, date unknown
3. *Olive Trees,* Vincent van Gogh, 1889

1

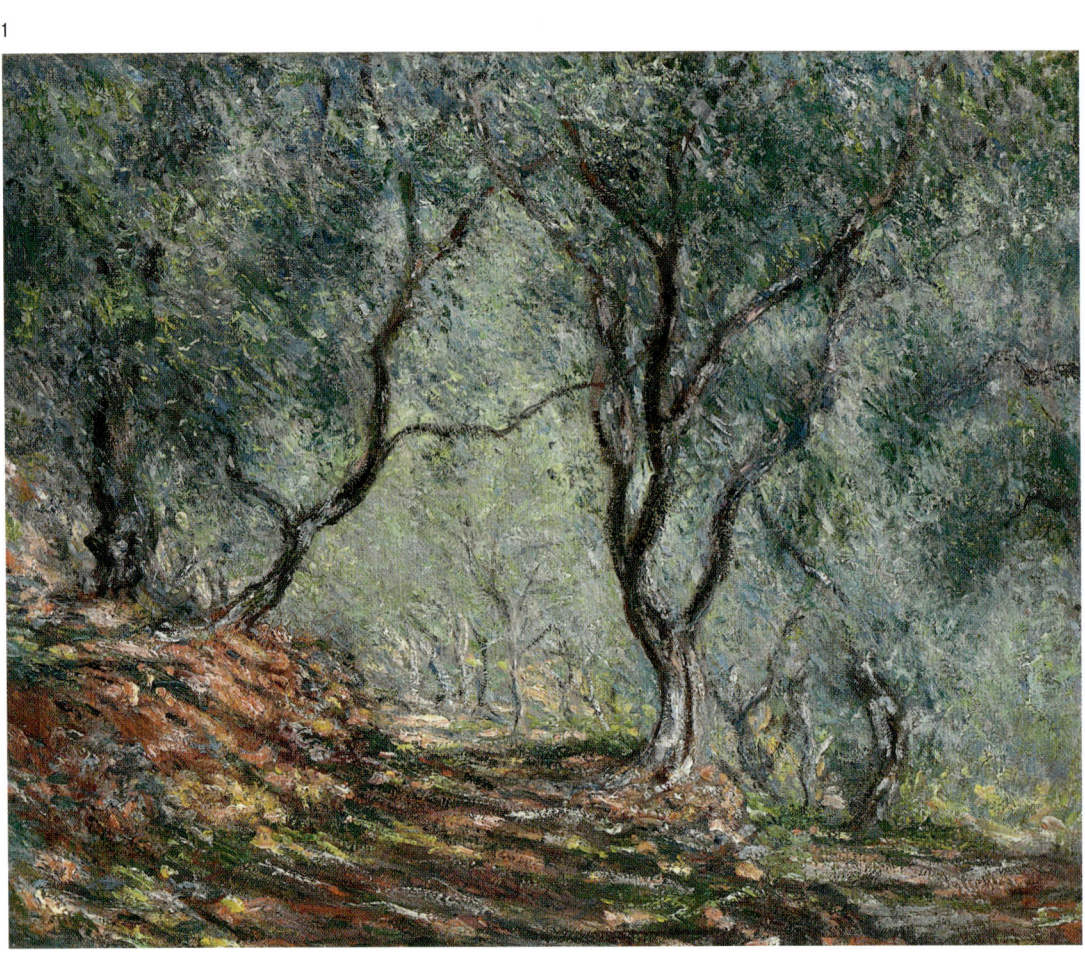

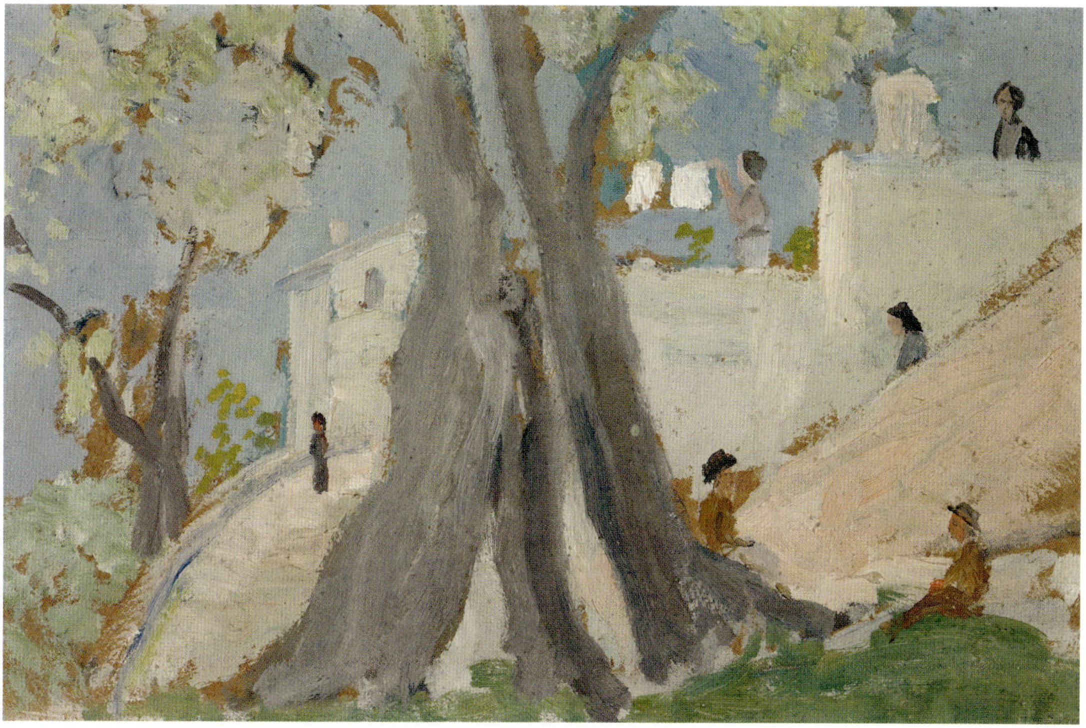

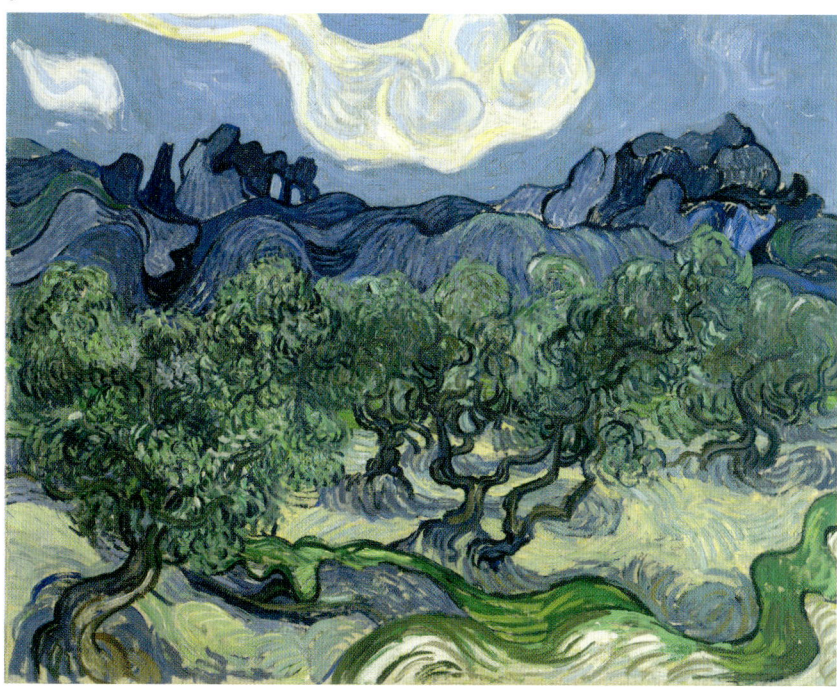

2

3

Fig

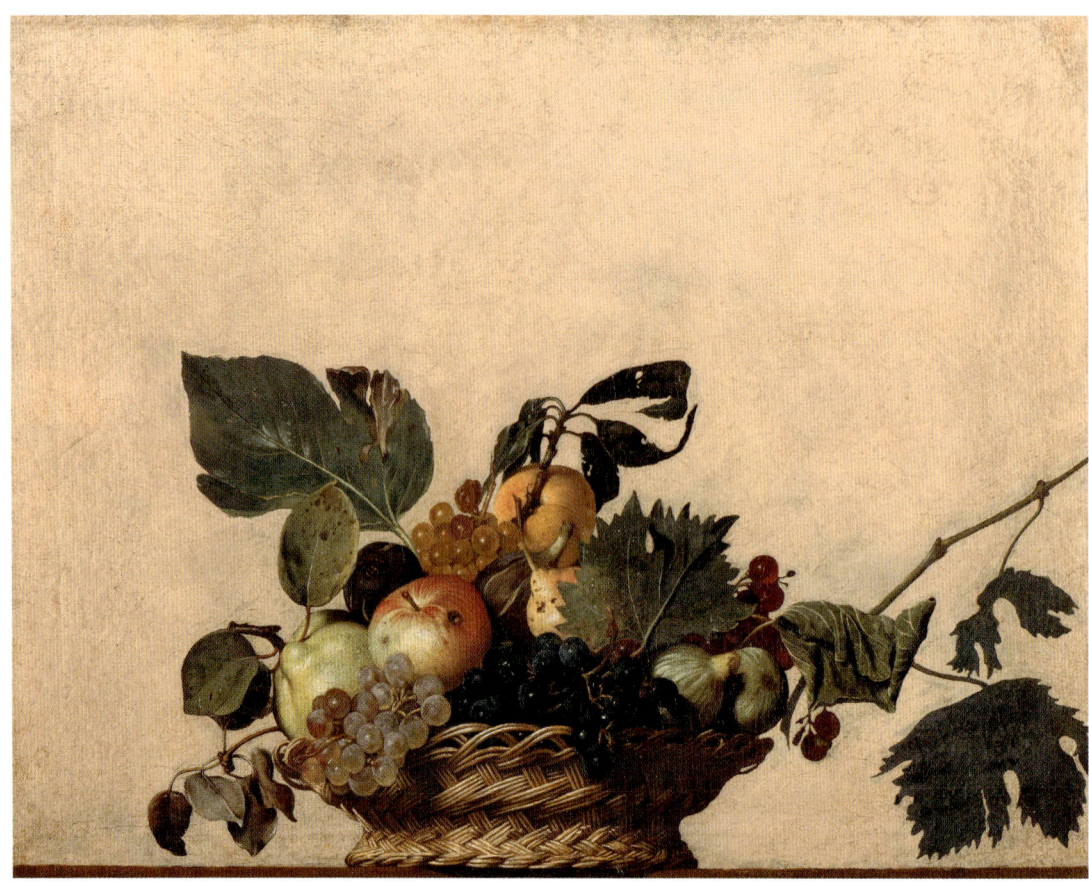

1

Rooted in ancient mythology, religion and cultural traditions, the fig's symbolism across art and cultures can be physical, moral or divine. In classical art, it often represents fertility, abundance and sensuality due to its sweet fruit and association with lush landscapes. It was linked to Dionysus and Bacchus, the gods of wine and pleasure in ancient Greece and Rome. In Jewish and Christian imagery, the fig holds special significance. After eating the forbidden fruit in the Garden of Eden, Adam and Eve used fig leaves to cover themselves, associating the fig tree with modesty, shame and the fall from innocence. From that idea, several artists used fig leaves as modest coverings on nude figures in Renaissance and Baroque paintings. Yet, unlike its associations with guilt, the fig also represents knowledge and enlightenment. In Eastern traditions, such as Buddhism, the fig tree, especially the Bodhi tree, symbolizes spiritual awakening.

Fig   49

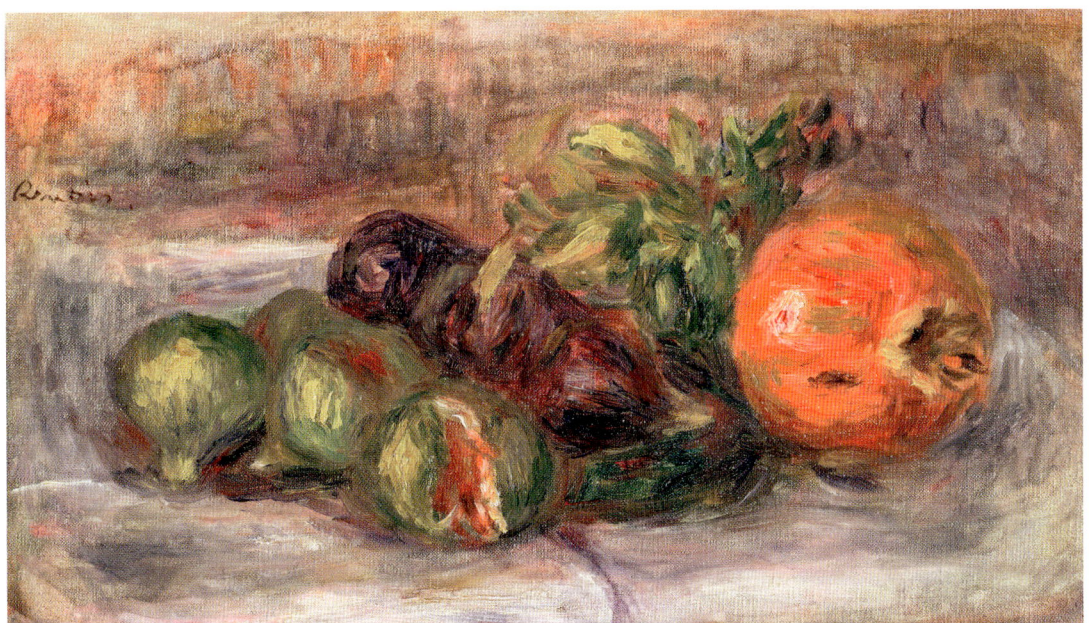

2

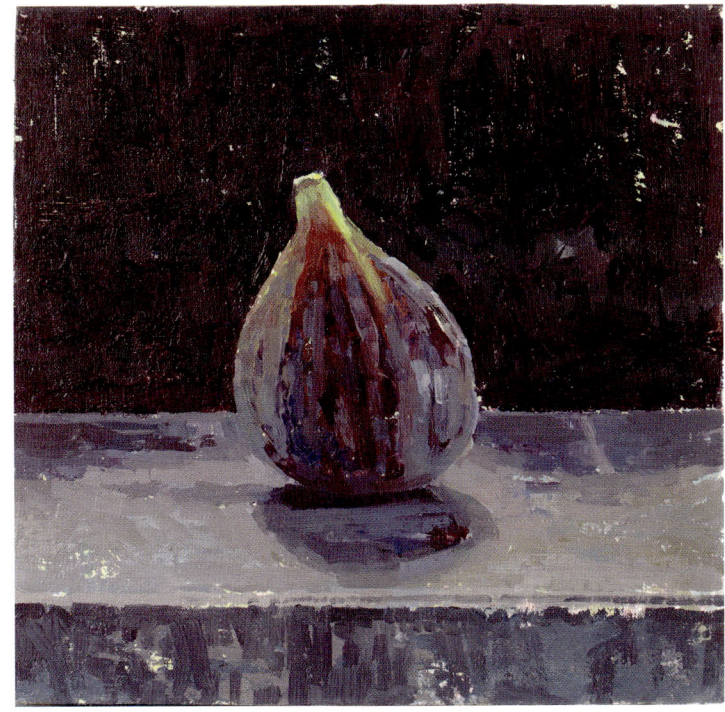

3

1. *Basket of Fruit*, Caravaggio, c. 1599
2. *Pomegranates and Figs,*
   Pierre-Auguste Renoir, 1917
3. *Fig,* Francis Hamel, 2010

Orange

Replacing the usual apple with an orange, the orange tree has sometimes been depicted as the Tree of Knowledge. The orange has also been associated with riches, fertility, protection and opulence. During the Northern Renaissance, as it was only accessible to the wealthy, it symbolized luxury and status. In contrast, in Spain, oranges represented the country's farming heritage and nature's abundance. The tree's white flowers have often epitomized chastity and beauty. In marriage portraits, oranges usually represent fertility. In Renaissance Italy, oranges were associated with the Medici family for several reasons. The golden fruit visually resembled coins, subtly reinforcing the Medici's origins in banking. The orange tree was associated with the golden apples of the Hesperides in classical mythology, suggesting divine favour, eternal life and cultural refinement. The Medici name means 'doctors' (from *medico*, Italian for physician), and oranges were used in Renaissance medicinal practices. As the colour can be associated with gold, in Chinese art, oranges symbolize good luck and prosperity.

1. *Still Life with Oranges,* Paul Gauguin, 1881
2. *La Primavera,* Sandro Botticelli, late 1470s–early 1480s
3. *Wrapped Oranges,* William J. McCloskey, 1889

1

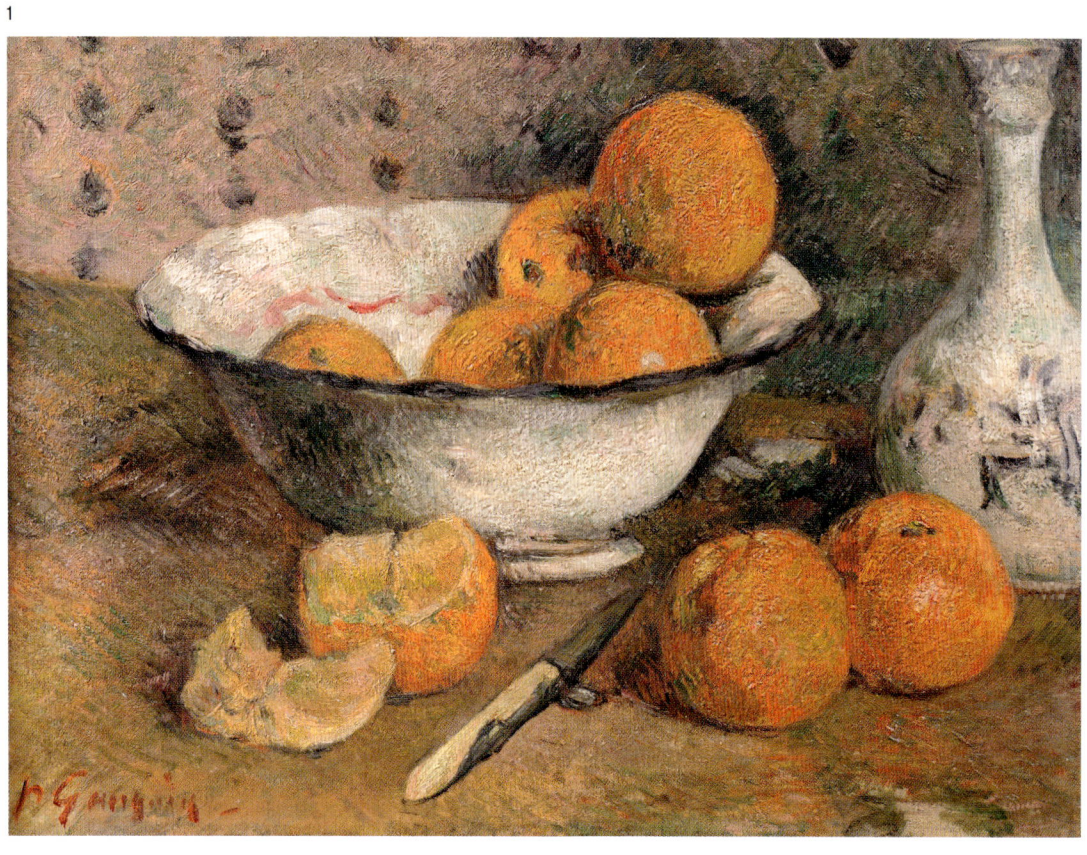

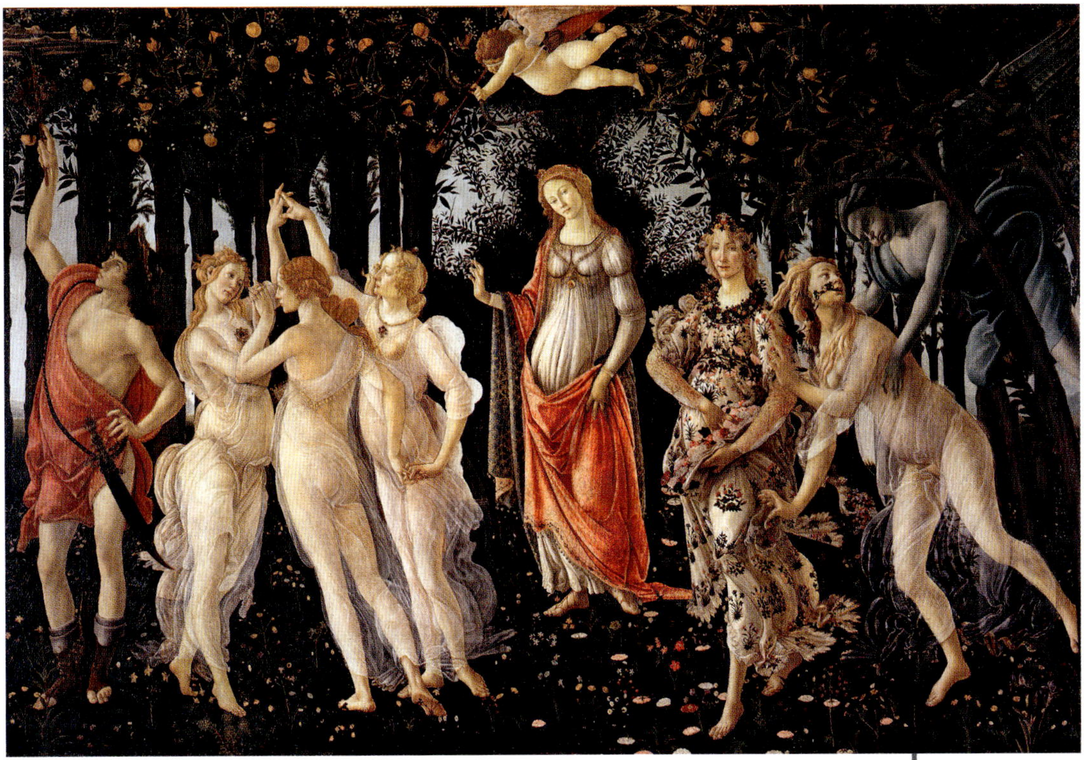

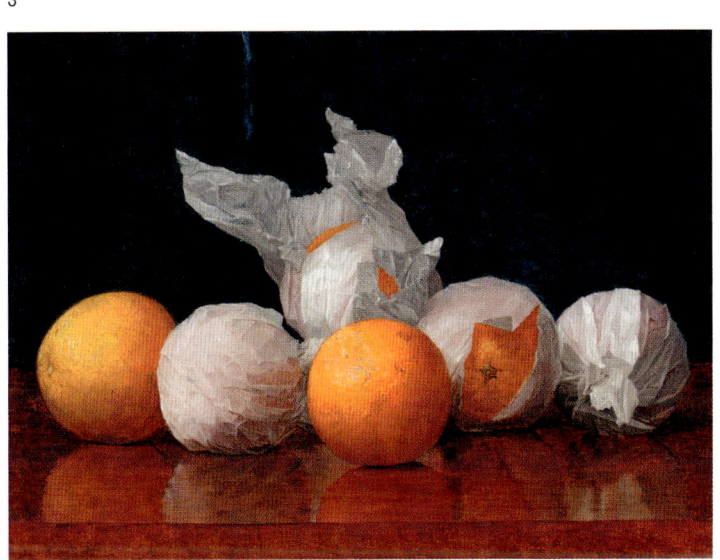

2

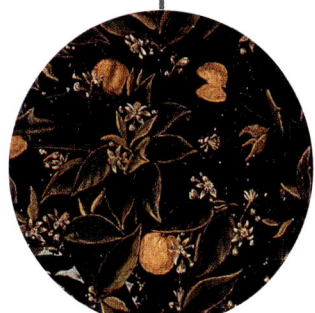

3

Watermelon

Watermelons in art often symbolize fertility, abundance and vitality. They were included in still-life paintings during the Renaissance to represent nature's bounty, abundance and sensual pleasures, such as in *Watermelons, Peaches, Pears and Other Fruit in a Landscape* (1645-72) by Giovanni Stanchi (1608-72). Watermelons also appeared in allegorical paintings to convey moral, religious or political messages and to celebrate the harvest season. *Still Life with Watermelon* (1822) by Raphaelle Peale (1774-1825) conveys sensuality, abundance and the fleeting nature of life. *The Merchant's Wife at Tea* (1918) by Boris Mikhailovich Kustodiev (1878-1927) features signs of abundance,

including a shiny samovar and sliced watermelon. The final painting of Frida Kahlo (1907-54), *Viva la Vida* (1954), painted just before her premature death, features watermelons to celebrate life and resilience while linking them to Mexico's Day of the Dead, symbolizing remembrance. The watermelon's vibrant colours and rich symbolism have made it a recurring motif across cultures, evolving from a simple fruit to a powerful emblem of life, struggle and celebration.

1. *Viva la Vida, Watermelons,* Frida Kahlo, 1954
2. *Watermelons, Peaches, Pears and Other Fruit in a Landscape,* Giovanni Stanchi, 1645-72
3. *The Merchant's Wife at Tea,* Boris Mikhailovich Kustodiev, 1918
4. *Watermelon Flag,* Khaled Hourani, 2007

1

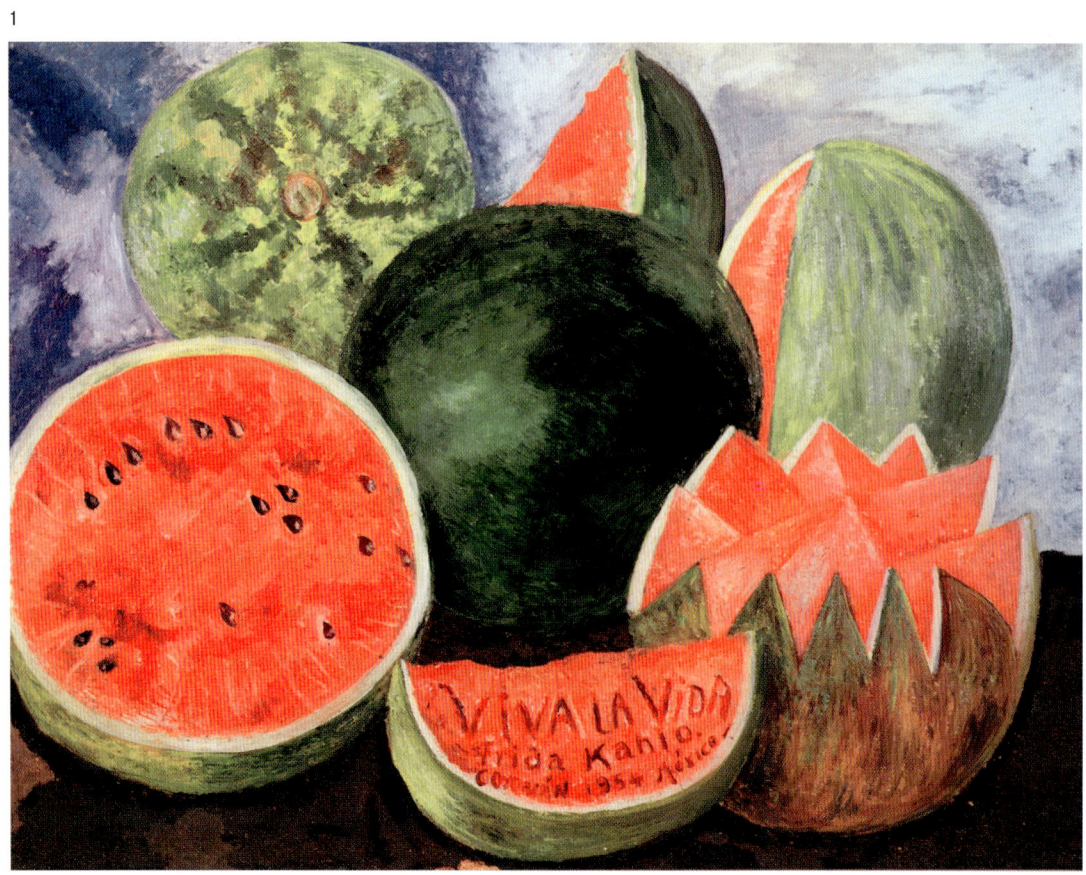

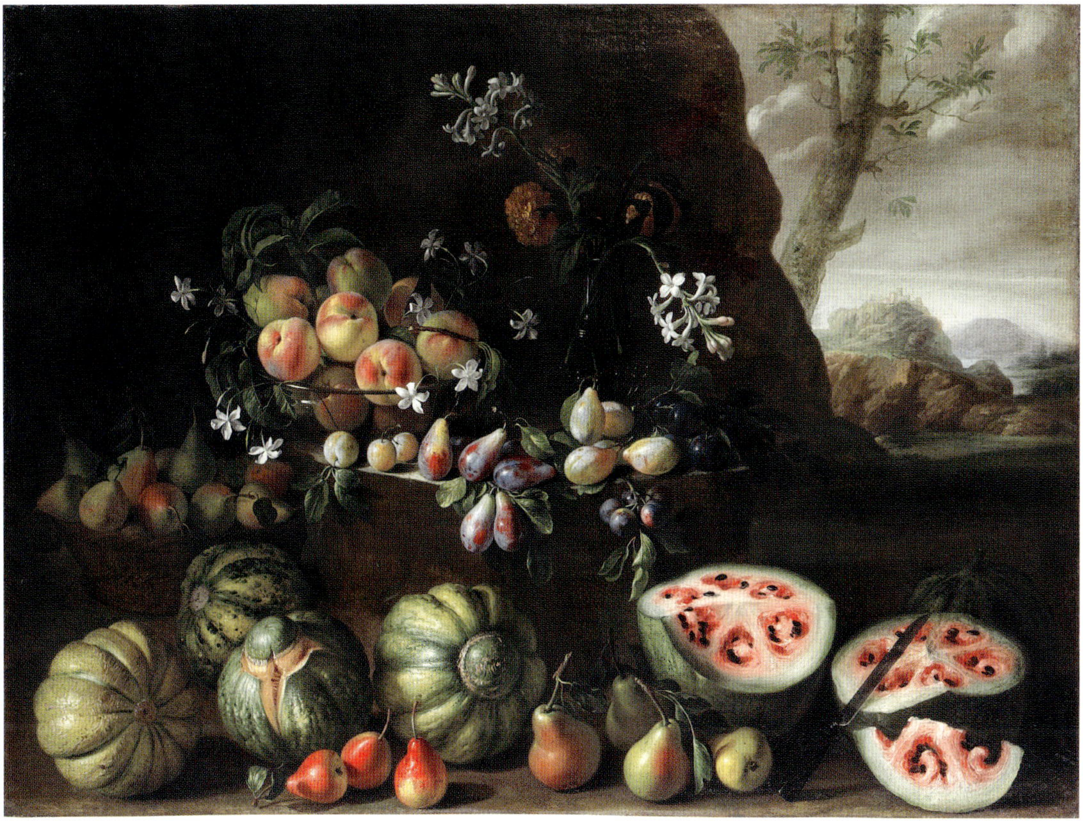

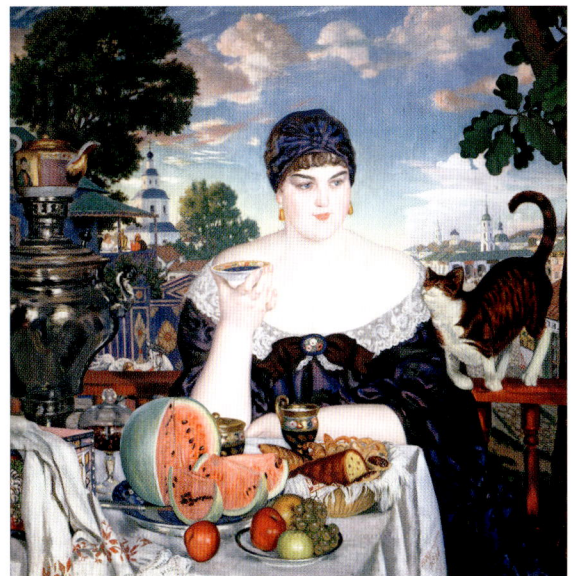

2

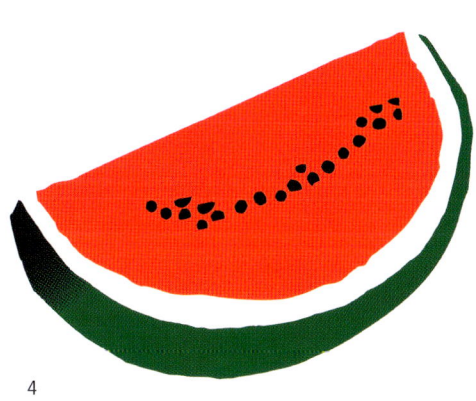

3

4

Lemon

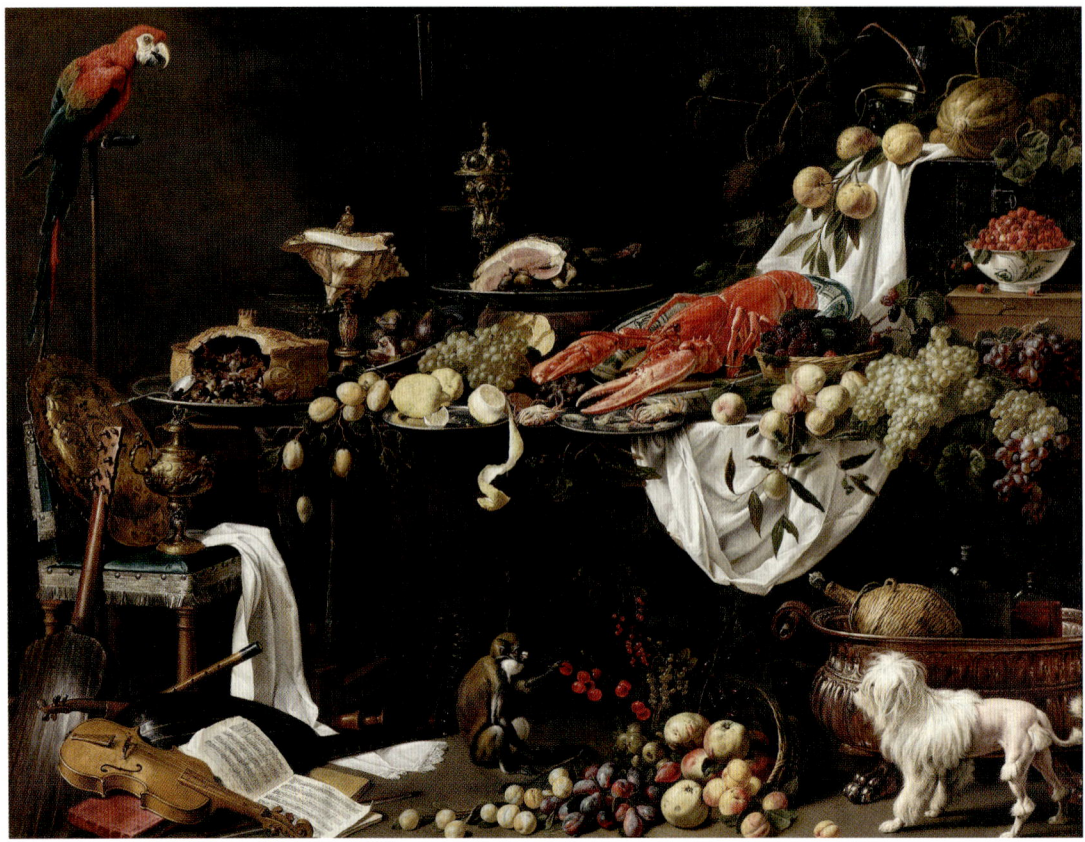

1

The lemon in art has often symbolized wealth, luxury and transience. In seventeenth-century Dutch still-life paintings, such as those by Willem Kalf (1619-93), lemons - usually partially peeled - highlighted artists' technical skill while symbolizing vanitas, the fleeting pleasures of life. The fruit's exotic origins and rarity in Europe made lemons a status symbol, and they were included in art to show the owner's wealth. In the Mediterranean, particularly in Spanish art, lemons reflected local abundance and vitality. The painting *Winter* (c. 1563) by Giuseppe Arcimboldo (1526-93) features lemons to reflect their limited availability in northern Italy during the winter. In Islamic art, citrus motifs, including lemons, adorned ceramics and textiles, symbolizing paradise and divine creation. In contemporary art, artists such as Wolfgang Tillmans (b. 1968) have used lemons to explore form, colour and everyday beauty. Overall, lemons have represented opulence and impermanence, bridging naturalistic detail with cultural and spiritual meaning.

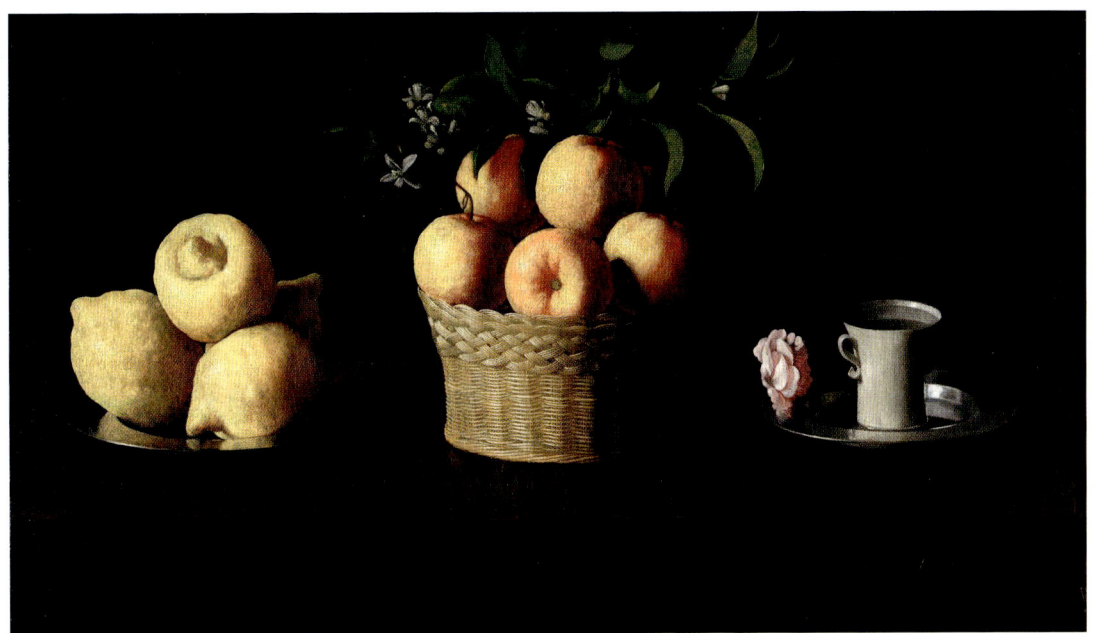

2

3

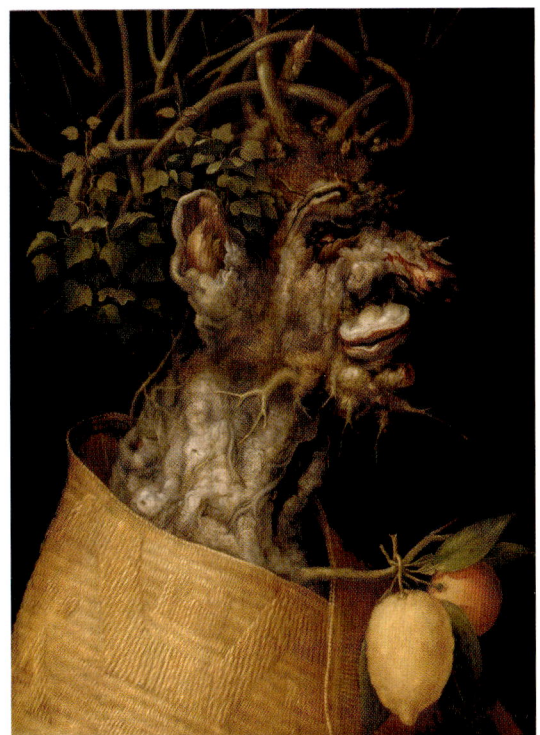

4

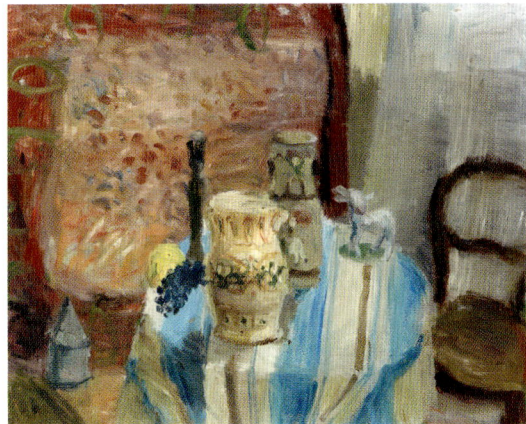

1. *Banquet Still Life,* Adriaen van Utrecht, 1644
2. *Still Life with Lemons, Oranges and a Rose*, Francisco de Zurbarán, 1633
3. *Winter*, Giuseppe Arcimboldo, c. 1563
4. *Still Life with Lemon and Grape,* Walter Kurt Wiemken, 1929

Banana

Although less prevalent in earlier art, bananas have become increasingly featured in modern and contemporary art. For example, *The Meal (The Bananas)*, painted by Paul Gauguin (1848-1903) in 1891, soon after he arrived in Tahiti, aimed to capture what he saw as a 'primitive' or 'pure' way of life. However, this was a European fantasy, as Tahitian culture had already been transformed by French colonization. The bananas symbolize natural abundance and self-sufficiency, while the bright yellow colour draws the viewer's eye. The bananas in *Bananas* (1952) by Lucian Freud (1922-2011) embody decay, sensuality, mortality and psychological tension. Through meticulous realism, Freud transforms simple fruit into a profound meditation on the human condition – fragile, physical, and transient. The fruit's tropical origin also associates bananas with colonialism and trade, as seen in artworks that critique imperial exploitation and global commerce. More recently, the controversial work *Comedian* (2019) by Maurizio Cattelan (b. 1960), a banana duct-taped to a wall, challenged notions of art, value and consumerism.

1. *The Meal (The Bananas),* Paul Gauguin, 1891
2. *Bananas,* Lucian Freud, 1952

1

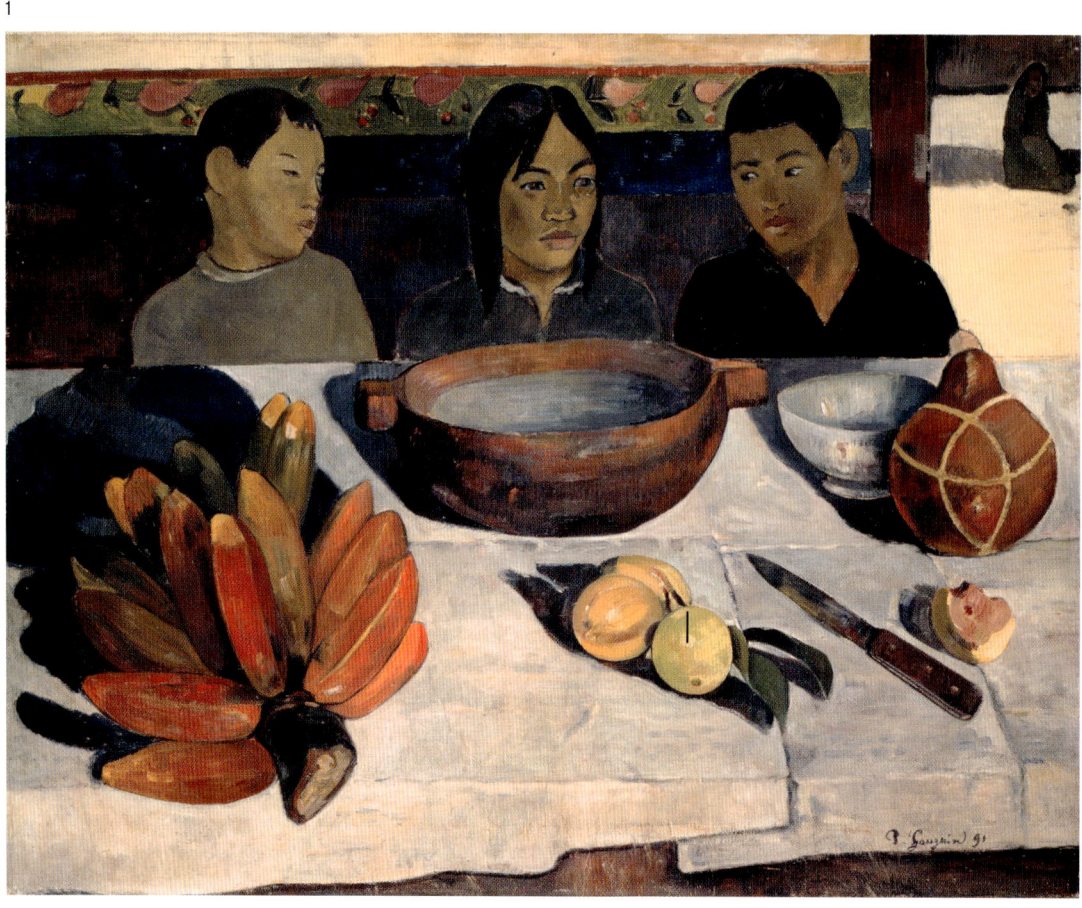

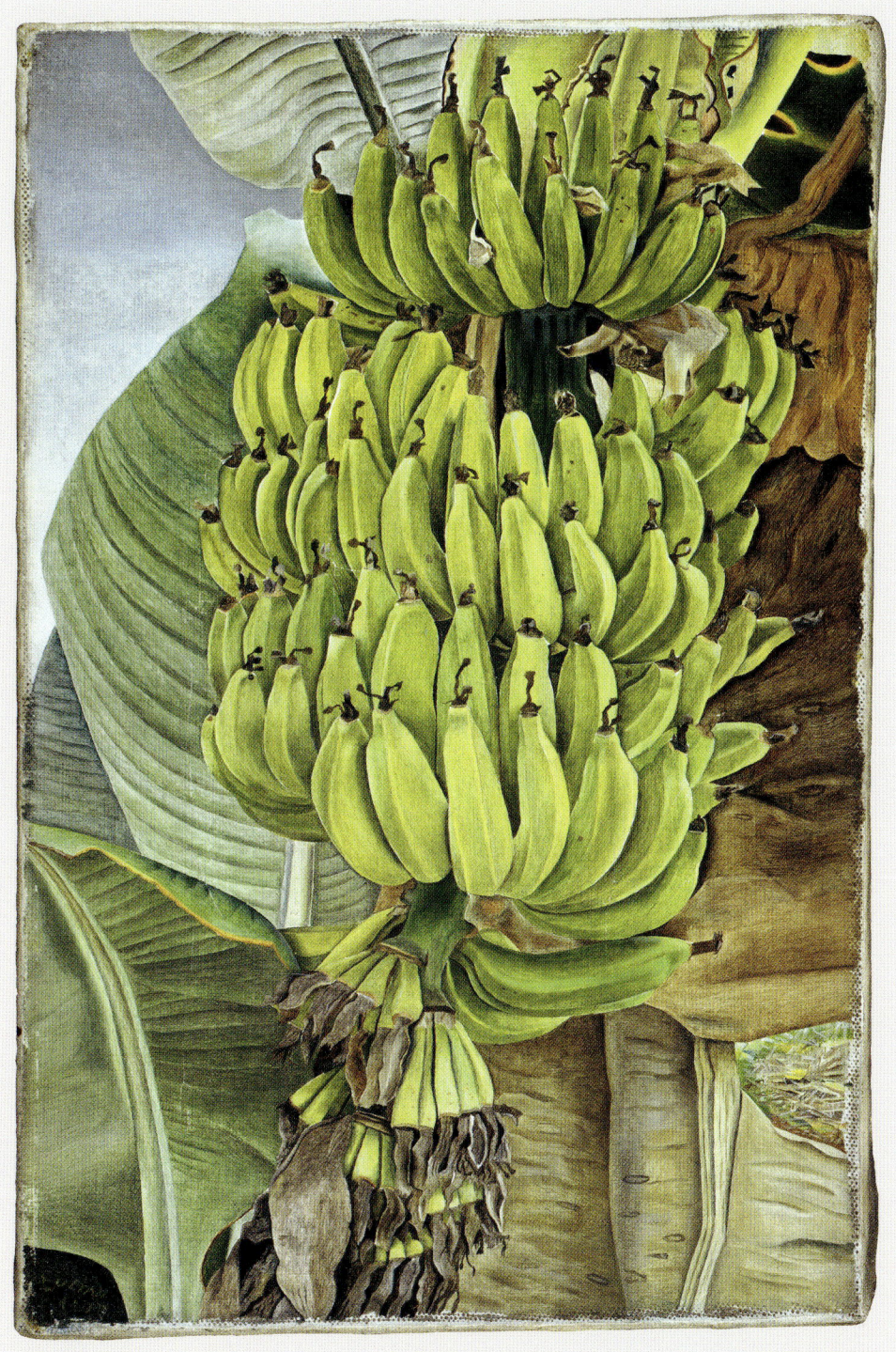

Pomegranate

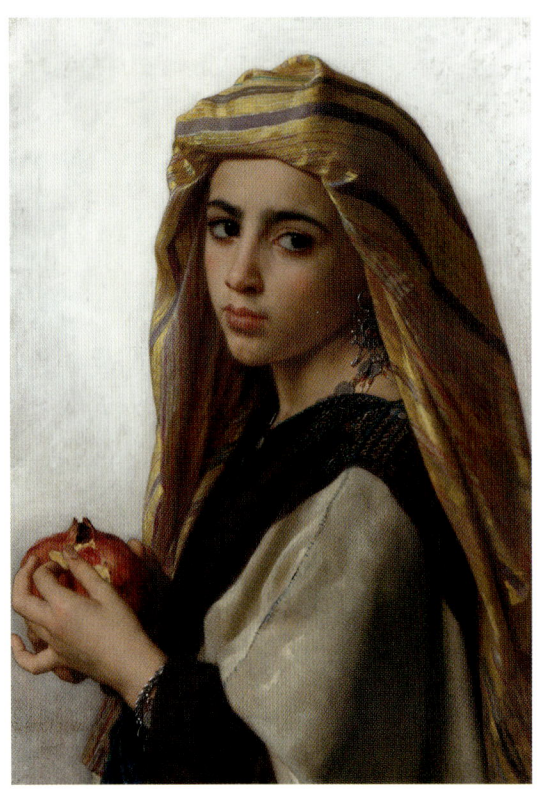

1

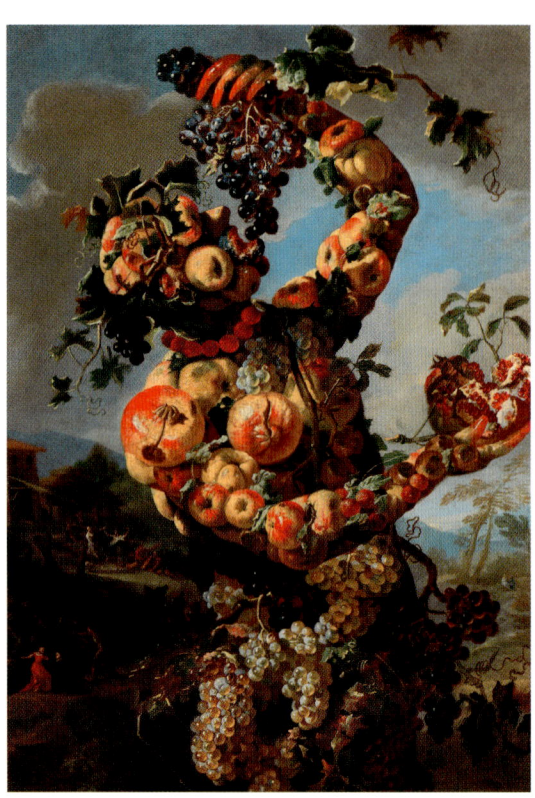

2

Among art's most symbolically charged fruits, pomegranates appear in paintings, sculpture, textiles, tiles and more, from ancient Persia to Renaissance Europe and beyond. Their many seeds make them symbols of fertility, abundance and eternal life. In Greek mythology, Persephone's consumption of pomegranate seeds binds her to the underworld, making the fruit emblematic of both life and death. In Christian iconography, pomegranates often appear in depictions of the Virgin and Child, with their many seeds in one skin, such as in the *Madonna of the Pomegranate* (c. 1487) by Sandro Botticelli (c. 1445–1510), symbolizing resurrection and the unity of the Church. In Islamic and Persian art, the pomegranate usually stands for

beauty, paradise and divine creation. Pomegranates in still-life painting may suggest sensual pleasure, mortality or spiritual richness. In general, artists exploit the fruit's vivid colours and complex forms, for instance, in *Still Life (Primroses, Pears and Pomegranates)* (1866) by Henri Fantin-Latour (1836–1904) and *Still Life of Fruit with a Wine Glass* (c. 1649) by Jan Davidsz. de Heem (1606–83/84).

1. *Girl with a Pomegranate,* William-Adolphe Bouguereau, 1875
2. *Allegory of Autumn,* Giovanni Paolo Spadino (attrib.), late seventeenth century
3. *Pomegranates,* Albert Joseph Moore, 1866
4. *Madonna of the Pomegranate,* Sandro Botticelli, c. 1487

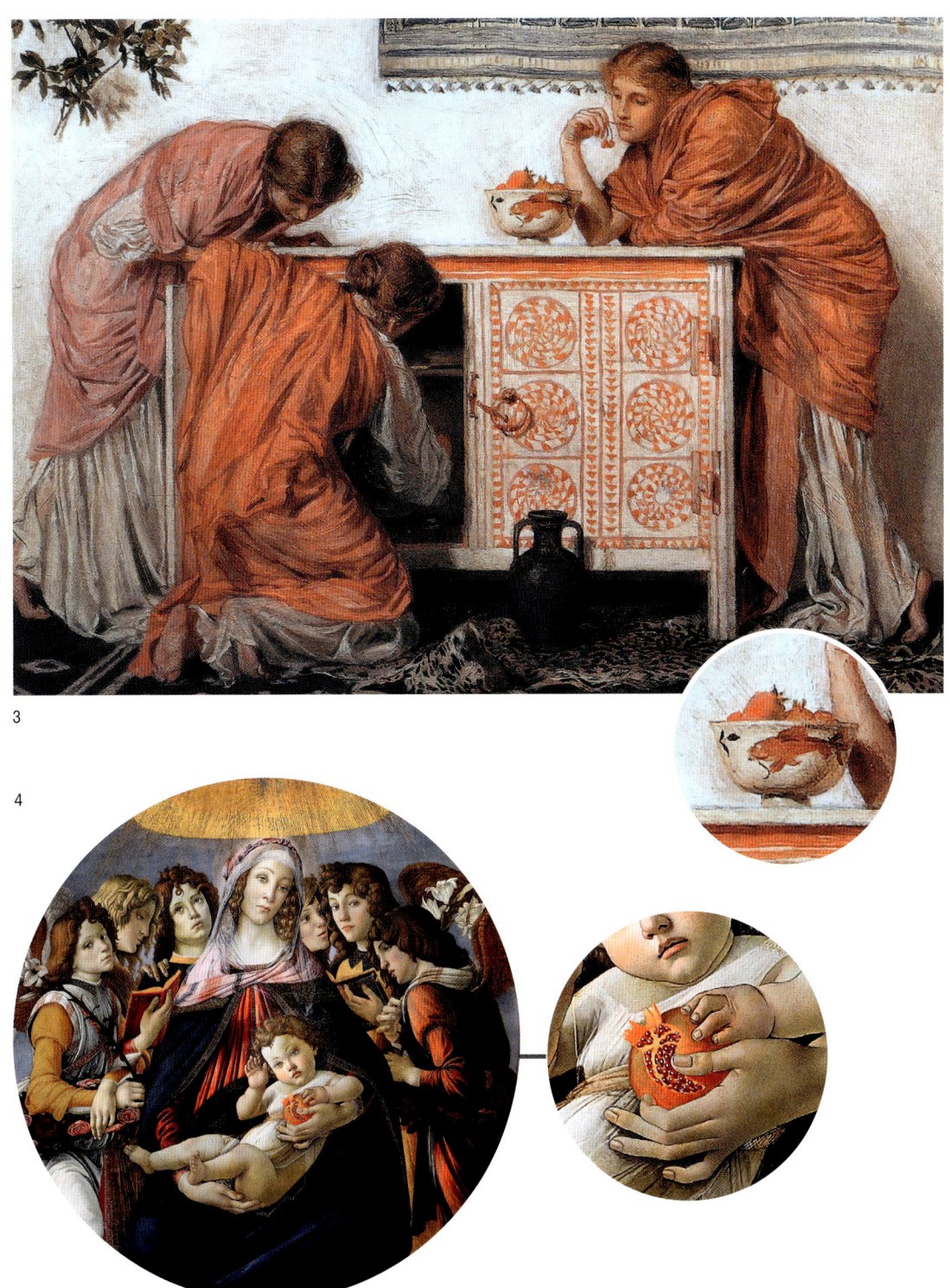

3

4

Strawberry

In secular Renaissance art, strawberries often represented ephemeral sensual delights and fleeting indulgence. At the same time, due to their association with the Virgin Mary and the Holy Trinity (through their tri-part leaves), they frequently suggested purity and righteousness, and were often depicted in garden depictions of Eden or Mary's *hortus conclusus* (enclosed garden). In some cultures, the wild strawberry's small size and fragility sometimes symbolized humility. From the Baroque to the Rococo, still lifes containing strawberries generally evoked natural abundance and momentary pleasures, celebrating the senses, balanced by an awareness of ephemerality. At the same time, the natural,

unspoiled sweetness of the fruit has been associated with innocence and rural virtue, as seen in *The Strawberry Girl* (1884) by Albert Anker (1831–1910). Other artists have incorporated them into paintings to suggest natural abundance and delicate or lingering pleasure, such as in *Strawberries* (c. 1882) by Édouard Manet (1832–83).

1. *Still Life with Cherries, Strawberries and Gooseberries,* Louise Moillon, 1630

2. *Strawberries,* Édouard Manet, c. 1882

3. *Madonna Among the Strawberries,* unknown artist, c. 1420

4. *The Strawberry Girl,* Albert Anker, 1884

1

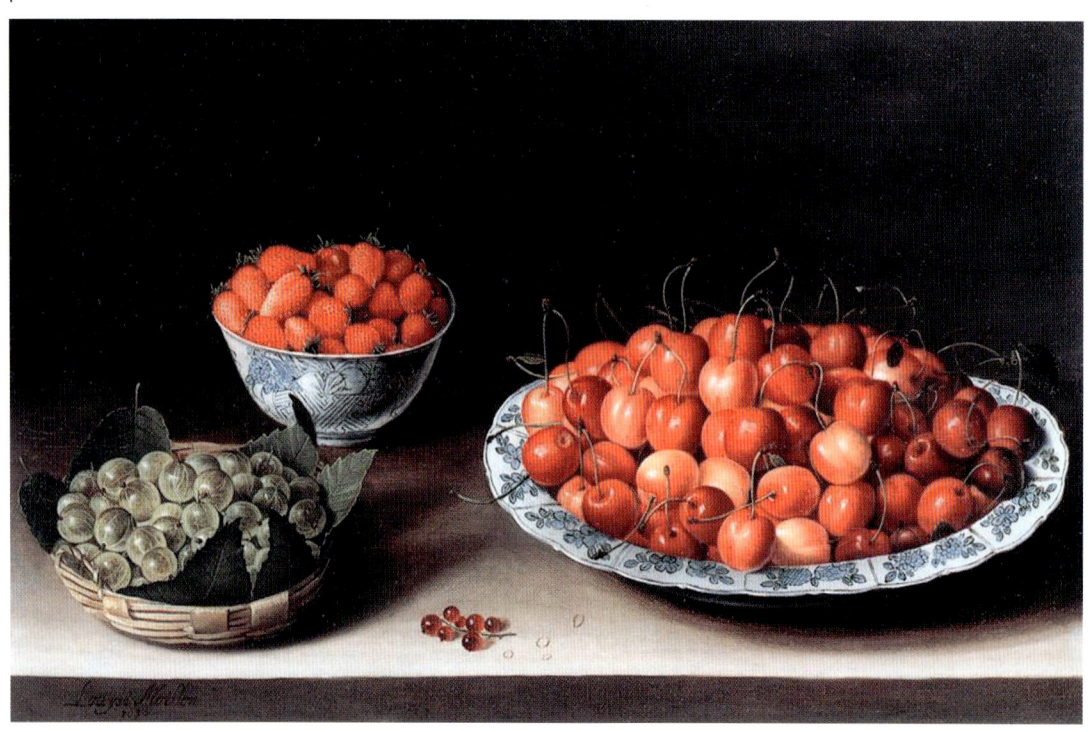

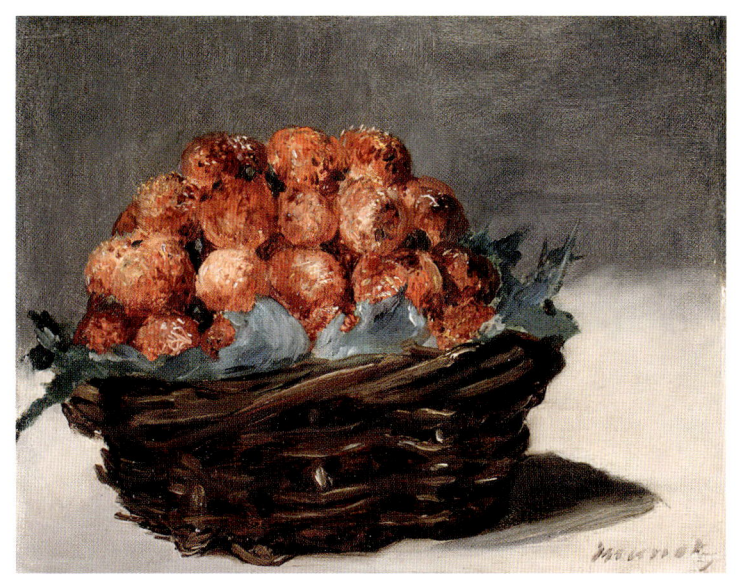

2

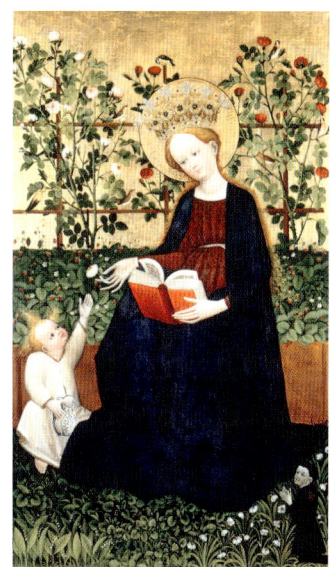

3

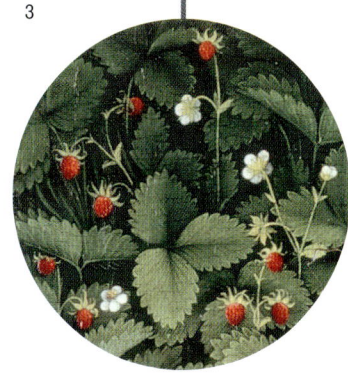

4

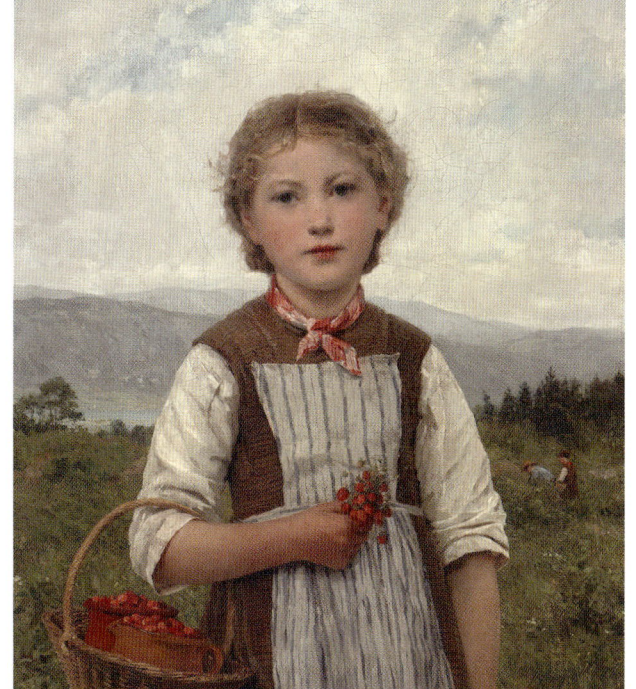

Cherry

Cherry blossoms, known as *sakura* in Japanese, hold special significance in Japanese culture as a symbol of renewal, impermanence and the fleeting nature of life. They are celebrated during the annual *hanami* tradition, when people gather to appreciate the beauty of cherry blossoms in bloom. Conveying this, numerous Japanese artists, such as Utagawa Hiroshige (1797–1858), have depicted cherry blossoms in various contexts and styles. In Christian art, cherries are sometimes featured to represent paradise or the fruit of heaven; however, as an alternative to the apple, they are also ambiguously linked to the concept of original sin. The ripe red cherry evokes the blood Christ will shed on the cross, while its round perfection alludes to resurrection and the ultimate reward of paradise. Meanwhile, in other art, cherries often symbolize sexual awakening, temptation or virginity. Their bright colour and juicy flesh contribute to interpretations of fertility and sensuality. During the eighteenth century Spanish Enlightenment, cherries were often depicted as signs of wealth, sensuality or the fragility of life.

1. *Still Life with Cherries and Peaches*, Paul Cezanne, 1885-87
2. *The Madonna of the Cherries,* Joos van Cleve, c. 1525
3. *Girl with Cherries,* unknown artist, c. 1820,
4. *Cherry Blossoms at Arashiyama,* Utagawa Hiroshige, c. 1834

1

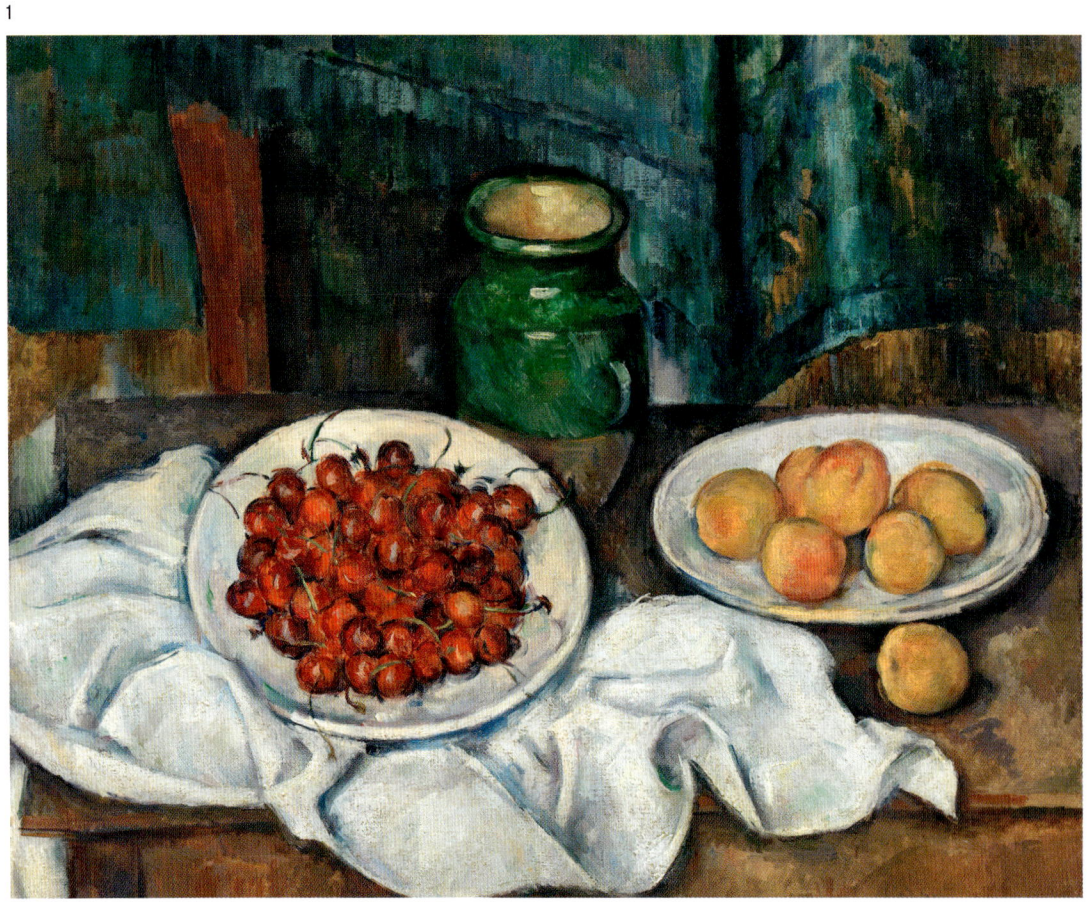

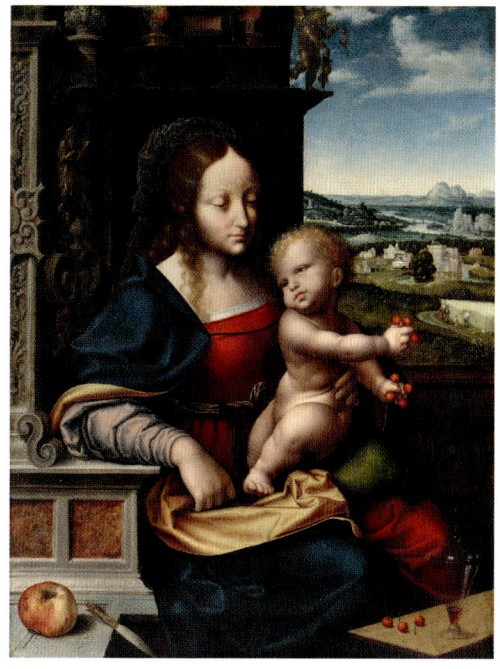

2

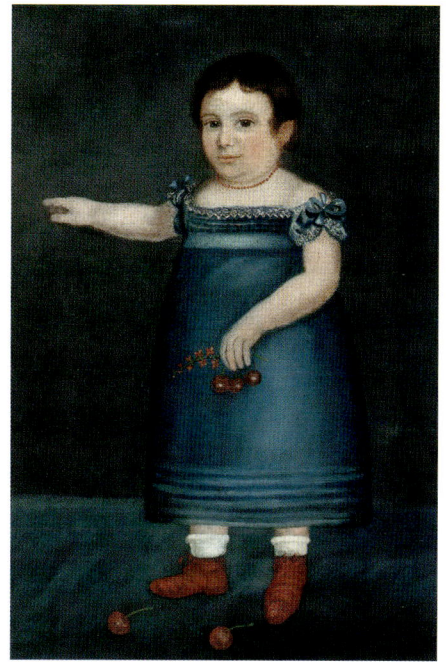

3

4

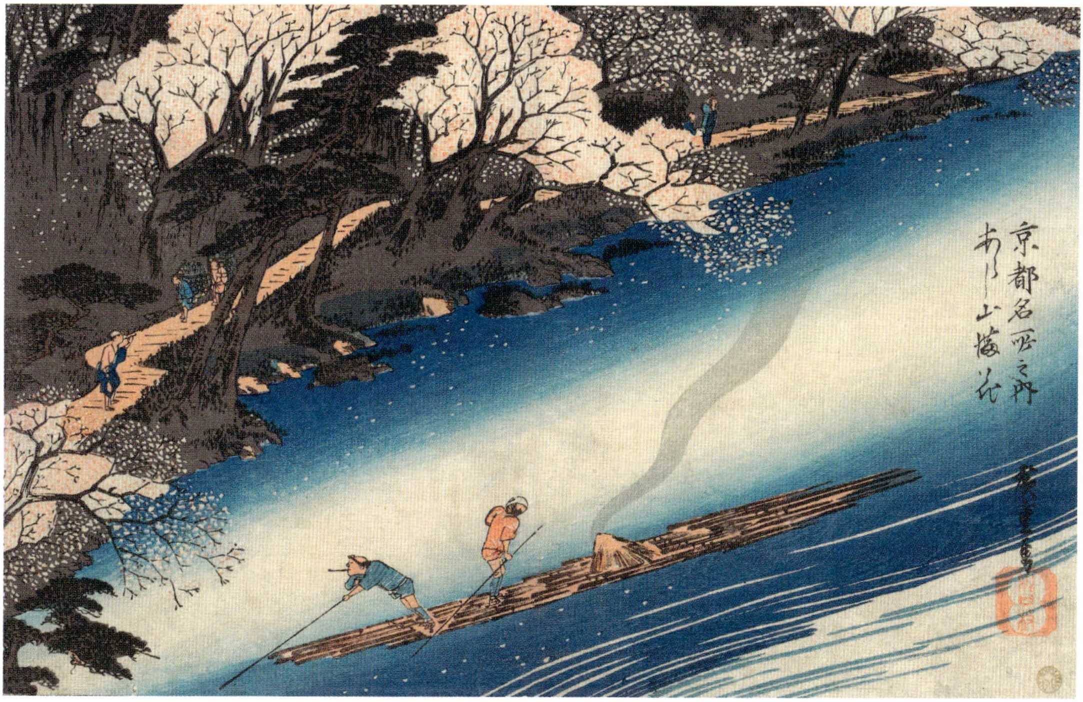

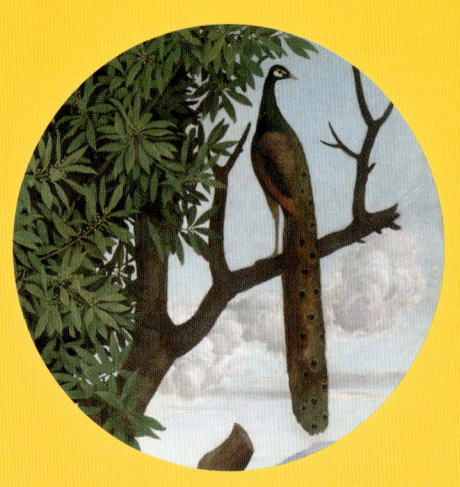

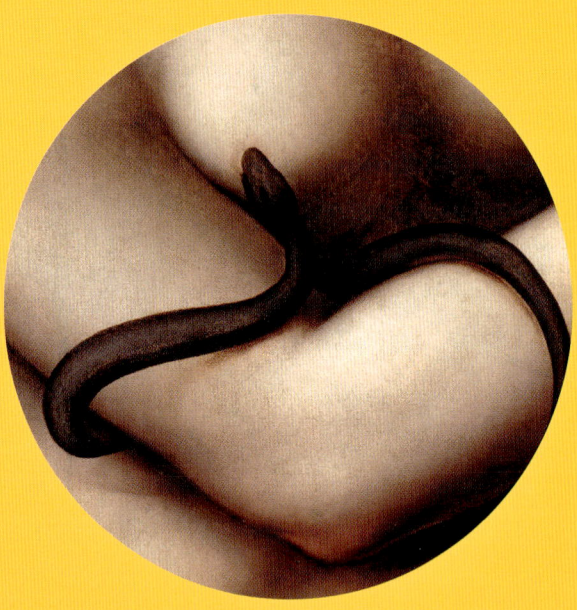

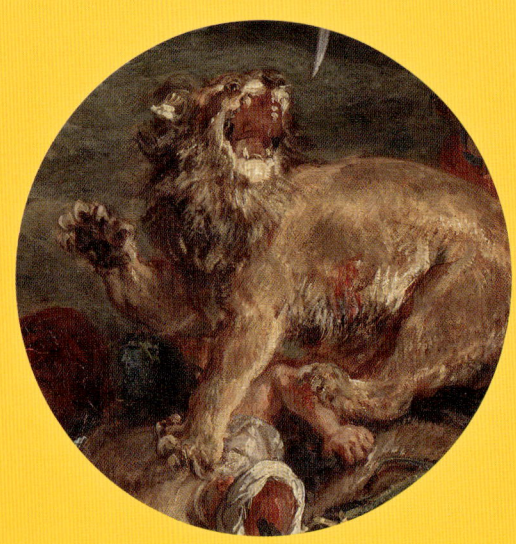

Animals

Horse

From prehistoric cave paintings, such as those at Lascaux and Pech-Merle, to contemporary art, horses have been illustrated to symbolize power, freedom, nobility, war and death. In Greco-Roman art, they were typically associated with gods, war and triumph, and featured in equestrian statues, where they asserted authority and control. In medieval and Renaissance religious art, white horses were frequently symbols of purity or divine intervention, while black horses often suggested death or danger. In battle scenes and historical art, horses have long represented power, dynamism, and even the personification of war or victory, as

seen in *The Battle of the Amazons* (c. 1618) by Peter Paul Rubens. *Whistlejacket* of 1762, painted by George Stubbs (1724-1806), embodies the horse's majesty, strength, vitality and beauty. Romantic and nineteenth-century artists, such as Théodore Géricault (1791-1824) and Eugène Delacroix (1798-1863), painted horses to convey emotional intensity and human struggle. In the early twentieth century, Wassily Kandinsky (1866-1944) and Franz Marc (1880-1916) painted blue horses to convey spirituality, freedom, intuition and masculinity. In Eastern art, horses can signify speed, loyalty and mysticism.

1

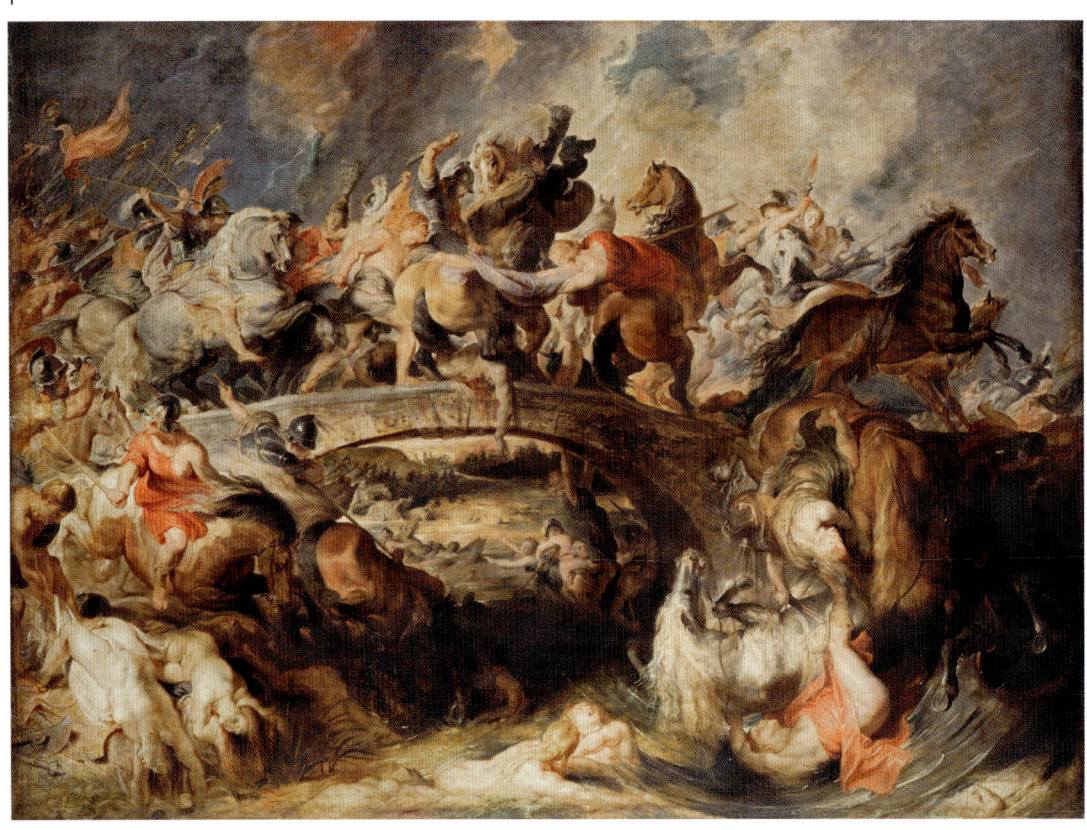

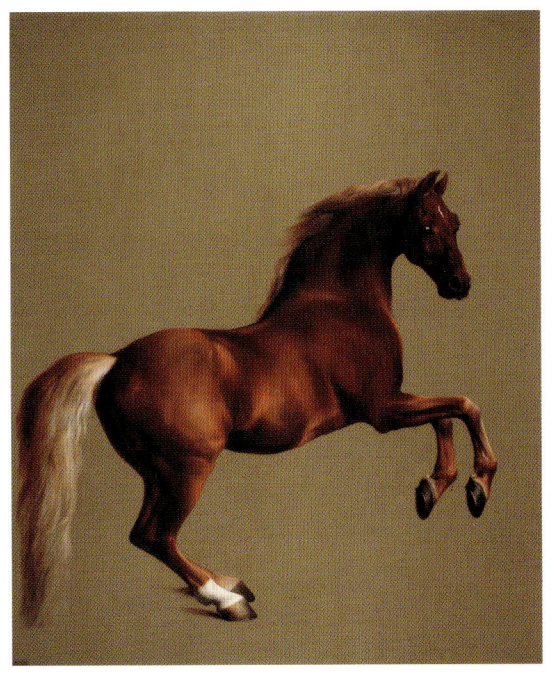

2

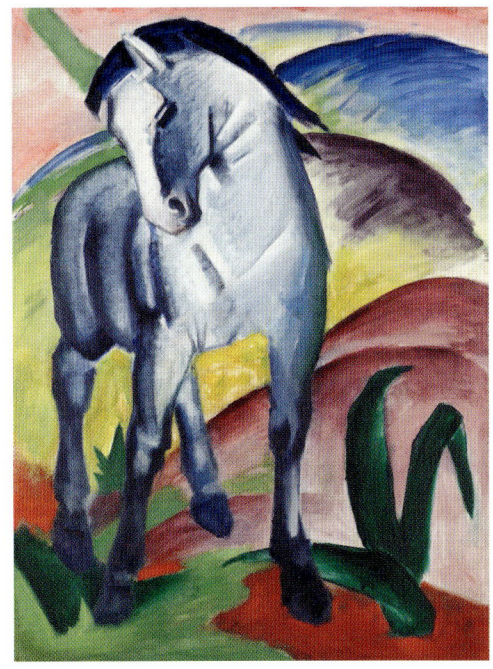

3

4

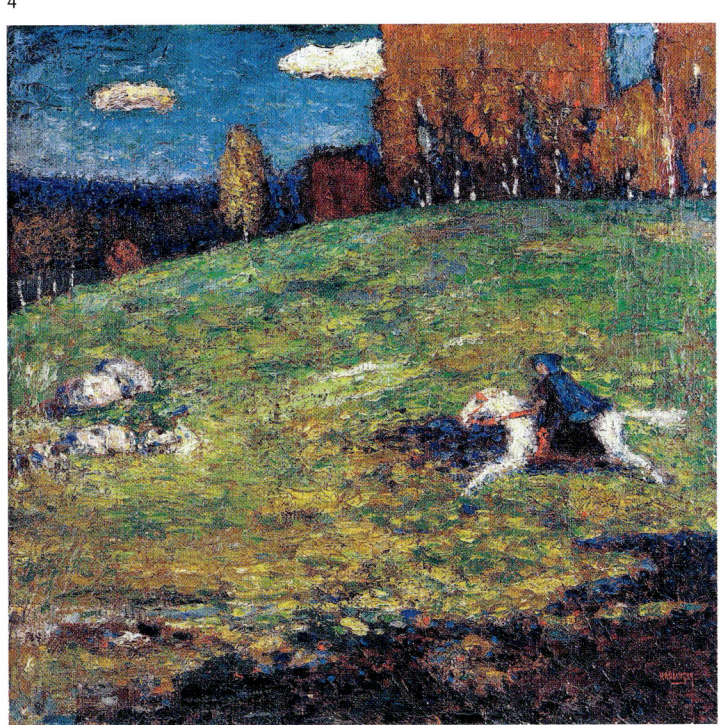

1. *The Battle of the Amazons,* Peter Paul Rubens, c. 1618
2. *Whistlejacket,* George Stubbs, 1762
3. *Blue Horse I,* Franz Marc, 1911
4. *The Blue Rider,* Wassily Kandinsky, 1903

Snake

In art, snakes embody both good and evil, life and
death, wisdom and temptation, rebirth and healing.
In Judeo-Christian tradition, the serpent in Eden
represents sin and seduction, becoming a powerful
symbol of moral fall and human frailty. This imagery
dominates medieval and Renaissance religious art.
Yet in classical mythology, snakes also signify
transformation and healing. Asclepius, the Greek
god of medicine, carries a staff entwined with a
serpent, a symbol still used in medicine today. In
Hindu and Buddhist art, snakes (nagas) are revered
as sacred and protective beings. In Mesoamerican
cultures, feathered serpent deities like Quetzalcoatl
represent rebirth and cosmic order. The snake's
ability to shed its skin makes it a natural metaphor
for regeneration, and artists often exploit its
sinuous form to introduce tension, sensuality or
danger. In modern art, the snake's ambiguous
symbolism can offer layers of psychological and
spiritual meaning, from the erotic to the esoteric.

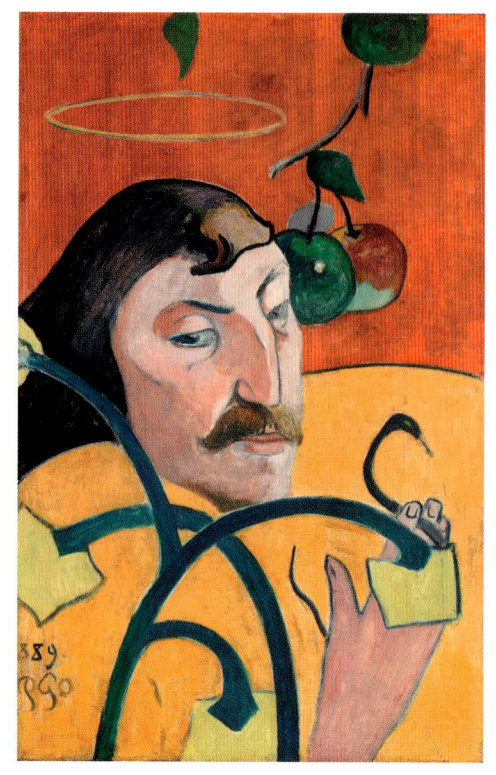

1

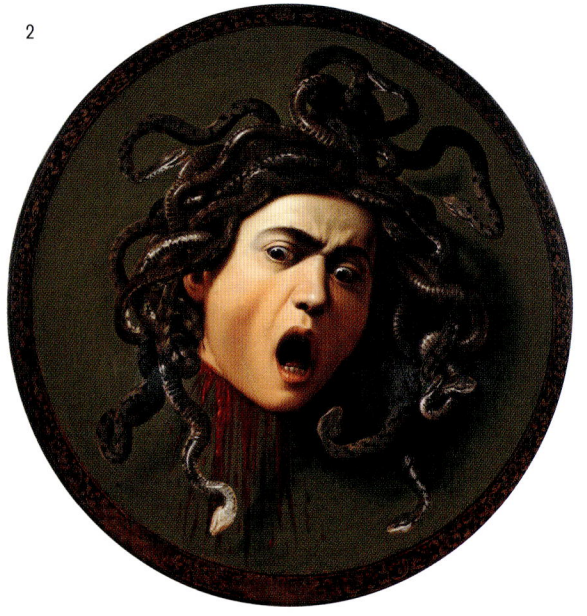

2

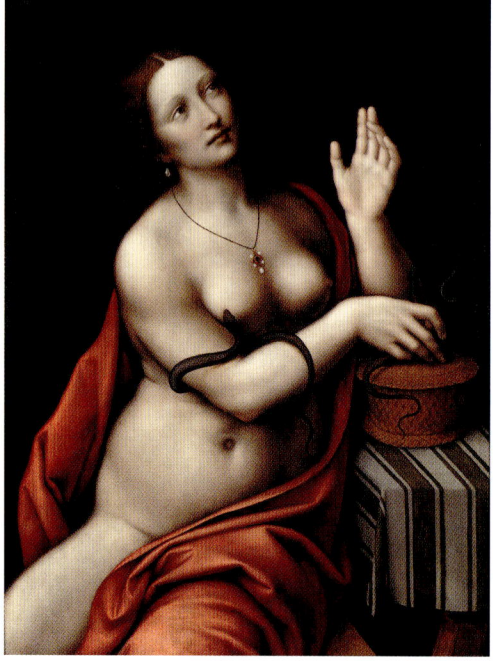

3

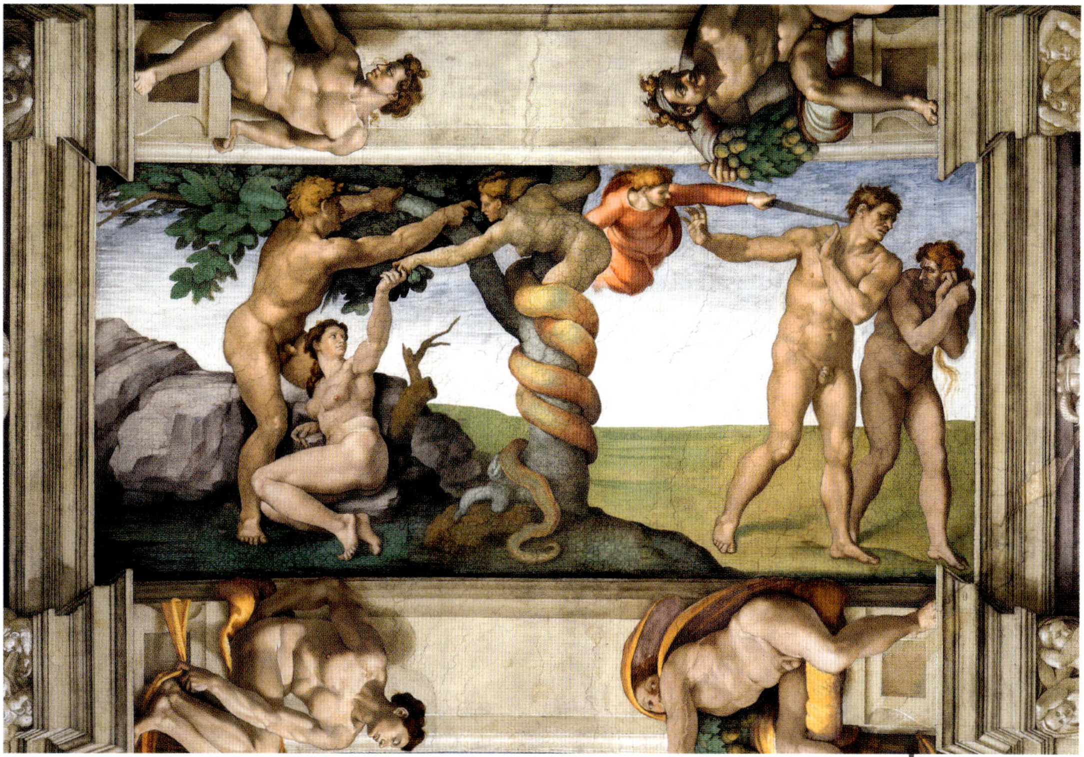

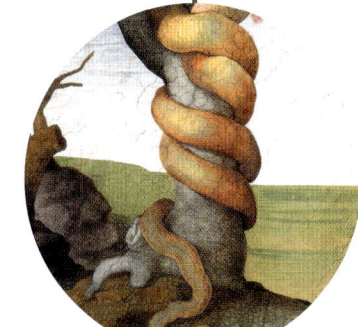

4

5

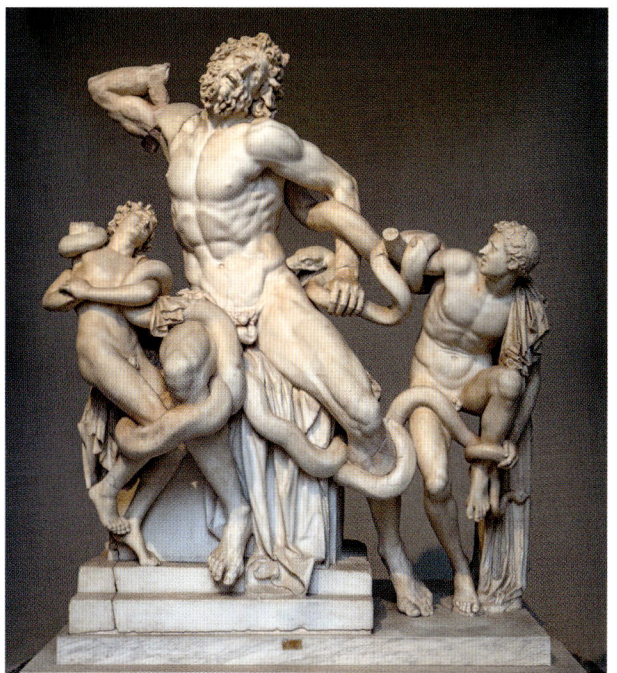

1. *Self-Portrait with Halo and Snake,* Paul Gauguin, 1889
2. *Medusa,* Caravaggio, 1595-96
3. *Cleopatra,* Giampietrino, 1524-26
4. *The Fall of Man,* Michelangelo, 1508-11
5. *Laocoön and His Sons,* Greece, (323 BCE-31 CE)

Monkey

Monkeys in art often serve as mirrors of human folly, curiosity or mischief. In medieval and Renaissance paintings, they can symbolize vice, vanity and irrationality; they are creatures driven by instinct rather than reason. The idea of *singerie* (French for 'monkey trick'), a genre of art in which monkeys are depicted imitating human behaviour, became especially popular in the sixteenth century. Artists who incorporated monkeys into allegorical scenes include Pieter van der Borcht (c. 1530–1608), Jan Brueghel the Elder (1568–1625), and David Teniers the Younger (1610–90) and his younger brother Abraham Teniers (1629–70), who portrayed monkeys as satirical substitutes for people, mocking social conventions. In Eastern traditions, monkeys often carry spiritual significance. In Chinese and Japanese art, they may symbolize cleverness or be linked to specific deities, such as the Monkey King in Chinese folklore. In modern art, monkeys sometimes embody the blurred line between nature and culture, or question the boundaries of civilization or the human condition.

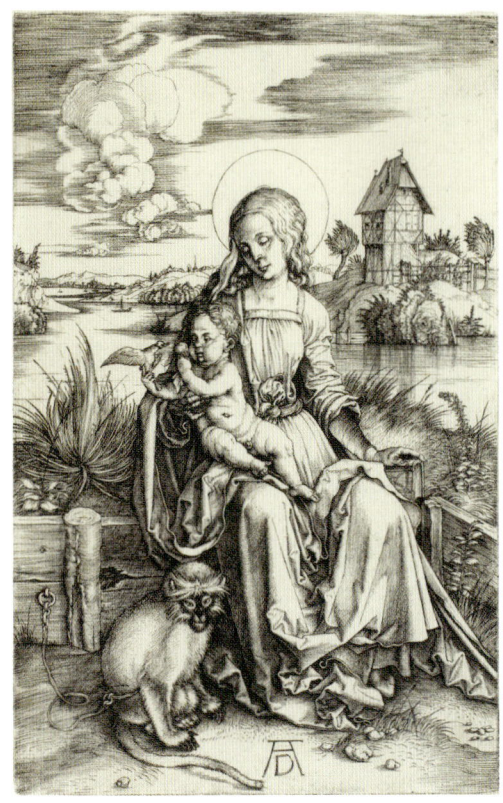

1

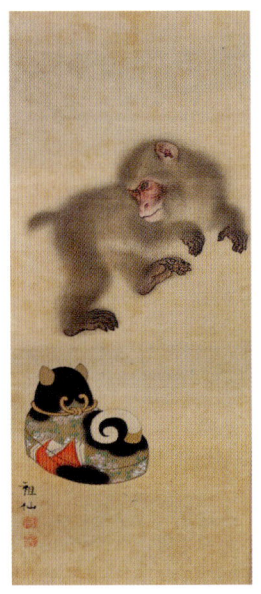

2

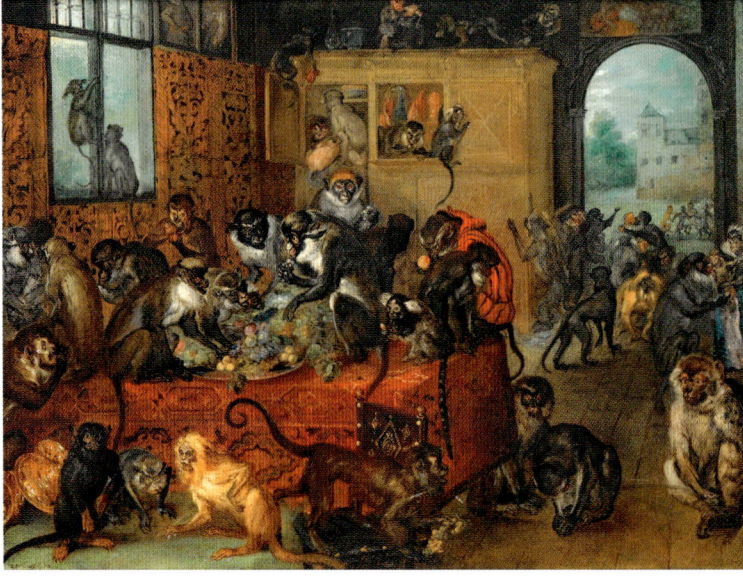

3

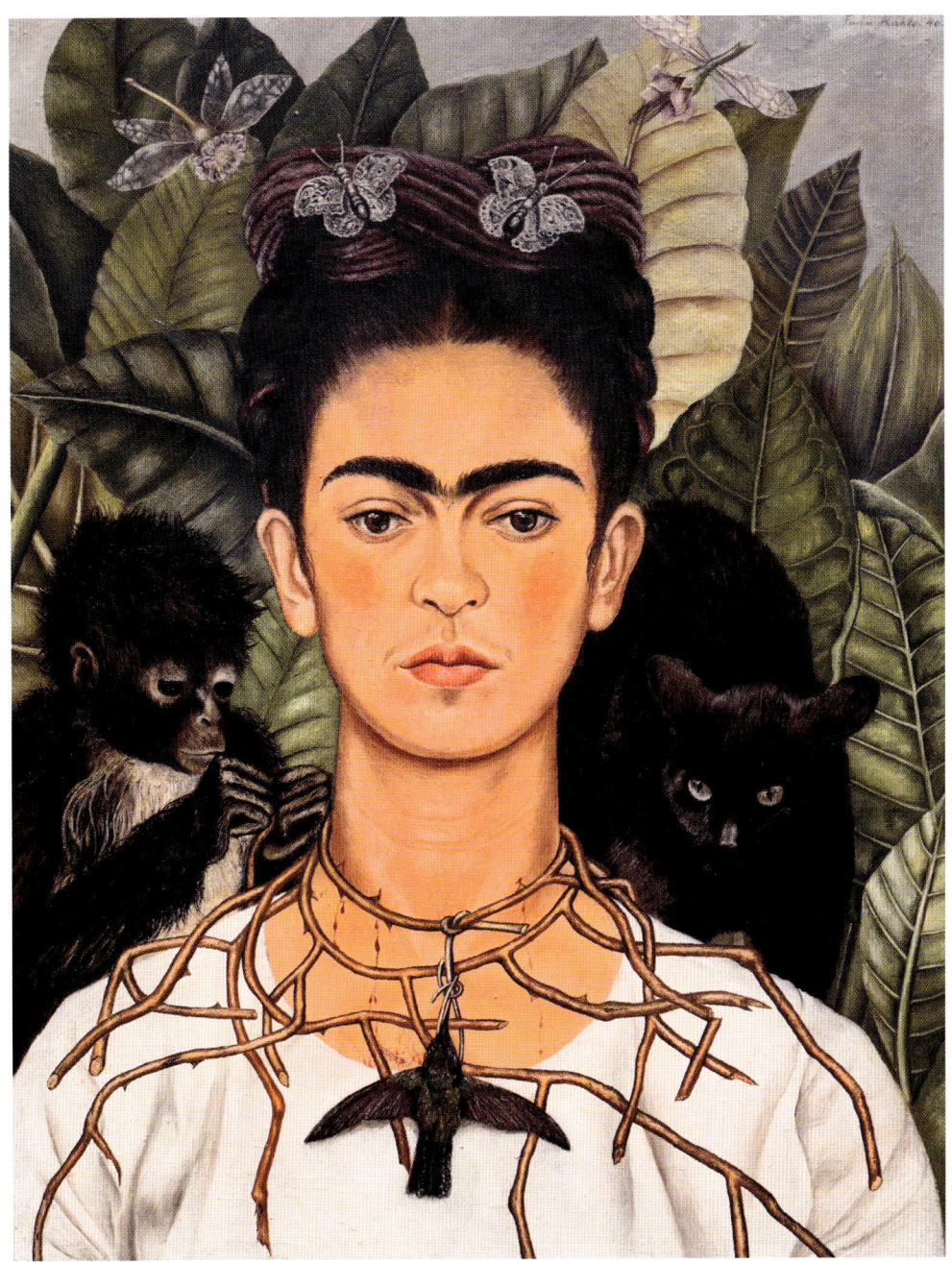

4

1. *Madonna with the Monkey,* Albrecht Dürer, c. 1498
2. *Monkeys at Play,* Mori Sosen, 1800
3. *Monkeys Feasting,* Jan Brueghel the Elder, 1620
4. *Self-Portrait with Thorn Necklace and Hummingbird,* Frida Kahlo, 1940

Lion

Lions have symbolized strength, courage, protection and magnificence for centuries in many societies. In ancient Mesopotamia, Assyria and Egypt, lions were often depicted as protectors or symbols of rulers, sometimes in scenes of lion hunts, which were intended to convey the king's power and authority. One of the gates leading to the city of Babylon featured various animals, including lions that embodied the goddess Ishtar. Lions in Christian art can symbolize Jesus, St Mark, majesty and resurrection. In medieval heraldry, they allude to nobility, bravery and lineage. Images of lions frequently flanked thrones, gates or coats of arms, guarding earthly and spiritual realms. In Hinduism and Buddhism, the lion is associated with divine power and cosmic authority. Later artists, such as Peter Paul Rubens and Eugène Delacroix, often portrayed lions to explore themes of nature, violence or exoticism. The lion's muscular, majestic form makes it an enduring artistic icon of power, spiritual might and heroic symbolism.

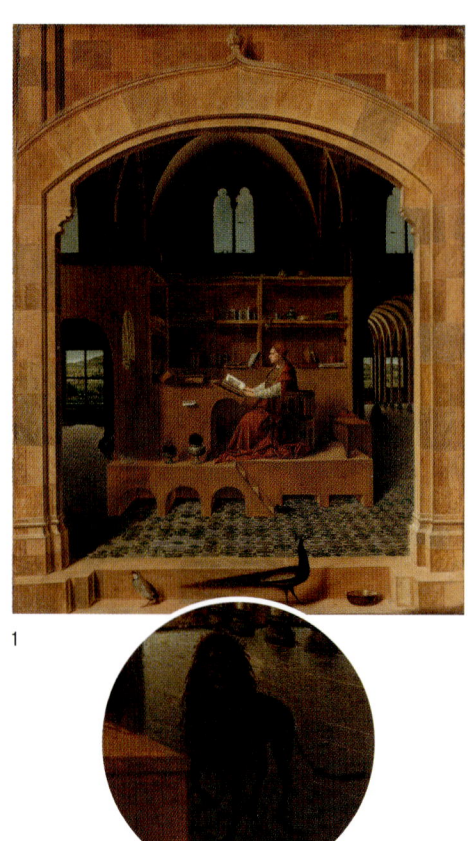

1

2

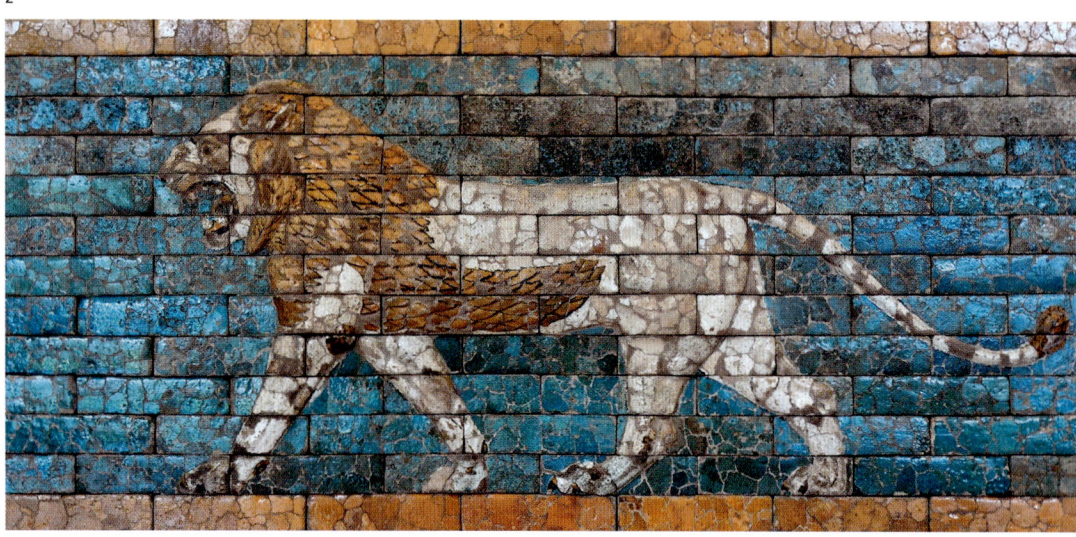

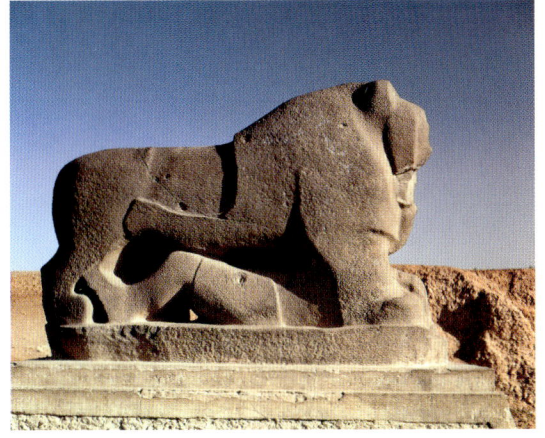

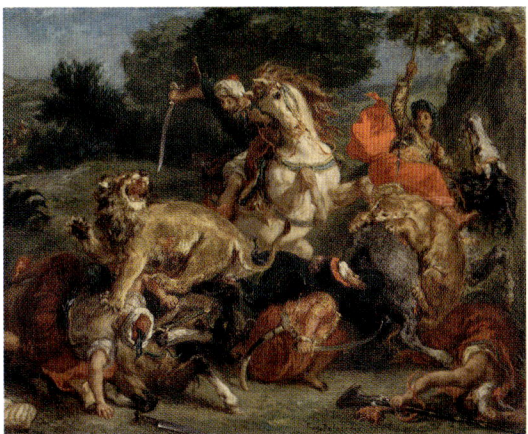

3

4

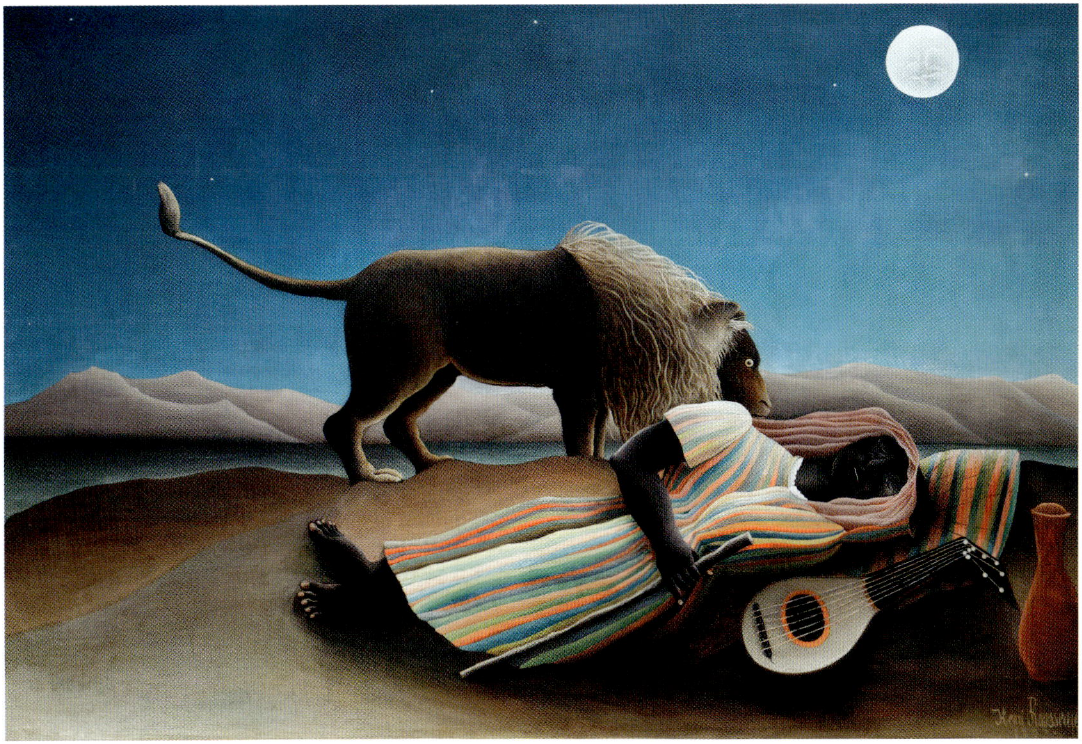

5

1. *Saint Jerome in His Study,* Antonello da Messina, c. 1475
2. *Detail from Ishtar Gate,* Iraq, c. 569 BCE
3. *Lion of Babylon,* Mesopotamia, 1595 BCE
4. *The Lion Hunt,* Eugène Delacroix, 1855
5. *The Sleeping Gypsy,* Henri Rousseau, 1897

Deer

In art, fawns and deer often symbolize gentleness, piety and spiritual renewal. Their graceful form, locomotion and elusive nature have made them powerful metaphors across religions and cultures. In Christian iconography, the deer sometimes represents the soul's longing for God. Saint Eustace and Saint Hubert are said to have seen visions of a crucifix between a deer's antlers, which is why they are often depicted as symbols of divine revelation. In Eastern art, especially in Buddhism, deer signify harmony and peace, frequently appearing in serene landscapes or alongside the Buddha to represent the deer park where he first taught. In medieval bestiaries, deer

were admired for their gentleness and moral purity. As their antlers are shed and regrown, they also represent regeneration. In Romantic and more modern art, deer may evoke wilderness, innocence or melancholy, continuing their role as gentle yet profound emblems of the natural and spiritual worlds. Frida Kahlo, who had a pet deer called Granizo, painted her as a symbol of resilience.

1. *The Vision of Saint Eustace,* Pisanello, c. 1438-42
2. *The Monarch of the Glen,* Sir Edwin Landseer, 1851
3. *Diana and Actaeon,* Titian, 1556-59
4. *The Hunt in the Forest,* Paolo Uccello, 1470

1

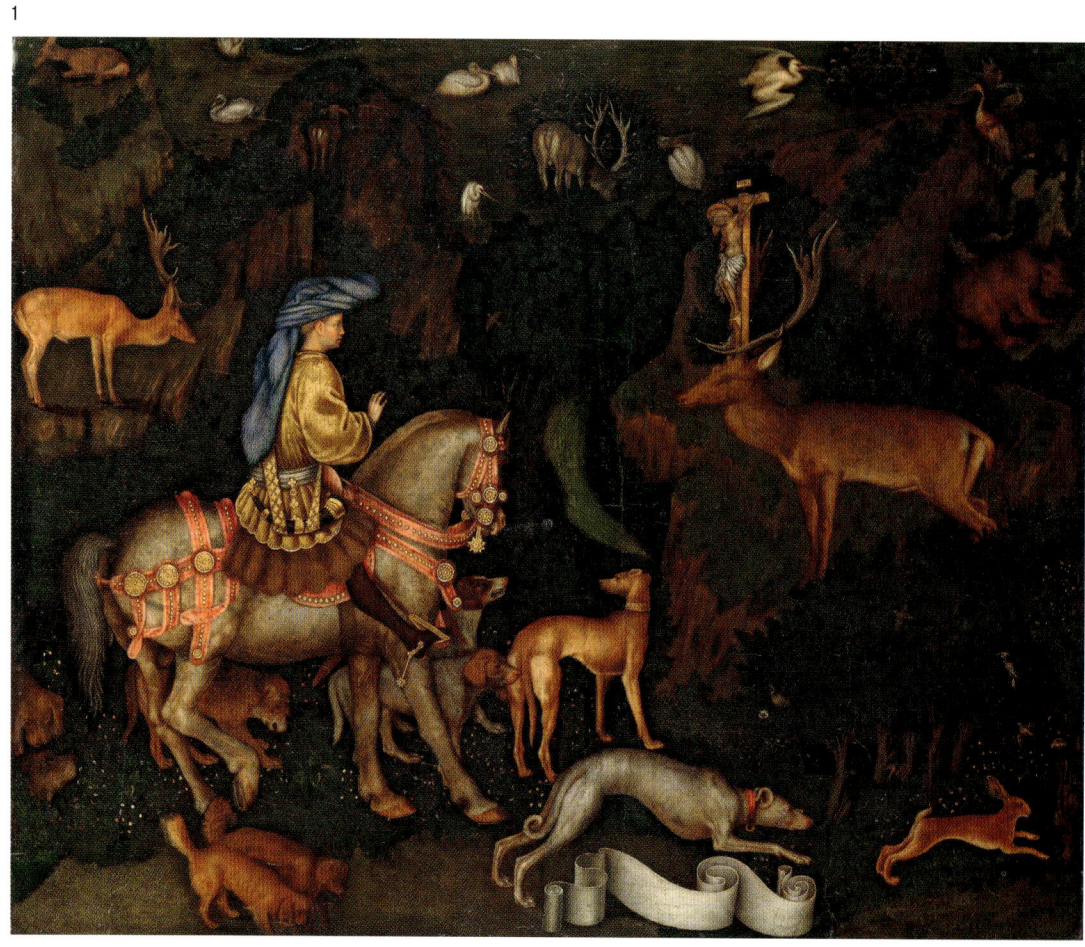

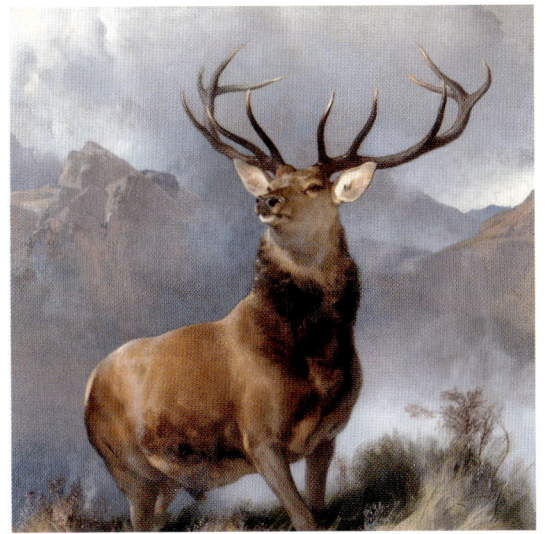

2

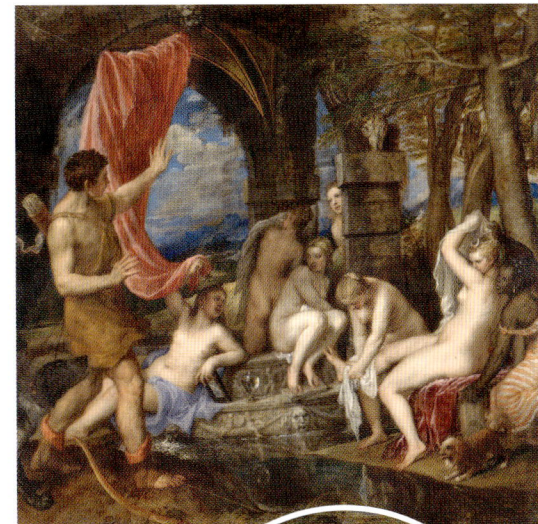

3

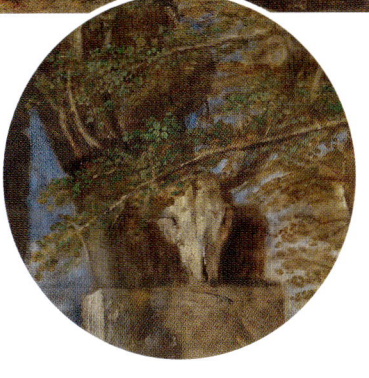

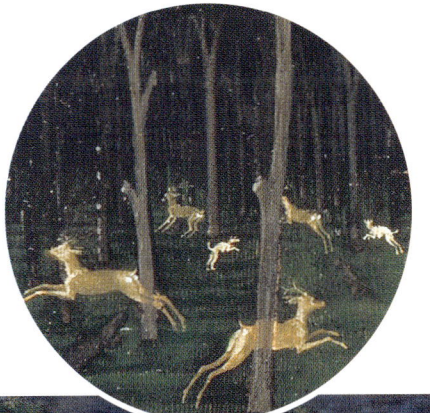

4

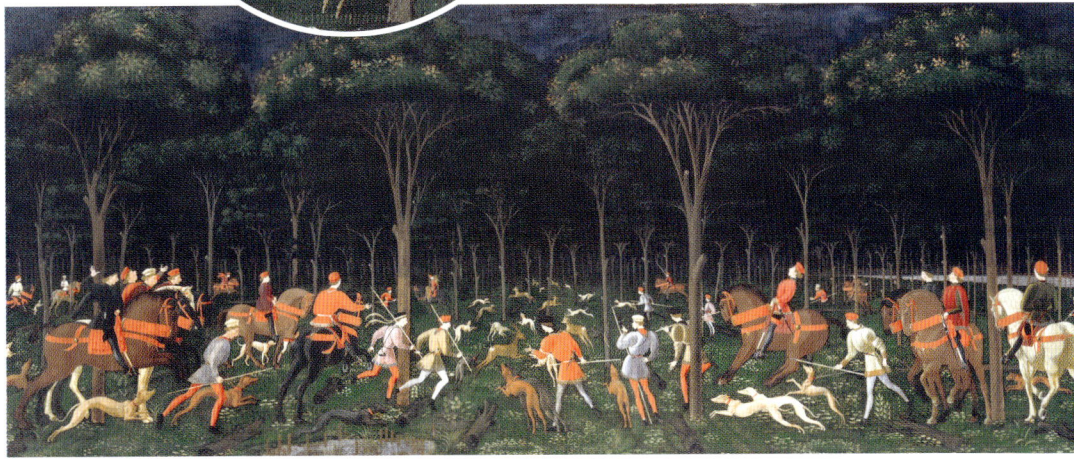

Cat

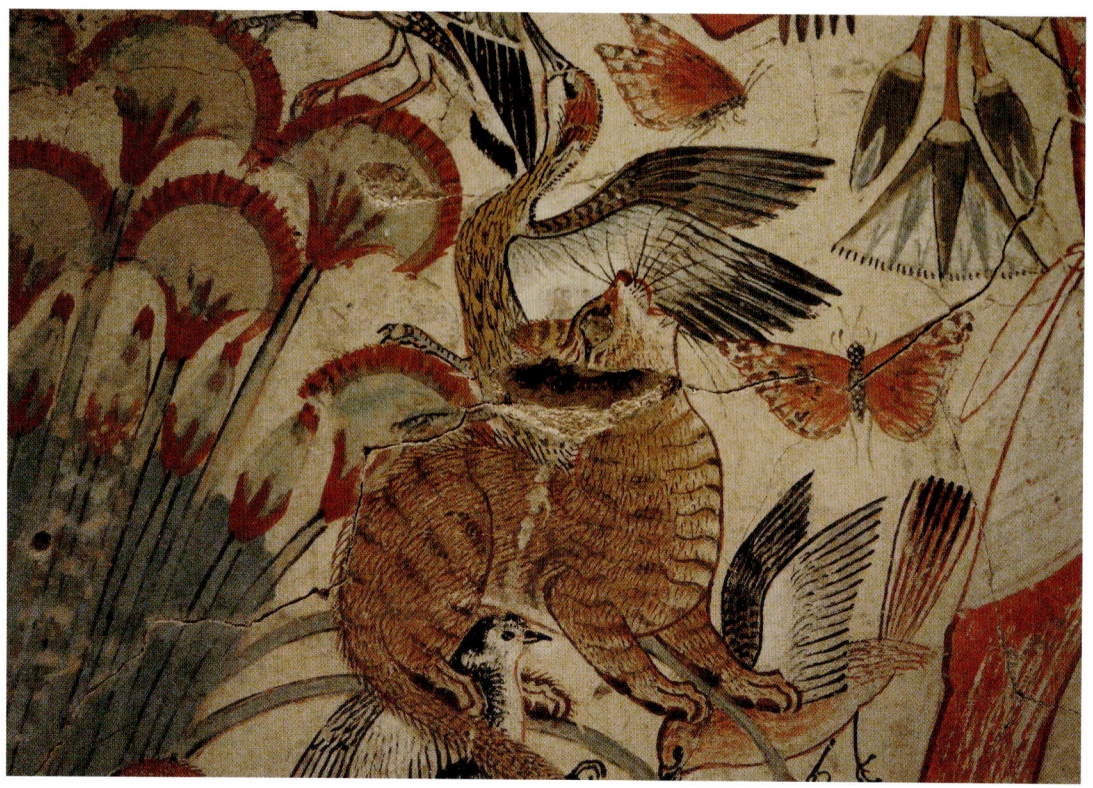

1

Cats have been featured as diverse symbols throughout art history, often embodying mystery, independence and the supernatural. In ancient Egypt, cats were sacred animals associated with the goddess Bastet, symbolizing protection, fertility and domestic harmony. Japanese art sometimes shows cats as lucky charms or spiritual beings. In medieval Europe, however, cats, especially black ones, became linked with witchcraft, magic and evil, reflecting societal fears and superstitions. In Renaissance and Baroque art, cats often symbolized sensuality, cunning or female sexuality. In general, cats in art can be depicted as either good or evil. For example, the cat in *The Awakening Conscience* (1853) by William Holman Hunt (1827–1910) is trying to catch a bird, representing the man in the painting who is trying to keep his mistress. The black cat in *Olympia* (1863) by Édouard Manet is a symbol of promiscuity. Contrastingly, the cats in *Cat at Play* (c. 1860–78) by Henriëtte Ronner-Knip (1821–1909) and *Gabrielle Arnault as a Child* (1815) by Louis-Léopold Boilly (1761–1845) denote innocence, softness and domestic harmony.

1. *Detail from the Tomb of Nebamun,* Egypt, 1400–1350 BCE
2. *Le Chat Noir,* Théophile Steinlen, 1896
3. *The Awakening Conscience,* William Holman Hunt, 1853
4. *Olympia,* Édouard Manet, 1863

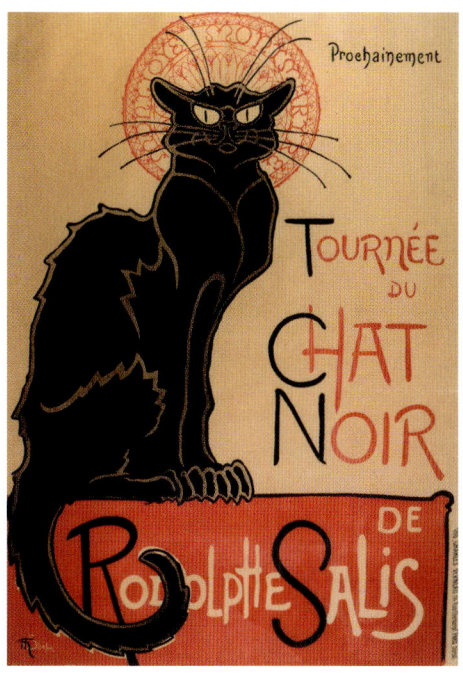

2

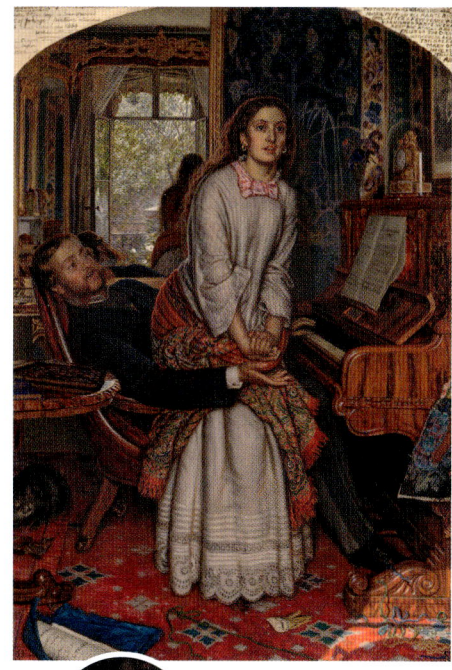

3

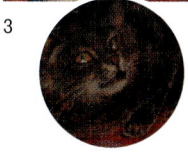

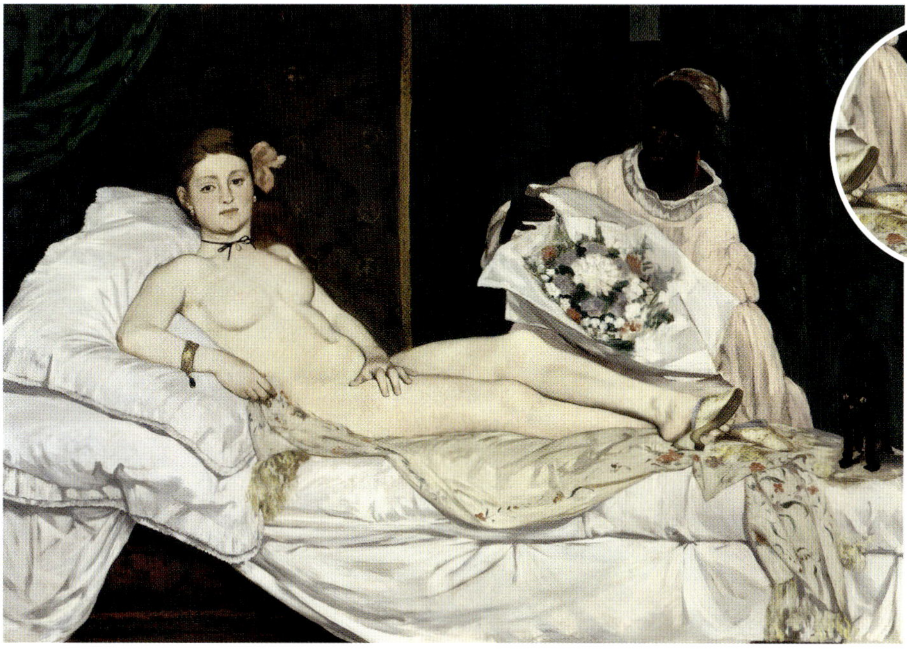

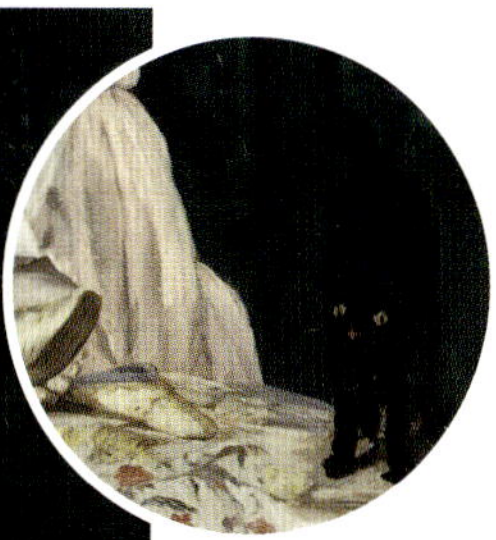

4

Dog

Dogs are longstanding symbols of loyalty, fidelity, protection, vigilance and companionship. For centuries, they have appeared alongside humans as faithful guardians or hunting partners. Dogs in ancient Egyptian tomb paintings embodied vigilance and served as guides to the afterlife. The ancient Sumerian goddess Gula was initially known as Bau (or Baba), the goddess of dogs, and was usually depicted with a canine companion or as a dog-like creature. In Renaissance portraits, dogs often symbolize marital fidelity; for instance, in *The Arnolfini Portrait* (1434) by Jan van Eyck (before 1390–1441) and *Venus of Urbino* (1534) by Titian. In various forms of religious art, dogs can signify guardianship or spiritual watchfulness. The Christian Saint Roch is often depicted with a dog, denoting healing and loyalty. In Baroque paintings, dogs often express the emotional bond between humans and animals. In the main, the dog's consistent presence across cultures and eras highlights its universal association with devotion, protection and the human-animal bond.

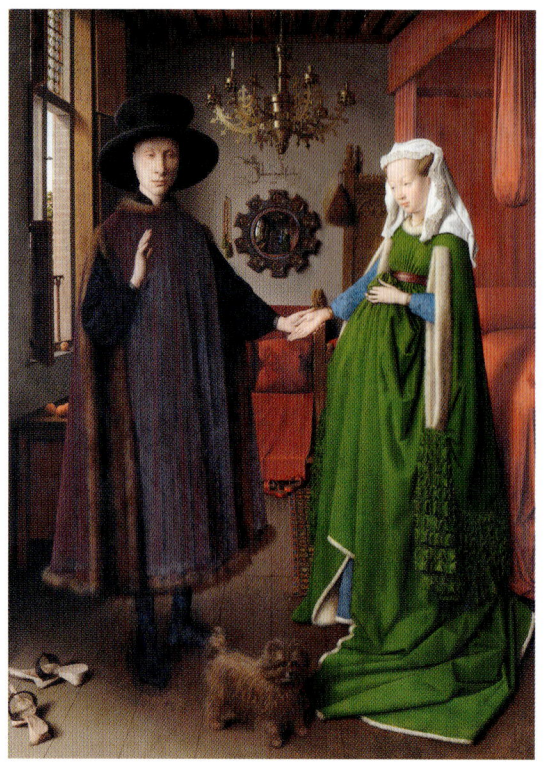

1

2

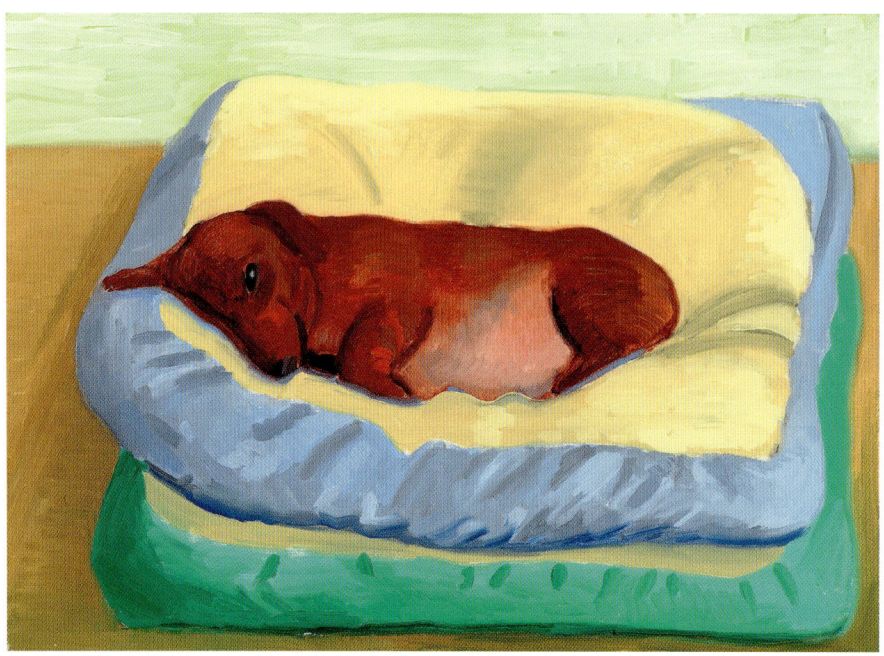

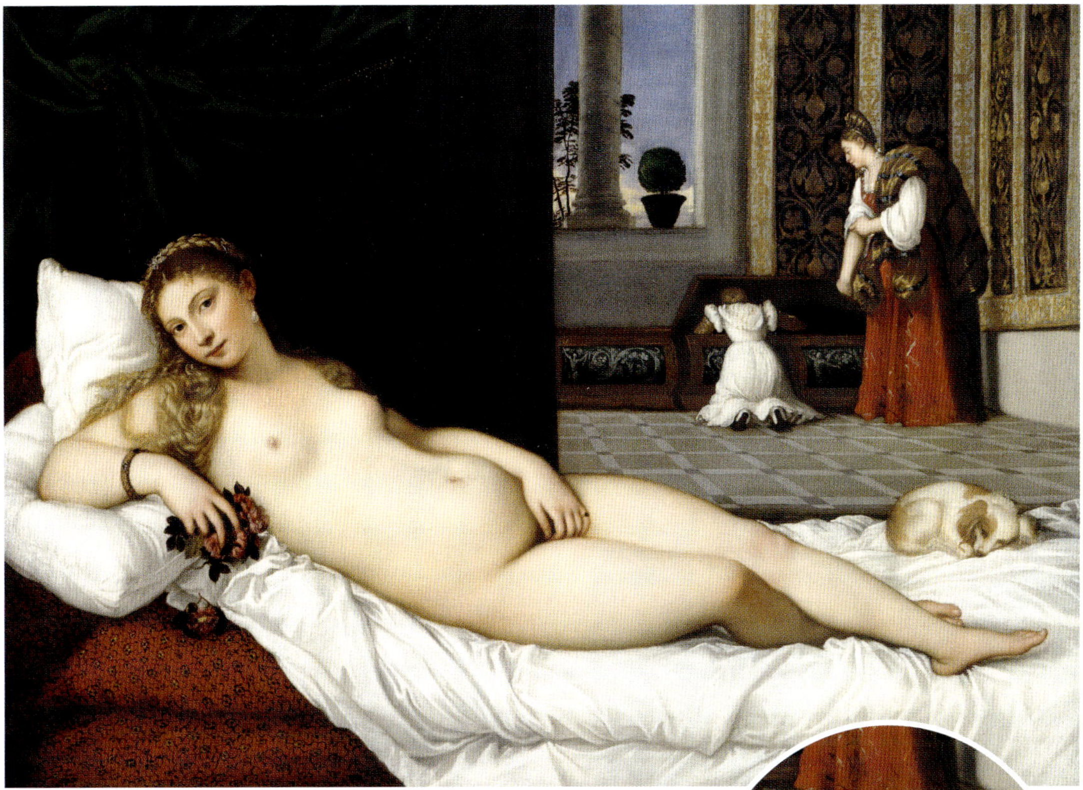

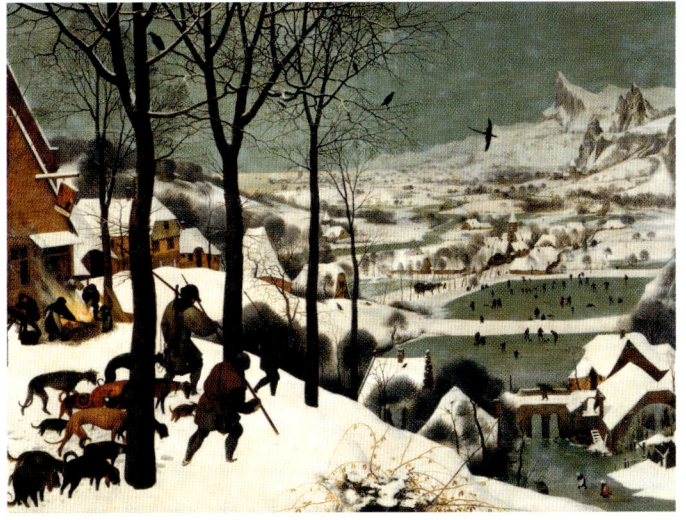

3

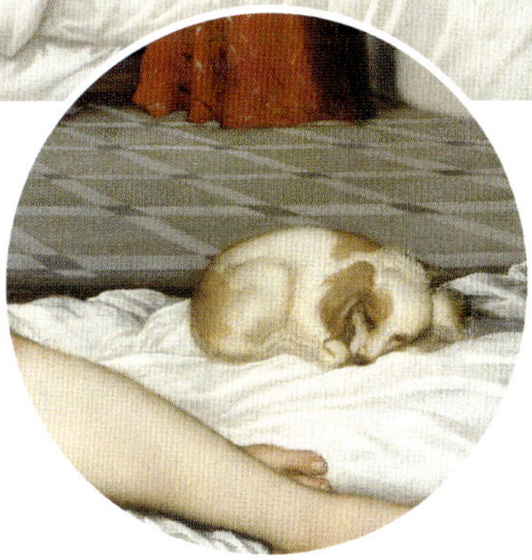

4

1. *The Arnolfini Portrait,* Jan van Eyck, 1434
2. *Dog Painting 44,* David Hockney, 1995
3. *Venus of Urbino,* Titian, 1534
4. *The Hunters in the Snow,* Pieter Bruegel
   the Elder, 1565

Fish

Fish symbolism in art is multifaceted and often tied to fertility, abundance, the unconscious and spirituality. In Christian iconography, the fish is usually used to represent Christ and his followers. The Greek word *ichthys* (fish) was a secret sign among early, persecuted Christians. Medieval and Renaissance religious art often includes fish to denote faith or baptism. In many cultures, fish symbolize fertility and prosperity due to their prolific reproduction and life-giving association with water. In East Asian art, the koi fish embodies perseverance, strength and good fortune. French artist Henri Matisse (1869–1954) was fascinated by Morocco, where he saw people relax by watching fish, so he painted nine versions of goldfish to achieve a similar effect. Odilon Redon often depicted fish, drawing inspiration from mythology, where fish symbolize transformation, wisdom or hidden realms beneath the surface of human consciousness.

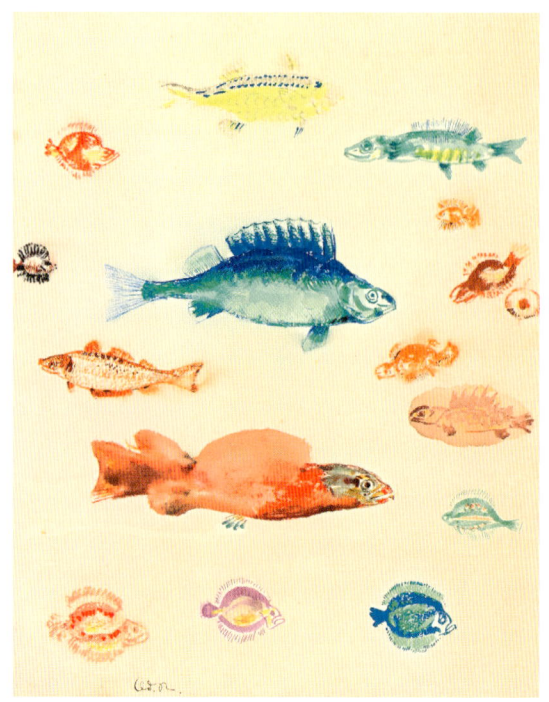

1

2

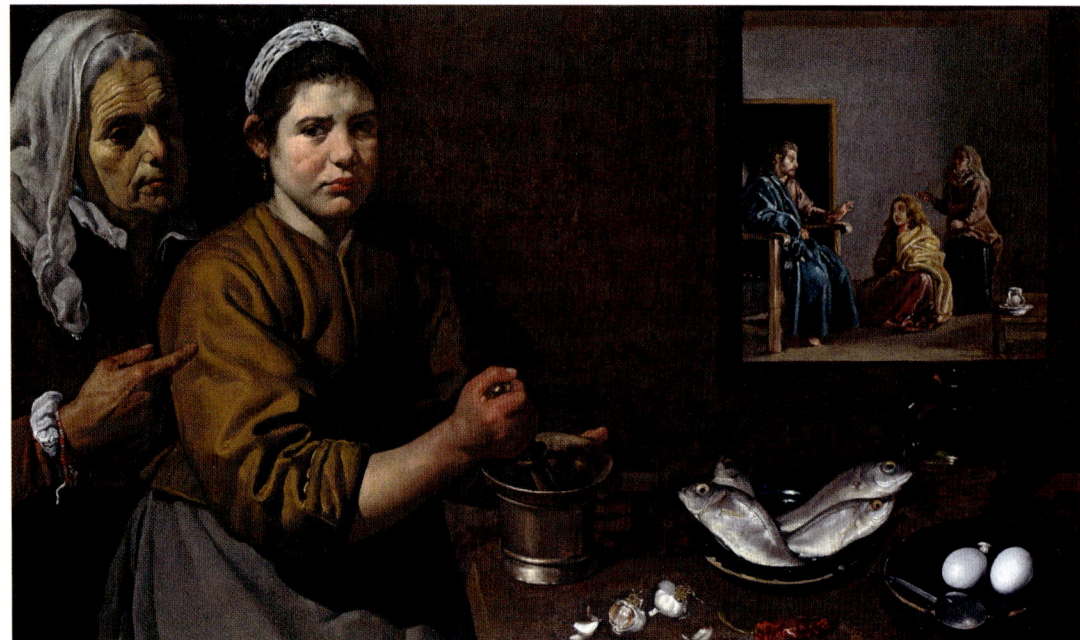

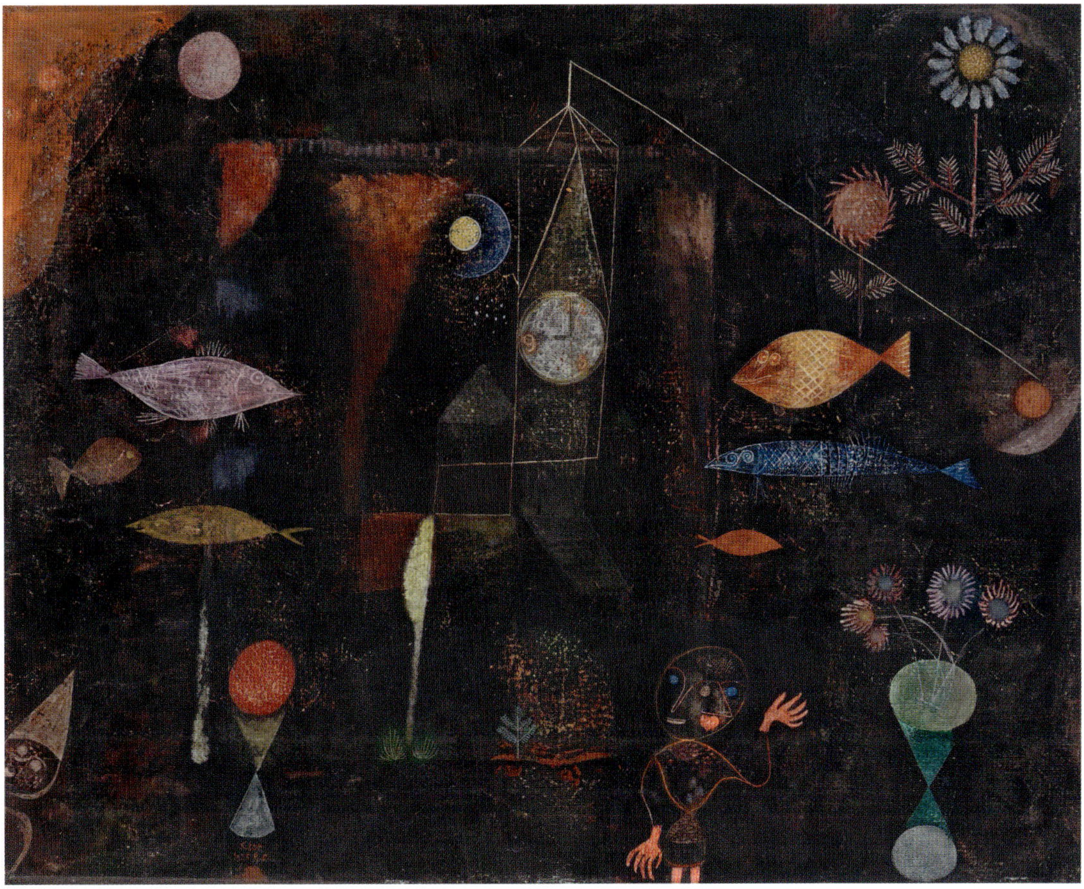

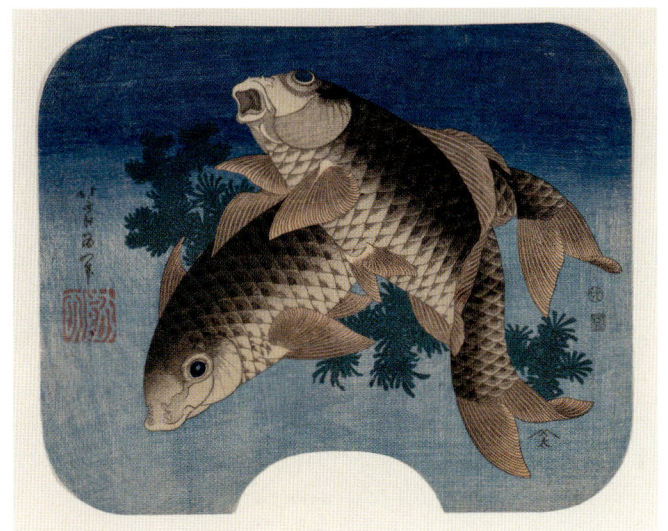

3

4

1. *Fish,* Odilon Redon, 1912
2. *Christ in the House of Martha and Mary,*
   Diego Velázquez, 1618
3. *Fish Magic,* Paul Klee, 1925
4. *Two Carp,* Katsushika Hokusai, 1831

Lobster

Representing various themes such as decadence, the subconscious, prosperity and mortality, the lobster in an artwork often adds layers of meaning and intrigue. In seventeenth-century Dutch still lifes, when lobsters appeared alongside silverware and exotic fruits, leaving vibrant reflections, they symbolized wealth, indulgence and mortality. In Japanese ukiyo-e images, artists including Utagawa Kuniyoshi (1798-1861) depicted lobsters as symbols of longevity and strength. Lobsters are sometimes associated with the uncanny or the irrational, as seen in the Surrealist three-dimensional artwork *Lobster Telephone* (1936) by Salvador Dalí (1904-89). In *The Illegal Operation* (1962), Edward Kienholz (1927-94) depicted a lobster

crawling out of a woman's purse, symbolizing themes of secrecy, danger and the unexpected consequences of clandestine actions. Lobsters have also appeared in the works of artists like Claes Oldenburg (1929-2022), who created large-scale sculptures of everyday objects, including a soft sculpture of a lobster, challenging traditional notions of materiality and form in art.

1. *Lobster Telephone,* Salvador Dalí, 1936
2. *Lobster and Phoenix,* Utagawa Kuniyoshi, c. 1837

1

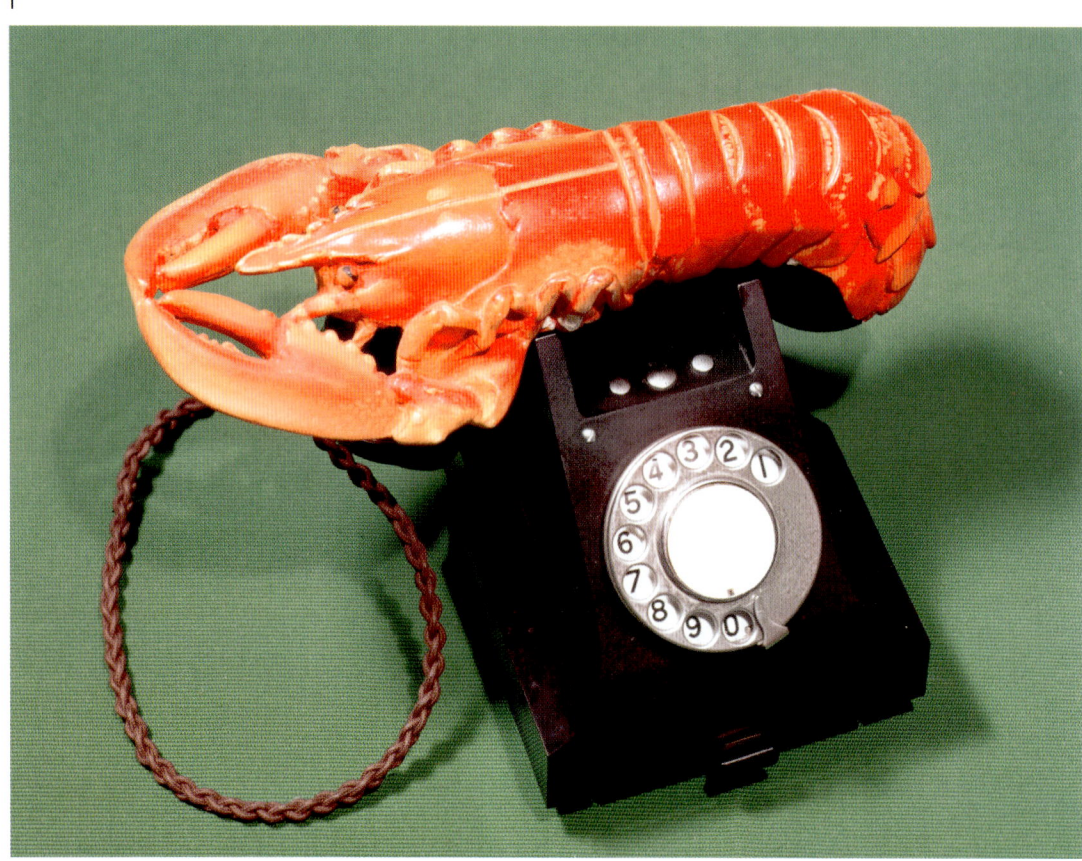

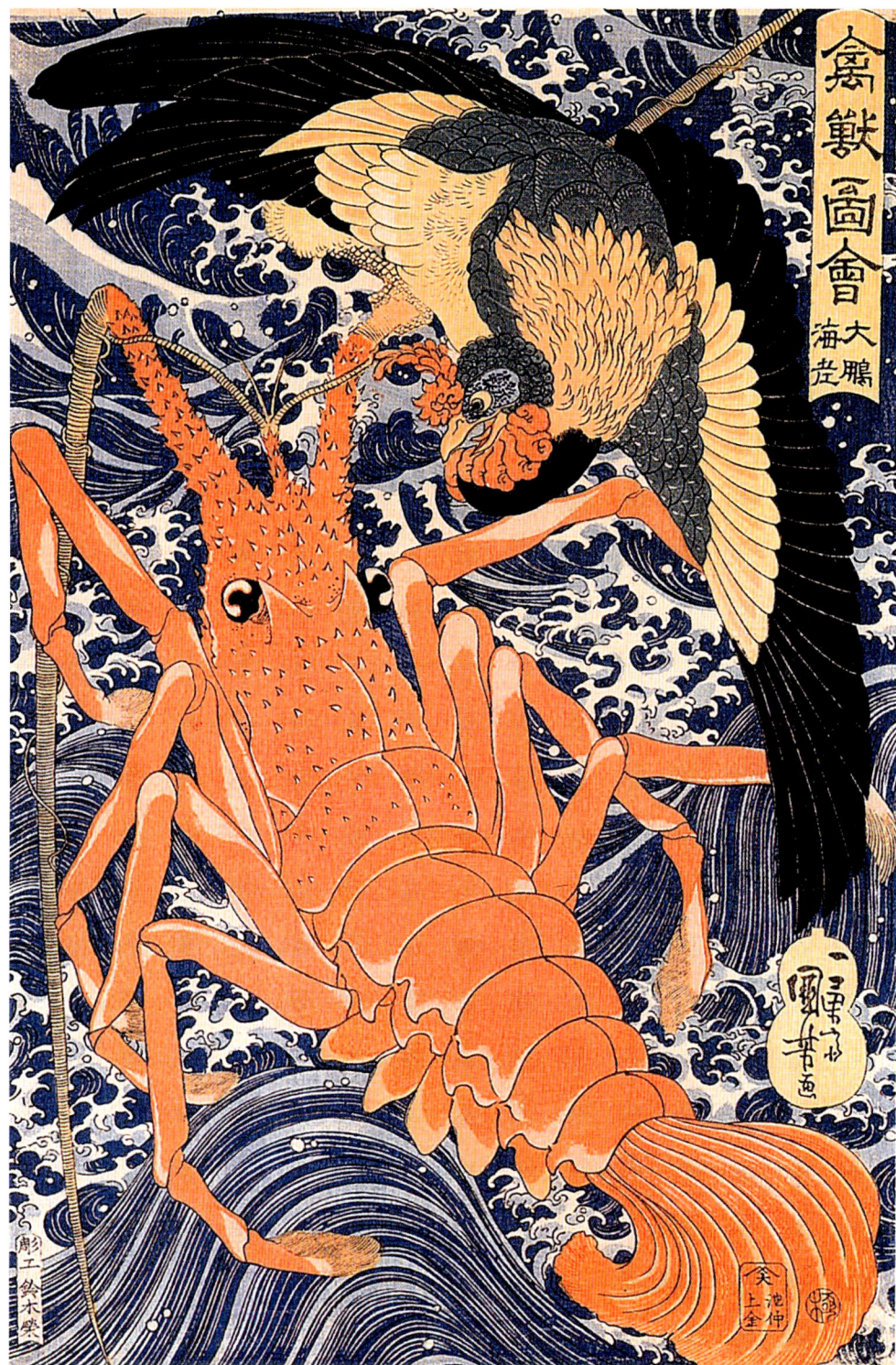

Dolphin

From Minoan frescoes to a 1987 bronze public sculpture in Puerto Vallarta, Mexico, dolphins have long symbolized intelligence, guidance, protection and harmony with nature. In art deriving from ancient Greek and Roman mythology, they were often linked to the gods Poseidon/Neptune and Aphrodite/Venus. For example, in *The Birth of Venus* (1879) by William-Adolphe Bouguereau (1825–1905), Venus stands nude on a scallop shell pulled by a dolphin. Dolphins also frequently appear in mosaics, pottery and sculptures as helpers of sailors and guides of souls, signifying safe passage. Renaissance artists revived classical dolphin imagery to convey notions of salvation and friendship. Dolphins also represent joy and playfulness. In Christian symbolism, dolphins occasionally appear as emblems of resurrection and redemption, echoing their role as protectors in pagan myths, or, for early sailors, as a symbol of Jesus himself. Throughout art history, dolphins have been associated with positive spiritual and social qualities, bridging the natural and divine worlds with their graceful presence.

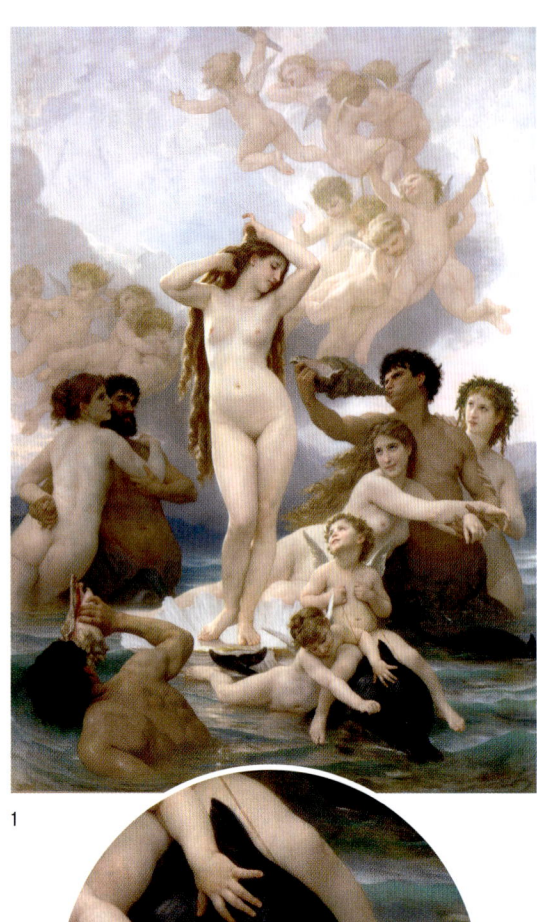

1

2

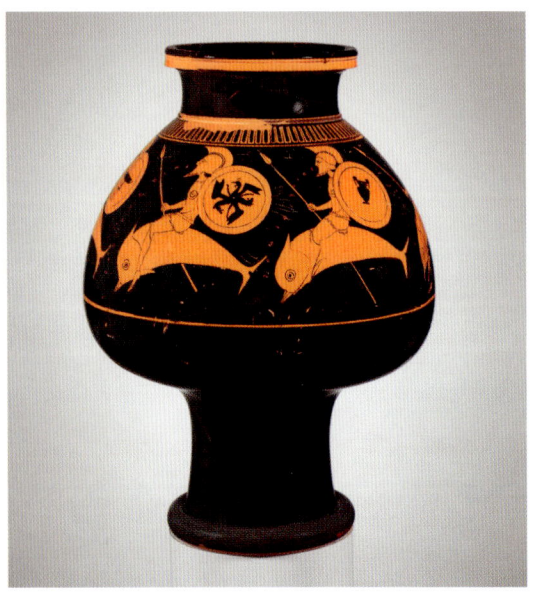

1. *The Birth of Venus,* William-Adolphe Bouguereau, 1879
2. Detail from Terracotta psykter (vase for cooling wine), attributed to Oltos, c. 520–510 BCE
3. *Detail from Dolphin Fresco,* Greece, 1600–1450 BCE
4. Roman floor mosaic in the House of Amphitrite, Tunisia, second century CE
5. *The Beautiful Friendship Fountain (Dancing Dolphins),* James 'Bud' Bottoms and Octavio González, 1987

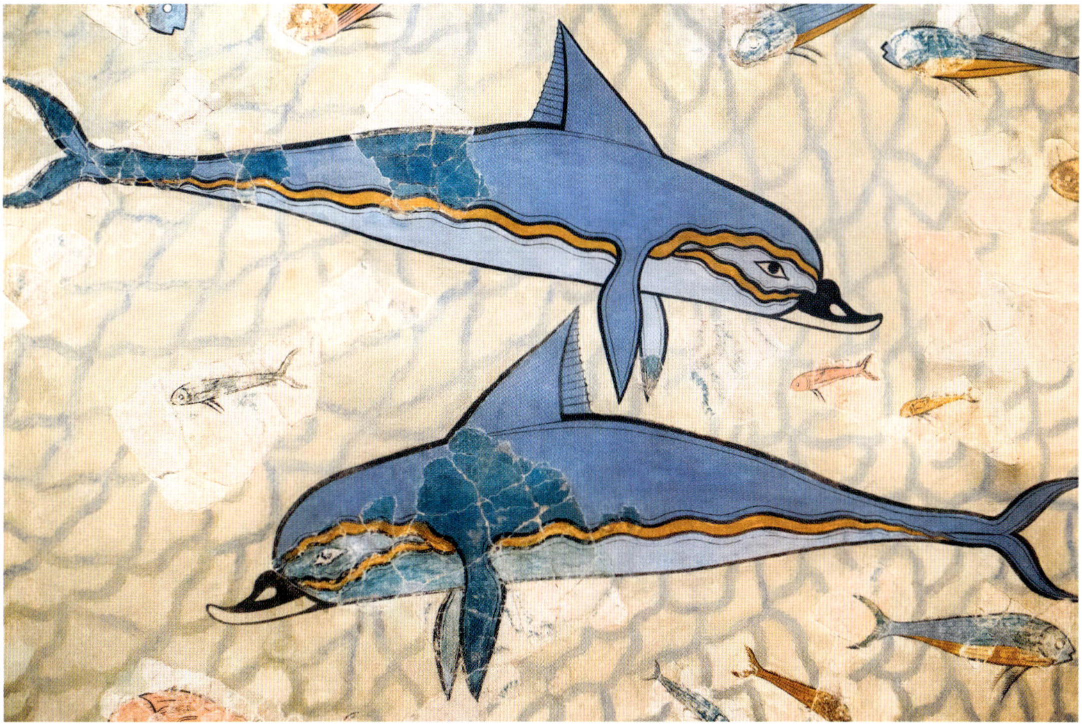

3

4

5

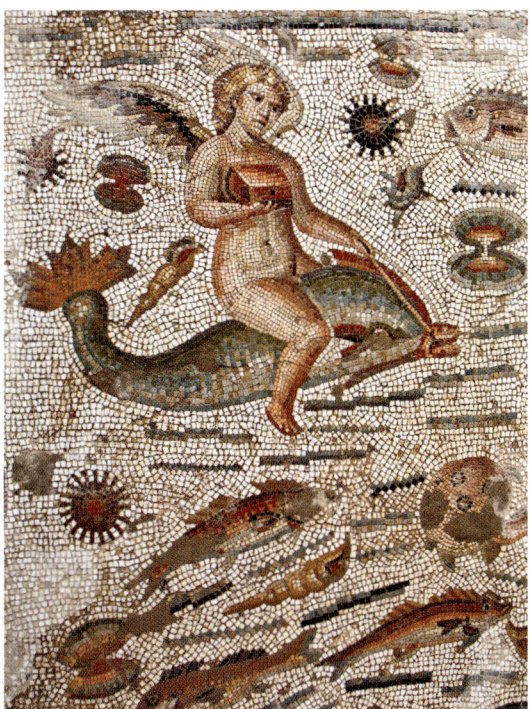

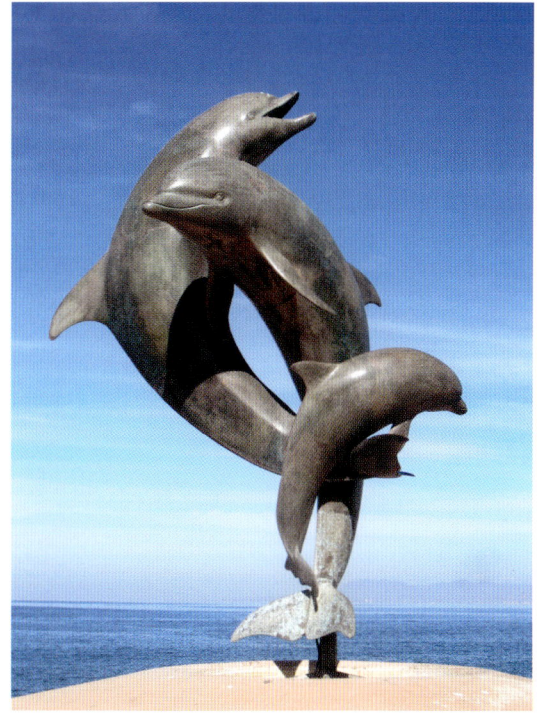

Seashell

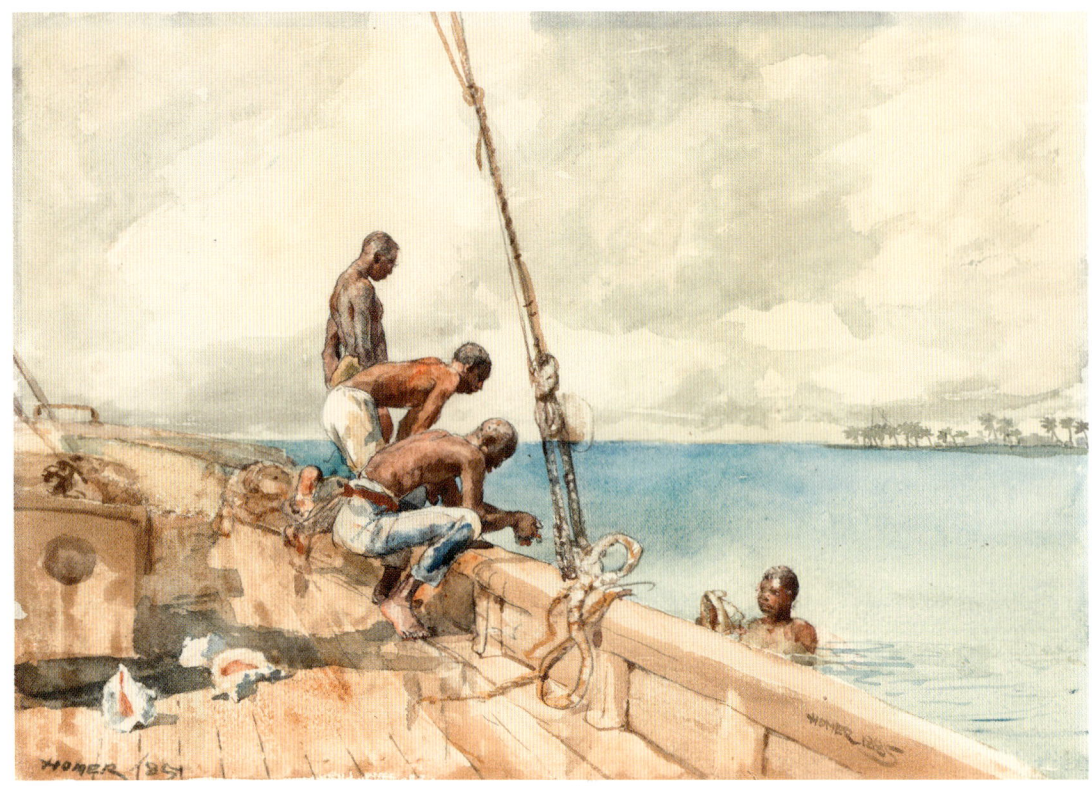

1

Embodying themes of fertility, femininity, rebirth, the divine, the mysteries of life, beauty and impermanence, seashells appear in a vast range of art. In ancient Greece and Rome, the scallop shell was associated with Aphrodite/Venus, the goddess of love, who was depicted arriving on the island of Cyprus on a seashell in Botticelli's *The Birth of Venus* (c. 1484-86). The scallop shell also occasionally appears in Christian art to represent spiritual awakening and faith. In Hinduism, the conch shell (shankha) symbolises purity and the sound 'Om', often used in meditation, while in Buddhism, the conch shell is emblematic of the dissemination of Buddha's teachings. Indigenous American and African cultures have used cowrie shells as symbols of fertility, wealth and protection, often incorporating them into ceremonial objects and jewellery. During the Renaissance and Baroque periods, shells appeared in religious and allegorical paintings, sometimes as architectural motifs symbolizing divine shelter. In seventeenth-century Dutch vanitas still lifes, empty shells evoked the transience of life.

1. *The Conch Divers,* Winslow Homer, 1885
2. *Still Life with Flowers, Insects and a Shell,* Maria van Oosterwijck, 1689
3. *Shells,* Edward Weston, 1927-30
4. *The Birth of Venus,* Sandro Botticelli, c. 1484-86

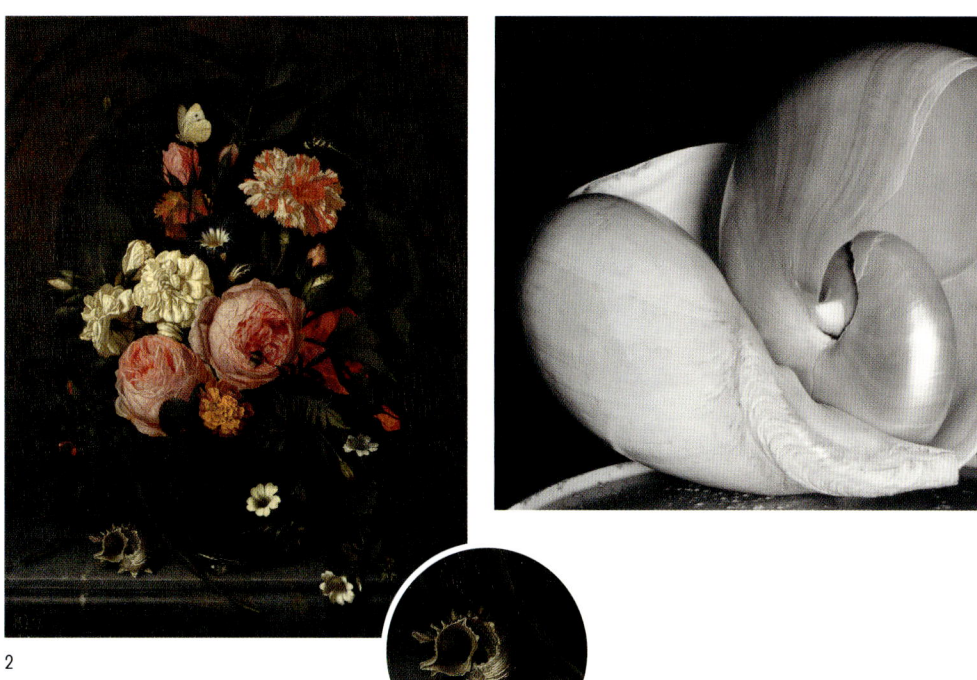

2

3

4

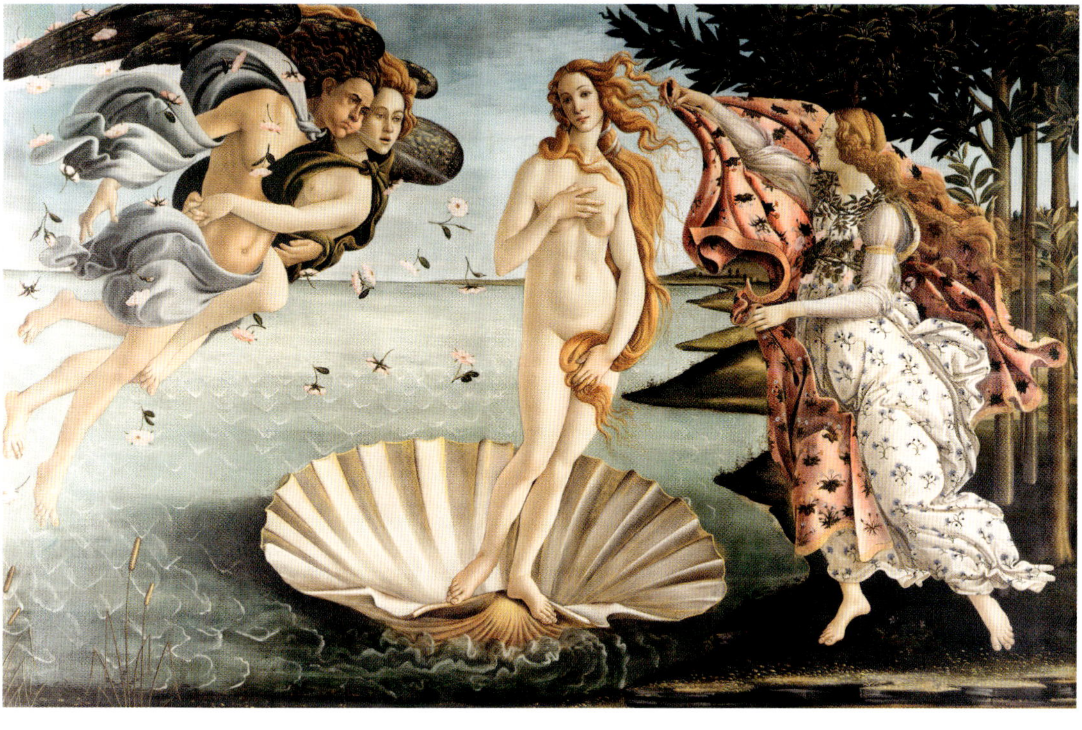

Crane

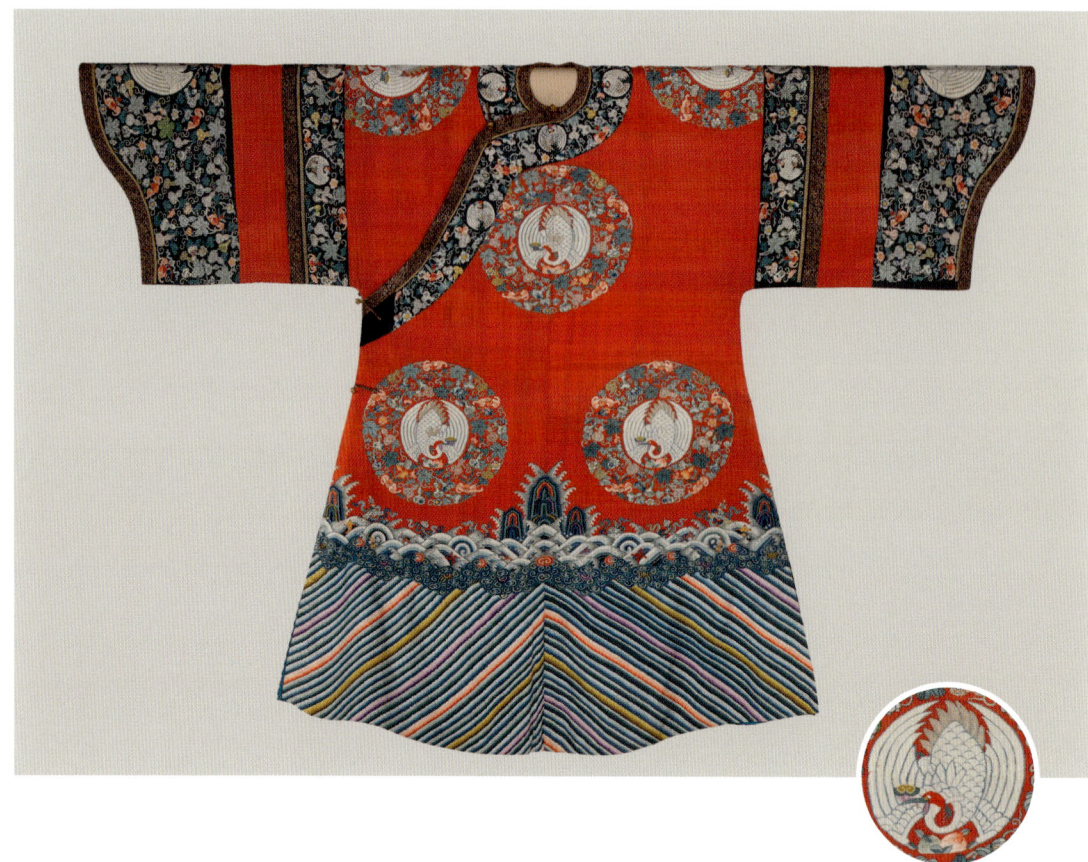

Especially in East Asian art, cranes are potent symbols of longevity, vigilance and wisdom. In Chinese and Japanese traditions, cranes represent immortality and good fortune, often depicted flying or standing in serene landscapes. Due to their elegant form and graceful demeanour, they are associated with scholars and sages. In Japanese art, cranes symbolize peace and fidelity; for example, origami cranes are associated with wishes for health and happiness, while painted screens, such as *Reeds and Cranes* (c. 1828–early 1830s), by Suzuki Kiitsu (1796–1858), were created to convey both the elegance of cranes and their perceived powers of eternal life and luck. In medieval European art, cranes sometimes implied watchfulness, as they were believed to hold stones in their claws to keep them alert even when resting. Cranes also appear in mythological stories and allegories, embodying themes of transformation and transcendence. Their distinctive stature and behaviour have made them enduring emblems of nobility and spiritual aspiration in art worldwide.

1. *Woman's Robe Decorated with Crane Medallions,* China, c. seventeenth–nineteenth century
2. *Reeds and Cranes,* Suzuki Kiitsu, c. 1828–early 1830s
3. *Portrait of an Imperial Censor and his Wife,* Qing China, c. 1767–1899
4. *Paper Cranes,* Sadako Sasaki, 1955

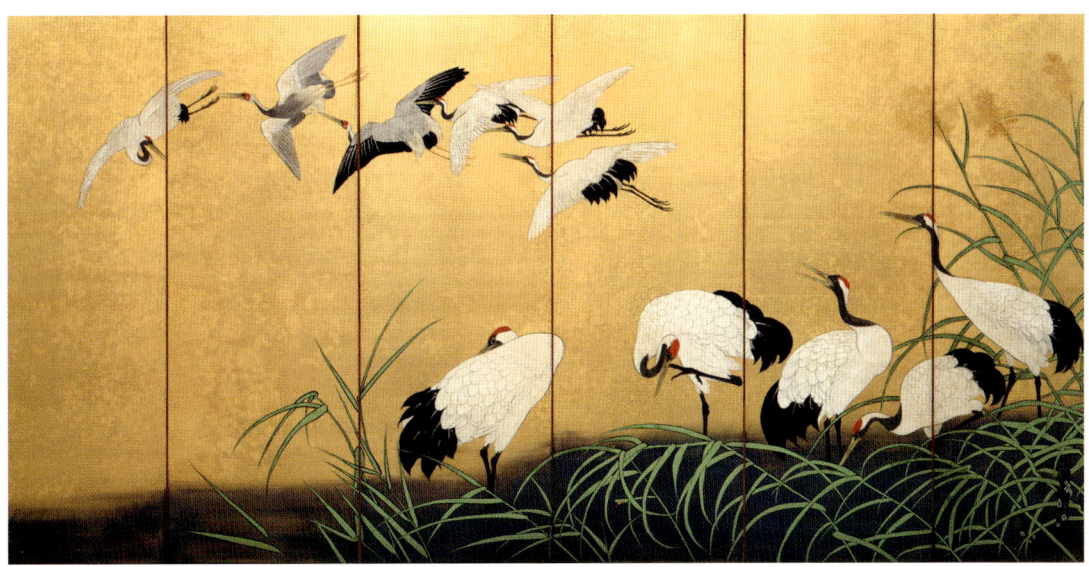

2

3

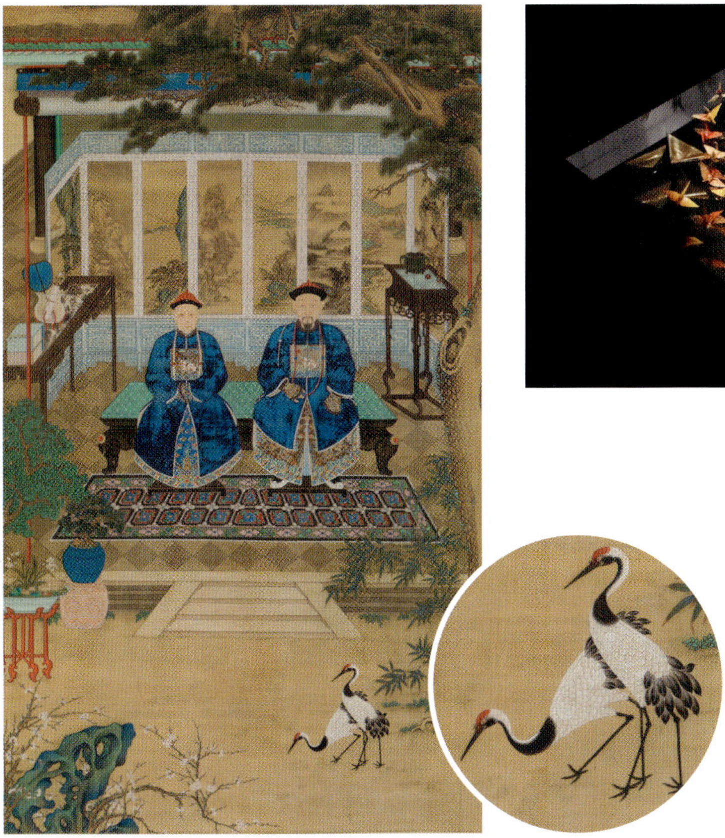

4

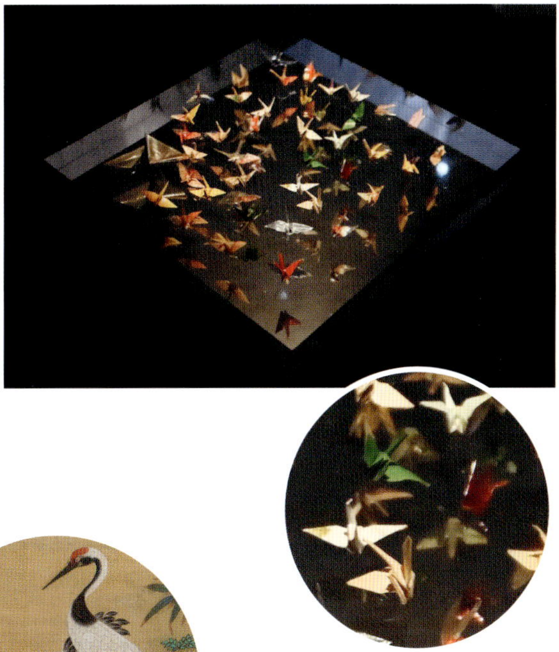

Peacock

The peacock has been illustrated as a symbol of beauty, pride, immortality, paradise, vanity and spiritual awakening. In ancient Greece and Rome, it was associated with Hera/Juno, the queen of the gods, symbolizing royalty and divine majesty. Its magnificent plumage, with 'eyes' on its feathers, has long represented the concept of all-seeing knowledge and protection. In Christian symbolism, the peacock signifies resurrection and eternal life because its feathers are thought to renew themselves each year and never decay. Medieval and Renaissance art frequently featured peacocks in religious scenes as symbols of immortality and incorruptibility, for example, in *The Annunciation with Saint Emidius* (1486) by Carlo Crivelli (c. 1430-c. 1495) and *The Origin of the Milky Way* (c. 1575) by Jacopo Tintoretto (1518-94). In Indian and Persian art, peacocks symbolize love, grace, and protection. Their striking appearance has made peacocks a favourite motif in decorative and allegorical art, representing both earthly splendour and spiritual truths.

1

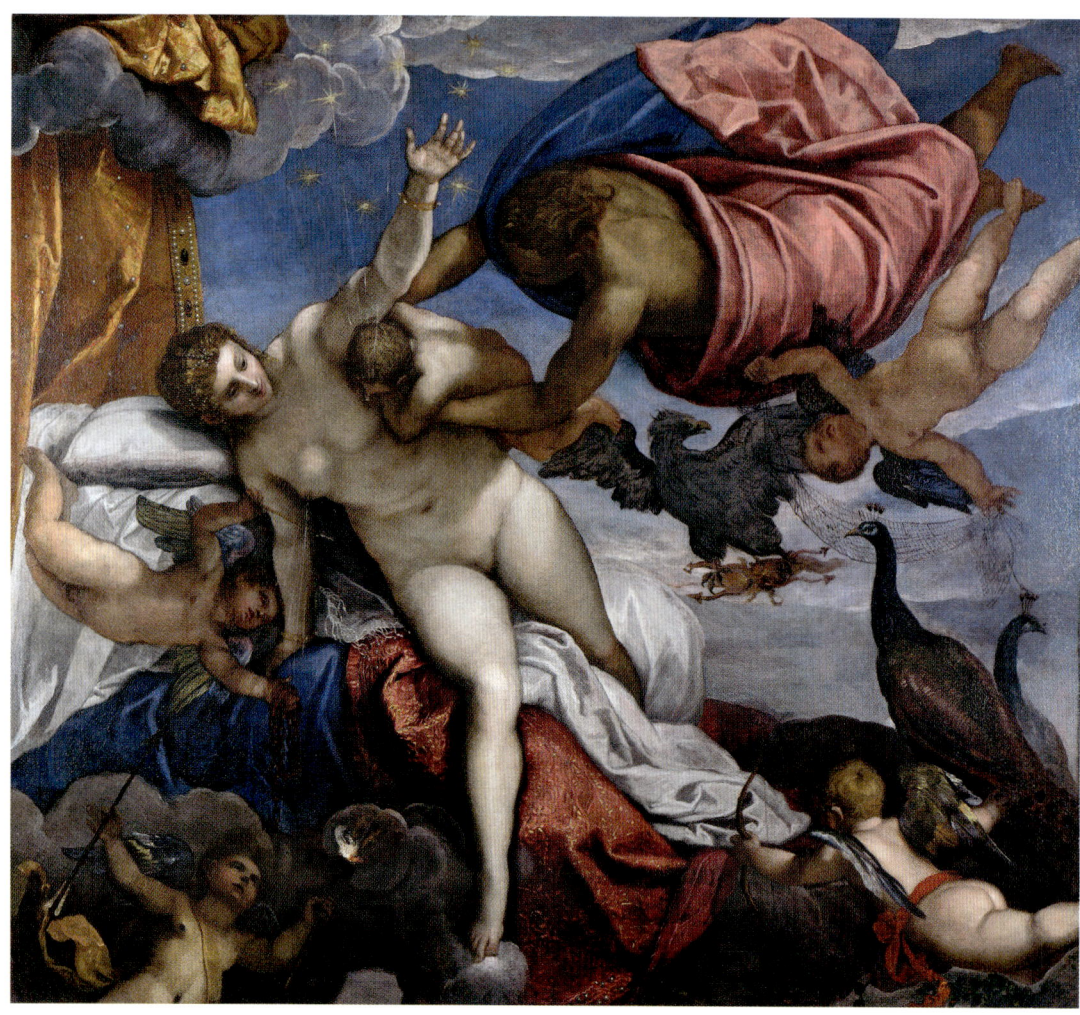

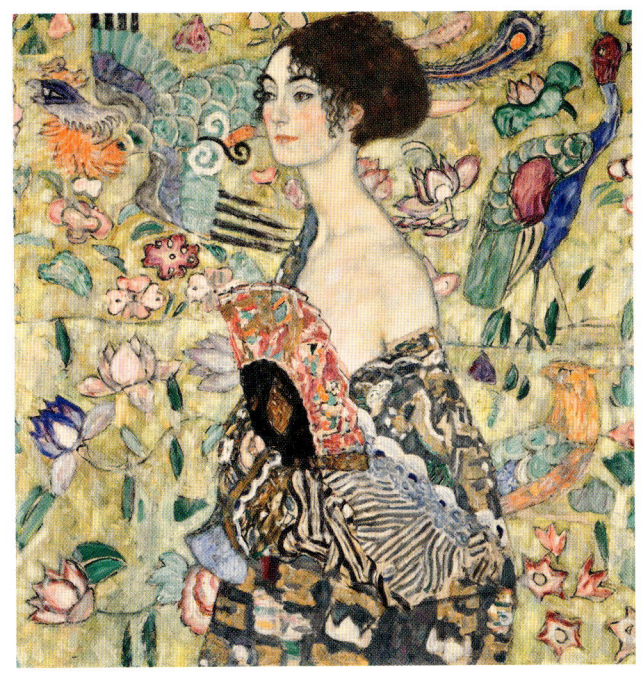

2

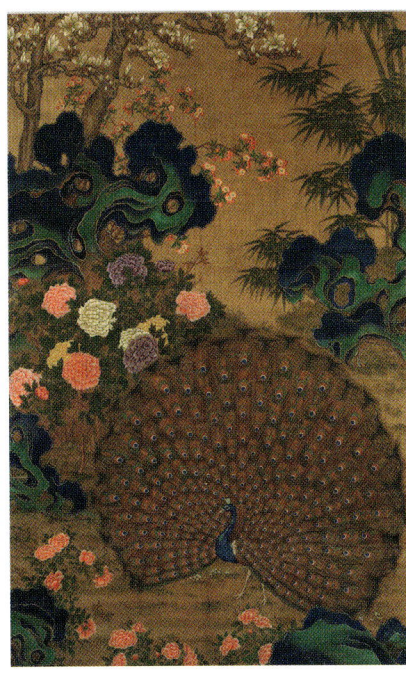

3

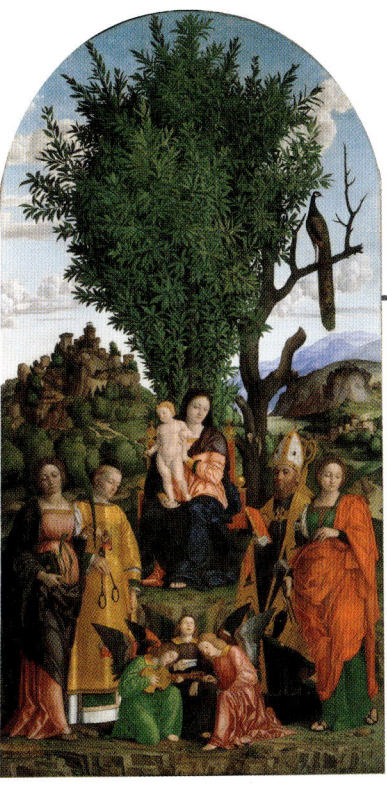

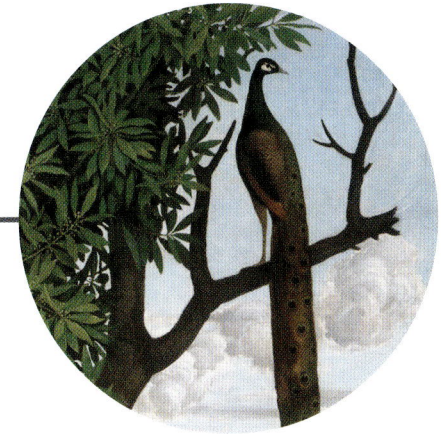

4

1. *The Origin of the Milky Way,* Jacopo Tintoretto, c. 1575
2. *Lady with a Fan,* Gustav Klimt, 1917-18
3. *Peacock with Flowers and Fantastic Rocks,* China, seventeenth century
4. *Madonna and Child with Saints,* Girolamo dai Libri, c. 1520

Falcon

In ancient Egypt, falcons represented the god Horus, embodying kingship and the sky. The monumental sculpture of Horus at the Temple of Edfu in Egypt depicts the falcon-headed god, a symbol of kingship, heavenly security and power. Egyptian pharaohs often wore falcon headdresses to symbolize their divine authority. In medieval European art, falconry was associated with aristocracy and skill, so falcons in art at that time conveyed nobility and hunting prowess. Renaissance portraits sometimes include falcons to emphasize the sitter's status, courage or strategic mind. Falcon imagery can also imply sharp vision and vigilance, linked to spiritual insight or power. Across cultures, falcons have been associated with swiftness and precision, making them enduring symbols of leadership and strength, as well as divine protection.

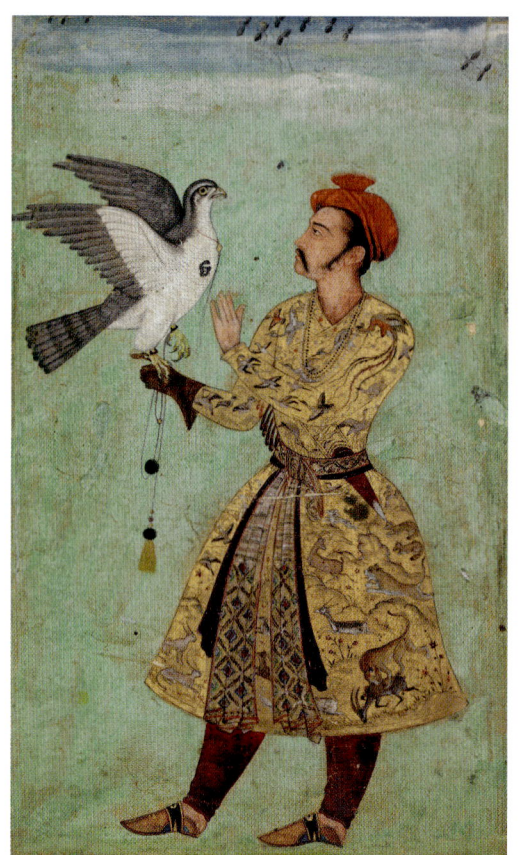

1

2

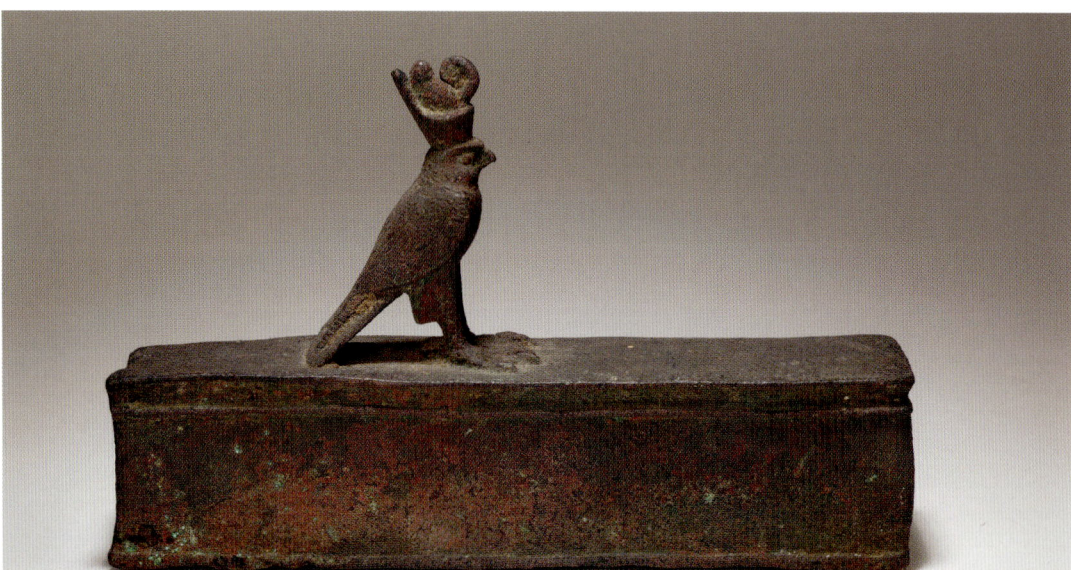

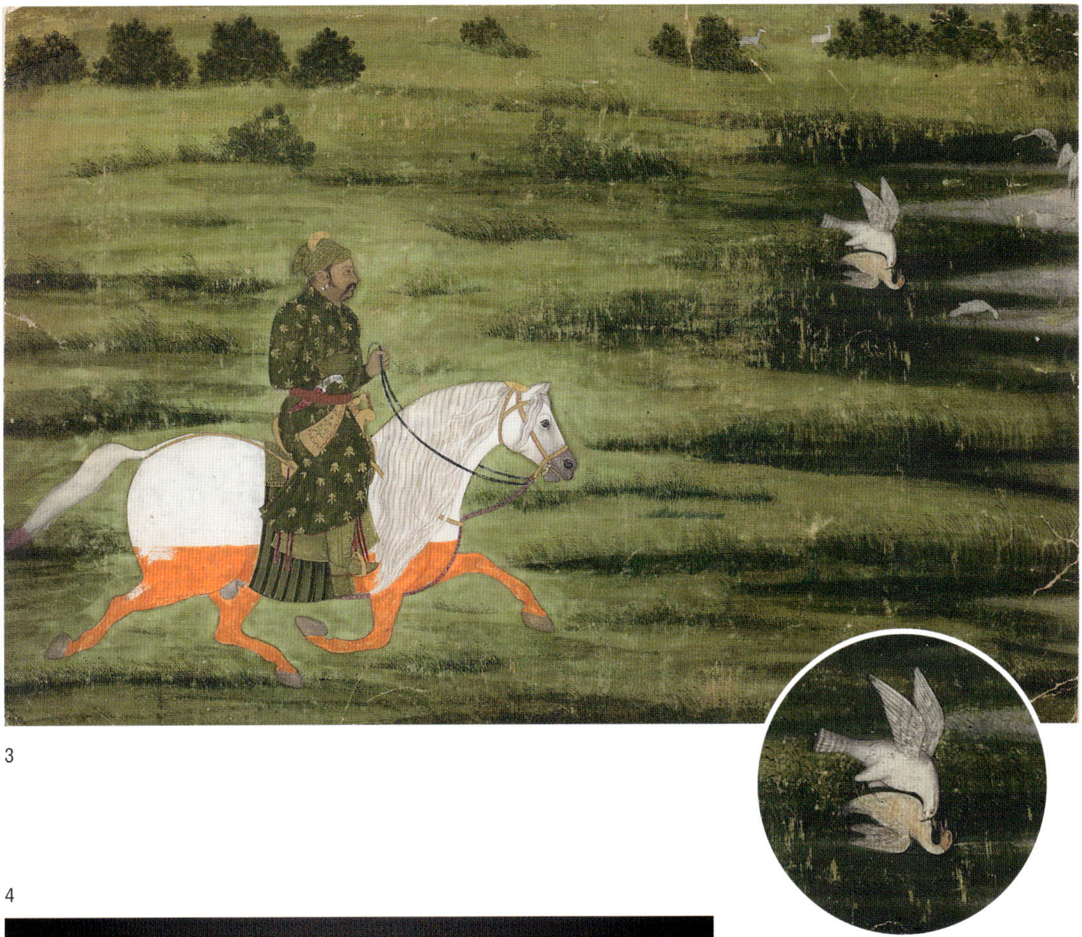

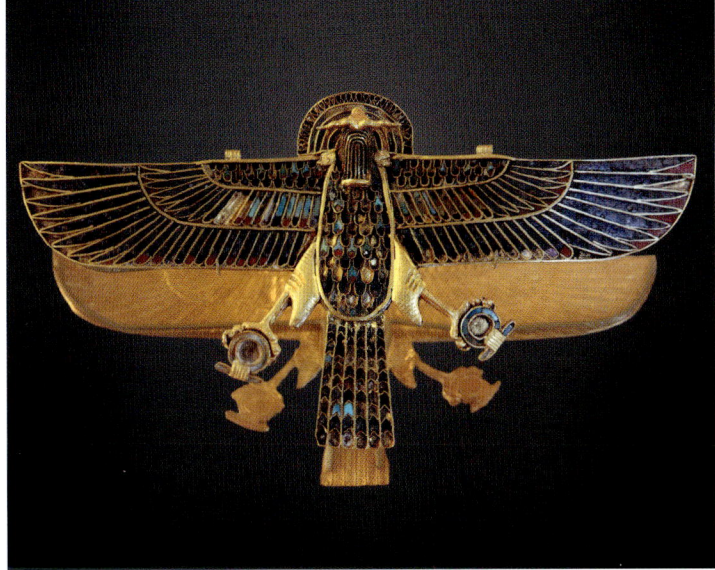

3

4

1. *Prince With a Falcon*, India, c. 1600-05
2. *Animal mummy case topped by a falcon*, Egypt, 664-30 BCE
3. *A Mounted Man Hunting Birds with a Falcon*, India, early eighteenth century
4. *Ram-Headed Falcon Pendant*, Egypt, c.1279-1213 BCE

Owl

Owls in art have long symbolized wisdom, mystery and sometimes night, death or the supernatural. In ancient Greece, the owl was sacred to Athena, the goddess of wisdom, and was frequently depicted as a symbol of knowledge and protection. The Little Owl (*Athene noctua*) became an enduring emblem of insight. In ancient Egypt, owls were associated with Thoth, the god of writing and the moon, denoting wisdom and protection against evil spirits. Some Indigenous American tribes view owls as guardians of sacred knowledge, while others see them as omens of death or transformation. During the Middle Ages in Europe, owls were often associated with witchcraft, death and the supernatural. They appeared in illuminated manuscripts and church carvings as warnings or symbols of hidden knowledge. In Japanese and Chinese folklore, owls are seen more positively as symbols of luck, protection and longevity. The owl's nocturnal nature and piercing vision often represent the ability to see what others cannot. Nowadays, owls can also symbolize the unconscious mind and spiritual awakening.

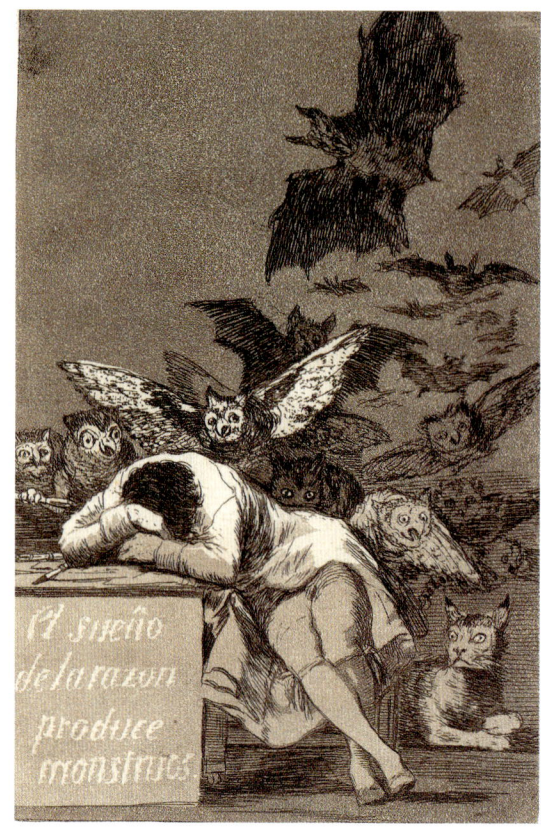

1

2

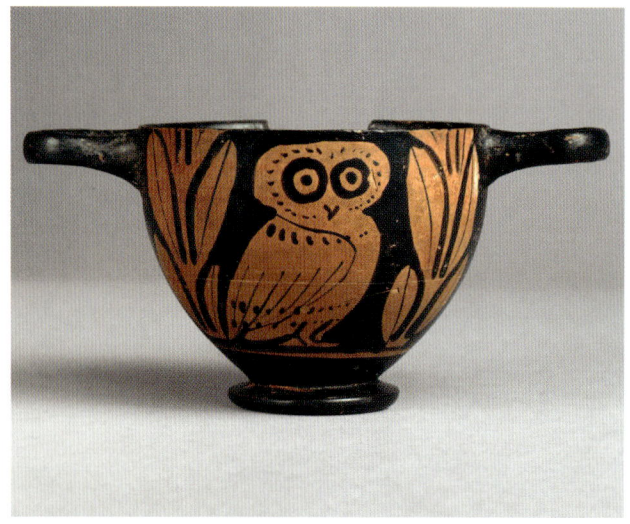

3

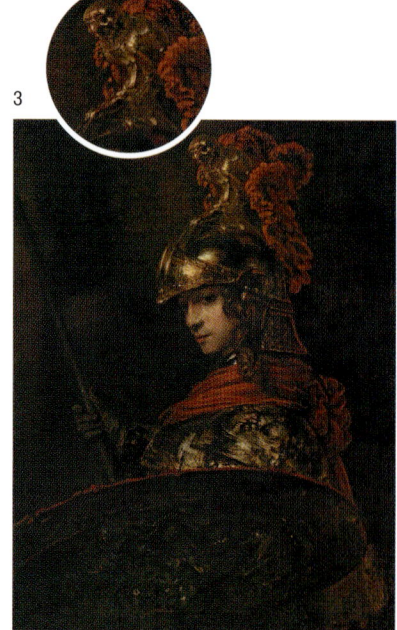

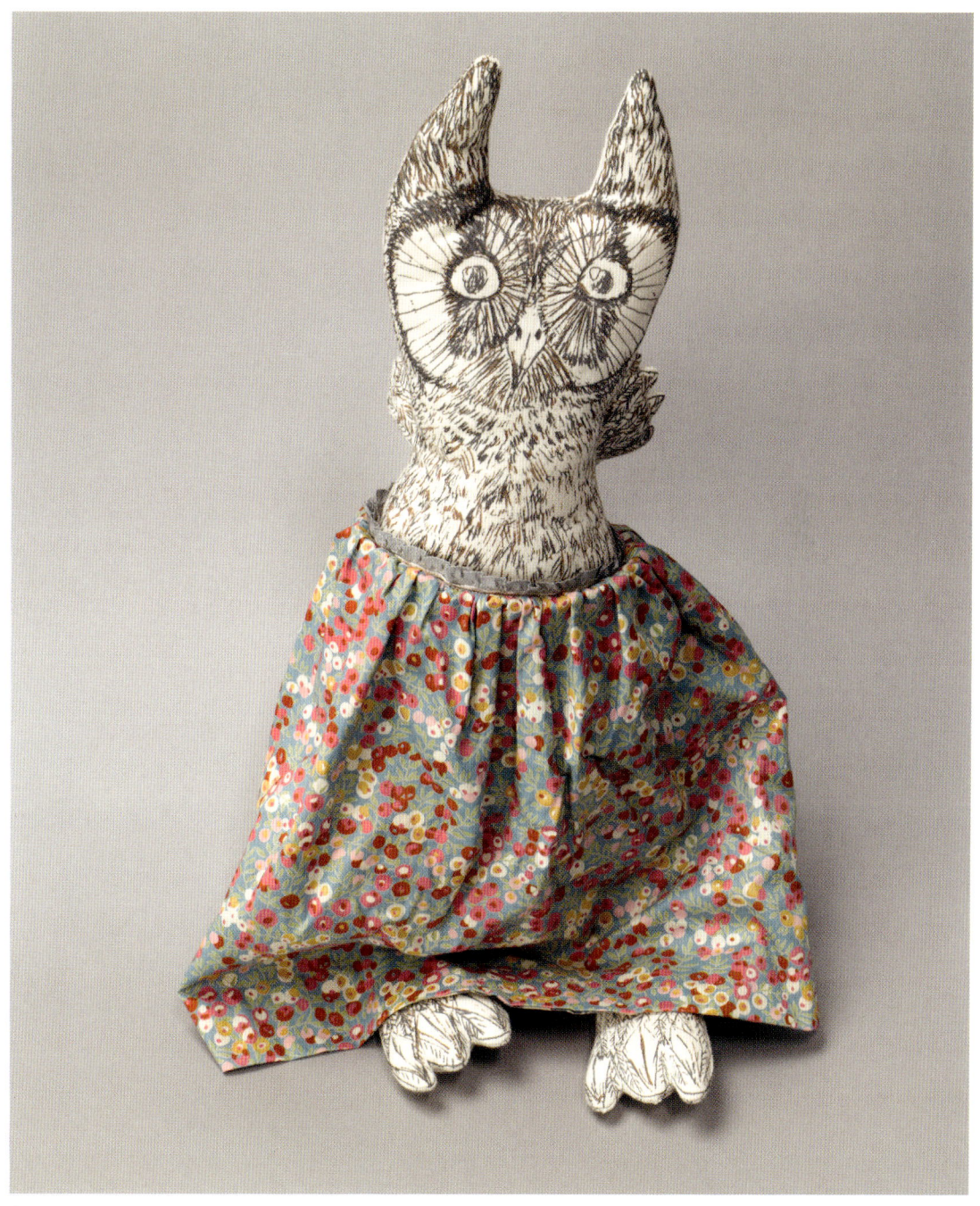

4

1. *The Sleep of Reason Produces Monsters,* Francisco Goya, 1799
2. Red-Figure Pot, Greece, c. 530–320 BCE
3. *Pallas Athena,* Rembrandt van Rijn, c. 1657
4. *Owl and Pussycat,* Kiki Smith, 2002

Eagle

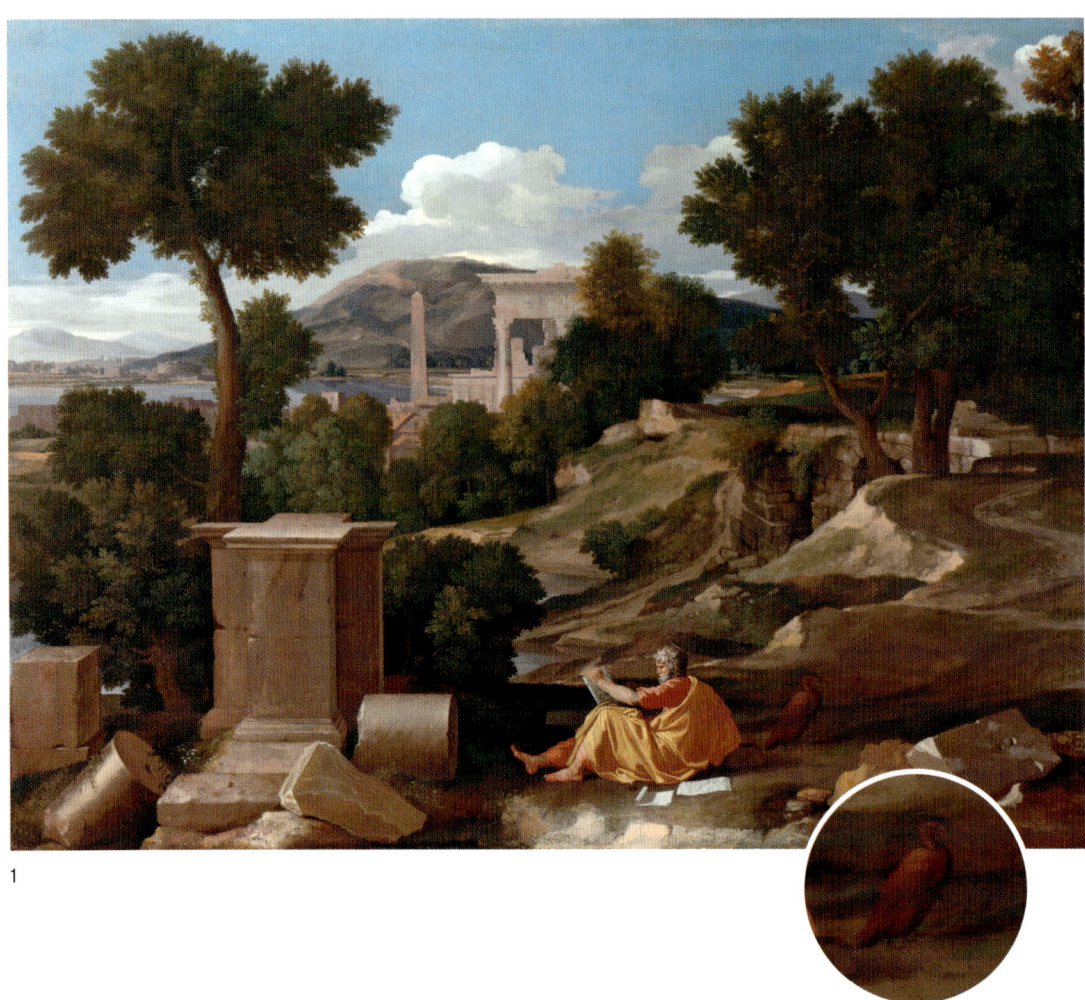

1

A universal symbol of power, courage and divine authority, the eagle, with its broad wingspan, keen eyesight and graceful flight, has been a potent symbol across many cultures and eras. In ancient Rome, they represented the empire and Jupiter, the king of the gods, conveying imperial strength and victory. They appeared on coins, standards and sculptures as emblems of rulership and military might. In Christian art, the eagle often represents John the Evangelist and spiritual ascension, due to its ability to soar high and look directly into the sun. Indigenous American cultures revere the eagle as a sacred messenger between heaven and earth, symbolizing freedom and vision. Renaissance and Baroque art also featured eagles to signify noble virtues and leadership. The bald eagle is one of the most powerful symbols of North American art, representing freedom, strength, resilience and vision. It has been the national bird and emblem of the United States since 1782, and appears on the Great Seal, clutching an olive branch for peace and arrows for war.

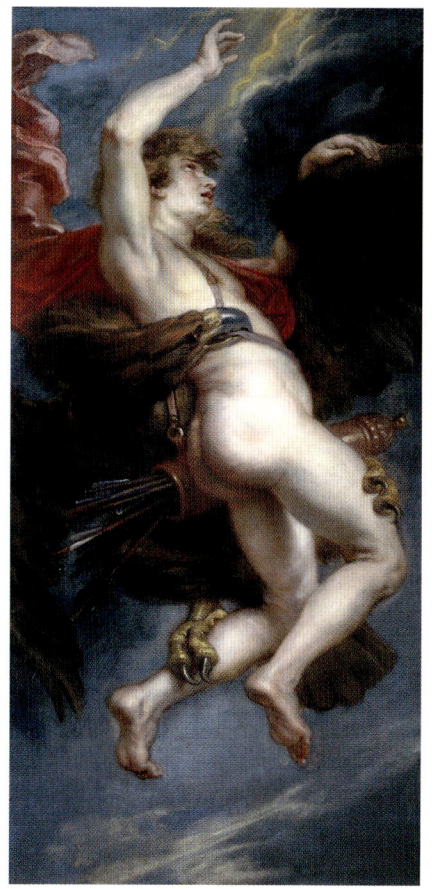

2

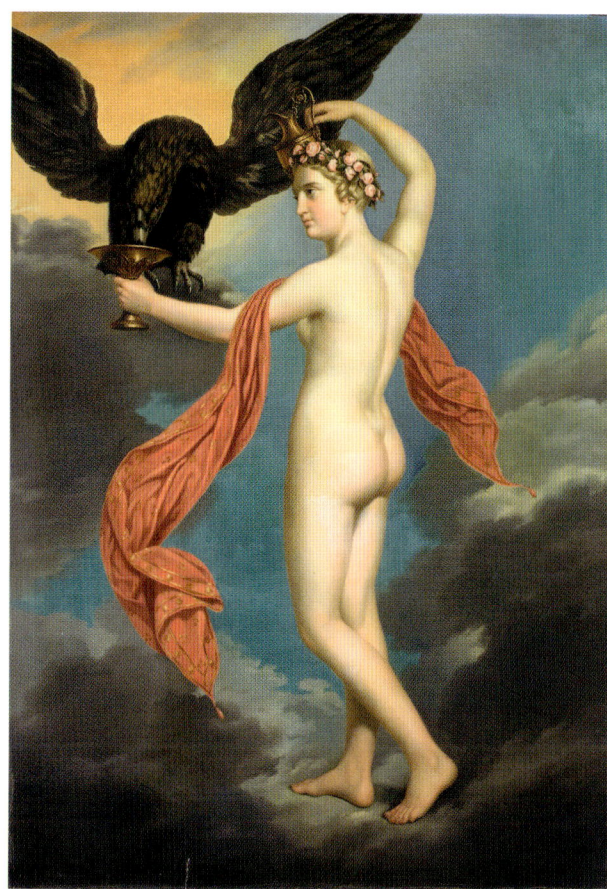

3

4

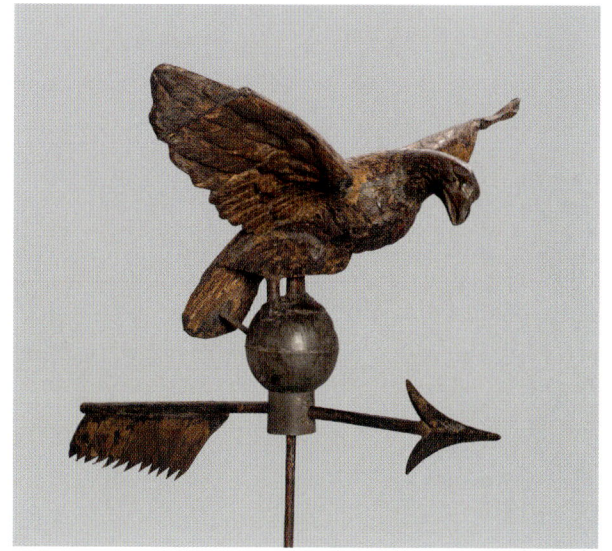

1. *Landscape with Saint John on Patmos,* Nicolas Poussin, 1640
2. *The Rape of Ganymede,* Peter Paul Rubens, 1636-38
3. *Hebe with Jupiter in the Guise of an Eagle,* Gustav-Adolphe Diez, 1820-26
4. *Eagle,* North America, 1800-30

Dove

One of art's most enduring symbols of peace, love and purity, the dove is often featured in Christian iconography to represent the Holy Spirit and is frequently depicted descending during the baptism of Christ or at Pentecost. Its whiteness symbolises innocence and divine presence. Beyond Christianity, doves are universal symbols of peace and hope, famously represented with an olive branch from the pre-Renaissance to the present day. In ancient cultures, doves were associated with the goddess Aphrodite/Venus, symbolizing romantic love and fidelity. Doves also appear in allegories of harmony and reconciliation. Their gentle nature and symbolic purity have made the bird a powerful and widely recognized motif in art, reflecting spiritual and social ideals. In *Child with Dove* (1901) by Pablo Picasso, a young child gently holds a white dove, symbolizing peace, innocence and hope. Painted during Picasso's Blue Period, the work contrasts melancholic tones with the dove's purity.

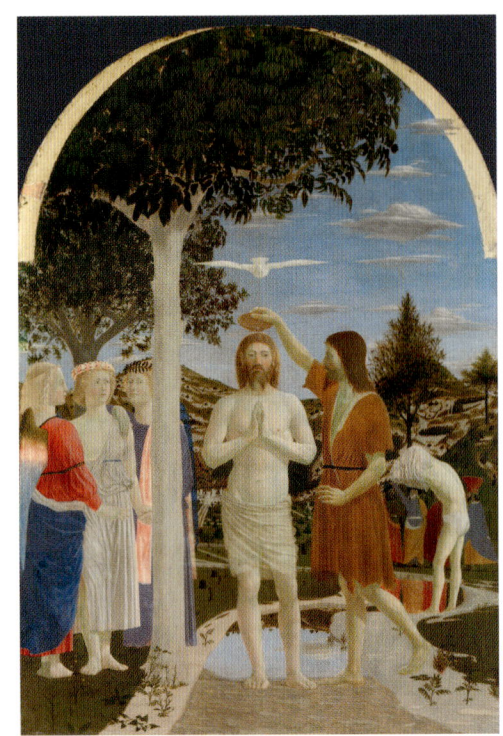

1

2

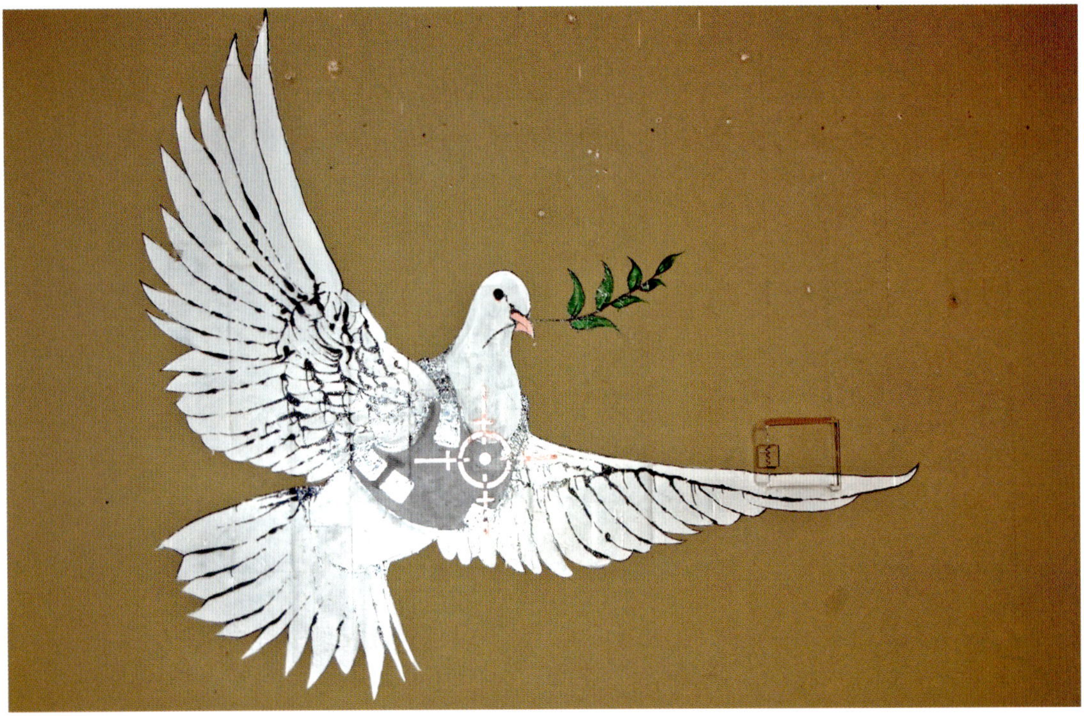

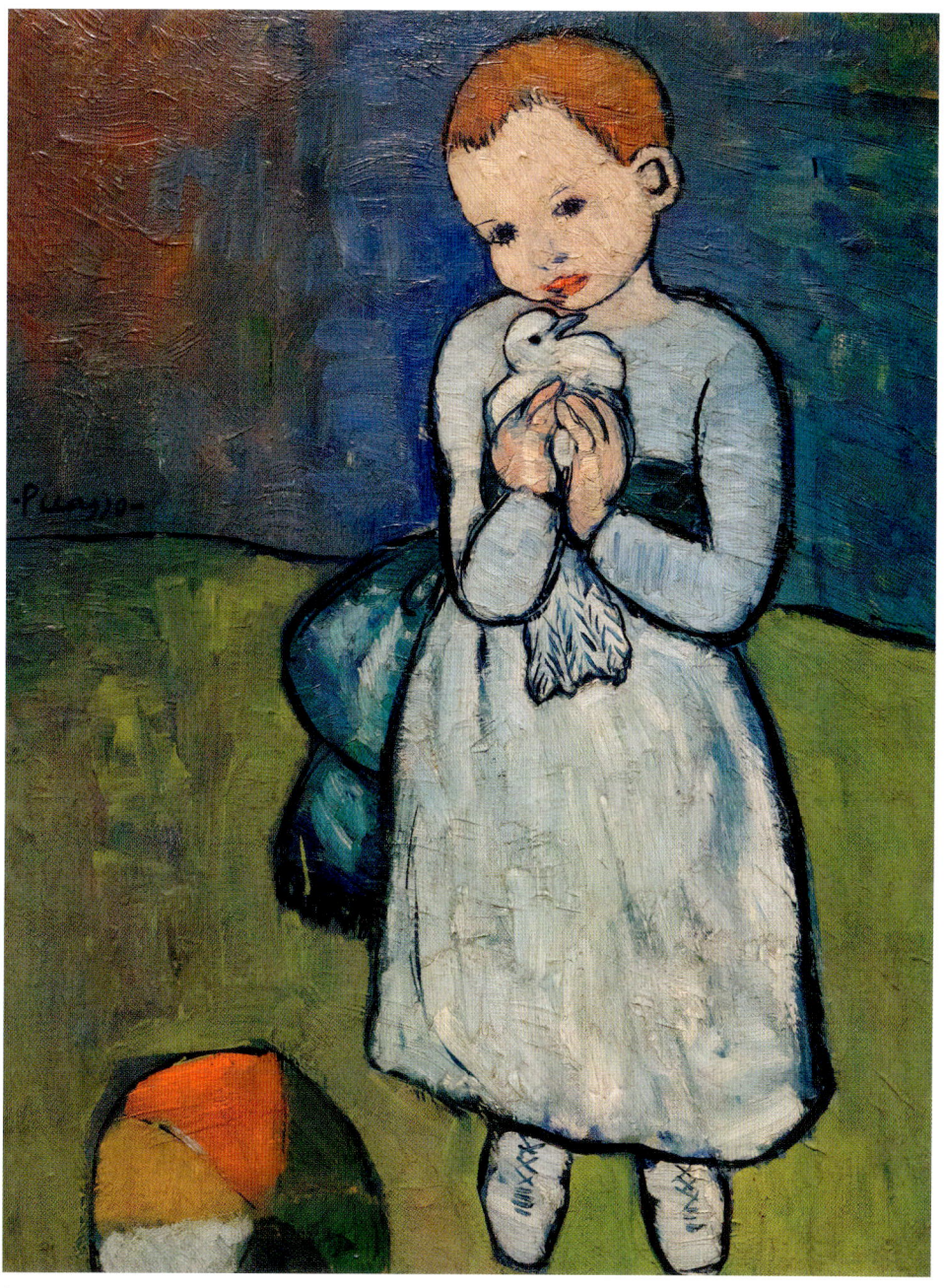

3

1. *The Baptism of Christ,* Piero della Francesca, 1448–50
2. *Armoured Peace Dove,* Banksy, 2005
3. *Child with Dove,* Pablo Picasso, 1901

Raven and Crow

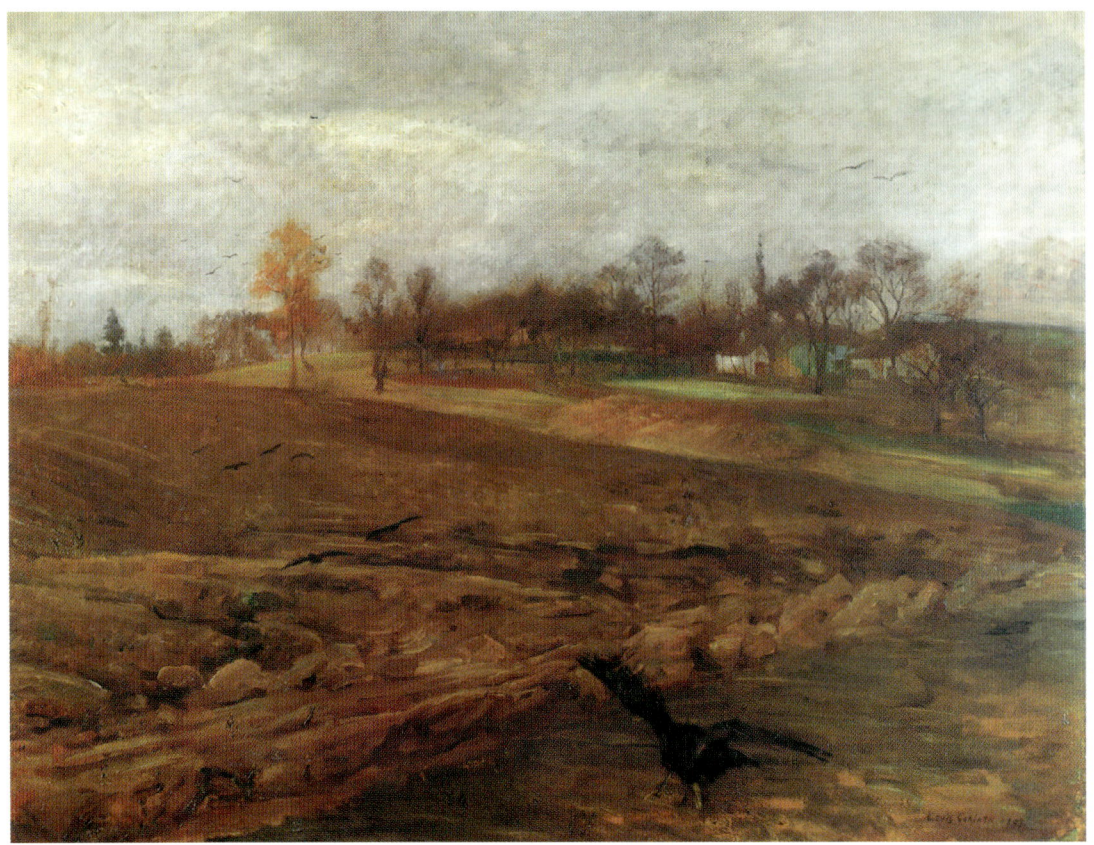

1

For centuries, ravens and crows have symbolized mystery, intelligence and transformation. In Norse mythology, Odin's ravens, Huginn and Muninn, represented thought and memory, acting as divine messengers. In Christian art, these birds sometimes symbolize sin or death, appearing in vanitas paintings alongside skulls and hourglasses to suggest mortality. The poem, *The Raven* (1845) by Edgar Allan Poe (1809-49), cemented the bird's association with sorrow and the supernatural. In Indigenous American traditions, ravens are often associated with wisdom and transformation. Their dark plumage and piercing gaze make them striking subjects in visual art, where they are frequently used to evoke a sense of foreboding or introspection. In paintings such as *Antigone Giving Burial Rites to the Body of Her Brother Polynices* (date unknown) by Marie Spartali Stillman (1844-1927), *Landscape with a Large Raven* (1893) by Lovis Corinth (1858-1925) and *Wheatfield with Crows* (1890) by Vincent van Gogh, it is generally assumed that the crows and ravens symbolize approaching death.

1. *Landscape with a Large Raven*, Lovis Corinth, 1893
2. *The Magic Circle*, John William Waterhouse, 1886
3. *Antigone Giving Burial Rites to the Body of Her Brother Polynices*, Marie Spartali Stillman, date unknown
4. *Kylix of Apollo*, Greece, c. 470 BCE
5. *Wheatfield with Crows*, Vincent van Gogh, 1890

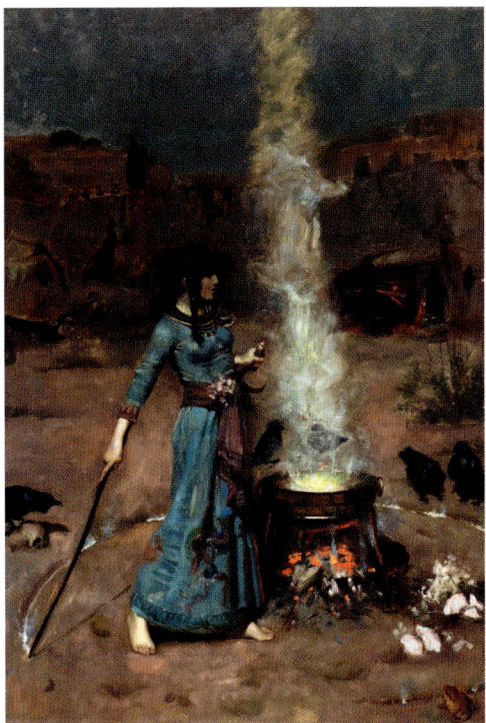

2

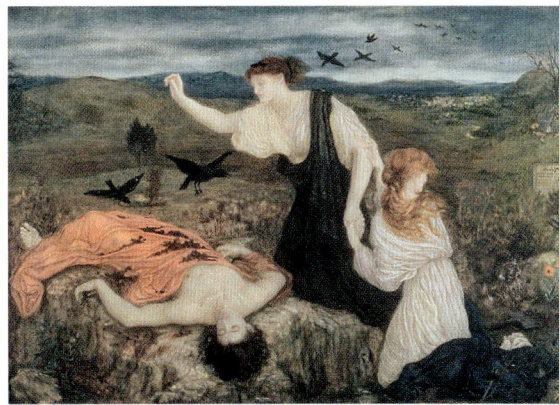

3

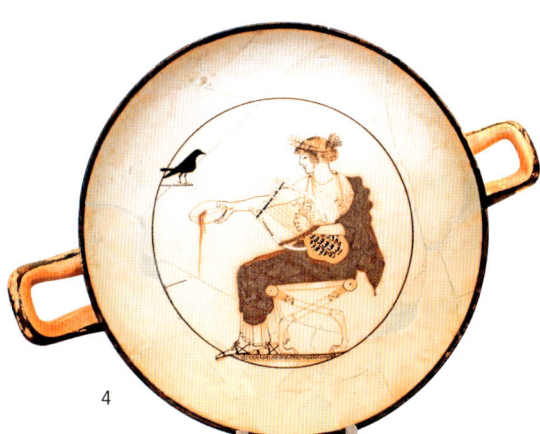

4

5

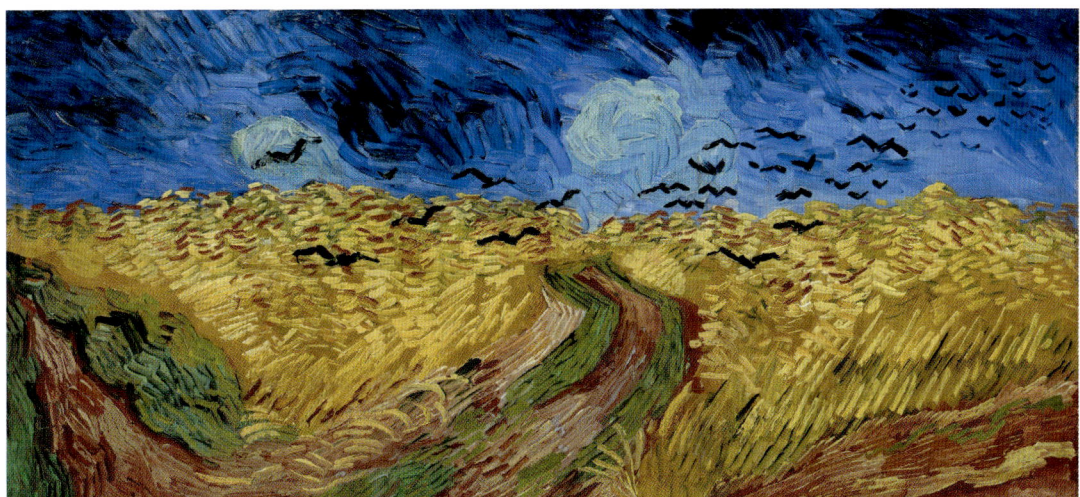

Feathers

Symbolizing freedom, spirituality, status, transformation and connection to the divine, feathers appear in a diverse range of art. In ancient Egypt, they were associated with Ma'at, the goddess of truth and justice, whose ostrich feather was used to weigh the souls of the dead. In Mesoamerican cultures, such as those of the Aztecs and Maya, feathers, especially those of the quetzal bird, adorned headdresses and ceremonial objects, signifying power, nobility and a link to the gods. Indigenous North American traditions hold eagle feathers sacred, representing honour, strength and spiritual communication, and they are often featured in regalia, dance and ritual art. Feathers have also been used symbolically in European art. In Christian iconography, angel wings composed of feathers signify purity and divine presence. Renaissance and Baroque artists frequently incorporated feathers into portraits to convey fashion, social status, exoticism or personal virtue. The peacock feather, in particular during that time, symbolized immortality and divine vision.

1. *Weighing of the Heart,* Papyrus of Hunefer, Egypt, c. 1275 BCE
2. *Air,* Giuseppe Arcimboldo, 1566
3. *The Winged Victory of Samothrace,* Greece, c. 190 BCE
4. *Feathered Panel,* Wari culture (Peru), 650–1000 CE

1

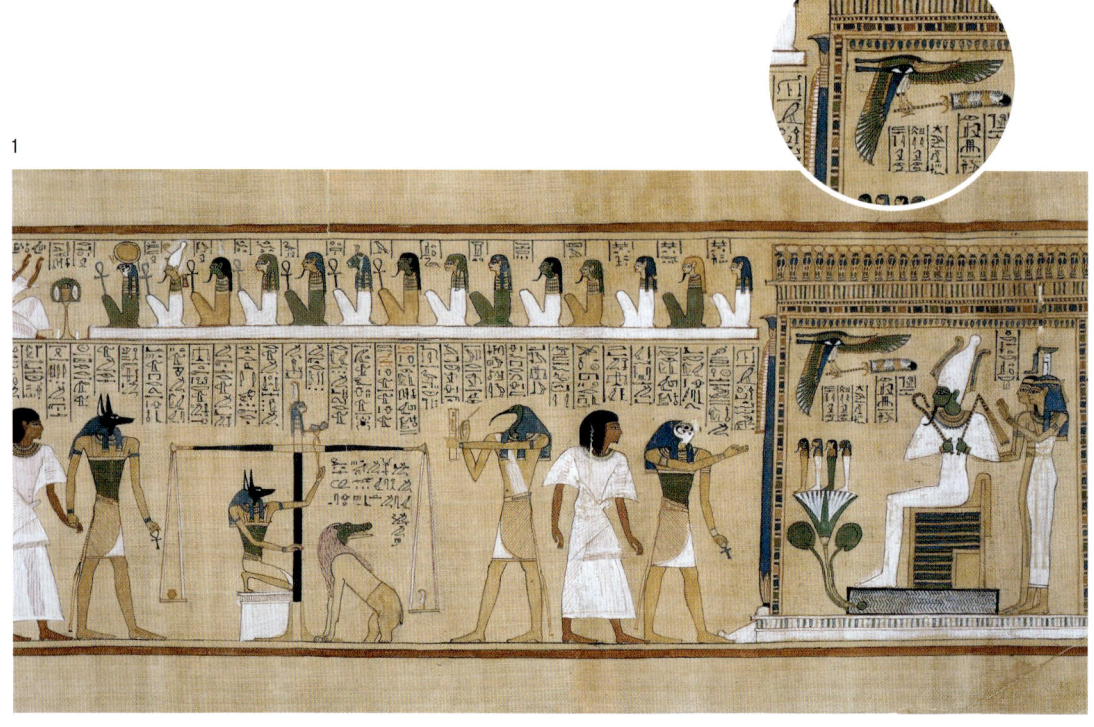

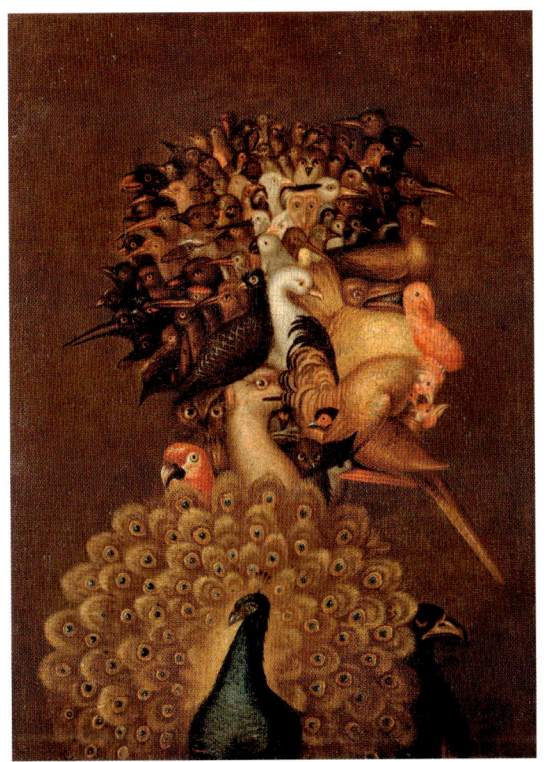

2

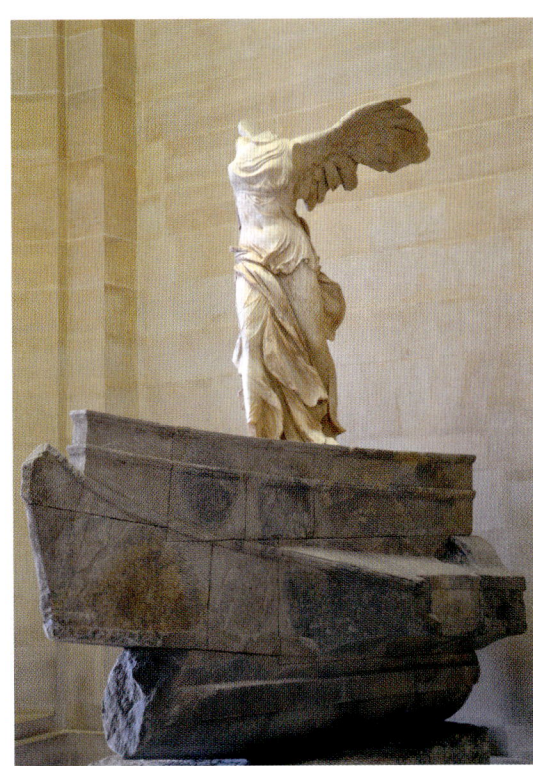

2

4

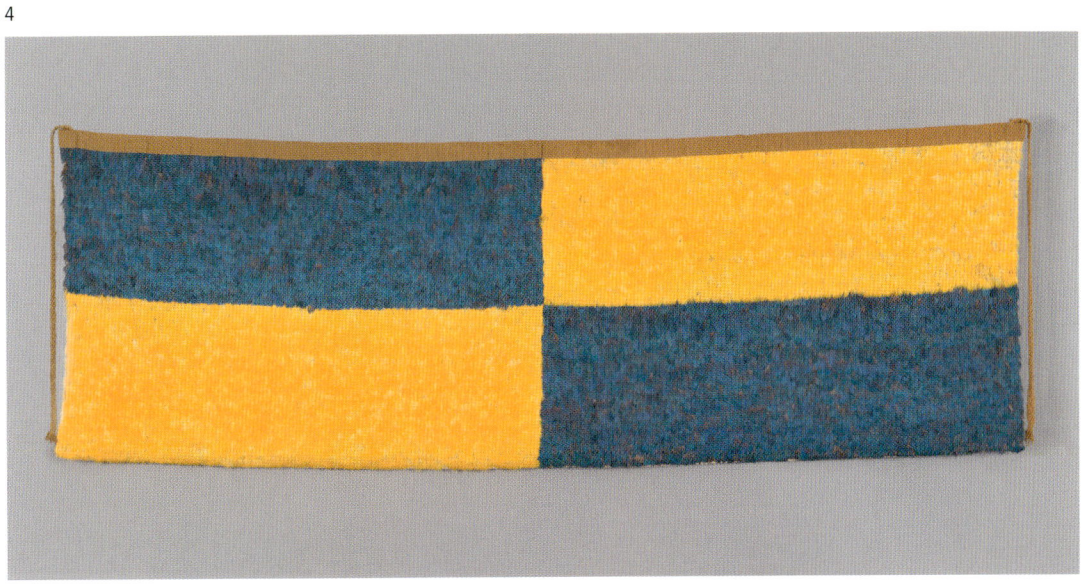

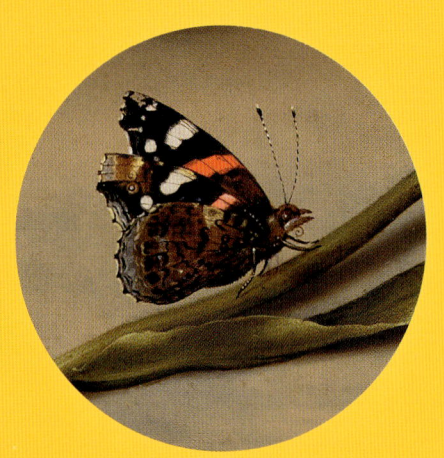

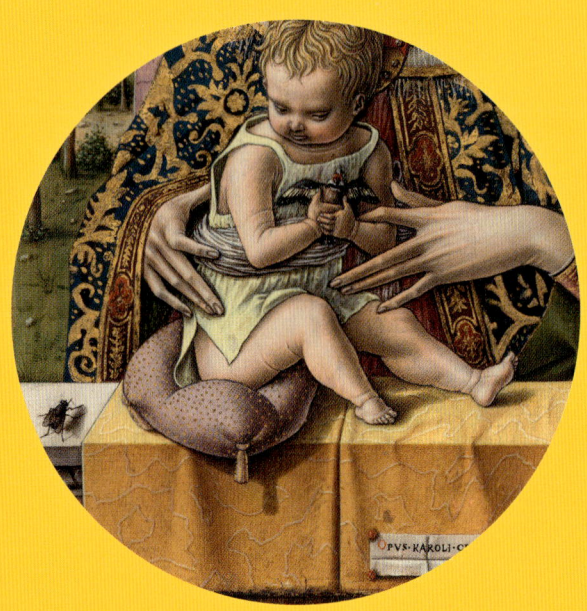

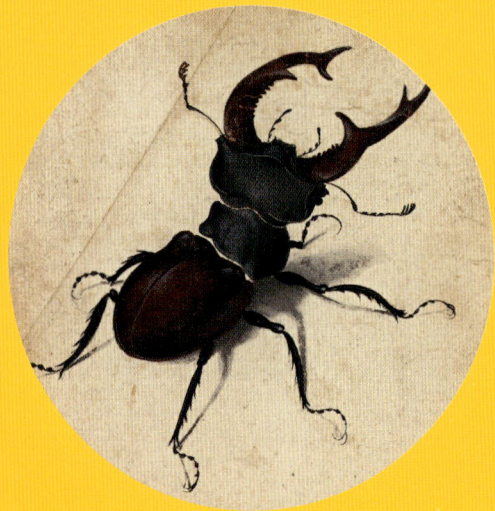

Insects

Butterfly

Across many art forms, butterflies have long symbolized transformation, resurrection and the fleeting nature of life. In ancient Greek art, they were associated with Psyche, the embodiment of the soul. Seventeenth-century Dutch painters incorporated butterflies into vanitas paintings as a symbol of the impermanence of beauty and earthly pleasures. As the metamorphosis of a caterpillar into a butterfly mirrors themes of rebirth, it has become a common motif in Christian art, often depicted to denote Christ's resurrection. In Japanese culture, butterflies represent the spirits of the departed, bringing comfort to the living. Several late works by Odilon Redon depict small, colourful elements of nature - such as butterflies, seashells, and flowers - as metaphors for the imagination. In May 1889, Vincent van Gogh wrote of his drawing of a large nocturnal moth. He later made several brightly coloured images from his drawing, each a deeply symbolic work that blends his intense observation of nature with his spiritual and emotional concerns during one of his most challenging periods.

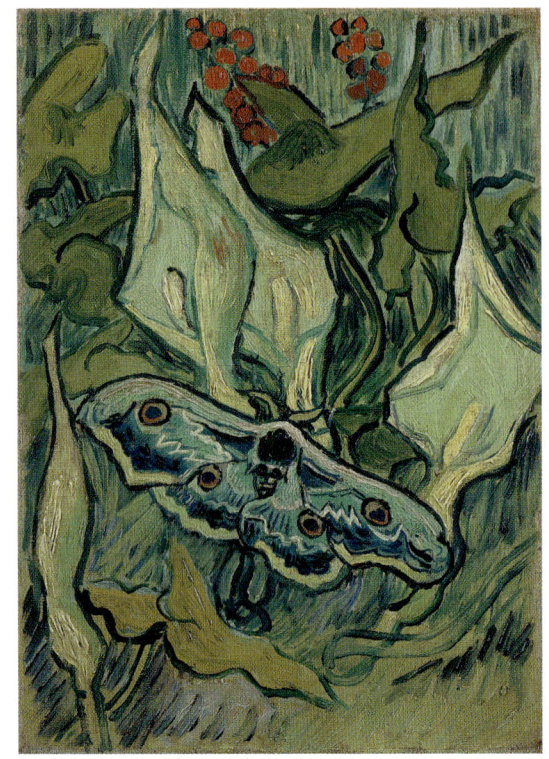

1

2

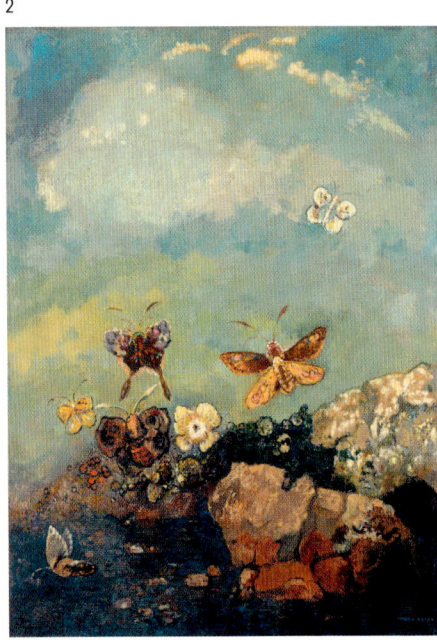

3

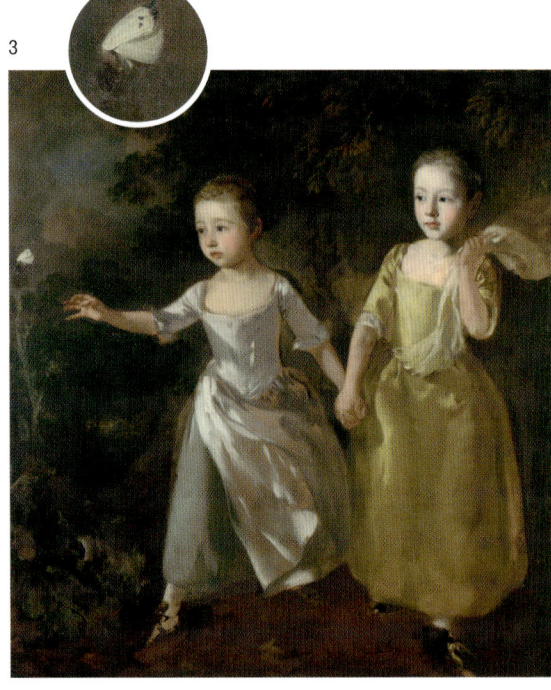

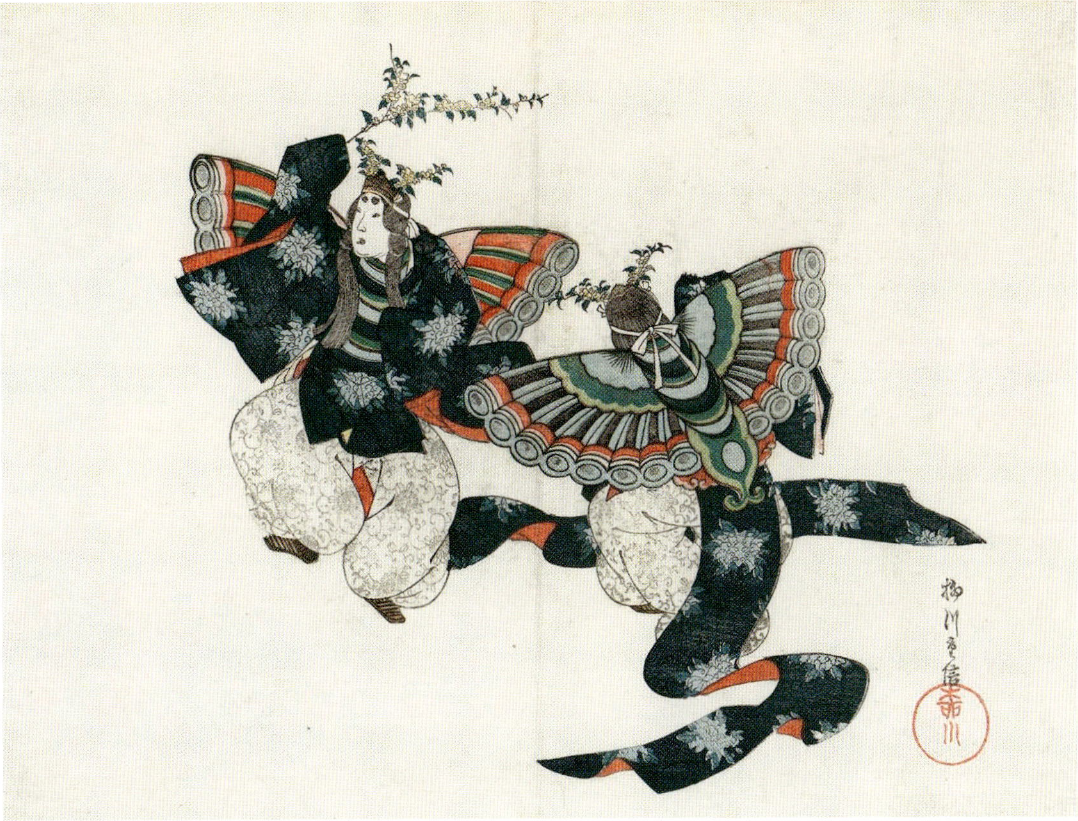

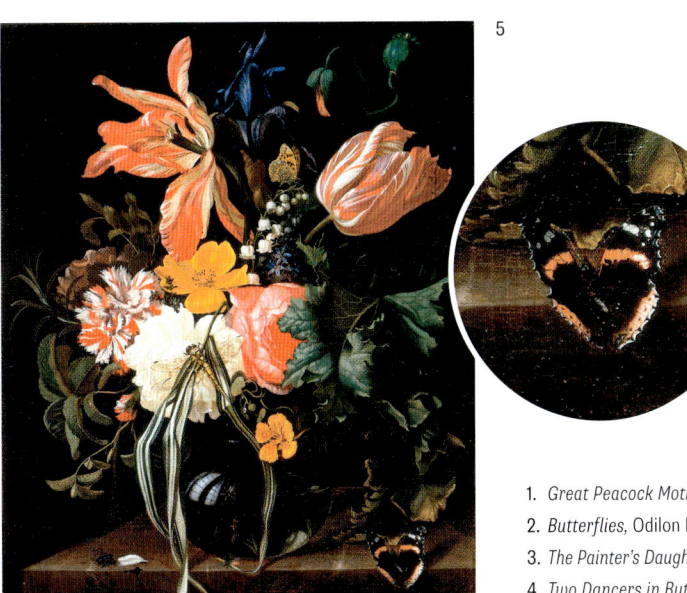

4

5

1. *Great Peacock Moth*, Vincent van Gogh, 1889
2. *Butterflies*, Odilon Redon, c. 1910
3. *The Painter's Daughters Chasing a Butterfly*, Thomas Gainsborough, 1756
4. *Two Dancers in Butterfly Costumes*, Yanagawa Shigenobu, c. 1820s
5. *Flower Still Life*, Maria van Oosterwijck, 1669

Bee

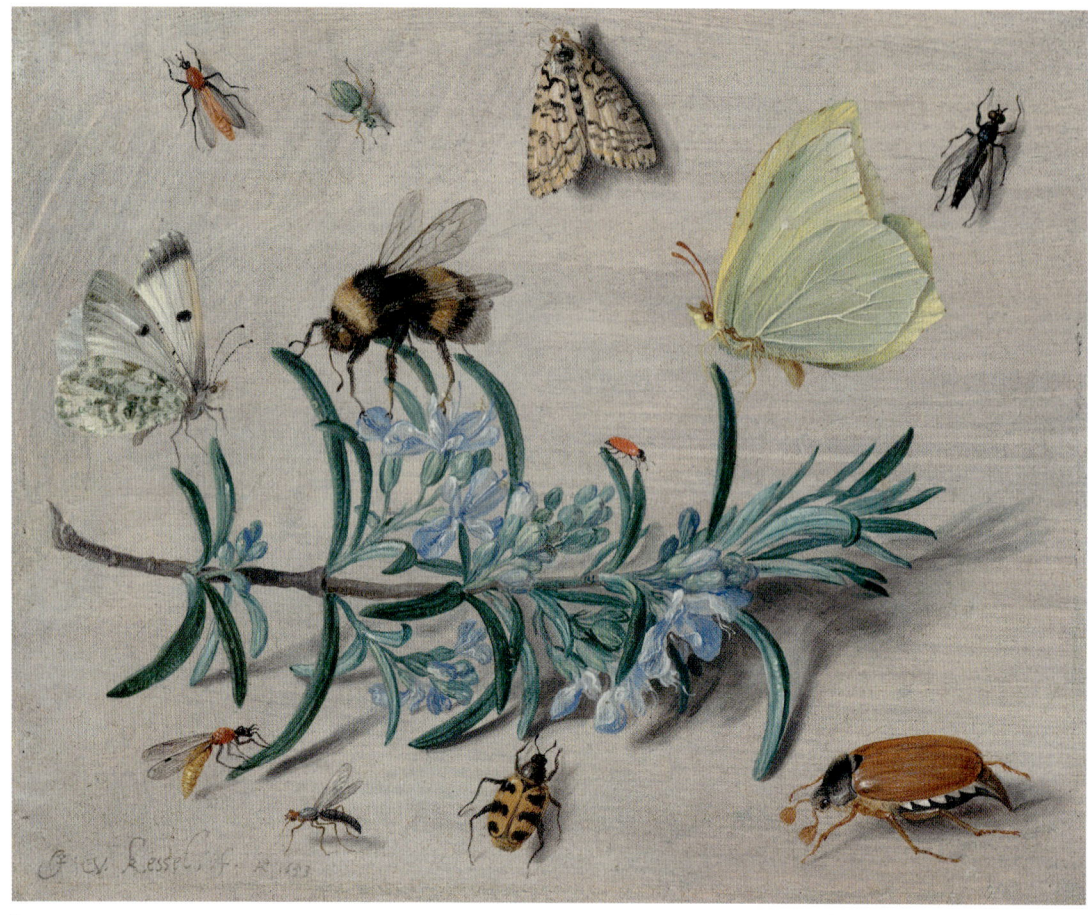

1

In most cultures, bees symbolize diligence, community and divine order. In ancient Egyptian art, bees were believed to be formed by the tears of the sun god Ra. In Christian iconography, bees represent virtues such as perseverance and hard work, while the beehive serves as a metaphor for organized teamwork, reflecting the importance of collective effort. Similarly, in feminist art, bees frequently symbolize shared labour and resilience, celebrating women's contributions to society. The role of bees in pollination and honey production has made them enduring symbols of productivity and harmony in nature-inspired artworks. They have also been incorporated into art and design

as emblematic of royalty, industry, community, fertility, and even death. Golden bees are embroidered on Napoleon's robes as symbols of imperial power, continuity and authority in *Portrait of Napoleon I in his Coronation Robes* (1805) by François Gérard (1770-1837). Napoleon adopted the bee as a personal emblem to evoke the Merovingian dynasty, associating his rule with industriousness and historical legitimacy.

1. *Insects and a Sprig of Rosemary,* Jan van Kessel the Elder, c. 1653
2. *Portrait of Napoleon I in His Coronation Robes,* François Gérard, 1805
3. *Cupid complaining to Venus,* Lucas Cranach the Elder, c. 1526-27
4. *The Tomb of Pabasa,* El Assasif, Egypt, c. 656-610 bce

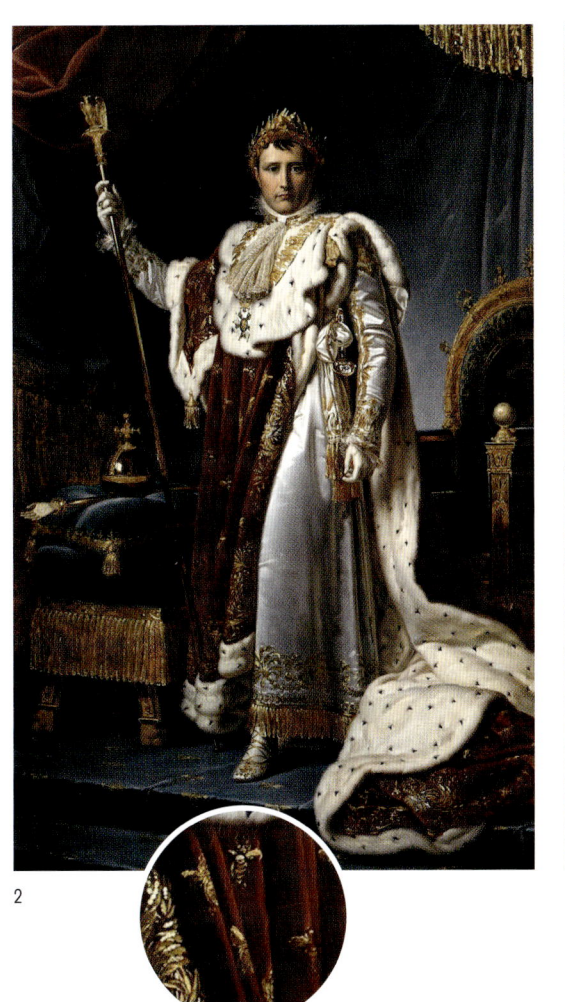

2

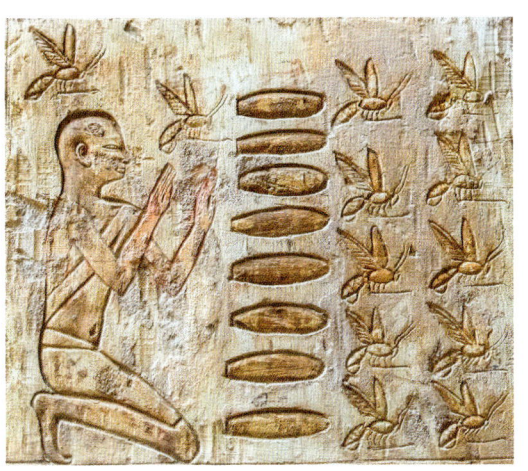

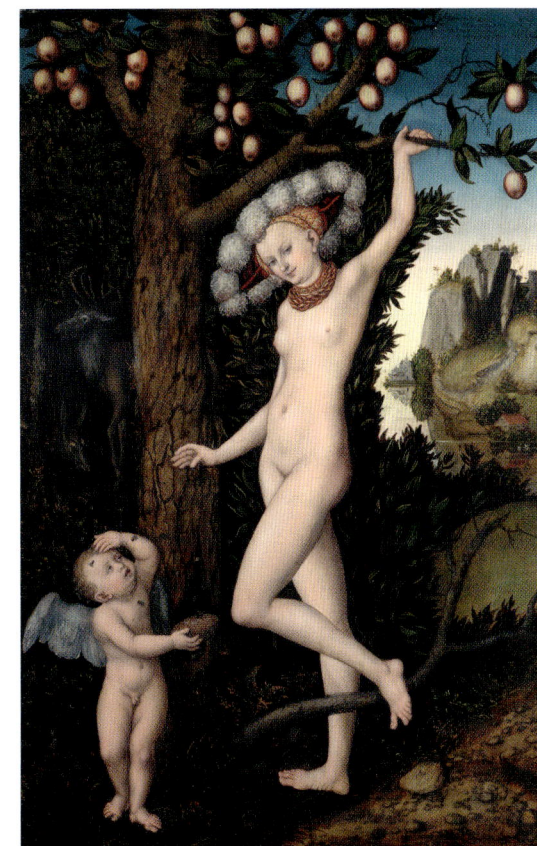

3

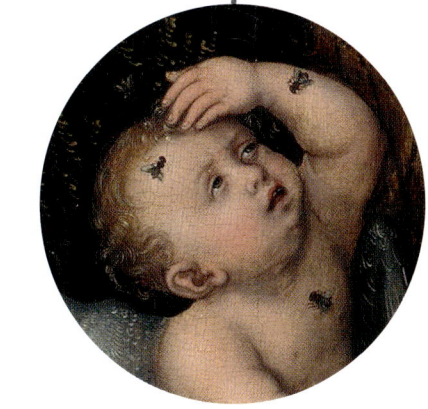

4

Dragonfly

Dragonflies have been used in art as symbols of transformation, personal growth, renewal and spiritual insight across numerous cultures. Many Indigenous traditions depict them as messengers of wisdom and change. Their agile flight and connection to water have often been used to symbolize resilience and adaptability. They have been depicted as messengers, connecting the natural and spiritual worlds. Their ability to move quickly and gracefully through the air is sometimes seen as a metaphor for the soul's journey towards enlightenment. In Japanese art, they frequently appear in traditional paintings, textiles and ceramics, representing courage, strength and happiness. In Chinese culture, they are usually associated with prosperity and fleeting beauty. During the Art Nouveau period (c. 1890-1910), René Lalique (1860-1945) incorporated dragonflies into jewellery and decorative arts, emphasizing their elegance, flowing natural forms and delicately iridescent wings. Some modern artists use dragonflies to explore themes of illusion, discernment, resilience and change, reflecting their ability to move swiftly and change direction mid-flight.

1

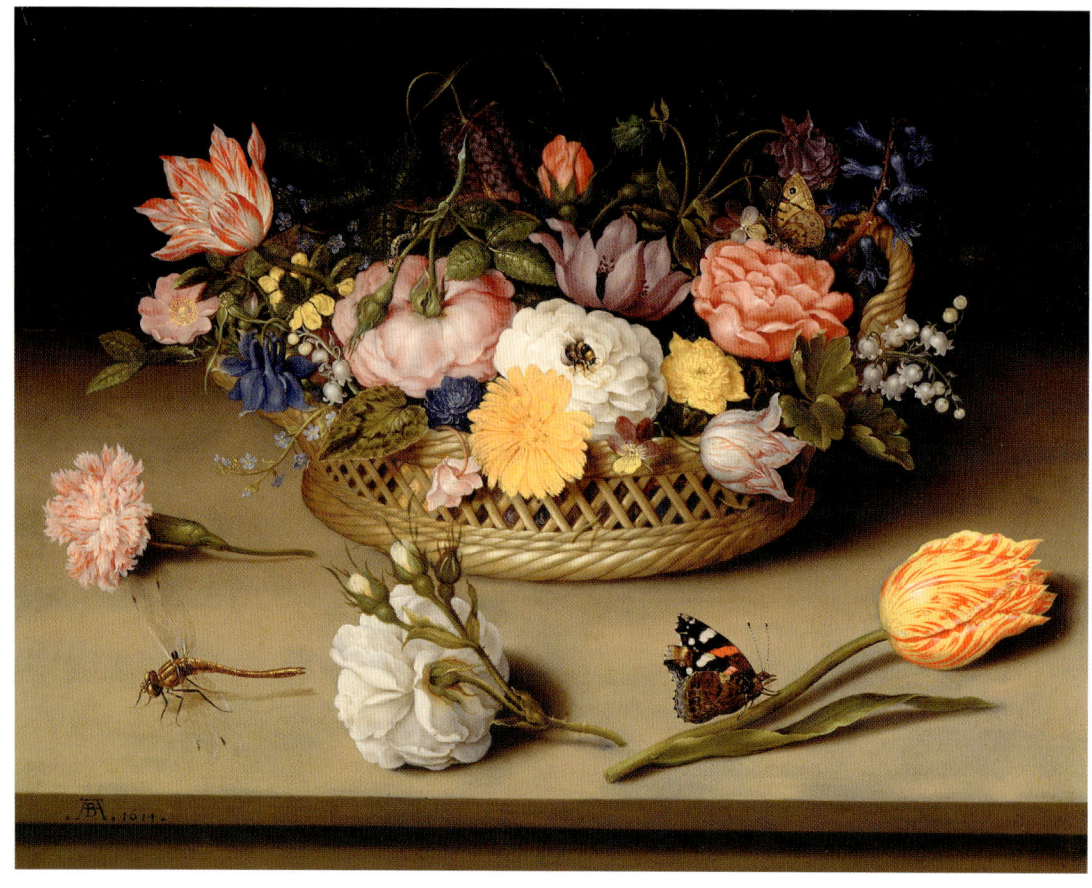

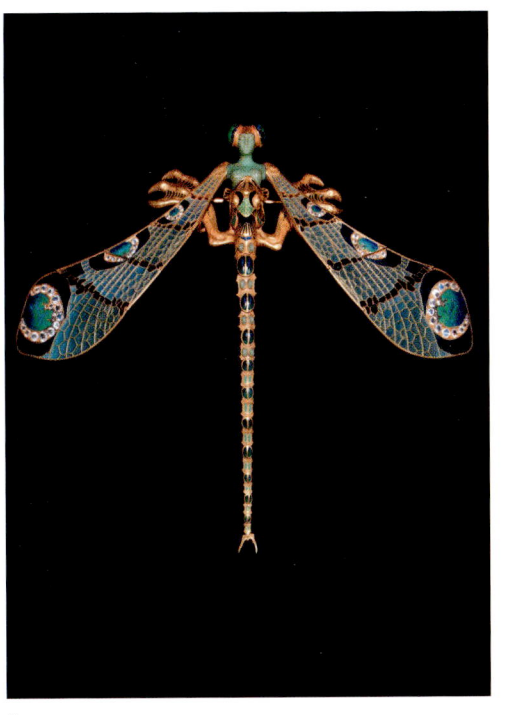

2

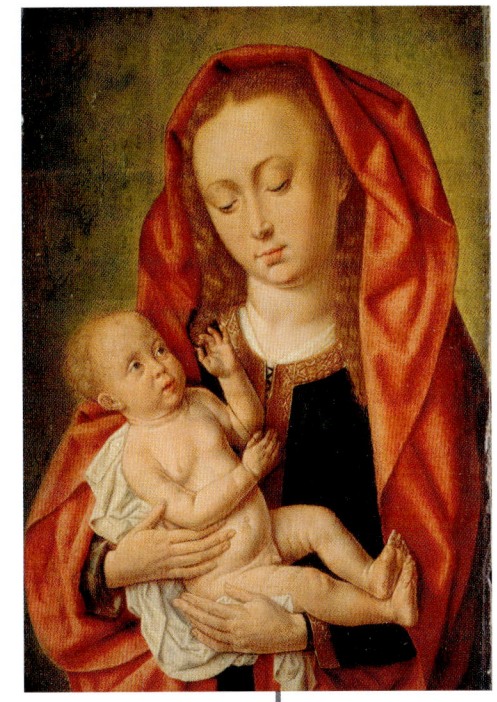

3

4

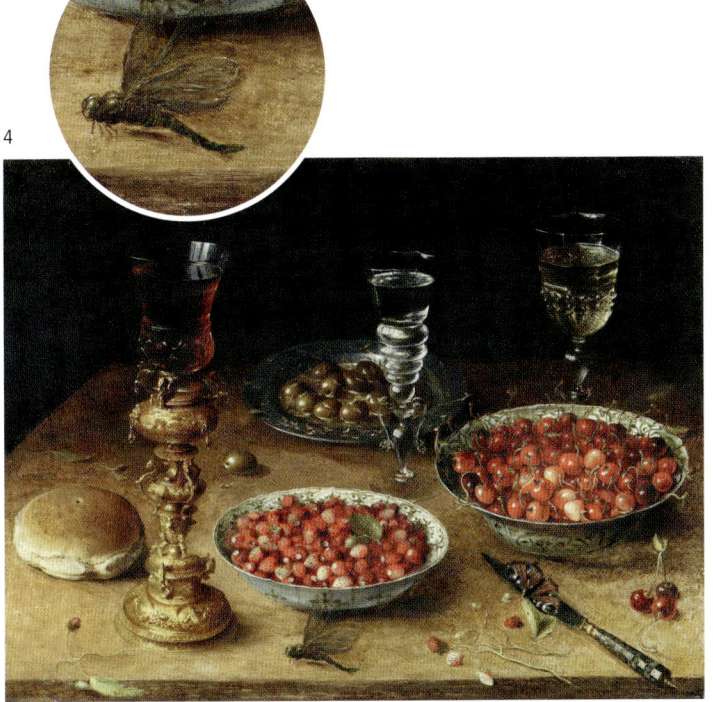

1. *Flower Still Life,* Ambrosius Bosschaert, 1614
2. *Dragonfly Woman Corsage Ornament,*
   René Lalique, c. 1897-98
3. *Virgin and Child with a Dragonfly,* Master
   of Saint Giles, 1500
4. *Still Life with Cherries and Strawberries in
   China Bowls,* Osias Beert, 1608

Beetle

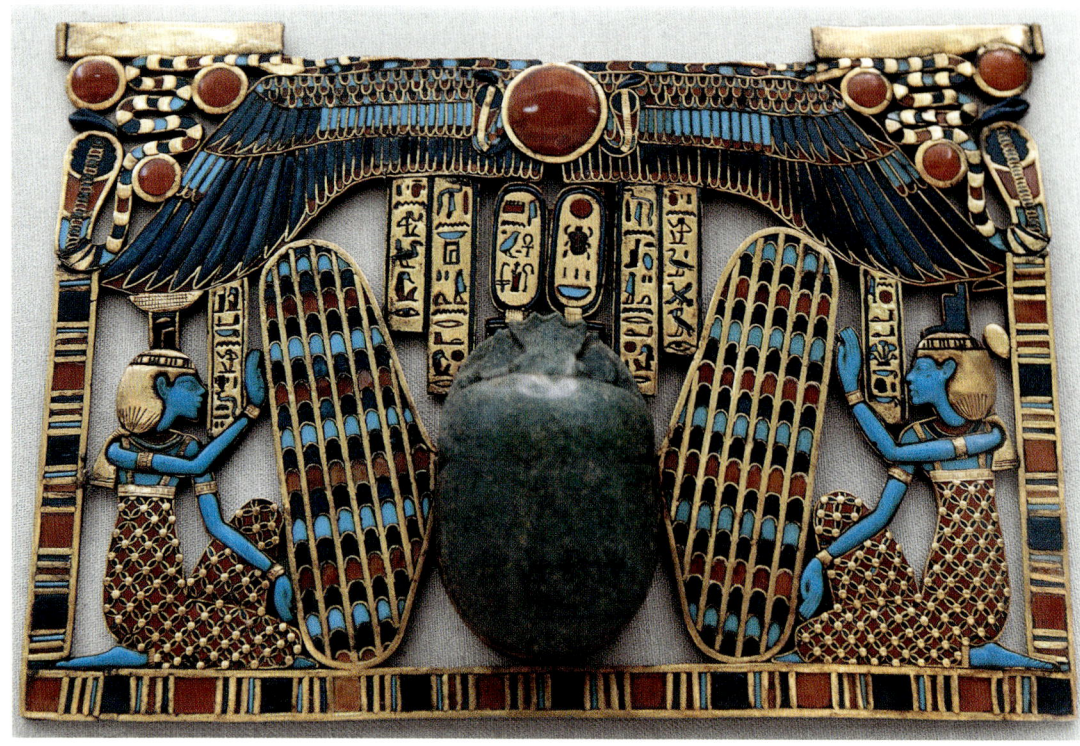

1

The ancient Egyptians depicted the sacred scarab beetle (*Scarabaeus sacer*) in funerary art and hieroglyphs. Scarabs carved in stone bore religious inscriptions from the Book of the Dead and were placed in tombs to ensure the immortality of the soul. Reflecting their metamorphosis from larva to adult, they have been depicted throughout history as symbols of the ephemeral nature of life, transformation, protection, rebirth, renewal, immortality, the sun's cycle and the divine. Alternatively, stag beetles were sometimes depicted in Northern European paintings of the sixteenth and seventeenth centuries with negative associations, often linked to the presence of evil, possibly connected to their role in decomposition, which suggests decay or death. One of the most notable examples of beetles in art is Albrecht Dürer's 1505 watercolour of the European Stag Beetle (*Lucanus cervus*). In contemporary art, Christopher Marley (b. 1969) uses real beetles in intricate, symmetrical compositions, blending natural history with design.

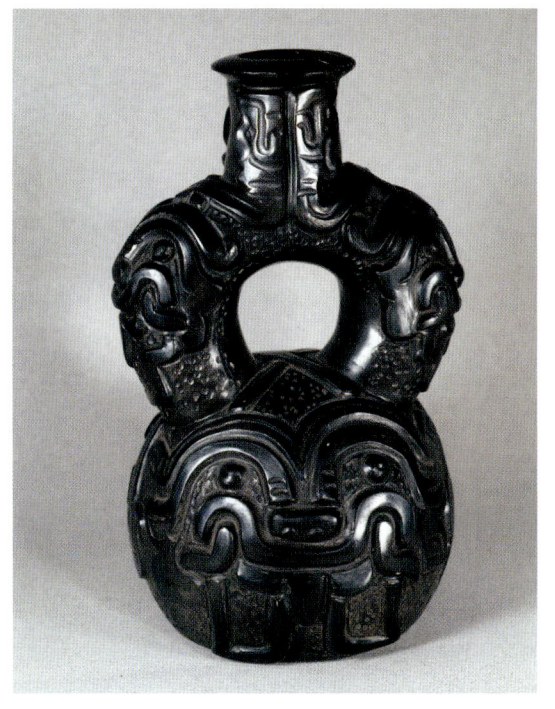

2

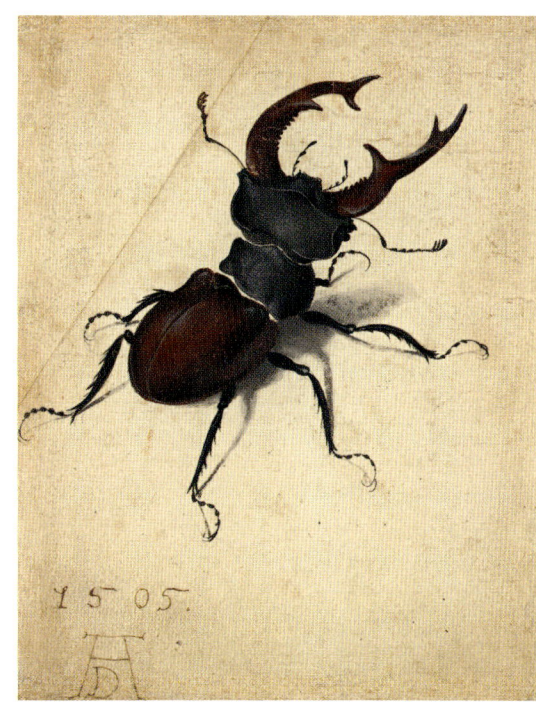

3

4

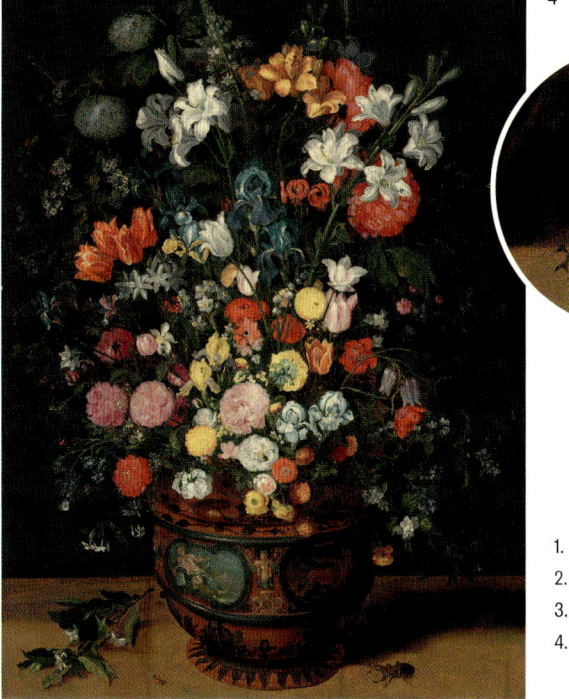

1. *Winged Scarab Pectoral of Tutankhamun,* Egypt, c. 133-1323 BCE
2. *Beetle-shaped Chavín black terracotta vase,* Peru, 900 BCE-200 CE
3. *Stag Beetle,* Albrecht Dürer, 1505
4. *Lilies, Irises, Roses and other Flowers in a Vase decorated with the figures of Amphitrite and Céres, on a Stone Ledge with a Stag Beetle and other insects,* Jan Brueghel II, 1618-20

Fly

Flies have buzzed through art history as symbols of decay, mortality and illusion. In trompe-l'œil paintings, flies were sometimes included as a test of artistic skill, appearing so lifelike that viewers might try to swat them away, while in Renaissance and Baroque vanitas paintings, the '*musca depicta*' (painted fly) often appeared as an unsettling reminder of death and impermanence, painted near skulls and rotting fruit, emphasizing life's fleeting nature. For example, Barthel Bruyn the Elder (1493–1555) painted *Vanitas* in 1524, adding a lifelike fly on a skull to remind viewers of life's fleeting nature and the inevitability of death. Petrus Christus (c. 1410/20–1475/76) painted *Portrait of a Carthusian* in 1446, adding a fly that rests on the trompe-l'œil frame, thereby blurring the line between reality and illusion. Carlo Crivelli frequently included flies in his religious works, such as *Madonna and Child* (c. 1480), where the insect disrupts the sacred scene, possibly symbolizing corruption.

1

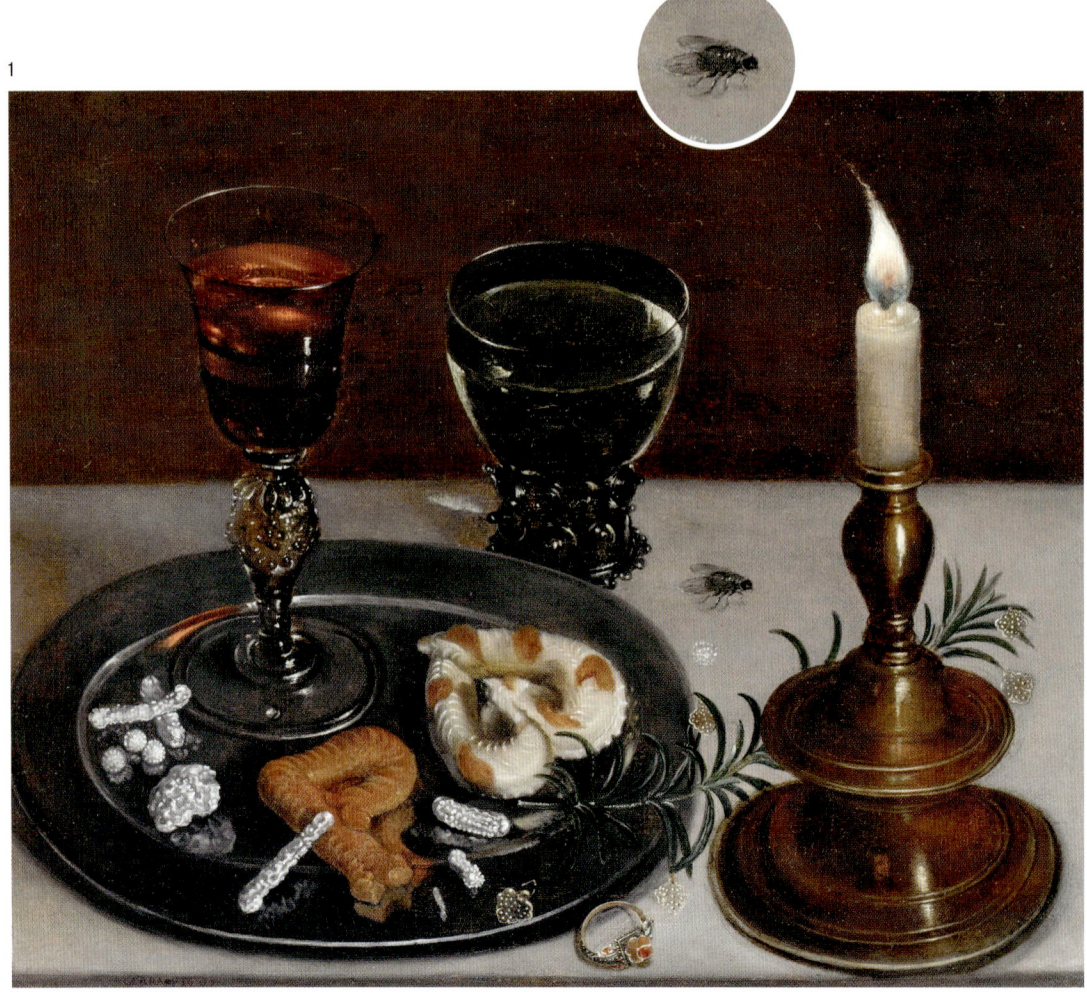

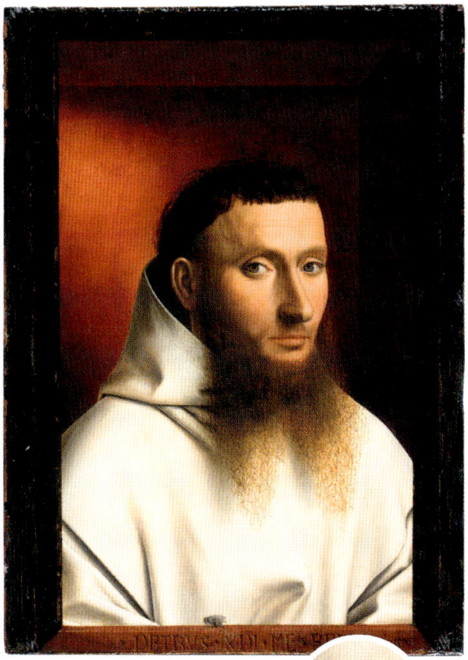

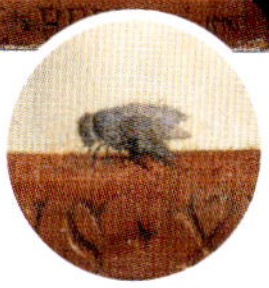

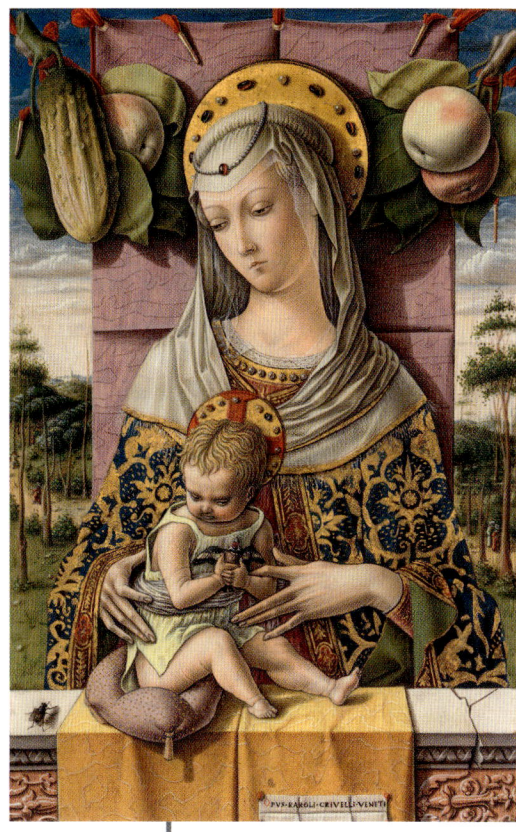

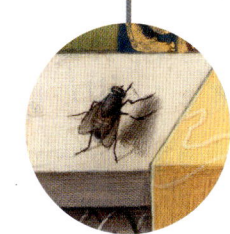

2

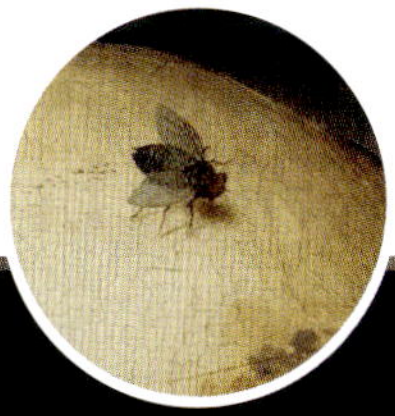

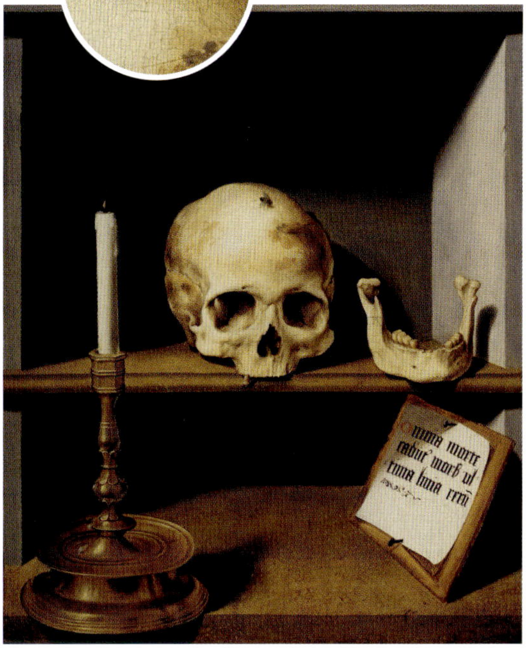

4

3

1. *Still Life with Dainties, Rosemary, Wine, Jewels and a Burning Candle,* Clara Peeters, 1607
2. *Portrait of a Carthusian,* Petrus Christus, 1446
3. *Madonna and Child,* Carlo Crivelli, c. 1480
4. *Vanitas,* Barthel Bruyn the Elder, 1524

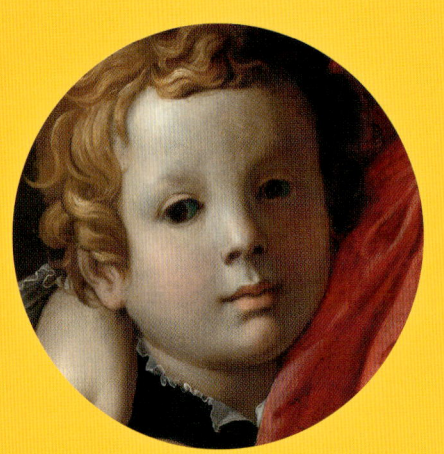

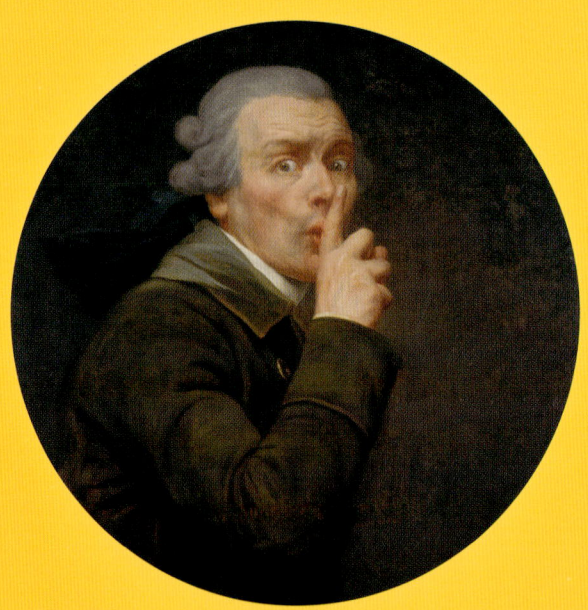

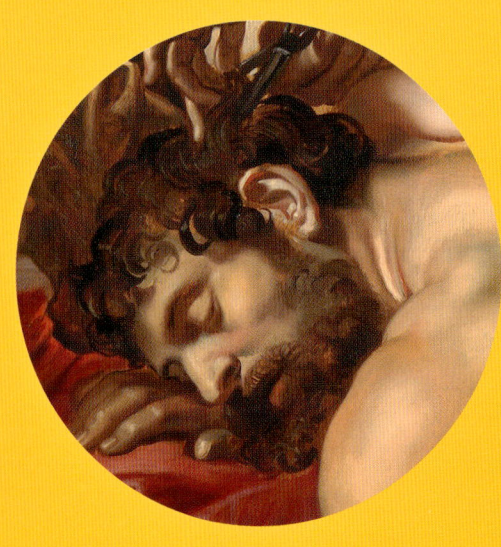

Bodies

Skull

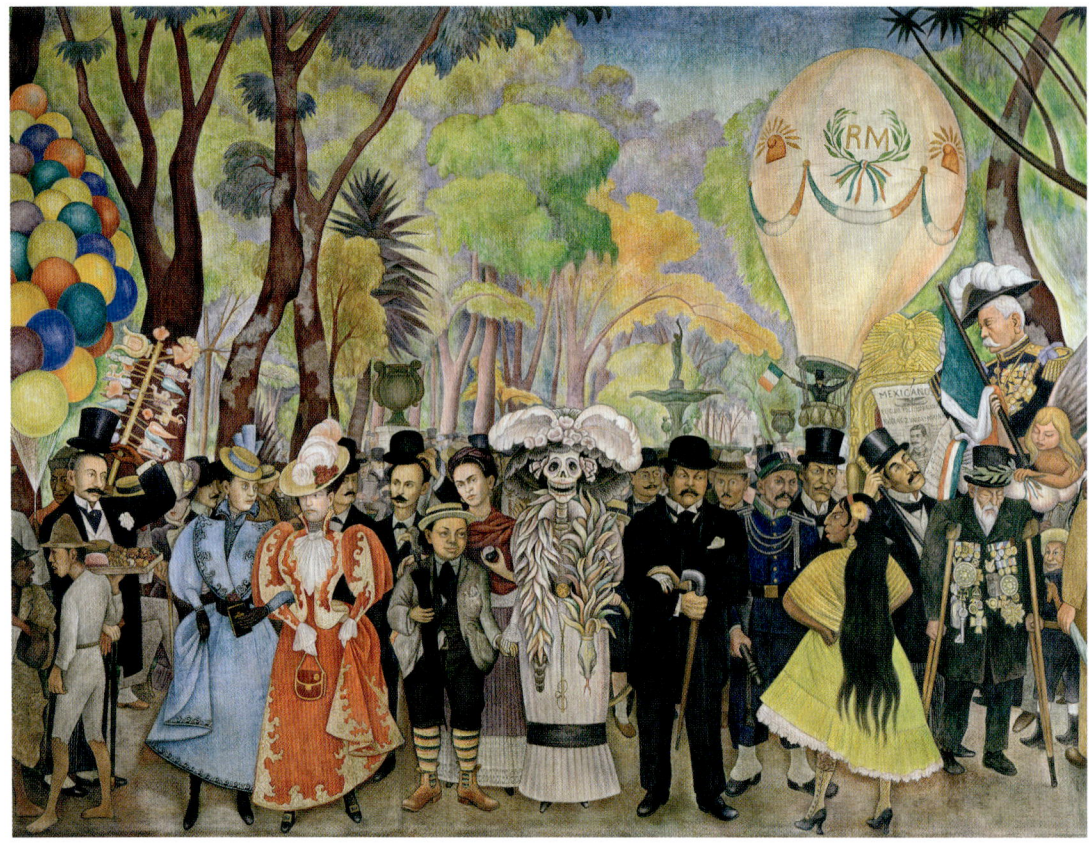

1

Mortality, transience and life cycles are just three of the meanings that have been attached to skulls in art. From ancient to modern times, the skull remains a versatile and compelling artistic motif, both ominous and celebratory, confronting the viewer with the truth of impermanence. In vanitas paintings of the sixteenth and seventeenth centuries, skulls were often placed alongside decaying fruit, extinguished candles or wilting flowers, to remind viewers of the fleeting nature of existence. *The Ambassadors* (1533) by Hans Holbein the Younger (c. 1497–1543) is famously known for featuring a distorted skull, visible only from a specific angle, which

reinforces themes of perspective and mortality. In Mexican folk art, skulls play a vibrant role in *Día de los Muertos* (Day of the Dead), where intricately decorated *calaveras* celebrate ancestors rather than mourn loss. Contemporary artists like Damien Hirst have used skulls to explore themes of rebellion, identity, wealth, power and the inevitability of death.

1. Detail from *Dream of a Sunday Afternoon at Alameda Central Park,* Diego Rivera, 1946-47
2. *For the Love of God,* Damien Hirst, 2007
3. *The Ambassadors,* Hans Holbein the Younger, 1533
4. *Death and Life,* Gustav Klimt, 1910

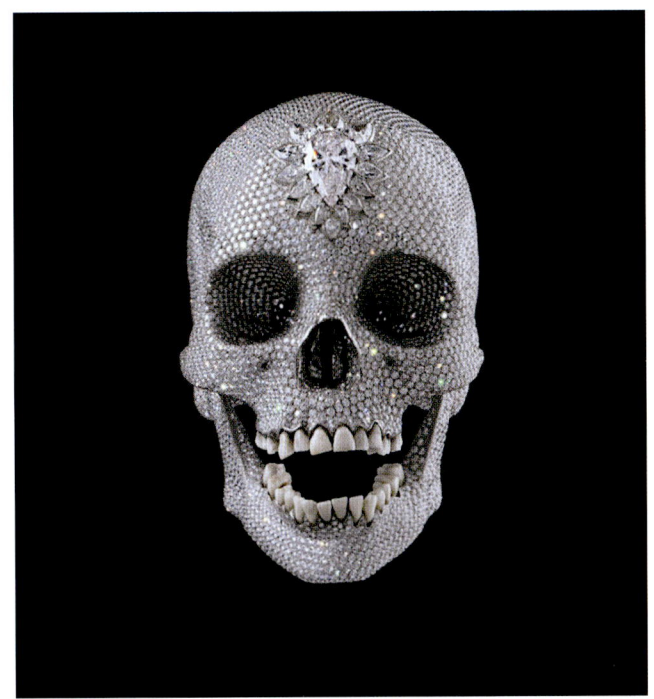

2

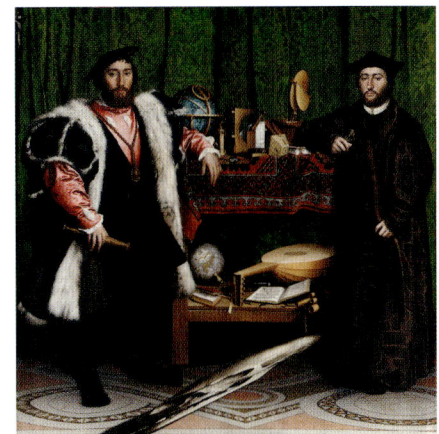

3

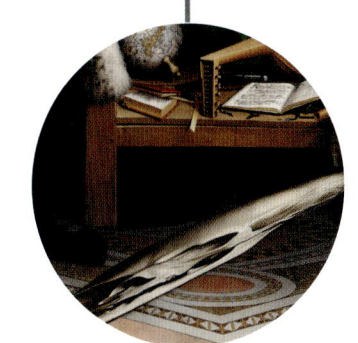

4

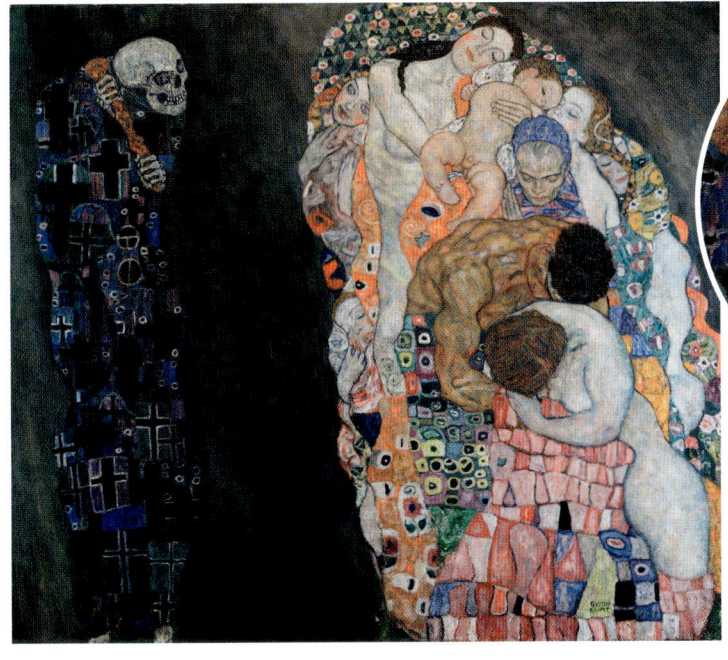

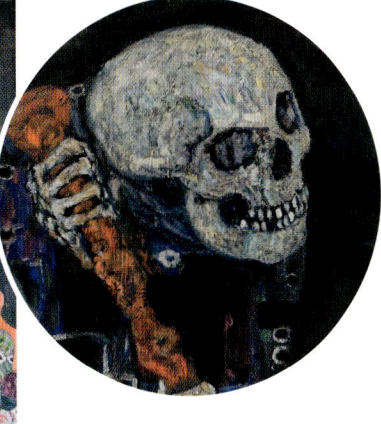

Blood

Blood has been depicted across civilizations to evoke themes of life, death, sacrifice and spiritual transformation. In ancient Mesoamerican cultures, particularly among the Maya and Aztecs, the depiction of blood emphasized the divine necessity of human sacrifice. Reliefs and murals portray priests offering blood to nourish the gods.
In Hindu and Buddhist iconography, blood is often depicted with wrathful deities, such as Kali or Mahakala. Blood is entwined with themes of redemption and sacrifice in Christian art. For example, *Descent from the Cross* (c. 1435) by Rogier van der Weyden (1399/1400–1464) features Christ's blood as a conduit for divine grace and human empathy. *Saturn Devouring His Son* (c. 1820-23) by Francisco Goya (1746–1828) reflects both his personal despair and his dark vision of humanity's capacity for self-destruction. In Frida Kahlo's *The Two Fridas* (1939), the shared artery and flowing blood symbolize her inner pain, emotional duality, and the life-giving yet wounding connection between her two selves and her lost love for Diego Rivera.

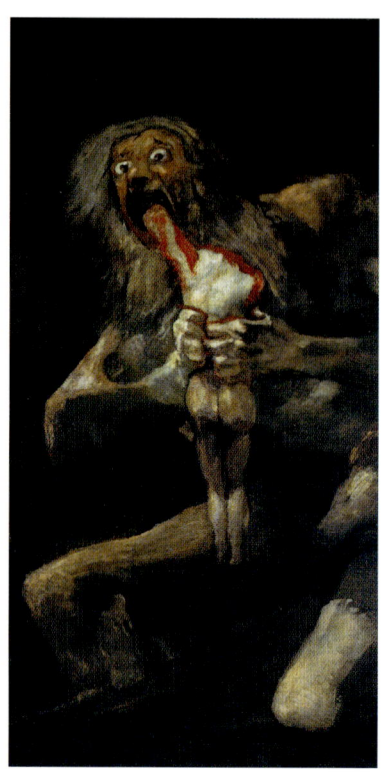

1

2

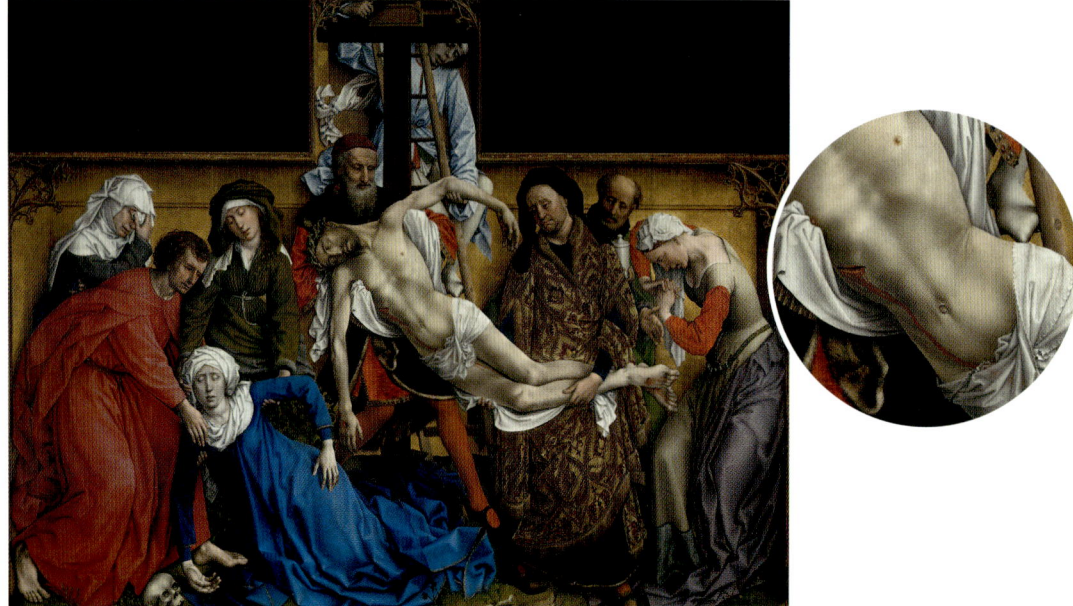

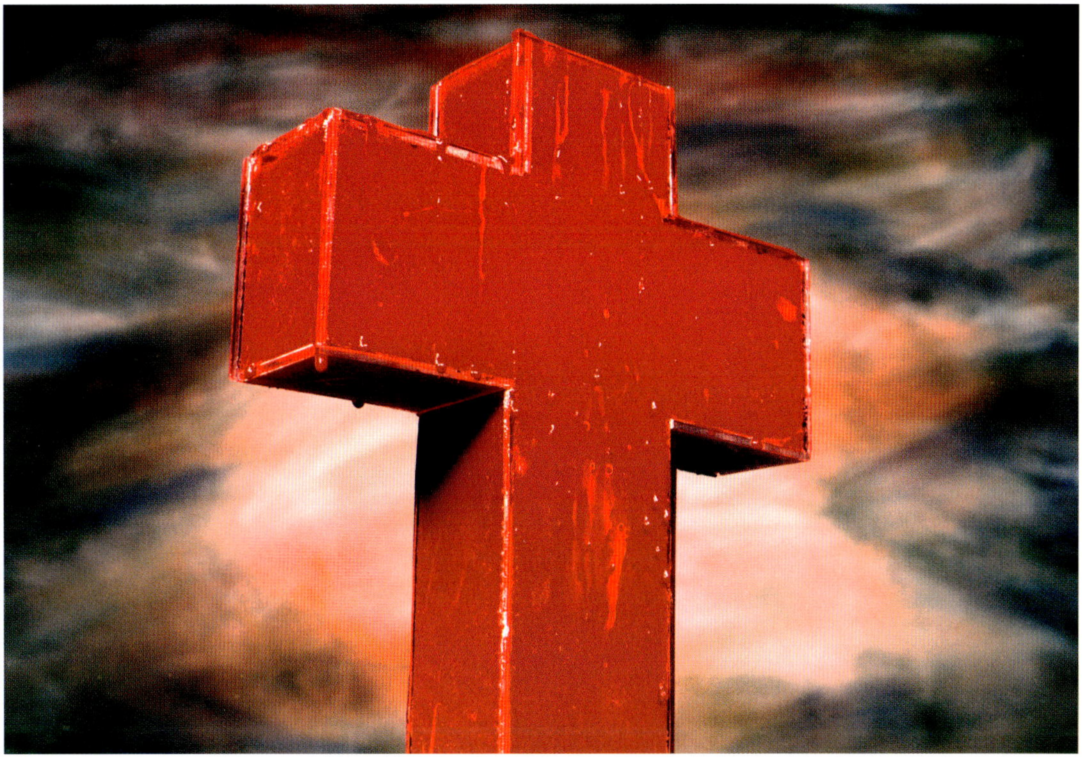

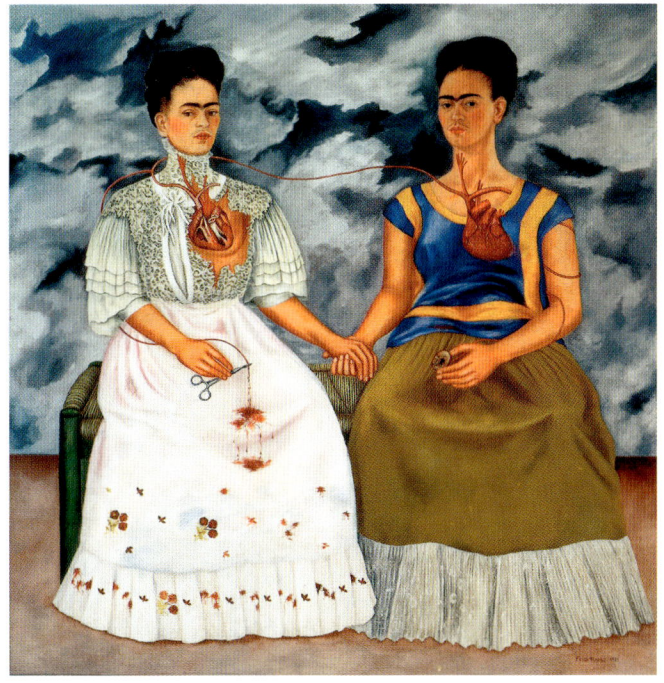

3

4

1. *Saturn Devouring His Son*, Francisco Goya,
   c. 1820-23
2. *Descent from the Cross,* Rogier van der Weyden,
   c. 1435
3. *Blood Cross,* Andres Serrano, 1990
4. *The Two Fridas*, Frida Kahlo, 1939

Heart

The heart has long served as a rich and powerful symbol in art, representing not just emotion but the essence of humanity itself. In ancient Egypt, it was central to the people's concept of the soul. Artists depicted hearts in funerary art as the organ weighed against the feather of Ma'at to determine a soul's worthiness in the afterlife. In classical antiquity, although the anatomical heart wasn't fully understood, philosophers like Aristotle viewed it as the basis of intellect and spirit, which inspired Greco-Roman art and sculpture. By the Middle Ages, the stylized, symmetrical heart shape began to emerge in Christian iconography, symbolizing divine love, and was often seen in depictions of the Sacred Heart of Jesus, for example, in the 1767 painting *Sacred Heart of Jesus* by Pompeo Batoni (1708–87). During the late fifteenth century, Leonardo da Vinci created some of the first anatomical drawings of the heart. In modern and contemporary art, the heart has been portrayed as a symbol of love, identity and resistance.

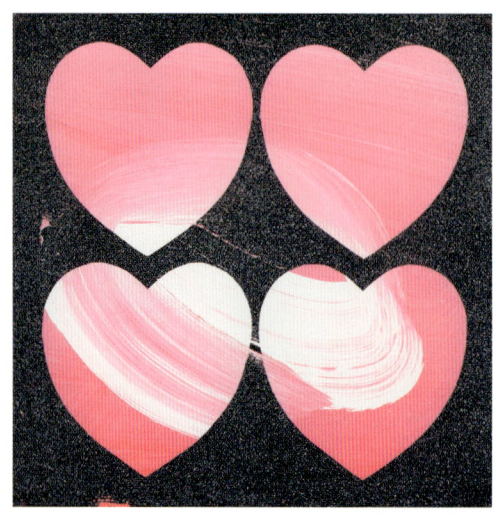

1

2

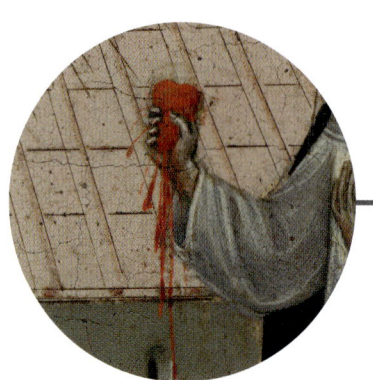

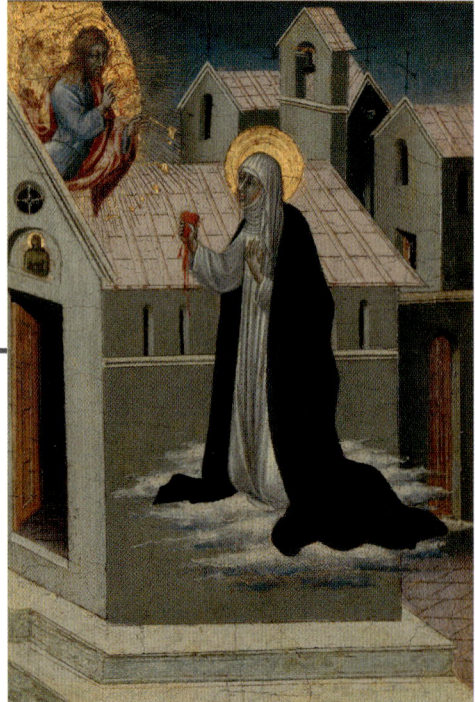

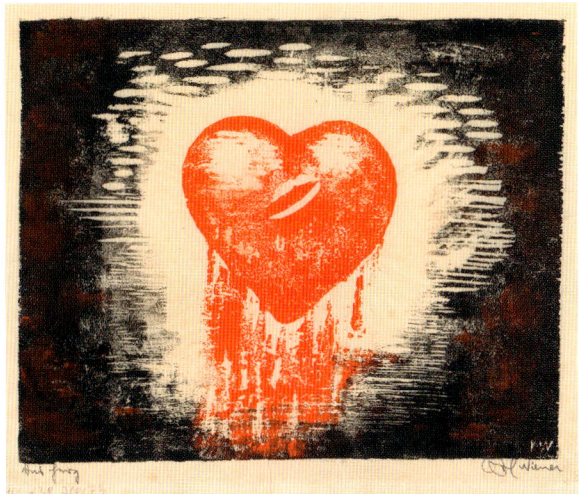

3

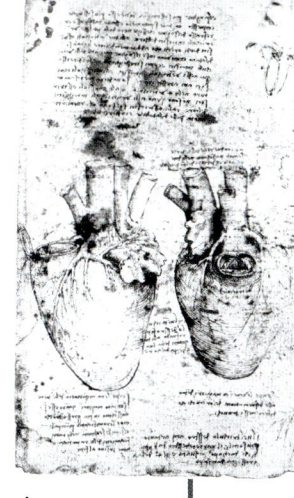

4

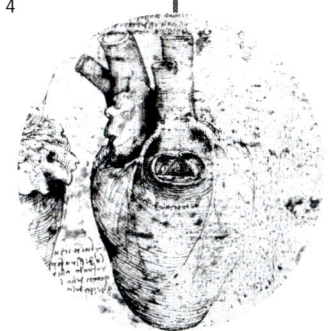

5

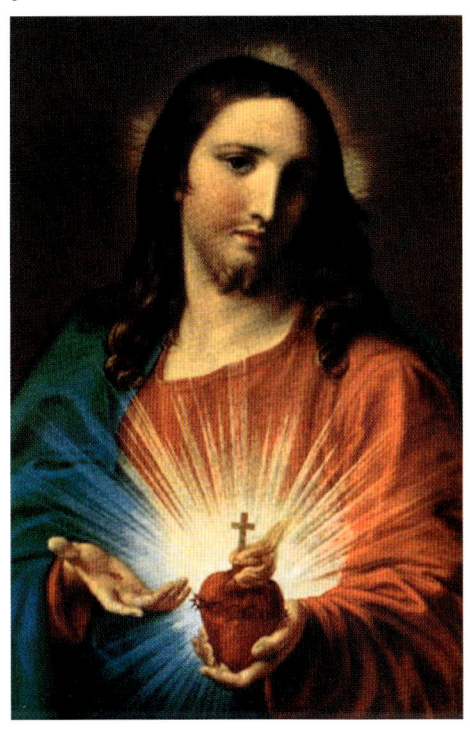

1. *Four Hearts,* Andy Warhol, 1981
2. *St Catherine of Siena Exchanging Her Heart with Christ,* Giovanni di Paolo, c. 1460
3. *The Heart,* Karl Wiener, c. 1930
4. *Anatomical drawings of the heart,* Leonardo da Vinci, c. 1490s
5. *Sacred Heart of Jesus,* Pompeo Batoni, 1767

Hands

From holding to praying, reaching to writing, clapping to signing, hands have historically represented a wide range of meanings, including power, creation, communication and spirituality. In ancient cave paintings in Lascaux, France, handprints are an early expression of human presence. In religious art, hands often convey divine authority or blessing, as seen in Michelangelo's *Creation of Adam* (1508-11), where God's outstretched hand bestows life upon Adam. In medieval and Renaissance art, gesture conveyed narrative and emotion; a raised hand, for instance, might indicate teaching or a benediction. In Eastern traditions, *mudras* (hand gestures) in Buddhist and Hindu art symbolize spiritual states and intentions. Modern and contemporary artists, such as Alberto Giacometti (1901-66) or Louise Bourgeois (1911-2010), utilized hands to explore themes of identity, vulnerability and human connection. In protest art, raised or clasped hands have signified solidarity and resistance. Across cultures and eras, the hand is capable of building, blessing, wounding or reaching out, making it a universal motif of human experience and expression.

1. *Golden Bridge-Bà Nà Hills,* unknown artist, 2018
2. *Le Discret (The Secret),* Joseph Ducreux, c. 1791
3. *Study of an Apostle's Hands (Praying Hands),* Albrecht Dürer, c. 1508
4. *The Creation of Adam,* Michelangelo, 1508-11

1

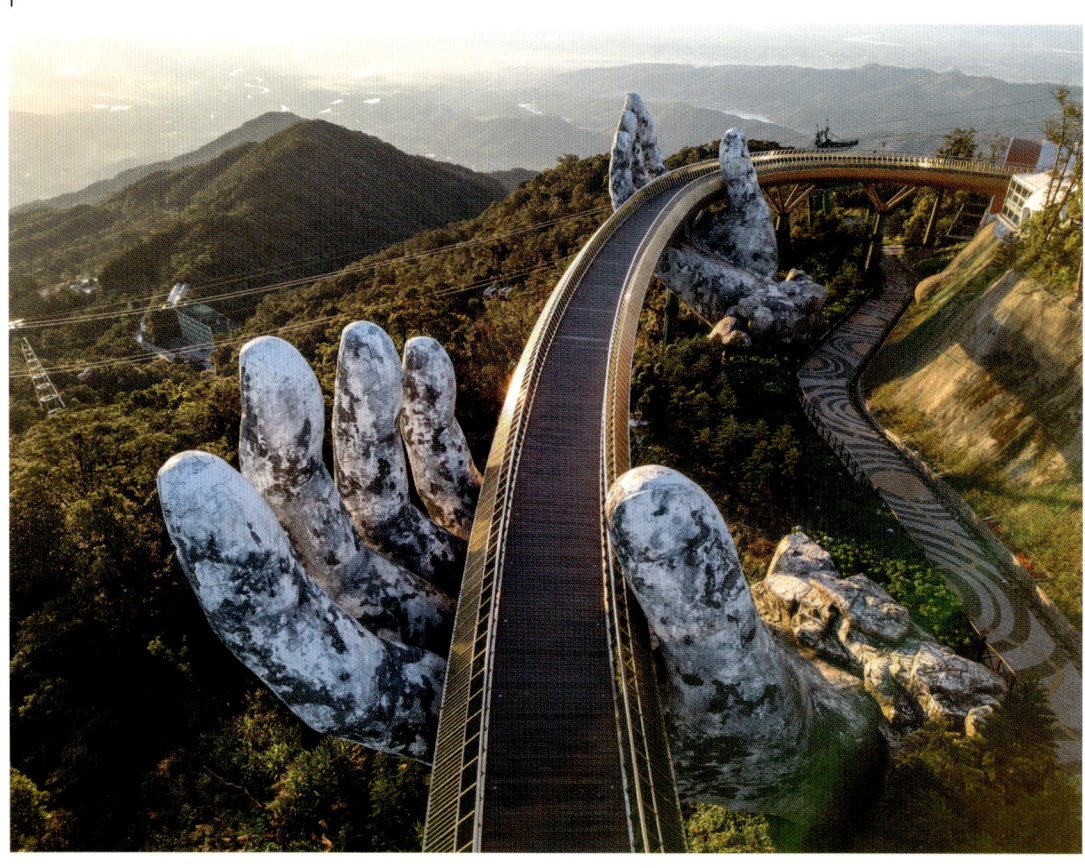

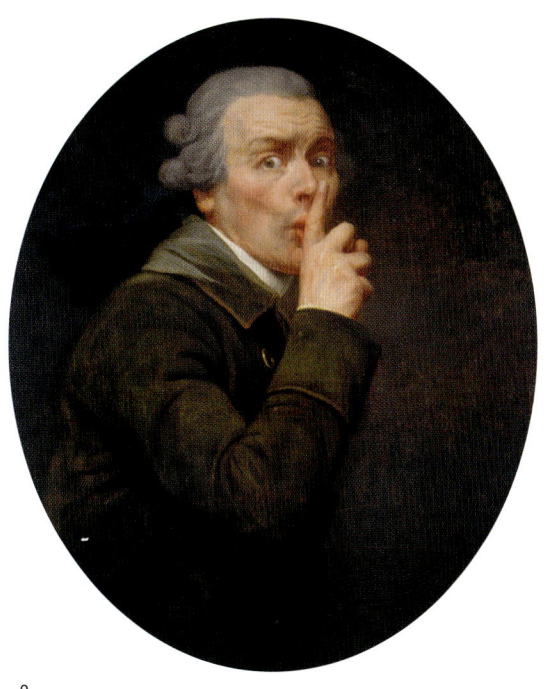

2

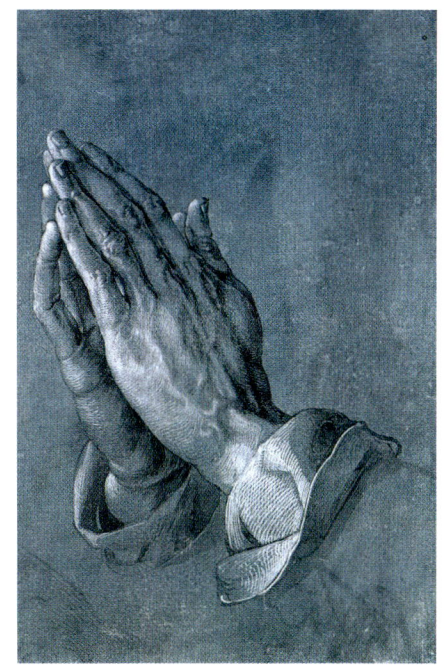

3

4

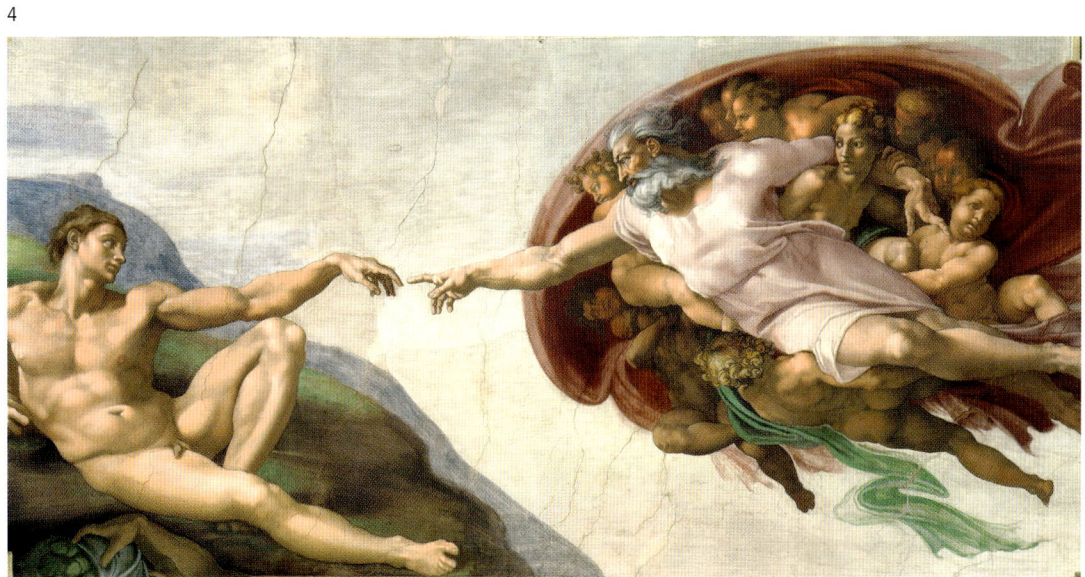

Eyes

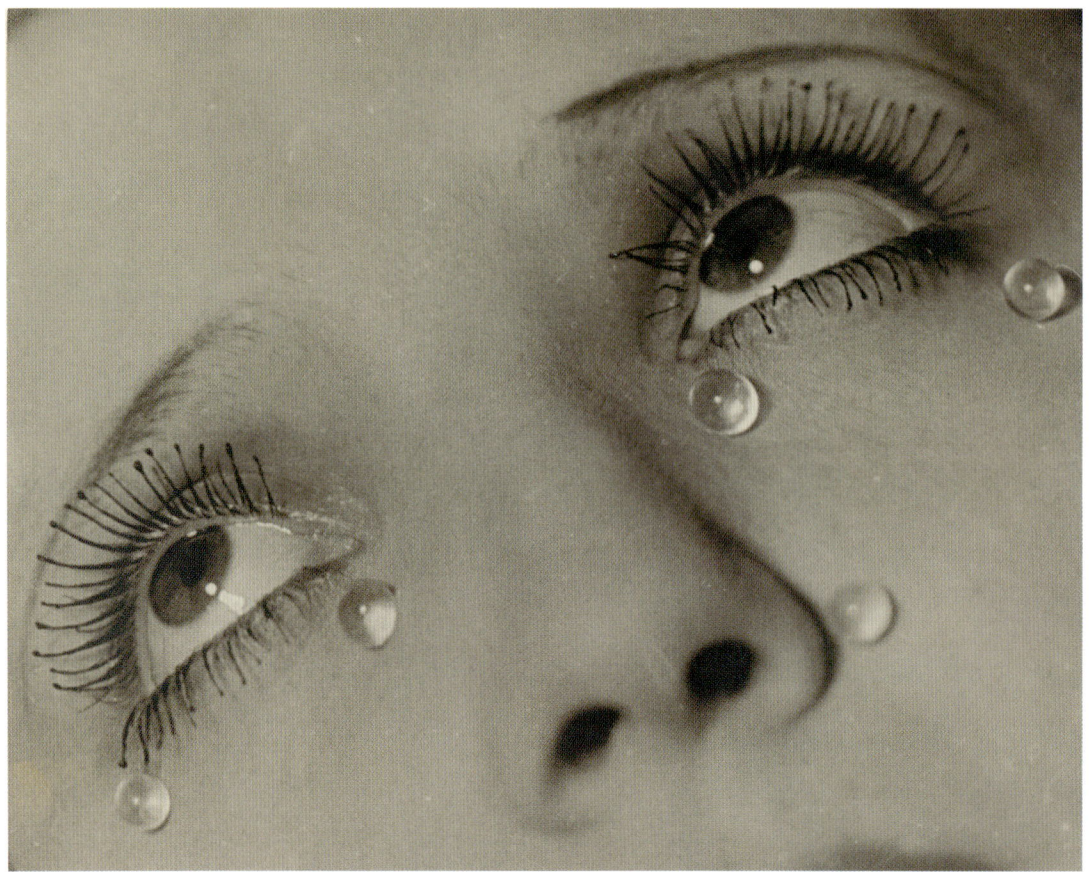

1

Since ancient times, eyes have served as powerful symbols, representing perception, knowledge, truth and the soul. The Eye of Horus symbolized protection, health and divine power in ancient Egyptian art. Similarly, in Greek and Roman art, eyes were often emphasized to reflect character and inner life. In Renaissance portraiture, artists like Leonardo da Vinci, Filippo Lippi and Giovanni Battista Moroni (c. 1520/24–78) used the eyes to convey emotion and psychological depth, for example, in the enigmatic gaze of the *Mona Lisa* (c. 1503–17). In Hinduism, the eye is often associated with the god Shiva, who is known as the destroyer of ignorance and the bringer of enlightenment. *The False Mirror* (1928) by René Magritte (1898–1967) presents an eye reflecting the sky, challenging our perception of reality. In contemporary art, eyes can symbolize surveillance, identity and introspection. Artists such as Jenny Holzer (b. 1950) have used eye motifs to evoke themes of control, awareness and vulnerability.

1. *Glass Tears*, Man Ray, 1932
2. *Madame Kisling,* Amedeo Modigliani, 1917
3. *Eye of Ra,* Egypt, c. 1323 BCE
4. *The False Mirror*, René Magritte, 1928

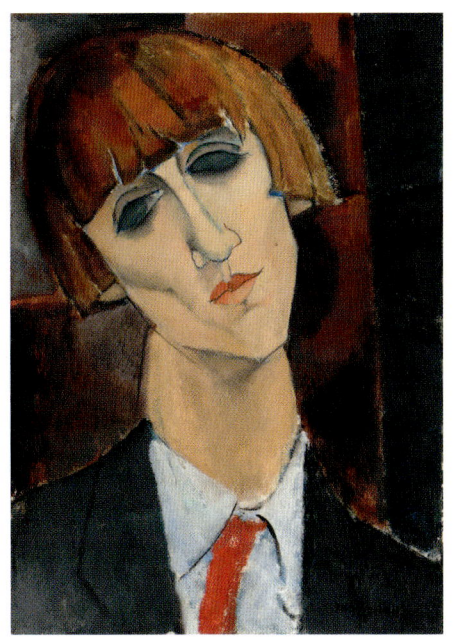

2

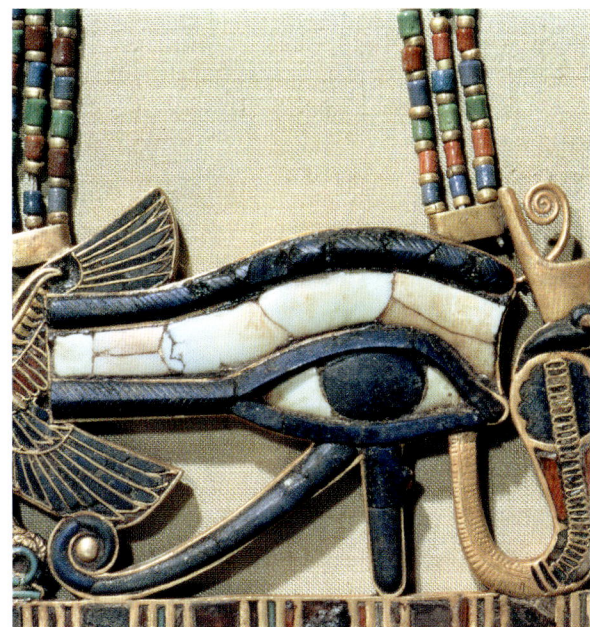

3

4

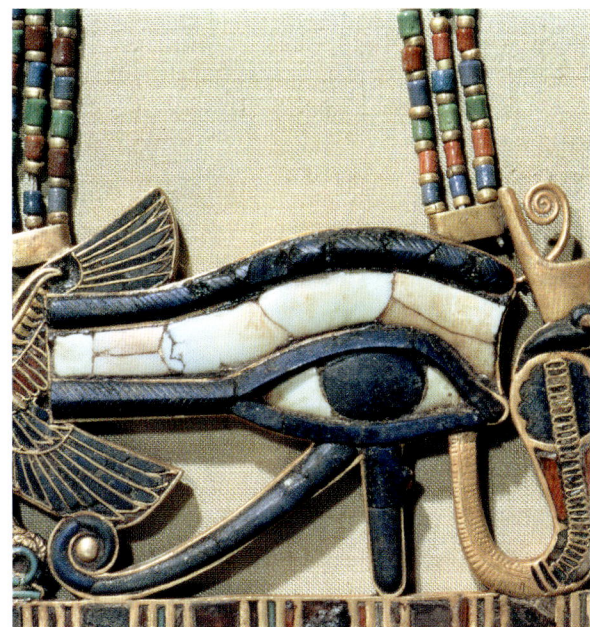

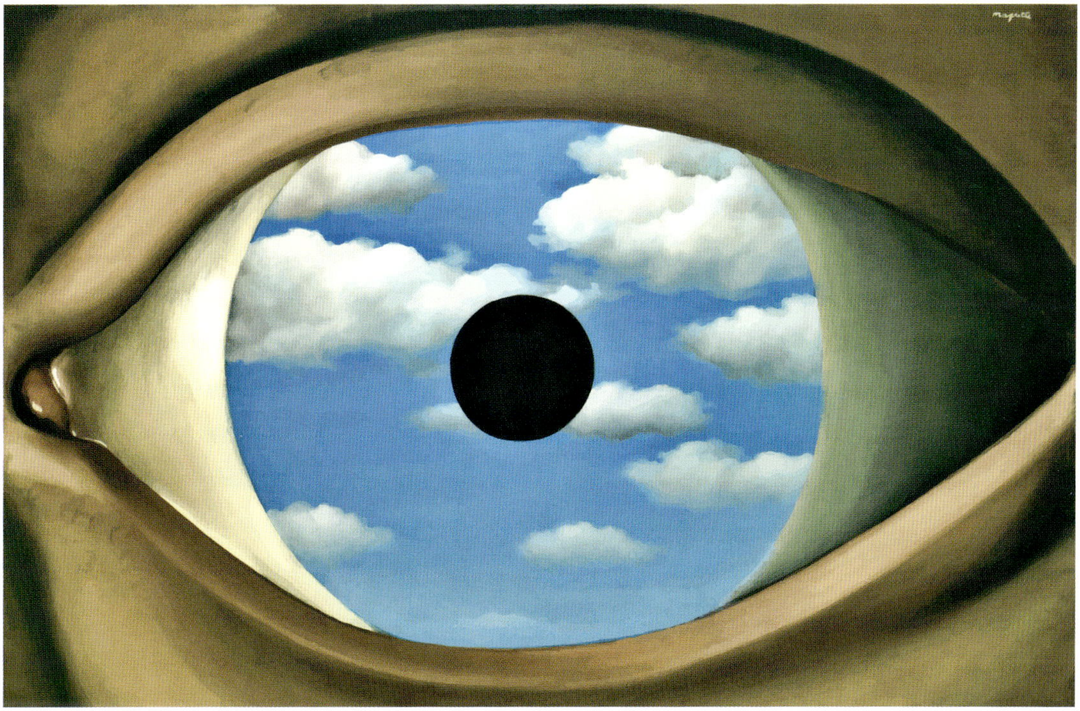

Ears

Listening, awareness and perception are just three of the many reasons that ears have featured in art. In several ancient cultures, ears were associated with divine communication; for example, in Mesopotamia, some gods were depicted with large ears to signify their ability to hear prayers. Similarly, in Buddhist sculpture, elongated earlobes on figures such as the Buddha signify wisdom, spiritual enlightenment and detachment from material concerns. Van Gogh's self-mutilation and depiction of his bandaged ear in *Self-Portrait with Bandaged Ear* (1889) poignantly symbolizes mental anguish, isolation and the tension between hearing and understanding. Hieronymus Bosch (c. 1450–1516) painted several ears in *The Garden of Earthly Delights* (1490–1510). In the right panel, he painted a giant pair of ears pierced by a knife, with a face-like shape formed by surrounding elements. This bizarre ear-knife hybrid is widely interpreted as a symbol of the dangers of sensory excess, particularly related to eavesdropping, and the consequences of succumbing to earthly temptations.

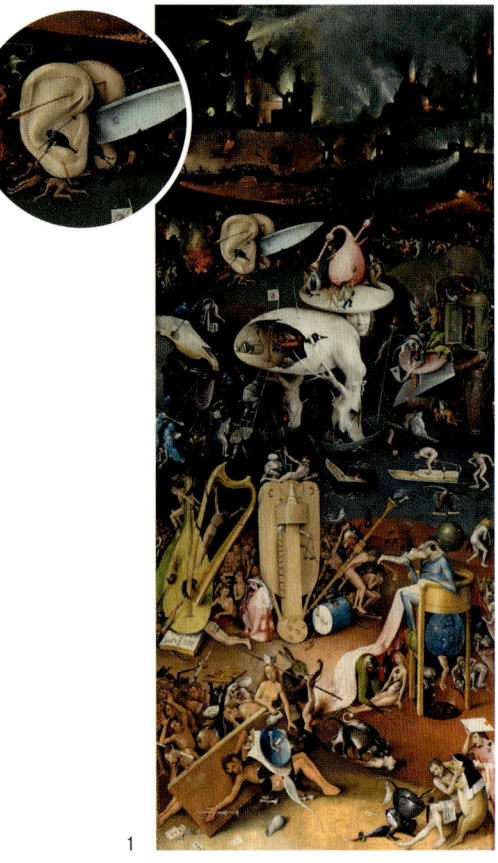

1

2

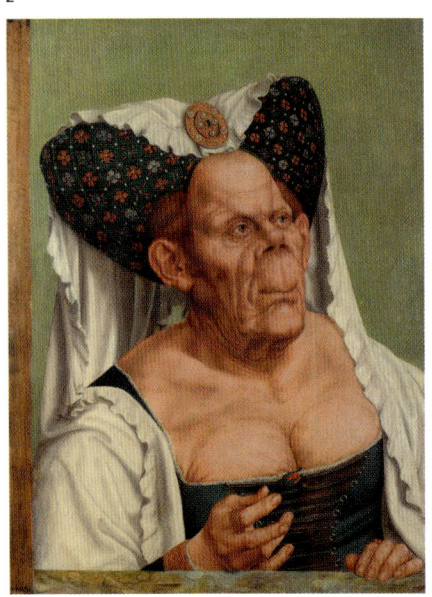

3

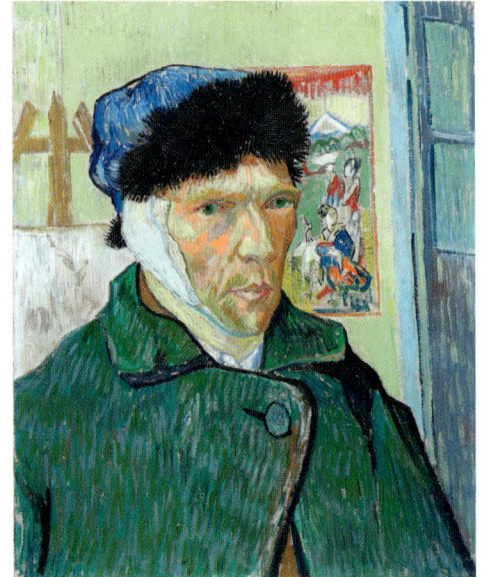

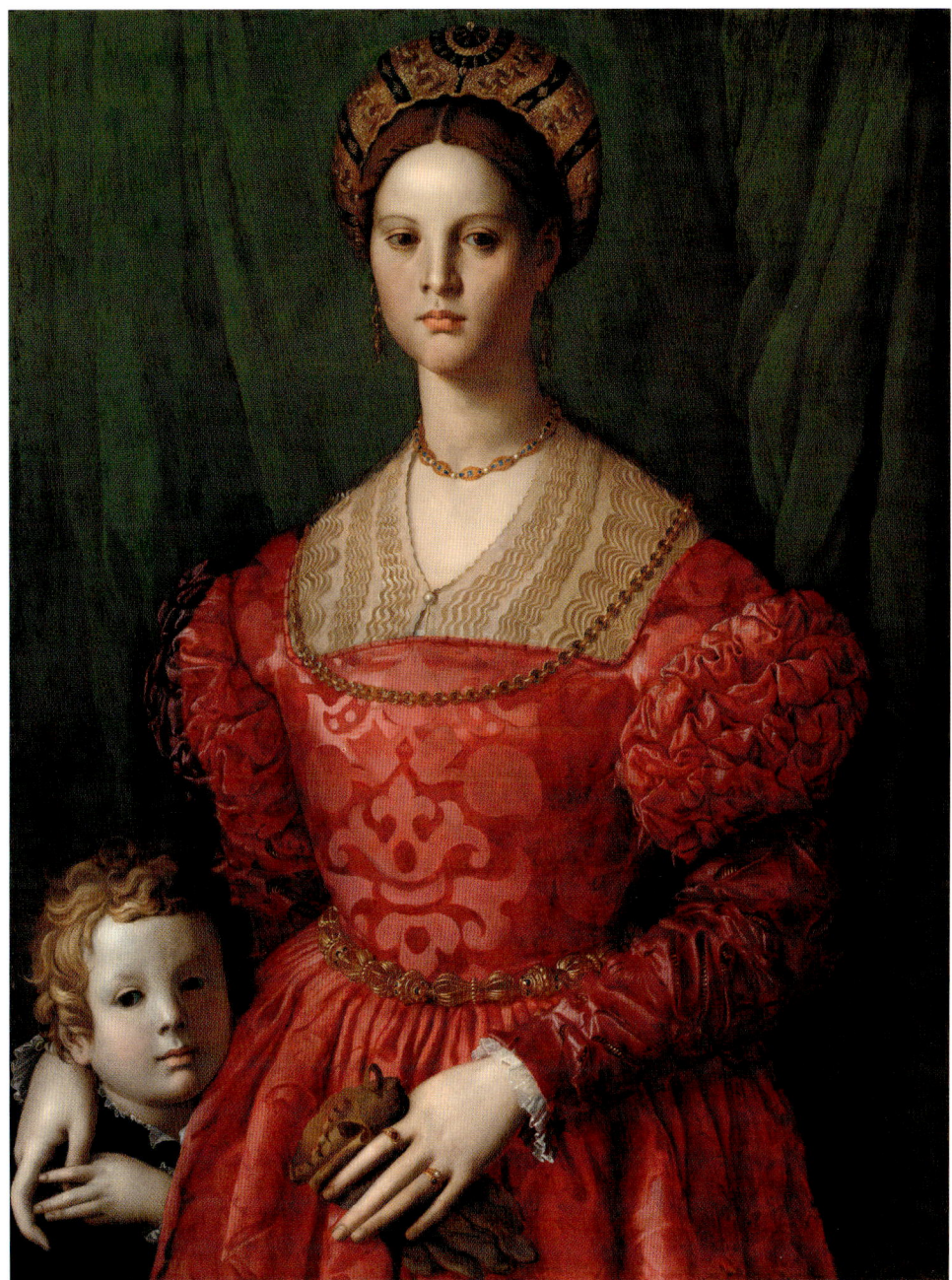

4

1. *Hell (detail from The Garden of Earthly Delights),* Hieronymus Bosch, 1490-1510
2. *An Old Woman (The Ugly Duchess),* Quinten Massys, c. 1513
3. *Self-Portrait with Bandaged Ear,* Vincent van Gogh, 1889
4. *A Young Woman and her Little Boy,* Agnolo Bronzino, c. 1540

Feet

As symbols of movement, humility, journeys, identity, the human condition and spiritual connections, feet have appeared in art across cultures. In ancient Egypt, feet in profile signified motion and status. Feet represent divinity and devotion in Indian art; touching a deity's feet is a sacred gesture, and Vishnu's footprints symbolize his cosmic presence. Classical Greek sculpture idealized the human form, including feet, as an expression of beauty and balance. Christian depictions of Jesus washing his disciples' feet, for example, *The Washing of the Feet* (1304-06) by Giotto di Bondone (c. 1267-1337), represent humility and service. In Hindu and Buddhist traditions, depictions of sacred footprints symbolize divine presence and enlightenment. During the Renaissance, artists such as Michelangelo used bare feet to humanize divine figures. In Japanese ukiyo-e prints, the exposed foot often implied sensuality. More recently, modern and contemporary artists have explored feet as symbols of journey, identity or vulnerability.

1

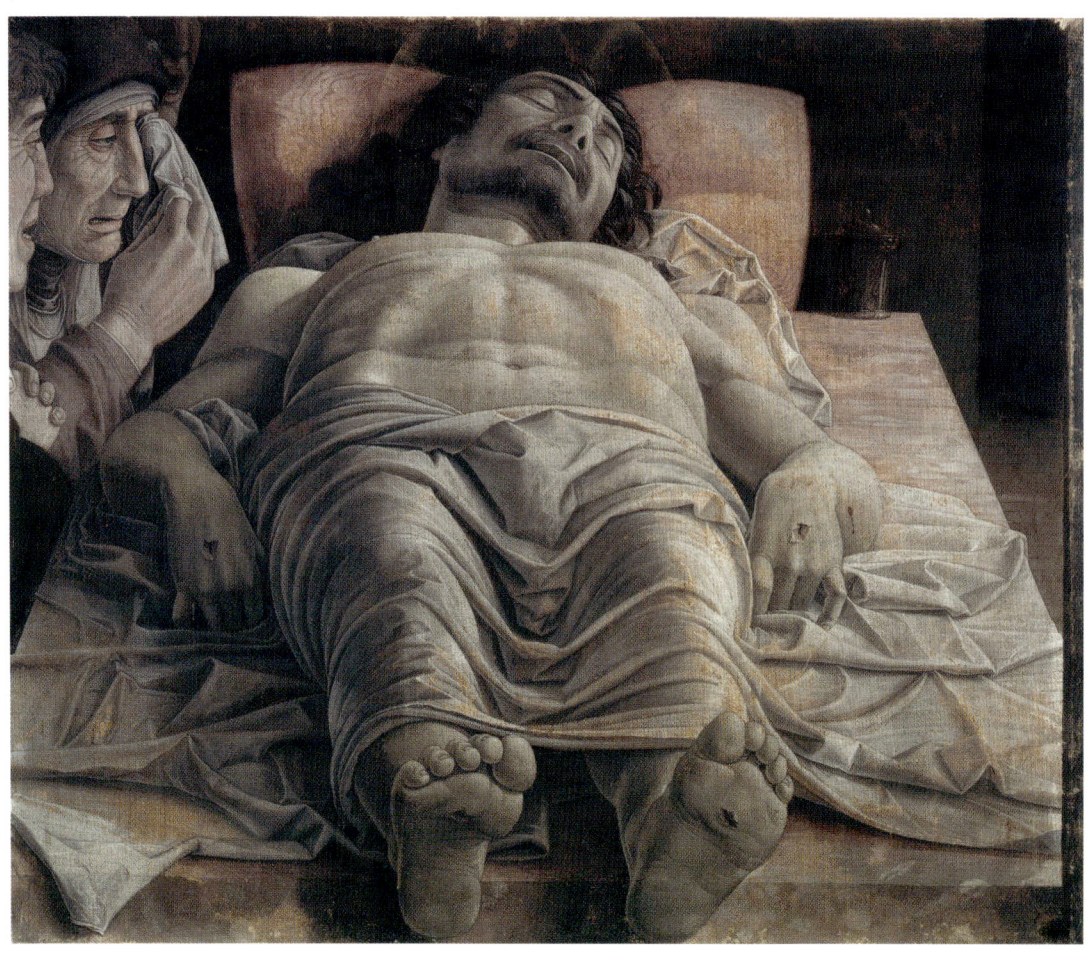

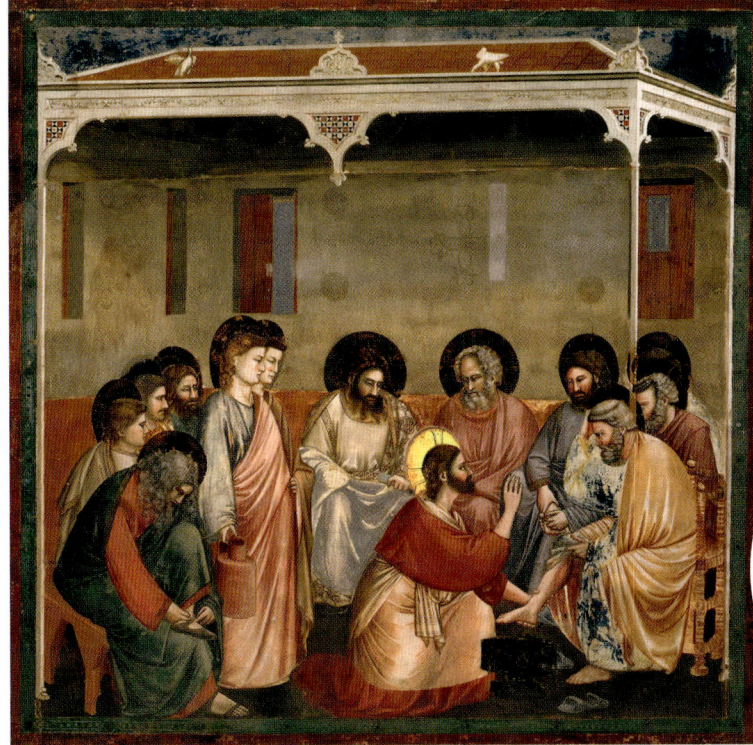

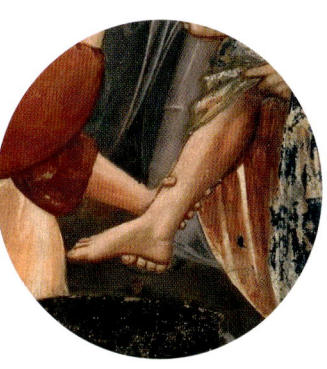

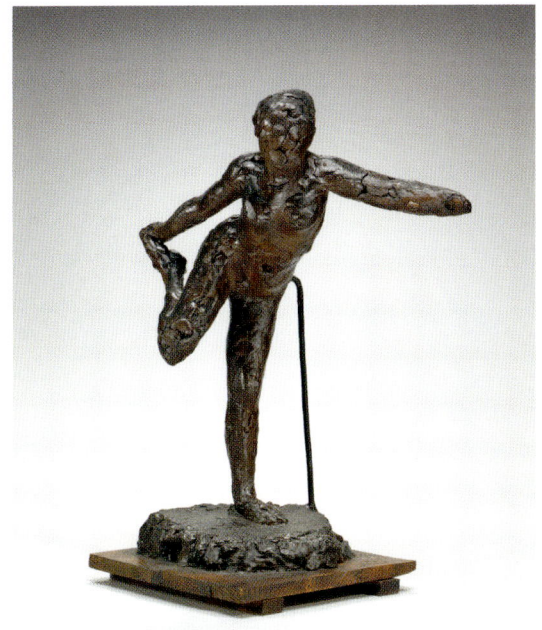

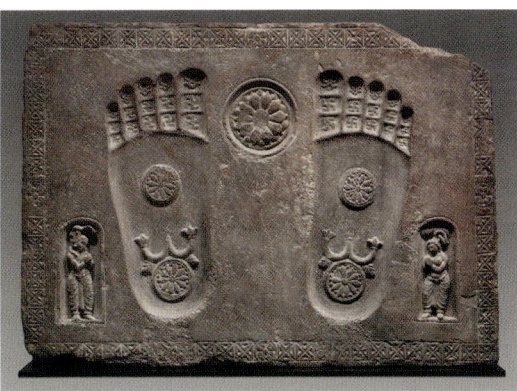

1. *Lamentation Over the Dead Christ*, Andrea Mantegna, c. 1470–74

2. *The Washing of the Feet*, Giotto di Bondone, 1304–06

3. *Dancer Holding her Right Foot in her Right Hand*, Edgar Degas, c. 1900–10

4. *Buddhapada (Footprints of the Buddha)*, Pakistan, second century CE

Hair

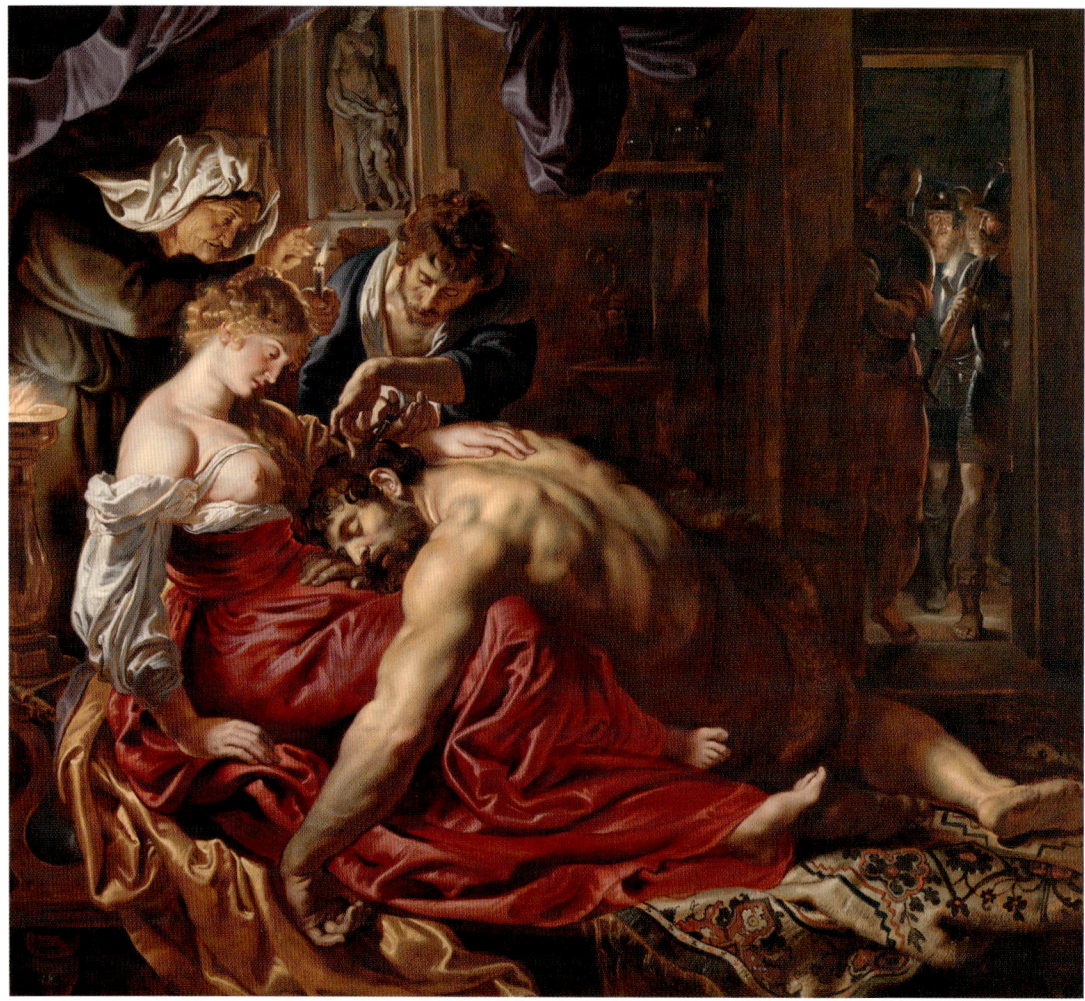

1

In ancient Egypt, elaborate wigs denoted status and divinity, while in Greek sculpture, flowing locks symbolized both beauty and heroism. During the Renaissance, hair in portraiture conveyed virtue or sensuality, depending on its style and the degree of exposure it received. The Benin Bronzes, created from the sixteenth century onwards, depicted intricate hairstyles to convey status, identity and cultural symbolism. Hair was linked to spiritual power. In Pre-Raphaelite paintings, such as *Proserpine* (1882) by Dante Gabriel Rossetti, flowing hair symbolizes femininity.

The Bridesmaid (1851) by John Everett Millais (1829-96) features golden hair to evoke innocence and longing. Edgar Degas (1834-1917) captured women combing their hair in intimate moments, as in *Woman Combing her Hair* (c. 1888-90), emphasizing the private self. Hair can also signify political and cultural identity. In *No Woman, No Cry* (1998) by Chris Ofili (b. 1968), the figure's braided hair references Black identity and mourning, while self-portraits by Zanele Muholi (b. 1972) feature elaborate hairstyles to challenge racial stereotypes.

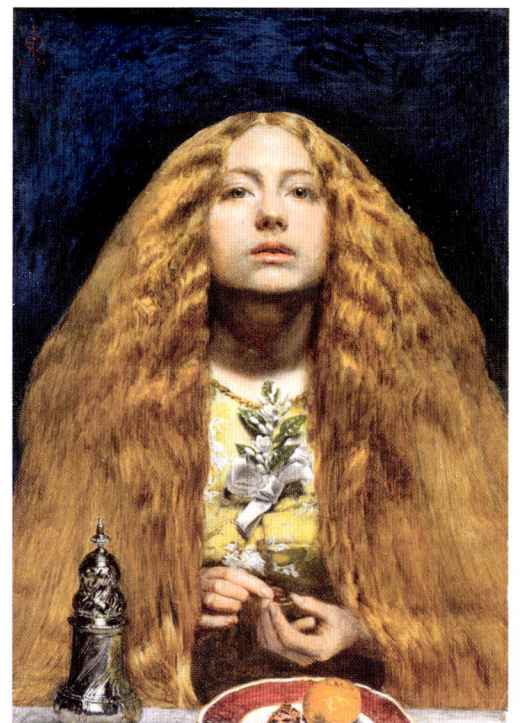

2

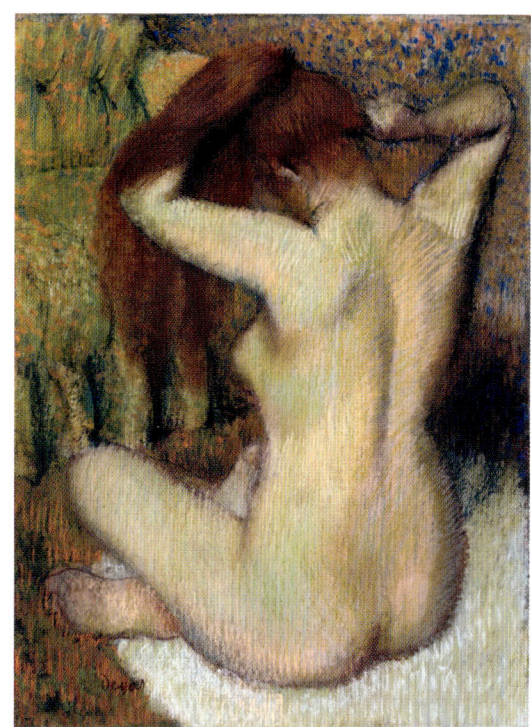

3

4

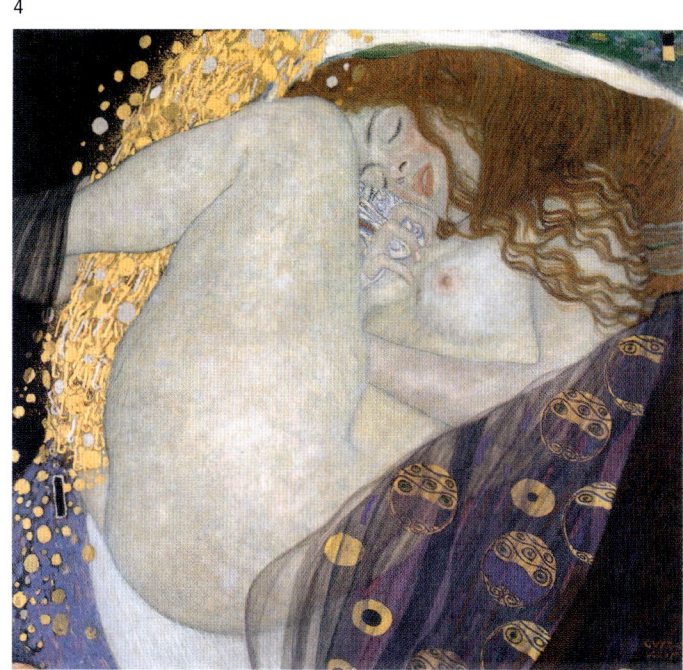

1. *Samson and Delilah*, Peter Paul Rubens, c. 1609-10

2. *The Bridesmaid*, John Everett Millais, 1851

3. *Woman Combing her Hair*, Edgar Degas, c. 1888-90

4. *Danaë*, Gustav Klimt, 1907-08

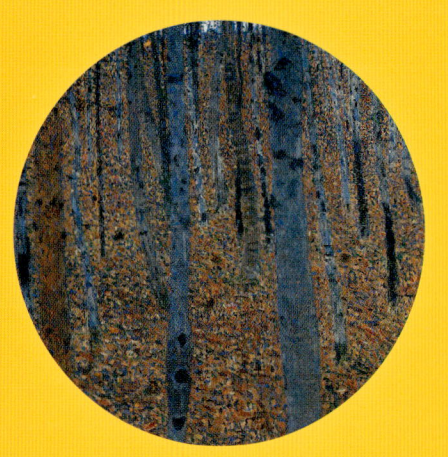

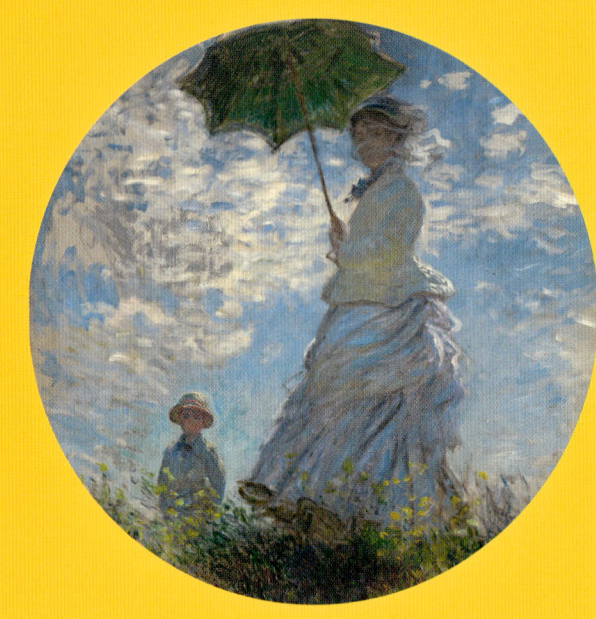

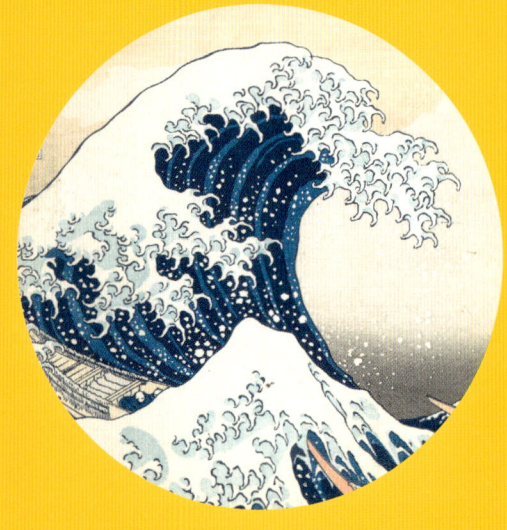

Land, Water
and Air

Mountains

From ancient Chinese scrolls and Japanese ukiyo-e to Romantic European landscapes, mountains in art have evoked feelings of spiritual ascent, isolation or awe. Artists often choose to depict them for their grandeur, but also to suggest obstacles, enlightenment or eternal truths, reflecting inner journeys, sacred realms or nature's sublime, timeless power. Mountains connect the earthly with the transcendent; they can represent permanence or divine presence. In East Asian art, such as traditional Chinese ink paintings, mountains symbolize harmony with nature and spiritual contemplation, often linked to Daoist and Buddhist ideals. In Western art, mountains frequently appear in religious contexts; for example, Renaissance artists placed biblical events on mountains to signify closeness to God. Romantic painters like Caspar David Friedrich (1775-1851) and J.M.W. Turner (1774-1840) evoked the awe-inspiring, overwhelming force of nature that overshadows human presence. Some indigenous and mythological art also depicts mountains as sacred sites or homes of deities, reflecting cultural reverence for nature.

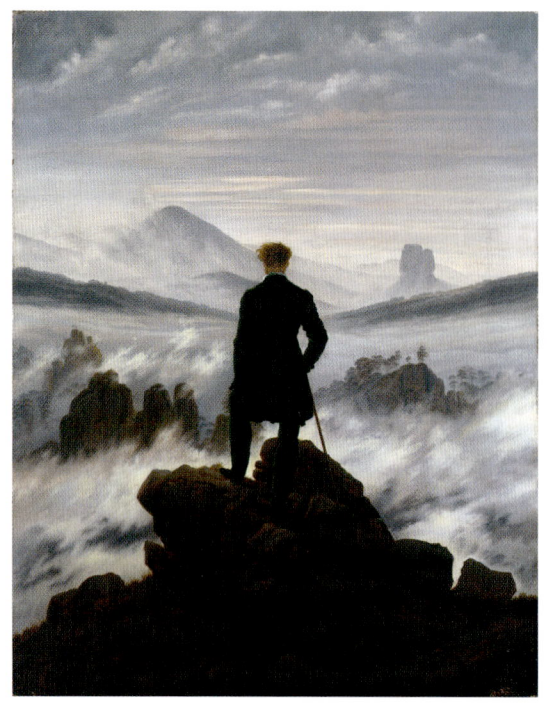

1

2

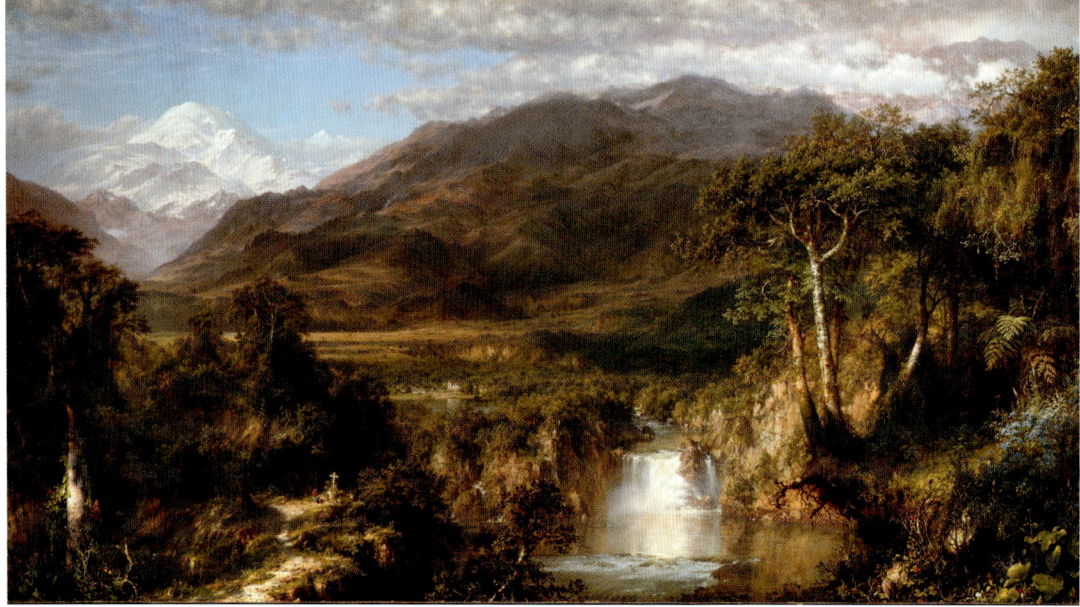

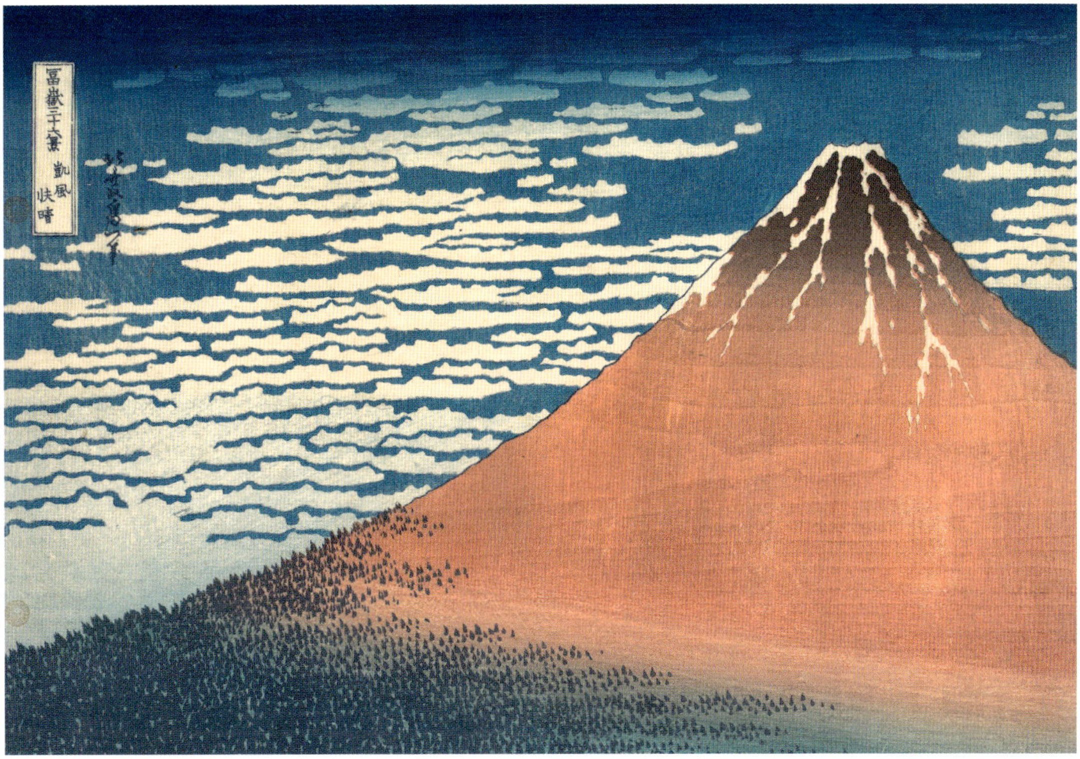

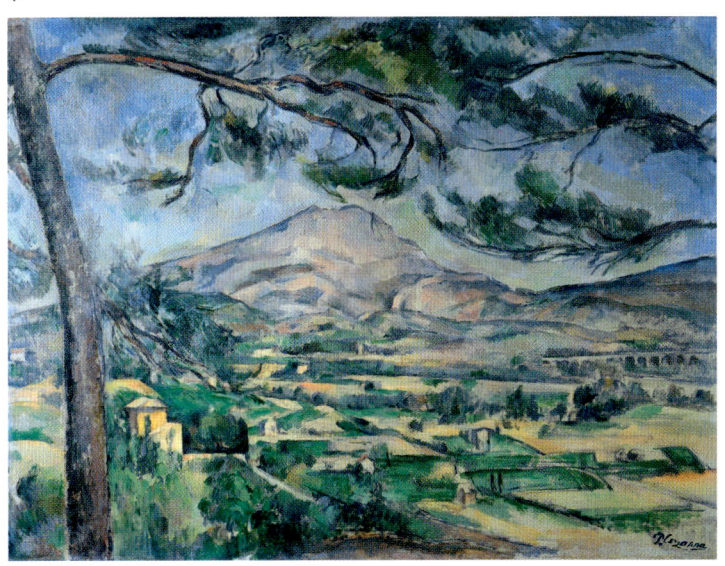

3

4

1. *The Wanderer Above the Sea of Fog,*
   Caspar David Friedrich, c. 1817-18

2. *The Heart of the Andes,* Frederic Edwin
   Church, 1859

3. *South Wind, Clear Sky (Red Fuji),*
   Katsushika Hokusai, c. 1830-31

4. *Mont Sainte Victoire with Large Pine,*
   Paul Cézanne, 1887

Woods and Forests

Woods and forests have often represented mystery, transformation, danger or the unconscious mind. Across cultures, they can also evoke journeys into the mind, hidden truths or a threshold between the human and the divine. In Indigenous and Eastern traditions, forests are often sacred spaces that represent harmony with nature or spiritual guardianship. Some medieval and Renaissance paintings depict forests as places of spiritual trial. For example, in *The Story of Nastagio degli Onesti I* (c. 1480s) by Sandro Botticelli. Hudson River School artists sought to capture the spiritual majesty and sublime beauty of the American landscape, promoting a sense of national identity and divine harmony between humanity and nature, as in *Giant Redwood Trees of California* (1874) by Albert Bierstadt (1830-1902). In the paintings, the monumental redwoods symbolize the sublime grandeur and divine majesty of the American wilderness, reflecting both national pride in the western frontier and reverence for nature's transcendent power.

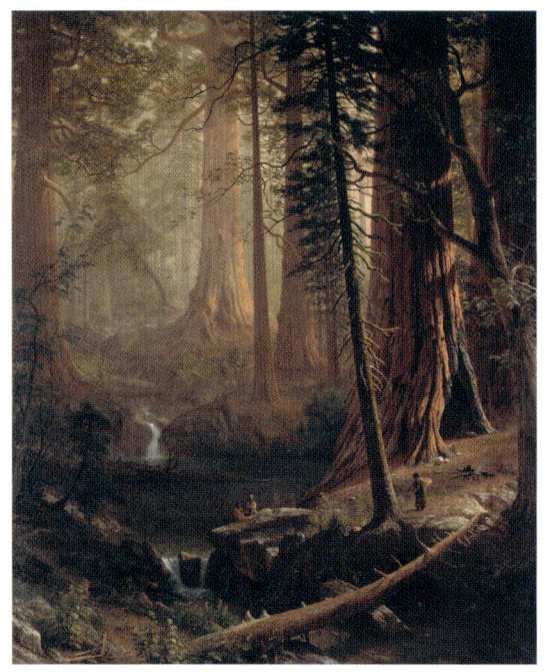

1

2

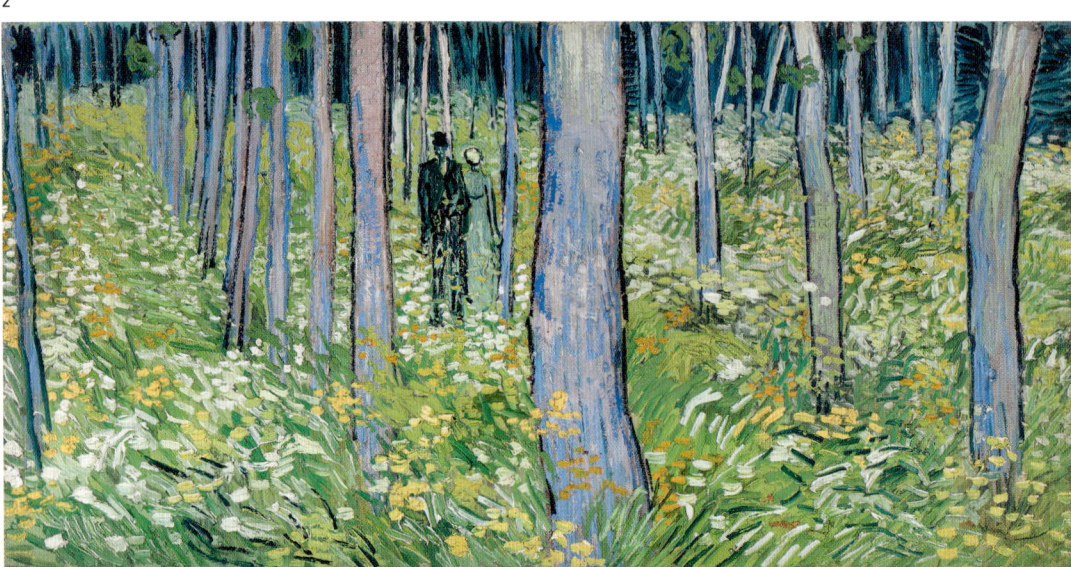

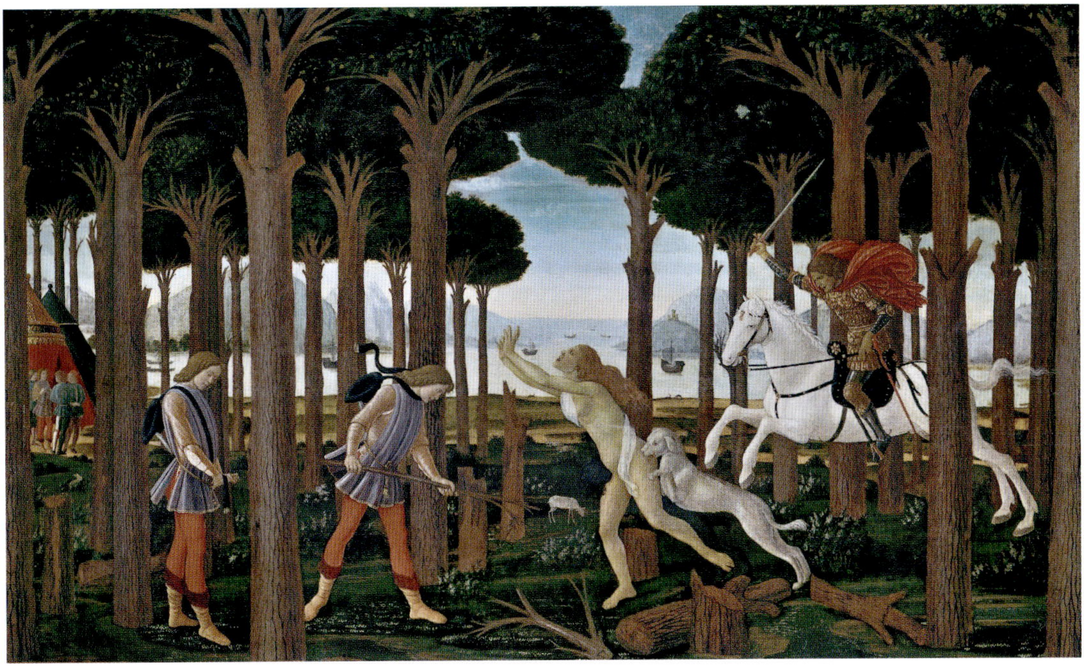

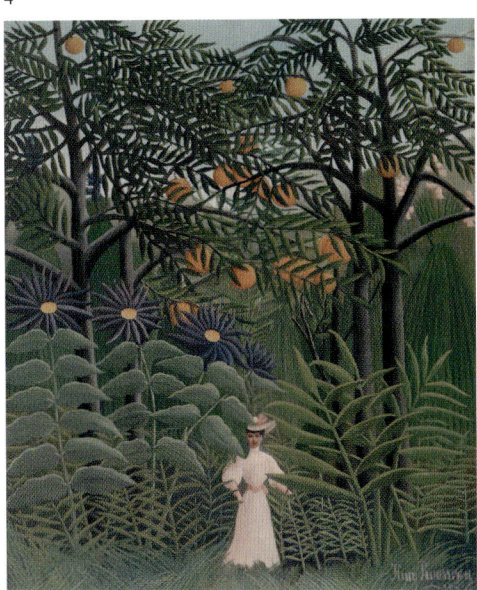

3

1. *Giant Redwood Trees of California,* Albert Bierstadt, 1874
2. *Undergrowth with Two Figures,* Vincent van Gogh, 1890
3. *The Story of Nastagio degli Onesti I,* Sandro Botticelli, c. 1480s
4. *Woman Walking in an Exotic Forest,* Henri Rousseau, 1905
5. *Beech Forest I,* Gustav Klimt, 1902

4

5

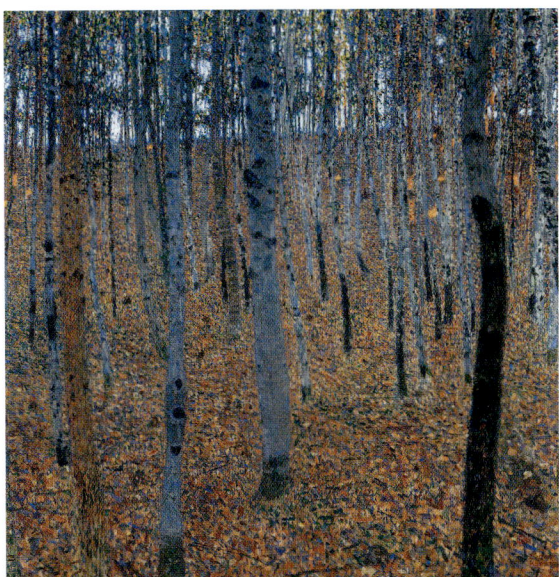

Rivers

Rivers in art can represent life, death, time, change, boundaries, movement, spiritual cleansing and more. The ancient Egyptians viewed the Nile as a divine, life-giving force, symbolizing rebirth, eternity, fertility, renewal and a connection with the afterlife; therefore, it was often depicted in tomb paintings and carvings. Chinese rivers, such as the Yangtze and Yellow River, symbolize cosmic harmony, longevity and the *Dao* (Way) in Daoist philosophy. Many traditional ink paintings of rivers evoke tranquillity, meditation and the flow of *qi* (life force), as seen in *Along the Riverbank at Dusk* (930s-960s) by Dong Yuan (c. 934-c. 962). In Christian art, rivers often symbolize baptism, spiritual purification and

moral boundaries. In the Dreamtime stories of Aboriginal art, rivers are linked to creation myths and spiritual maps of the land. J.M.W. Turner used the River Thames as a metaphor for transition in *The Fighting Temeraire* (1839). Similarly, the river's bend in *The Oxbow* (1836) by Thomas Cole (1801-48) separates the untamed wilderness and cultivated land.

1. *The Fighting Temeraire,* J.M.W. Turner, 1839
2. *Washington Crossing the Delaware,* Emanuel Leutze, 1851
3. *A Sunday Afternoon on the Island of La Grande Jatte,* Georges Seurat, 1884

1

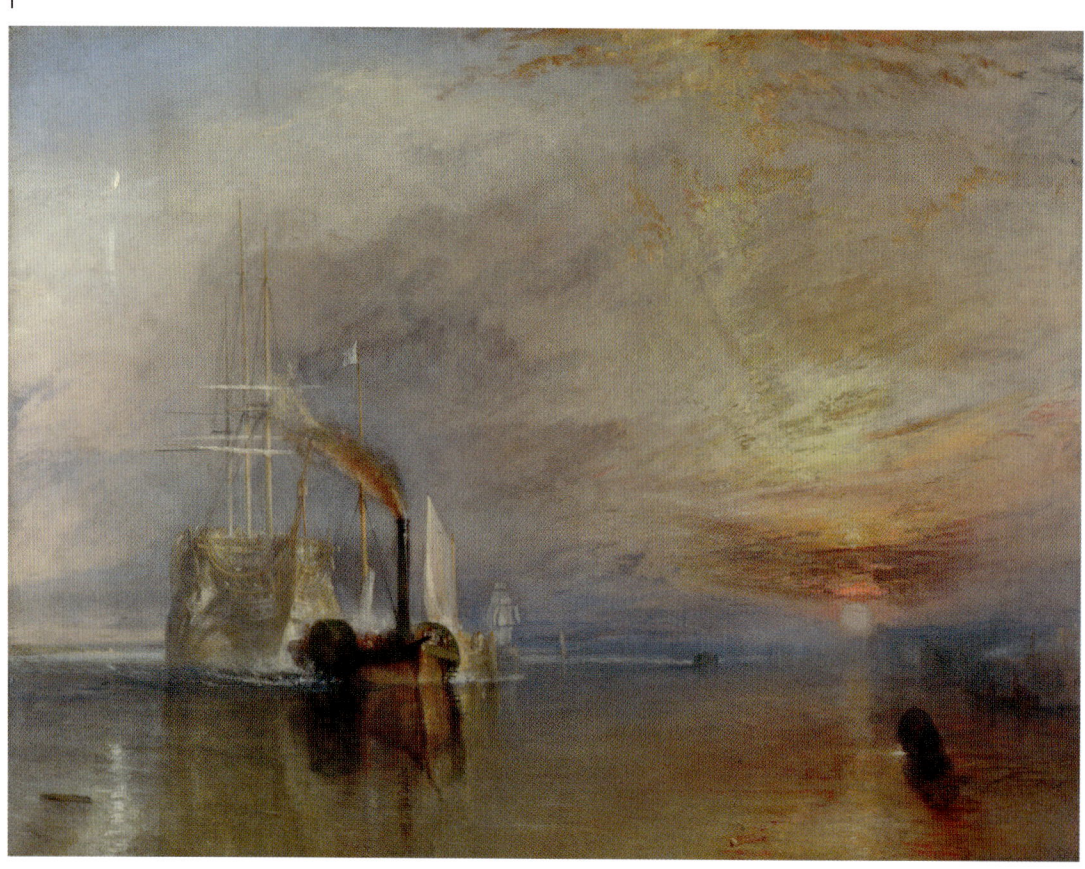

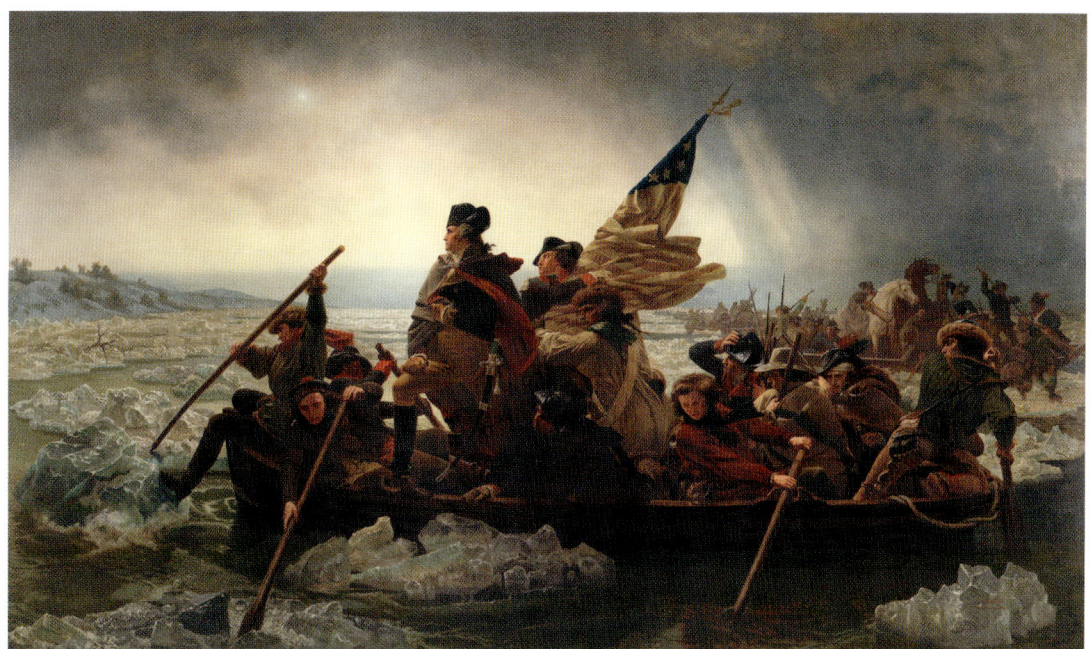

2

3

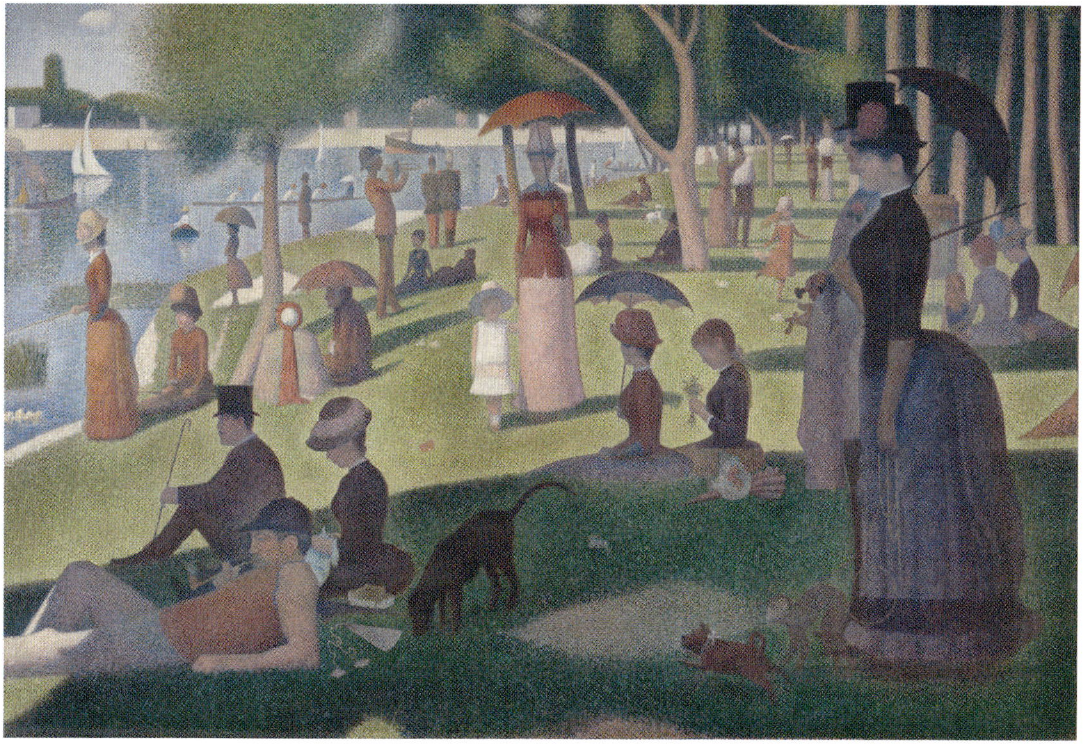

Sea

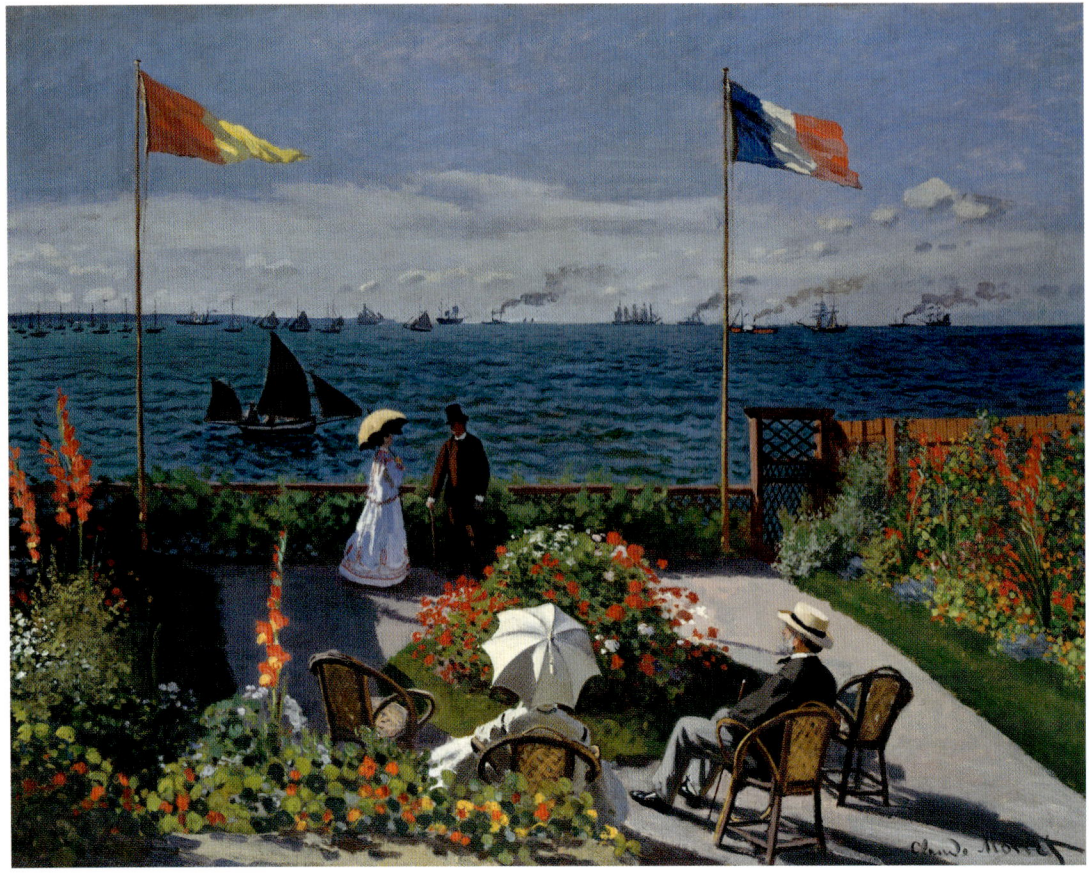

1

In mythology, the sea is often linked to creation and destruction, appearing in ancient Greek and Japanese art as a realm of gods and mythical creatures. It has also been used to represent mystery, power and transformation. One of the most well-known images of the sea, *Under the Wave Off Kanagawa* (1830-32) by Katsushika Hokusai, captures the sea's raw force, symbolizing nature's dominance over humanity. Caspar David Friedrich and other Romantic painters often depicted vast, turbulent waters to evoke existential themes. The sea is also a symbol of journeys and the unknown, as seen in marine paintings by Winslow Homer (1836-1910) and J.M.W. Turner, who painted swirling oceans that

evoke nature's majesty and terror, reflecting moments when human identity was reshaped by industrialization and existential uncertainty. Sandro Botticelli's *The Birth of Venus* depicts the sea as a metaphor for purity and divine beauty, reinforcing its role as a source of life and transformation. In modern art, the sea can sometimes signify freedom, isolation and introspection.

1. *Garden at Saint-Adresse,* Claude Monet, 1867
2. *Under the Wave off Kanagawa (Kanagawa oki nami ura),* also known as The Great Wave, Katsushika Hokusai, c. 1830-32
3. *The Gulf Stream,* Winslow Homer, 1899

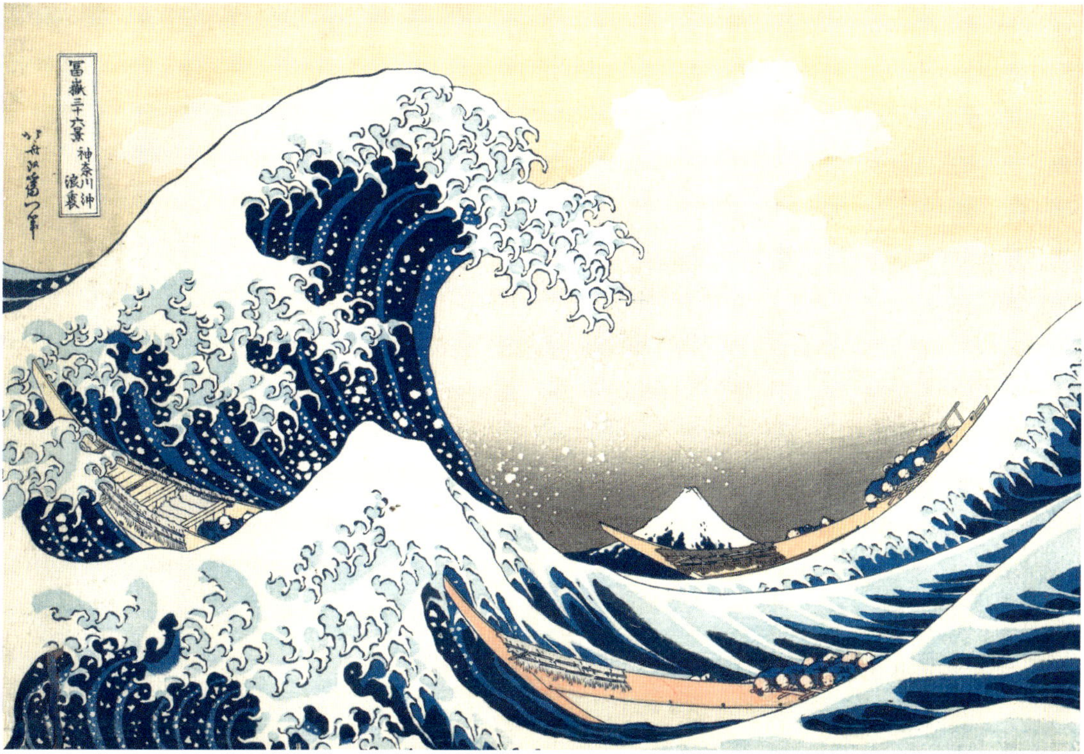

2

3

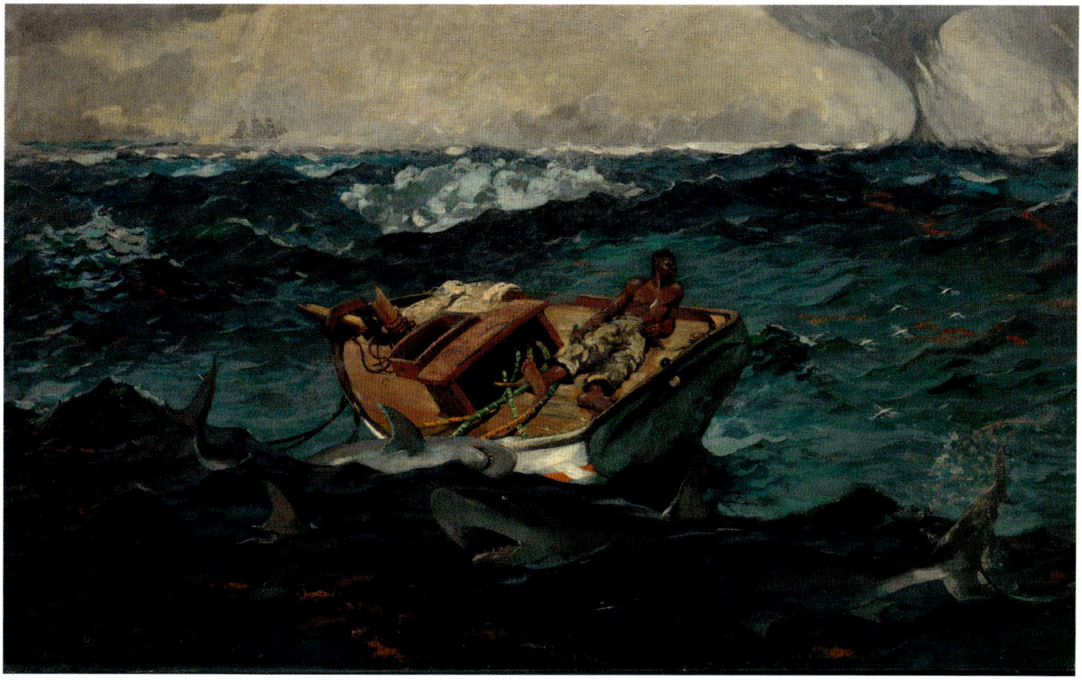

Clouds

As they constantly change, clouds can symbolize the transient nature of life, the passage of time and uncertainty. They can also convey emotions, dreams and the imagination, signifying creativity and the subconscious. In religious art, clouds can represent the divine realm, heavenly beings or a connection to the spiritual world. For example, John Constable (1776-1837) made many studies of clouds, which he saw as suggesting the ever-changing, living spirit of nature, reflecting his belief in the divine presence. In *View of Toledo* (1599-1600) by El Greco (1541-1614), turbulent clouds similarly signify divine energy and spiritual revelation, turning the city beneath them into a mystical bridge between earth and heaven. The clouds in the oculus of *Camera degli Sposi* (1465-74) by Andrea Mantegna (1431-1506) denote the sky opening above the mortal realm, uniting the earthly courtly space below with the divine and celestial world above. In Chinese and Japanese art, stylized clouds often symbolise spiritual energy and transformation, frequently accompanying dragons or deities. Contemporary artists frequently use clouds to explore themes of climate change, impermanence and emotional depth.

1. *Study of Clouds*, John Constable, 1822
2. *Woman with a Parasol, Madame Monet and Son*, Claude Monet, 1875
3. *View of Toledo*, El Greco, 1599-1600
4. *Camera degli Sposi*, Andrea Mantega, 1465-74

1

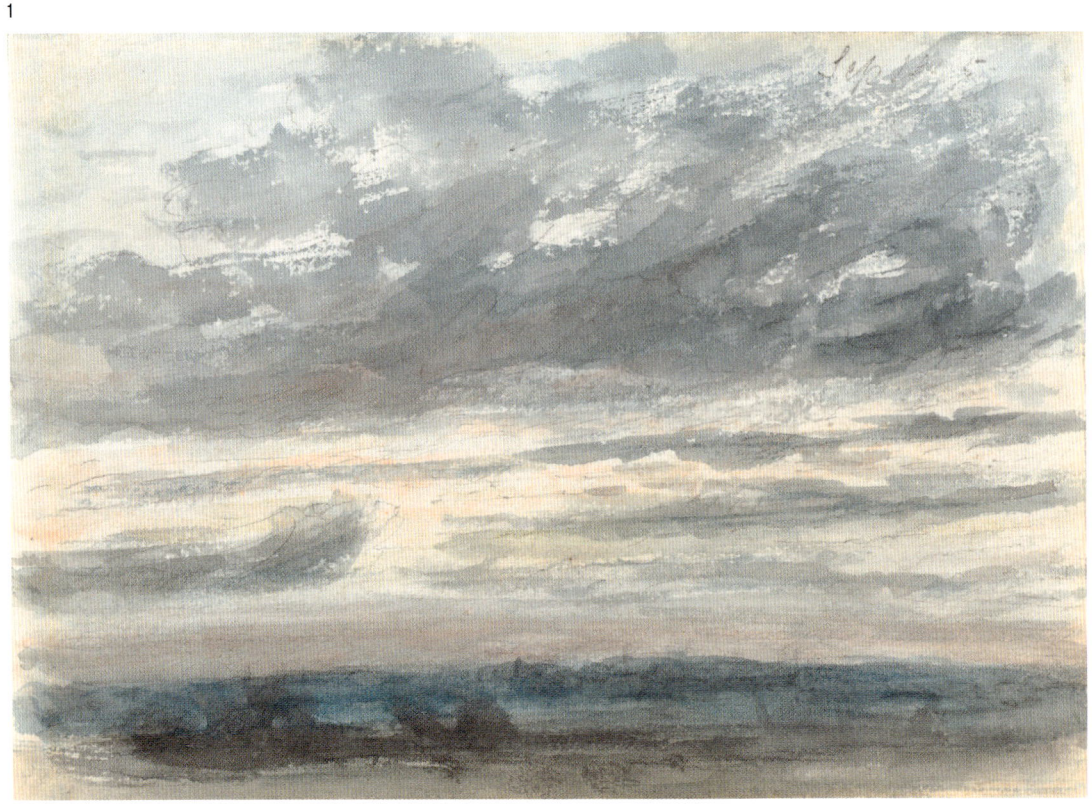

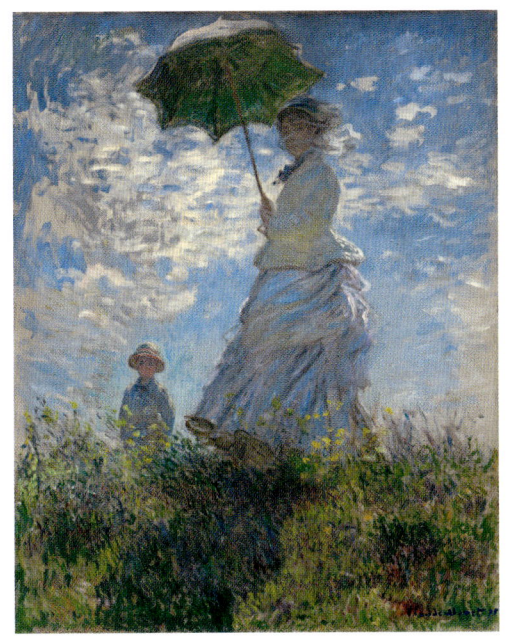

2

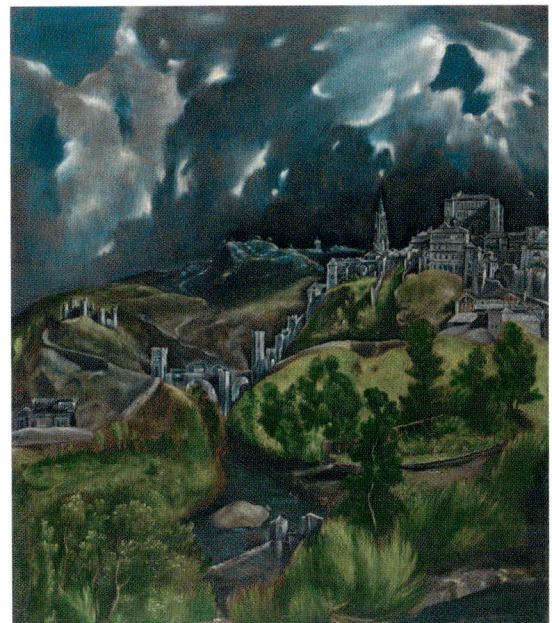

3

4

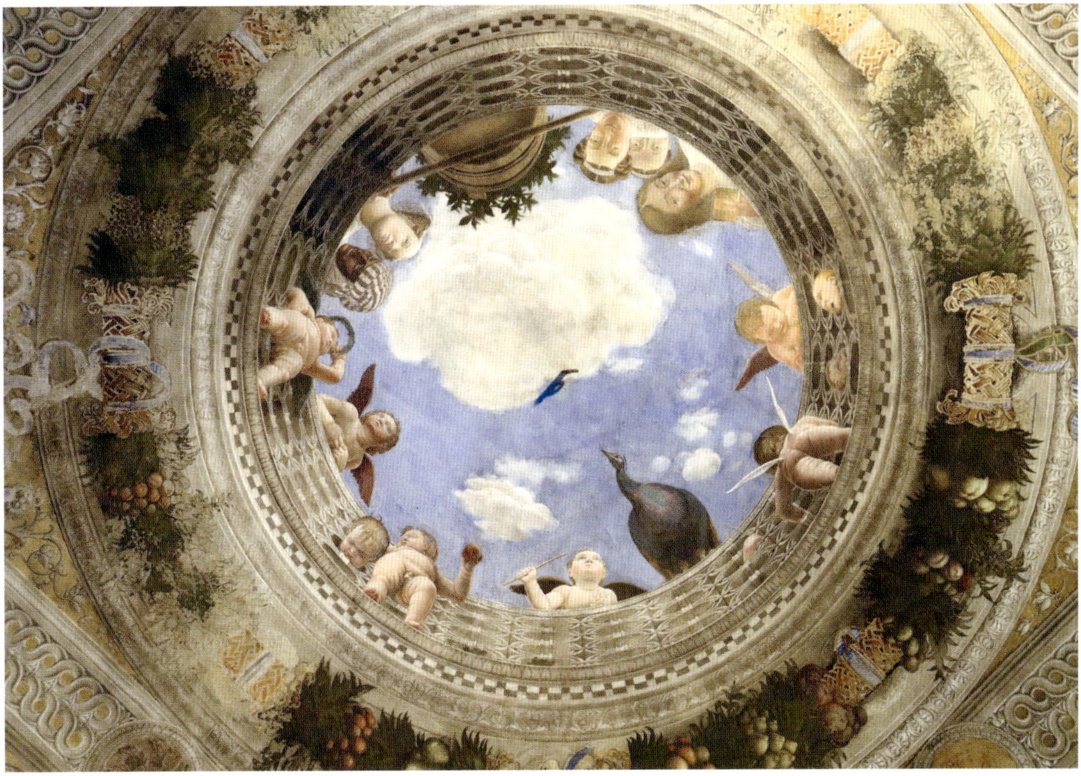

Rain

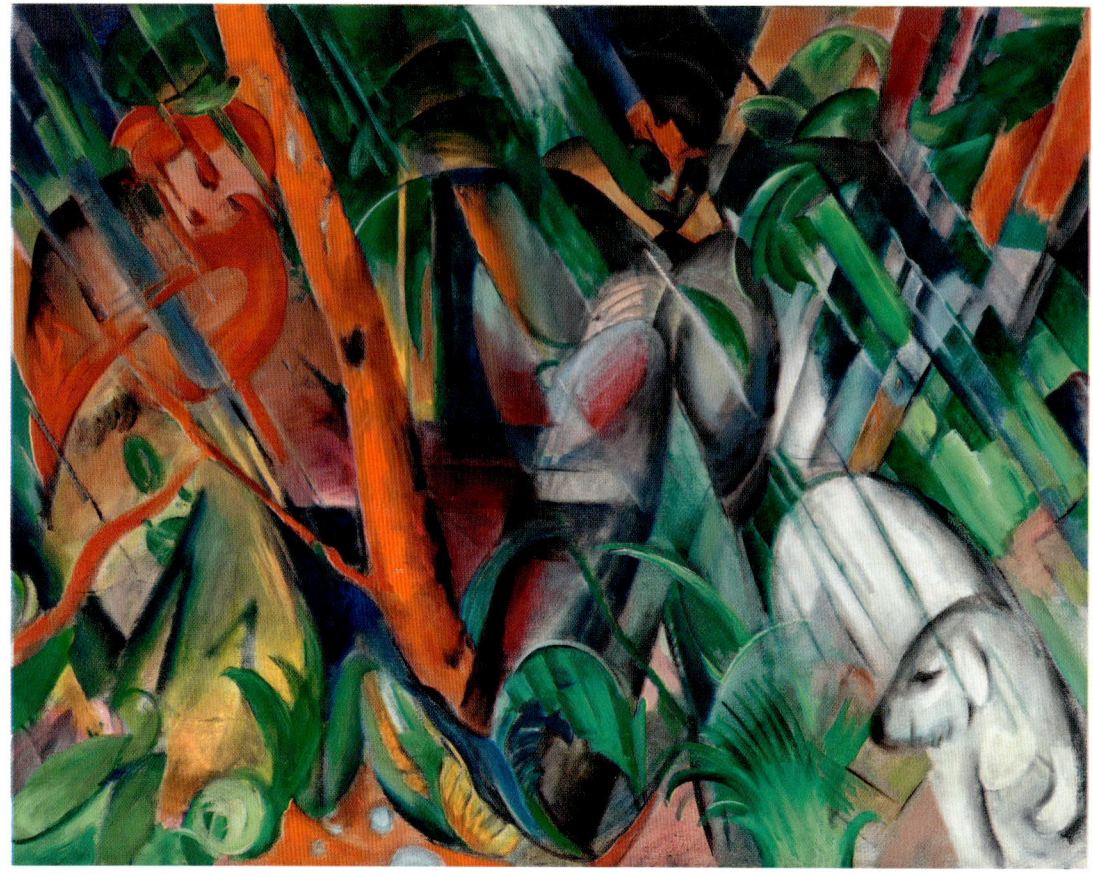

1

Crucial for crops, rain has often been linked with divine blessings and fertility. It has also symbolized melancholy, renewal and drama. One of the earliest artists to depict rain was Flemish artist Jan van der Straet, also known as Giovanni Stradano (1523-1605), who engraved *The Gluttons* in 1587. The engraving illustrates part of Dante's Inferno, featuring diagonal lines that represent rain, hail and snow. Japanese artist Utagawa Hiroshige produced the woodblock print *Sudden Shower over Shin-Ōhashi Bridge and Atake* in 1857, conveying rain with broken, dark, diagonal lines. Dutch artist Jacob van Ruisdael (c. 1628-82) painted dramatic skies, clouds and storms, often suggesting rain as a force of nature more than mere background. *Rain, Steam and Speed* (1844) by J.M.W. Turner features blurring rain over a speeding train, conveying the speed of industrial progress. In contrast, *Rain* (1889) by Vincent van Gogh evokes a sense of movement and creates atmospheric depth, reinforcing notions of solitude and introspection.

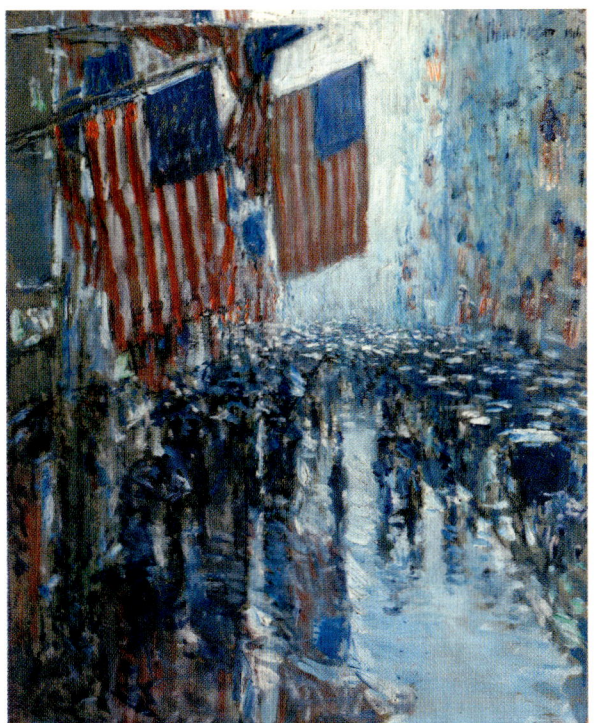

2

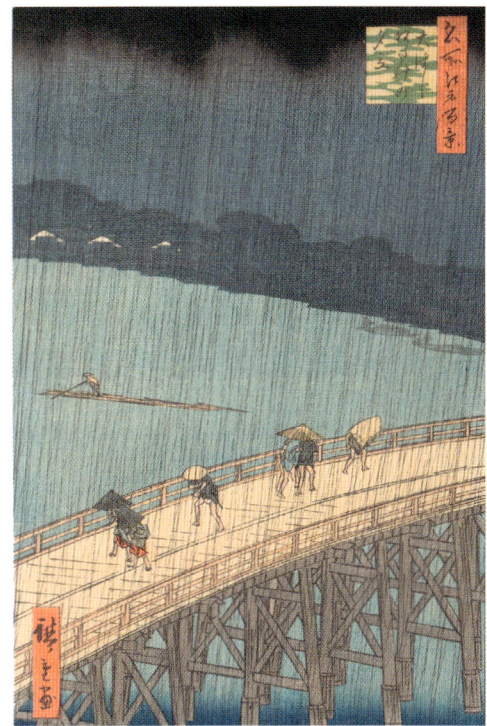

3

4

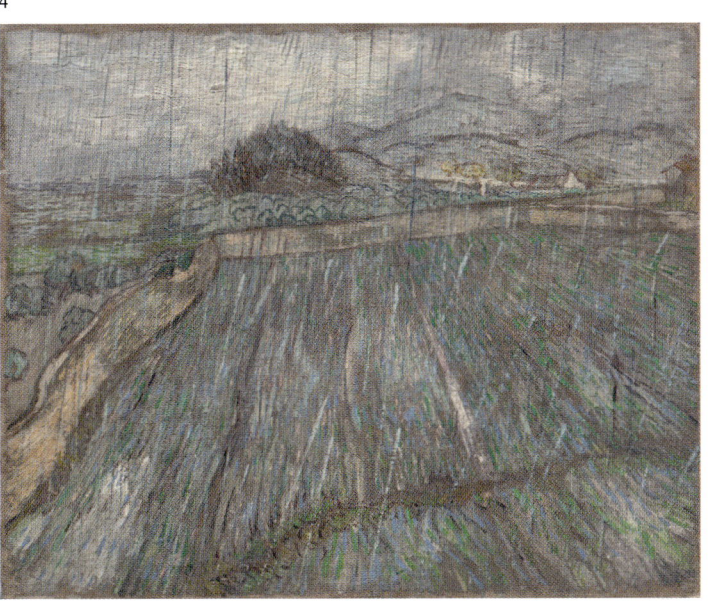

1. *In the Rain*, Franz Marc, 1912
2. *Rainy Day, Fifth Avenue*,
   Childe Hassam, 1893
3. *Sudden Shower over Shin-Ōhashi Bridge
   and Atake*, Utagawa Hiroshige, 1857
4. *Rain*, Vincent van Gogh, 1889

Sun

Many diverse cultures have depicted the Sun as a symbol of life, divinity and enlightenment. The Mesoamerican Aztec Sun Stone (c. 1502–20) embodies cosmic power and timekeeping, reflecting the Sun's role in structuring human existence. In Christian iconography, the Sun is frequently associated with rebirth and transcendence, as seen in depictions of Christ's resurrection. During the Renaissance, sun-like halos were painted around the heads of holy figures to signify divine presence and symbolize spiritual illumination. In Baroque and Romantic art, the Sun was often depicted as a source of drama and revelation, casting strong contrasts between light and shadow. The 'Sun King' Louis XIV adopted the Sun as a symbol of absolute monarchy. Impressionist artists like Claude Monet and J.M.W. Turner captured the Sun's fleeting light, emphasizing its role in perception and emotion. In *The Red Vineyard* (1888), Vincent van Gogh represented the Sun to convey God, hope, vitality and warmth. In contemporary art, the Sun is usually used to represent climate change, energy and human connection to nature.

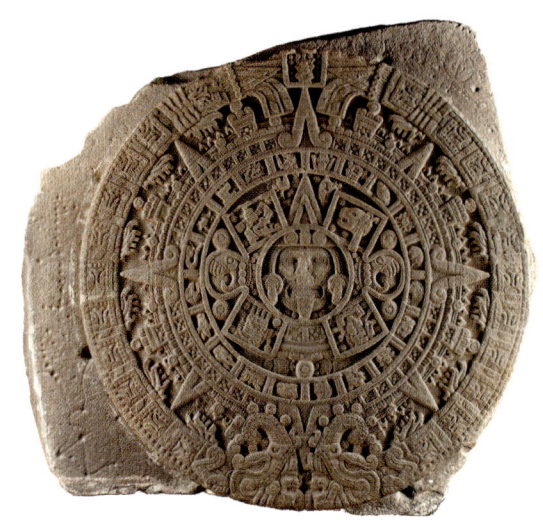

1

2

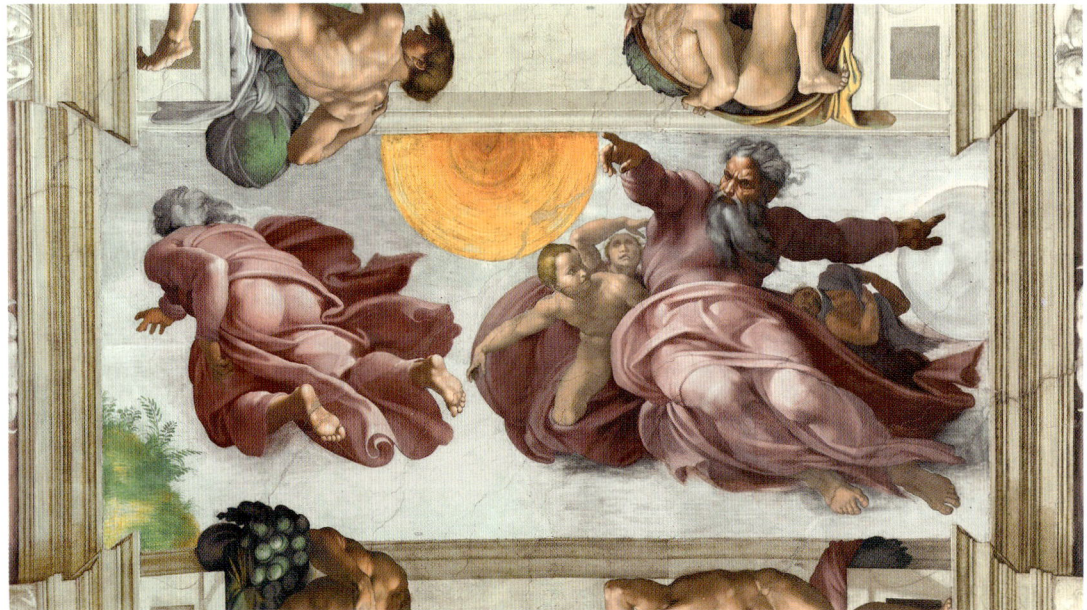

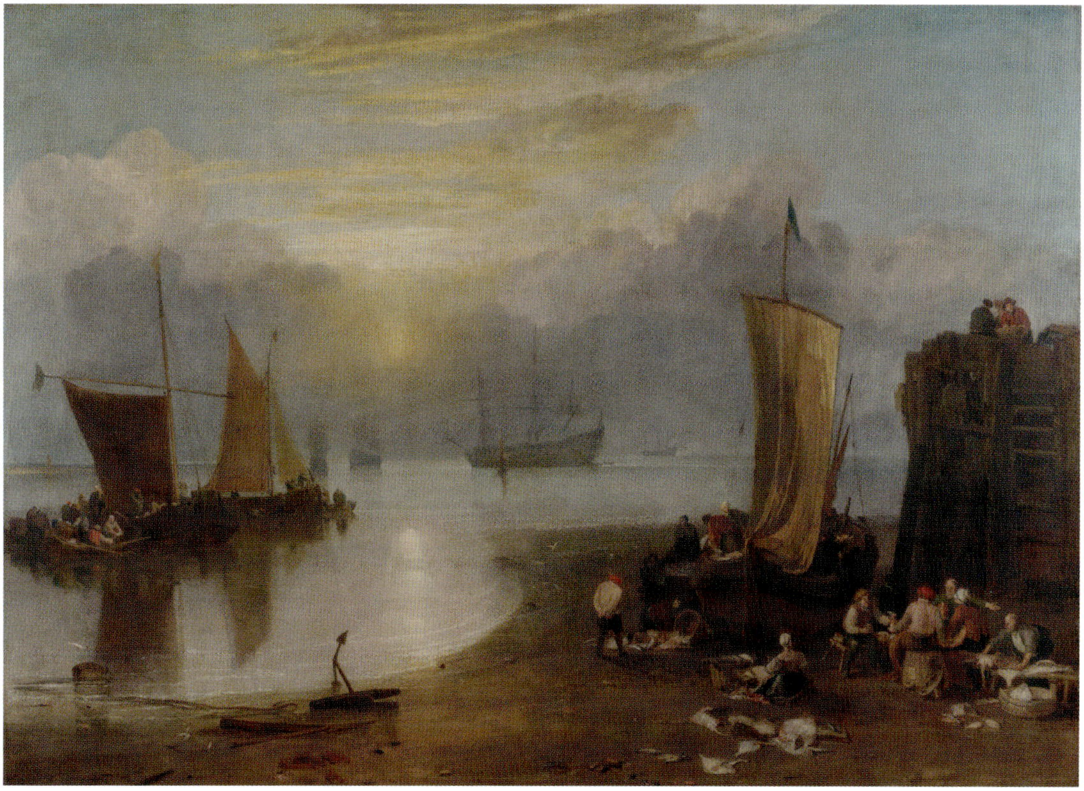

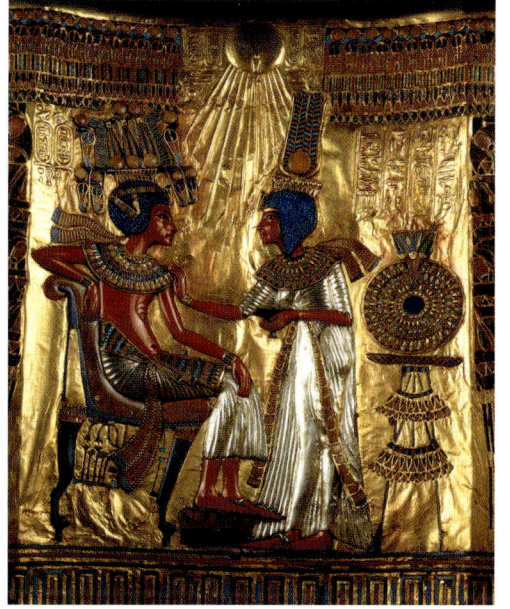

3

4

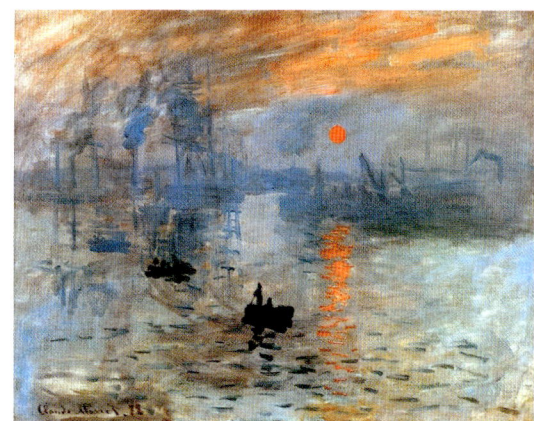

5

1. *Aztec Sun Stone*, Mexico, c. 1502-20

2. *The Creation of the Sun, Moon and Vegetation*, Michelangelo, 1511

3. *Sun Rising through Vapour*, J.M.W. Turner, 1807

4. *Queen Ankhesenamun and Tutankhamun,* back of Tutankhamun's throne, Egypt, c. 1323 BCE

5. *Impression, Sunrise*, Claude Monet, 1872

Moon

As a symbol of mystery, femininity and cycles, the Moon has been featured in a range of art forms for various purposes. For example, Vincent van Gogh's *Road with Cypress and Star* (1890) portrays the Moon as a source of wonder and introspection. In Japanese ukiyo-e prints, the Moon often signifies solitude and fleeting beauty. Artists such as Caspar David Friedrich employed moonlit landscapes to evoke melancholy and contemplation, for example, in his *Two Men Contemplating the Moon* (1819-20).

The Moon's phases are also often symbolically associated with change and renewal. In ancient Egyptian and Greek art, it was depicted as a celestial force guiding human fate. Surrealists like René Magritte utilized the Moon to explore themes related to the subconscious, reinforcing its enigmatic nature. The Moon is also linked to goddesses and femininity, appearing in depictions of Selene, Artemis and other lunar deities. In modern art, the Moon is often used to explore themes of dreams, illusion and the passage of time.

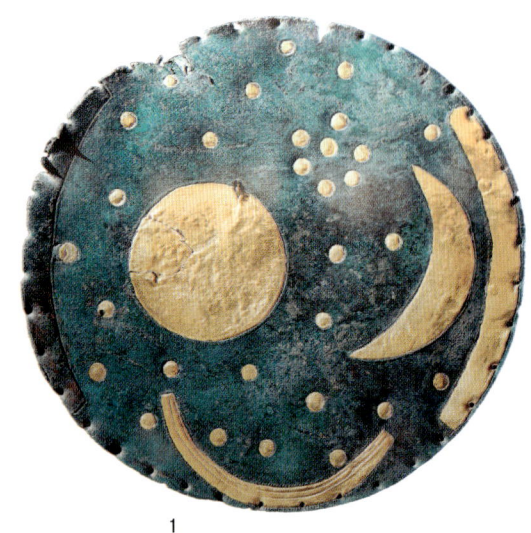

1

2

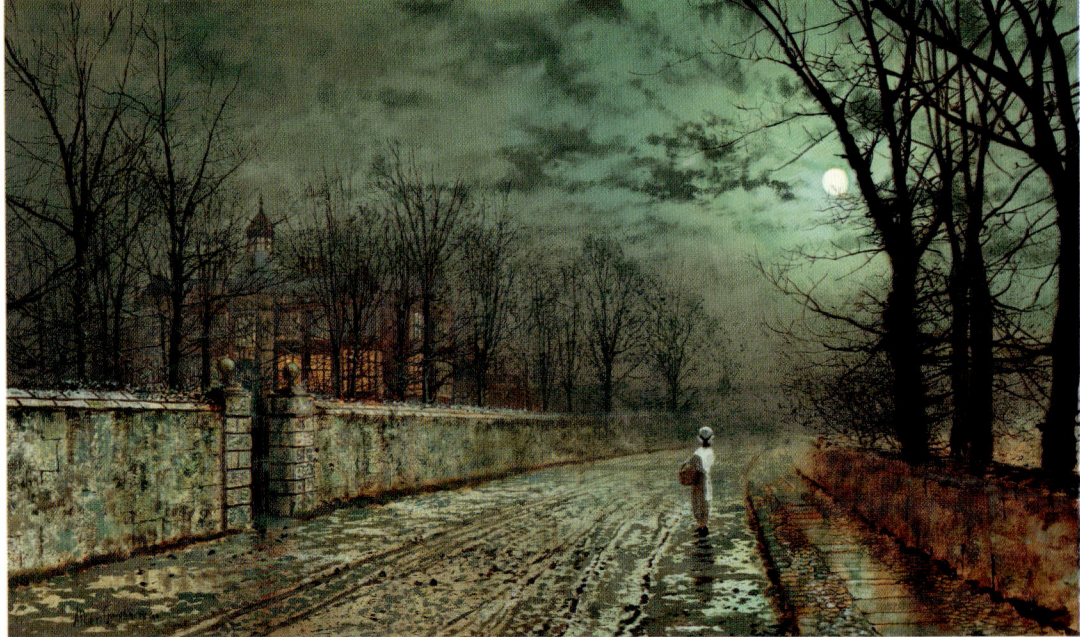

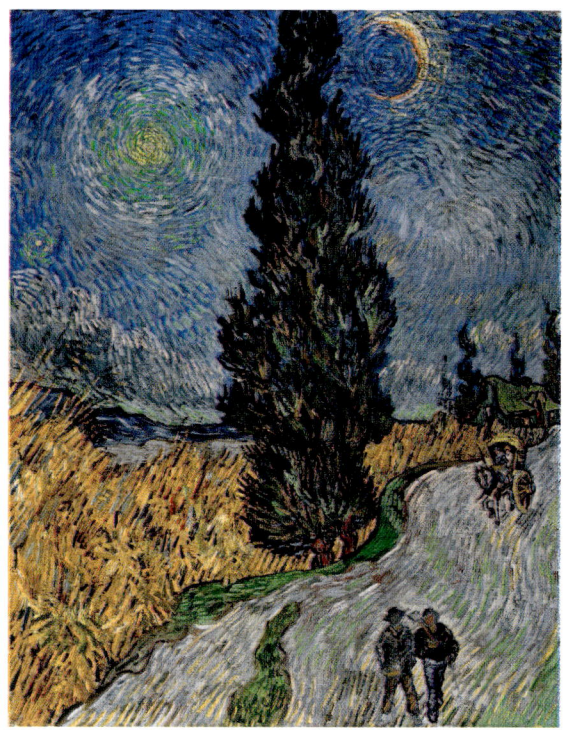

3

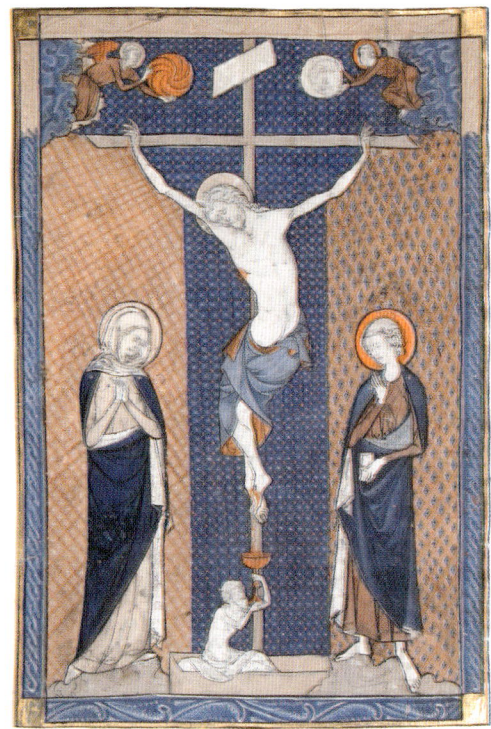

4

5

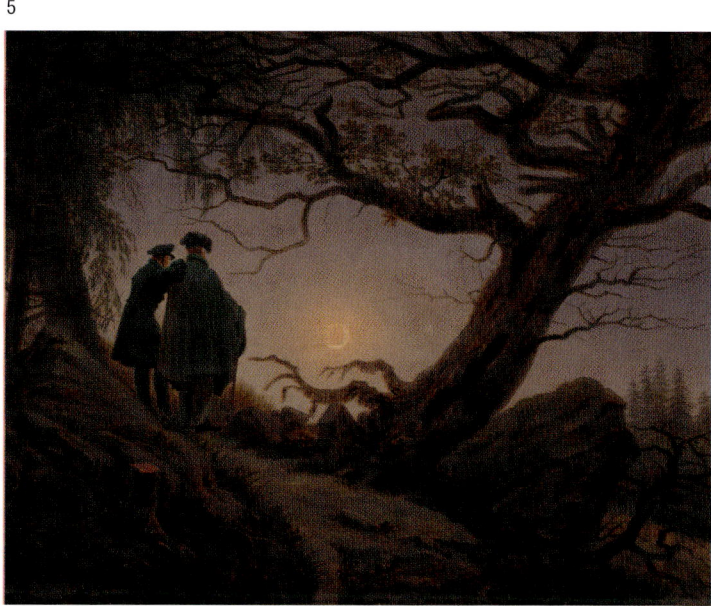

1. *The Nebra Sky Disc*, Germany, 1600 BCE

2. *A Moonlit Evening*, John Atkinson Grimshaw, 1880

3. *Road with Cypress and Star*, Vincent van Gogh, 1890

4. *Manuscript Leaf with the Crucifixion from a Missal*, France c. 1270-80

5. *Two Men Contemplating the Moon*, Caspar David Friedrich, 1819-20

Stars

Stars in art have often represented wonder, mystery, guidance, divinity, fate or the vast unknown. In ancient Mesopotamian and Egyptian art, stars were frequently associated with gods and the concept of celestial order. In Indigenous Australian art, star constellations are often integral to ancestral stories and cosmic maps. Several Christian paintings have included the Star of Bethlehem to symbolize divine guidance and the birth of Christ, such as *The Star of Bethlehem* (c. 1887–91) by Edward Burne-Jones (1833–98). Islamic art features star-based geometric patterns to reflect a sense of the infinite and the divine. In *The Starry Night* (1889), Vincent van Gogh featured stars to express awe and inner turmoil, while Japanese ukiyo-e artists, such as Utagawa Hiroshige, often incorporated stars to heighten the atmosphere of night scenes, evoking a sense of solitude, as in his print *Bamboo Yards, Kyobashi Bridge* (1857).

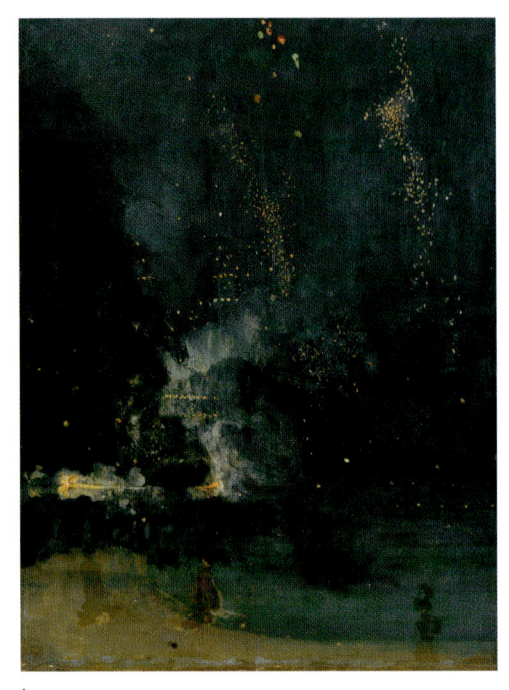

1

2

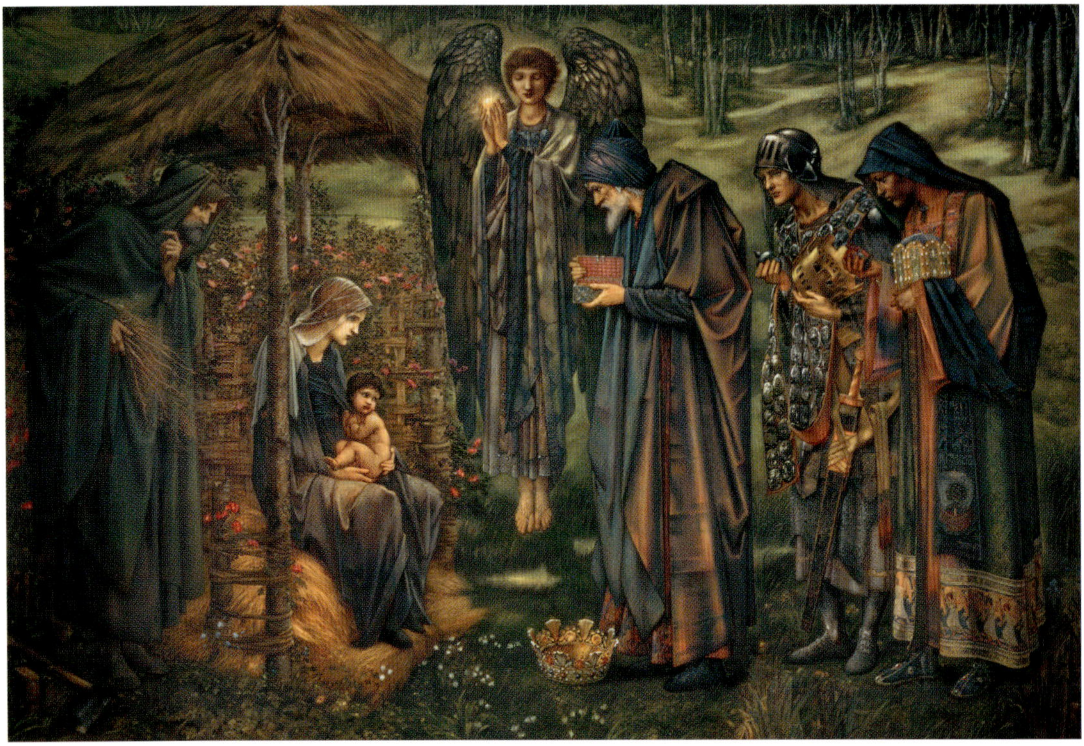

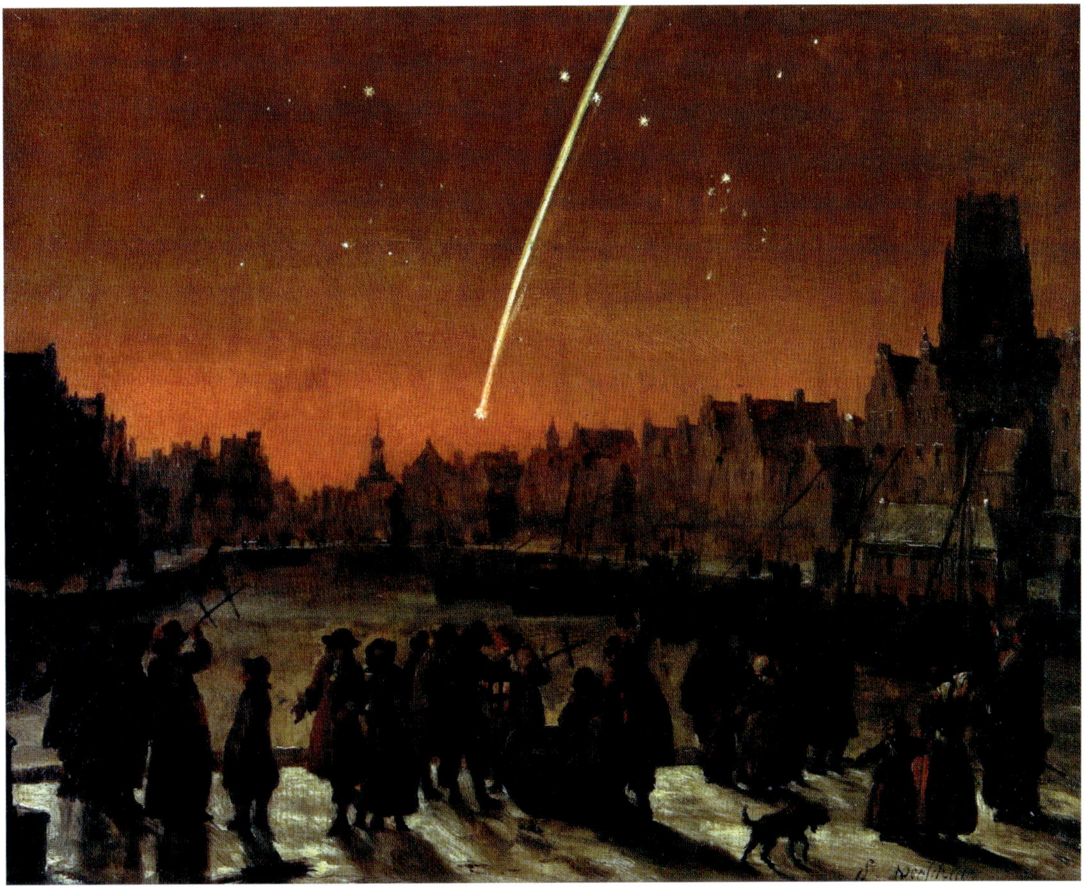

3

4

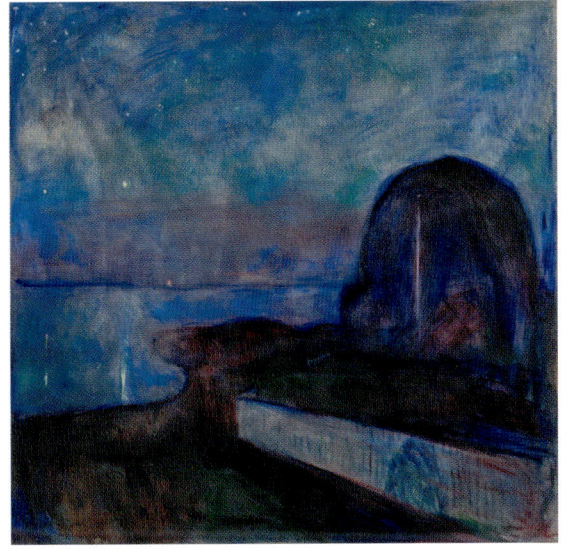

1. *Nocturne in Black and Gold: The Falling Rocket*, James Abbott McNeill Whistler, 1875
2. *The Star of Bethlehem*, Edward Burne-Jones, c. 1887-91
3. *Tailed Star (Comet) over Rotterdam,* Lieve Verschuier, c. 1680
4. *Starry Night*, Edvard Munch, 1893

The Manmade World

From the earliest cave paintings to contemporary installations, the human impulse to shape the world has always extended beyond the physical into the realm of the symbolic. The manmade world - including tools, furniture, architecture, clothing, machines, musical instruments, even balloons - has long served as a mirror of our values, fears, ambitions and identities. In art, these creations are often depicted not only for their utility or aesthetic appeal but also imbued with layered meanings that transcend their material form.

The following section of the book examines how artists across historical periods and cultural traditions have explored the imagery of the manmade world to convey complex ideas and meanings, such as power, progress, alienation, conformity and the human condition itself.

The symbolic use of manmade objects in art is as ancient as art itself. In Mesopotamian reliefs, the ziggurat - part temple, part tower - was more than a feat of engineering; it symbolized the *axis mundi*, the bridge between heaven and earth. Egyptian tomb paintings depicted boats, tools, food and furniture, not only as possessions of the deceased but as metaphors for the journey to the afterlife. In these early civilizations, the built environment and crafted objects were deeply entwined with spiritual and cosmological beliefs. They were not passive backdrops to human life, but active participants in the sacred narrative.

Manmade objects depicted in art can be either familiar or mysterious. For example, a chair is something we sit on, but in art, it can also signify power, absence or identity. A clock tells the time, but it can also evoke feelings of mortality, urgency or memory. Shoes are worn to protect the feet, but they can also represent ambition, journeys or identity. These objects are embedded in daily life, yet when placed in a visual composition - whether a medieval altarpiece, a Dutch still life, a Renaissance painting or a contemporary installation - they take on new resonance, frequently becoming signposts in a symbolic landscape, guiding the viewer towards deeper layers of meaning.

In religious art, manmade objects often serve as allegorical devices. For instance, a book may represent divine wisdom or a key might have the ability to reveal spiritual truths. In secular contexts, these objects can signify status, intellect or moral character. The symbolic charge of these objects is never static; it changes with time, place and cultural perspective. A mirror in a seventeenth-century painting, for example, might serve as a warning against vanity, while in a modern self-portrait, it might explore themes of individuality and self-perception. A globe might once have symbolized imperial ambition or travel, while now it evokes globalization or environmental fragility.

Over the years, still-life painting has allowed artists to lavish attention on the textures and surfaces of manmade objects, such as books, instruments, vessels or timepieces, not merely to display technical skill, but to invite contemplation of their deeper meanings. These artworks often functioned as vanitas – meditations on the fleeting nature of life and the futility of material wealth. Yet even in their celebration of the ephemeral, they affirmed the symbolic richness of the human-made world. In the modern era, as industrialization and mass production transformed the material landscape, artists responded by reimagining the symbolic role of objects. The readymades of Marcel Duchamp (1887-1968), the assemblages of Joseph Cornell (1903-72) and the installations of contemporary artists like Mona Hatoum (b. 1952), for a few instances, all challenge viewers to reconsider the meanings of the manmade world. A light bulb might become a symbol of fragile enlightenment; a set of scales, a commentary on justice or imbalance; a key, a meditation on access and exclusion.

The following pages examine how artists have utilized manmade objects to explore themes of time, knowledge, power, identity and mortality. Whether humble or grand, utilitarian or ornamental, the objects we make and the ways we represent them offer profound insights into who we are, what we value and how we make sense of the world around us. The following pages trace some of these symbolic threads across cultures and centuries, examining how the manmade world in art reflects not only our external environments but also our deepest internal landscapes.

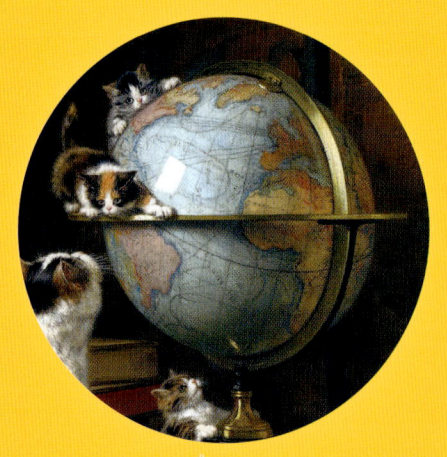

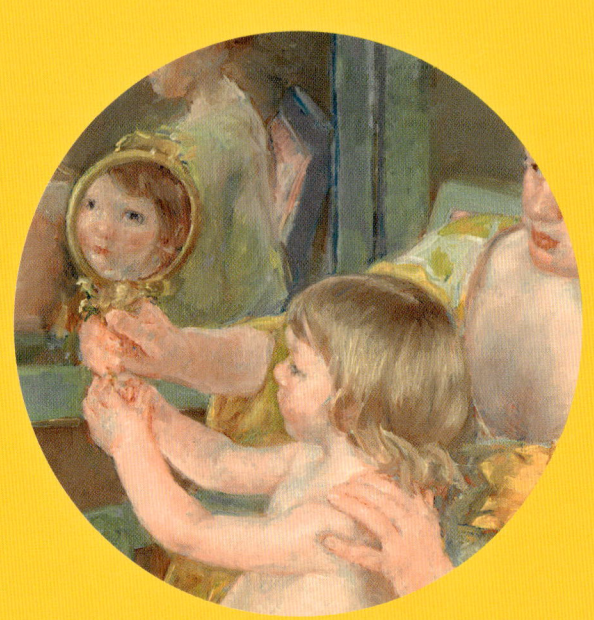

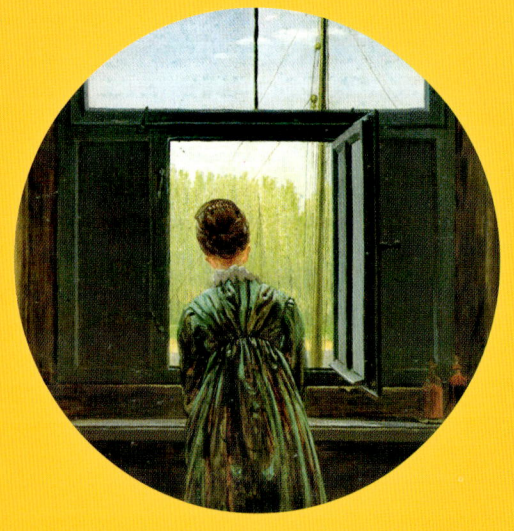

The Home

Bed

Whether a cradle of life, a site of death or a threshold of dreams, the bed has been an enduring motif in art, constantly reinterpreted to explore the human condition in all its contradictions. Beds have often been depicted to convey concepts of intimacy, vulnerability, power and mortality. In ancient Egyptian tomb paintings, they symbolized the journey to the afterlife, frequently showing the dead resting on them, accompanied by protective gods. In medieval Christian art, beds signified the sanctity of marriage or divine revelation, as seen in depictions of the Annunciation or the Virgin Mary's deathbed. In the *Arnolfini Portrait* (1434) by Jan van Eyck, the ornate bed in the living room shows wealth and a comfortable domestic life. In 1952, Edward Hopper (1882–1967) painted *Morning Sun*, a symbol of isolation and introspection, depicting a solitary figure confronting the quiet emptiness of modern life. Both *Le Lit (In Bed)* (1893) by Henri de Toulouse-Lautrec (1864–1901) and *Le Sommeil (The Sleepers)* by Gustave Courbet (1819–1877) in 1866, depict female intimacy, but they were created within a nineteenth-century male-dominated context that often eroticized women for male viewers. Either way, they symbolize sensuality, tenderness and refuge.

1

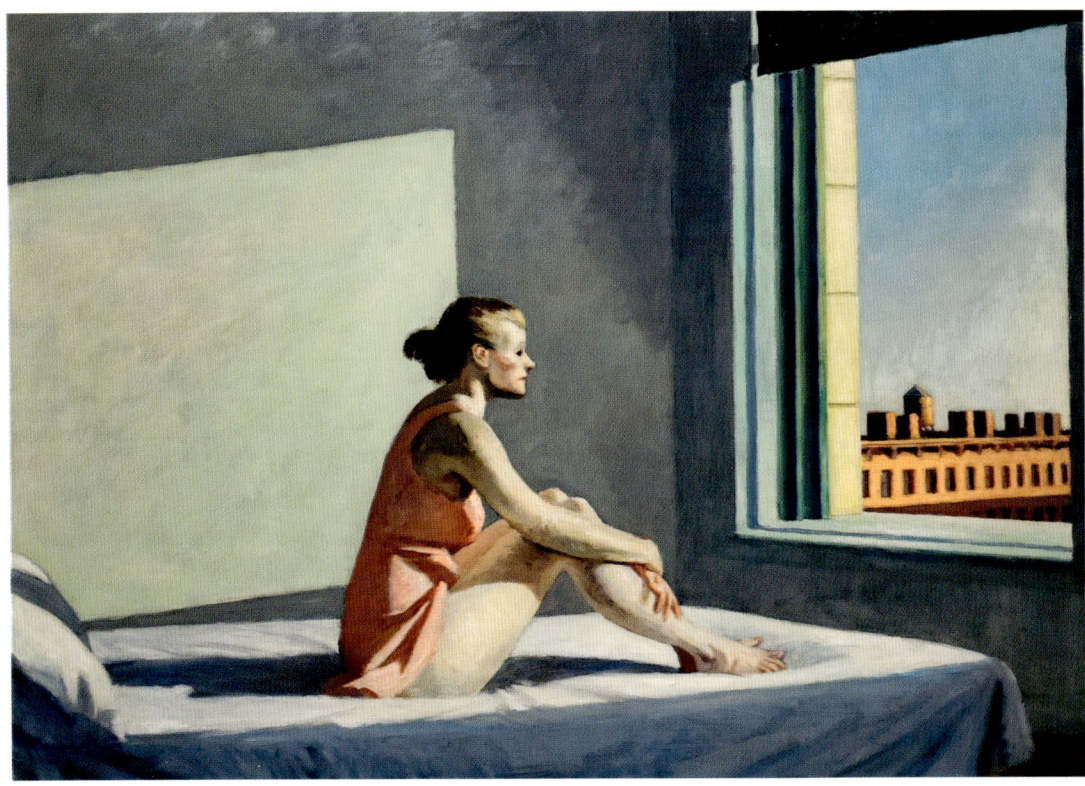

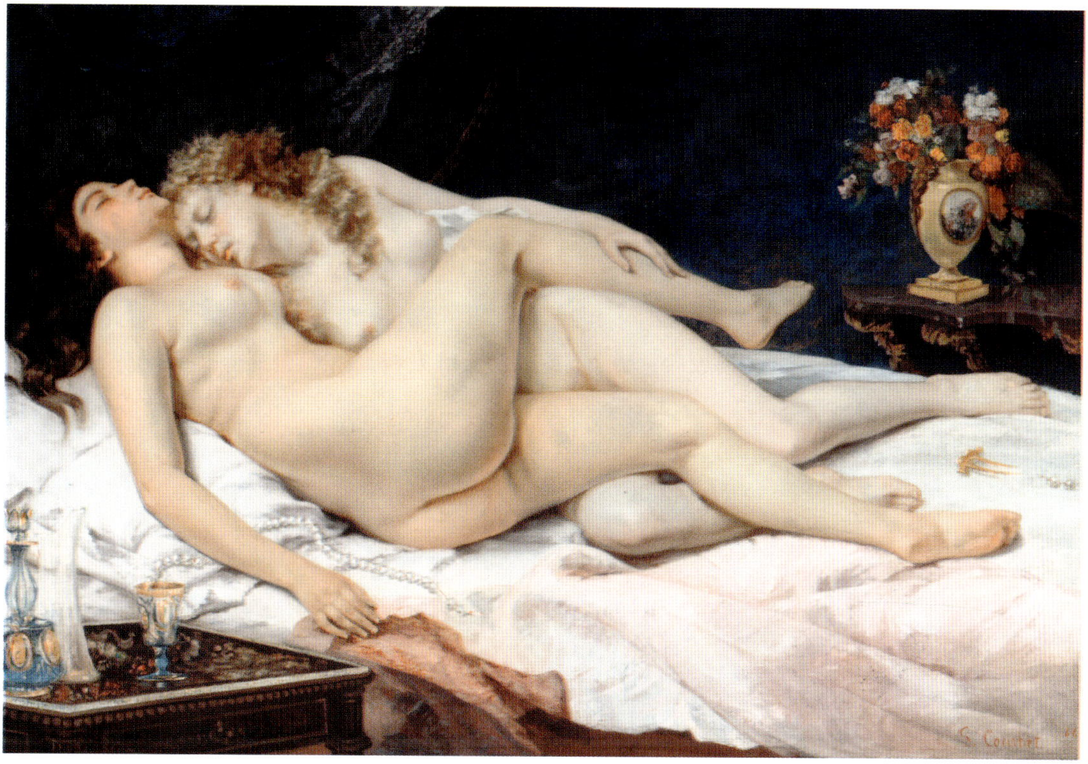

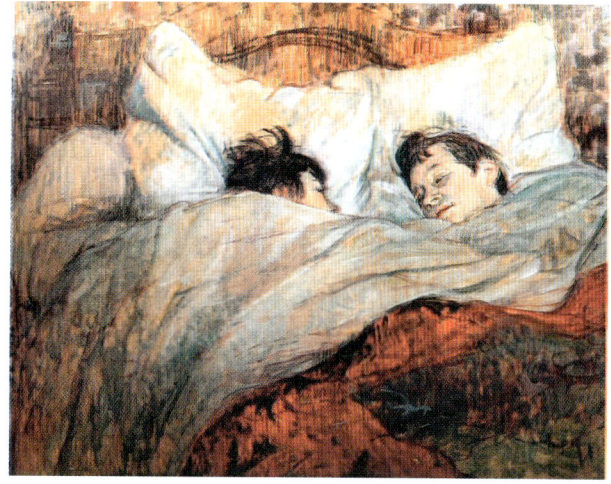

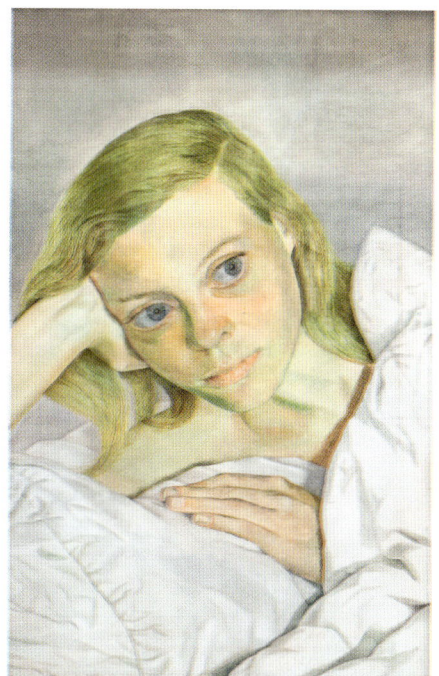

2

3

4

1. *Morning Sun*, Edward Hopper, 1952

2. *Le Sommeil (The Sleepers)*, Gustave Courbet, 1866

3. *Girl in Bed*, Lucian Freud, 1952

4. *Le Lit (In Bed)*, Henri de Toulouse-Lautrec, 1893

Chair

Often signifying power, status or identity, chairs have appeared in art ever since they conveyed divine power in ancient Egypt; seen for example in the ornate Golden Throne of Tutankhamun (c. 1332–1323 BCE). Similarly, in Byzantine icons and Renaissance altarpieces, the enthroned Madonna and Christ denote holiness and spiritual authority, often flanked by saints or angels. Chairs have also served as personal devices. In Dutch portraits during the seventeenth century, for example, sitters are frequently posed beside or on chairs, their stances suggesting virtue, wealth, importance or moral character. In these instances, the chair is often seen as an extension of identity. In 1888, Vincent van Gogh painted his own and *Gauguin's Chair*, aiming to embody the character of his friend and fellow artist, Paul Gauguin (1848–1903). Later, conceptual works, such as *One and Three Chairs* (1965) by Joseph Kosuth (b. 1945), questioned representation by juxtaposing a physical chair, a photograph of a chair and a dictionary definition of a chair, inviting viewers to contemplate meaning.

1

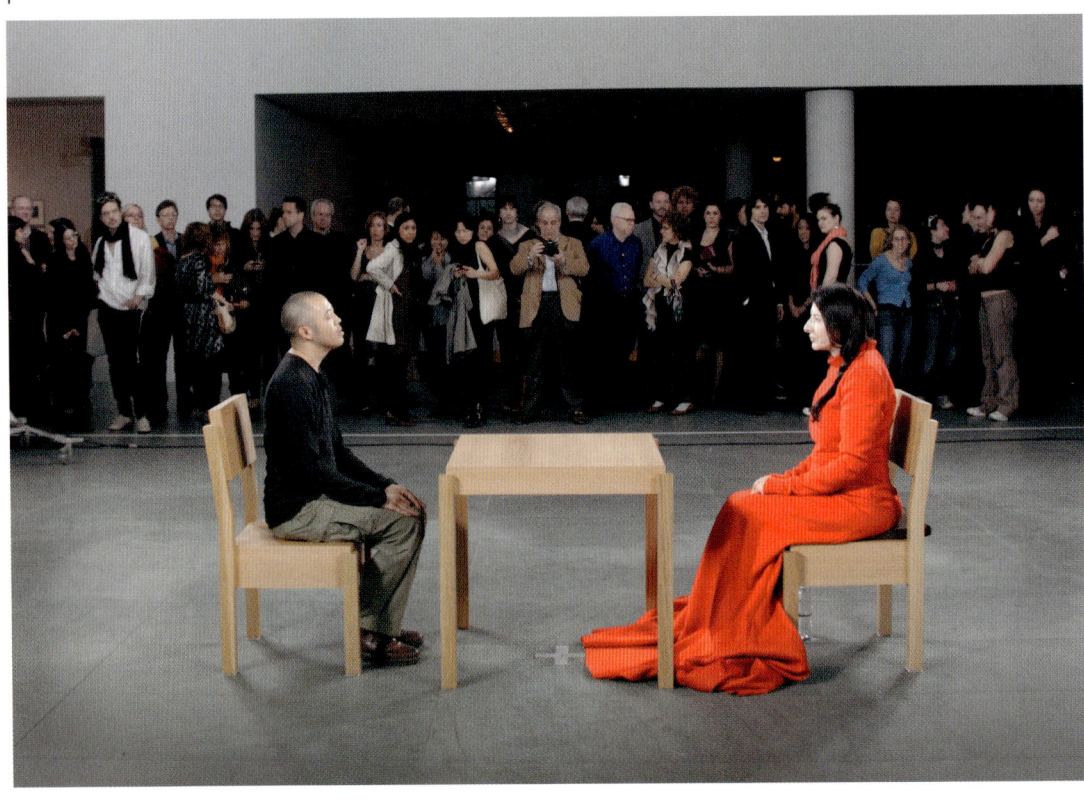

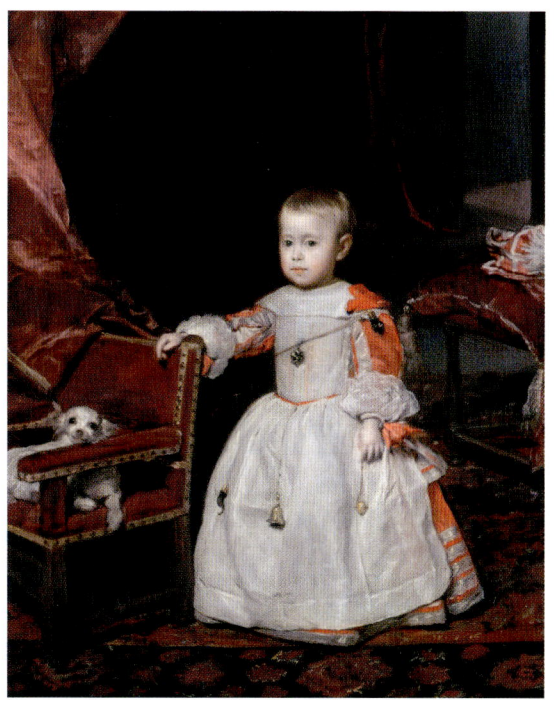

2

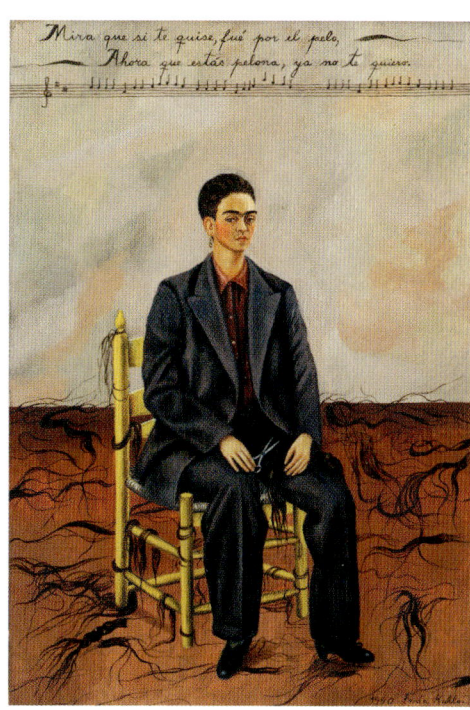

3

4

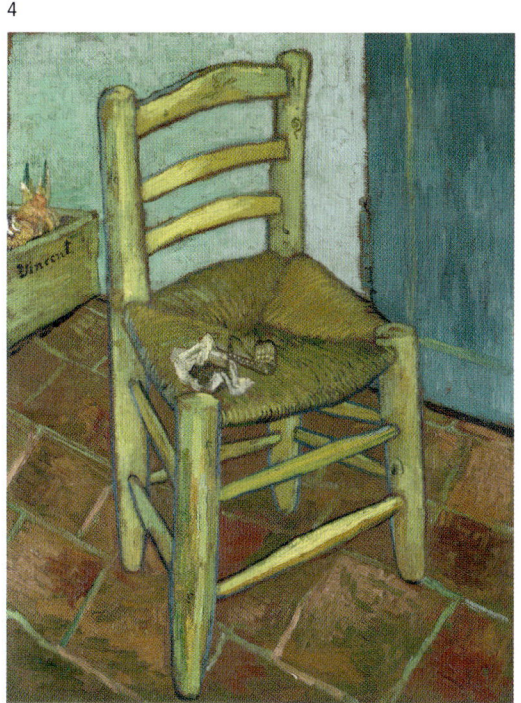

1. *The Artist is Present*, Marina Abramović, 2010
2. *Portrait of Prince Philip Prospero*, Diego Velázquez, 1659
3. *Self-Portrait with Cropped Hair*, Frida Kahlo, 1940
4. *Van Gogh's Chair*, Vincent van Gogh, 1888

Mirror

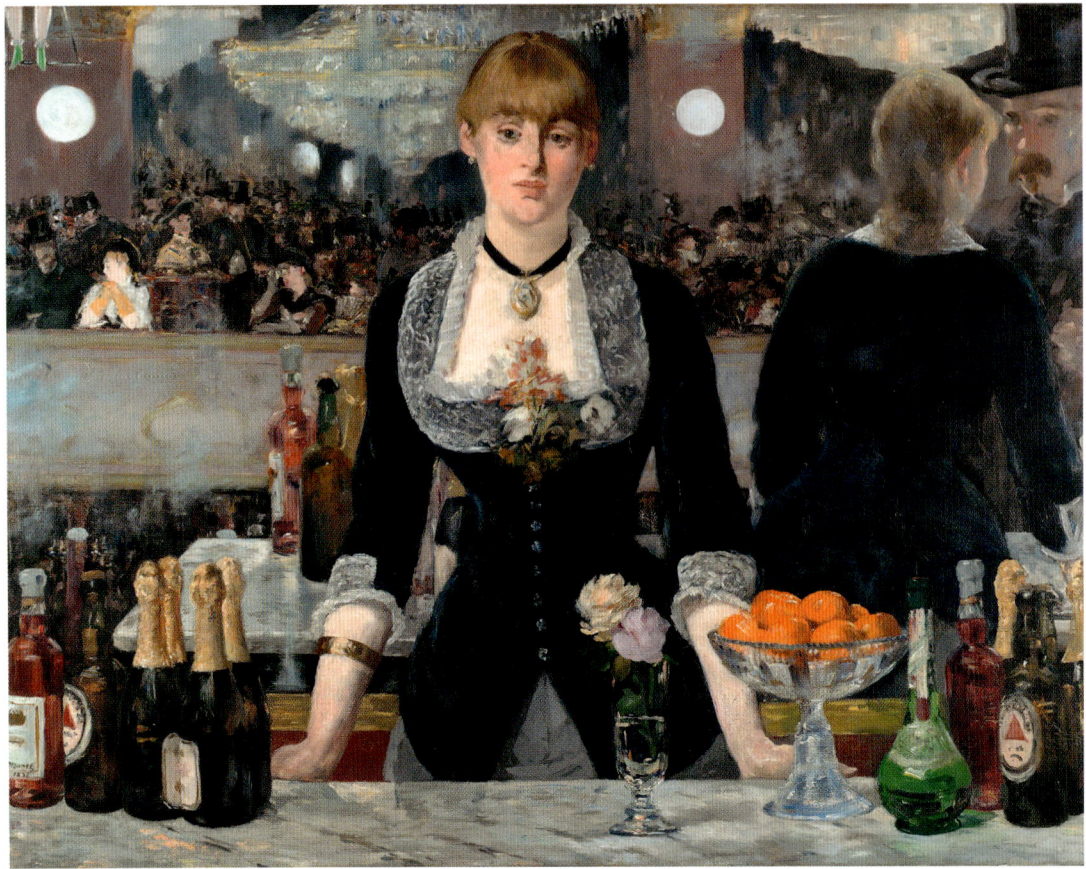

1

The depiction of mirrors in art often adds layers of meaning, inviting viewers to contemplate deeper philosophical or psychological concepts. Mirrors have been featured in art to convey themes of beauty, vanity, self-reflection, introspection, illusion, selfhood and the duality of appearance and reality. In ancient Egyptian art, mirrors were sometimes depicted in the hands of goddesses like Hathor, symbolizing beauty, vanity and the reflection of inner qualities. Mirrors were often used in Greek and Roman art to denote self-reflection, introspection and the idea of inner contemplation. They were also associated with the goddess Aphrodite/Venus, representing love

and beauty. In medieval and Renaissance art, mirrors were sometimes featured to signify spiritual reflection, moral introspection, vanity, self-awareness and the idea of reflecting on one's mortality. The mirror in A *Bar at the Folies-Bergère* (1882) by Édouard Manet conveys the tension between appearance and reality, while in 2006, Anish Kapoor (b. 1954) created *Cloud Gate* to mirror both individuals and the environment.

1. *A Bar at the Folies-Bergère*, Édouard Manet, 1882
2. *Girl Before the Mirror*, Titian and workshop, c. 1515
3. *Woman with a Sunflower*, Mary Cassatt, 1905
4. *Cloud Gate*, Anish Kapoor, 2004

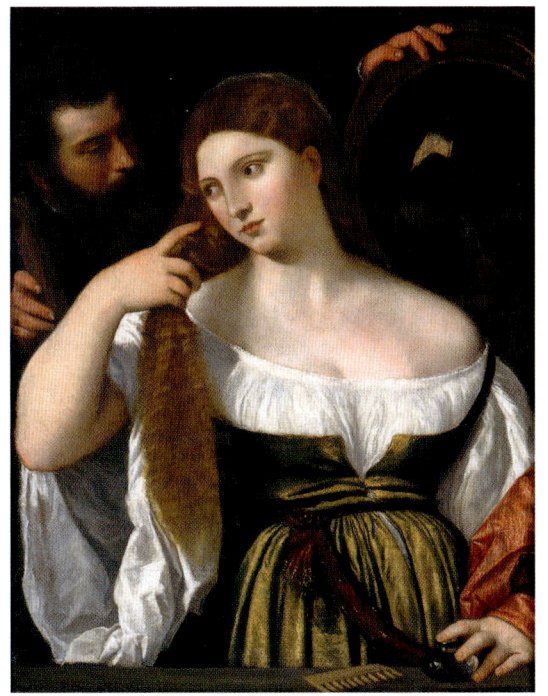

2

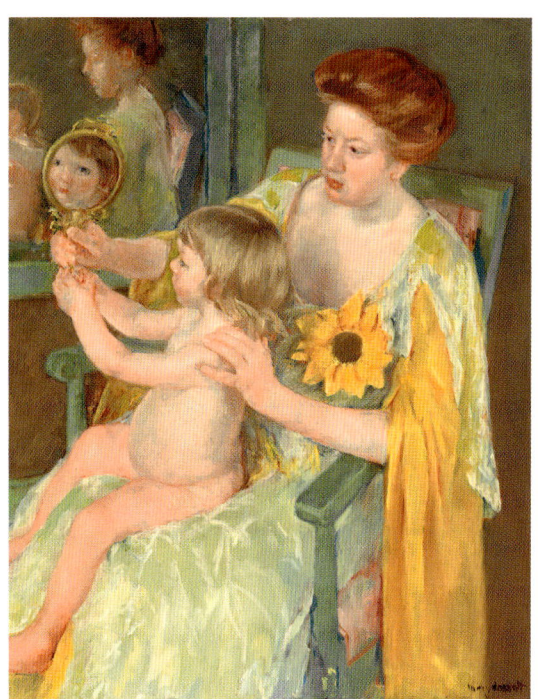

3

4

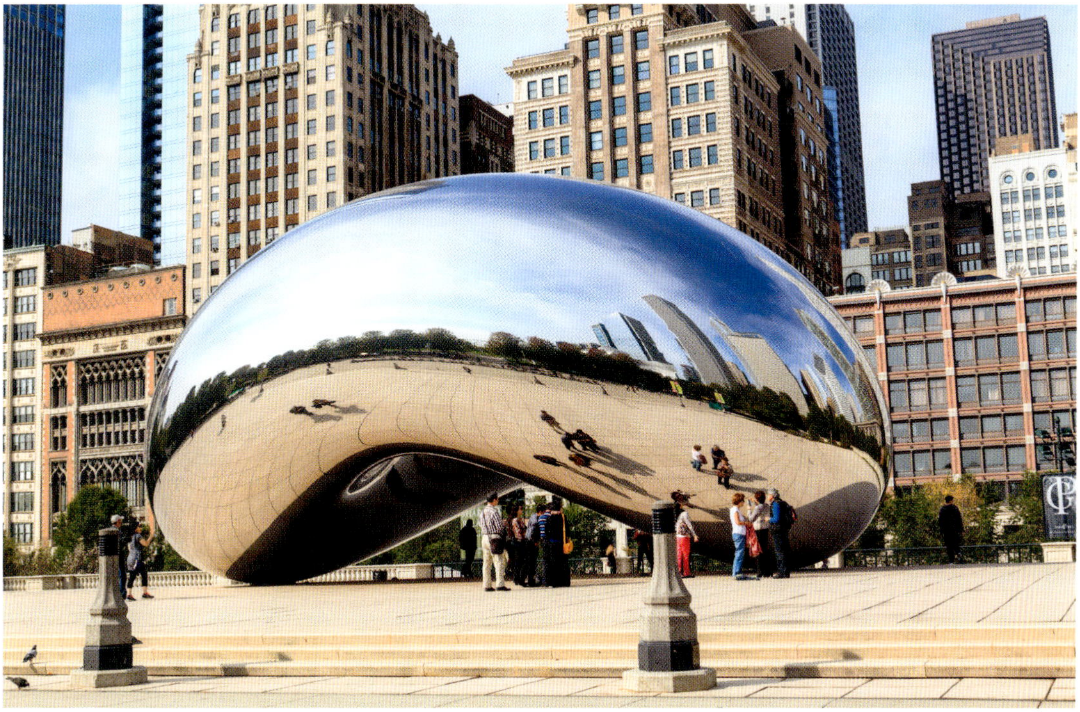

Clock

Time, mortality and the transient nature of existence have all been represented by clocks in a wide range of art. Examples can be found in seventeenth-century vanitas paintings, where clocks or hourglasses frequently appeared alongside skulls and withering flowers, reminding viewers of life's fleeting nature. The melting clocks in *The Persistence of Memory* (1931) by Salvador Dalí evoke the fluidity of time and question the concept of reality itself. Clocks can also symbolize urgency or inevitability. In contemporary art, digital clocks and fragmented timepieces often explore themes of technology, modern anxiety and the artificial measurement of life. *The Clock* (2010) by Christian Marclay (b. 1955) is a 24-hour video installation composed of thousands of film and television clips, each featuring a clock or reference to time, meticulously edited to be a reminder of mortality, highlighting the shared rhythms of daily life and exploring how cinema shapes our perception of the present. Clocks can symbolize continuity and rhythm, reflecting the cyclical nature of existence.

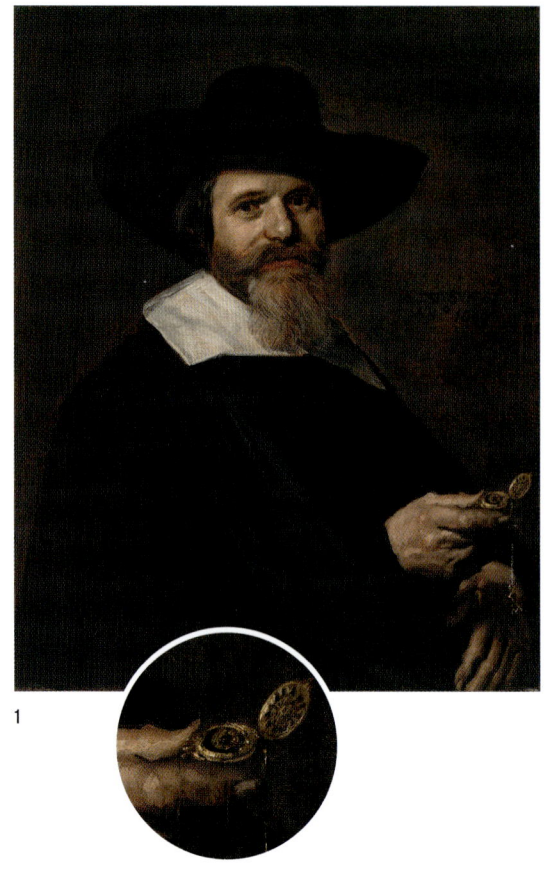

1

2

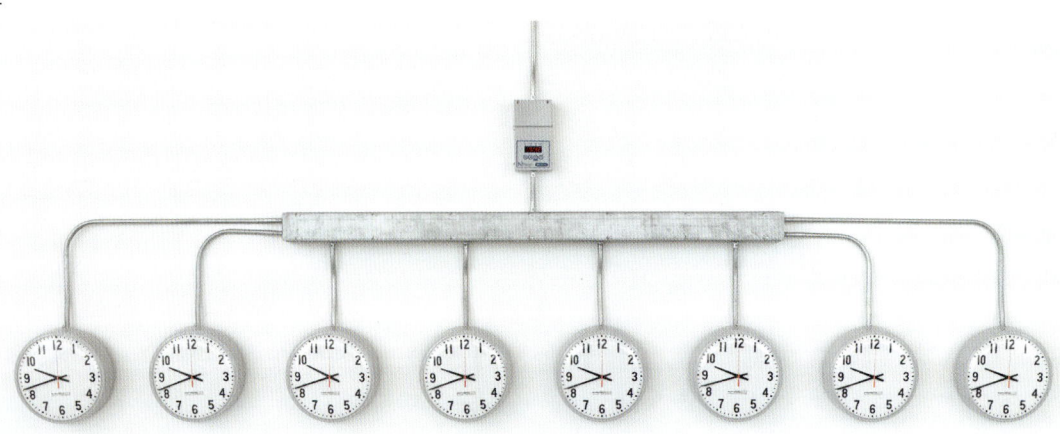

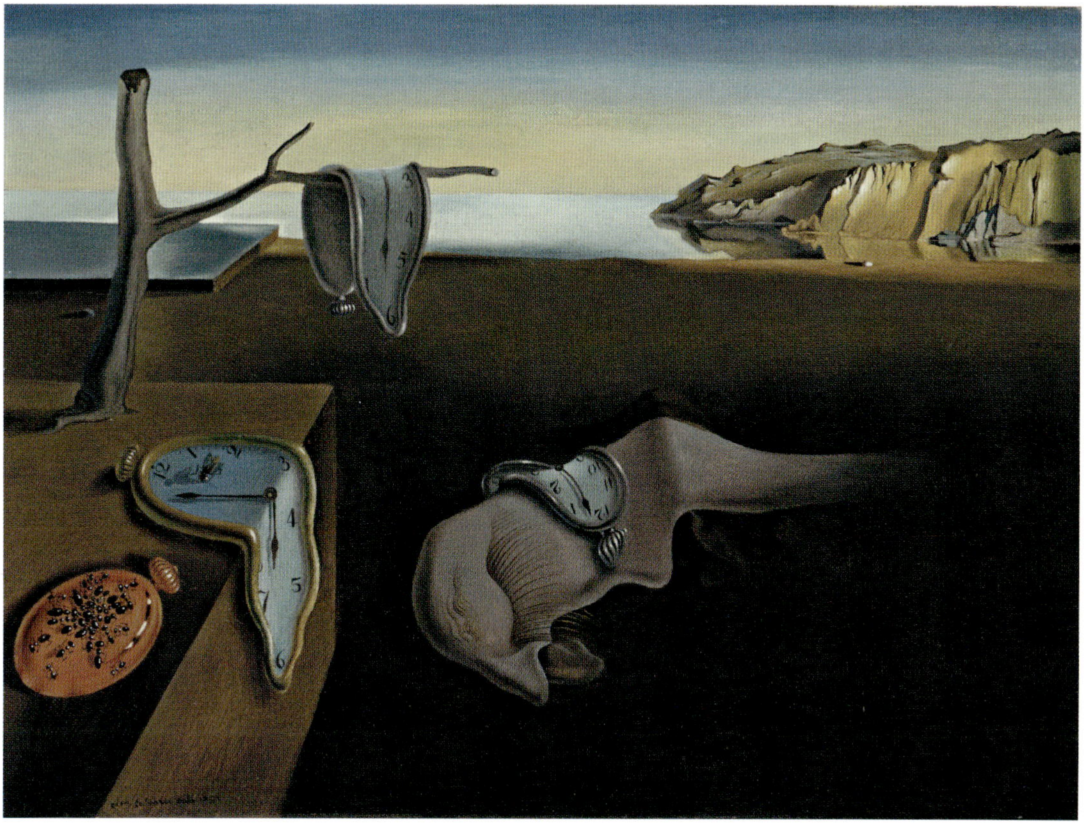

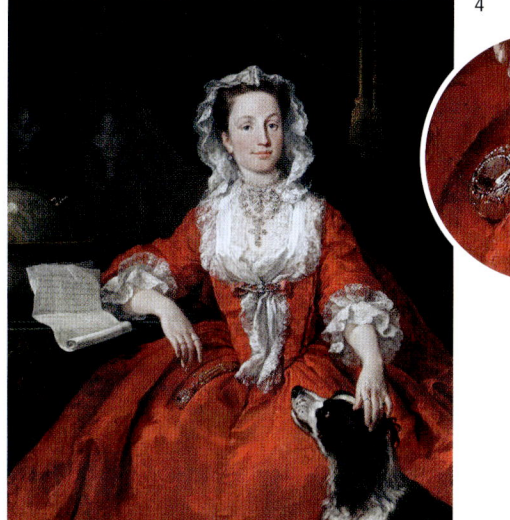

3

4

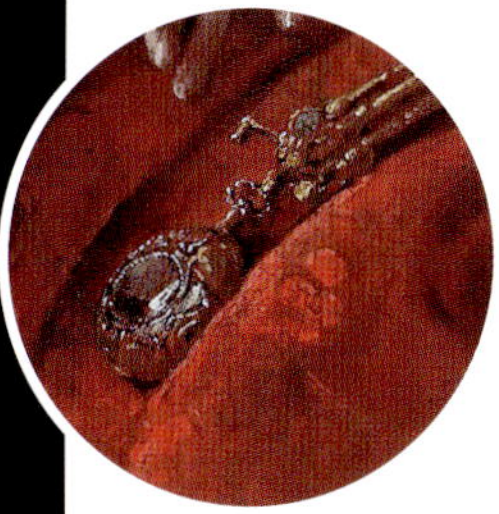

1. *Portrait of a Man Holding a Watch,* Frans Hals, 1643
2. *National Times,* Agustina Woodgate, 2019
3. *The Persistence of Memory,* Salvador Dalí, 1931
4. *Miss Mary Edwards,* William Hogarth, 1742

Hourglass

Although similar to the clock, which also measures time, the hourglass differs in its function. For example, the hourglass with its sand in the glass represents time as a physical substance. In memento mori and vanitas paintings, the hourglass is sometimes featured to remind viewers of life's brevity. For instance, in *The Three Ages of Man and Death* (c. 1540) by Hans Baldung Grien (c. 1484–1545), the hourglass marks the relentless passage of time and human mortality. The hourglass often reminds the viewer that time is constantly moving, urging meditation on spiritual concerns over material ones. In *Allegory of Vanity* (c. 1632–36), Antonio de Pereda (c. 1611–78), the hourglass highlights the fleeting nature of earthly beauty and material wealth, emphasizing life's transience. The slow, silent movement of the hourglass invites contemplation and evokes a sense of inevitability. Because the hourglass can be turned, it also captures the rhythm of nature, of seasons, of lives, and humanity's complex relationships with the world and the universe.

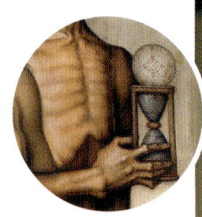

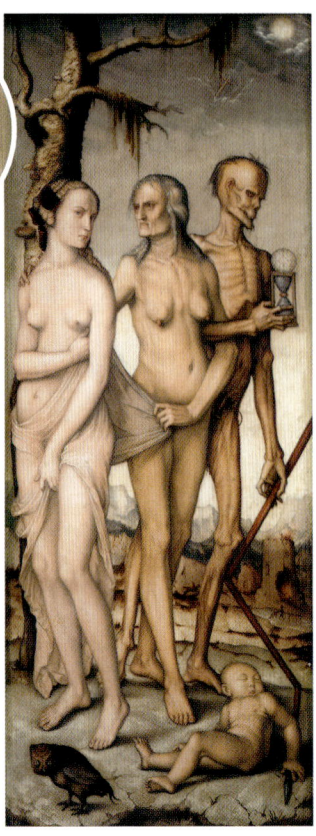

1

2

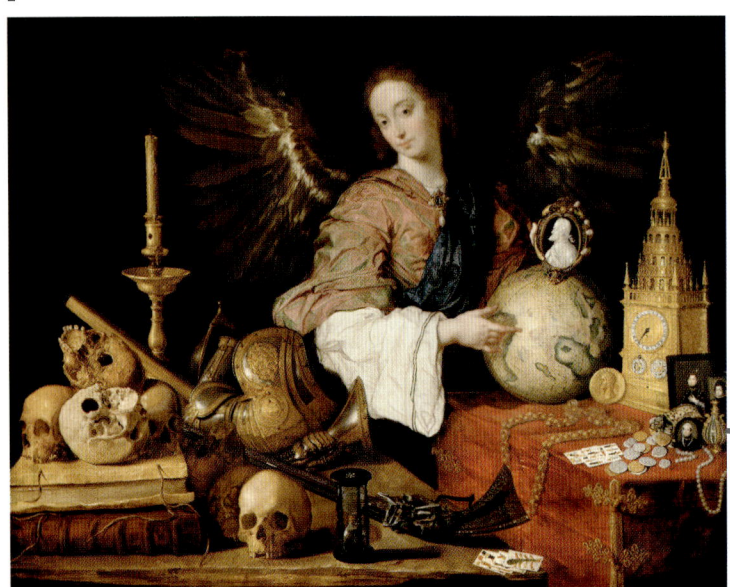

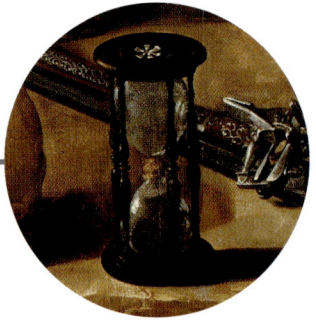

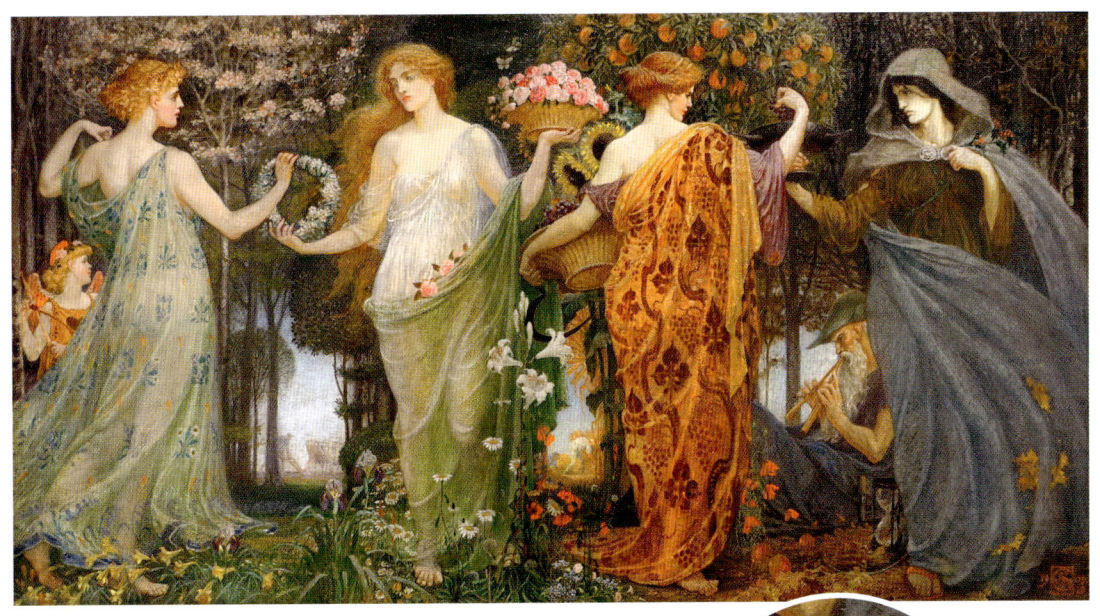

3

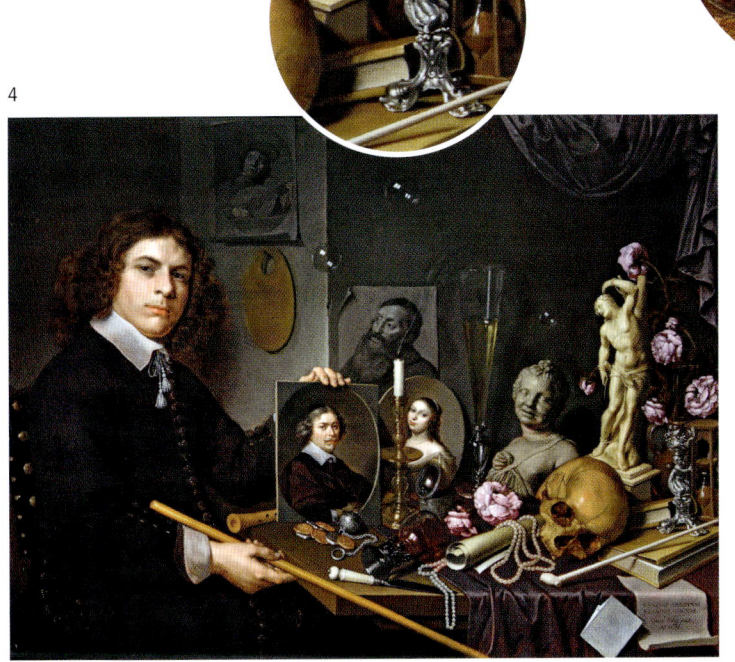

4

1. *The Three Ages of Man and Death,*
   Hans Baldung Grien, c. 1540

2. *Allegory of Vanity,* Antonio de
   Pereda, c. 1632–36

3. *A Masque for the Four Seasons,*
   Walter Crane, 1905–09

4. *Self-Portrait with Vanitas Symbols,*
   David Bailly, 1651

Book

Books in art symbolize knowledge, spirituality, wisdom and authority. In Christian art, books often appear in the hands of saints, apostles and the Virgin Mary, representing the Word of God. Artists like Giotto di Bondone and Fra Angelico (c. 1395-1455) often incorporated open books in their paintings to convey sacred texts or divine revelation. Islamic books, especially the Qur'an, frequently feature exquisite manuscript illumination to reflect the holiness of written knowledge. During the Renaissance, books were often depicted as status symbols and symbols of divine wisdom and sacred scholarship. *The Library* (1960) by Jacob Lawrence (1917-2000), *Reading* (1873) by Berthe Morisot (1841-95) and *Piles of French Novels* (1887) by Van Gogh all convey introspection and the richness of inner life. Modern artists, such as Anselm Kiefer (b. 1945), have utilized books to evoke memories, destruction and history. Whether sacred or secular, books in art represent the enduring human reverence for knowledge and learning.

1

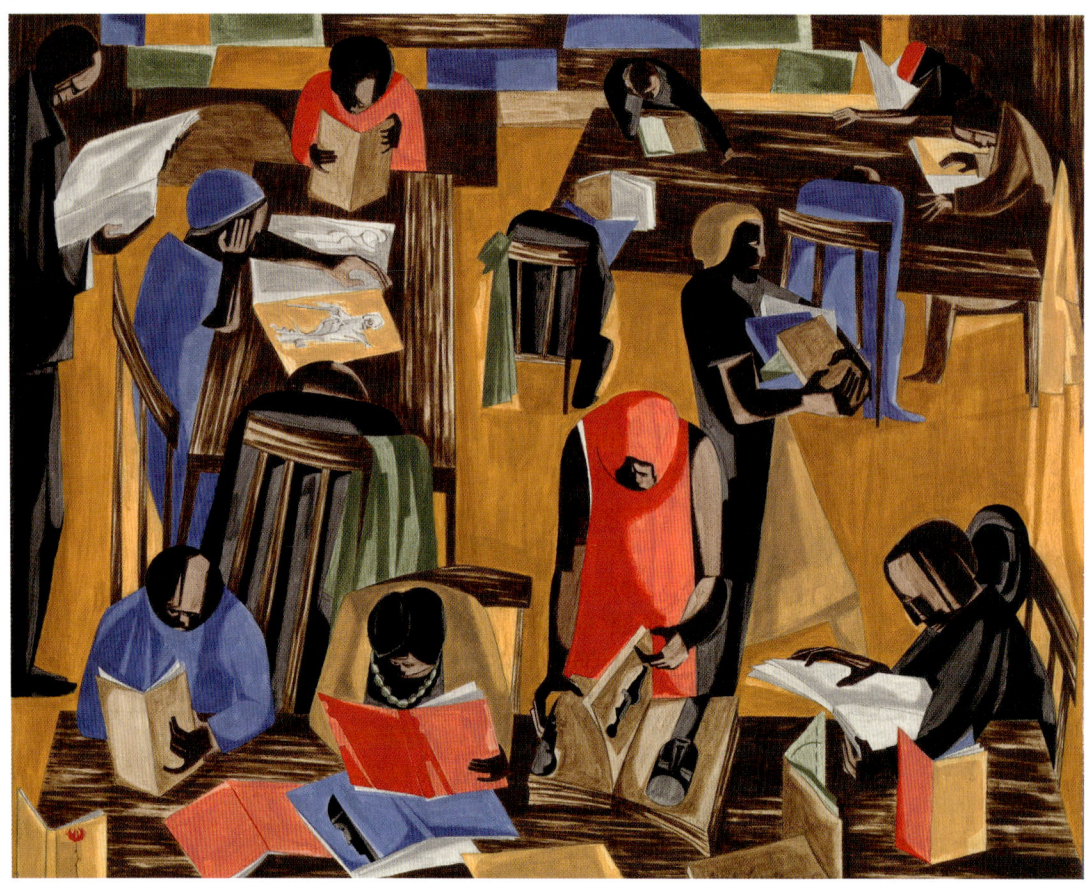

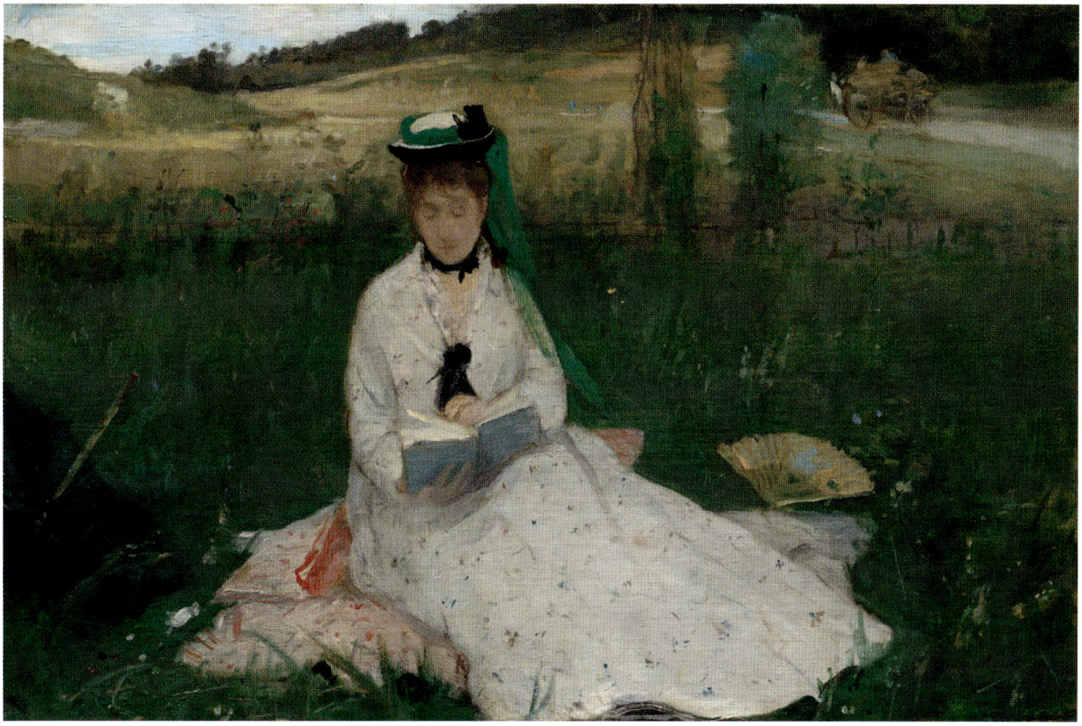

2

3

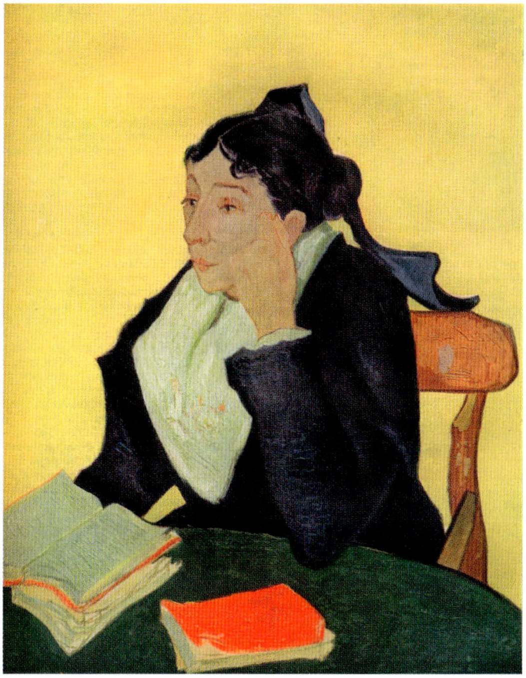

4

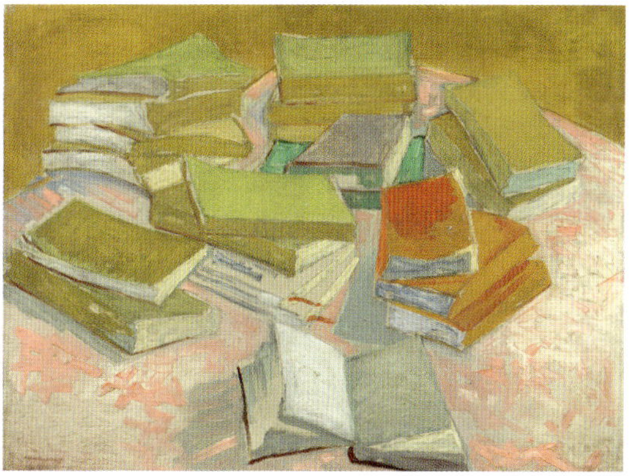

1. *The Library,* Jacob Lawrence, 1960
2. *Reading,* Berthe Morisot, 1873
3. *L'Arlésienne,* Vincent van Gogh, 1890
4. *Piles of French Novels,* Vincent van Gogh, 1887

Globe

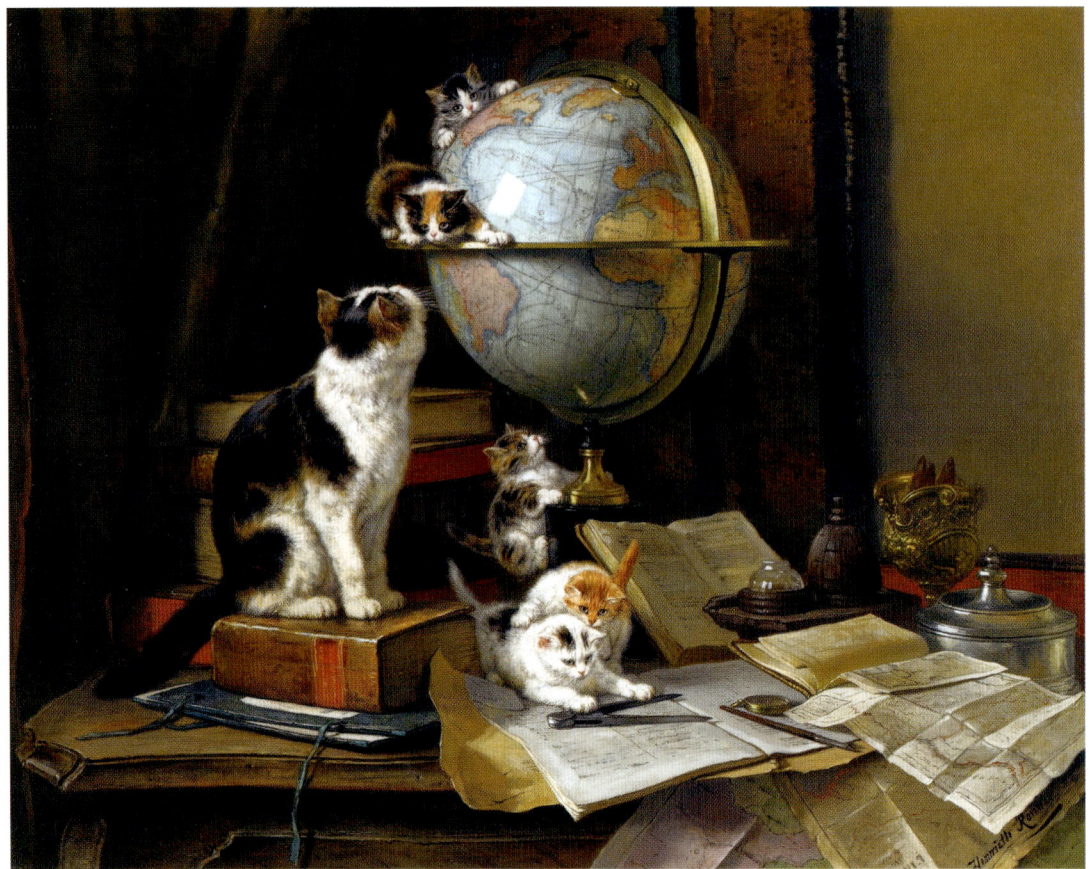

1

The globe in art generally symbolizes exploration, knowledge, power and humanity's place in the cosmos. In Hans Holbein the Younger's *The Ambassadors* (1533), a terrestrial globe appears among scientific instruments and luxury objects, reflecting the Renaissance fascination with exploration and intellectual mastery. During the sixteenth and seventeenth centuries, European portraits often depicted scholars or aristocrats with globes to emphasize worldly awareness or colonial ambitions. Johannes Vermeer (1632-75) also used globes in *The Geographer* (c. 1668-69) and *The Astronomer* (c. 1668) to evoke intellectual curiosity and national pride. In *Allegory of the Catholic Faith* (c. 1670-72), he placed a globe beneath a woman's foot to symbolize Catholic authority and Dutch colonial reach. Meanwhile, Islamic art and cartographic manuscripts celebrated geographic and astronomical precision, with ornate globes reflecting both spiritual and scientific insights. In modern works, the globe can signify globalization, environmental awareness, or unity. For example, *Globe Head Ballerina* (2012), by Yinka Shonibare (b. 1962), critiques imperial histories while invoking shared cultural legacies.

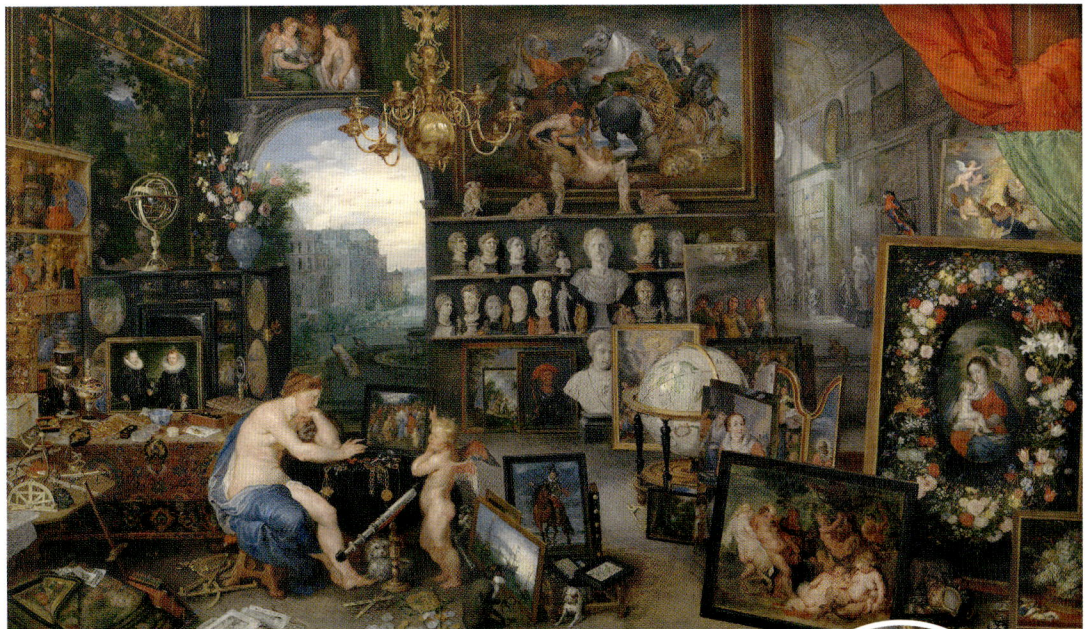

2

3

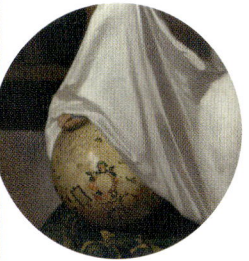

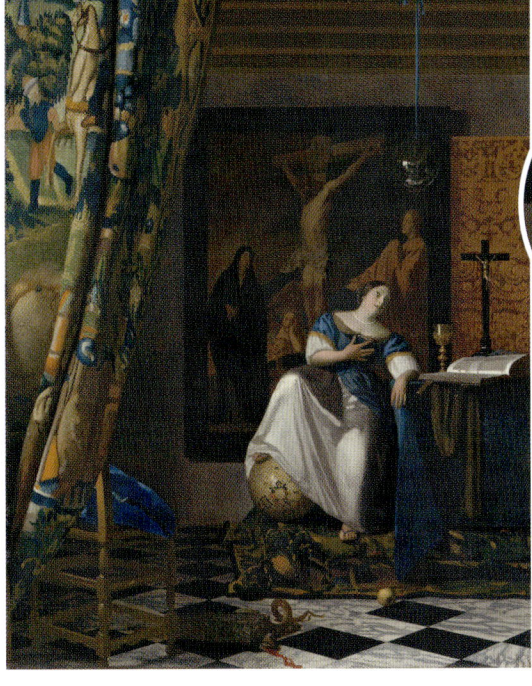

1. *The Globetrotters,* Henriëtte Ronner-Knip, 1883
2. *The Sense of Sight,* Jan Brueghel the Elder and Peter Paul Rubens, 1617
3. *Allegory of the Catholic Faith,* Johannes Vermeer, c. 1670-72

Window

Bridging interior and exterior worlds, both physically and symbolically, windows have been depicted to suggest hope, confinement, transition, revelation and possibility, the threshold between internal and external worlds, or as a metaphor for the human soul. The glass can represent the barrier between the earthly and unearthly realms or transparency and truthfulness. Caspar David Friedrich's *Woman at the Window* (1822) employs the motif to evoke longing and introspection, with the woman gazing out towards the unknown. In 1913, Marc Chagall (1887–1985) painted *Paris Through the Window*, blending dreamlike imagery with urban reality and using the window as a portal to imagination. Henri Matisse used windows to merge interior and exterior spaces, as in *Open Window, Collioure* (1905), where vibrant colours and flattened perspective reflect emotional liberation. Windows invite viewers to look beyond the surface, into other worlds, or deeper within themselves. In 1952, Edward Hopper (1882–1967) painted *Morning Sun*, using windows to explore themes of alienation and the inner life of his subjects.

1. *Street Story Quilt*, Faith Ringgold, 1985
2. *Open Window, Collioure*, Henri Matisse, 1905
3. *Woman at the Window*, Caspar David Friedrich, 1822
4. *Une fenêtre (A Window)*, Robert Delaunay, 1912
5. *Girl Reading a Letter at an Open Window*, Johannes Vermeer, c. 1657–59

1

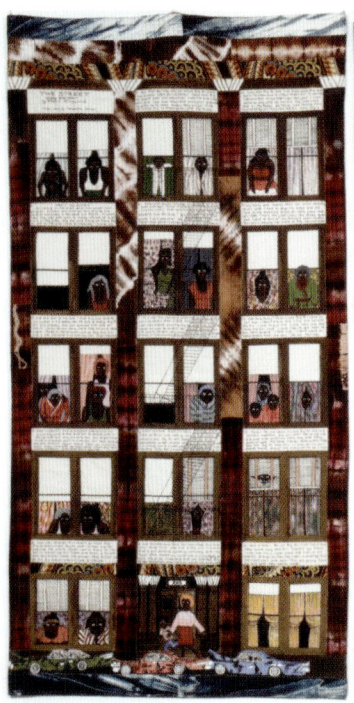 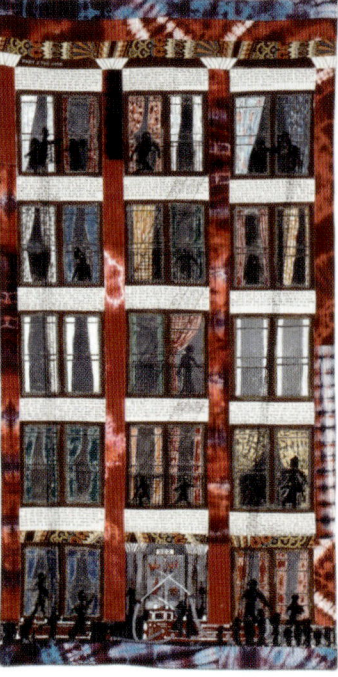 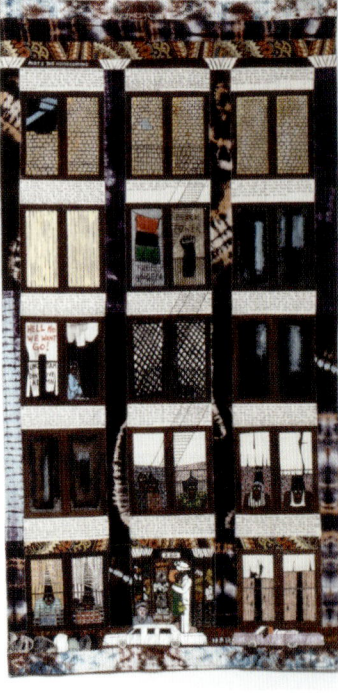

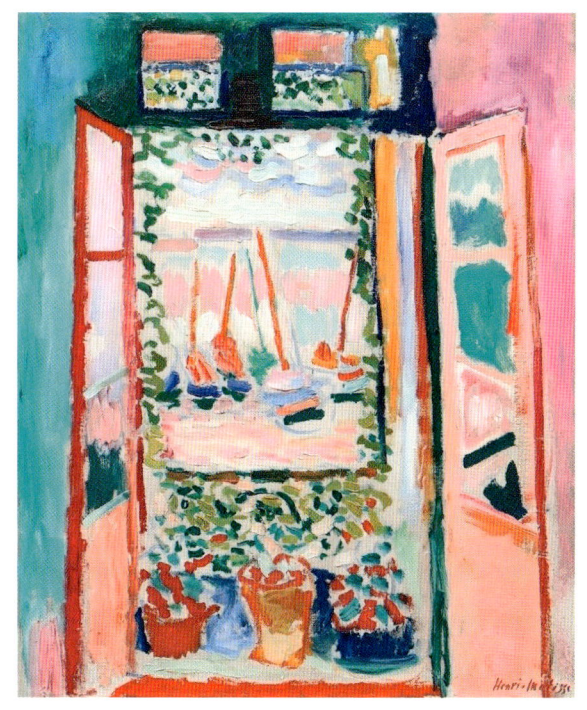

2

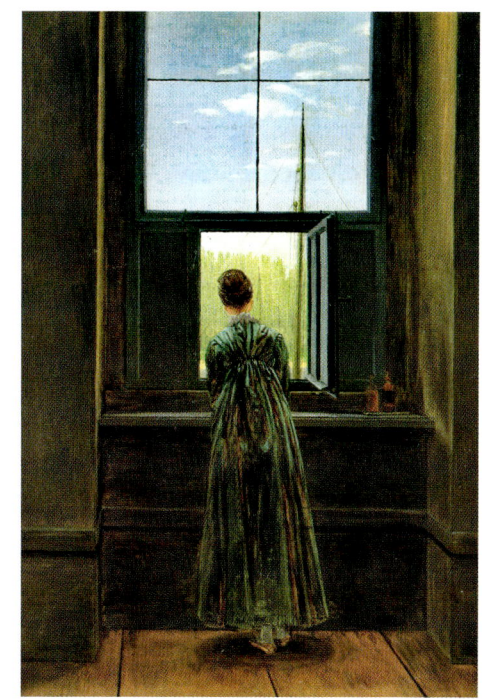

3

4

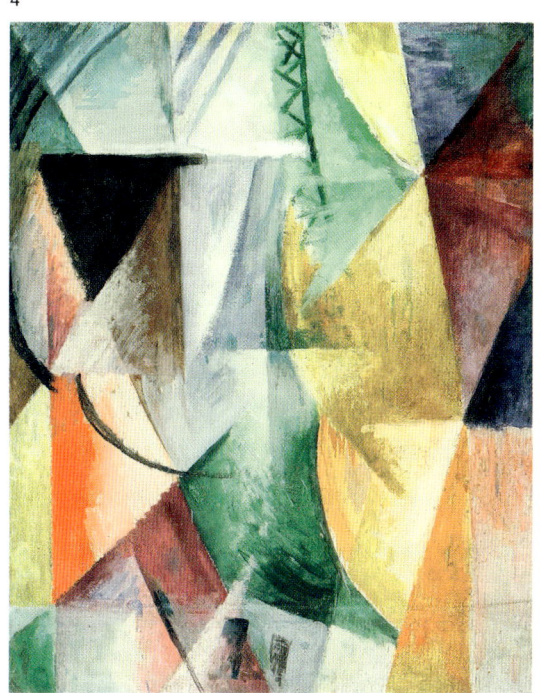

5

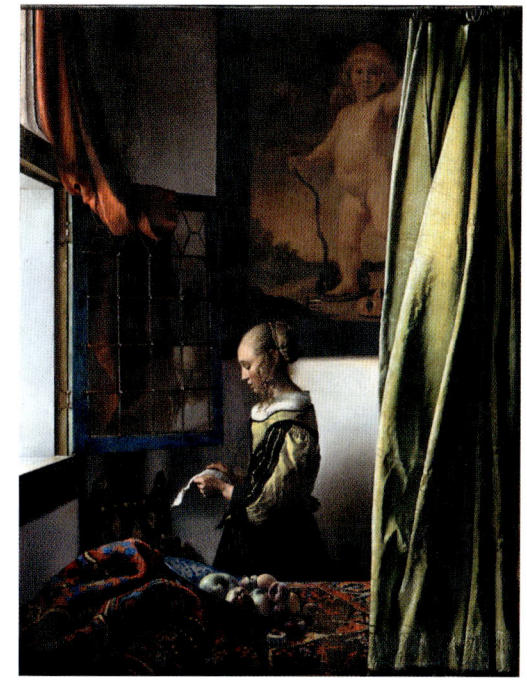

Door

Some ancient Egyptian tombs featured painted doorways that represented passages to the afterlife. Similarly, later Christian artists sometimes incorporated doors as divine thresholds, symbolizing entry into holy spaces, spiritual awakening or the boundary between earthly and celestial realms. For example, in the San Marco fresco *The Annunciation* (c. 1440–45), Fra Angelico (c. 1395–1455) included an open door to emphasize divine invitation and self-realization. In nineteenth-century Symbolism and Romanticism, doors in paintings frequently served as metaphors for an artist's inner turmoil, spiritual longing, or a need to escape the industrial developments of the time. Artists such as Gustave Moreau, Arnold Böcklin and René Magritte utilized doorways to evoke mystery and transcendence, while artists more grounded in realism, such as Edward Hopper, sometimes incorporated doors in interiors to suggest isolation and emotional distance. Across Asia, paintings and prints sometimes feature doors and gates to symbolize seasonal changes or emotional boundaries. In art, doors universally invite reflection on what lies beyond. They are metaphors for choice, opportunity and the unknown.

1. *The Annunciation (San Marco fresco),* Fra Angelico, c. 1440–45
2. *La Victoire (The Victory),* René Magritte, 1939

1

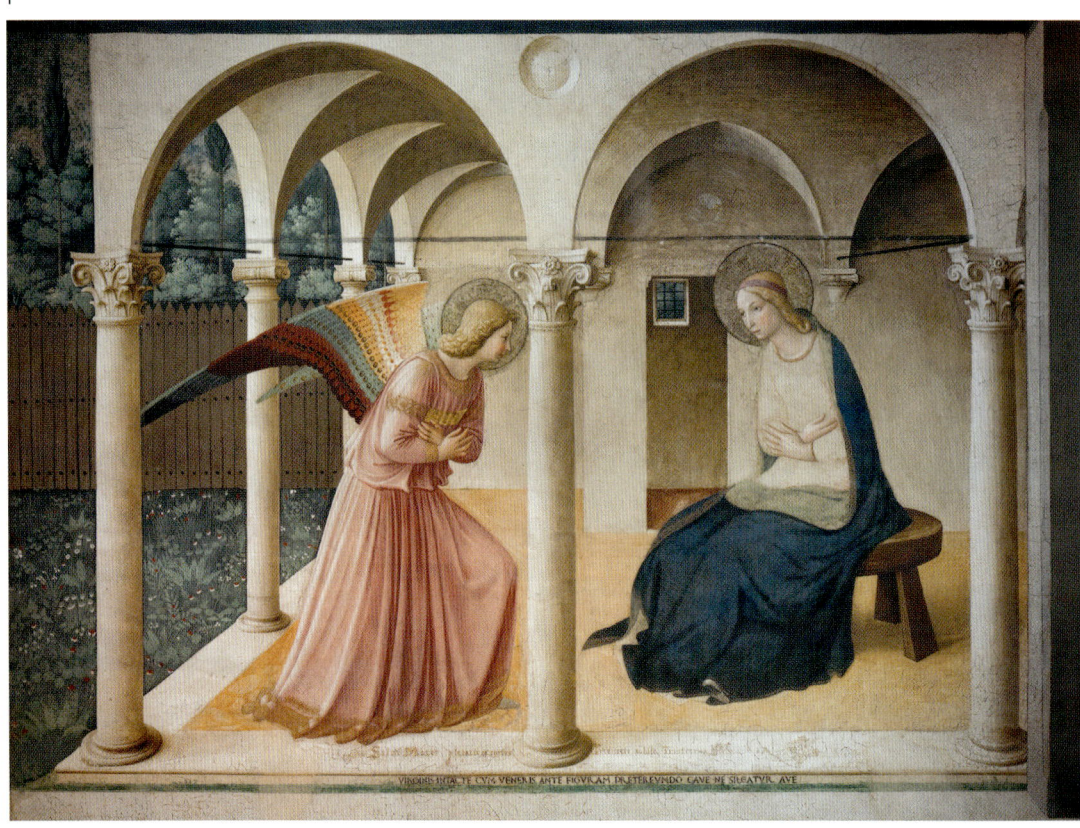

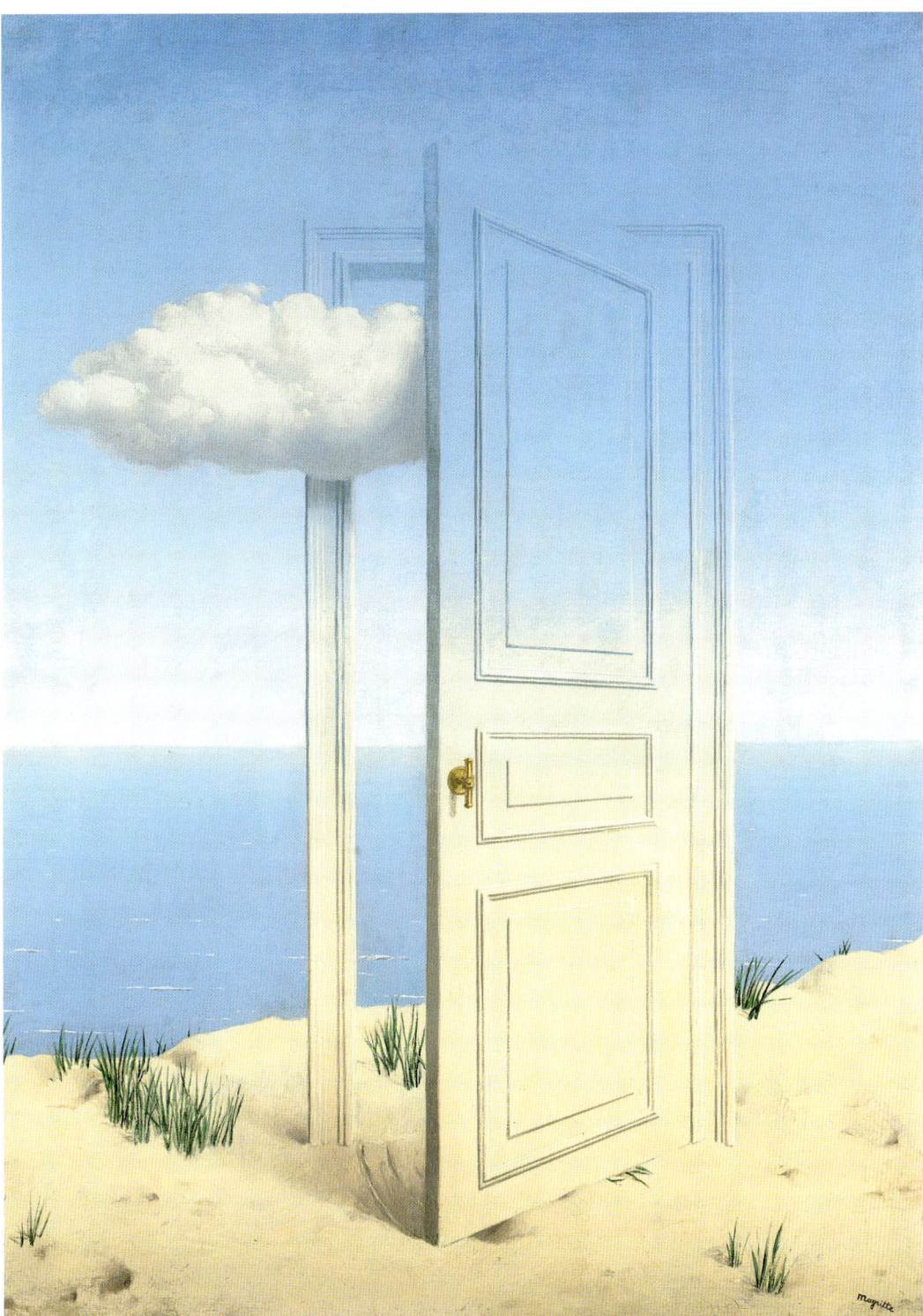

2

Scales

For millennia, scales or balances have symbolized justice, moral equilibrium, the balance between good and evil, excess and restraint, truth and deception, and morality and immorality. Ancient Egyptian funerary art often featured the 'Weighing of the Heart' ceremony, where Anubis weighed the deceased's heart on scales against a feather, determining its worthiness for the afterlife. In Western art, scales held by Lady Justice symbolize the balance between truth and fairness. In c. 1467-71, Hans Memling (c. 1430-94) painted the archangel Michael holding a pair of scales to weigh souls, a classic medieval depiction of the divine judgement. Over 300 years later, in 1808, William Blake (1757-1827) painted *A Vision of the Last Judgement* to portray the same theme. During the Renaissance, artists such as Raphael and Titian depicted justice as a cardinal virtue, often holding a balanced scale. *Woman Holding a Balance* (c. 1664) by Vermeer reflects personal introspection and moral choice.

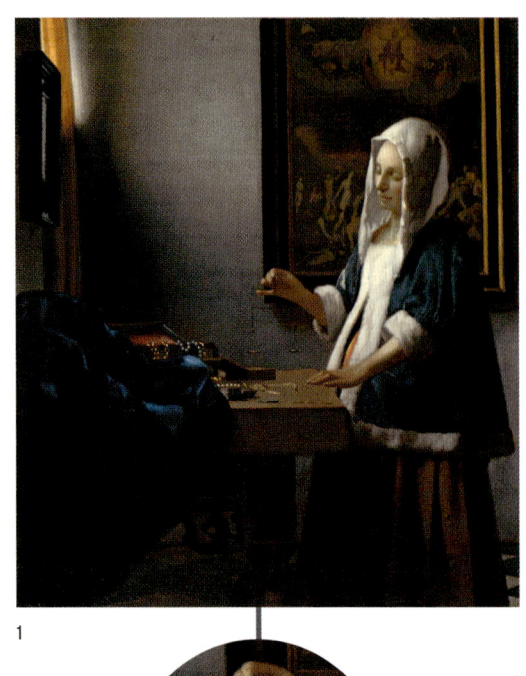

1

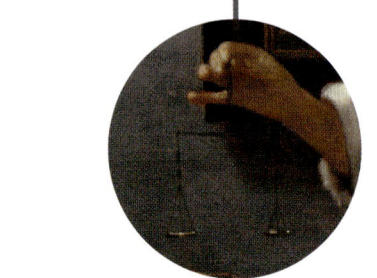

2

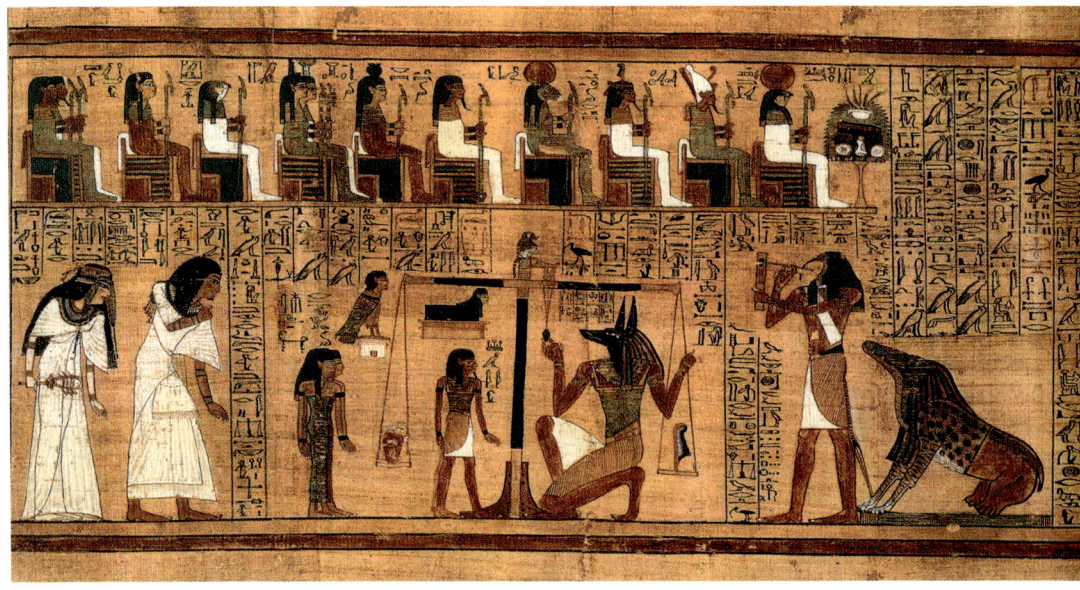

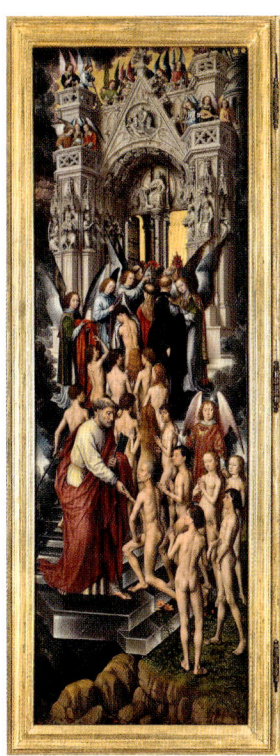
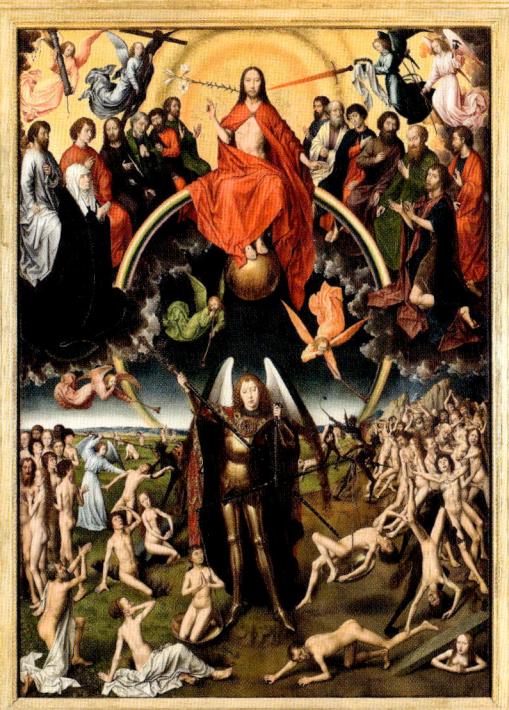
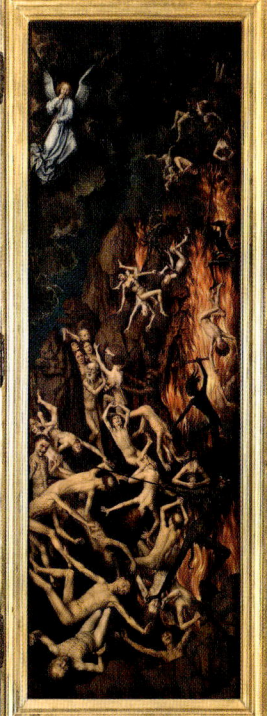

3

4

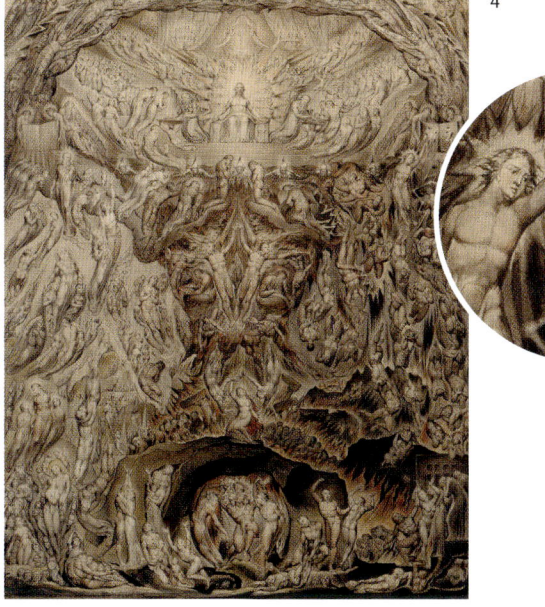

1. *Woman Holding a Balance*, Johannes Vermeer, c. 1664
2. Detail from *Papyrus of Ani, Book of the Dead*, Egypt c. 1250 BCE
3. *The Last Judgement*, Hans Memling, c. 1467-71
4. *A Vision of the Last Judgement*, William Blake, 1808

Key

Powerfully symbolic objects, keys often represent knowledge, authority, secrecy, or transition, and their meanings shift across cultures and periods. In Christian iconography, keys are strongly associated with Saint Peter, to whom Christ gave the 'keys to the kingdom of heaven'. This symbol appears often in Christian art, for example, in *Christ Giving the Keys to Peter* (c. 1626) by Guido Reni (1575–1642), where the key confers divine authority and spiritual leadership, signifying papal authority. In ancient Egyptian and Greek art, keys were often associated with protection and guardianship. Actual keys were frequently buried with the dead, meaning access to the afterlife.

Similarly, in Japanese netsuke and woodblock prints, keys sometimes denote hidden knowledge or the unlocking of fate. René Magritte sometimes used keys as metaphors for mystery and the unconscious. In contemporary sculpture, artists such as Louise Bourgeois incorporated keys to represent memory, personal history or access to psychological spaces. Keys also appear in political and protest art, as symbols of freedom or restriction, openings or containment.

1. *Traditio Clavium mosaic*, Italy, c. 350 CE
2. *Christ Giving the Keys to Peter*, Guido Reni, c. 1626

1

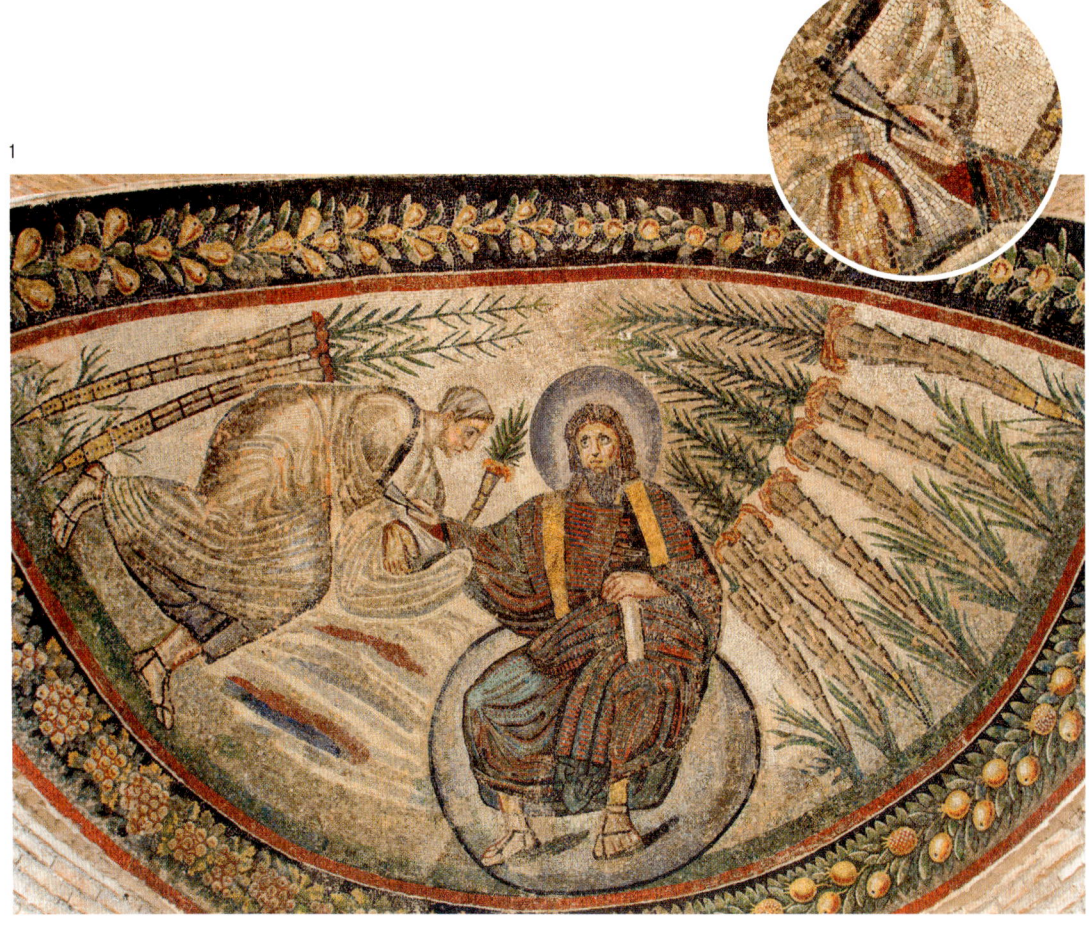

2

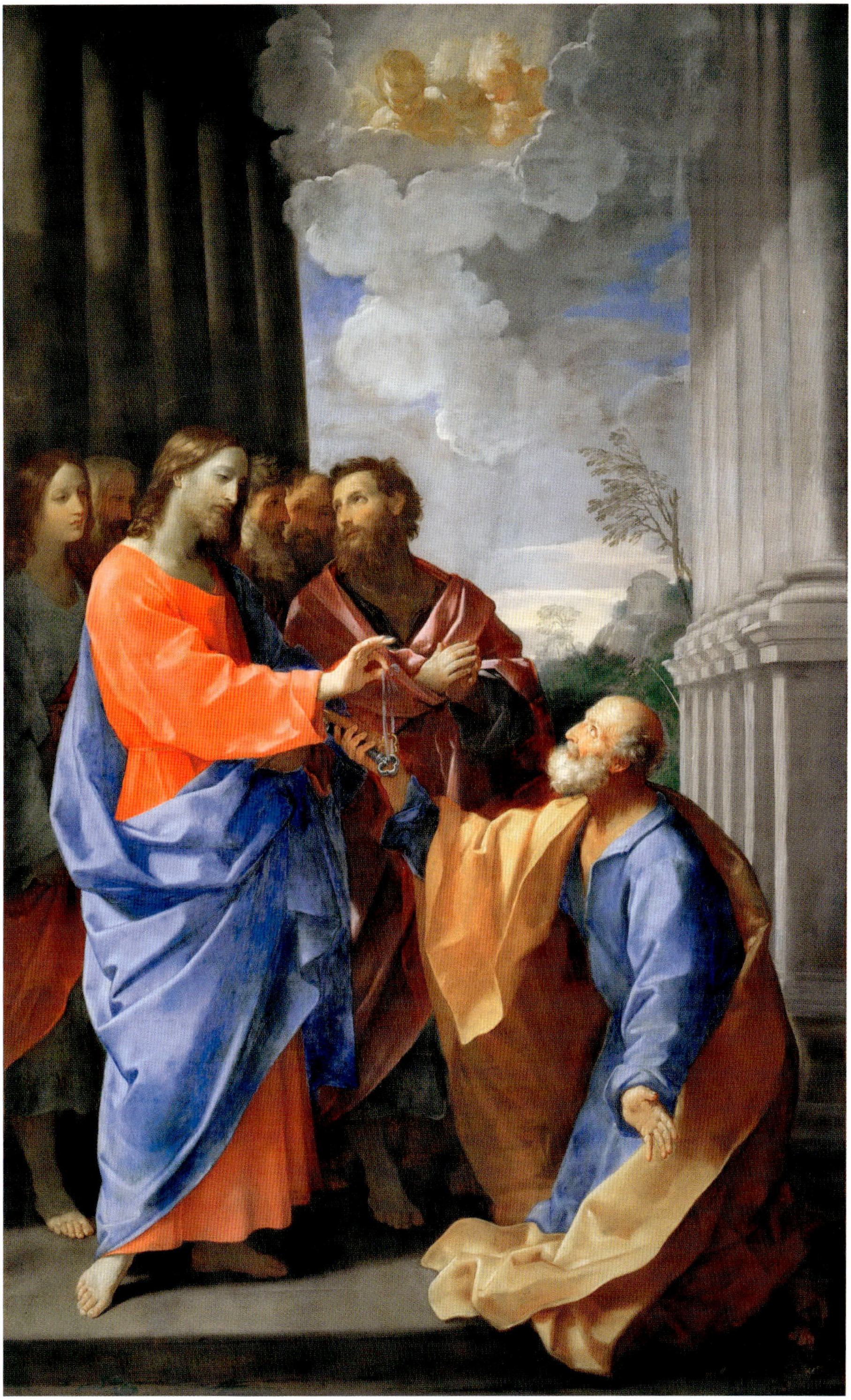

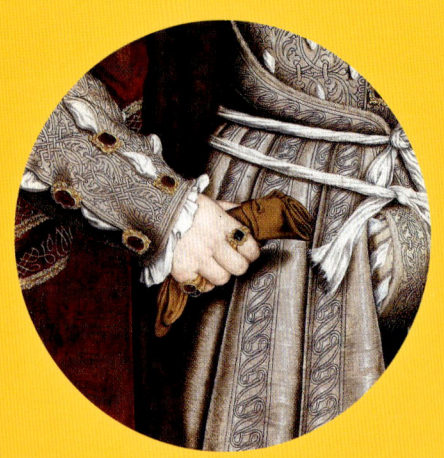

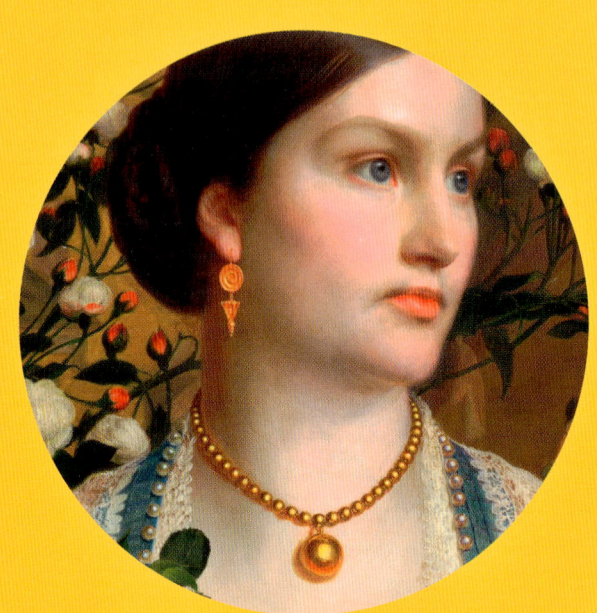

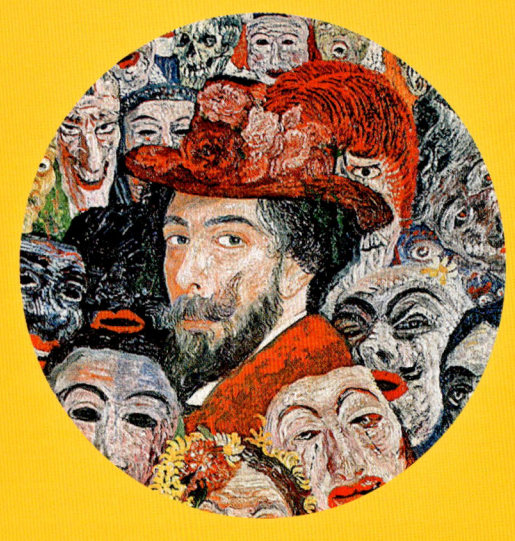

Clothing

Shoe

Throughout history, shoes have been depicted as symbols of identity, journey, poverty, power and absence. In Vincent van Gogh's *Shoes* (1888), a worn out pair evoke the labour of the working class and Van Gogh's empathy for everyday struggle. In *The Swing* (1767), Jean-Honoré Fragonard (1732–1806) uses a discarded shoe as a symbol of eroticism and flirtation, suggesting playful seduction between the figures. It also conveys a sense of carefree abandon, reflecting the Rococo era's frivolity and sensuality. In 1980, Andy Warhol (1928–87) produced a series of screenprints featuring diamond dust. His *Diamond Dust Shoes* symbolize glamour, consumer desire, and the glorification of luxury, reflecting both the cult of celebrity and the commodification of fashion in late twentieth-century America. The sparkling diamond dust elevates the mundane object into an icon of status, aspiration, and superficial allure, emphasizing Warhol's fascination with mass culture and the spectacle of materialism. In 1993, Doris Salcedo (b. 1958) created *Defiant (Atrabiliarios)*, an installation of shoes that belonged to individuals (primarily women) who 'disappeared' in Colombia.

1

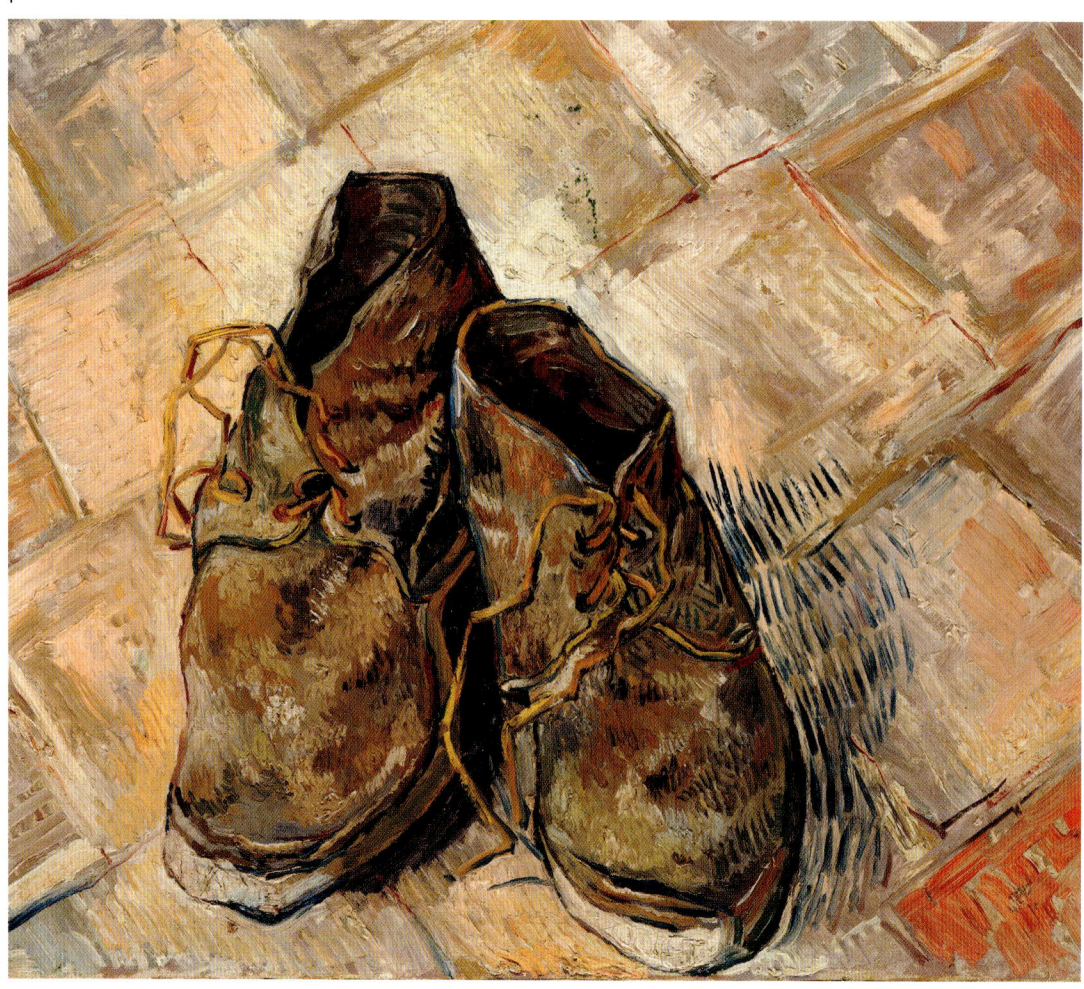

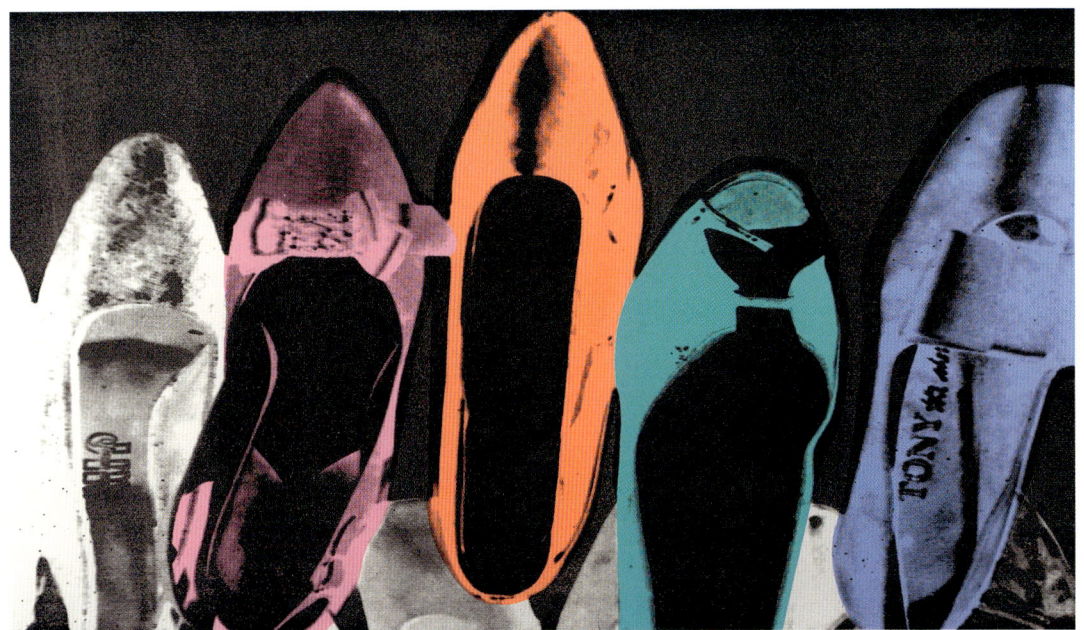

2

3

1. *Shoes,* Vincent van Gogh, 1888
2. *Diamond Dust Shoes*, Andy Warhol, 1980
3. *The Swing*, Jean-Honoré Fragonard, 1767

Gloves

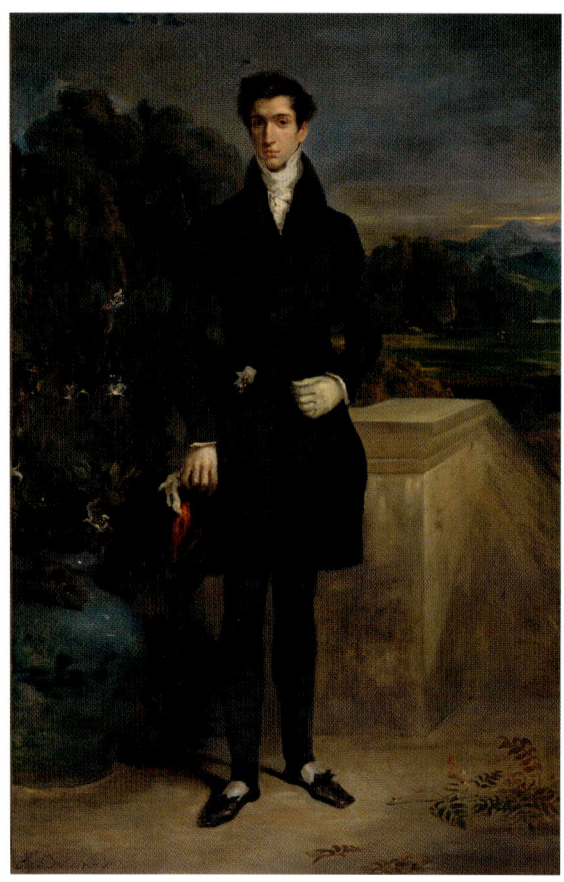

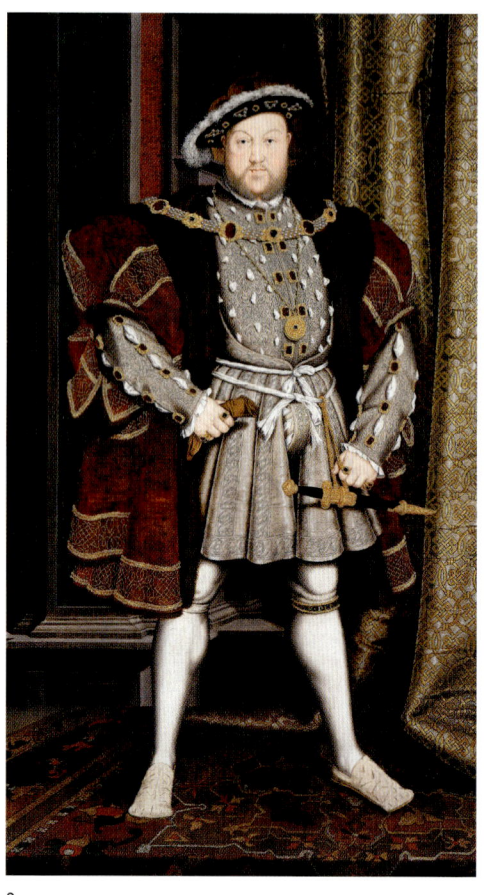

1

2

Status, purity, intimacy and concealment are just some of the reasons that artists include gloves in their art. Even during a period when gloves were necessary for the genteel, their presence in portraits and allegorical works often transcended fashion, offering insight into societal values and personal identity. In Renaissance and Baroque portraiture, gloves frequently signified wealth and refinement. For instance, in *Portrait of Henry VIII* (1536–37), by Hans Holbein the Younger (c. 1497–1543), the depiction of the king holding gloves conveys power, control and royal authority, suggesting mastery over both courtly manners

and political dominion. Gloves also conveyed moral or emotional undertones. In sixteenth- and seventeenth-century paintings, a discarded glove might suggest vulnerability or the shedding of worldly attachments. In *Portrait of Hester Crispe*, c. 1620, by an unknown English artist, the gloves symbolize virtue, modesty and gentility, reflecting early seventeenth-century ideals of feminine decorum and moral propriety. In religious art, gloves worn by clergy suggest spiritual purity. Meanwhile, in twentieth-century art, when gloves were no longer worn for decorum in the West, they often evoke sensuality or mystery.

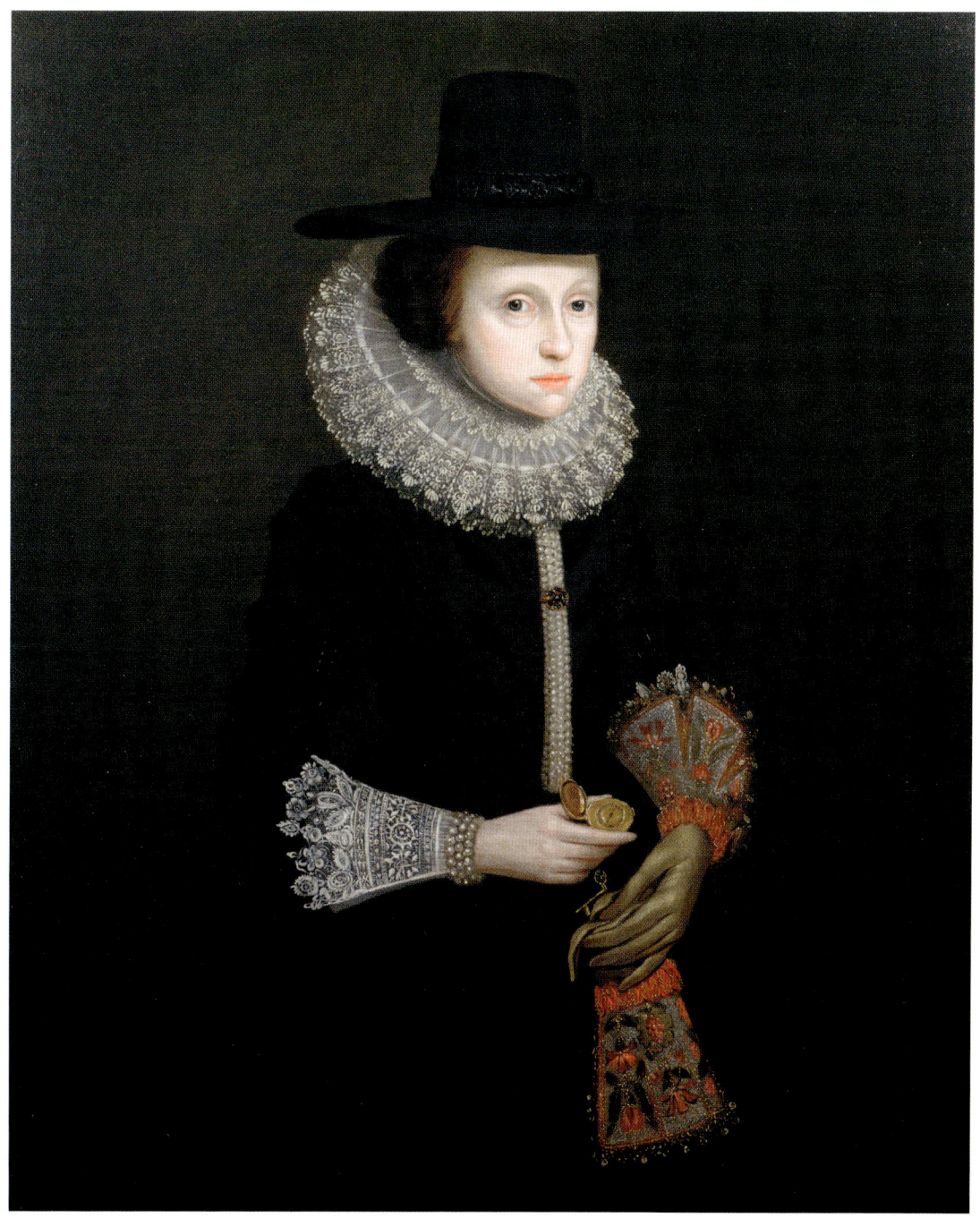

1. *Louis-Auguste Schwiter*, Eugène Delacroix, 1826–30
2. *Portrait of Henry VIII*, Hans Holbein the Younger, 1536–37
3. *Portrait of Hester Crispe*, unknown English artist, c. 1620

Mask

As vessels of transformation, concealment and revelation, masks occupy a decisive role in visual and performance art. In African ritual art, masks are worn during rituals, believed to become the spirit they represent. For example, a Dan or Baule mask is used in ceremonies where an ancestral presence replaces the wearer's identity. This concept recurs globally: in Japanese Noh theatre, masks convey a character's emotion and essence, whether divine, ghostly, or comic. In the Mexican *Mask of Malinaltepec*, of 300–550 CE, transformation and spiritual power serve as a conduit between the human and divine realms in Mesoamerican ritual practice. Whether sacred, theatrical or satirical, masks in art express the human urge to shape-shift into gods, monsters, ideals or reflections of ourselves. In modern Western art, masks take on metaphorical significance. In *Self-Portrait with Masks* (1899), James Ensor (1860–1949) suggests the hypocrisy and hidden nature of society, reflecting his sense of alienation and the tension between actual self and public façade.

1

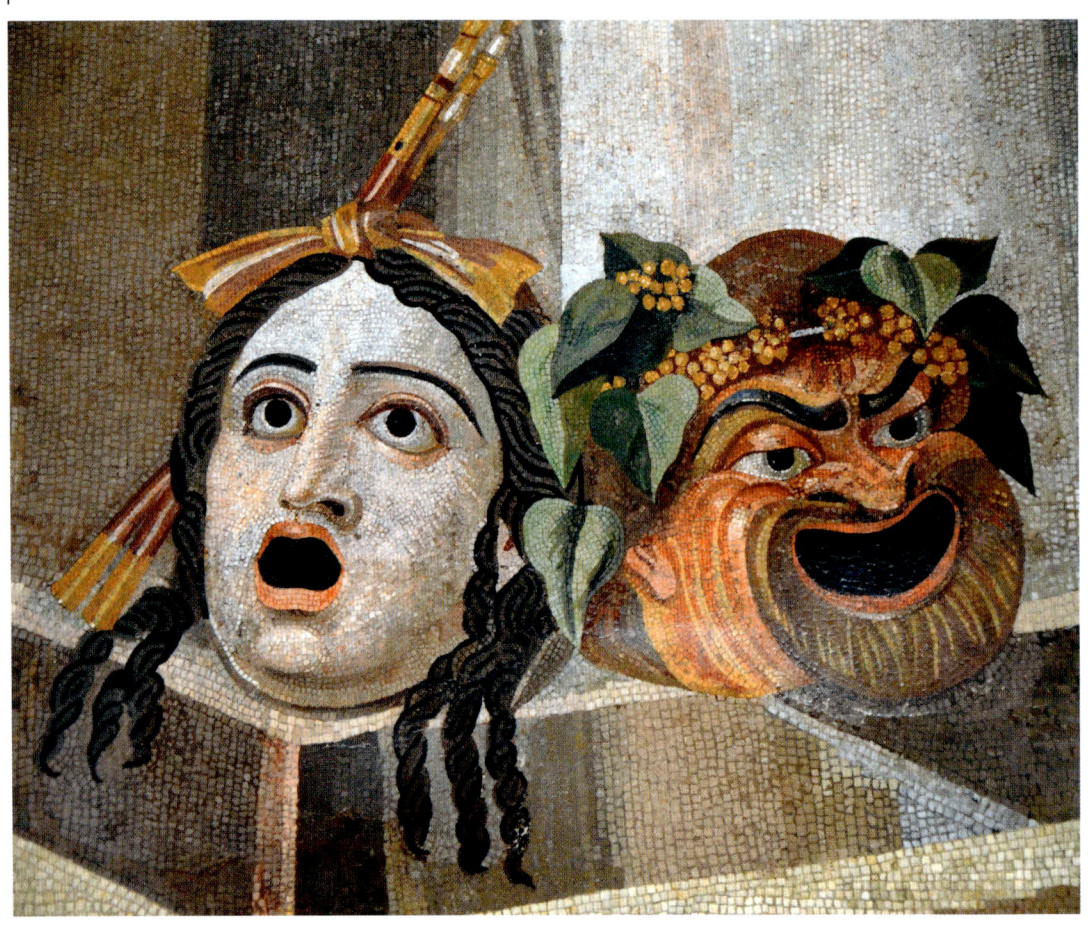

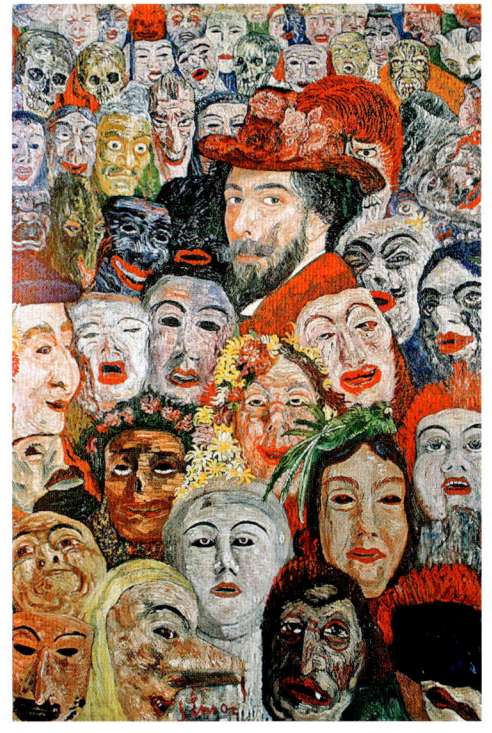

2

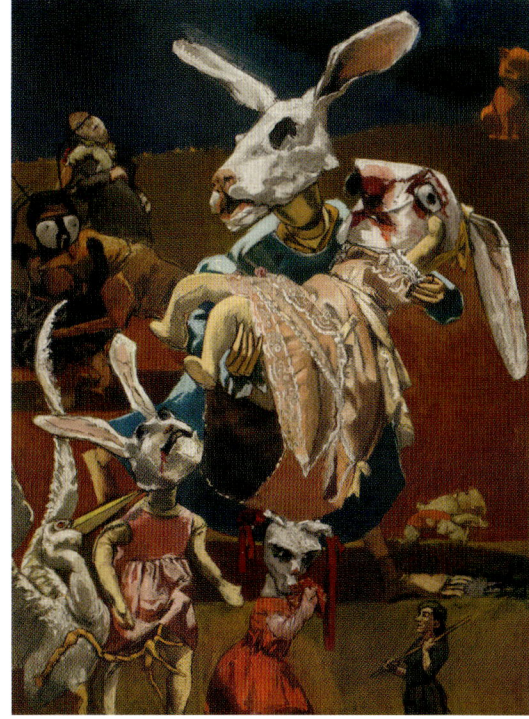

3

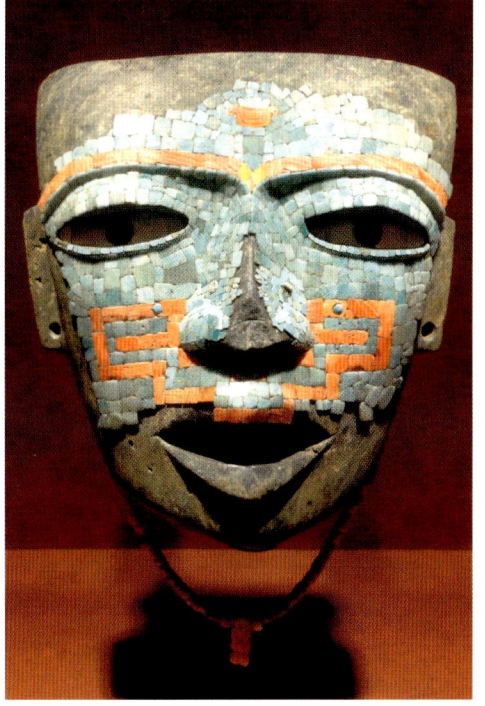

4

1. *Mosaic showing theatrical masks of Tragedy and Comedy,* Italy, second century CE

2. *Self-Portrait with Masks,* James Ensor, 1899

3. *War,* Paula Rego, 2003

4. *Mask of Malinaltepec,* Mexico, 300-550 CE

Jewellery

Reaching far beyond adornment, jewellery in art can convey themes of identity, hierarchy and transcendence. Jewellery in African sculpture, especially in Yoruba and Akan traditions, often symbolizes lineage, wisdom or spiritual potency, with gold and beads representing not merely material riches, but sacred vessels of ancestral power. In medieval Christian art, jewels on reliquaries and bishops' regalia signify purity, martyrdom or heavenly glory. In Mughal Indian miniature paintings, emperors and deities alike are adorned with elaborate gem-studded necklaces, earrings and crowns, reflecting divine right and cosmic authority. In *Portrait of Adele Bloch-Bauer I* (1907) by Gustav Klimt (1862–1918), the subject is enveloped in a golden mosaic of jewels and spirals, an extension of sensuality, status and the divine. In Johannes Vermeer's *Girl with a Pearl Earring* (c. 1665), the girl's enormous, tear-shaped pearl earring possibly symbolizes that young women should only hear chaste words, or 'pearls of the gospel'.

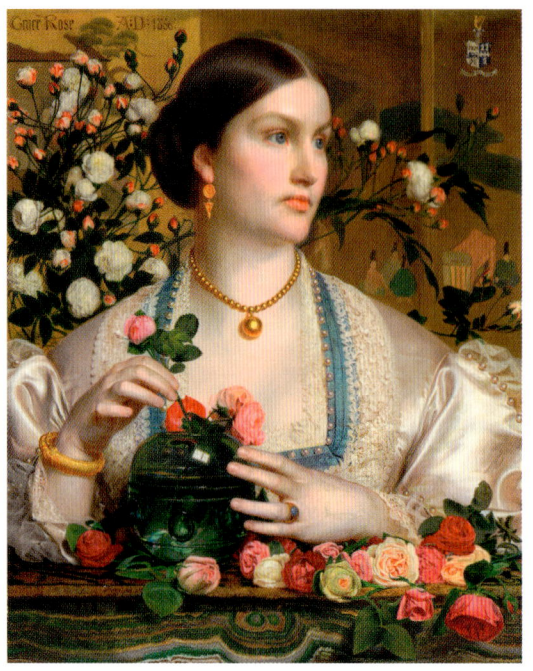

1

2

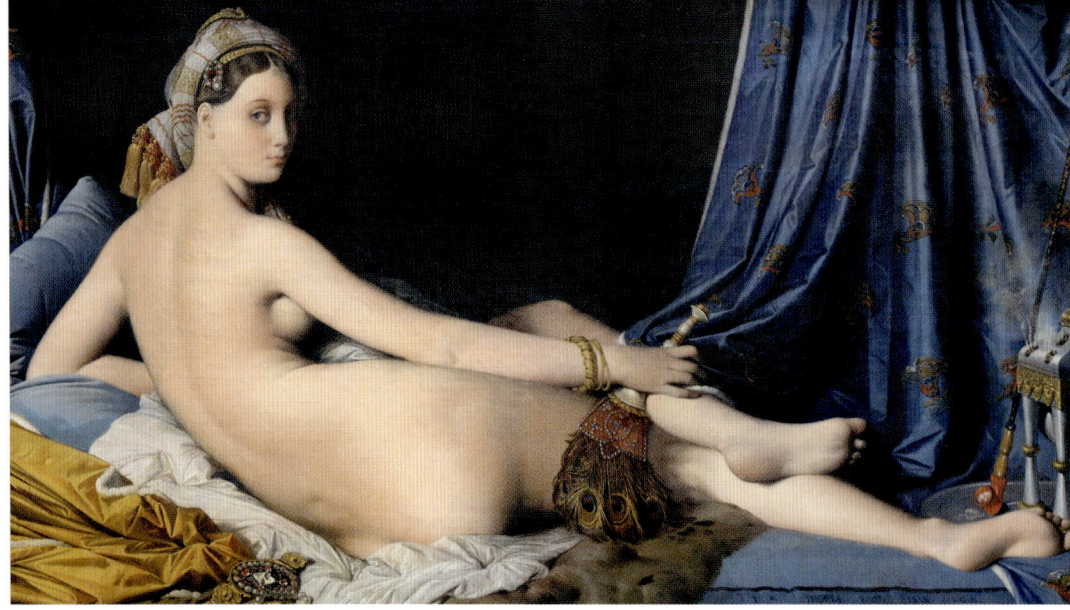

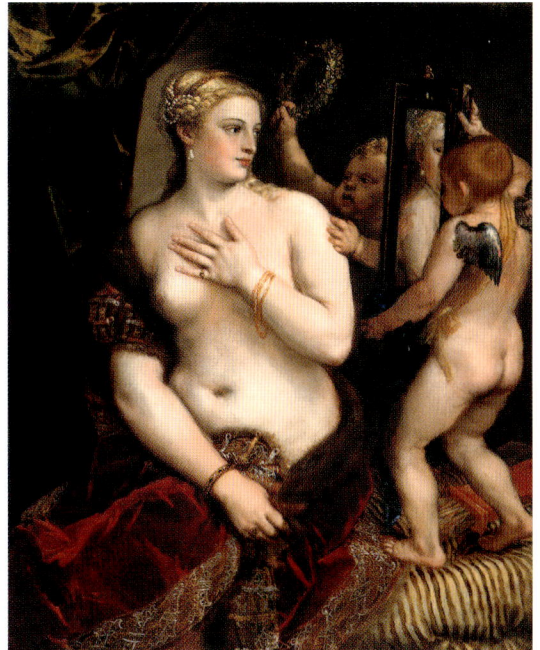

3

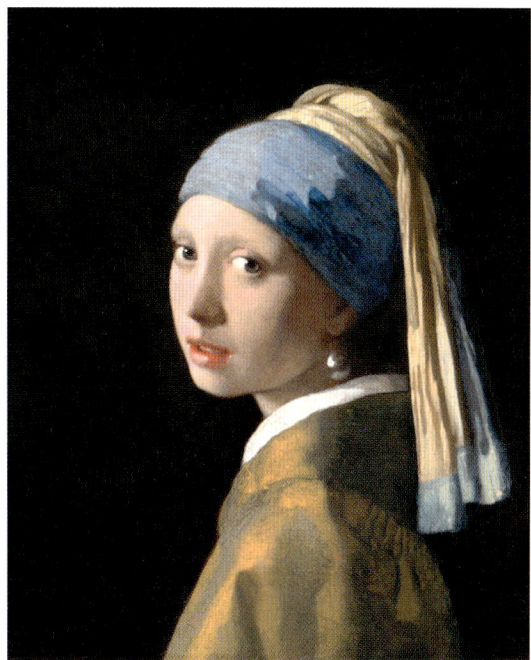

4

5

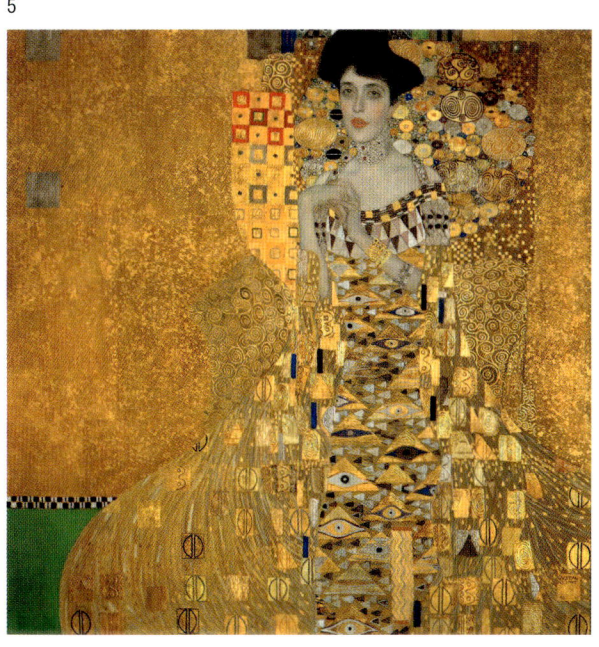

1. *Grace Rose,* Frederick Sandys, 1866
2. *The Grande Odalisque,* Jean-Auguste-Dominique Ingres, 1814
3. *Venus with a Mirror,* Titian, c. 1555
4. *Girl with a Pearl Earring,* Johannes Vermeer, c. 1665
5. *Portrait of Adele Bloch-Bauer I,* Gustav Klimt, 1907

Umbrella

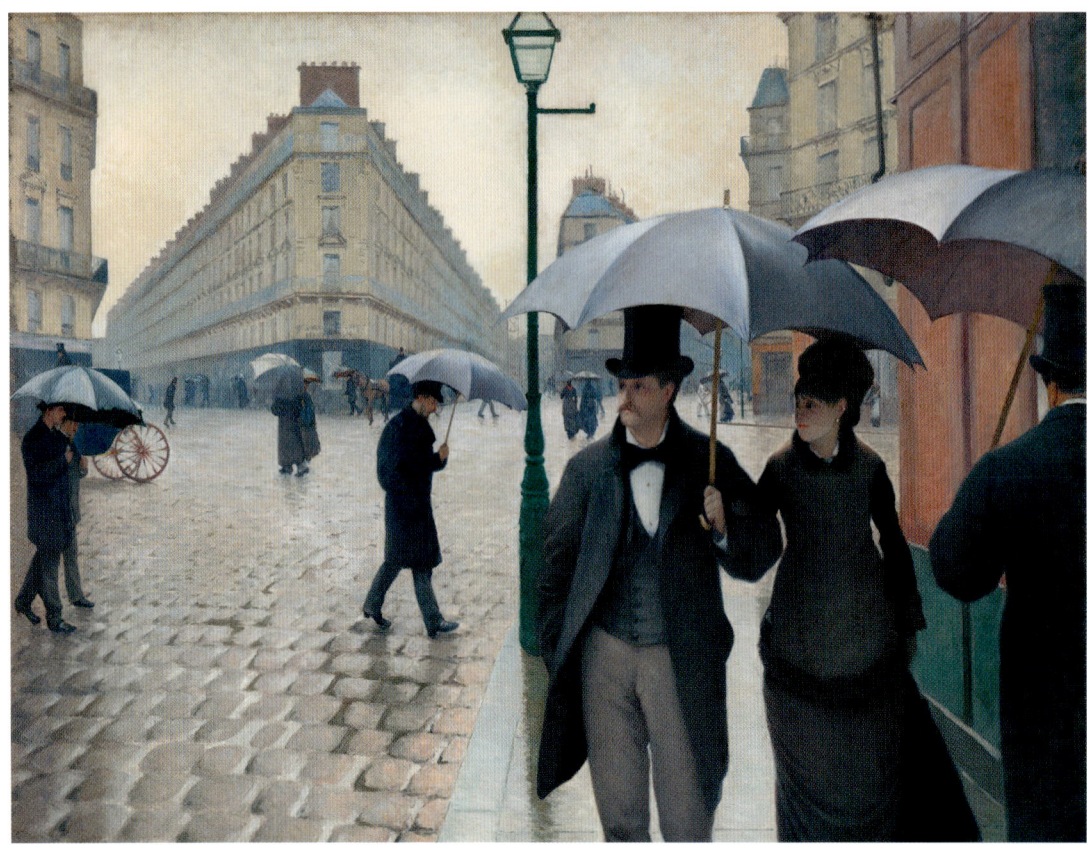

1

Appearing in art for millennia, umbrellas and parasols have often symbolized power, protection or the divine. In ancient Egypt, some reliefs and wall paintings depict attendants protecting pharaohs with parasols, conveying eminence and reverence. Similarly, in classical Indian art, umbrellas (or *chatras*) are recognized symbols of divinity and kingship, often depicted over deities and Buddha figures as signs of spiritual sovereignty. In Chinese and Japanese art, umbrellas carry multiple meanings. They may symbolize rank in ceremonial processions or evoke romantic or transient moods. For example, the umbrella in *Lovers Walking in the Snow* (1764–72) by Suzuki Harunobu (c. 1725–70) suggests intimacy and a fleeting moment in time. In Western art, umbrellas were depicted during the late nineteenth century by artists such as Pierre-Auguste Renoir, Édouard Manet and Gustave Caillebotte (1848–94) to convey aspects of modern urban life. Even in the twenty-first century, Banksy used the umbrella as a symbol of false security, ironically harming rather than protecting the girl, as he commented on misplaced trust and modern disillusionment.

1. *Paris Street; Rainy Day*, Gustave Caillebotte, 1877
2. *The Umbrellas,* Pierre-Auguste Renoir, 1881-86
3. *Under the Parasol*, Édouard Manet, 1881
4. *Umbrella Girl*, Banksy, 2008
5. *Lovers Walking in the Snow*, Suzuki Harunobu, c. 1764-72

2

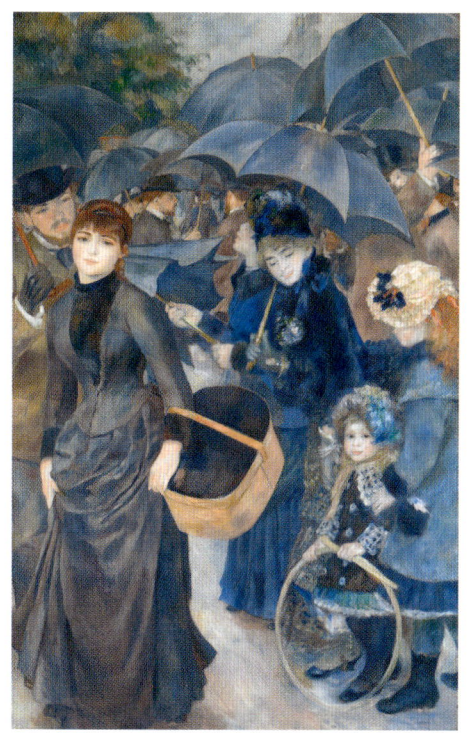

3

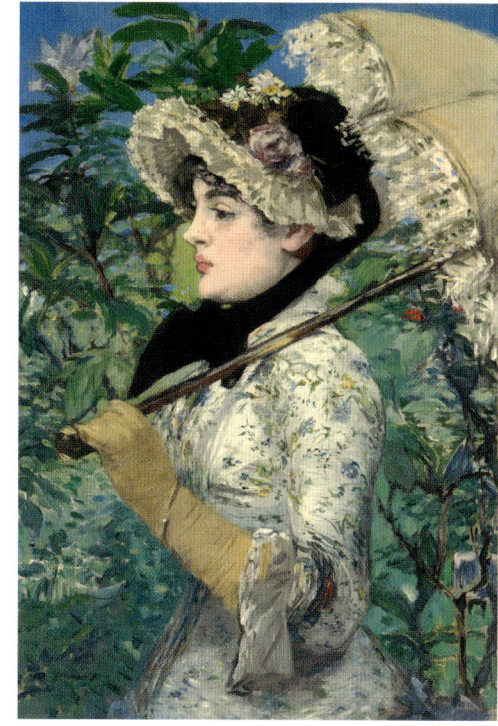

4

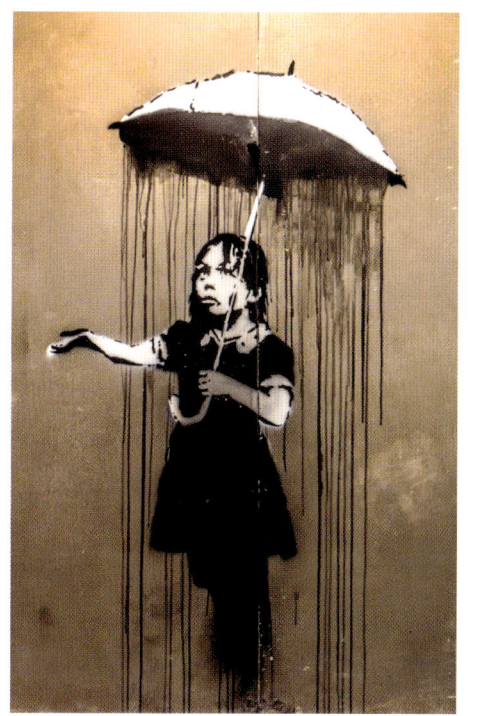

5

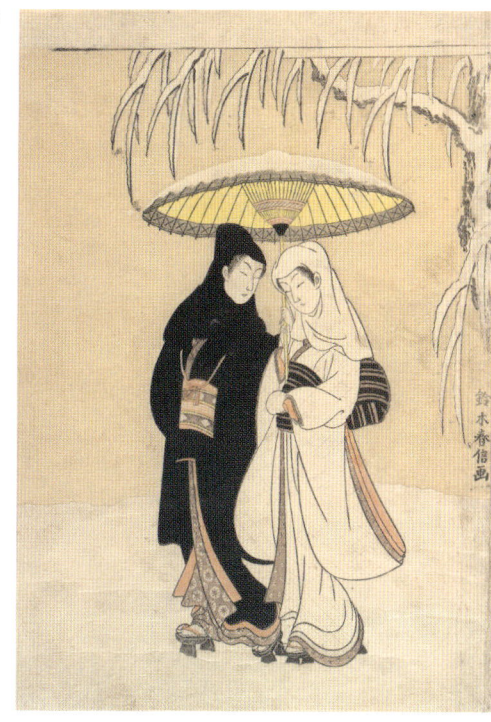

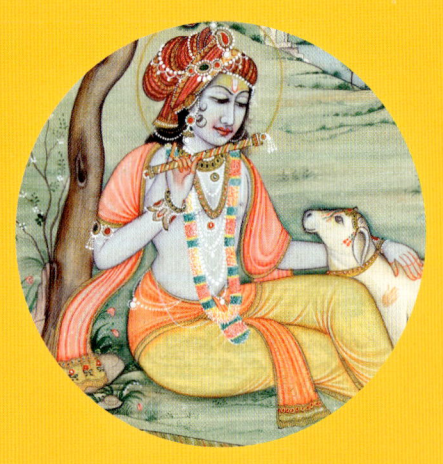

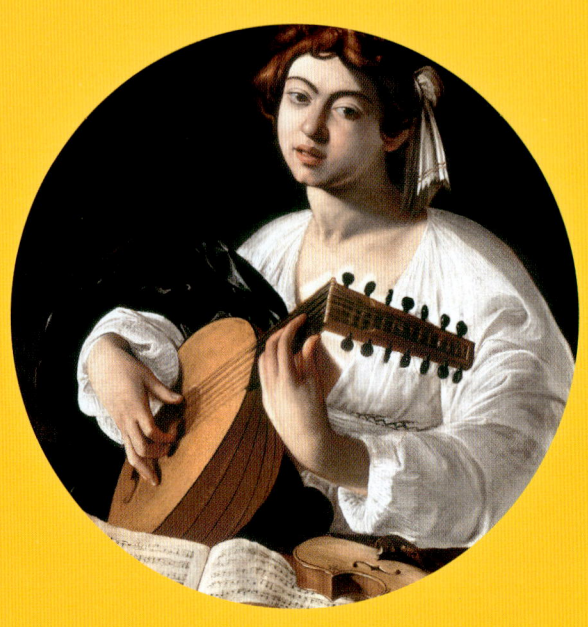

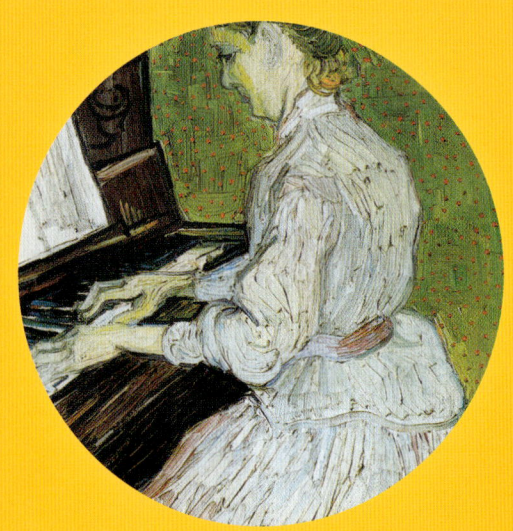

Music

Trumpet

Resonating through art history as harbingers of divine power, authority and revelation, trumpets have frequently signified the Apocalypse or divine judgement, such as in *The Judgement Day* (1939) by Aaron Douglas (1899-1979). In ancient Egypt, trumpets appeared among the treasures of Tutankhamun, where they were believed to summon divine attention or accompany the soul to the afterlife. Echoing the Book of Revelation, where seven trumpets sound divine catastrophes, Albrecht Dürer's *The Four Horsemen of the Apocalypse* (1498) created a dramatic scene with celestial trumpeters initiating chaos. In Classical antiquity, trumpets symbolized military might; depictions on Roman triumphal arches celebrate victories with trumpeters accompanying returning generals. In Baroque allegorical paintings, trumpets are often held by winged figures as emblems of fame or eternal glory. In each context, the trumpet is more than an instrument; it signals a transition: from life to death, from silence to proclamation, from worldly to divine.

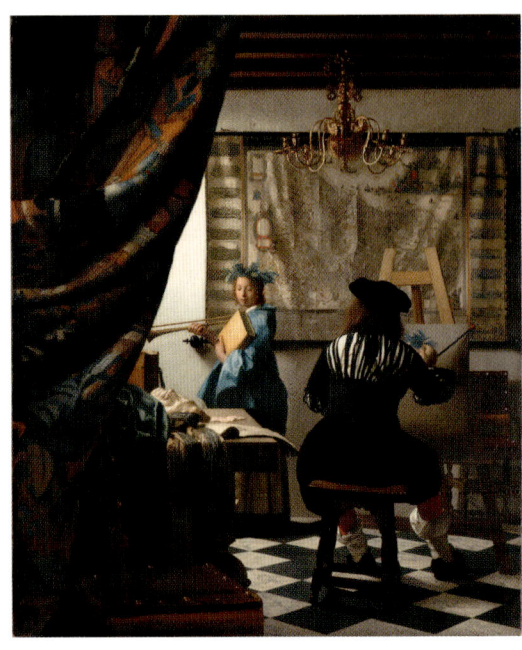

1

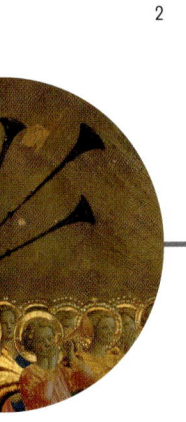

2

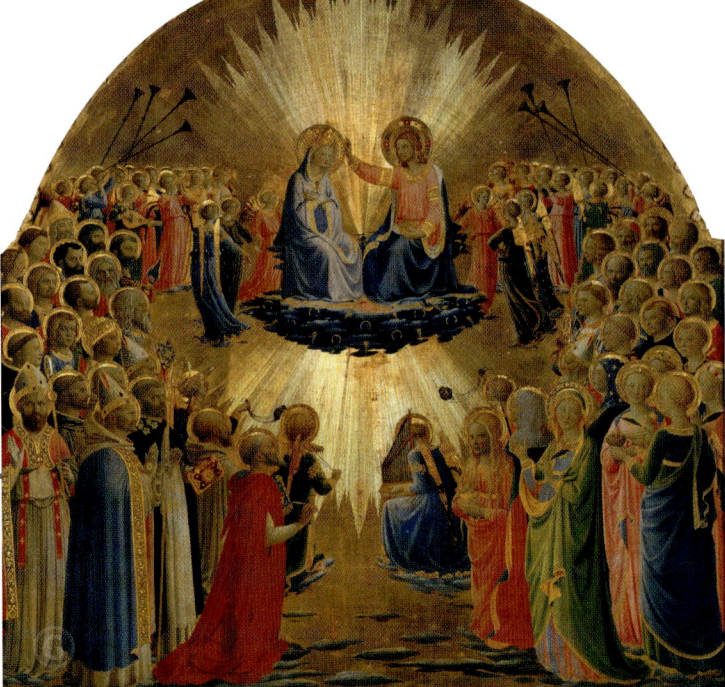

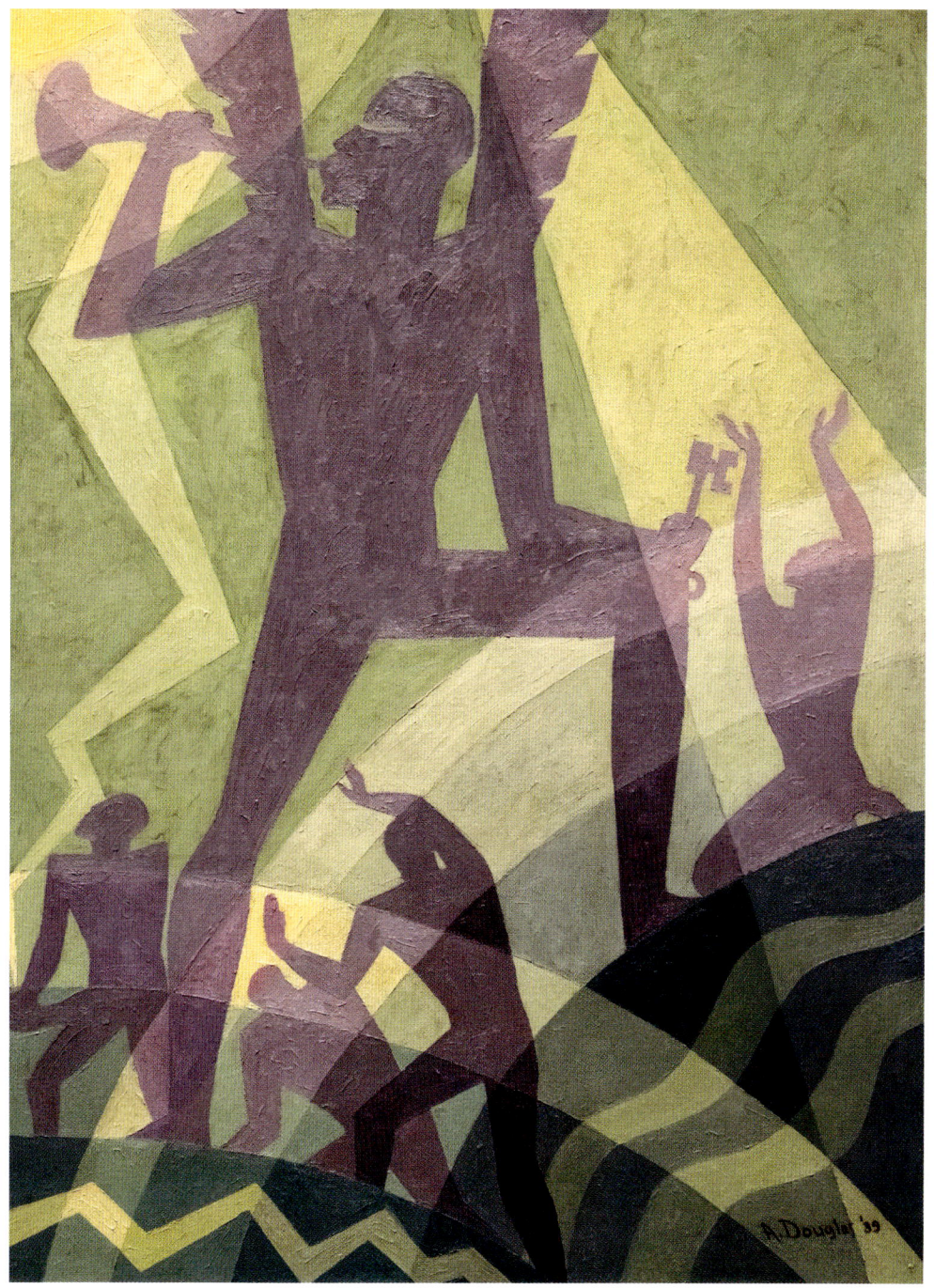

1. *The Art of Painting,* Johannes Vermeer, c. 1662-68
2. *The Glorification of the Virgin,* Fra Angelico, 1434-35
3. *The Judgement Day,* Aaron Douglas, 1939

Lute

Whether in sacred, romantic or educational contexts, the lute's presence in art conveys the human desire to connect through music. With its gentle, evocative tone, the lute has long symbolized emotional complexity, from romantic desire to intellectual refinement. The similar Chinese *pipa* has been associated with feminine refinement and often appeared in Tang dynasty murals, where heavenly beings or elegant courtesans frequently played it. In Persian miniature painting, the lute (or *barbat*) serves as a conduit of love and mysticism, often played by lovers in intimate gardens. In Dutch sixteenth- to seventeenth-century painting, the lute frequently appears in courtship scenes or allegories of harmony, such as Vermeer's *Young Woman with a Lute* (c. 1662–63), which symbolizes longing and inner harmony, suggesting the woman's yearning for love or spiritual connection beyond her domestic confines. *The Lute Player* (c. 1596) by Caravaggio (1571–1610) conveys sensuality, the harmony between music and desire, and the fleeting nature of pleasure and youth. In many traditions, the lute's curved body and delicate strings have served as visual metaphors for femininity, fragility and human emotion.

1

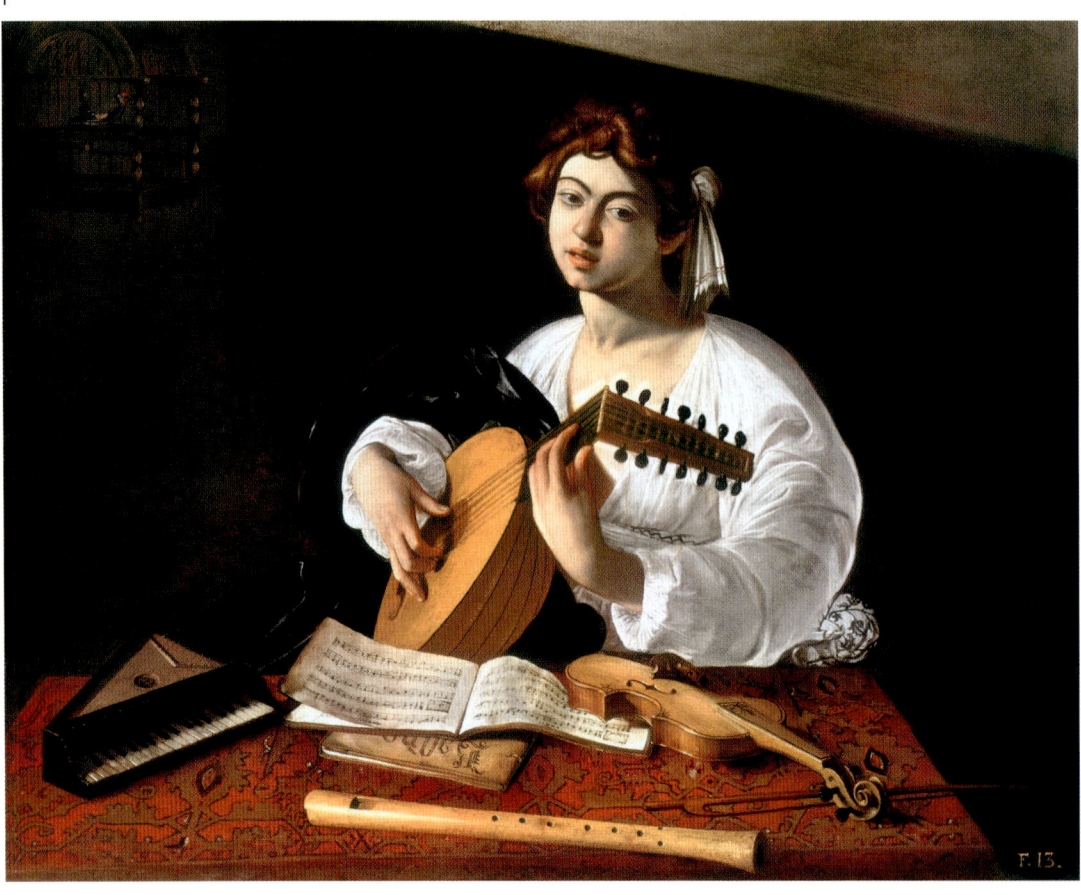

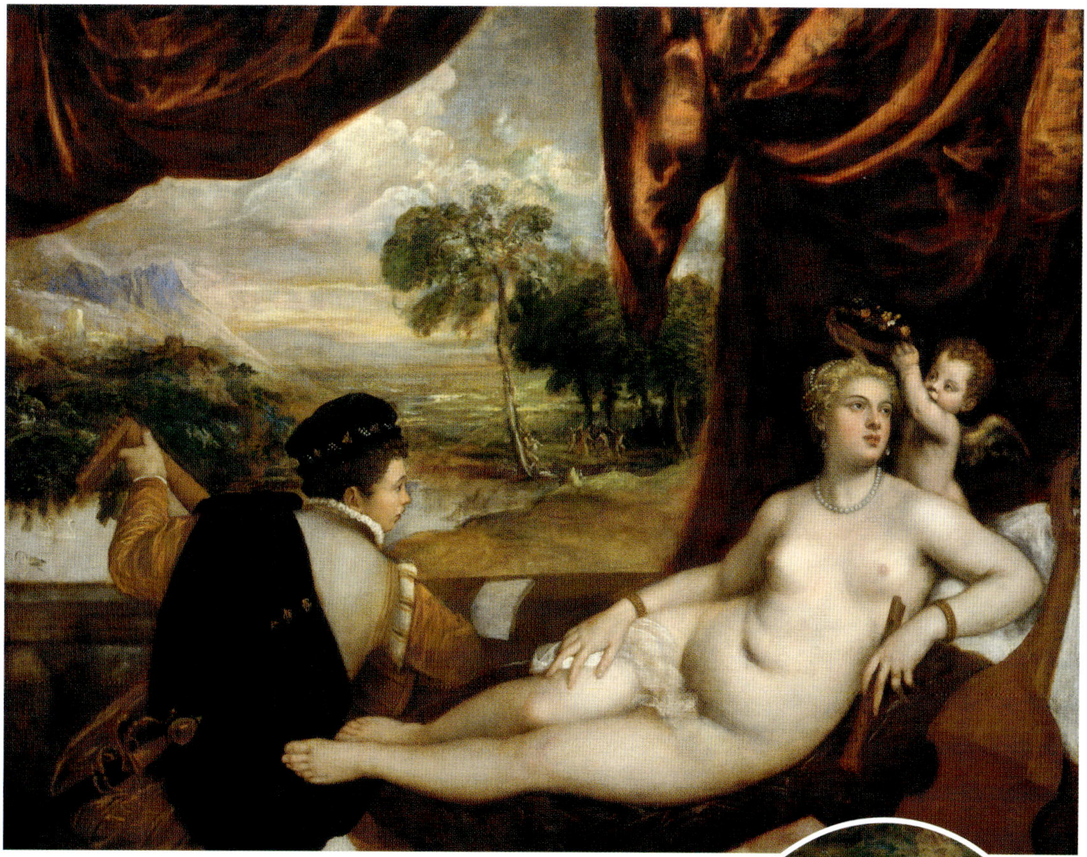

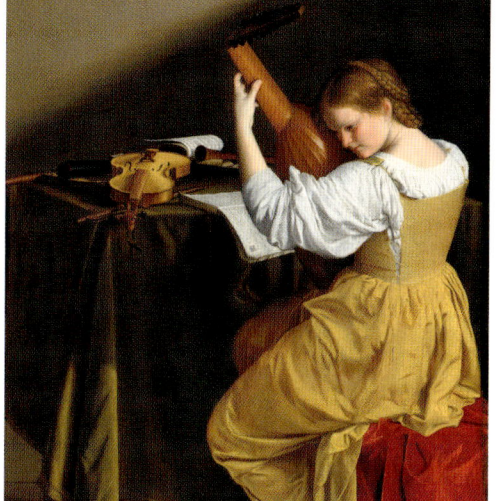

1. *The Lute Player*, Caravaggio, c. 1596
2. *Venus and the Lute Player*, Titian, c. 1565-70
3. *The Lute Player*, Orazio Gentileschi, c. 1612-20

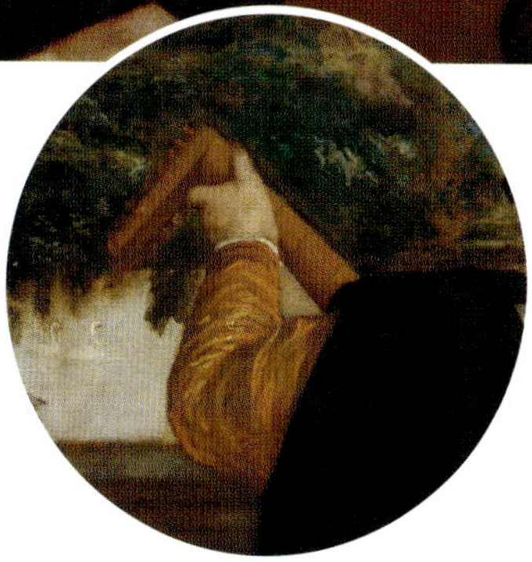

Flute

Spirituality, the divine, emotional expression, life force, longing and the unseen are just a few of the secondary meanings that have been attributed to the flute in art. In Hinduism, it is linked to Lord Krishna, whose playing symbolizes divine love and the call of the soul towards transcendence. In Indigenous American traditions, the flute is a sacred instrument used in healing ceremonies and courtship, denoting a connection to nature and the spirit world. In Western art, especially during the Baroque and Rococo periods, flutes often appear in pastoral and genre scenes to evoke innocence, sensuality or idyllic harmony. A large number of seventeenth-century Netherlandish paintings featured the theme of music, with the flute being one of the most popular instruments. Music was an integral part of daily life and one of the main ways to brighten up leisure time, as epitomized in *Concert* (1626) by Hendrick ter Brugghen (1588–1629).

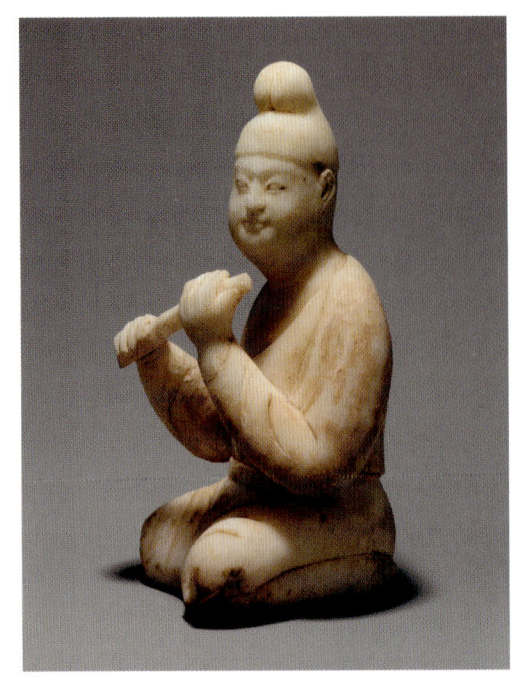

1

2

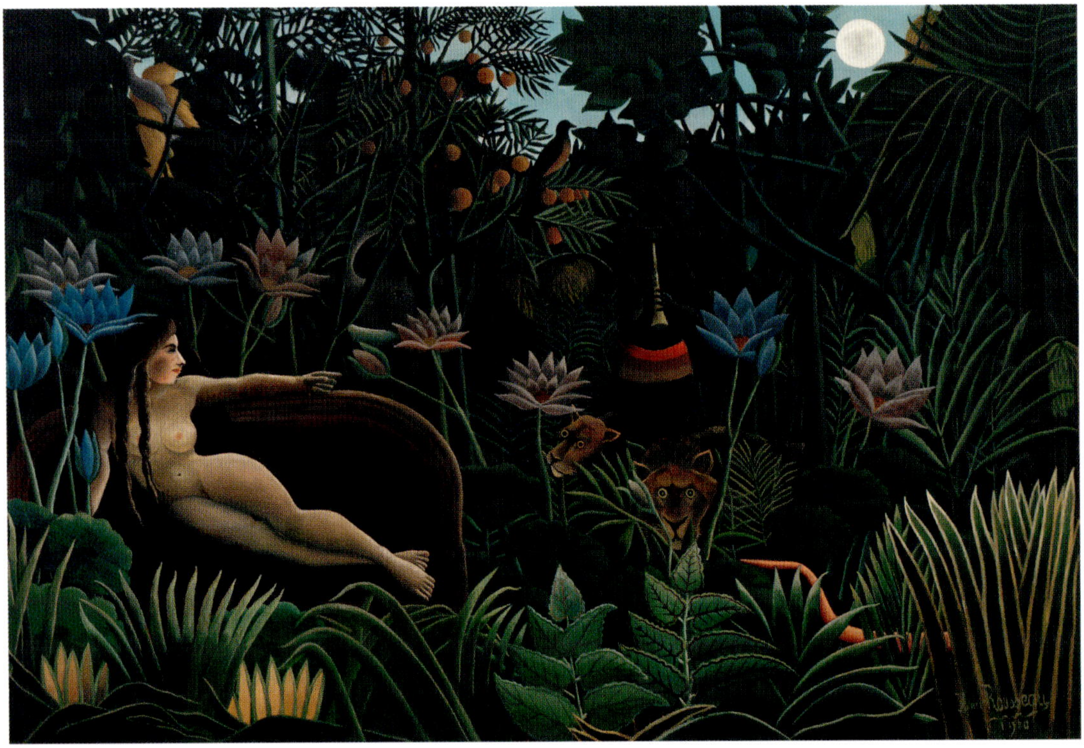

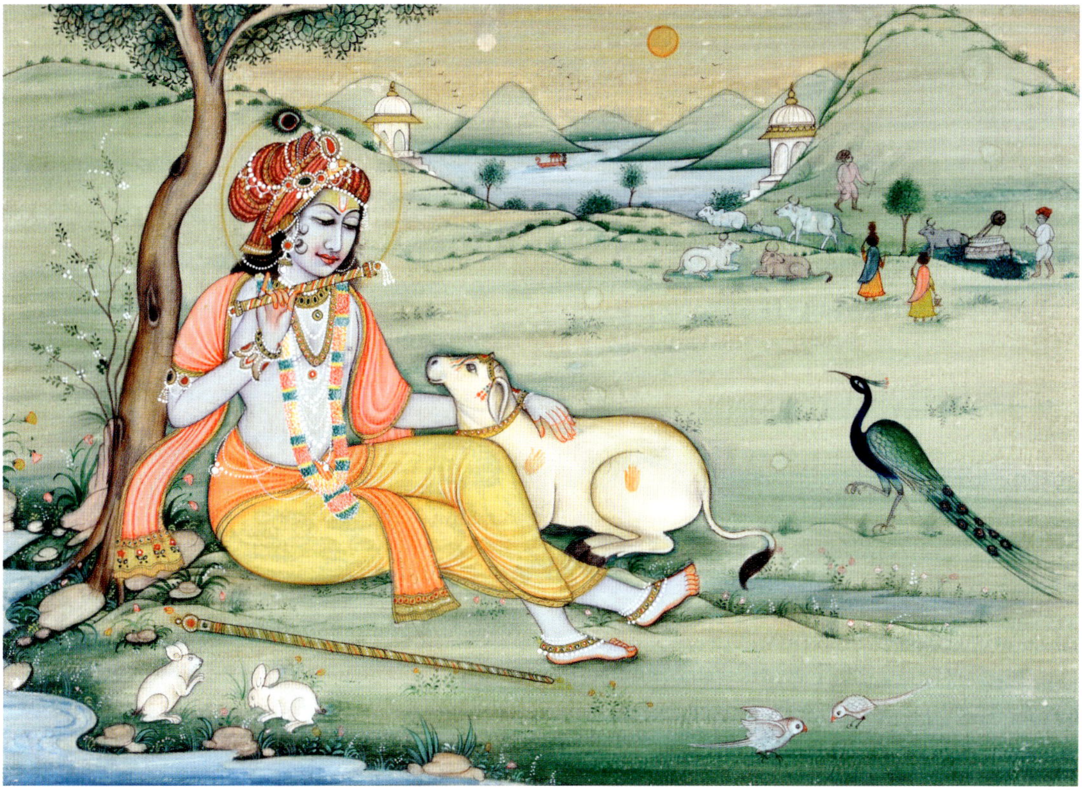

3

4

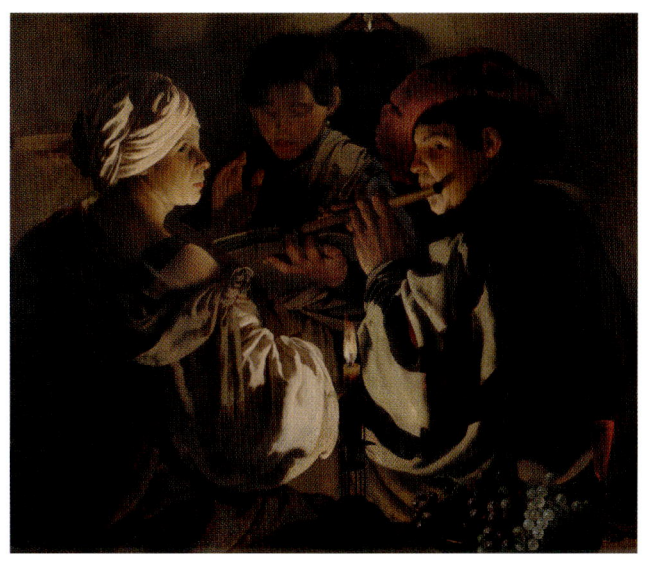

1. *Flute Player*, China, eighth century CE
2. *The Dream*, Henri Rousseau, 1910
3. *Krishna Playing the Flute*, various Indian artists,
   c. seventeenth–nineteenth centuries
4. *Concert*, Hendrick ter Brugghen, 1626

Piano

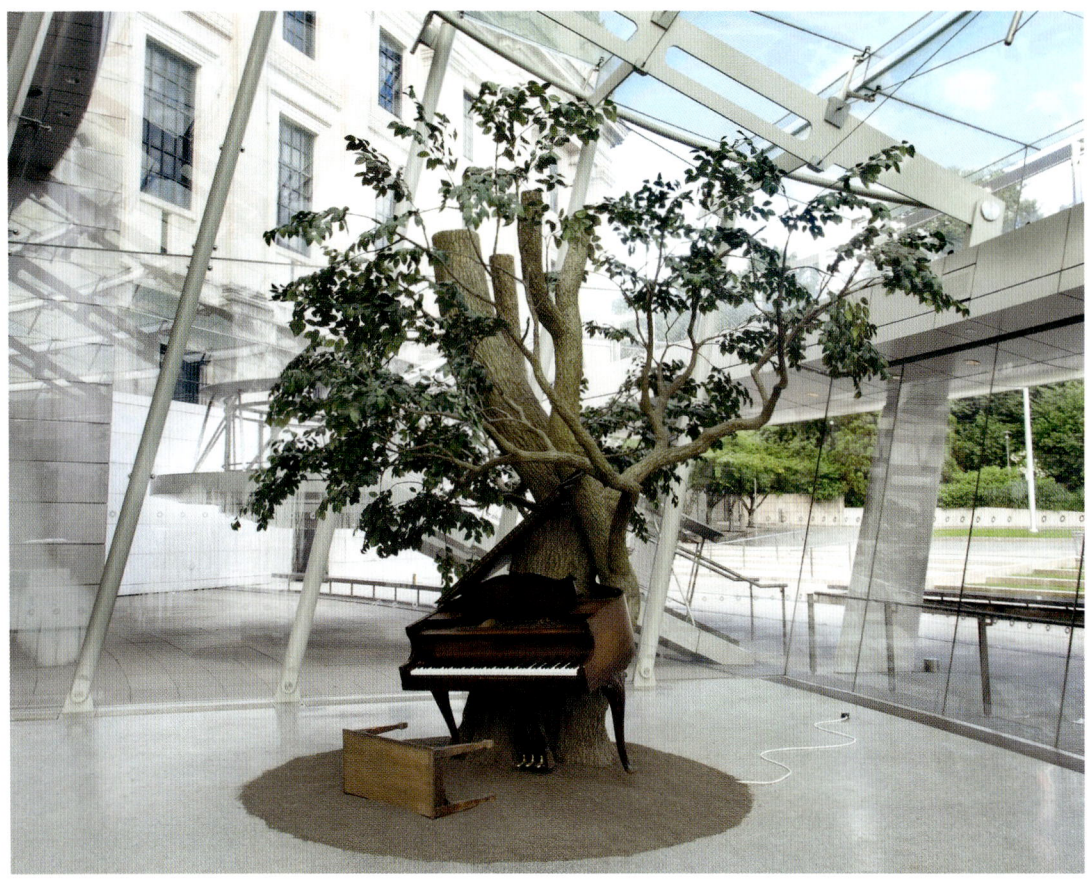

1

Since the eighteenth century, pianos in art have often symbolized emotional depth, social refinement, nostalgia, domestic intimacy and personal introspection. In late nineteenth-century paintings, such as those by Édouard Manet, Pierre-Auguste Renoir and Mary Cassatt), the piano often represents feminine education, bourgeois culture and domestic intimacy, such as in Renoir's *Young Girls at the Piano* (1892). In Vincent van Gogh's *Marguerite Gachet at the Piano* (1890), the instrument conveyed unspoken emotion and longing. *The Awakening Conscience* (1853) by William Holman Hunt depicts a young unmarried woman sitting on the lap of her married lover as they play the piano together. The lyrics of the song have pricked her conscience, and she realizes the error of her ways. In 2007, Sanford Biggers (b. 1970) produced *Blossom*, merging a piano with a tree to convey cultural memory, resilience and rebirth. Johannes Vermeer, who often included musical instruments in his paintings, suggested that music can bring both happiness and solace in his painting featuring a virginal, *The Music Lesson* (c. 1662-65).

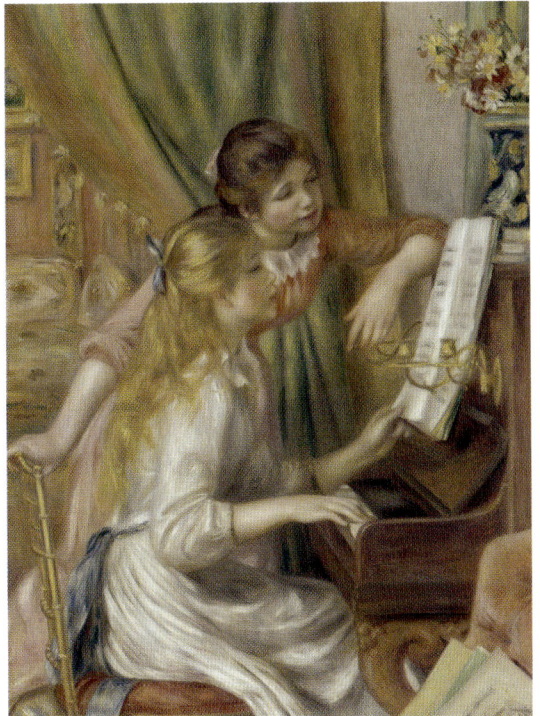

2

4

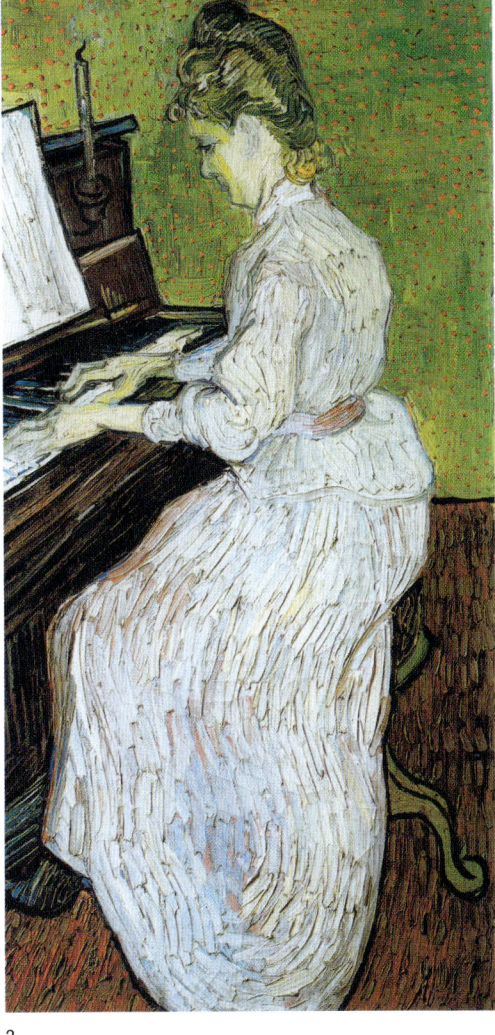

3

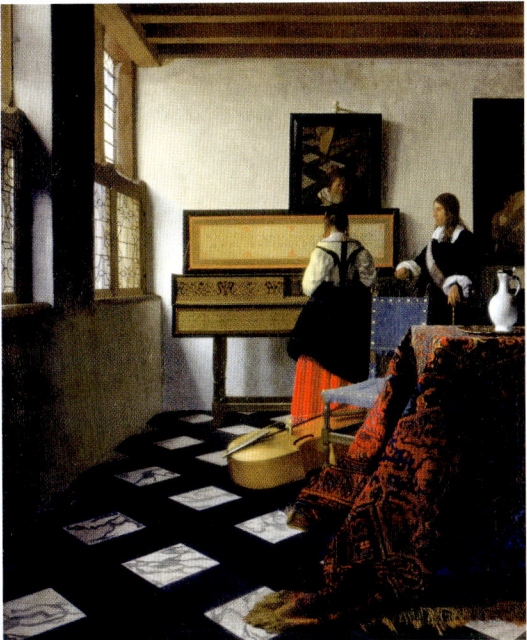

1. *Blossom* (installation), Sanford Biggers, 2007
2. *Young Girls at the Piano,* Pierre-Auguste Renoir, 1892
3. *Marguerite Gachet at the Piano,* Vincent van Gogh, 1890
4. *The Music Lesson,* Johannes Vermeer, c. 1662–65

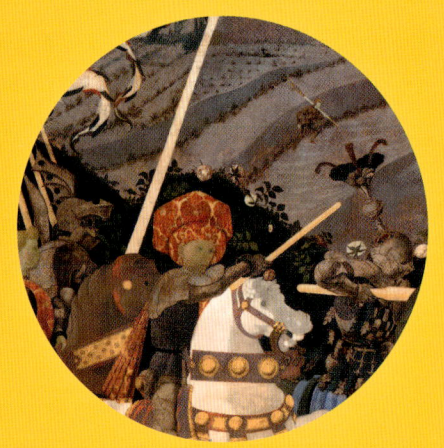

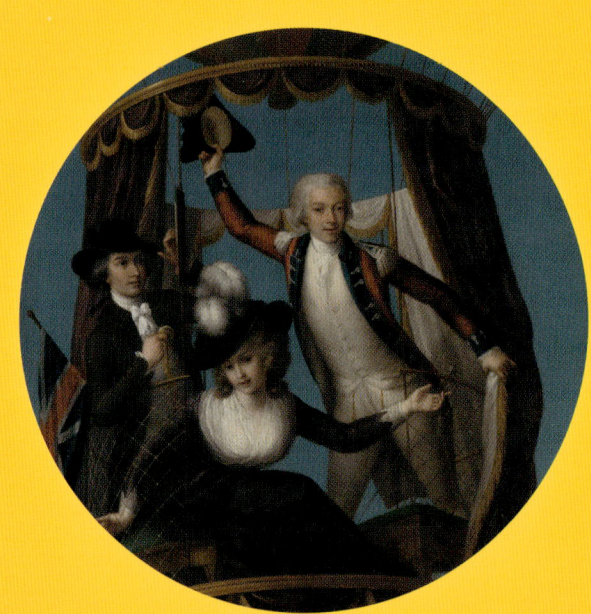

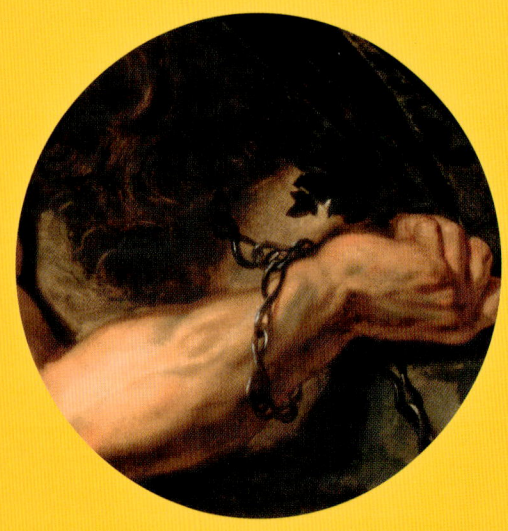

Objects

Weapons

Weapons in art have long served as potent symbols of power, honour, conflict and identity. In ancient civilizations, they often denoted divine authority or heroic virtue, as in Greek vase paintings, where spears and shields accompany gods and warriors, and in Egyptian tomb art, where daggers and bows indicate protection in the afterlife. In medieval and Renaissance Europe, swords and armour, such as the gleaming lances and swords in *The Battle of San Romano* (c. 1435-40) by Paolo Uccello (1397-1475), convey chivalric order and human ambition, turning warfare into a display of perspective, geometry, and the pursuit of heroic idealism. Japanese samurai portraits reflect the 'Bushidō code', in which the sword embodies spiritual discipline and social status. Weapons also appear as divine justice and moral triumph. For example, *The Archangel Michael Defeating Satan* (1635) by Guido Reni (1575-1642) embodies the victory of heavenly virtue over sin and darkness. In 1937, Pablo Picasso painted a broken sword in *Guernica*, as a symbol of human suffering and an anti-war protest. Weapons have also been depicted to signify protection, justice, betrayal, violence, virtue and cultural identity.

1

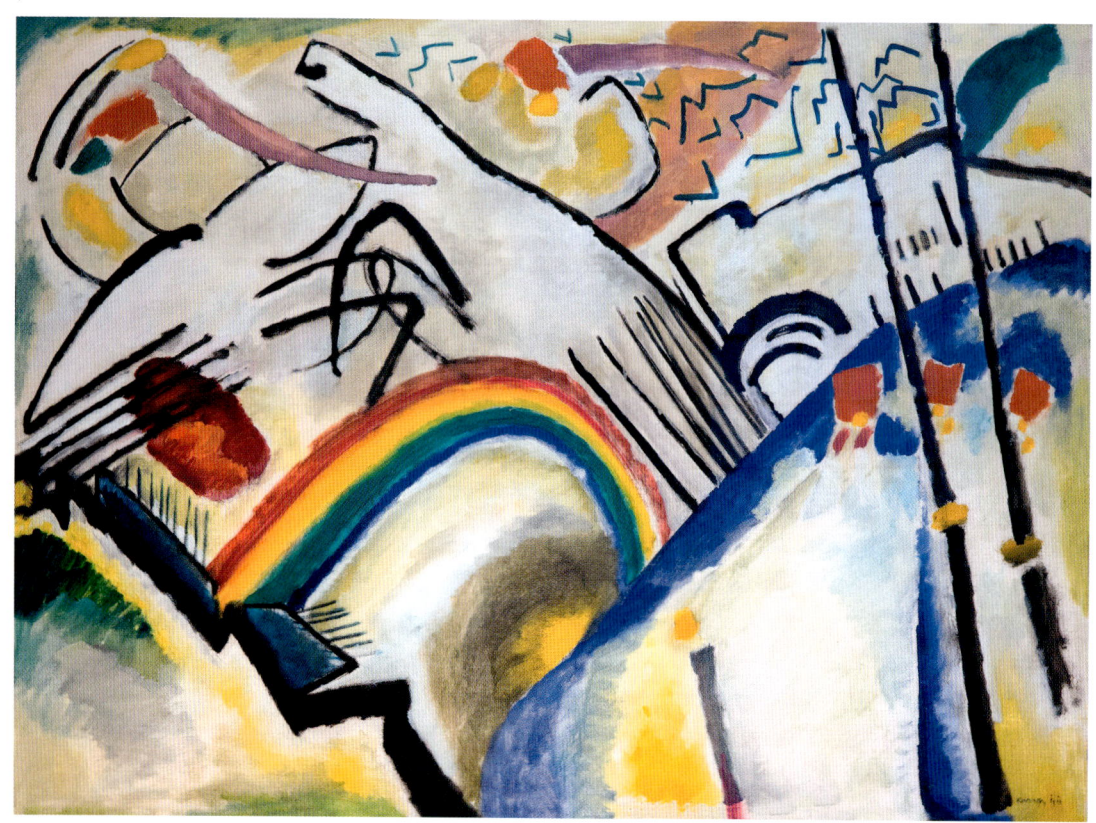

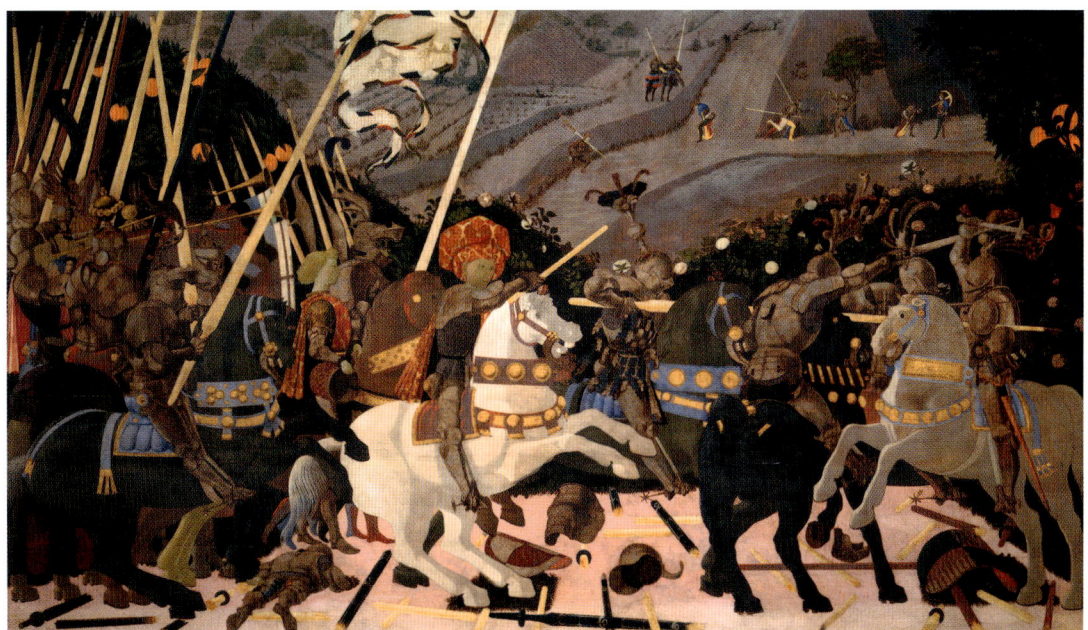

2

3

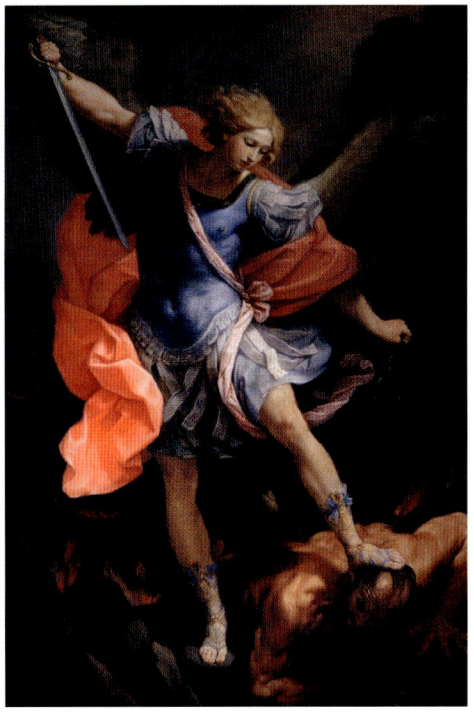

4

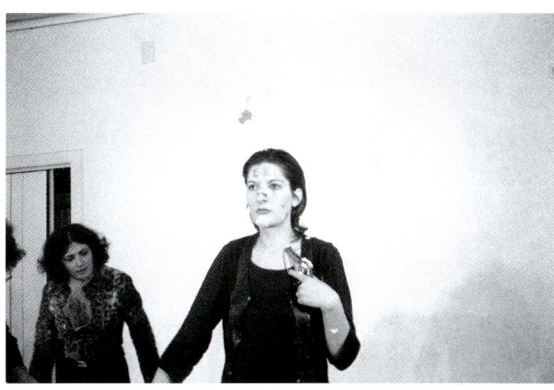

1. *Cossacks,* Wassily Kandinsky, 1911
2. *The Battle of San Romano,* Paolo Uccello, c. 1435-40
3. *The Archangel Michael Defeating Satan,* Guido Reni, 1635
4. *Rhythm 0,* Marina Abramović, 1974

Chains

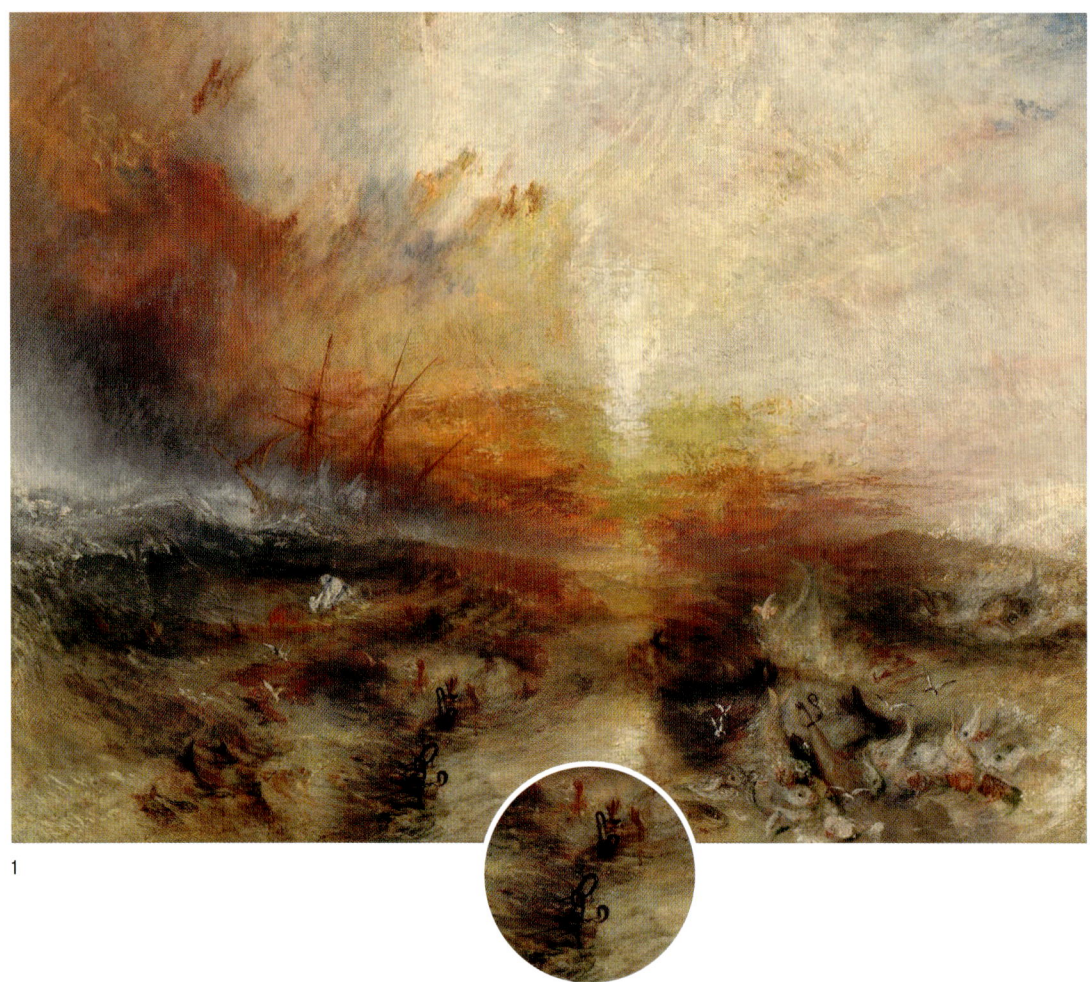

1

Confinement and struggle are the main reasons for chains being depicted in art, and they have often also conveyed oppression, bondage and connections. In ancient Egypt and Greece, chains were shown restraining prisoners or slaves. In Greek mythology, Prometheus was famously chained as punishment, and paintings depicting this story symbolize both suffering and defiance. Chains can represent the bondage of sin or the trials of saints, such as the Apostle Paul, who was imprisoned for his faith. During the revolutions in France, Russia and America, broken chains became iconic symbols of liberation and resistance. The representation of chains has evolved. While intact chains may still signify oppression or limitation, broken chains often denote freedom, resilience and transformation. Some communist art features chains to represent solidarity, with each link serving as a metaphor for collective strength. Overall, chains have appeared in visual culture as metaphors for the human condition, capturing the tension between captivity and liberation, isolation and unity, burden and strength.

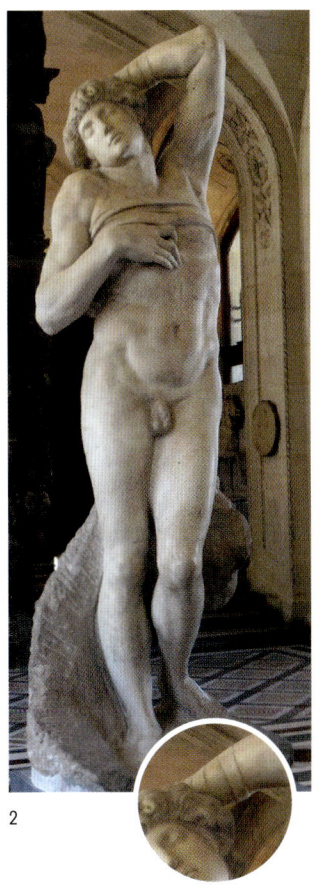

2

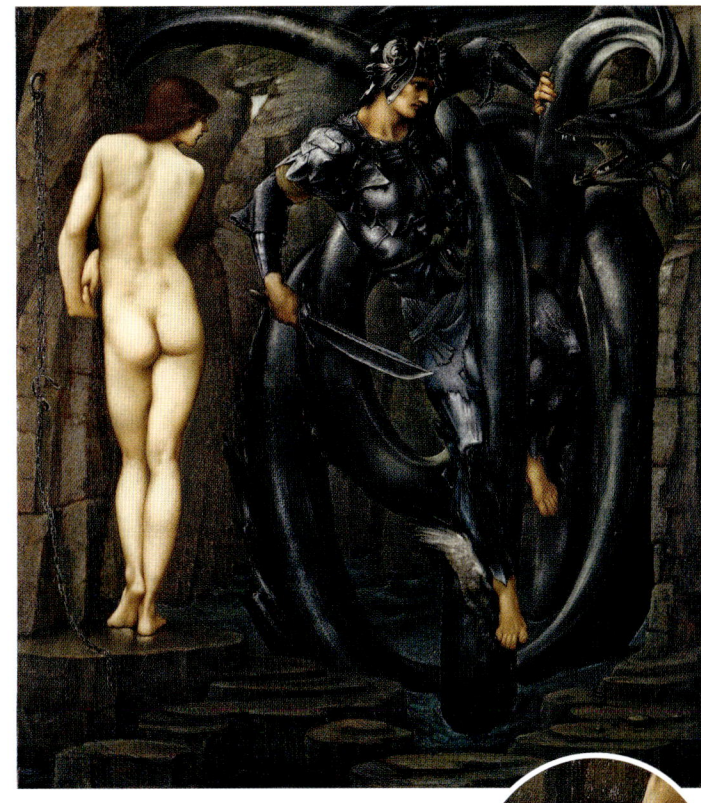

3

4

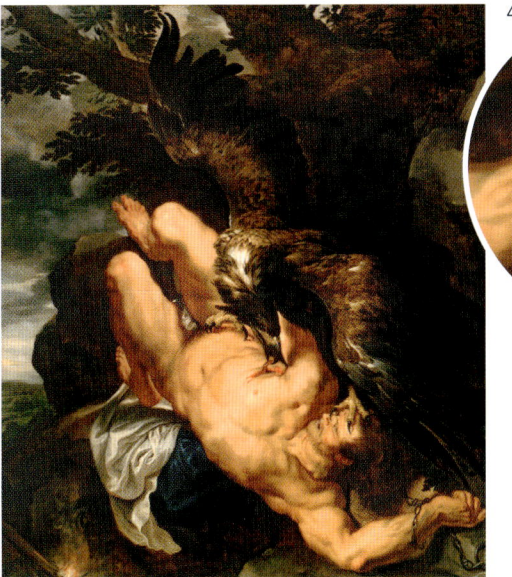

1. *The Slave Ship,* J.M.W. Turner, 1840
2. *The Slave,* Michelangelo, 1513-16
3. *The Doom Fulfilled,* Edward Burne-Jones, 1888
4. *Prometheus Bound,* Peter Paul Rubens, c. 1611-12

Cross

One of the most enduring and multifaceted symbols in global art, the cross has embodied themes of sacrifice, divinity, balance and cosmic order. Long before its Christian associations, the cross shape appeared in prehistoric carvings and ancient Egyptian art, such as the ankh, which symbolizes life and immortality. In Mesopotamian and Celtic cultures, the cross represented the four cardinal directions and the union of earth and sky. Variations such as the Latin cross, Greek cross and Celtic cross each carried distinct theological and cultural meanings. In Christianity, the cross became the central icon of faith, redemption and divine love. In works such as *Christ Crucified* (1632) by Diego Velázquez (1599-1660), it symbolized Christ's sacrifice and the promise of salvation. In modern and contemporary art, the cross has been reinterpreted, sometimes reverently, sometimes provocatively, as a symbol of identity, suffering or resistance. Artists like Andres Serrano (b. 1950) and Tracey Emin (b. 1963) have used it to explore themes of faith, trauma and personal history.

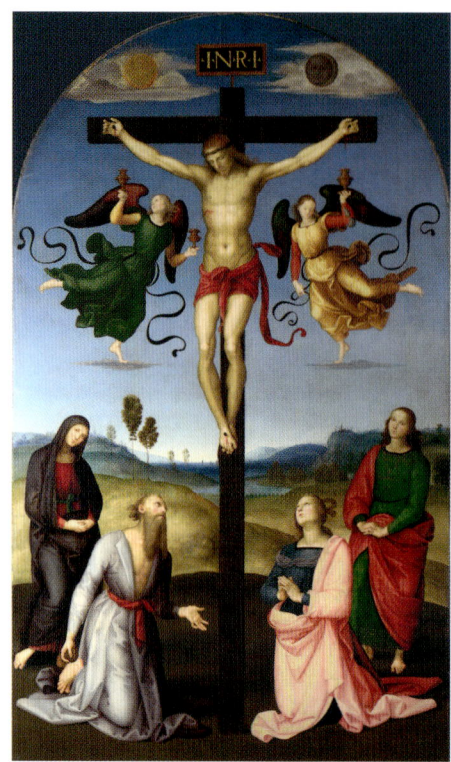

1

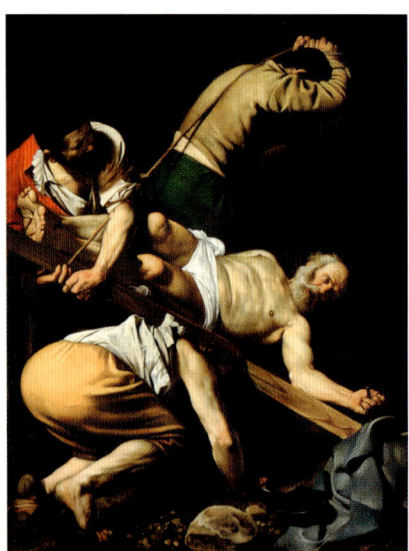

2

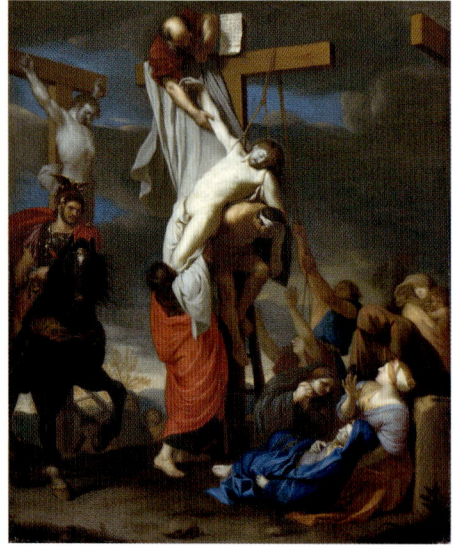

3

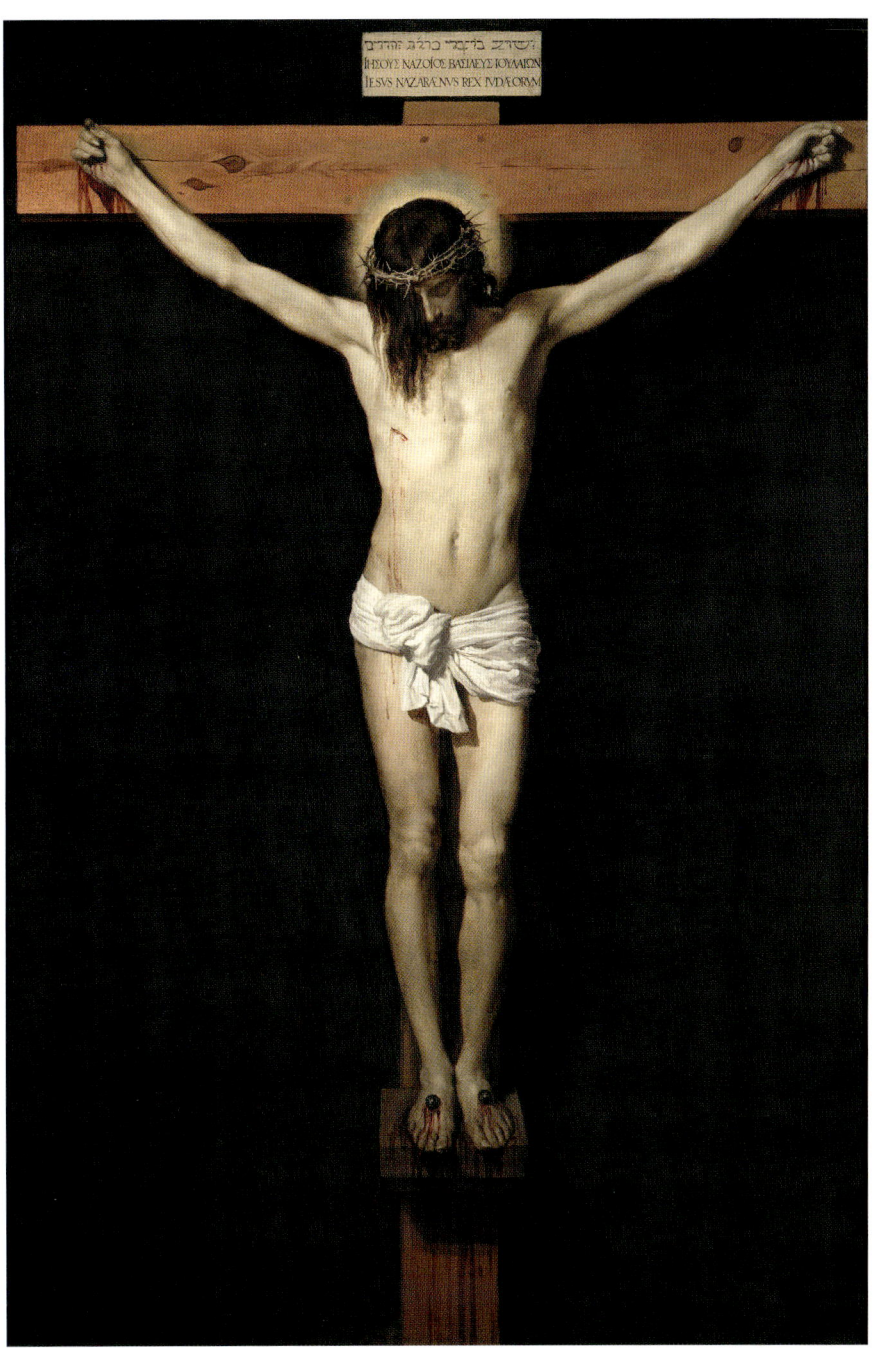

4

1. *Crucifixion (Città di Castello Altarpiece),* Raphael, 1502-03

2. *Crucifixion of Saint Peter,* Caravaggio, 1600

3. *The Deposition,* Charles Le Brun, c. 1647-48

4. *Christ Crucified,* Diego Velázquez, 1632

Balloon

Symbols of freedom, imagination and the ephemeral, balloons, although a relatively modern invention, have inspired artists across cultures to explore themes of transcendence and transience. In Western art, early depictions of hot air balloons in the eighteenth and nineteenth centuries celebrated human innovation and the spirit of exploration. *Ascent of a Montgolfier Balloon at Aranjuez* (c. 1784) by Antonio Carnicero (1748-1814), for example, presents human innovation, celebrating the spirit of discovery and the triumph of reason and progress during the Age of Enlightenment. Similarly embodying the Enlightenment ideal of exploration and human achievement, in 1785, John Francis Rigaud (1742-1810) painted *Captain Vincenzo*

Lunardi with his Assistant George Biggin and Letitia Anne Sage in a Balloon, implying ambition and the courage to transcend earthly boundaries. At other times, artists have featured balloons to suggest innocence, aspiration, society's complexity, hope and resilience. Contemporary art has often embraced balloons as playful, yet poignant symbols.

1. *Balloon Girl,* Banksy, 2002
2. *Ascent of a Montgolfier Balloon at Aranjuez,* Antonio Carnicero, c. 1784
3. *Captain Vincenzo Lunardi with His Assistant George Biggin and Letitia Anne Sage in a Balloon,* John Francis Rigaud, 1785
4. Detail from *A Bouquet of Love I Saw in the Universe,* Yayoi Kusama, 2021

1

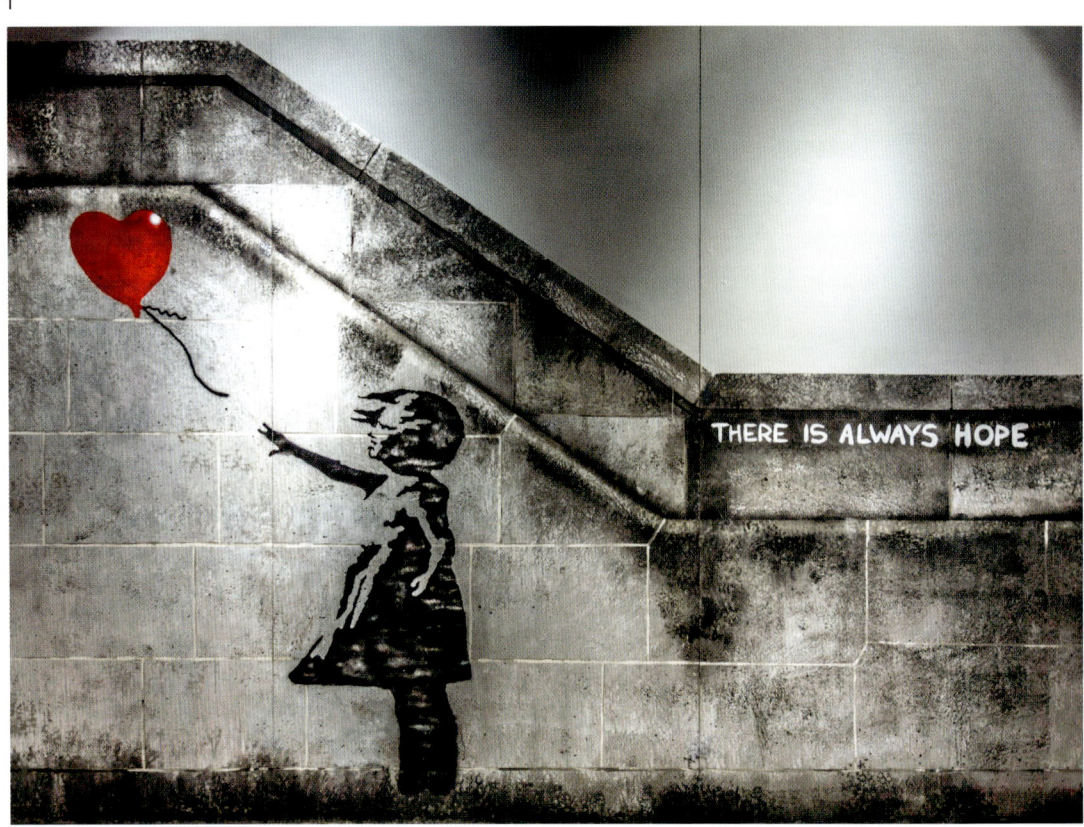

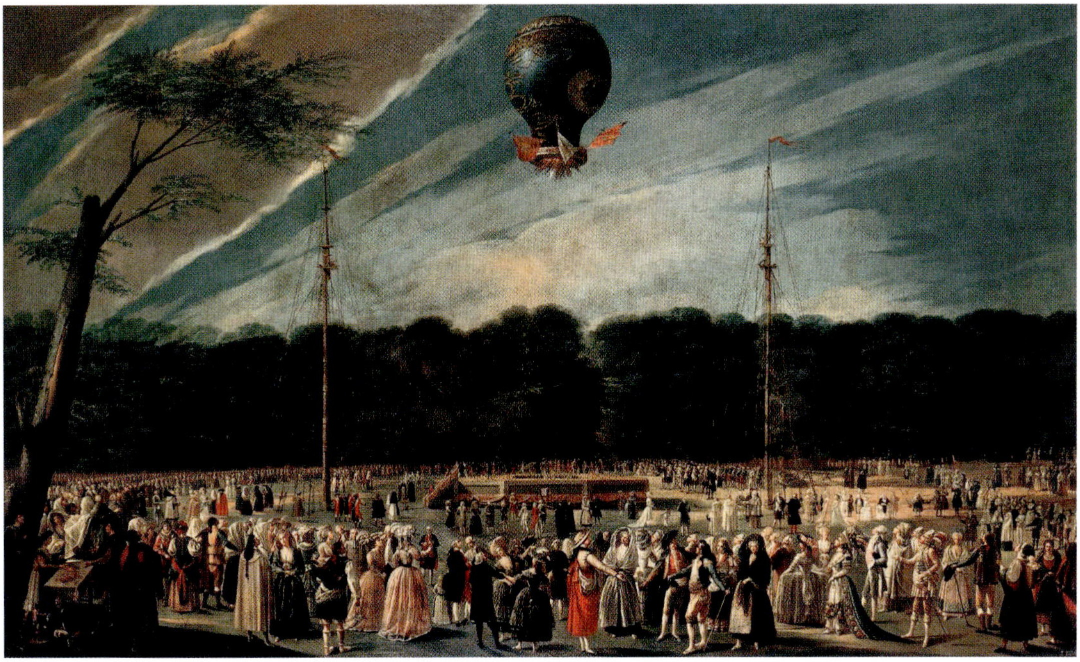

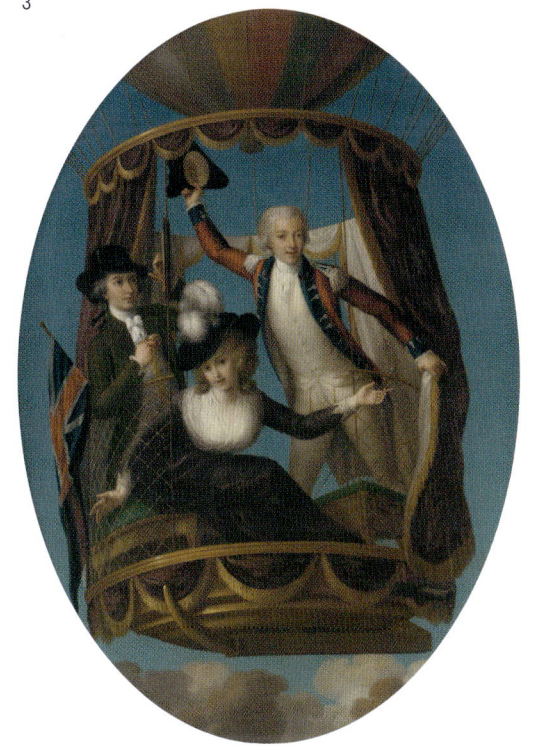

2

3

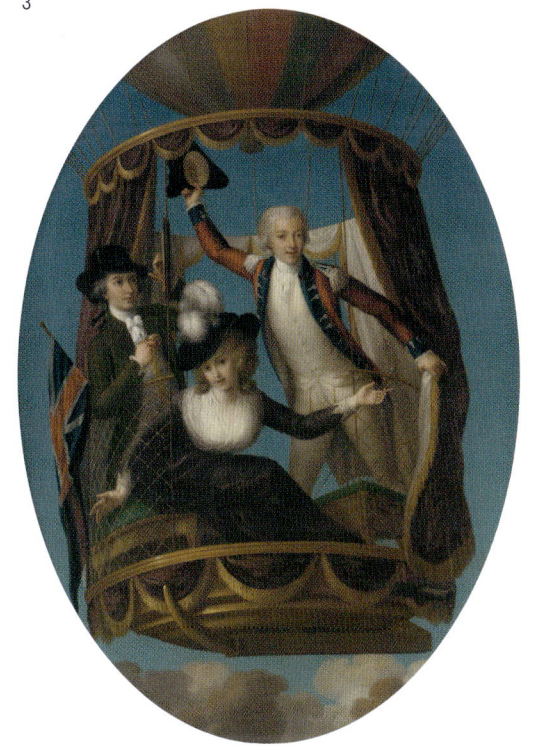

4

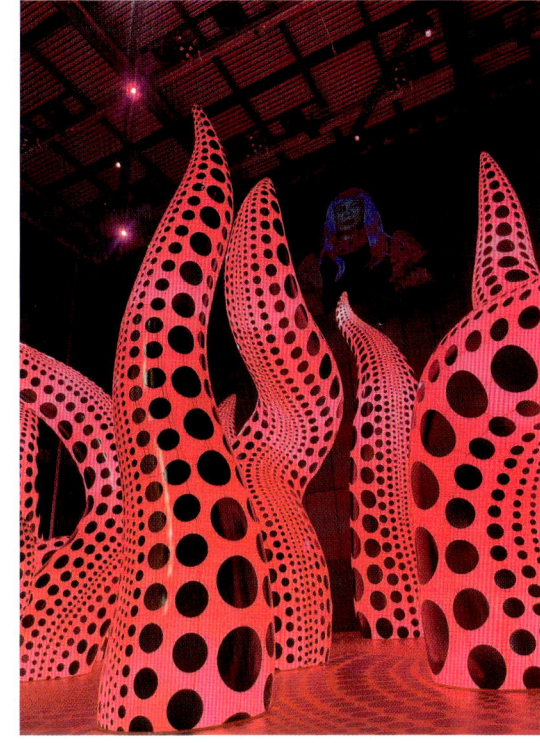

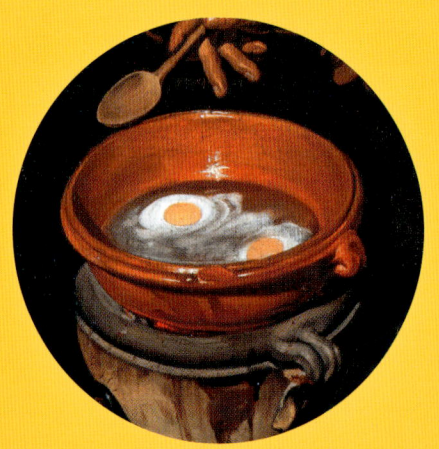

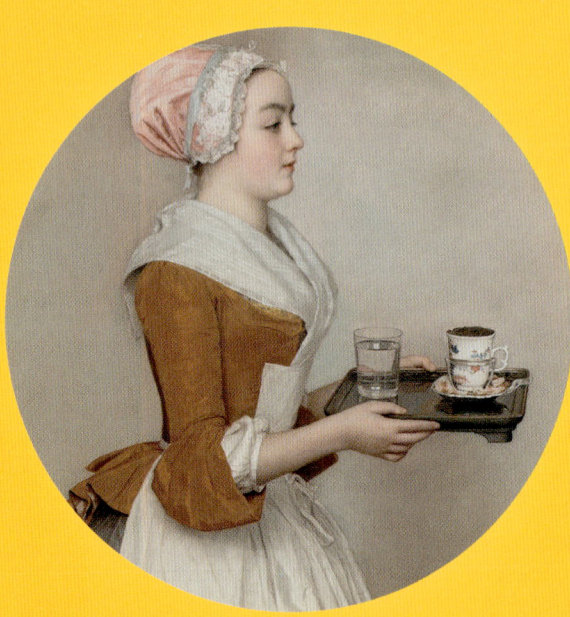

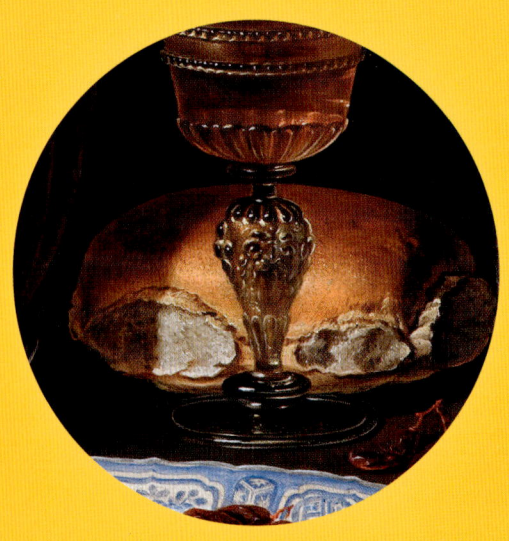

Food

Bread

As one of humanity's oldest staples, bread often appears in visual art not merely as food, but as a metaphor for life itself. Whether depicted as sacred or secular, it remains a powerful symbol of life's fragility, ritual, hospitality, community and sustenance. In ancient Egyptian tomb paintings, it was often depicted to ensure eternal nourishment. In Christian art, bread frequently appeared in depictions of the Last Supper, such as Leonardo da Vinci's fresco (c. 1495-98), where bread represents the body of Christ and symbolizes spiritual communion. Similarly, artists such as Pieter Claesz (1597-1661) used bread to signify humble abundance, mortality or divine grace. In modern art, bread has been used to represent themes of mortality, ritual and introspection, such as in Antony Gormley's *Bed* (1980-81), made from 8,640 slices of bread. Tatsumi Orimoto (1946-2025) created 'Bread Man' performances, using bread as a surreal mask, to explore identity, absurdity and social connections.

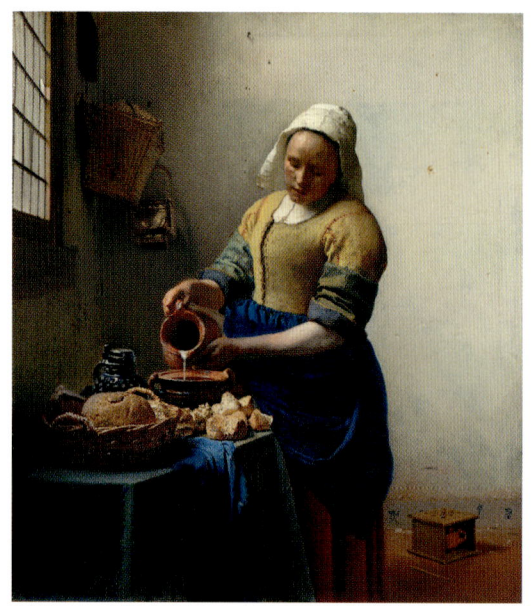

1

2

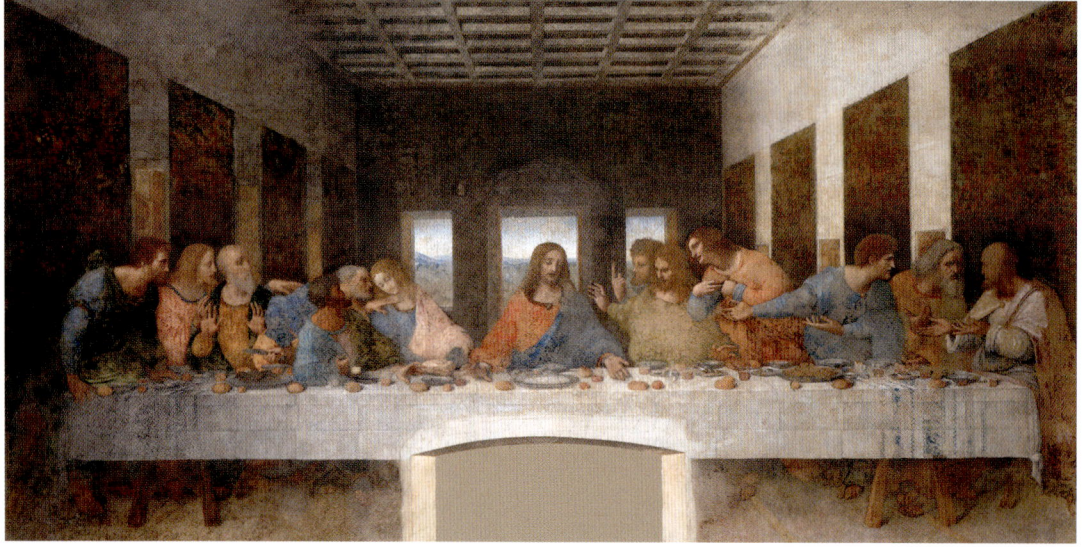

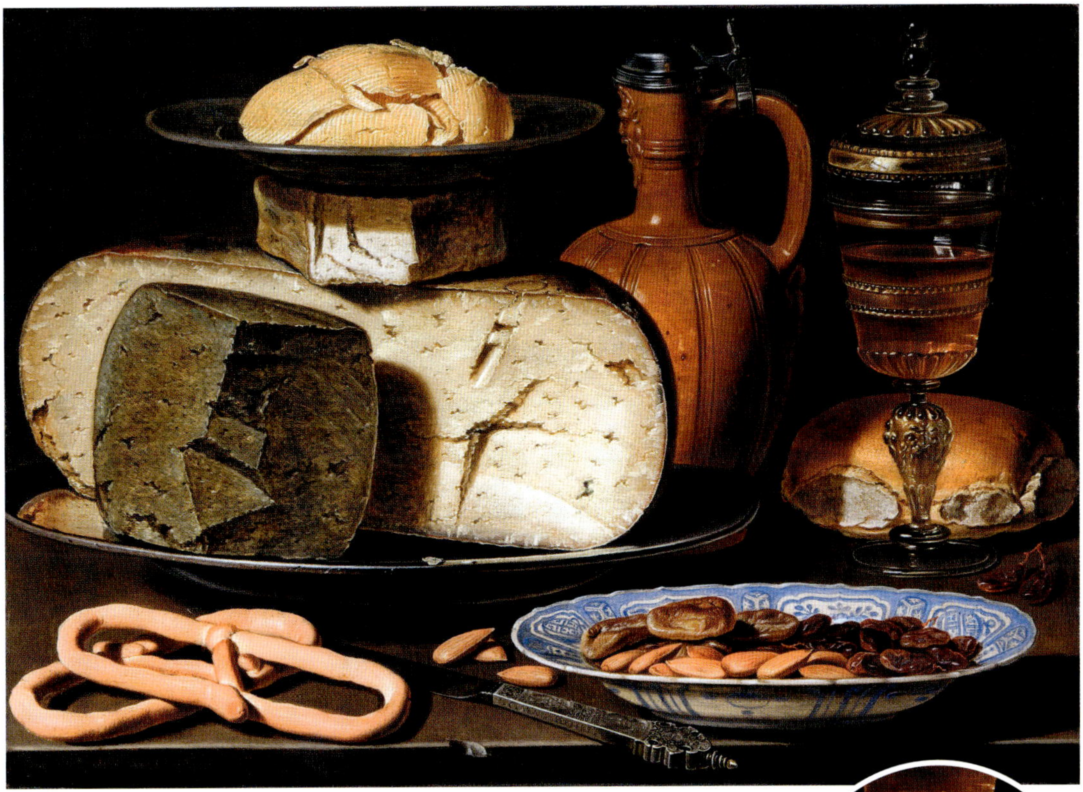

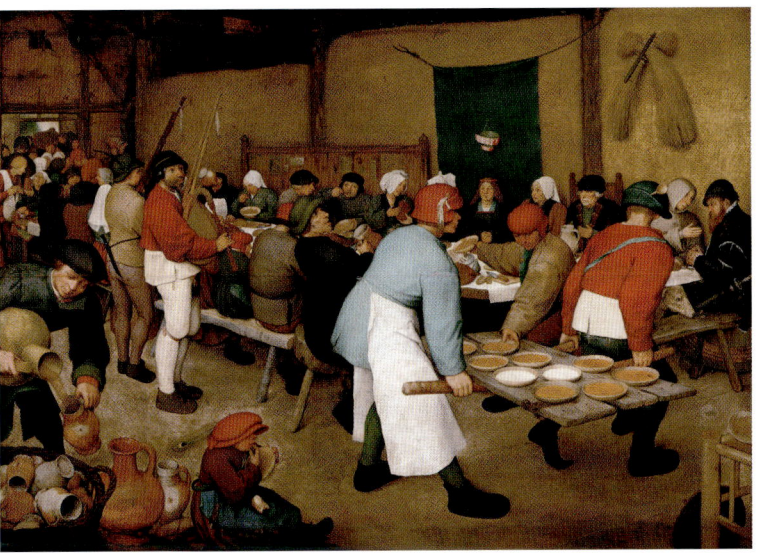

3

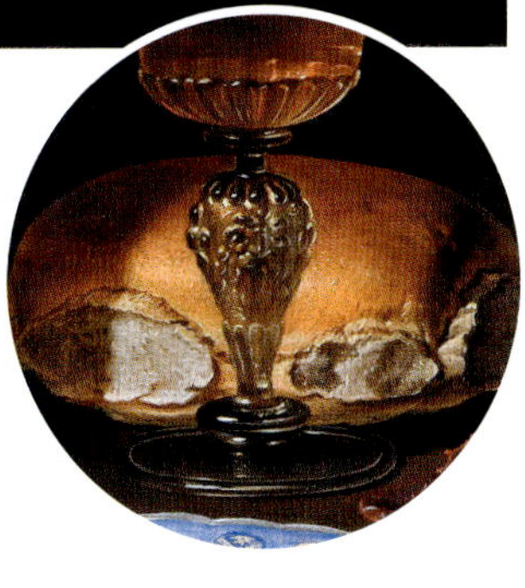

4

1. *The Milkmaid,* Johannes Vermeer, c. 1657-58
2. *The Last Supper,* Leonardo da Vinci, 1495-98
3. *Still Life with Cheeses, Almonds and Pretzels,* Clara Peeters, 1615
4. *The Peasant Wedding,* Pieter Bruegel the Elder, 1567

Egg

Symbolizing creation, fertility, rebirth, beginnings, transformation and mystery, the egg is often also used to suggest the origin of life. In Hindu, Egyptian and Greek traditions, the universe was believed to have hatched from a primordial egg. In Christian art, the egg is a metaphor for resurrection and eternal life. *The Brera Madonna* (1472–74) by Piero della Francesca (1415–92) features a suspended ostrich egg over the Virgin and child, symbolic of Mary's purity and Christ's miraculous birth. Fabergé eggs, symbols of opulence and craftsmanship, were created under the supervision of Peter Carl Fabergé (1846–1920) between 1885 and 1917. Tjalf Sparnaay (b. 1954) said of his 2018 painting *Golden Egg*: 'To paraphrase Magritte, this is not an egg. In actual fact, it's an illusion of an egg, which instantly opens up a whole range of different interpretations: life, the sun, a mandala and geological analogies. It's suddenly about archetypal and universal metaphors deeply rooted in our identities.'

1

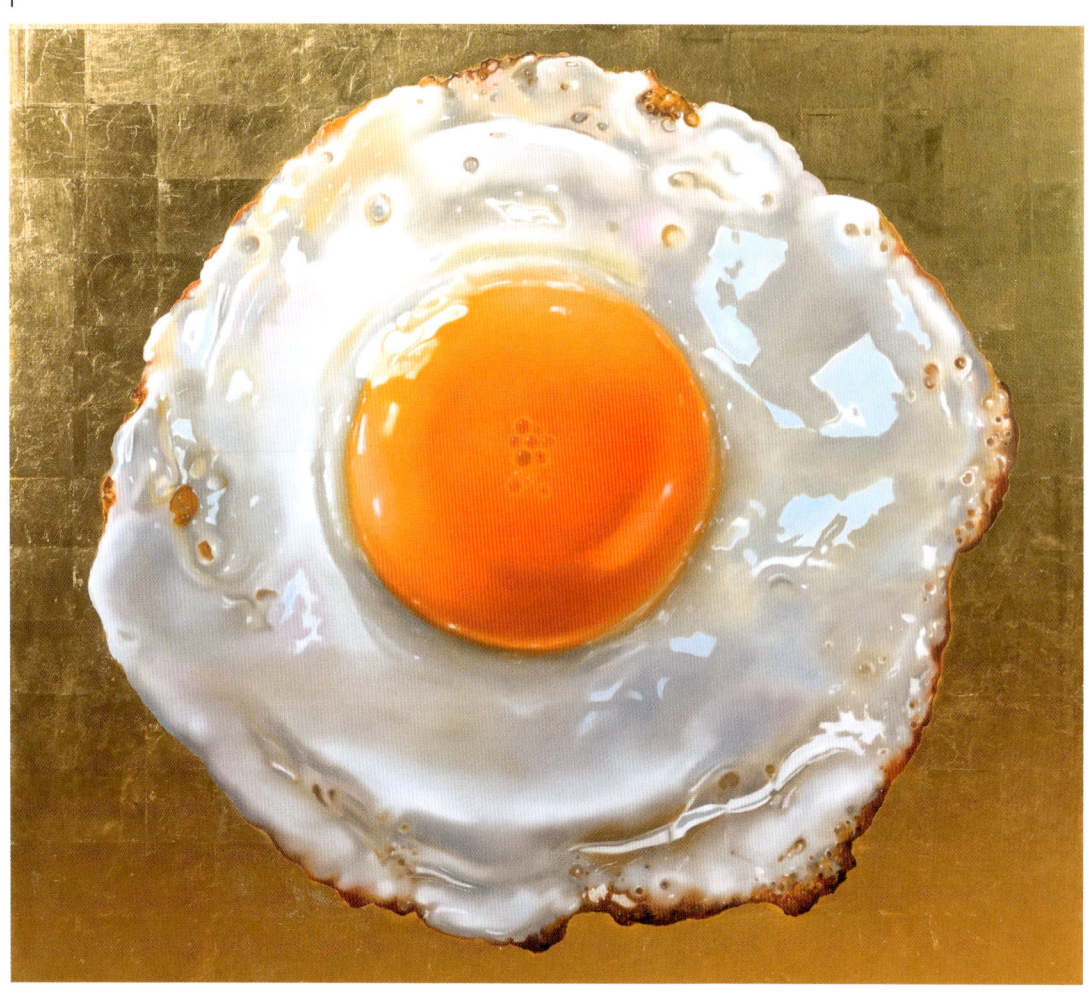

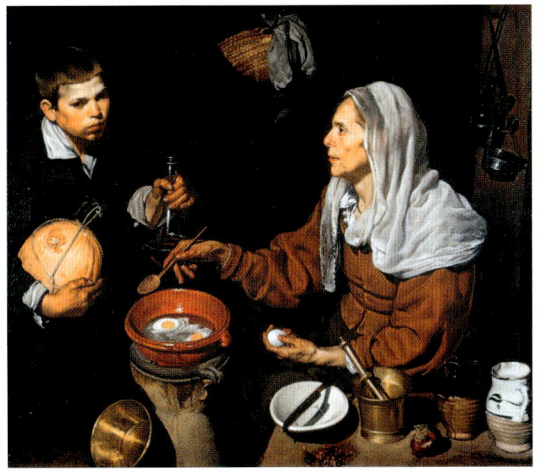

2

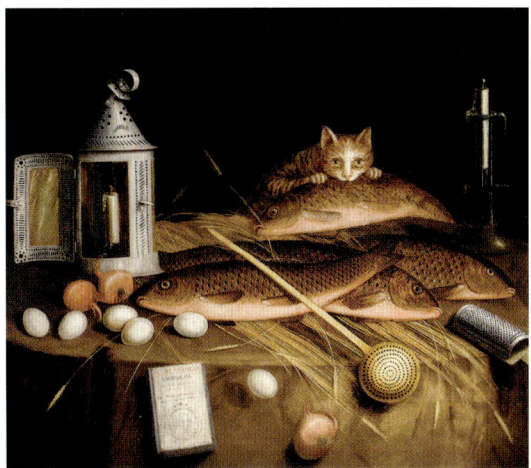

3

4

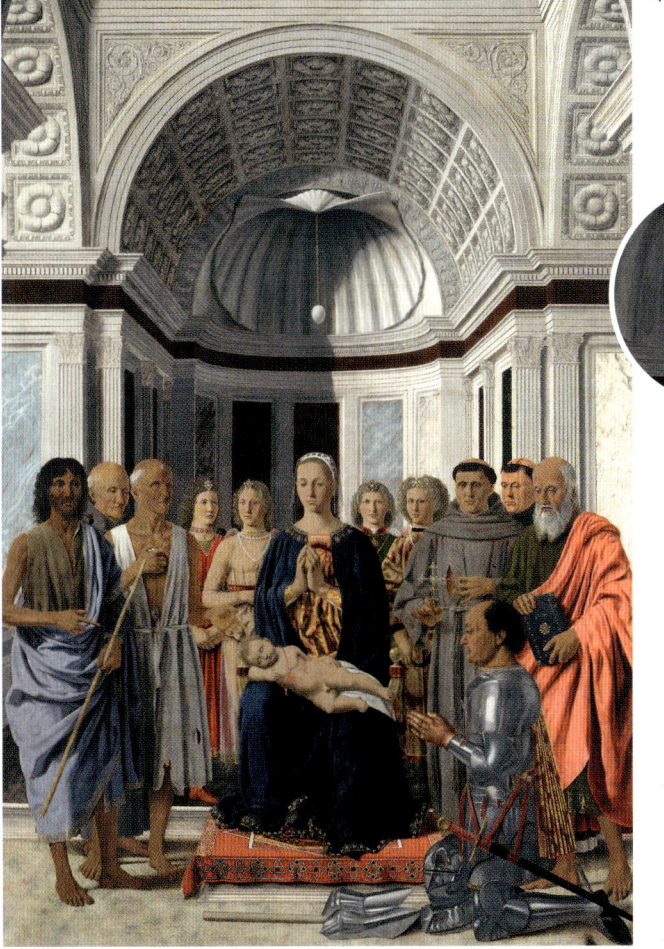

1. *Golden Egg,* Tjalf Sparnaay, 2018, 120 x 120 cm, oilpaint and 24 krts pure goldleave on linen

2. *Old Woman Frying Eggs,* Diego Velázquez, c. 1618

3. *Kitchen Still Life with Fish and Cat,* Sebastian Stoskopff, c. 1650

4. *The Brera Madonna,* Piero della Francesca, 1472-74

Chocolate

Signifying luxury, desire, colonial power and sensuality, chocolate traverses cultures and eras. Originating in Mesoamerican civilizations, cacao held sacred status among the Maya and Aztecs, and was often depicted in ancient ceramics and murals as offerings to the gods. After its introduction to Europe in the sixteenth century, chocolate became associated with the aristocracy and notions of indulgence. *The Chocolate Girl* (1744) by Jean-Étienne Liotard (1702-89) uses chocolate as a symbol of domestic virtue and refined service, reflecting Enlightenment ideals of civility, gentility, and the emerging culture of European luxury. In the nineteenth century, chocolate began to appear in commercial art and advertising, symbolizing comfort, sensuality and the rise of consumer culture. In his poster *Chocolat Idéal* (1897), Alphonse Mucha (1860-1939) symbolized chocolate through a young woman and two children, evoking luxury and sensual indulgence, using Art Nouveau elegance to link consumer pleasure with beauty, femininity, and refined taste.

1

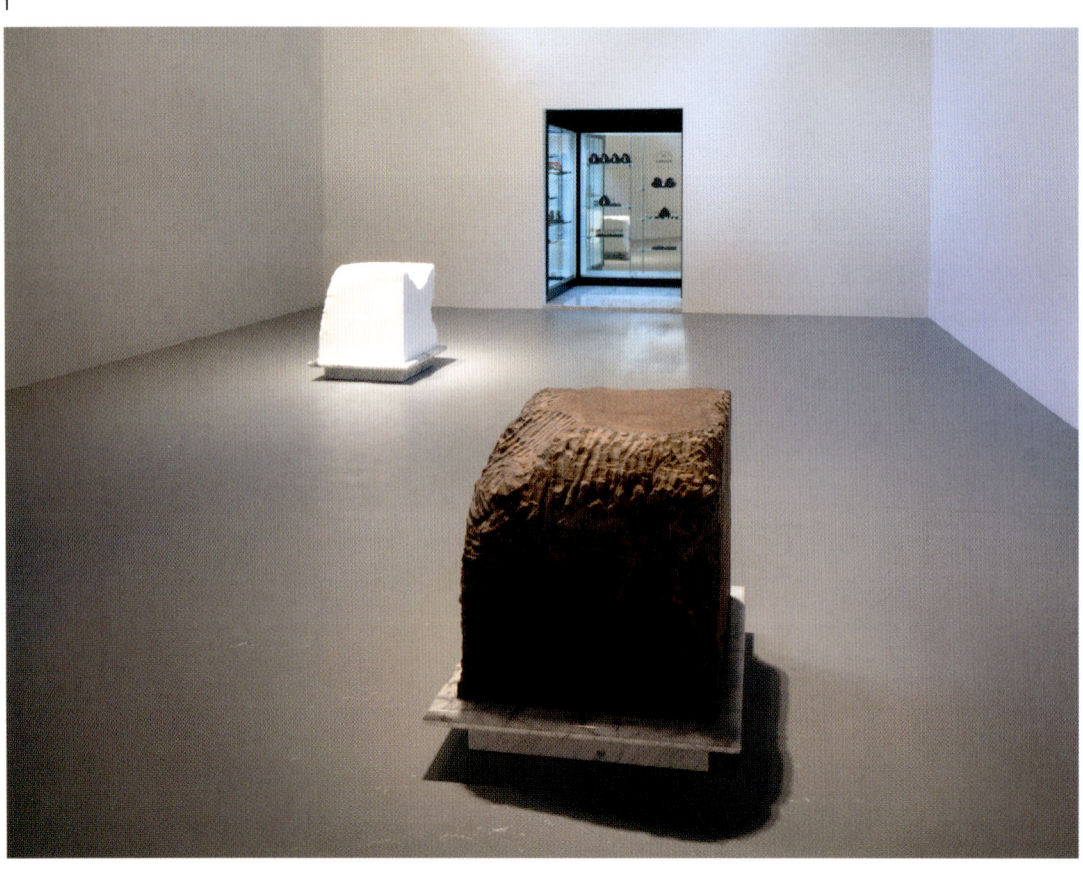

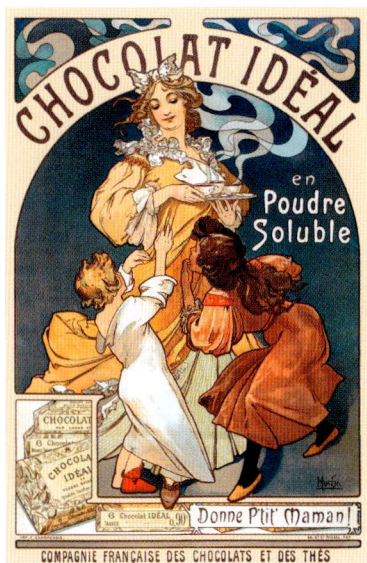

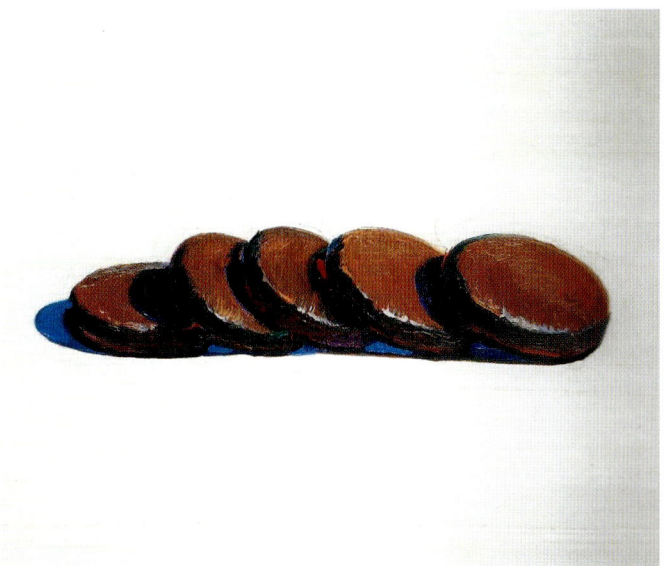

2

3

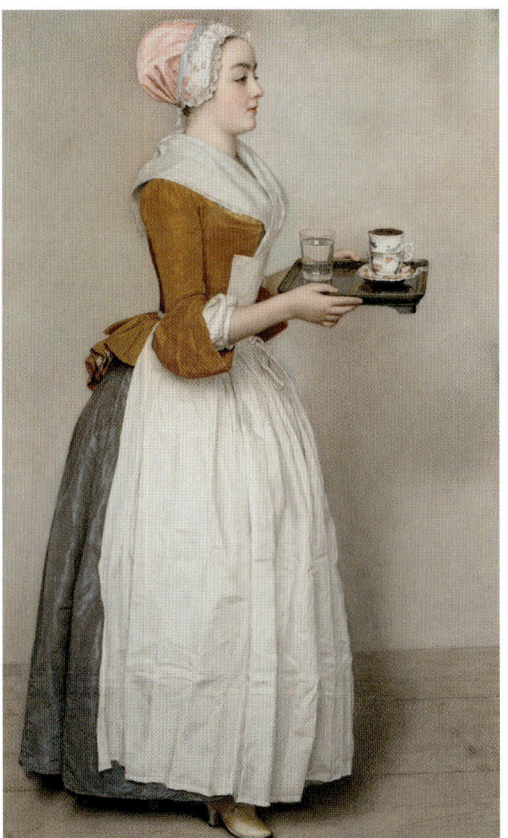

4

1. *Gnaw,* Janine Antoni, 1992
2. *Chocolat Idéal* (advertisement poster), Alphonse Mucha, 1897
3. *Five Chocolate Cookies,* Wayne Thiebaud, 1989
4. *The Chocolate Girl,* Jean-Étienne Liotard, 1744

Onion and Garlic

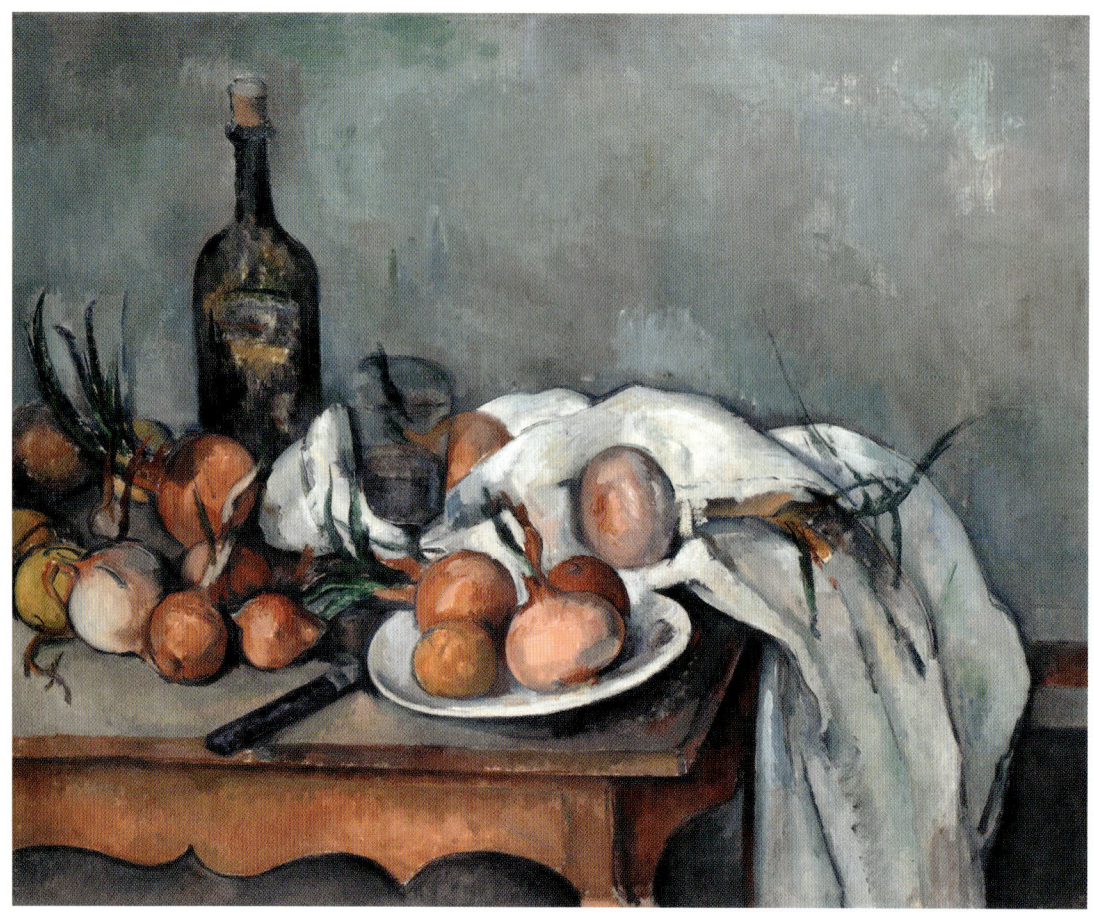

1

Onions and garlic have been depicted in art as symbols of protection, healing and the complexities of human experience. From Renaissance religious paintings to Dutch genre scenes, garlic has often symbolized protection, healing and spiritual defence. It was even believed to ward off evil spirits and disease. In *Still Life with Bream, Oranges, Garlic and Kitchen Utensils* (1772) by Luis Egidio Meléndez (1716–1780), garlic and onions are included to symbolize sustenance and humble labour, contrasting earthly nourishment with the spiritual richness of daily life. With their translucent layers, onions and garlic have also often represented emotional depth, truth and revelation, frequently appearing in still lifes to evoke specific human experiences. In *Still Life with Onions* (c. 1896–98), Paul Cézanne (1839–1906) painted humble onions to symbolize simplicity, honesty and his search for truth in everyday forms, reflecting his effort to reveal enduring structure within the ordinary. Contrastingly, *The Pink Onions* (1906) by Henri Matisse (1869–1954) conveys vitality and sensory abundance, their intense colour and form embodying his belief in emotional expression through the energy of pure colour.

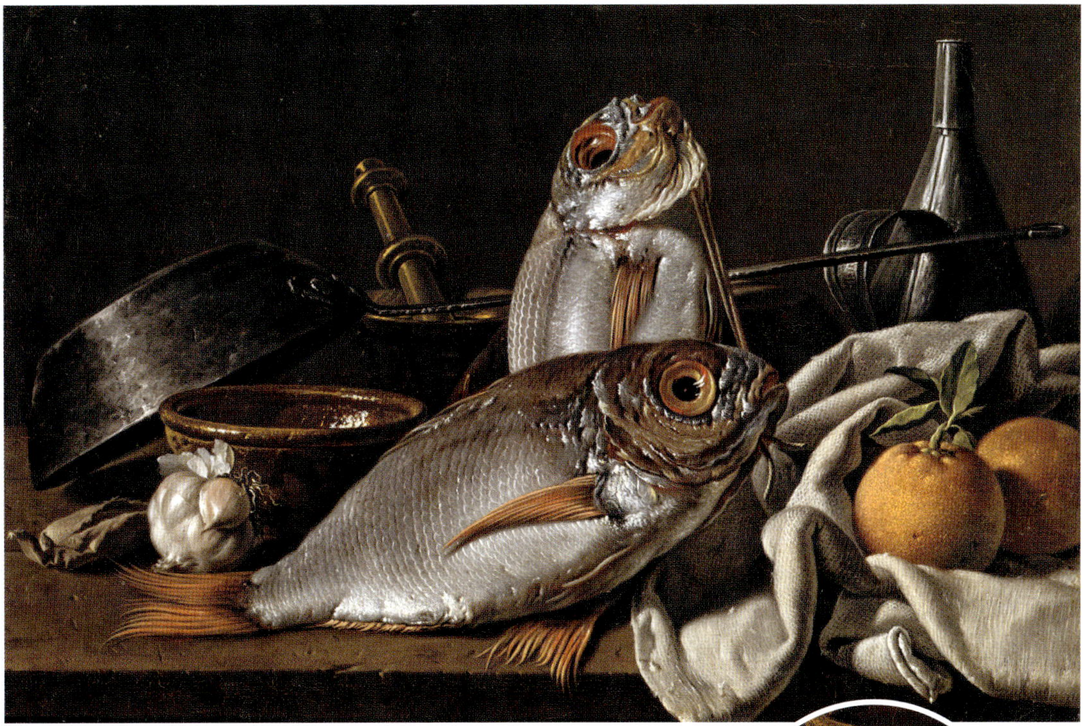

2

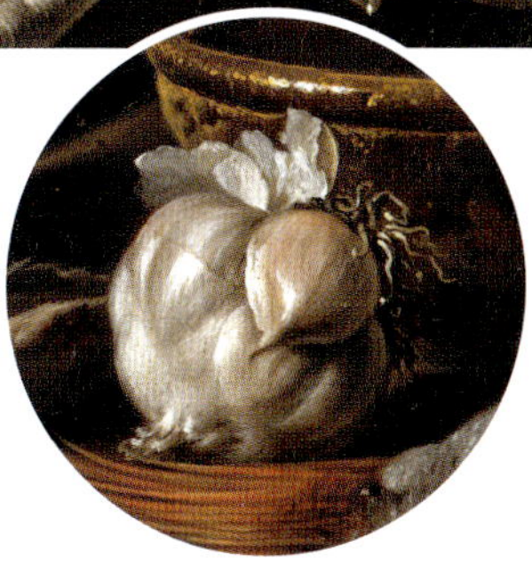

3

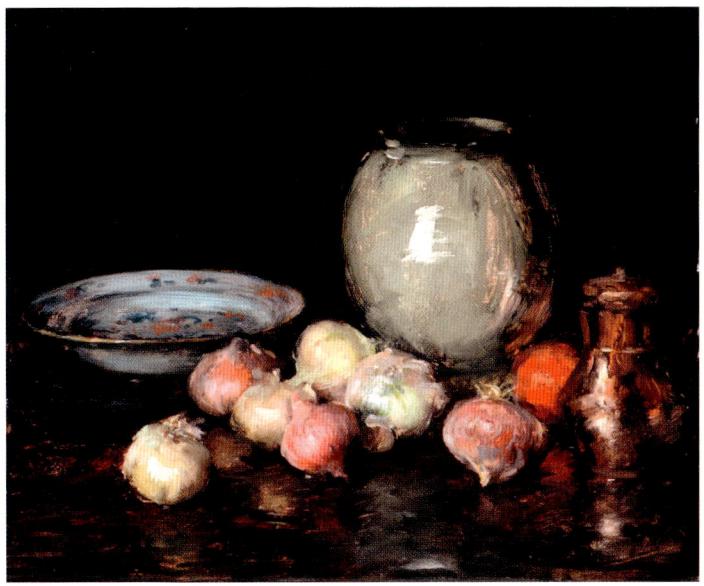

1. *Still Life with Onions,* Paul Cézanne,
    c. 1896-98
2. *Still Life with Bream,* Oranges, Garlic and
    Kitchen Utensils, Luis Egidio Meléndez, 1772
3. *Just Onions,* William Merritt Chase, 1912

Corn

Artists have featured corn in their artworks as a powerful symbol of life, fertility and abundance, often transcending its role as food to become a metaphor for community and continuity. In Mesoamerican civilizations, such as the Maya and Aztecs, corn (maize) was revered as a sacred gift from the gods. The Maya Popol Vuh creation myth describes humans as being formed from corn dough, and maize gods and corn motifs abound in murals, pottery and codices. In Indigenous American art, especially among the Navajo and Hopi, corn appears in weaving, pottery, sand paintings and ceremonial masks, symbolizing nourishment, strength and spiritual balance. More recently, Cherokee artist Jimmie Durham (1940-2021) has used corn in installations to critique colonialism and celebrate Indigenous resilience. Similarly, Diego Rivera (1886-1957) depicted corn in some of his murals as a symbol of Mexican identity and agrarian pride. Artists like Damián Ortega (b. 1967) use corn to explore economic systems, labour and cultural memory, often blending satire with political critique.

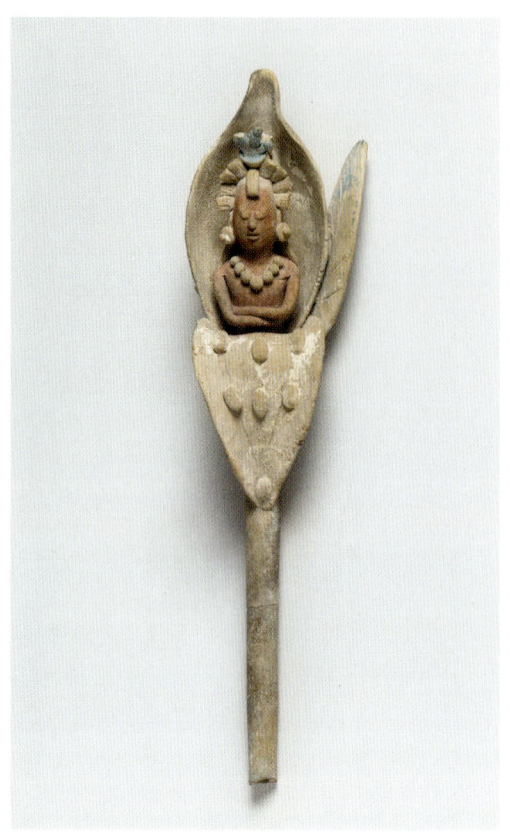

1

2

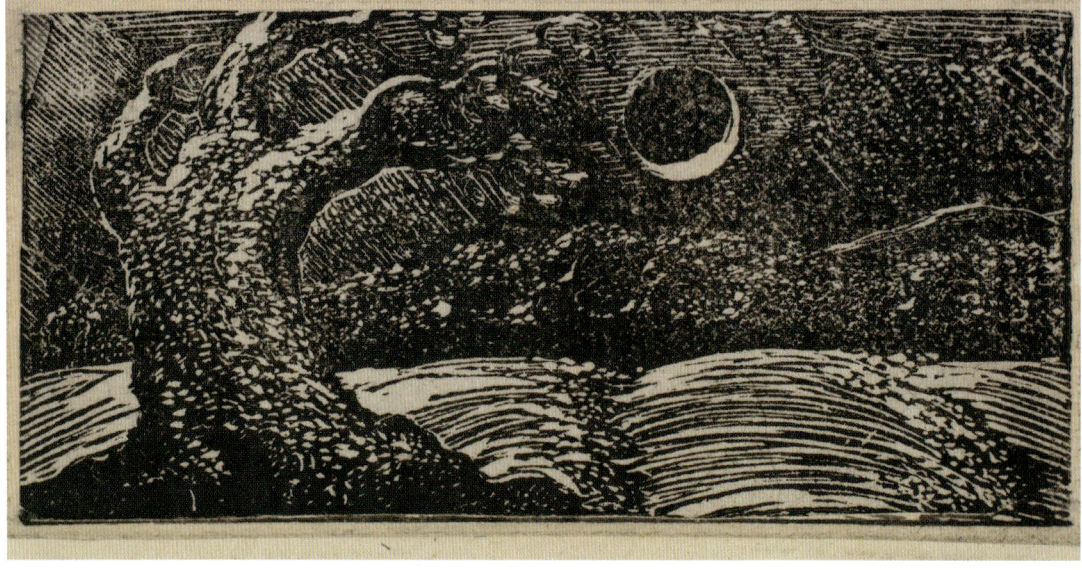

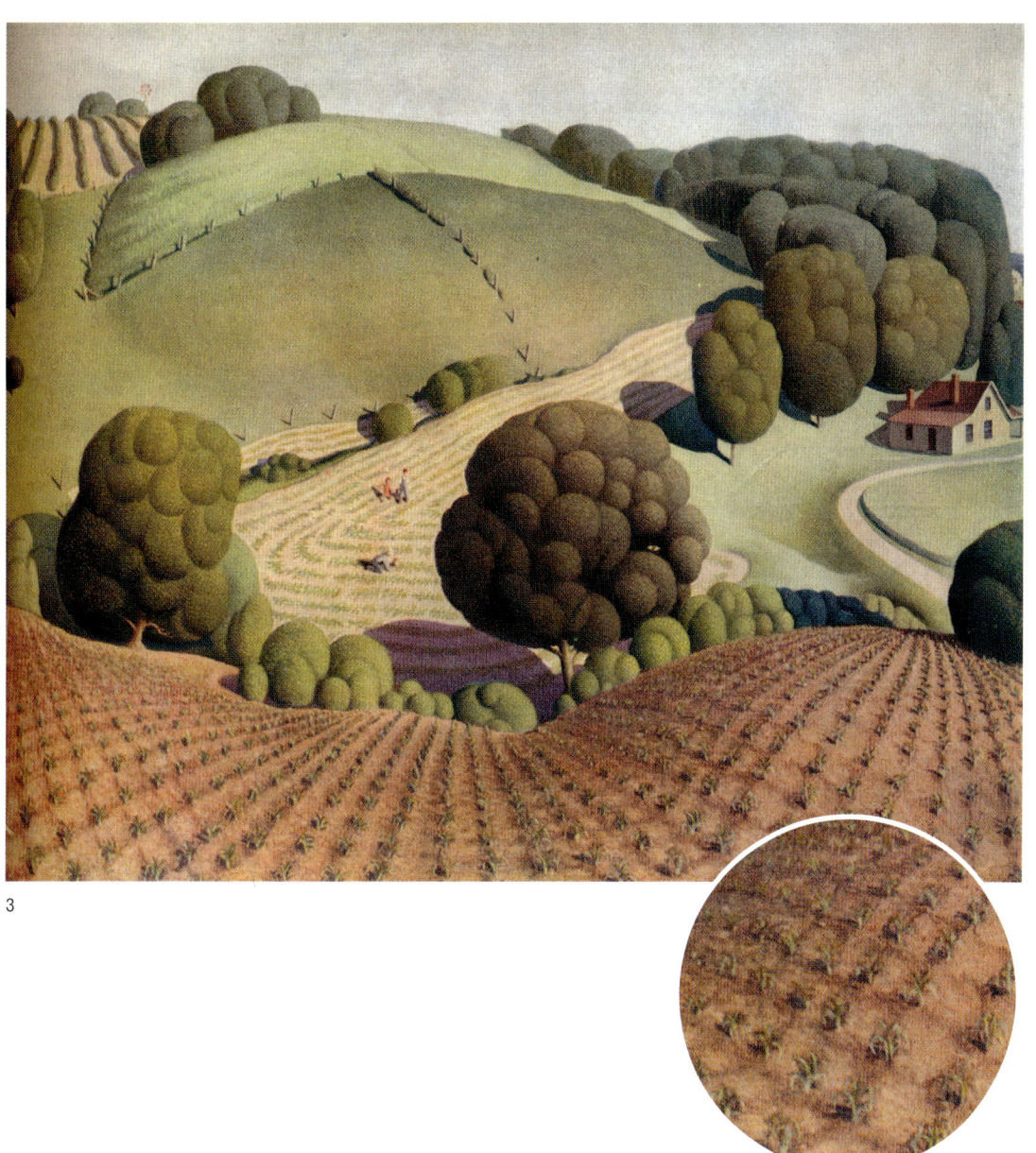

3

1. *Maize God in Corn Husk,* Mexico, seventh-ninth century CE
2. *The Blighted Corn,* William Blake, 1821
3. *Young Corn,* Grant Wood, 1931

The Supernatural World

In almost every culture, the supernatural has been depicted for its symbolic meanings. From celestial beings to mythical beasts, from radiant halos to fiery phoenixes, the paranormal world has provided artists with a rich vocabulary for expressing the inexpressible, including divine presence, moral struggle, spiritual transformation, and the mysteries of existence. These symbols transcend the boundaries of the visible world, and the next section explores the enduring human fascination with forces beyond the material.

Often serving as a bridge between the human and the divine, imagery of the supernatural is frequently decorative or symbolic. In many traditions, supernatural beings are believed to embody moral or metaphysical truths. Angels, for instance, appear across Abrahamic religions (Judaism, Christianity and Islam) as messengers of God, their wings symbolizing transcendence and their shining halos signifying sanctity. In Christian iconography, the halo became a visual shorthand for holiness, encircling the heads of saints, martyrs and divine figures to indicate their spiritual elevation. The use of gold leaf in medieval, Byzantine and Early Renaissance art was there to evoke the supernatural. As candlelight flickered against the shining golden surfaces, it transformed them into luminous, seemingly divine images.

In Western traditions, dragons often represent chaos, evil or the untamed forces of nature — enemies to be conquered by saintly heroes, such as Saint George. Their curving bodies, glowing eyes, pointed claws and tails, and fiery breath seem terrifying, and their defeat symbolizes the success of good over evil. In many East Asian cultures, however, dragons are seen as embodying luck and the emperor's power. Chinese dragons are generally associated with rain, fertility and heaven. These cultural variances illustrate how the same symbol can carry completely different underlying interpretations.

In ancient Egypt, the Bennu bird, an early precursor to the phoenix, was associated with the sun, rebirth and the cyclical nature of time. In Greco-Roman mythology, the phoenix was said to burst into flames at the end of its life, only to rise anew from its ashes, a powerful metaphor for immortality and regeneration. Early Christians adopted the phoenix as a symbol of resurrection and eternal life, often incorporating it into funerary art. Across all these traditions, the phoenix embodies the same hope that destruction leads to rebirth.

Supernatural symbols often serve to articulate the unseen forces that shape human destiny. In Hindu and Buddhist art, celestial beings such as *devas* and *apsaras* populate heavenly realms, their graceful forms and elaborate adornments symbolizing spiritual bliss and divine favour.

In Indigenous and animist traditions, the mystical is often inseparable from the natural world. Spirits inhabit animals, trees, rivers and mountains, and art is one method to communicate with these unseen presences. In Indigenous American, Aboriginal Australian and African art, supernatural beings are frequently illustrated in stylized, symbolic forms that encode cosmological knowledge, ancestral memory and ritual power. These works are active participants in spiritual life, serving as tools for healing, storytelling and communion with the sacred.

In modern and contemporary art, symbolism featuring supernatural characters has evolved. Surrealists often drew on myth, dreams and the occult to explore the unconscious mind. Contemporary artists continue to reimagine supernatural motifs, such as angels, demons, dragons and spirits as metaphors for identity, trauma, resistance and transcendence. In an age of scientific rationalism, the supernatural remains a vital symbolic language for grappling with the unknown.

The following section journeys through some of these diverse expressions of the supernatural, tracing how symbols like dragons, halos, phoenixes and angels have been used to visualize the invisible and give form to the indefinable. Whether as protectors or adversaries, guides or omens, these supernatural figures reflect humanity's enduring desire to understand its place in our wondrous, terrifying and sublime cosmos.

Dragon

Chaos, destruction, wisdom, divine protection, cosmic harmony and moral conflict are just some of the concepts that dragons have expressed in art. In East Asia, particularly in China, dragons have long been revered as benevolent, celestial beings, symbolizing power, prosperity and good fortune, and often associated with rain, rivers and imperial authority. Chinese emperors were considered 'Sons of the Dragon,' and dragons frequently appear in traditional paintings, carvings and architecture, portrayed as guardians of cosmic balance. In contrast, in the Middle Ages in the West, dragons were depicted as terrifying creatures, personifying evil, underlying fears and the unknown. In Christian art, Satan is often depicted as a fearsome dragon to symbolize ultimate evil, chaos and rebellion against divine order. Christian art features saints slaying winged, fire-breathing dragons, implying the triumph of good over evil. These conveyed the challenges of moral struggle. Other cultures used dragon imagery to express divine authority, natural forces and national identity, such as the Aztecs with Quetzalcoatl (the Feathered Serpent) and the Bhutanese with the Thunder Dragon Druk.

1

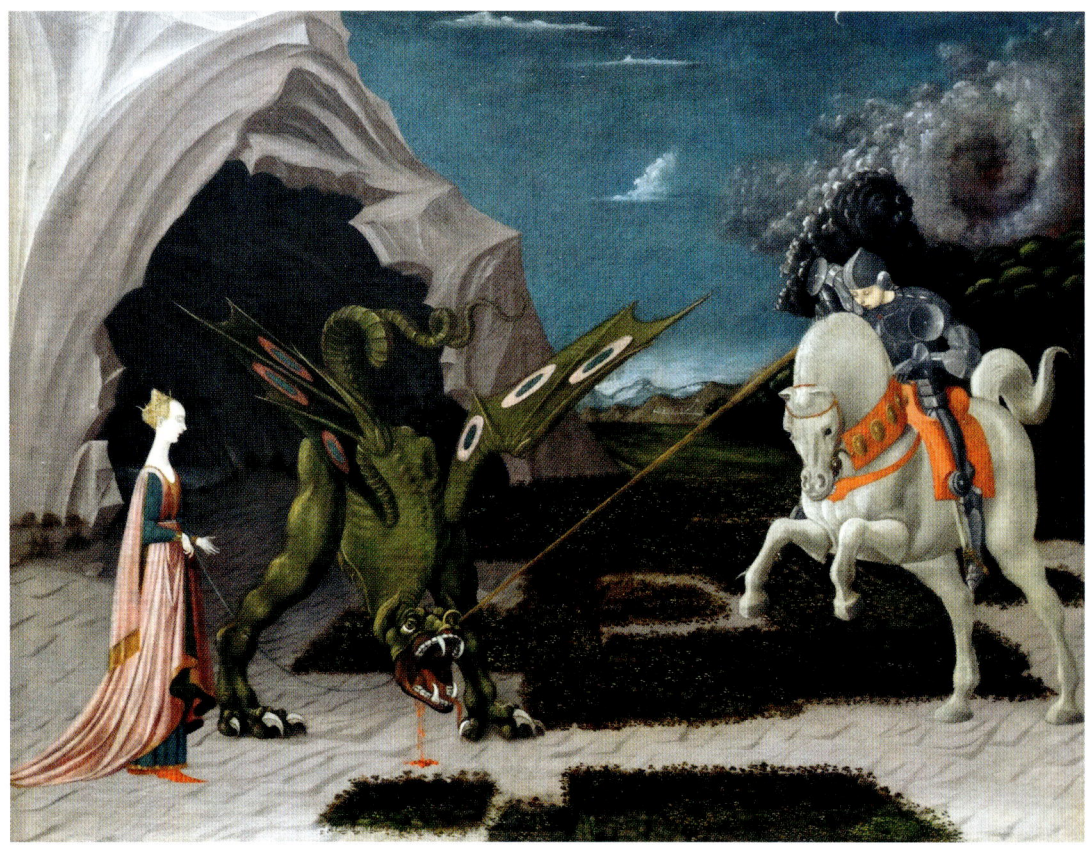

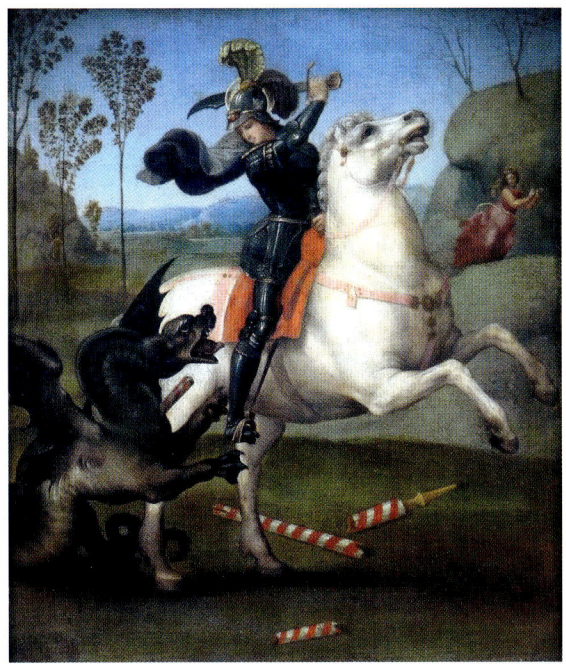

2

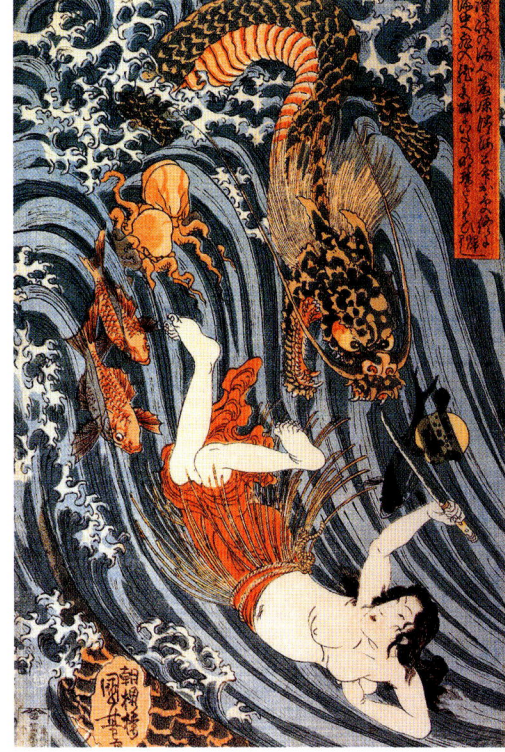

3

4

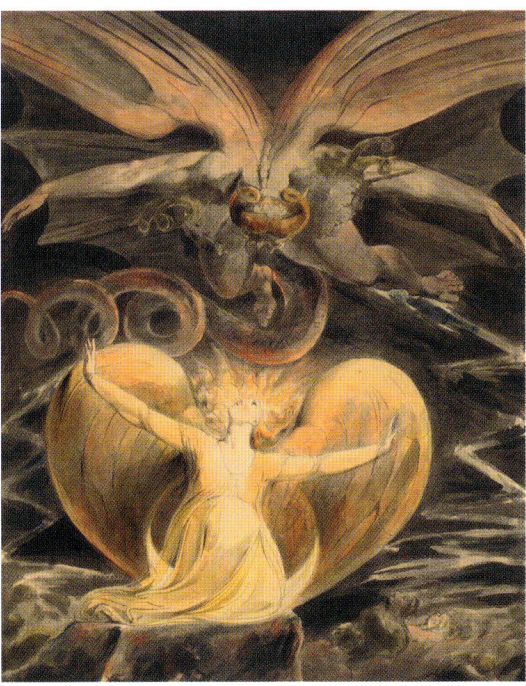

1. *St George and the Dragon,* Paolo Uccello, c. 1470
2. *St George and the Dragon,* Raphael, c. 1505
3. *Tamatori Escaping from the Dragon King,* Utagawa Kuniyoshi, mid-nineteenth century
4. *The Great Red Dragon and the Woman Clothed with the Sun,* William Blake, 1805–10

Halo

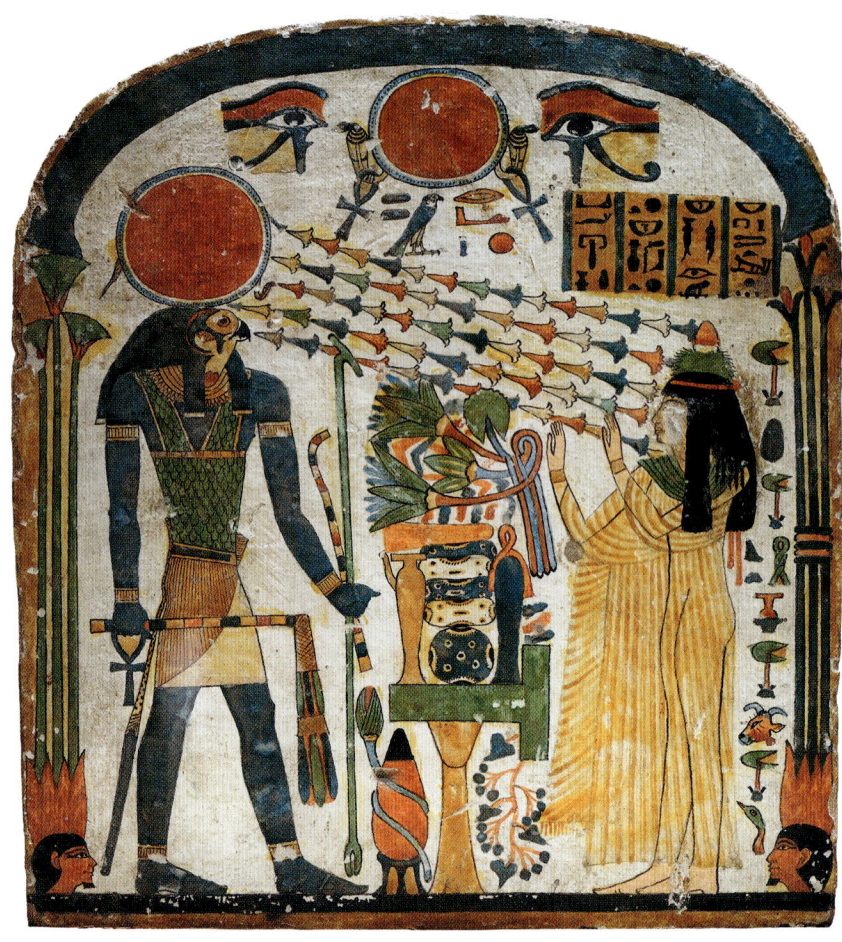

1

Across cultures and centuries, the halo has served as a radiant symbol of divinity, sanctity, virtue, the sacred and enlightenment. Its origins trace back to ancient civilizations including Egypt, Mesopotamia and Persia, where radiant discs or auras signified divine power or royal authority. In Christian art, halos became prominent from the fourth century CE, initially used to denote Christ and later extended to saints and angels. For instance, in Giotto di Bondone's frescoes in the Scrovegni Chapel (c. 1305), halos emphasize the sacred nature of biblical figures.

During the Renaissance, some artists depicted golden circles, either filled or as rings, as halos to signify spiritual purity. However, later artists abandoned them in favour of more naturalistic light effects. In Buddhist and Hindu art, halos – often elaborate and flame-like – represent enlightenment and spiritual radiance. Even in Greek and Roman art, gods like Helios and emperors were depicted wearing radiant crowns, linking them to the concept of divine light.

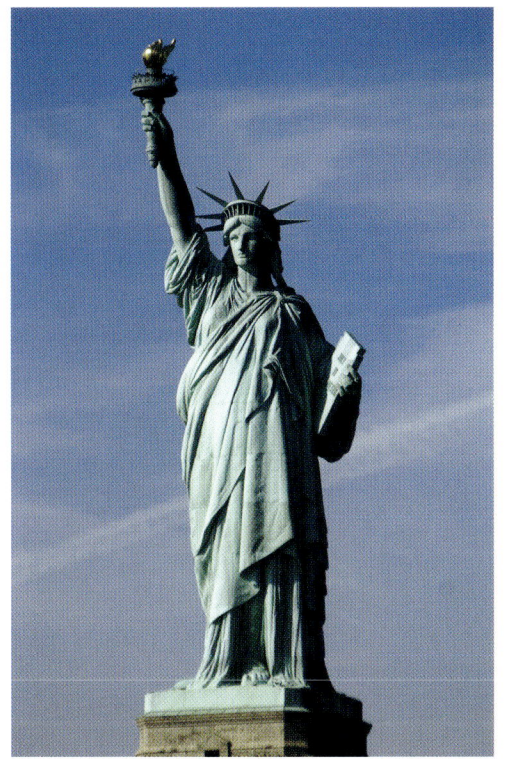

2

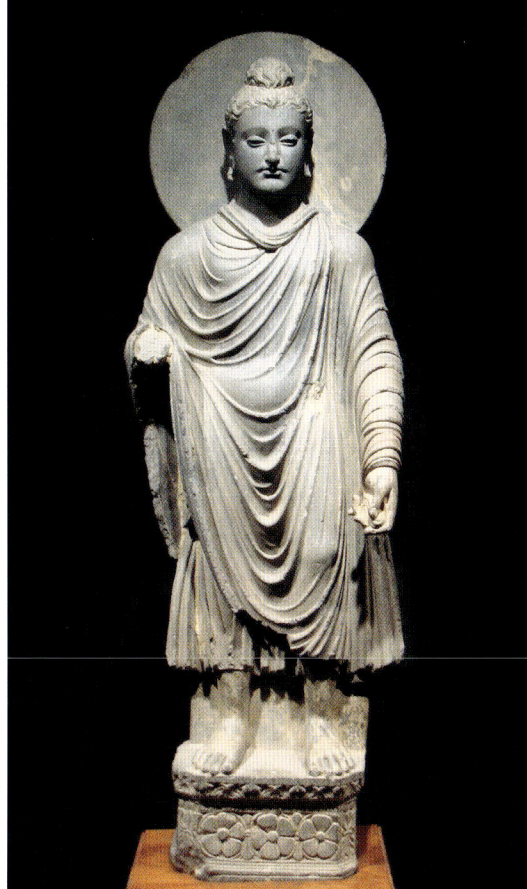

3

4

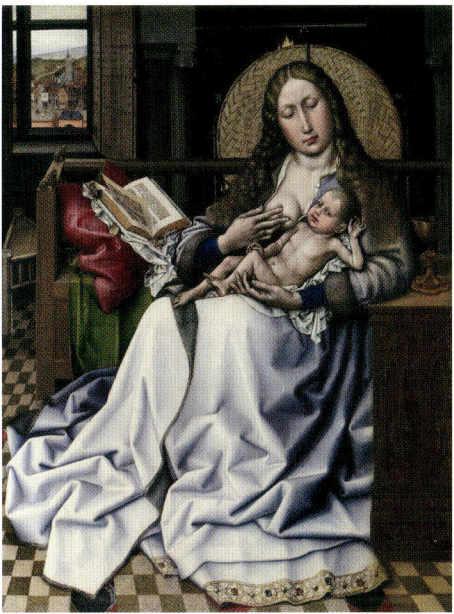

1. *Ra and Imentet,* The tomb of Nefertari, Egypt, thirteenth century BCE
2. *Statue of Liberty,* Frédéric Auguste Bartholdi, 1886
3. *Standing Buddha,* Pakistan, first-second century CE
4. *The Virgin and Child before a Firescreen,* follower of Robert Campin, c. 1440

Phoenix

Originating in ancient Egyptian and Greek mythology, the phoenix was believed to regenerate, rising from its own ashes after death. Its red and gold wings were often depicted to suggest the rising sun. In Greek and Roman mosaics and sculptures, it was frequently portrayed to express the concept of eternal life. Similarly, the phoenix became a metaphor for Christ's resurrection, and medieval illuminated manuscripts portrayed phoenixes engulfed in flames, then rising again to convey the idea of divine renewal. Meanwhile, in Chinese culture, the *fenghuang* (mythological birds usually equated to the phoenix, which feature in traditions throughout East and South-East Asia) symbolizes harmony, virtue and the union of yin and yang. Artists depicted it in intricate silk paintings and imperial robes, often alongside the dragon to represent the empress and emperor. Across time, the phoenix has remained a potent visual metaphor for resilience, hope and new beginnings. Whether in Renaissance tapestries, Japanese woodblock prints or contemporary digital art, its fiery rebirth continues to inspire artists.

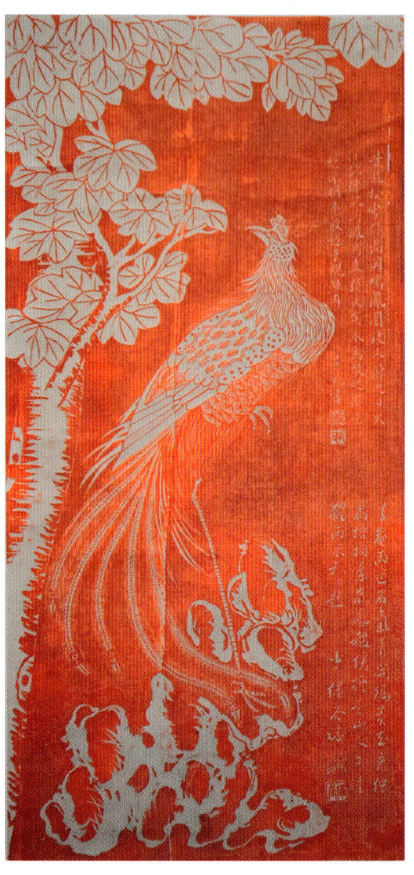

1

2

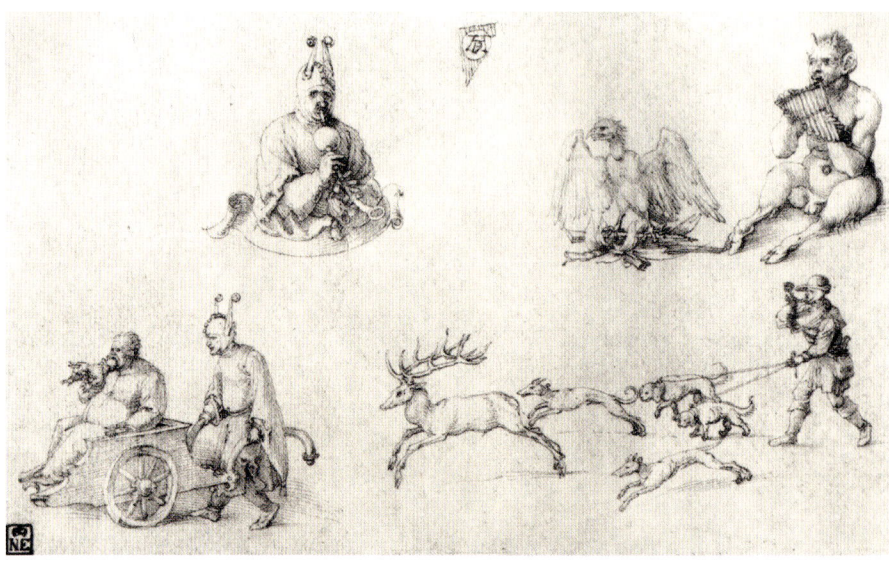

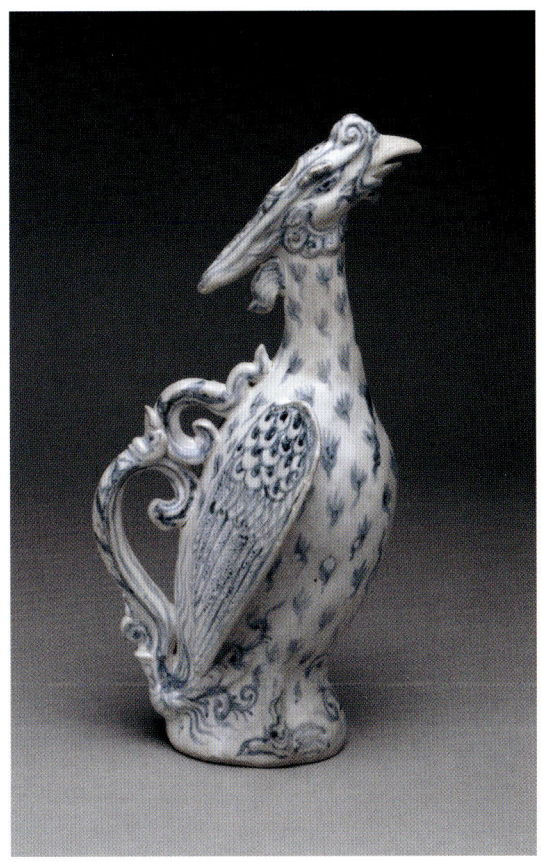

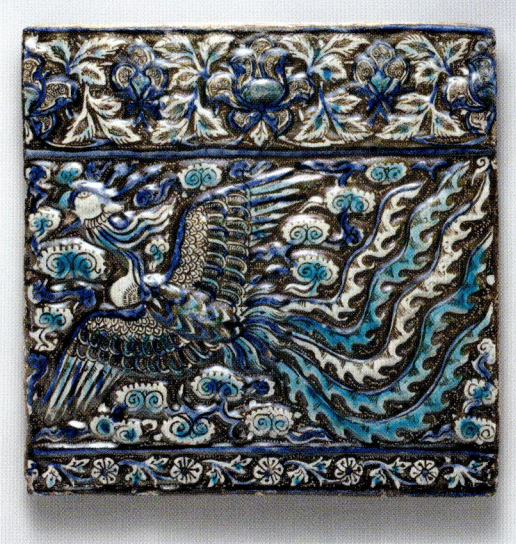

4

3

5

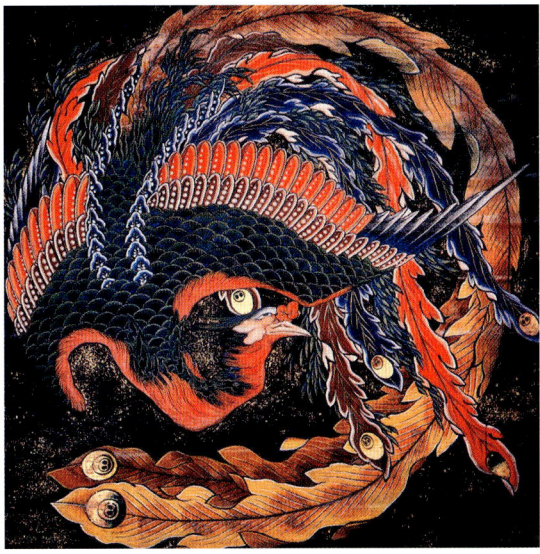

1. *Phoenix,* China, nineteenth or twentieth century
2. *Study sheet with fools, Faun, Phoenix and Deer Hunting,*
   Albrecht Dürer, 1515
3. *Ewer in the Form of a Phoenix,* Vietnam, c. fifteenth-sixteenth century
4. *Tile with Image of Phoenix,* Iran, late thirteenth century
5. *Phoenix Glaring in All Directions,* Katsushika Hokusai, 1843

Angel

Rooted in Abrahamic religions (Judaism, Christianity and Islam), angels are often portrayed as messengers between heaven and earth, embodying purity, guidance and the unseen forces of the cosmos. Their depiction became especially prominent during the Renaissance and Baroque eras. For example, *Annunciation* (1608) by Caravaggio is a dramatic portrayal of the archangel Gabriel visiting Mary, symbolizing divine intervention and grace. Raphael's *The Sistine Madonna* (1512) features two cherubic angels, representing innocence and contemplation, which have become one of the most iconic images of angels in Western art. *Fallen Angel* (1847) by Alexandre Cabanel (1823–89) presents a more humanized, emotional portrayal of a cast-out angel, symbolizing loss, rebellion and the complexity of divine justice. Beyond Christianity, winged figures like Nike in Greek art or the Hindu Garuda represent victory, divine will or cosmic order. Believing that women's virtues should be admired over their bodies, Abbott Handerson Thayer (1849–1921) painted *Angel* in 1887, modelled by his daughter Mary, who he believed epitomized this.

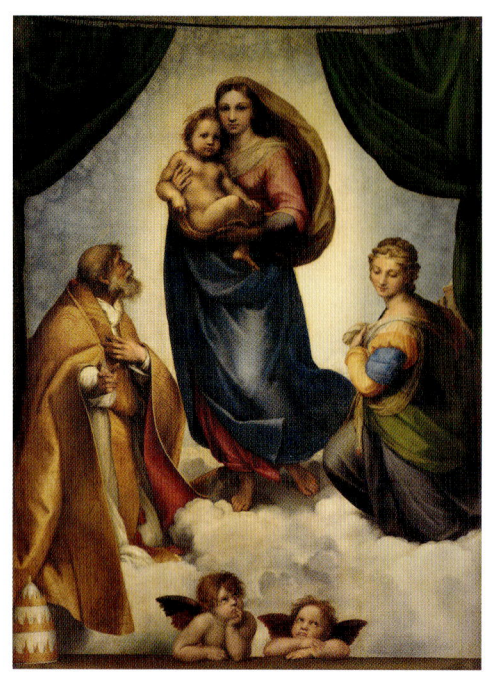

1

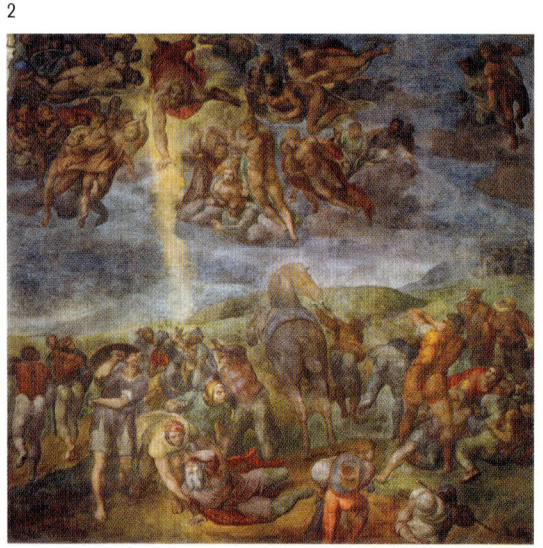

2

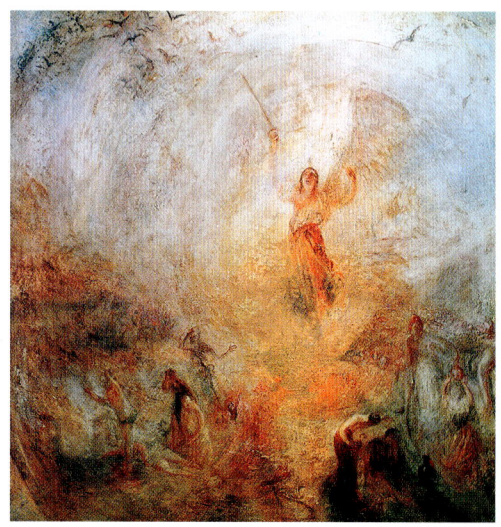

3

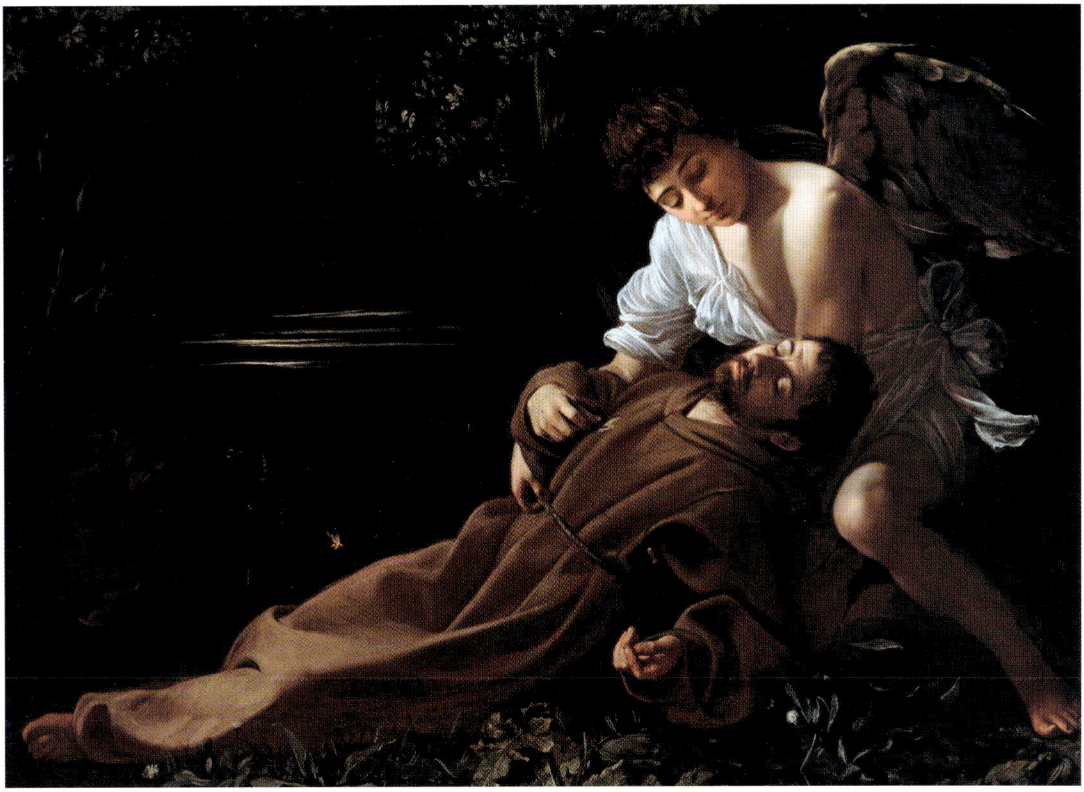

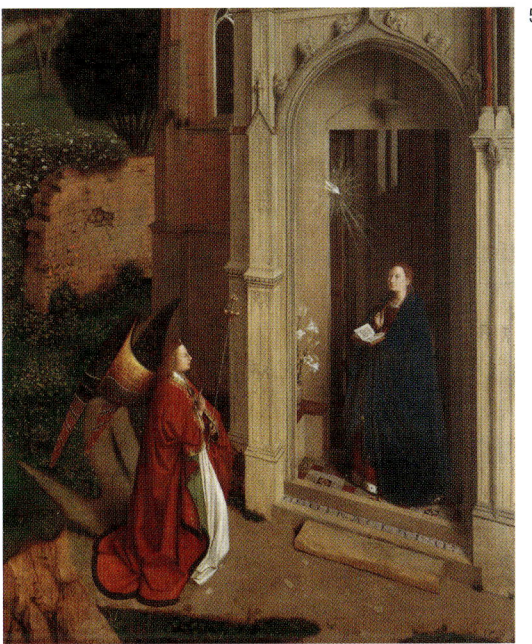

4

5

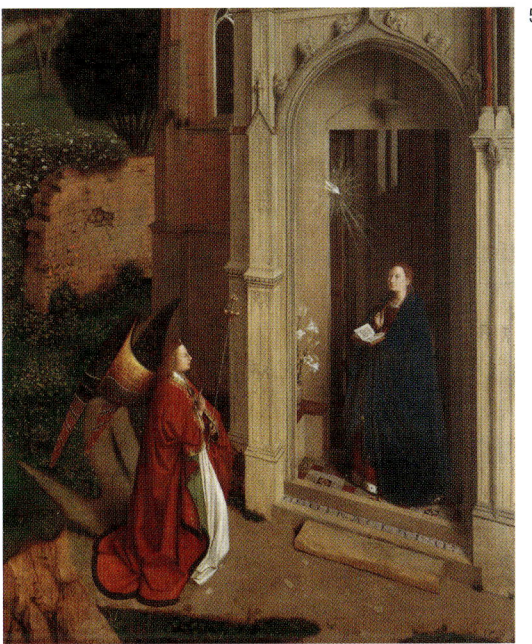

1. *The Sistine Madonna,* Raphael, 1512
2. *The Conversion of Saul,* Michelangelo, 1545
3. *The Angel Standing in the Sun,* J.M.W. Turner, 1846
4. *St Francis of Assisi in Ecstasy,* Caravaggio, 1595
5. *The Annunciation,* Petrus Christus, c. 1450

Colours and Shapes

Long before written language, humans communicated through visual forms – lines etched into stone, pigments smeared across cave walls, circles, spirals and other symbols that spoke volumes without a single word. Among the most enduring and universal elements of this visual language are colours and shapes. These fundamental building blocks of art are usually symbolic, shaped by cultural context, spiritual beliefs, psychological associations and historical traditions. They reveal how artists have evoked emotions, conveyed ideologies and expressed the undefinable. Colour, perhaps more than any other element, can stir the senses and the soul. Yet its meanings are far from fixed. In Western art, white is often associated with purity, innocence and divinity, as seen in the robes of angels or the lilies of the Virgin Mary. But in many Eastern cultures, white is the colour of mourning and death, worn at funerals and symbolizing the passage into the afterlife. Similarly, red can signify love, passion and vitality in one context, and danger, violence or sacrifice in another. In Chinese tradition, red is considered a symbol of luck and joy. In Christian iconography, it may represent the blood of Christ or the fires of hell.

Associated with the sky and the sea, blue often symbolizes divinity, tranquillity and wisdom. In ancient Egypt, blue was associated with the god Amun. In Hindu art, the gods Shiva and Krishna are depicted with blue skin. In Renaissance Europe, costly ultramarine was typically reserved for the robes of the Virgin Mary, signifying both her blessedness and the wealth of the person paying for the painting. Green, the colour of nature, has similarly complex meanings: it can represent fertility and growth, or envy and decay. Black, too, has multiple secondary meanings, symbolizing death and evil in some traditions, but also power, elegance, drama and the unknown in others.

Like colours, shapes can carry deep symbolic weight. The circle, with no beginning or end, is a universal symbol of unity, eternity and the divine. In Hindu and Buddhist mandalas, circular forms represent the cosmos and the path to enlightenment. In Christian art, halos encircle the heads of saints, signifying their spiritual perfection. The square, by contrast, suggests stability, order and the material world. Squares have shaped temples, altars and cities, imposing human logic on the natural world. Triangles, with their three points, often signify power, hierarchy and transformation, but also masculinity and femininity. In Christian symbolism, the triangle represents the Holy Trinity. In alchemy, it can denote the elements of fire (upright), water (inverted), air (upright with a line) and earth (inverted with a line).

Geometric shapes are a significant feature in Islamic art, where repeating, tessellated patterns of stars, polygons and other shapes are frequently used to convey God's infinity. In African art, shapes are usually encoded with cultural meanings. For example, zigzags may represent ancestral journeys and spirals suggest cycles of life and rebirth. In Indigenous Australian art, concentric circles, lines and dots map sacred landscapes and Dreamtime stories, serving as both visual language and spiritual cartography.

Modern and contemporary artists have continued to explore the symbolic potential of colours and shapes, often in radically new ways. Wassily Kandinsky, a pioneer of abstract art, thought that colours and shapes had spiritual vibrations. For him, yellow was warm and eccentric, blue was deep and inward, circles were peaceful, and angles were aggressive. Piet Mondrian (1872-1944) used grids of squares and primary colours to express a utopian vision of harmony and balance. Even in abstract art, the symbolic resonance of colour and shape persisted. A red or black square on a white canvas may evoke revolution, purity or tension. A dark coloured circle may suggest a cavity, a doorway, a nucleus or even a stone. These interpretations are formed not only by the artist's aims but also by the viewer's background, personal experiences and emotional responses. Symbolism, after all, is not static. It is a living dialogue between image and observer.

The following pages trace the symbolic language of colours and shapes across civilizations and centuries, revealing how they continue to shape our understanding of the world, offering a visual shorthand for the most profound truths of human experience.

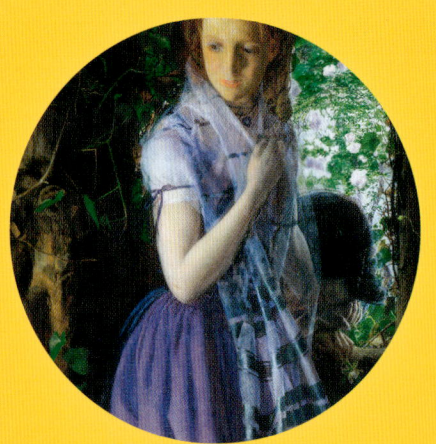

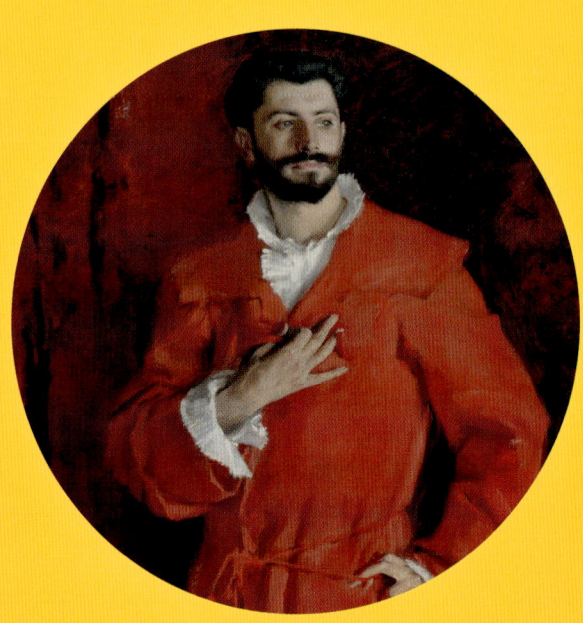

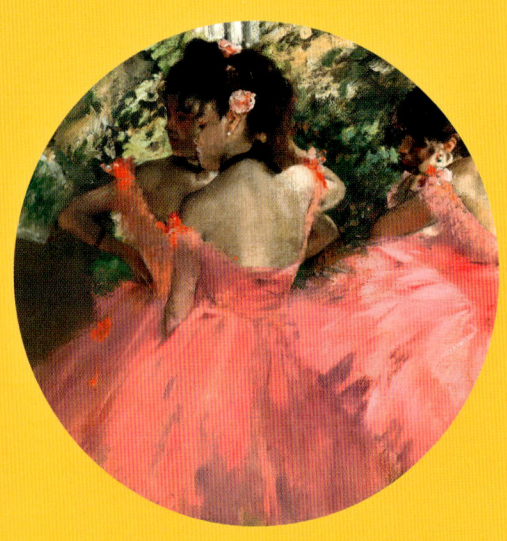

Colours

Red

Throughout history, artists have used the colour red to embody emotion, power and transformation. One of the most visually arresting colours, it is often associated with passion, love, danger, warmth and sacrifice. In ancient Egypt and China, red symbolized life, vitality and good fortune, appearing in tomb paintings, imperial robes and ceremonial objects. In Christian art, red often represents the blood of Christ and martyrdom, as seen in Christ's red robe in *The Disrobing of Christ* (1577-79) by El Greco (1541-1614). During the Renaissance and Baroque periods, red was used to convey wealth and authority, often worn by cardinals and nobility in portraits. In his *Colour Field* paintings, Mark Rothko (1903-70) used red to evoke profound emotional states such as grief, ecstasy or existential dread. In political art, notably in Soviet propaganda posters, red has symbolized revolution and resistance. Matisse painted *The Red Studio* in 1911. His studio was actually white, and the intense reds dominating the painting represent his inner world, imagination, energy and passion.

1

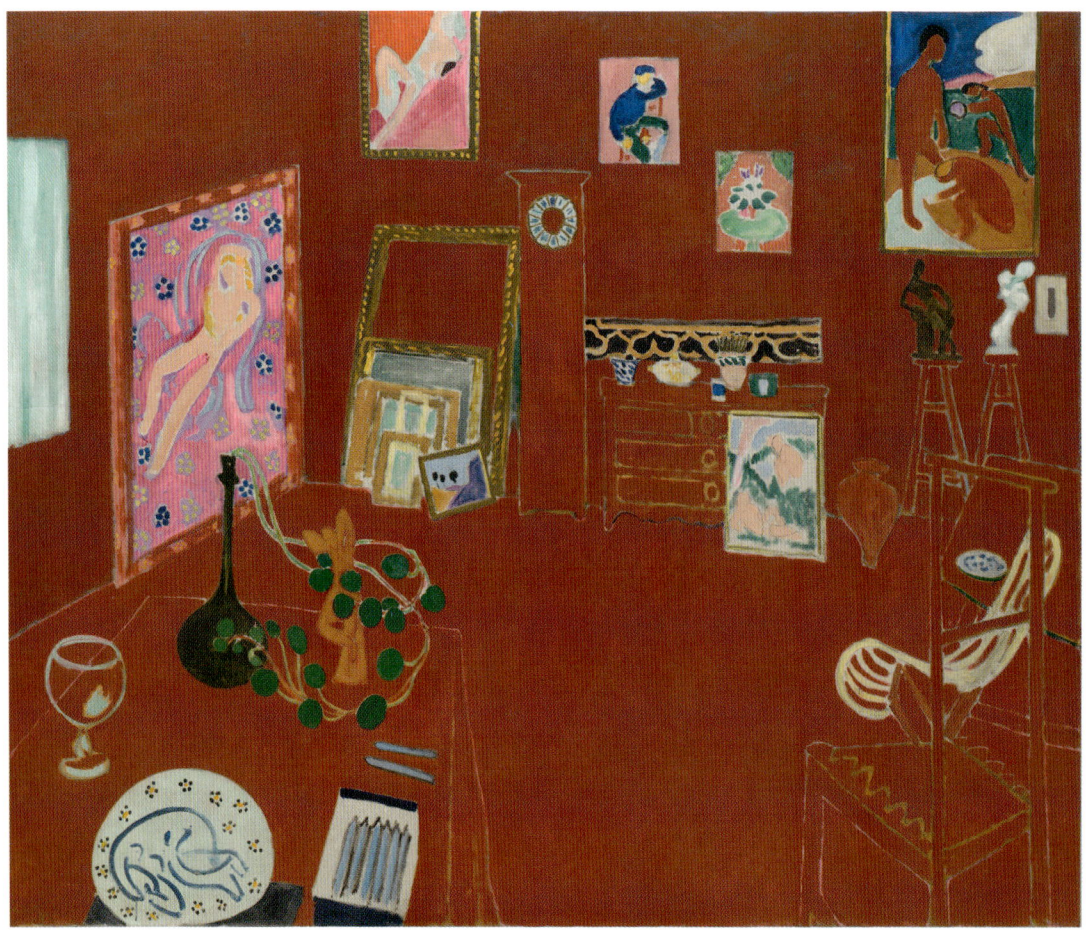

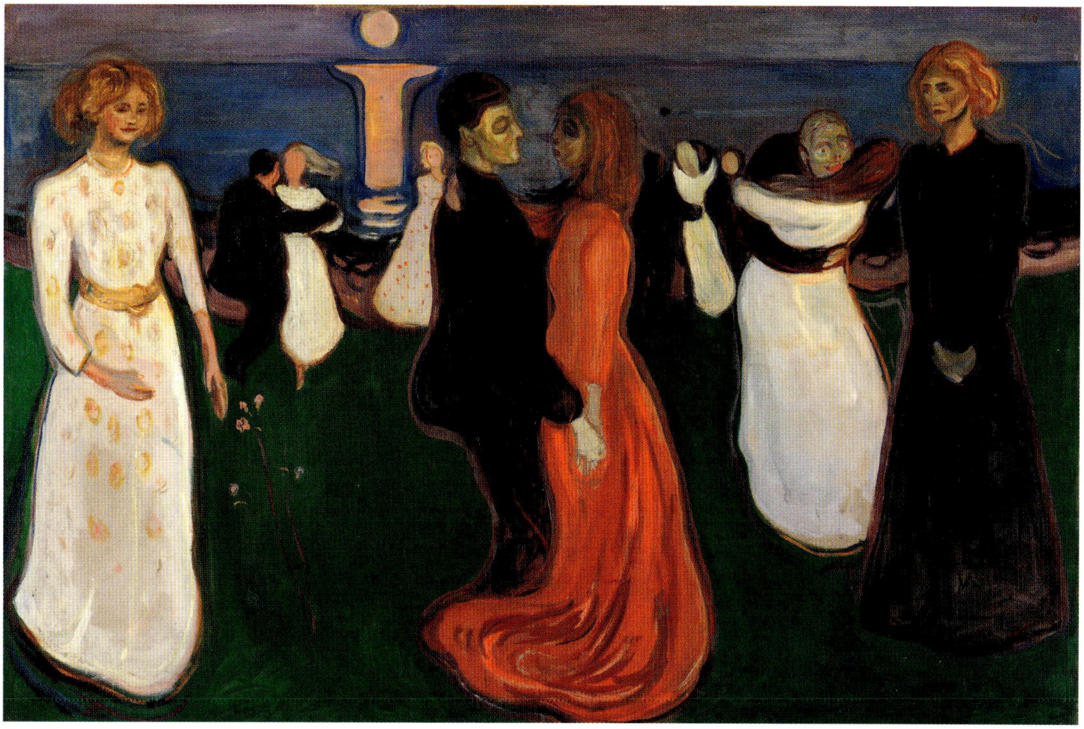

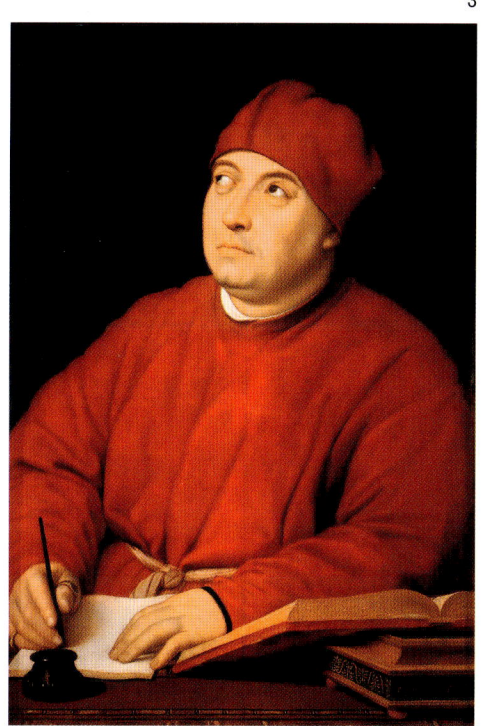

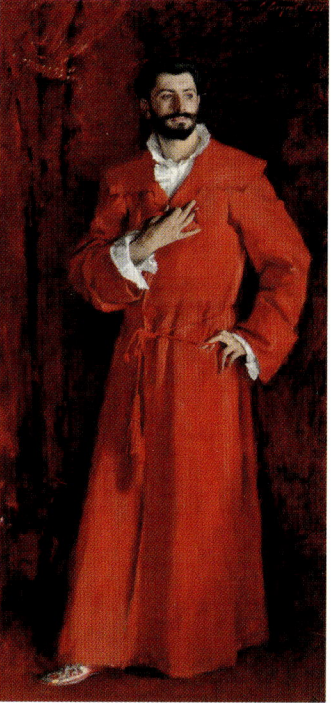

1. *The Red Studio,* Henri Matisse, 1911
2. *The Dance of Life,* Edvard Munch, 1899
3. *Portrait of Tommaso Inghirami,* Raphael, 1509
4. *Dr Pozzi at Home,* John Singer Sargent, 1881

Yellow

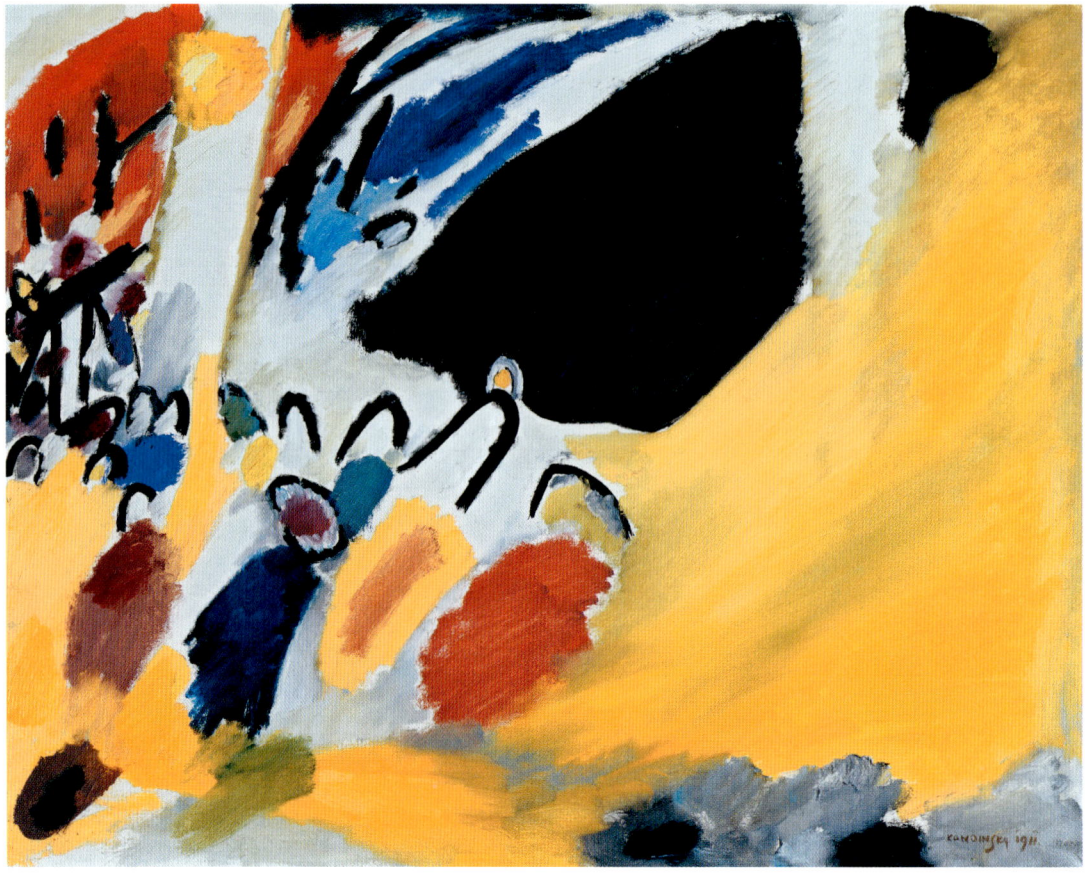

1

From divine light and joy to illness and deceit, yellow has been featured in art to convey a wide range of meanings. In ancient Egypt and China, it was associated with the sun, immortality and majestic power. Egyptian artists used yellow ochre to depict gods and eternal life, while Chinese artists employed yellow to symbolize the authority of the emperor, sacredness and yin. In medieval Europe, it was sometimes linked to betrayal or disease. Indian artists have used it to represent gold, glory and wisdom. Van Gogh used vibrant yellows in his paintings *Sunflowers* (1888) and *The Yellow House* (1888) to express optimism, hope, emotional intensity and happiness. Klimt's *The Kiss* (1907-08), with its golden-yellow palette, evokes notions of sensuality and transcendence, blending love with divine bliss. However, yellow also carries darker connotations. Gauguin used yellow for his emaciated looking *The Yellow Christ* (1889) to symbolize spiritual illumination as well as suffering and sacrifice.

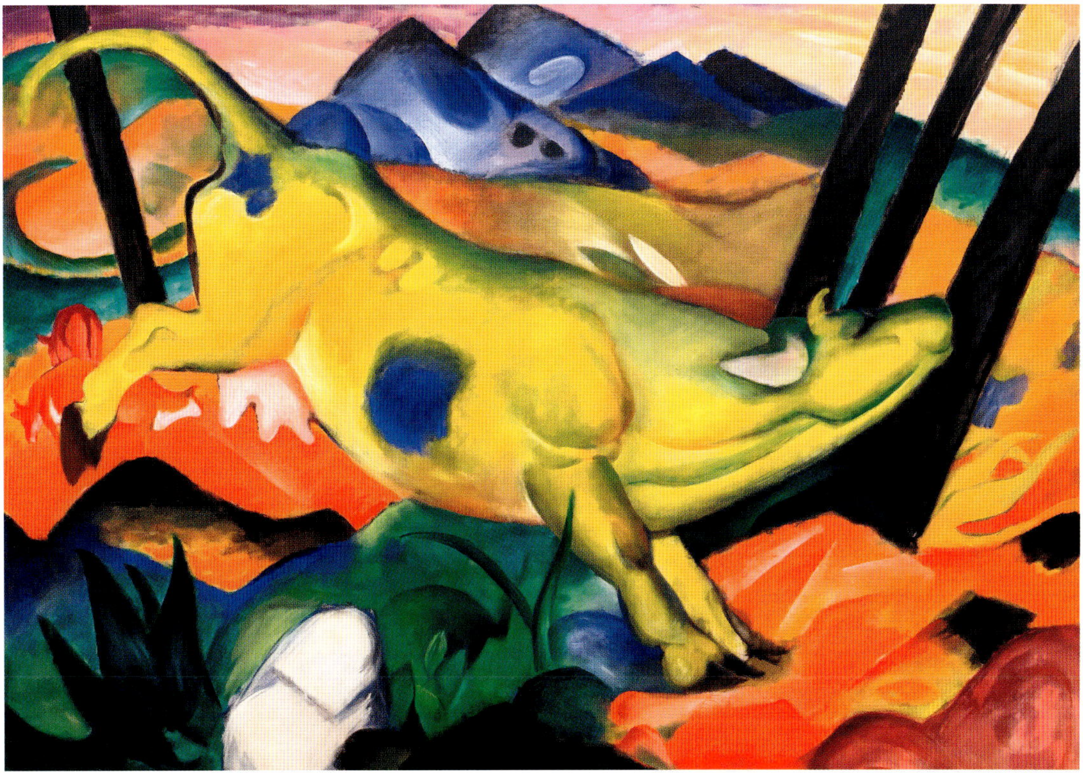

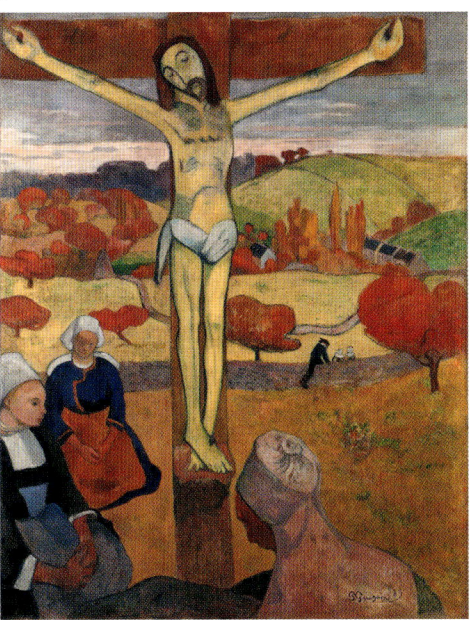

2

3

1. *Impression III (Concert),* Wassily Kandinsky, 1911
2. *Yellow Cow,* Franz Marc, 1911
3. *The Yellow Christ,* Paul Gauguin, 1889

Blue

Often evoking spirituality, power and introspection, the colour blue has held deep symbolic meaning in art throughout history. In ancient Egypt, blue was associated with the heavens and the divine, frequently used in depictions of gods and funerary art to symbolize protection and rebirth. The first synthetic blue pigment, known as Egyptian blue, was created around 2200 BCE in Egypt. It became a staple in Egyptian art and decoration. Pigment made from lapis lazuli, a rare and precious stone from Afghanistan, became known in Europe as ultramarine ('beyond the sea'). The Virgin Mary was often depicted wearing ultramarine robes, symbolizing purity, humility and heavenly grace. In East Asian art, blue appears in porcelain and textiles, evoking immortality and the vastness of nature. In Japanese ukiyo-e prints, blue waves and skies often reflect tranquillity and impermanence. Picasso's Blue Period (1901–04) employed muted blues to convey melancholy, sorrow and introspection. 'International Klein Blue' or IKB was invented by Yves Klein (1928–62) to explore the infinite and the immaterial.

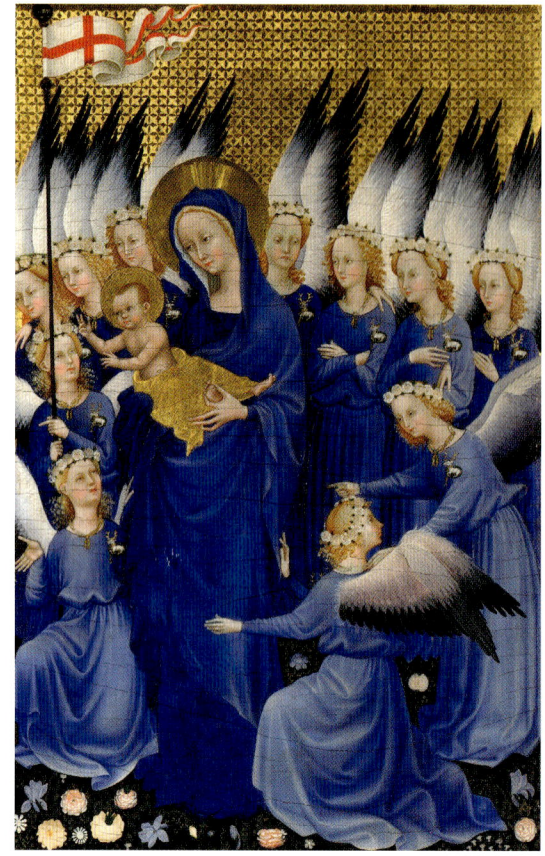

1

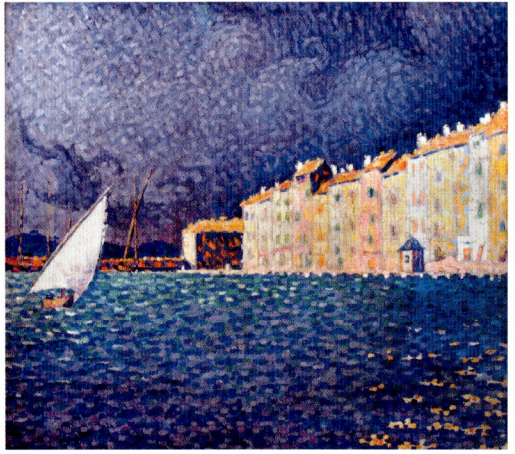

2

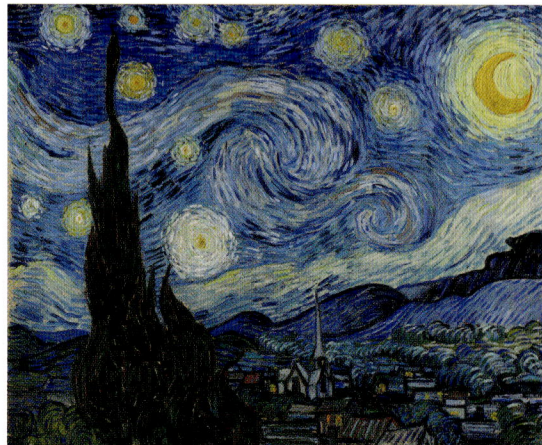

3

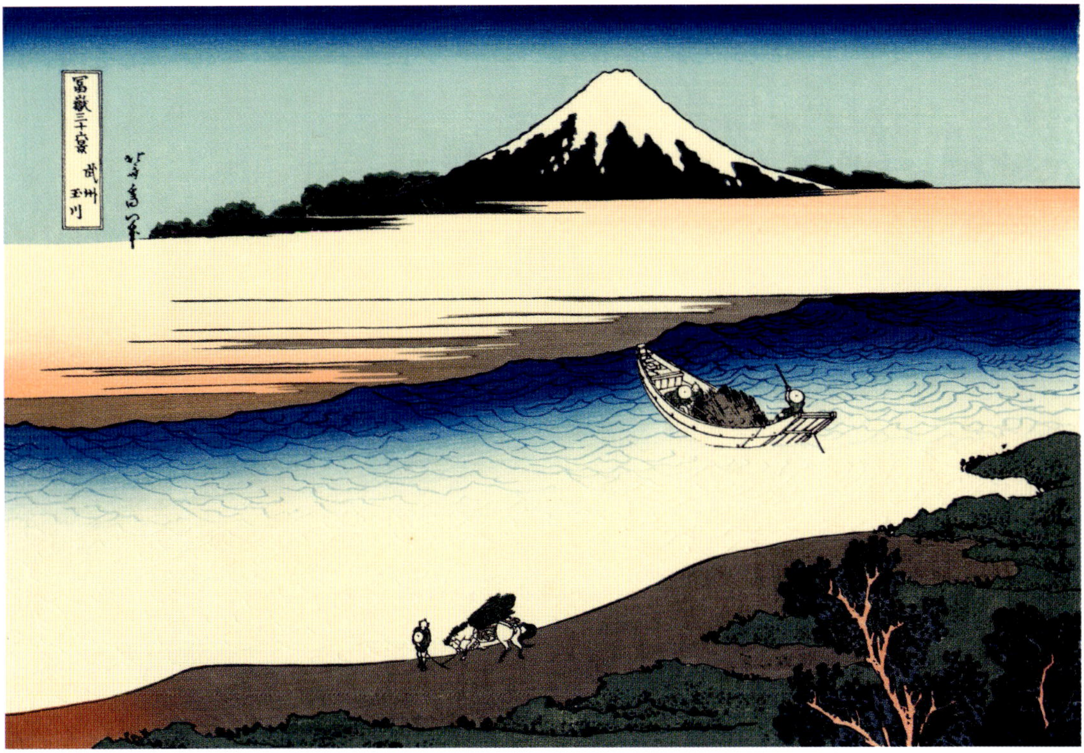

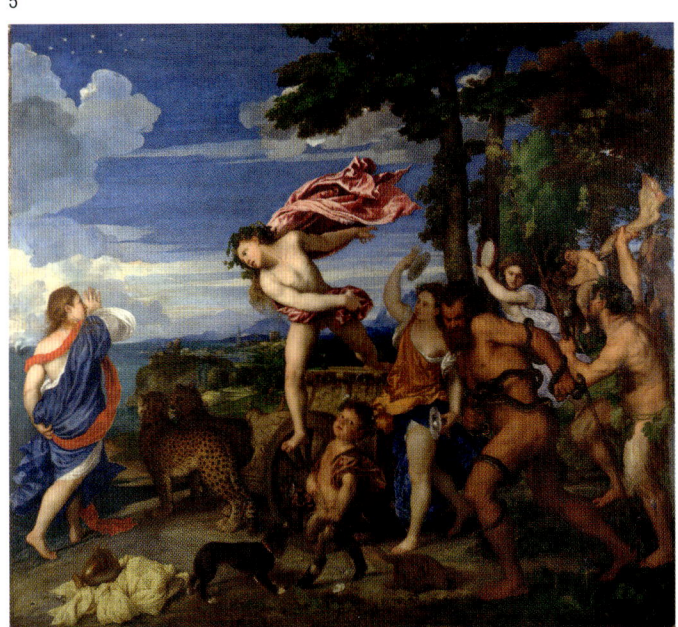

4

5

1. Detail from *The Wilton Diptych,* unknown artist, c. 1395-99
2. *Saint Tropez, Storm,* Paul Signac, 1895
3. *The Starry Night,* Vincent van Gogh, 1889
4. *Tama river in the Musashi province,* Japan, c. 1830
5. *Bacchus and Ariadne,* Titian, 1523

Green

Universally associated with nature, growth and renewal, green is frequently used in art to signify life and fertility. In ancient Egypt, green was linked to rebirth and the god Osiris, who was often depicted with green skin to symbolize resurrection and vegetation. In medieval European tapestries and illuminated manuscripts, green represented youth, love and springtime. During the Renaissance, green was used to signify harmony, freshness and fertility. In Islamic art, green holds sacred significance, as a symbol of paradise and divine blessing, while in Chinese art, green signifies health, wealth and harmony. Various artists have used green for individual reasons. For example, John Constable used it to express his connection to the English countryside. For him, green evoked the lushness of rural life, which was being destroyed by industrialization. In *At the Moulin Rouge* (1892–95), Henri de Toulouse-Lautrec (1864–1901) used an eerie green to evoke a sense of artificiality, alienation and psychological tension. The green reflects the decadent, absinthe-soaked atmosphere of the Belle Époque cabaret culture.

1

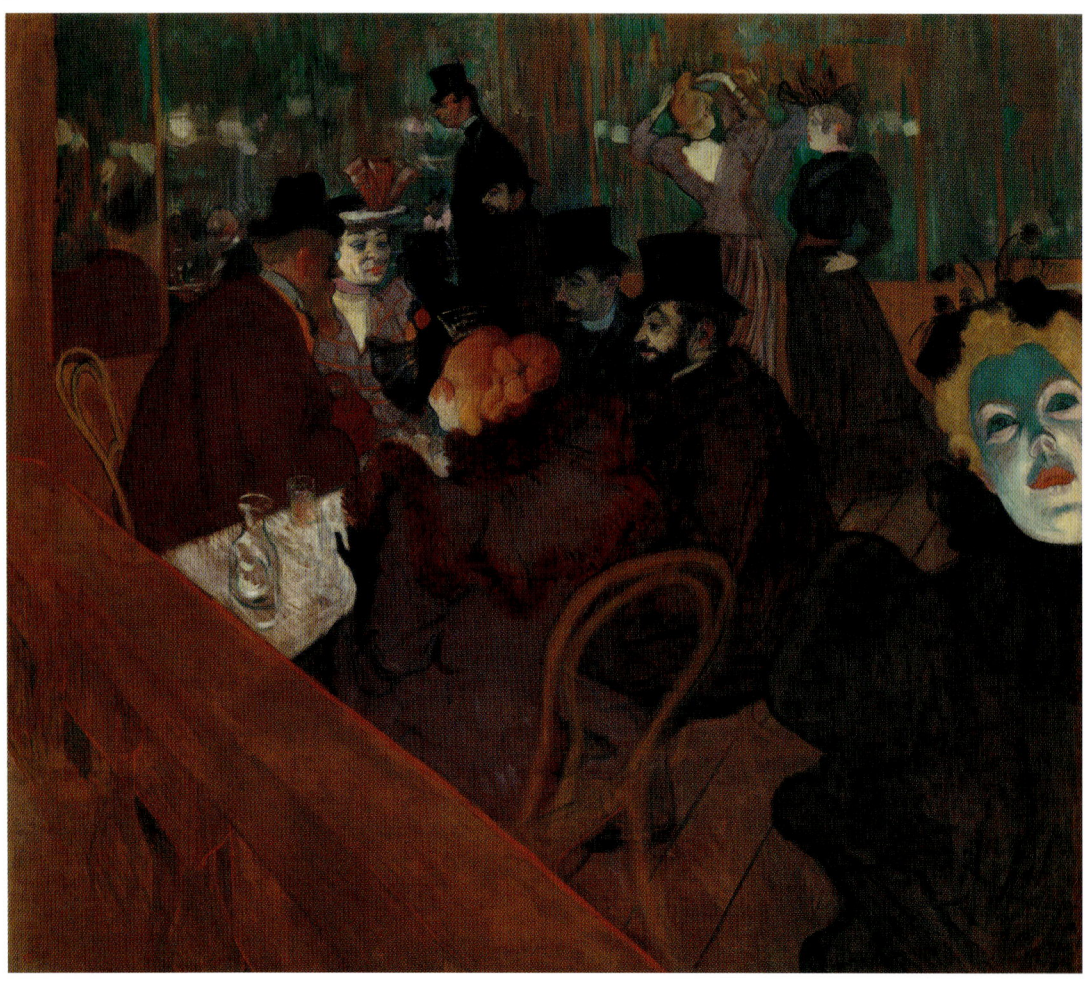

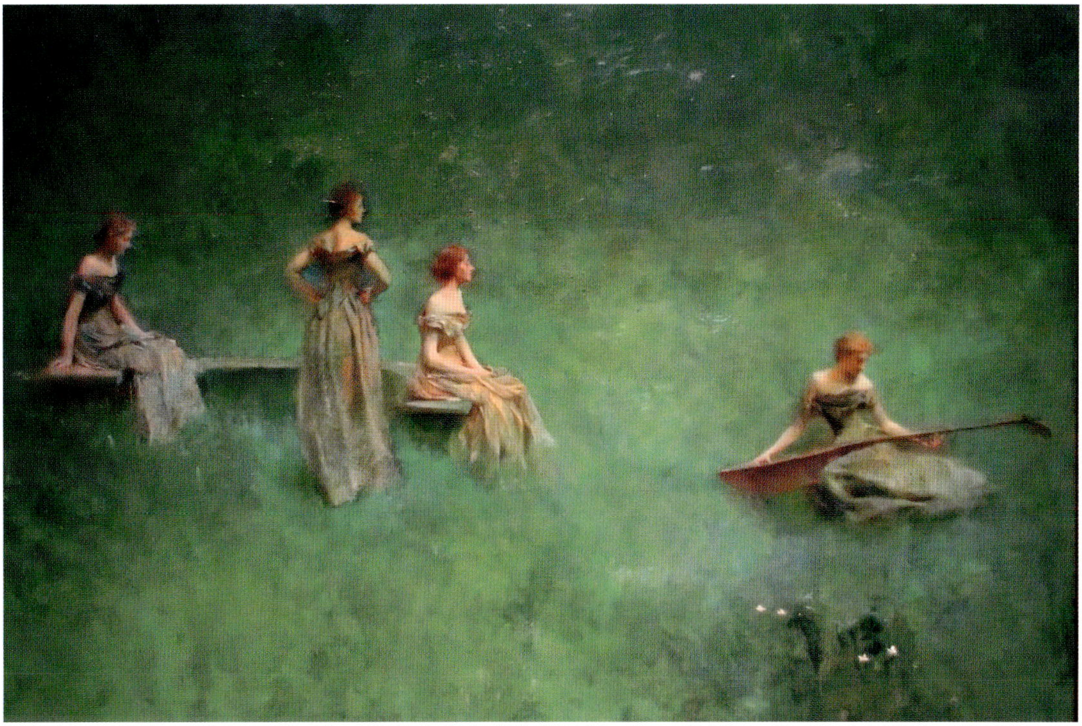

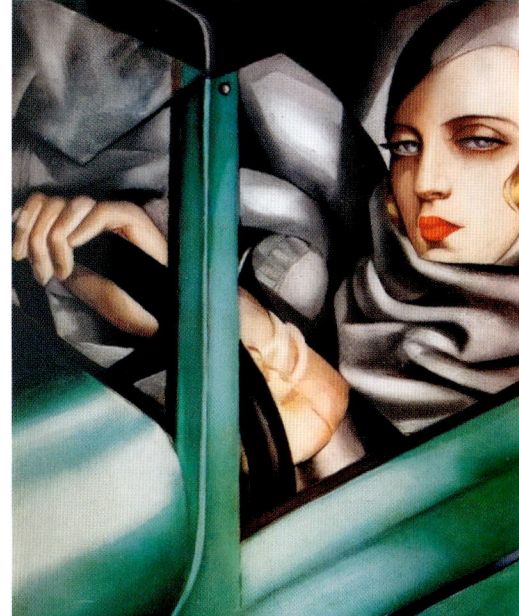

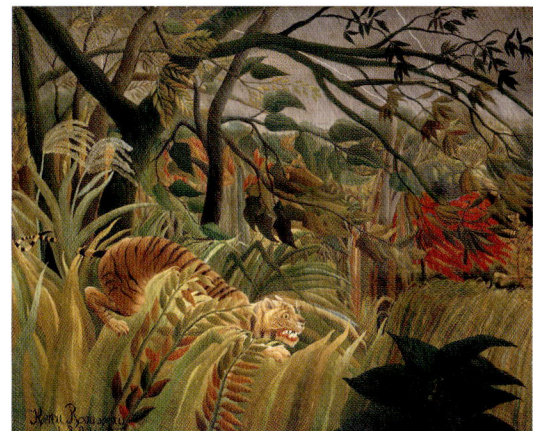

1. *At the Moulin Rouge,* Henri de Toulouse-Lautrec, 1892–95
2. *The Lute,* Thomas Wilmer Dewing, 1904
3. *Autoportrait (Tamara in a Green Bugatti),* Tamara de Lempicka, 1929
4. *Tiger in a Tropical Storm (Surprised!),* Henri Rousseau, 1891

Purple

Due to the rarity and cost of Tyrian purple dye, historically extracted from Mediterranean sea snails, purple became the colour of royalty. In ancient Rome and Byzantium, only emperors and high-ranking officials were permitted to wear it, and in religious art, purple often signified divine authority. Across eras, artists used purple to evoke emotion and depth. In *April Love* (1855-56) by Arthur Hughes (1832-1915), he mixed organic red madder with cobalt blue for the female figure's purple dress. Until then, purple had been used for mourning clothes. After that, purple came to be associated with love and passion. Also in 1856, the chemist William Henry Perkin (1838-1907) invented the synthetic dye mauveine. From that time, mauve became a fashionable colour in clothing, interior design and visual culture, denoting refinement and modernity. Artists of the Symbolist and Aesthetic movements, such as James McNeill Whistler, used mauve to create the atmosphere of mystery and sensuality. Mauve became associated with decadence, melancholy and the ephemeral beauty of modern life, and the 1890s came to be called the Mauve Decade.

1

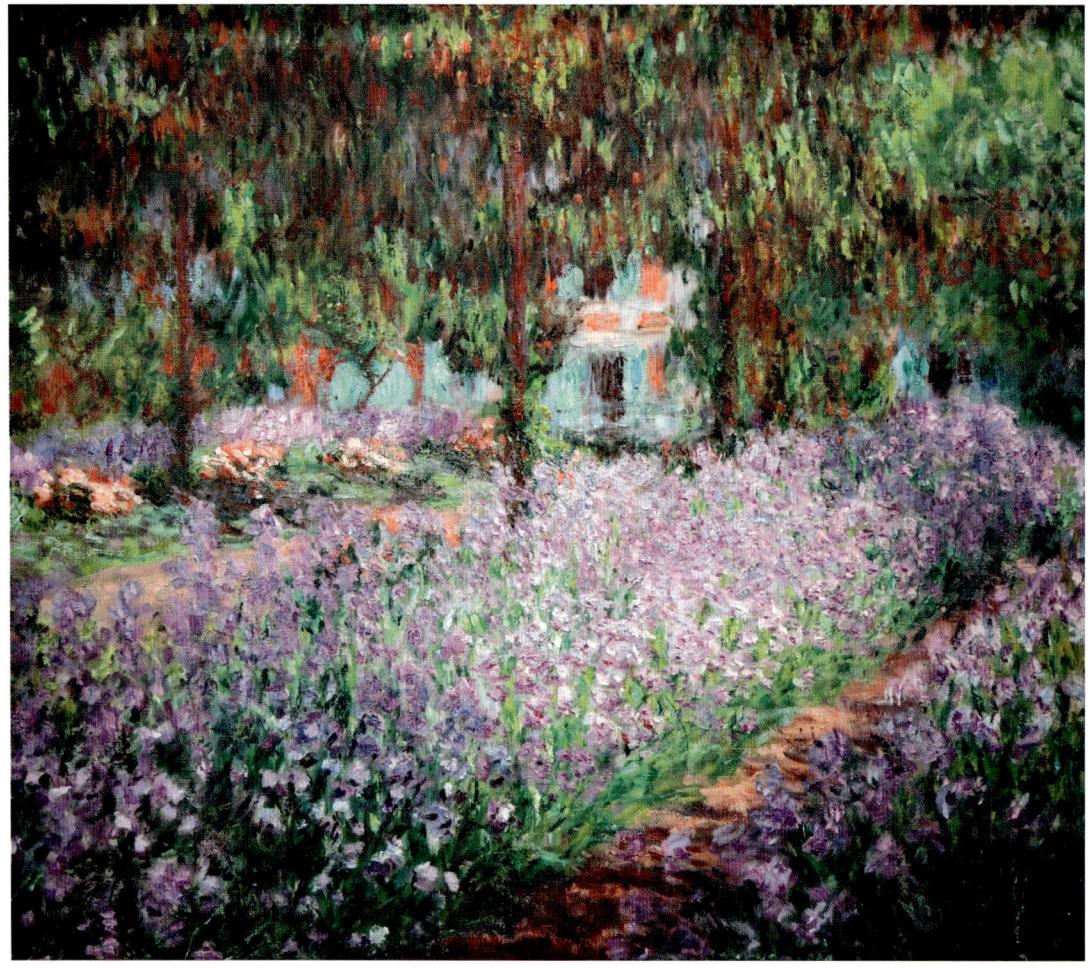

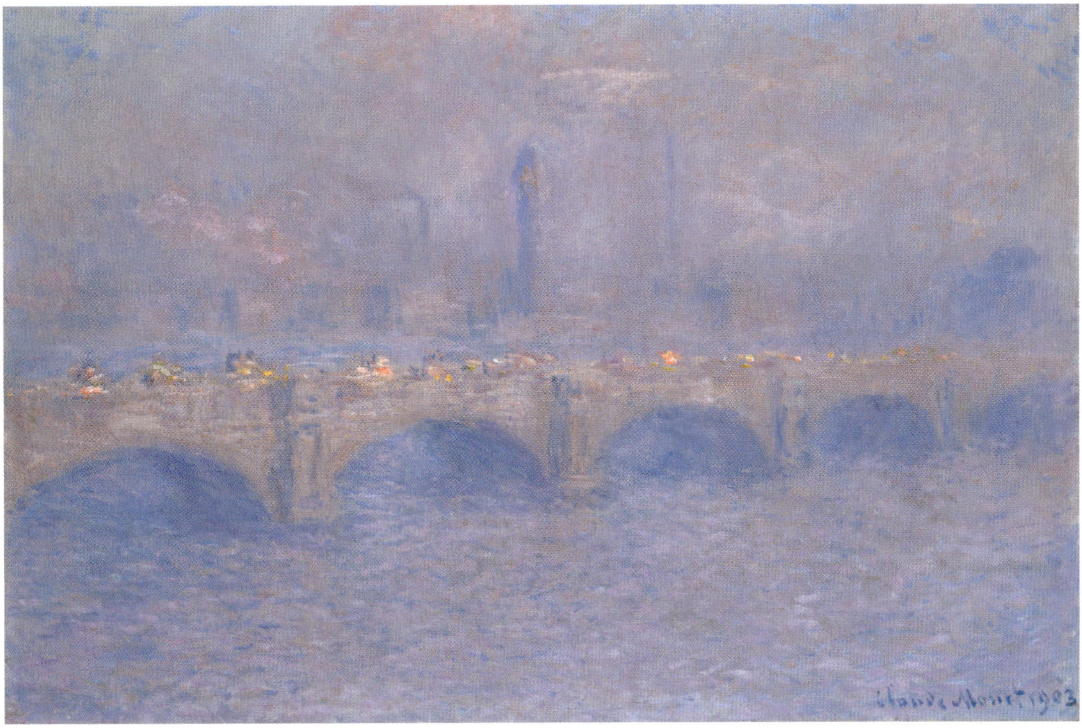

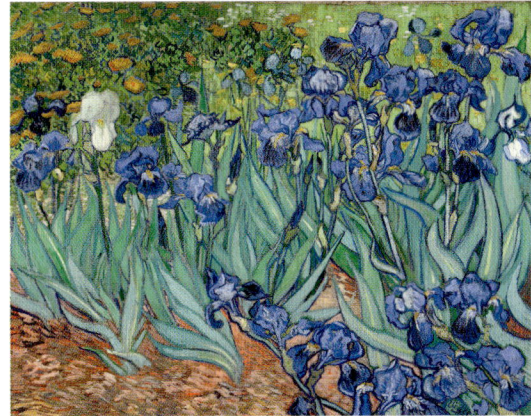

2

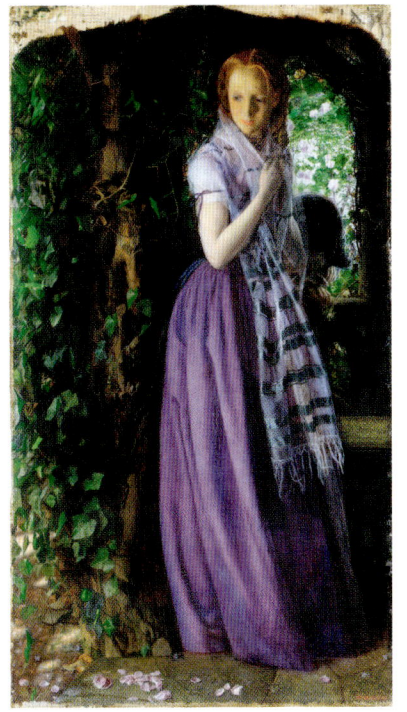

3

4

1. *The Artist's Garden at Giverny*, Claude Monet, 1900
2. *Waterloo Bridge, Sunlight Effect*, Claude Monet, 1903
3. *April Love*, Arthur Hughes, 1855-56
4. *Irises*, Vincent van Gogh, 1889

Orange

Often reflecting energy, transformation and vitality, orange is also associated with warmth, creativity, spiritual enlightenment, excitement and enthusiasm. As a colour of sunsets and autumn, orange can symbolize impermanence, emotion or the beauty of fleeting moments. In 1888, Van Gogh painted *Basket of Oranges* to denote warmth, vitality and the radiance of southern light, reflecting his belief in colour's power to convey spiritual and emotional intensity. Albert Joseph Moore (1841-93) painted *Midsummer* in 1887, using orange to evoke sensuality and warmth, suggesting the fullness and ripeness of summer and in 1895, Frederic Leighton (1830-1896) painted *Flaming June*, with brilliant orange drapery that conveys passion, energy and the fleeting vibrancy of life, contrasting his figure's tranquil repose with the burning intensity of the sun. Impressionists used orange in changing light to symbolize the passage of time, especially in paintings of dawn and dusk. In 1956, Mark Rothko (1903-70) painted swathes of orange evoking transcendence and spiritual ecstasy, using colour as a vehicle for emotional depth and a meditative encounter with the sublime.

1

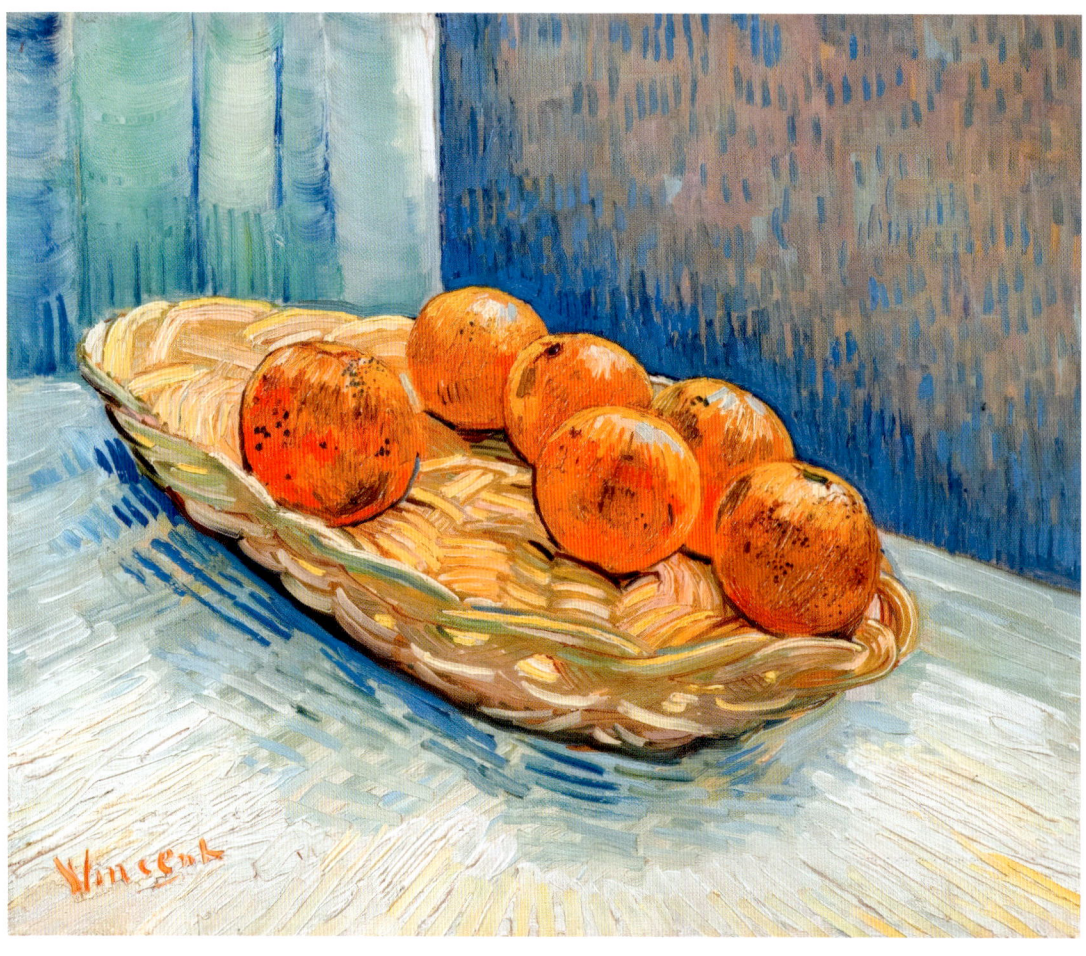

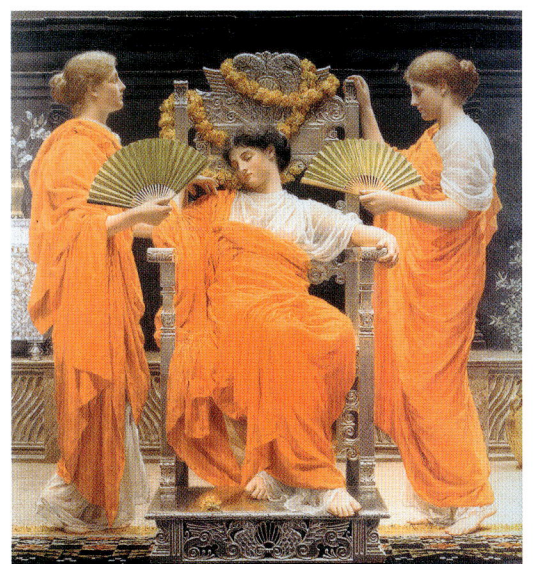

2

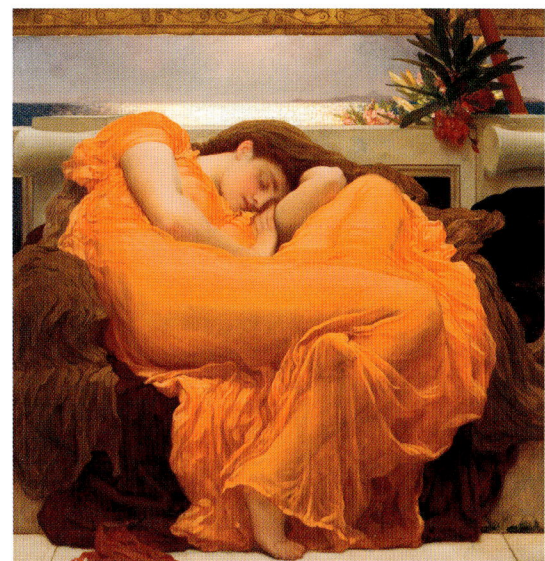

3

4

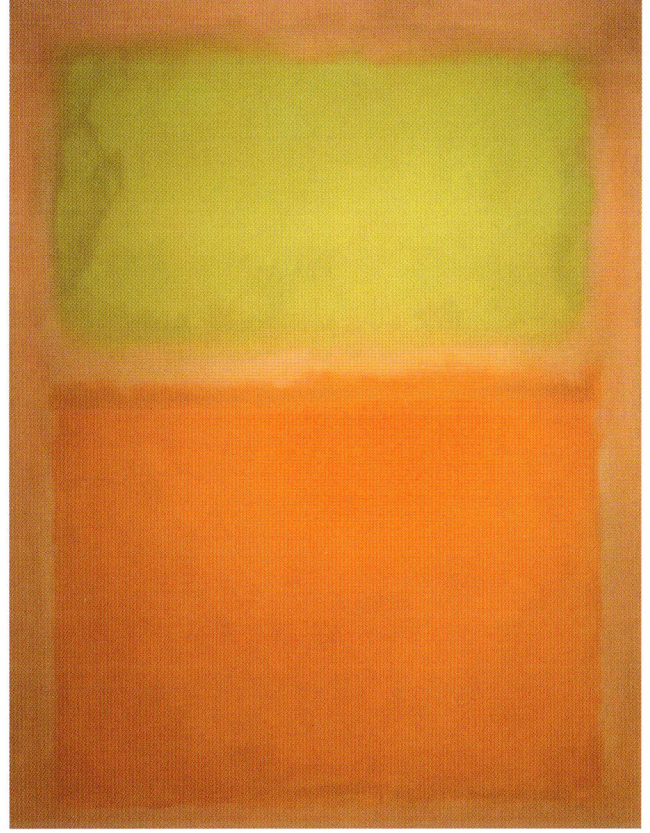

1. *Basket With Six Oranges,* Vincent van Gogh, 1888
2. *Midsummer,* Albert Joseph Moore, 1887
3. *Flaming June,* Frederic Leighton, 1895
4. *Orange and Yellow,* Mark Rothko, 1956

Pink

Whether a rosy daybreak sky, the flush of a cherub's cheeks, an eager dog's tongue, a velvety rose, or a delicate cherry blossom, the colour pink in art has symbolised innocence, romance, protest, and more. Pink was notably popularized in the eighteenth century by Madame de Pompadour, who inspired the creation of 'Pompadour pink' in Sèvres porcelain. In this era, pink became a symbol of luxury, refinement, femininity, erotic playfulness and aristocratic taste. In Japanese art, pink often denotes the transience of life, tied to Buddhist ideas of impermanence. Japanese ukiyo-e artist Kikukawa Eizan (1787-1867) created *The Courtesan Hanazome of the Ogiya Reading a Letter and Grinding Ink* in c. 1810-15, using delicate pink to symbolize youthful beauty, sensual refinement, and the fleeting charm of the courtesan world, reflecting the ukiyo-e ideal of life's transient pleasures. In 1876, Edgar Degas painted in vibrant pink to create *Dancers in Pink*, evoking youthful vitality and the artifice of performance, and capturing both the elegance and the underlying strain of the dancers' disciplined grace.

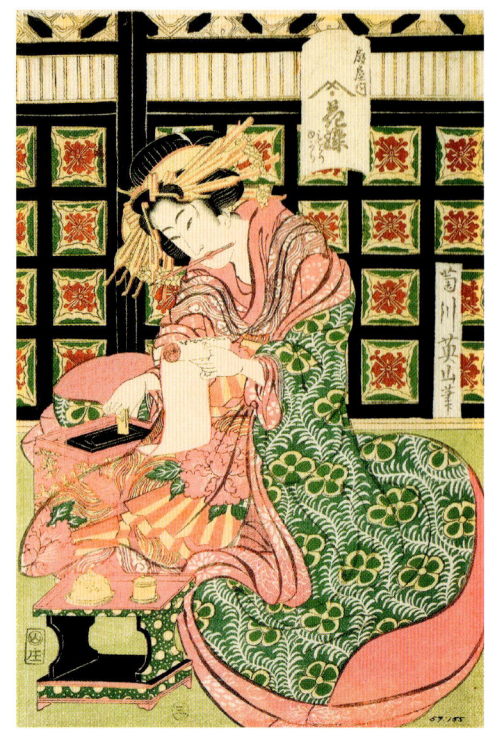

1

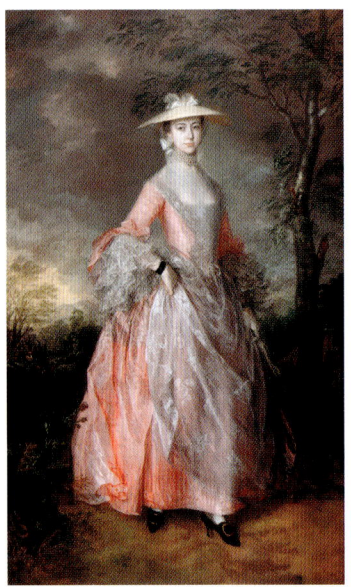

2

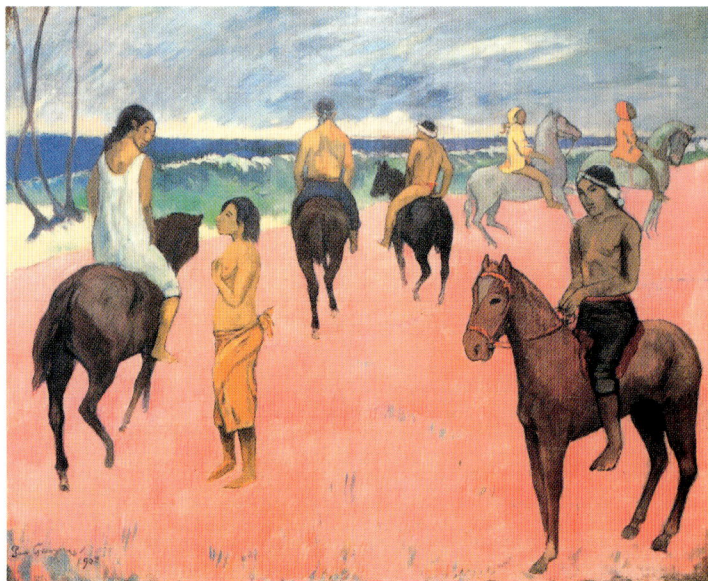

3

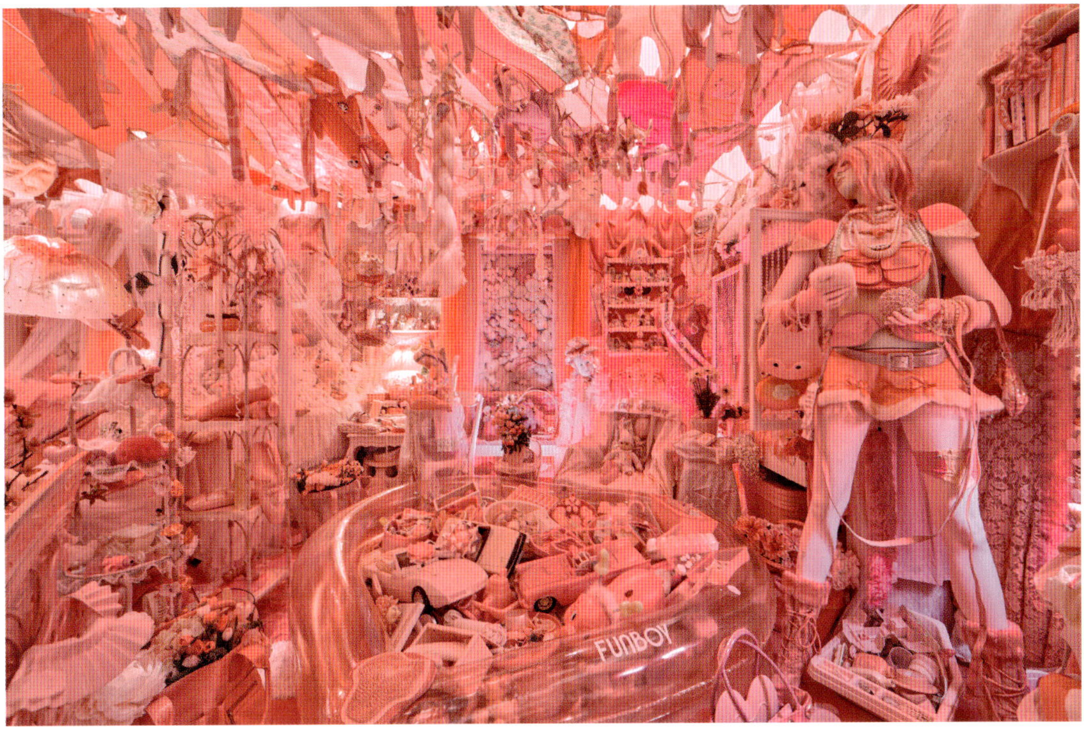

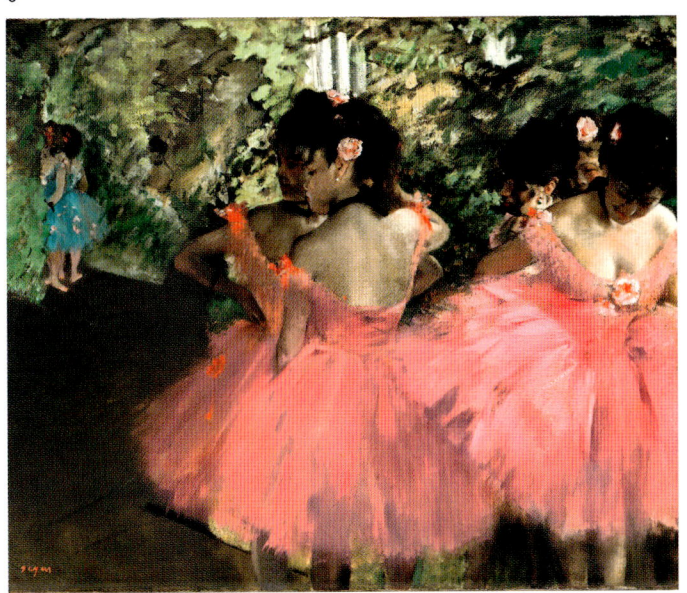

1. *The Courtesan Hanazome of the Ogiya Reading a Letter and Grinding Ink,* Kikukawa Eizan, c. 1810–15

2. *Mary, Countess Howe*, Thomas Gainsborough, c. 1764

3. *Riders on the Beach,* Paul Gauguin, 1902

4. *Pink Project,* Portia Munson, 1995

5. *Dancers in Pink,* Edgar Degas, 1876

White

From purity and divinity to emptiness and mourning, white conveys many underlying ideas. In ancient Egypt, it was associated with the sacred and the divine; pharaohs wore white linen to signify their spiritual authority. In Christian art, white often symbolizes purity, innocence and resurrection, seen in depictions of angels and Christ's robes. In contrast, in Eastern cultures such as China and India, white is the colour of mourning, representing death, transition and spiritual release. *White on White* (1918) by Kazimir Malevich (1879-1935) features white to explore spiritual transcendence and the reduction of form. Robert Ryman (1930-2019) built his career on white-on-white paintings, using the colour to question the nature of painting itself. White can also evoke notions of serenity, sterility or the sublime. *White Flag* (1955) by Jasper Johns (b. 1930) was a reinterpretation of the American flag that expunges its familiar colours. By rendering the recognizable image in shades of white, he challenged viewers to reconsider what the flag represents: national pride, identity or perhaps surrender.

1. *Corfu, Lights and Shadows*, John Singer Sargent, 1909
2. *York Street Leading to Charles Street, Manchester,* Pierre Adolphe Valette, 1913
3. *White on White,* Kazimir Malevich, 1918
4. *Strolling Along the Seashore,* Joaquin Sorolla, 1909
5. *Symphony in White, No. 1: The White Girl*, James McNeil Whistler, 1863

1

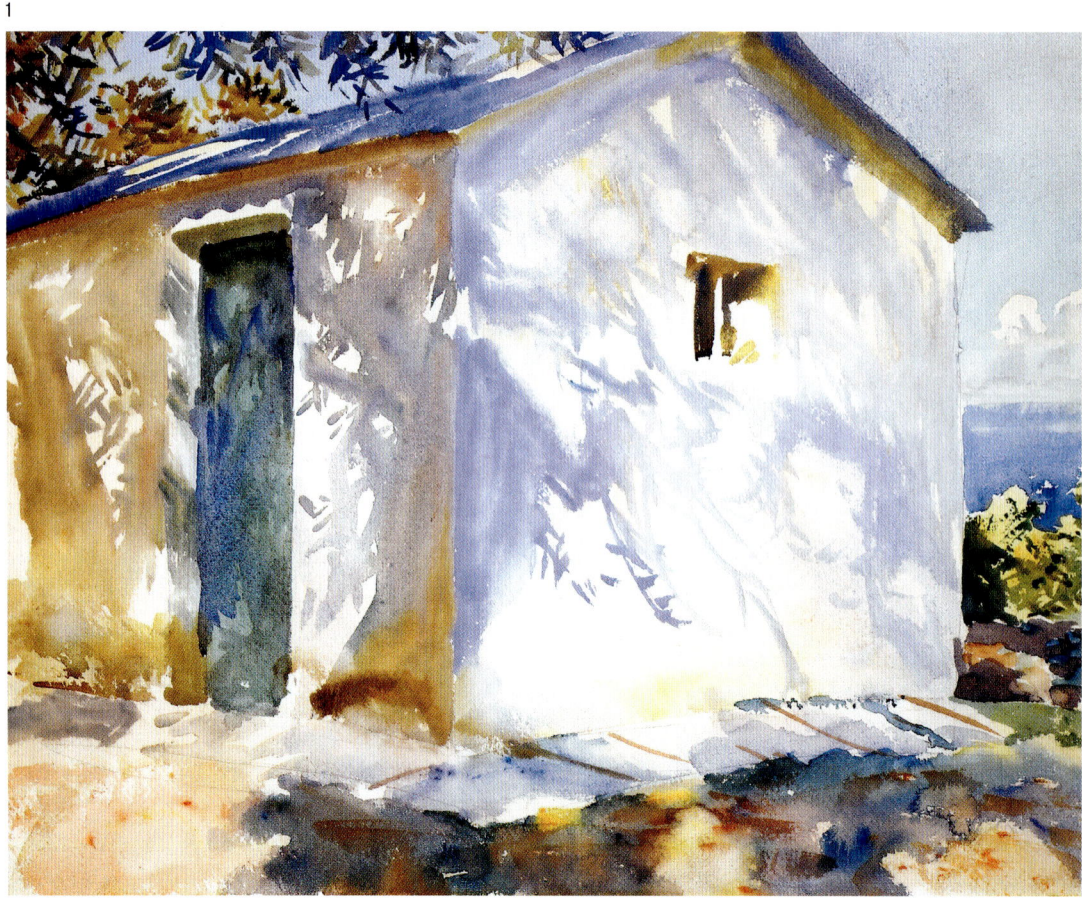

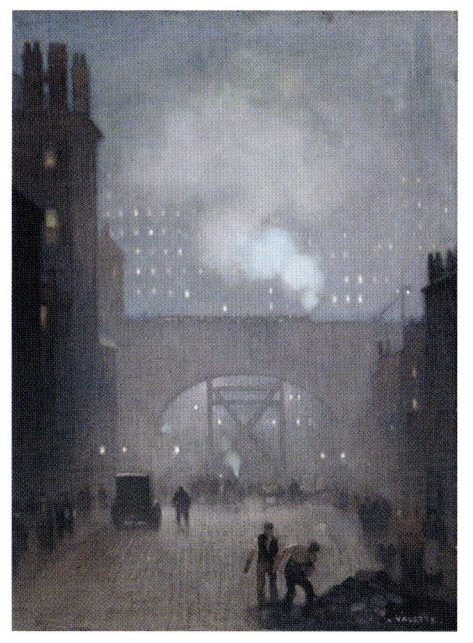

2

3

4

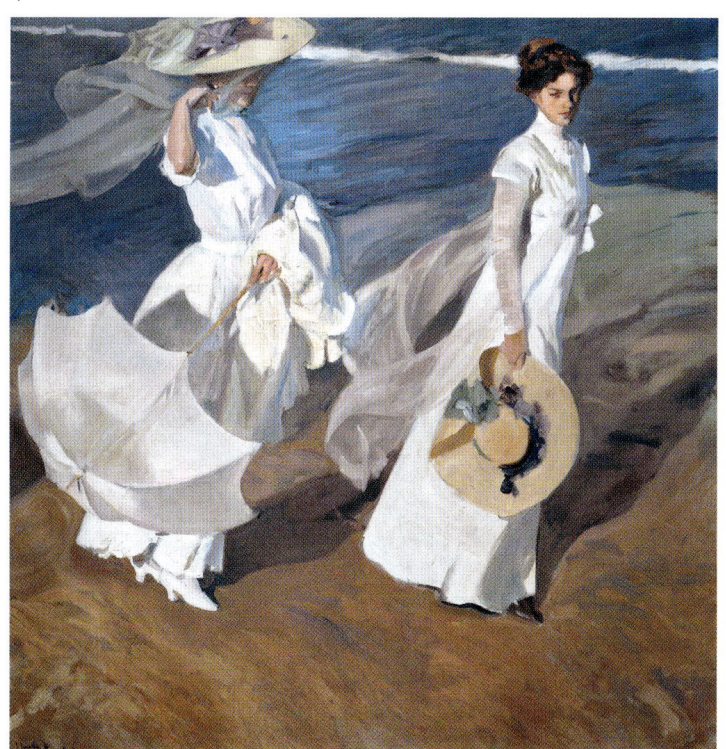

5

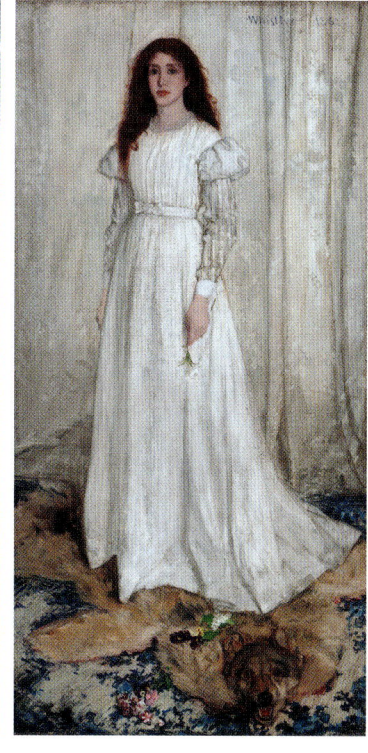

Black

Black has been used in art to symbolize a wide range of meanings, including power, mystery, mourning, drama, elegance and the unknown. In ancient Egypt, it denoted fertility and resurrection, linked to the rich soil of the Nile and the god Osiris. In ancient Rome, it was associated with mourning and death, a tradition that continues in many Western cultures to this day. In traditional African art, black represents spiritual power, maturity and a connection to the ancestral past. It appears in masks, textiles and sculptures to invoke the unseen forces of the universe. In Western art, black has often been used to convey drama, depth and sophistication. Artists like Francisco Goya (1746–1828) used black to express psychological darkness, as seen in his haunting *Black Paintings* (1819–23). In the twentieth century, Kazimir Malevich's *Black Square* (1915) used black as a radical symbol of pure abstraction and the void.

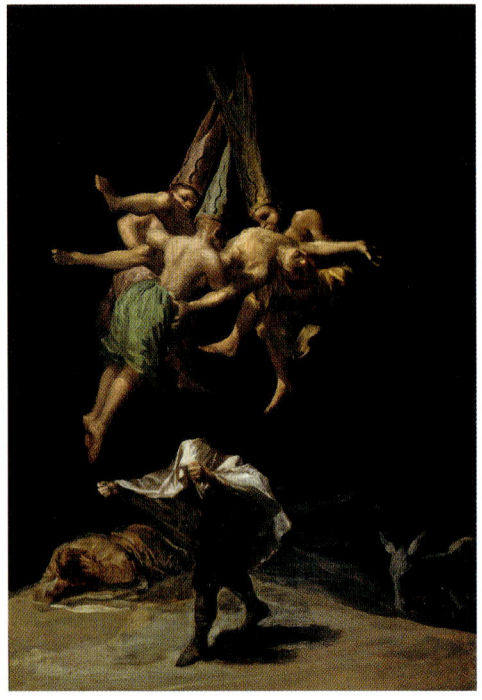

1

2

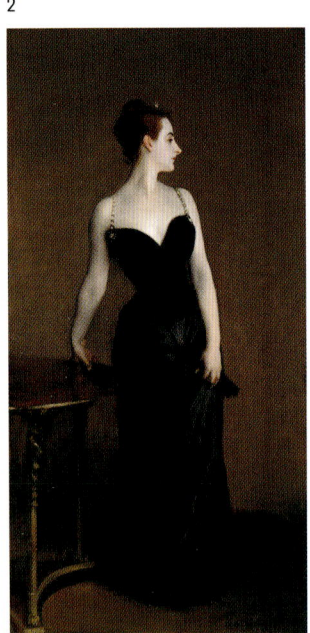

3

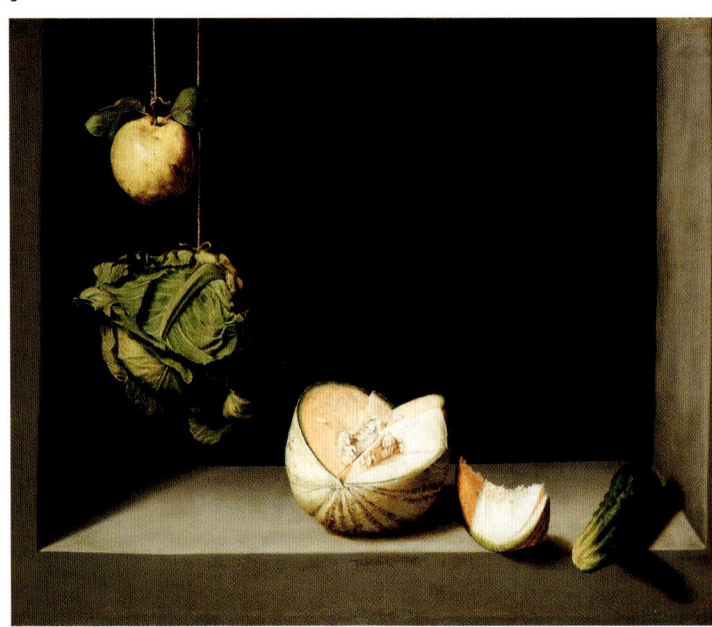

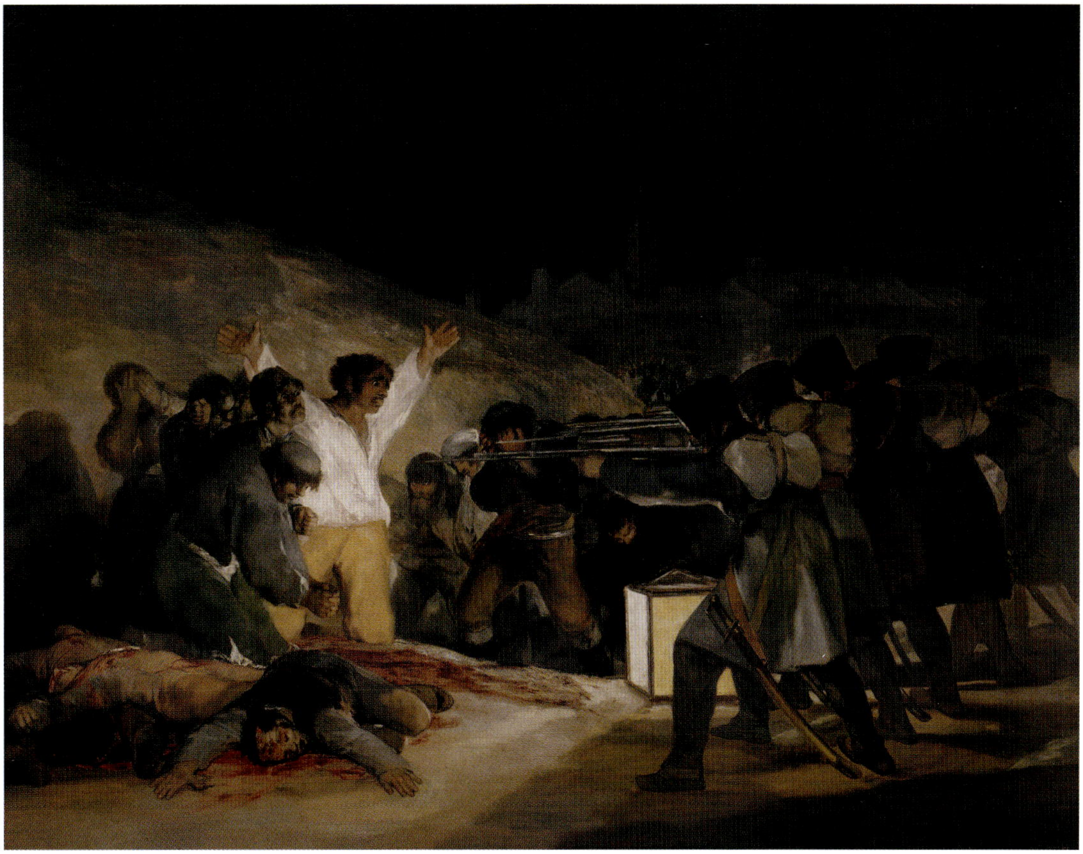

4

5

1. *Witches' Flight,* Francisco Goya, 1798
2. *Madame X,* John Singer Sargent, 1883-84
3. *Quince,* Cabbage, Melon and Cucumber,
   Juan Sánchez Cotán, c. 1602
4. *The Third of May 1808,* Francisco Goya, 1814
5. *Non-Object Black,* Anish Kapoor, 2021-22

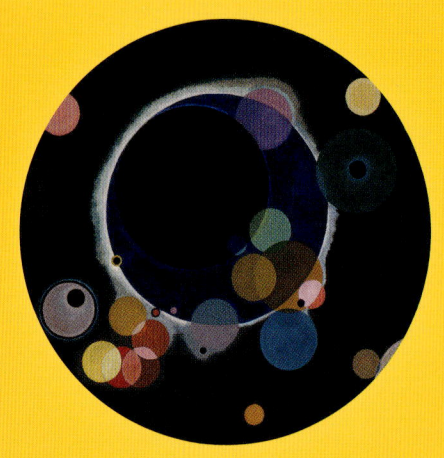

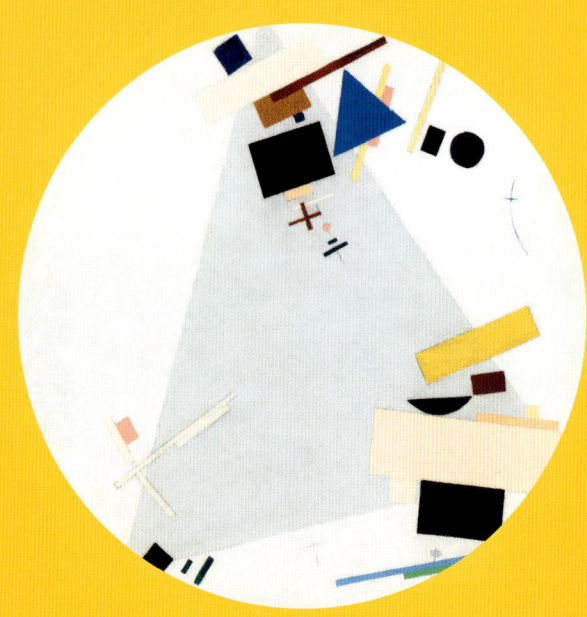

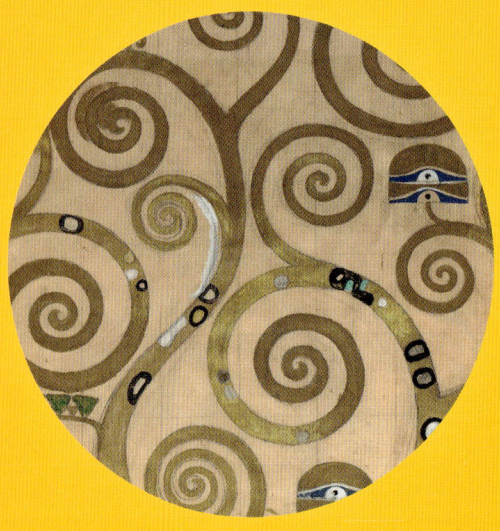

Shapes

Triangle

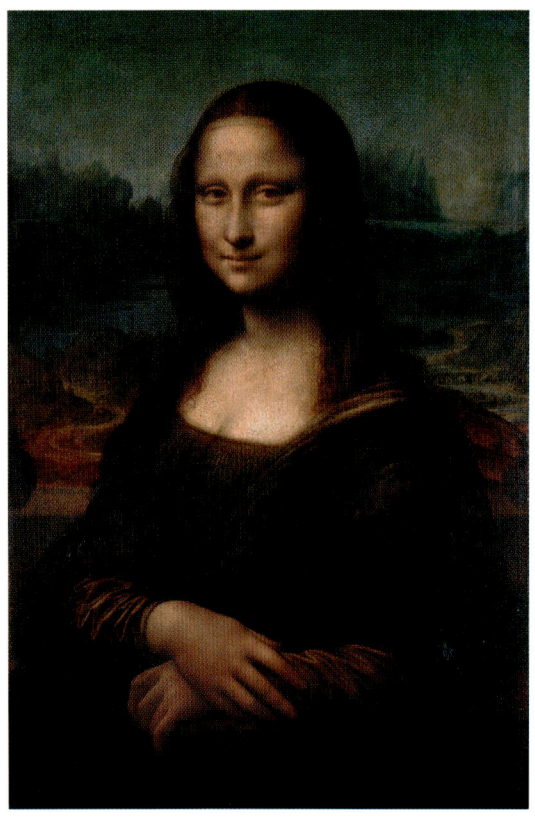

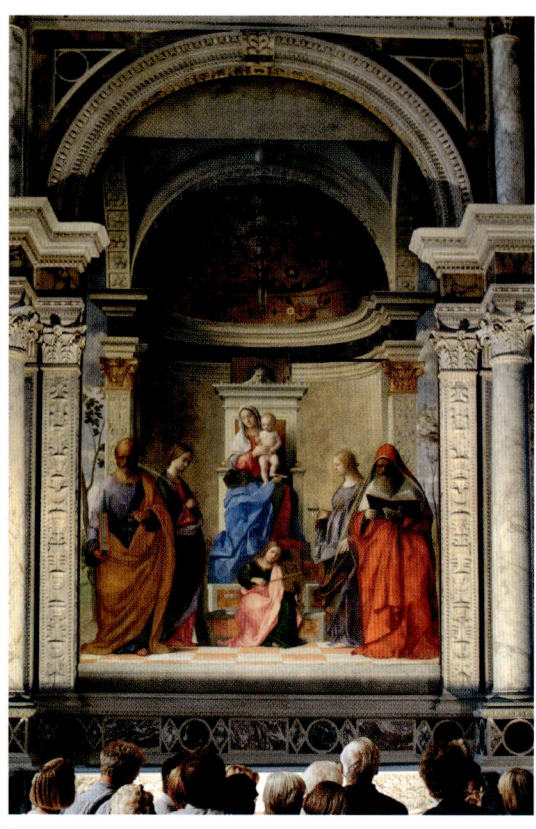

1

2

Spirituality, stability, divinity, balance, structure, transcendence and transformation are just a few of the meanings bestowed on triangles in art. Its earliest emblematic use appeared in ancient Egypt, where the triangular form of the pyramids symbolized the connection between earth and the divine, and the soul's ascent to the afterlife. In ancient Greece, triangles symbolized harmony, cosmic order and perfection - central to geometry, philosophy and art - appearing in Pythagorean mysticism, Platonic theory and sacred architecture, like temple pediments. Christian art frequently employed the triangle to represent the Holy Trinity, comprising the Father, the Son and the Holy Spirit. In Hinduism, upward and downward triangles symbolize masculine (Shiva) and feminine (Shakti) energies, and their union forms the Shatkona, a symbol of creation and balance. Indigenous American cultures used triangles in textiles and sand paintings to represent change, unity and direction. In general, triangular compositions in art convey balance and harmony, as seen in Leonardo da Vinci's *Mona Lisa* (c. 1503-17). Wassily Kandinsky and Kazimir Malevich used triangles in paintings to explore spiritual and geometric purity.

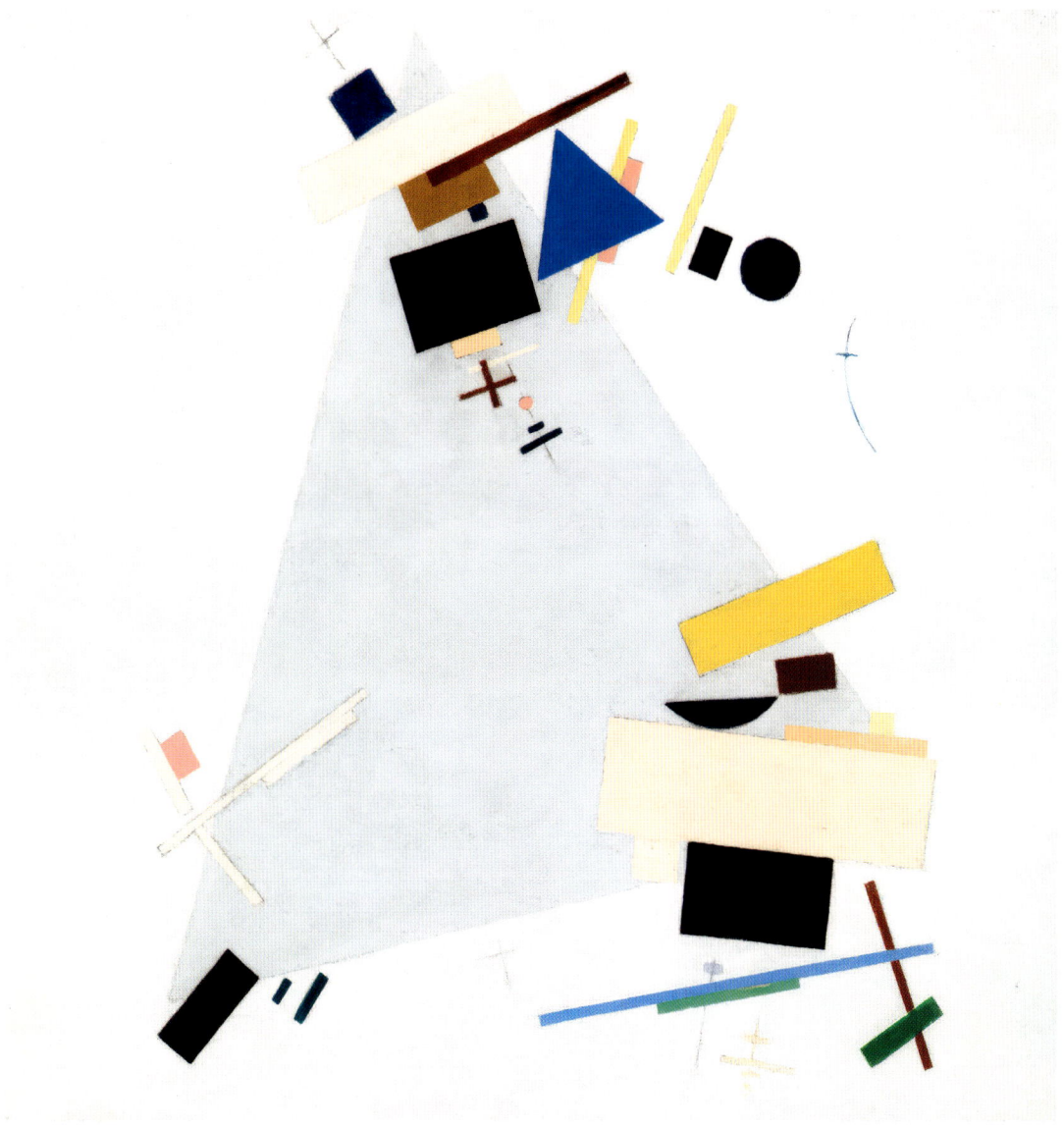

3

1. *Mona Lisa,* Leonardo da Vinci, c. 1503–17
2. *San Zaccaria Altarpiece,* Giovanni Bellini, 1505
3. *Dynamic Suprematism,* Kazimir Malevich, 1915/1916

Circle

With no beginning or end, the circle has come to
symbolize eternity, perpetuity and interconnection,
and has been depicted by artists across cultures to
represent perfection, heaven and the cosmos. Since
ancient times, the circle has been a symbol of
eternity, unity, wholeness and the cyclical nature
of life. It is often used as a powerful metaphor for
the infinite and the divine. Circular mandalas are
Hindu and Buddhist designs that are emblematic
of the world, the universe and spiritual harmony.
Similarly, Christian artists depicted circular halos
to signify holiness and divine light. The rose
windows of Gothic cathedrals evoke a sense
of cosmic order and spiritual transcendence.
In Native American belief, the circle is related to
the medicine wheel or sacred hoop that symbolizes
the cycles of life. Wassily Kandinsky used circles to
express spiritual resonance and cosmic harmony,
while Yayoi Kusama's polka-dotted installations
use circular repetition to evoke infinity and
self-obliteration. Among the theories about
Rembrandt's *Self-Portrait with Two Circles*
(1665–69) is that the circles may have
kabbalistic significance.

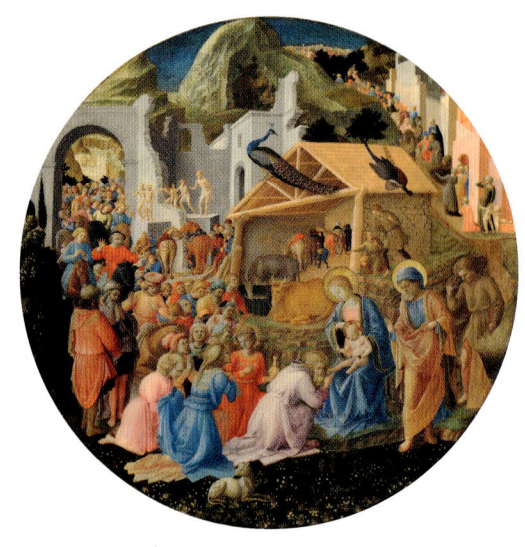

1

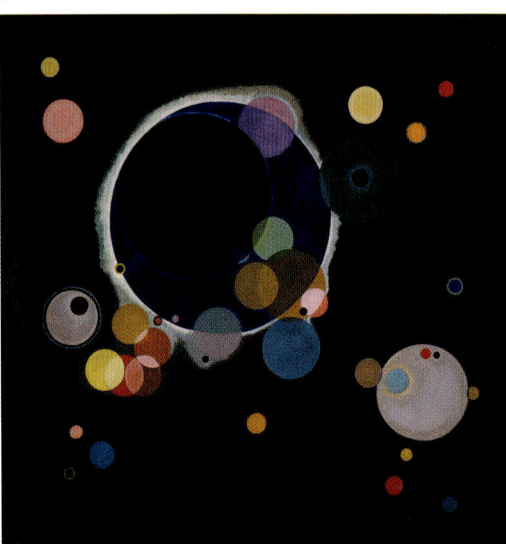

2

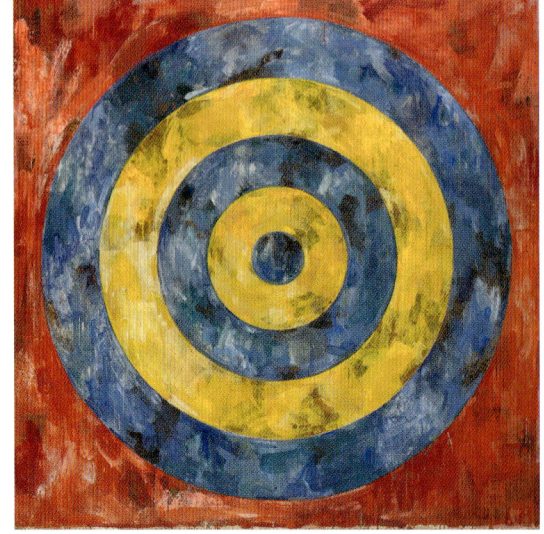

3

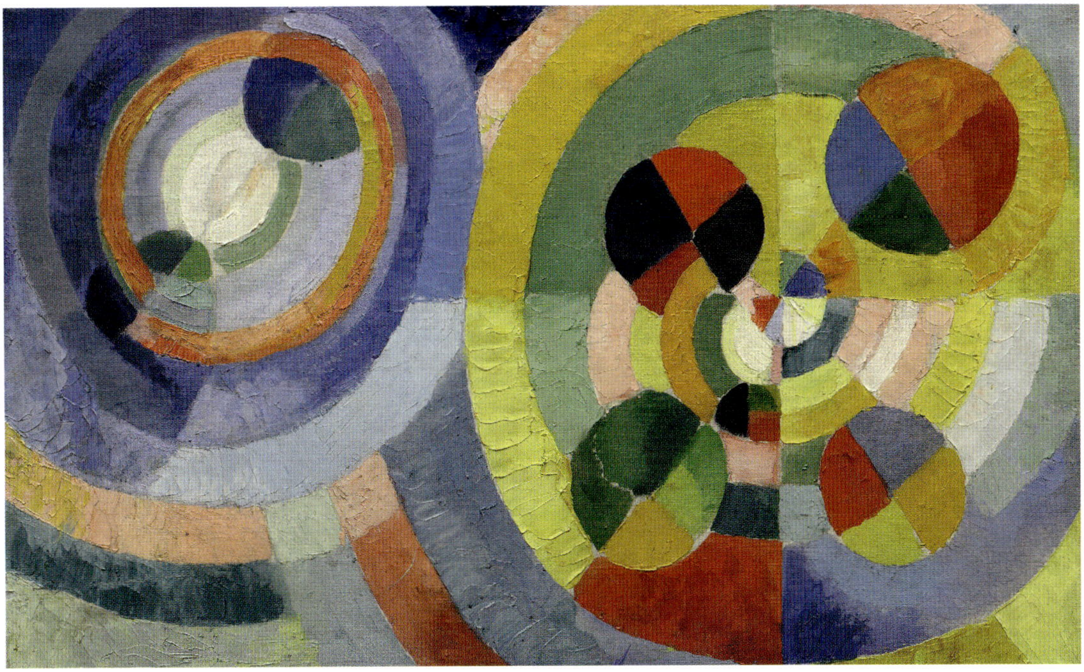

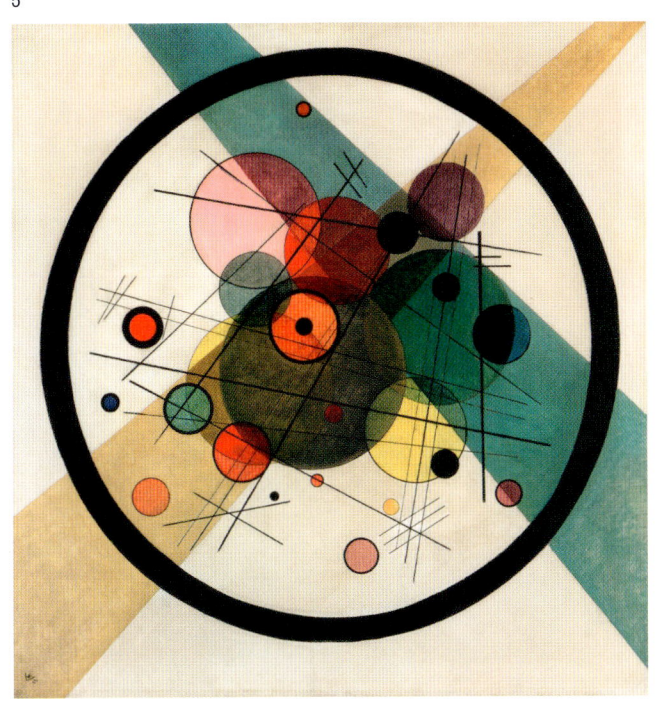

4

5

1. *Adoration of the Magi,* Fra Angelico, c. 1440-60
2. *Several Circles,* Wassily Kandinsky, 1926
3. *Target,* Jasper Johns, 1961
4. *Circular Forms,* Robert Delaunay, 1930
5. *Circles in a Circle,* Wassily Kandinsky, 1923

Square

Representing stability, order, balance and the material world, the four equal sides and right angles of the square have made it an emblem of structure. Contrasting with the circle, the square often symbolizes the earth, matter and stability. In ancient Mesopotamia, ziggurats were built on square bases to represent the four cardinal directions and the cosmic order. In ancient Egypt, the square was associated with the concept of *ma'at*, which encompasses truth, balance and divine order, often featured in temple layouts and sacred geometry. In Islam, the square is said to represent the heart of a normal person. Indigenous American cultures also used squares in textiles and sand paintings to define community, balance and the four elements. In modern Western art, the square became a symbol of abstraction and purity. Kazimir Malevich's *Black Square and Red Square* (1915) marked a radical break from representation, using the square to express spiritual transcendence and the concept of the void. Piet Mondrian used grids of squares and rectangles to explore universal harmony and order in his De Stijl compositions.

1

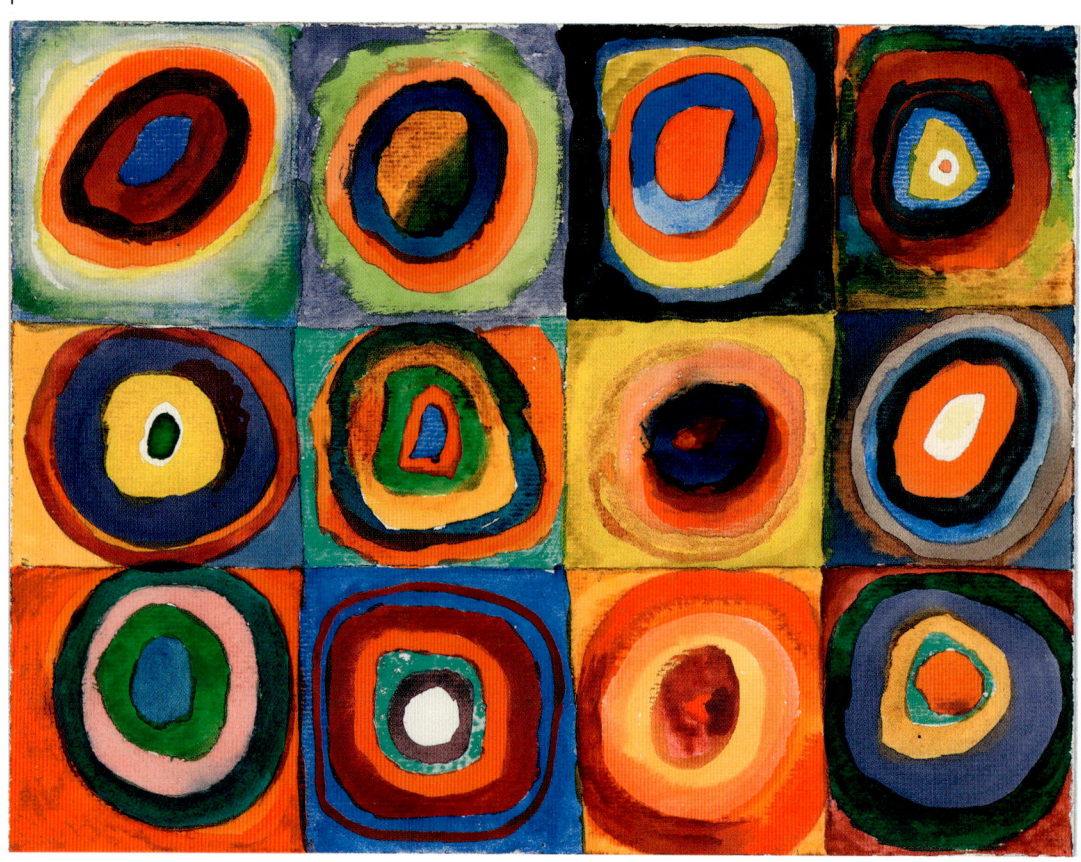

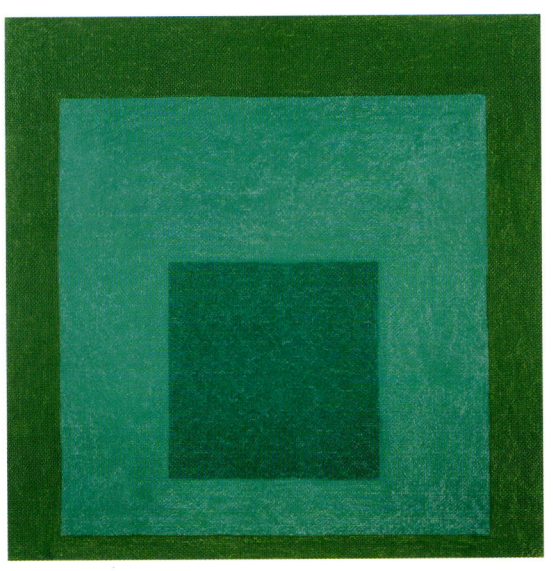

2

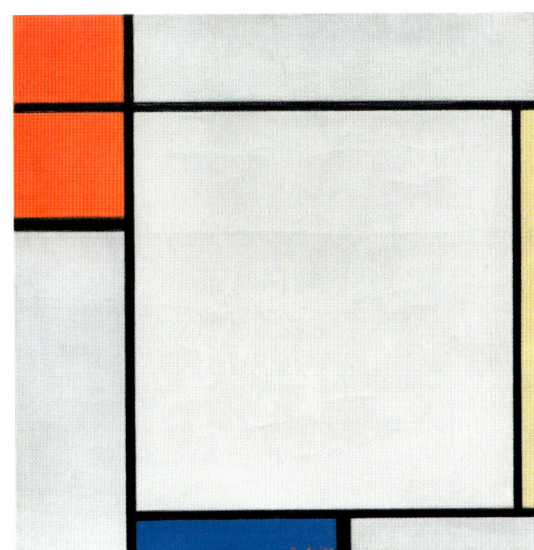

3

4

1. *Squares with Concentric Circles,* Wassily Kandinsky, 1913
2. *Homage to the Square,* Josef Albers, 1964
3. *Composition with Red, Yellow and Blue*, Piet Mondrian, 1927
4. *Black Square and Red Square,* Kazimir Malevich, 1915

Spiral

From growth and transformation to cosmic forces and the cycle of life, spirals have been a recurring motif in art since at least the Neolithic period, as seen in the entrance stones at Newgrange in Ireland (c. 3200 BCE). The spirals there are believed to represent the sun, life cycles or spiritual journeys. Spirals symbolized wind, water and the life force for the Aztecs and Maya. In ancient Greek art, spirals evoked infinity and harmony. In Polynesian and Maori cultures, spiral motifs like the *koru* represent new life, based on the unfurling fern frond. Widely used in Oceanic art, spirals represent the act of creation or the key to immortality. In Celtic art, the triple spiral or *triskele* is a symbol of life, death and rebirth. Spirals also feature in Buddhist mandalas, guiding meditation and representing spiritual awakening. In 1970, Robert Smithson (1938-73) created *Spiral Jetty* (1970), a monumental earthwork in Utah, using the spiral form to evoke environmental change, time, entropy and the natural world.

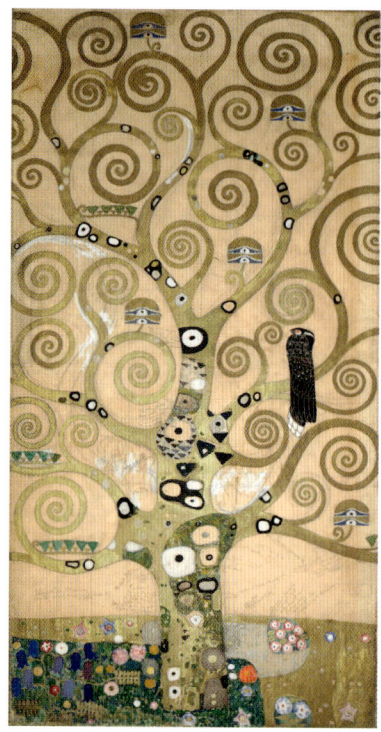

1

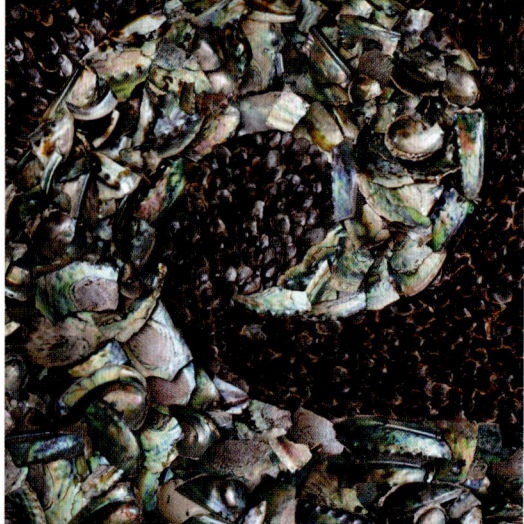

2

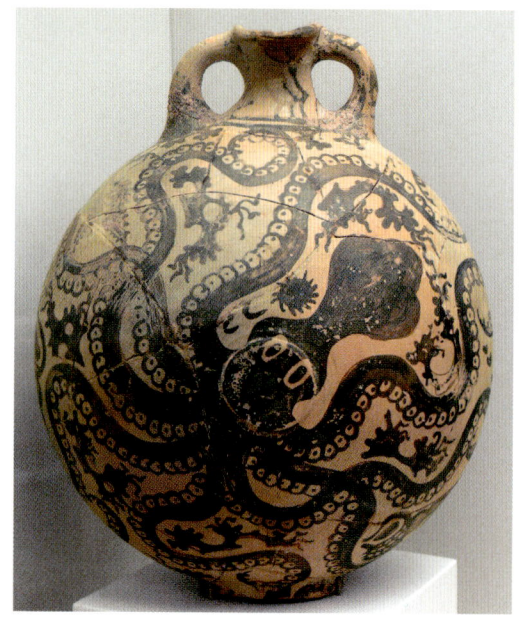

3

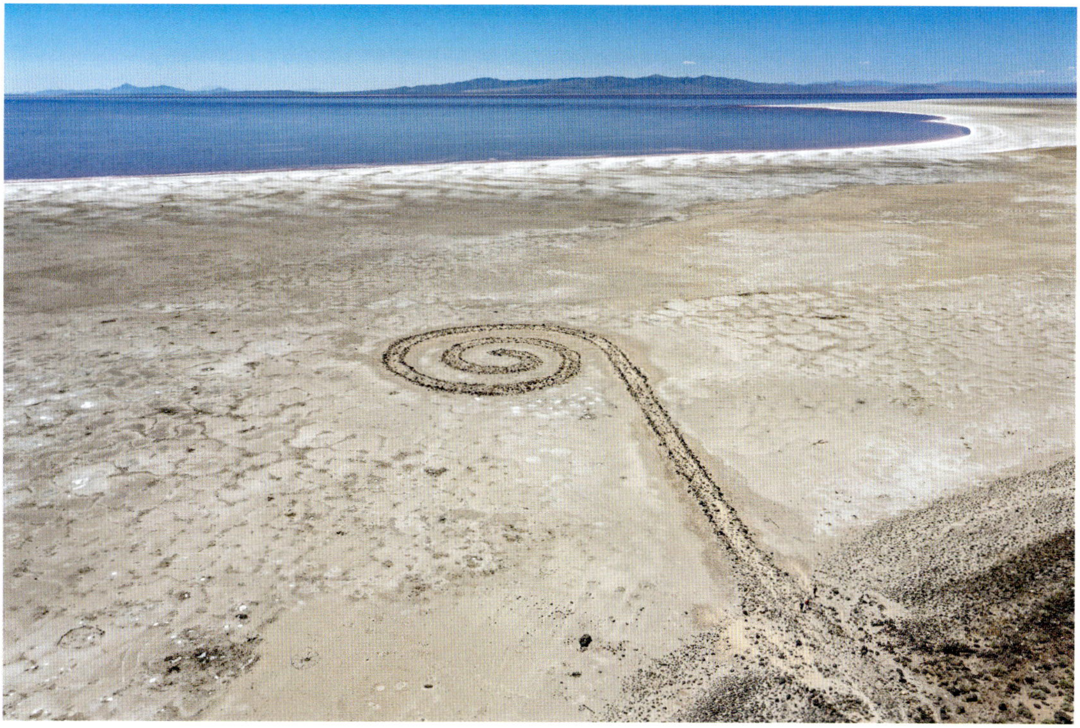

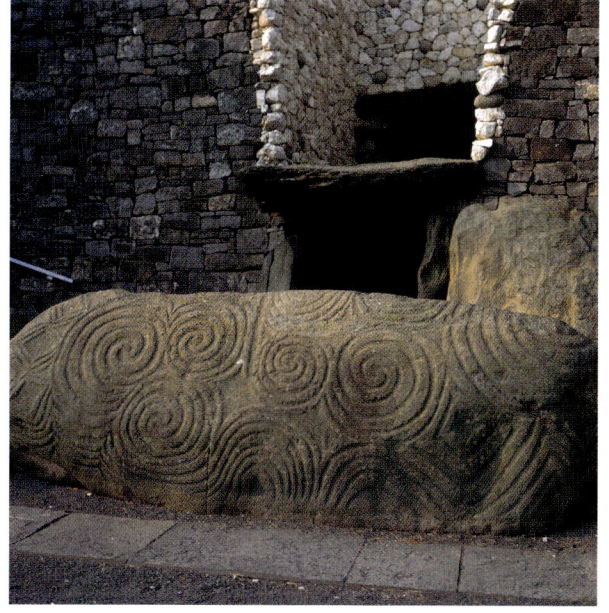

4

5

1. *The Tree of Life,* Gustav Klimt, 1909
2. *Koru Design,* unknown artist
3. *Pottery Jar with Octopus Design,* Greece, c. 1450-1400 BCE
4. *Spiral Jetty,* Robert Smithson, 1970
5. *Entrance Stone,* Newgrange, Ireland, c. 3200 BCE

Index

Credits

Acknowledgements

Thank you to everyone whose steady support helped bring this book to completion. I'm grateful to the whole team at Quarto - always a pleasure to work with - and especially to Philip Cooper and Izzy Toner, whose commitment to the project made the process both straightforward and enjoyable. Thanks also to Leonardo Collina for the beautiful and uplifting design. And, as ever, my thanks to family and friends, who remain endlessly patient with me and my decidedly antisocial habits whenever I'm deep in a book.